INTERNATIONAL LAW STUDIES

Volume 88

Non-International Armed Conflict in the Twenty-first Century

Kenneth Watkin and Andrew J. Norris
Editors

Naval War College
Newport, Rhode Island
2012

EDITORIAL OFFICE
International Law Studies
International Law Department
Naval War College (36)
686 Cushing Road
Newport, RI 02841-1207
Telephone: +1-401-841-4949
Fax: +1-401-841-3989
DSN: 841-4949
E-mail: ILD@usnwc.edu
Website: http://www.usnwc.edu/ild

The International Law Studies ("Blue Book") series was initiated by the Naval War College in 1901 to publish essays, treatises and articles that contribute to the broader understanding of international law.

OPNAVINST 5450.207 (series) formally tasks the Naval War College with publishing the "Blue Book" series. The thoughts and opinions expressed in this publication are those of the authors and are not necessarily those of the U.S. government, the U.S. Department of the Navy or the Naval War College.

INTERNATIONAL LAW STUDIES

Volume 88

IN MEMORIAM

This book is dedicated to the memory of Professor Leslie C. Green (1920–2011)—soldier, scholar of international law, independent thinker, mentor to many, dear friend, loving husband and father, a man who loved life and lived it with grace, dignity and active intellect to the very end.

Table of Contents

Non-International Armed Conflict in the Twenty-first Century

PART IV: LEGAL STATUS OF THE ACTORS IN NON-INTERNATIONAL ARMED CONFLICTS

PART V: MEANS AND METHODS IN NON-INTERNATIONAL ARMED CONFLICTS

PART VI: RECENT AND ONGOING NON-INTERNATIONAL ARMED CONFLICTS

Foreword

The historic International Law Studies ("Blue Book") series was initiated by the Naval War College in 1901 to publish essays, treatises and articles that contribute to the broader understanding of international law. This, the eighty-eighth volume of the "Blue Book" series, is a compilation of scholarly papers and remarks derived from the proceedings of a conference hosted at the Naval War College on June 21–23, 2011 entitled "Non-International Armed Conflict in the 21st Century."

The purpose of the June 2011 International Law Conference was to examine the legal issues surrounding non-international armed conflict (NIAC) in the modern era. To this end, renowned international academics and legal advisers, both military and civilian, representing military, diplomatic, non-governmental and academic institutions from the global community, were invited to the War College to analyze a variety of legal topics related to NIAC. Specifically, the panelists undertook an examination of the types of NIACs and the law applicable to each; the legal statuses of actors in NIAC; means and methods of warfare in NIAC; recent and ongoing NIACs; detention in NIAC; and enforcement of international law in NIAC. In addition, the Honorable Harold H. Koh, Legal Adviser of the U.S. Department of State, presented a luncheon address at the Naval Station Newport Officers' Club on the second day of the conference.

The distinguished panelists were invited to contribute articles to this volume to further develop their thoughts offered at the conference, and this "Blue Book" is largely comprised of these articles. Readers and researchers will find within this volume a detailed study of the law pertaining to non-international armed conflicts as it is interpreted and applied in the post–September 11 world, and its effect on State actions, particularly military operations.

The conference and the "Blue Book" were made possible with generous support from the Naval War College Foundation, the *Israel Yearbook on Human Rights*, the International Institute of Humanitarian Law, and the Lieber Society on the Law of Armed Conflict, American Society of International Law.

On behalf of the Secretary of the Navy, the Chief of Naval Operations and the Commandant of the Marine Corps, I extend our thanks and gratitude to all the participants, contributing authors and editors for their invaluable contributions to this project and to the future understanding of the law applicable in non-international armed conflicts, the predominant form of warfare during the last several decades and the type of conflicts in which military forces are most likely to be engaged in the twenty-first century.

JOHN N. CHRISTENSON
Rear Admiral, U.S. Navy
President, Naval War College

Introduction

During the past half century, non-international armed conflicts have far outnumbered those that are international in character. Indeed, as the conference that provided the basis for this volume was underway, the United States was engaged with its NATO allies in a non-international armed conflict in Afghanistan and was winding down its long participation in one in Iraq. The nation was also "at war" with various transnational terrorist groups in what many characterize as non-international armed conflict.

Yet, the *lex scripta* governing international armed conflict dwarfs that addressing non-international armed conflict. Moreover, although international tribunals have handled many cases involving the latter, their decisions often prove controversial, especially when applying the law of international armed conflict to non-international conflicts. Unfortunately, even the academic community pays less attention to the law of non-international armed conflict than merited by its legal complexity and the frequency and human consequences of the conflicts to which it applies.

This reality is unsurprising. International armed conflict self-evidently affects international stability. As history has demonstrated time and again, the risks of escalation and of spread are high whenever such conflicts occur. These and other factors motivate the members of the international community to agree upon norms limiting the effects of State-on-State conflict lest they find themselves involved therein. In doing so, States not only accept limitations on their battlefield actions, but also secure protection for, *inter alia*, their civilians, civilian property and soldiers *hors de combat*. The key to the system is the reciprocity inherent in the treaty and customary law regimes that encompass opposing belligerents. Since the law of international armed conflict is more robust than its non-international counterpart, so too is the attention paid it.

Non-international armed conflict is of a fundamentally different nature. In most cases, States are facing organized groups of lawbreakers from whom reciprocity cannot be expected. Therefore, there is often little incentive for States to limit their scope of action by agreeing to legal norms with which only they will abide. Moreover, as the conflict is "internal," the risk of spread is limited, while the involvement of other States is a matter of their discretion.

However, the context in which non-international armed conflict occurs is undergoing transformation. Transnational terrorism has become a globally pervasive phenomenon, one that the international community seems increasingly willing to classify as non-international, at least to the extent it rises to the level of "armed conflict" as a matter of law. Further, as illustrated by the conflicts in the Balkans, Afghanistan and the Great Lakes region of Africa, the likelihood of spillover into neighboring countries is very real, especially when a conflict is ethnically or religiously based or when adjacent territory is poorly governed. And the rise of criminal groups with capabilities equaling those of government forces, as in Colombia and Mexico, raises the question of whether the hostilities they engage in qualify as armed conflict.

The International Law Department of the Naval War College, long noted for exploring new legal challenges in its annual conferences, accordingly decided that a closer examination of the law governing non-international armed conflict was opportune. Held in June 2011, the resulting conference brought together many of the key legal practitioners and scholars in the field to consider both the state of the law and where it might be headed. Certain of the participants were invited to expand on their presentations in this volume, the eighty-eighth in the Naval War College's International Law Studies ("Blue Books") series. It delves into such complicated topics as the scope of non-international armed conflict, the legal status of actors, specific limitations on methods and means of warfare, detention and enforcement. The volume also offers several firsthand descriptions of particular non-international armed conflicts. Hopefully, the various contributions will assist those tasked with providing legal advice during future non-international armed conflicts, as well as make a measurable contribution to the scholarship on the subject.

Appreciation is owed to many who made the conference and this volume of the "Blue Books" possible. Rear Admiral John Christenson, President of the Naval War College, and Ambassador Mary Ann Peters, its Provost, provide the leadership that enables the International Law Department to undertake these cutting-edge studies. Professor Robert "Barney" Rubel, Dean of the Center for Naval Warfare Studies, consistently affords the International Law Department the material support necessary to engage in meaningful research, as well as the vision that undergirds all of its activities. Professor Dennis Mandsager, former Chairman of the International Law Department, was at the helm as the Department developed the topic and executed the conference. Lieutenant Colonel George Cadwalader ably served as Conference Director, an oft-thankless duty, but one that is the key to success. Finally, Brigadier General Kenneth Watkin, Canadian Forces (Ret.), the War College's 2011–12 Stockton Professor of International Law, and Captain Andrew Norris, U.S. Coast Guard, edited this important volume with substantive aplomb and editorial finesse. They are to be congratulated.

The Naval War College has engaged in international law study and writing since the late nineteenth century. Indeed, the first volume of the "Blue Book" series was authored in 1901 by Professor John Bassett Moore, who would go on to serve as the first U.S. judge on the Permanent Court of International Justice. It is our commitment to continue this proud tradition in the years to come.

PROFESSOR MICHAEL N. SCHMITT
Chairman, International Law Department
United States Naval War College

Preface

From June 21 to 23, 2011, the U.S. Naval War College hosted distinguished international scholars and practitioners, both military and civilian, representing government and academic institutions, to participate in a conference examining the evolving law in non-international armed conflict (NIAC) in the twenty-first century. Panelists discussed their views on how the law will develop as the world continues to struggle with the changing nature of the threats to national and international security posed by failed and failing States, insurgencies, and transnational criminal and terrorist organizations. The conference featured opening, luncheon and closing addresses, as well as six panel discussions.

The conference summary that follows was prepared by Commander Christian P. Fleming, JAGC, U.S. Navy, a member of the Navy Reserve unit that supports the Naval War College's International Law Department. The summary recapitulates the highlights of each conference speaker's presentation. As co-editors, we are deeply indebted to Commander Fleming for his attention to detail and assistance in facilitating the publication of this "Blue Book." We would also be remiss if we did not thank Captain Ralph Thomas, JAGC, U.S. Navy (Ret.), for his outstanding support and dedication in editing the submissions for this volume of the International Law Studies series. We also extend our sincere appreciation to Susan Meyer of the Naval War College's Desktop Publishing Division for expertly preparing the page proofs. Additionally, we would like to thank Albert Fassbender and Shannon Cole for their excellent work in proofreading the conference papers. The quality of this volume is a reflection of their professionalism and outstanding expertise.

This "Blue Book" would not have come to fruition had it not been for the enormously successful conference made possible in large measure by the conference committee under the leadership of Lieutenant Colonel George Cadwalader, U.S. Marine Corps, working with Mrs. Jayne Van Petten of the International Law Department, and the support provided by the Naval War College Foundation, the International Institute of Humanitarian Law, the Lieber Society on the Law of Armed Conflict (American Society of International Law) and the *Israel Yearbook on Human Rights*. We thank these individuals and organizations for their enduring support and generosity.

We hope that the thought-provoking articles published in this "Blue Book" will add to—and help shape—the debate on the multiple complex emerging legal issues presented by the changing character of war. The insights offered to legal practitioners and scholars should assist them as they address these and other issues that may evolve in future conflicts.

Opening Address

Professor Ken Watkin delivered the opening address. After introductory remarks, Professor Watkin began his discussion of law in NIAC by quoting Colonel Caldwell, who in 1906 defined a form of NIAC known as "small wars" as being "campaigns undertaken to suppress rebellion and guerilla warfare in all parts of the world where organized armies are struggling against opponents who will not meet them in the open field." The 1940 Small Wars Manual of the U.S. Marine Corps indicated that "small wars represent the normal and frequent operations of the Marine Corps."

Because States have been hostile to clarifying the law, there has been limited success in articulating the law of NIAC. The concern is that non-State actors will be given legitimacy. Given the lack of consensus on what law applies to small war, a dialogue has been left open as to how and to what degree human rights law governs the use of force, the treatment of detainees and the accountability process in NIACs. Gaps remain and the law governing NIAC needs to be clarified for a number of reasons.

First, NIACs have been and will remain the dominant form of warfare. NIACs will not disappear and pure international wars are becoming rare. International armed conflicts (IACs) can change to NIACs overnight. This occurred in Afghanistan. Did troops on the ground notice the change? Did the legal advice change? As a result, for most practitioners the key question to be asked is whether there is an armed conflict rather than whether it is IAC or NIAC. Ironically, the Lieber Code, written during the American Civil War, a NIAC, was a starting point for codifying rules in an armed conflict. Unfortunately, the law applied in NIACs has become muddier since then.

Second, the lack of clarity regarding the law of NIAC can have a profound and sometimes negative effect not only on the victims of conflict, but also on States in terms of whether their actions are viewed as being legitimate. For example, in post-9/11 detainee operations, the dialogue would have been much different if there had been greater clarity in the law. An application of the policy of treating captured personnel under prisoner of war standards, without providing that status, or as security detainees under Geneva Convention IV could have been a practical, defensible and ultimately helpful approach. However, even today, an internationally agreed-upon framework governing detainees in NIAC is lacking.

Third, there is a belief that the law applicable to NIAC has no real relevance to conflicts between States. However, there can be significant cross-pollination of legal issues, such as when dealing with an insurgency during belligerent occupation.

Finally, the unwillingness of States to clarify what law applies to NIAC has negatively impacted their ability to influence how that law is being shaped. Gaps, both real and perceived, are being filled by restatements and manuals of international organizations instead of by States. One example is the International Committee of the Red Cross's 2009 *Interpretive Guidance on the Notion of Direct Participation in Hostilities*, which deals with an issue that States appear to have been either unwilling or unable to address. The *Guidance* is representative of a trend suggesting that States should be held to a higher standard than their non-State opponents. Adding new inequity to the existing law is not likely to aid in reaching consensus among such significant stakeholders in international law as States.

At the same time, States cannot complain about new manuals if they do not get fully engaged in the processes being used to clarify the law. Civilians must be protected and the question is the degree to which States want to influence that process.

Panel I: Types of NIACs and Applicable Law

Panel I, moderated by Commander James Kraska, JAGC, U.S. Navy, of the Naval War College's International Law Department, consisted of Mr. David Graham of the U.S. Army's Judge Advocate General's Legal Center and School, Professor Geoffrey Corn of South Texas College of Law, Professor Charles Garraway of the Royal Institute of International Affairs (Chatham House) and Mr. Karl Chang of the U.S. Department of Defense Office of General Counsel.

Mr. Graham established the framework for the discussion by posing these questions: How do we recognize a NIAC? Are there different types of NIAC? How does the United States decide whether a NIAC exists or not? Mr. Graham commented that the law of armed conflict (LOAC) provides no definition of NIAC, nor does Common Article 3 of the Geneva Conventions of 1949. It is not clear what level of violence must exist and how protracted that violence needs to be for there to be a NIAC. States have been reluctant to recognize NIACs within their own borders for fear of legitimizing belligerent groups. Additional Protocol I to the 1949 Geneva Conventions does not aid in defining NIAC; Additional Protocol II (AP II) narrows the number of NIACs to which it would apply. The U.S. practice would appear to be that of making no official determination as to whether a NIAC exists, but, instead, to state that all U.S. personnel involved in a conflict will comply with LOAC, regardless of how such a conflict might be characterized. While perhaps self-serving, this is a practical approach with a proven track record.

Professor Corn focused on the issue of willful blindness in conflict determination and why this is a dangerous approach. When States invoke powers under LOAC—namely, to kill and detain—then States should be estopped from neglecting to provide protections under Common Article 3. Said differently, if a State is going to use the tools of war, then it must be bound by the rules of war. When a State enters an armed conflict, it cannot label it as a NIAC or IAC to game the system. Turning to the U.S. conflict against al Qaeda, Professor Corn believes the Bush administration attempted to use a gap in the law to justify an exception to Common Article 3. The United States attempted to use the inherent right of self-defense to justify the use of force, but pretended to not need to address *jus in bello* considerations. There was willful blindness to suggest that when invoking self-defense, the question of the legal framework governing the conflict did not have to be addressed.

Professor Garraway spoke from the European standpoint, and addressed the border between law enforcement and NIAC. Prior to 1949, there was either war or peace. In 1949, everything changed, and the spectrum of violence over the last fifty to sixty years has been like a rainbow, with difficulty in determining where the colors merge. The main issue for many years was the line between NIAC and IAC, but the underlying problem is determining the line between law enforcement and NIAC. Human rights law and LOAC are reasonably compatible insofar as "prohibitions" are concerned. The problem comes with the "permissions" inherent in "Hague law" on the conduct of hostilities. The challenge is that if human rights law and LOAC are not to collide, there need to be compromises where they differ, such as in targeting. There is a need to know what law applies in which circumstances. The answer might lie in the intensity of the violence. Where the intensity is similar to IAC, LOAC has priority; where the level is less, human rights law has priority.

Mr. Chang observed that people are troubled by a dearth of law pertaining to NIAC. He argued that attempts to fill this perceived void by drawing from human rights law or from law relating to IAC were unpersuasive and often an exercise in applying law to situations for which it was not intended. Instead, Mr. Chang proposed that the law of neutrality, which governs the relations between belligerents and neutrals, gave principled limits on transnational NIACs. In IAC, we know whom we are fighting and where we want to fight. But in transnational NIAC, the fighting often takes place in neutral or non-belligerent States against citizens of such States. The framework of neutrality law is needed to determine when persons have forfeited their neutral immunity and acquired enemy status. Similarly, neutrality law is needed to determine where the State may use force, i.e., when other States are unable or unwilling to address threats emanating from their territories.

Panel II: Legal Status of Actors in NIAC

The International Law Department's Commander Andrew Norris, U.S. Coast Guard, moderated this panel, which consisted of Durham University professor Michael Schmitt, Creighton University School of Law professor Sean Watts and Mr. Stephen Pomper of the U.S. Department of State. The panel delved into the legal status of actors in NIAC, focusing on the categorization of those fighting for and against the State. Mr. Pomper commented on various U.S. legal policy positions regarding NIAC.

Professor Schmitt discussed the law pertaining to opposition forces in NIAC, noting that treaty law directly on point is sparse. A threshold issue is determining whether the persons are actually members of the opposition or merely individual criminals or members of criminal gangs taking advantage of the instability that exists during conflict. The latter cannot be parties to the conflict unless they are acting in support of rebel forces, and operations conducted against them are governed by domestic and human rights law. Professor Schmitt cautioned, however, that there is a possible change in the wind for well-organized armed criminal gangs competing with the State for control and authority over territory when the State must resort to the military in response. As to opposition forces in a NIAC, the easiest case is that of dissident armed forces, which are clearly targetable at all times. Other groups must display some level of structure and coordination and engage in "armed" actions (or support thereof) against the State before attaining the status of an "organized armed group," that is, a party to the conflict and therefore subject to targeting as such. Individuals who act against the State without membership in an organized armed group may qualify as "direct participants in hostilities" depending on the nature of their activities. When they qualify, they become targetable for such time as they participate in the conflict. Professor Schmitt argued that if they engage in recurring acts of hostility, their targetability extends throughout the period of the acts.

Professor Watts addressed the status of government forces in NIAC, and clarified that "status" was being discussed in the classic sense as combatant status, i.e., one's exposure to hostilities and one's authority to engage in hostilities. Initially, Professor Watts observed that States have not turned to international law to define the status of government forces in NIAC. There is no customary international law in this area and very little by way of treatment in scholarly journals. States have not seen a need for international law to speak to the issue of government forces in NIAC, because they are committed to domestic law in this area and have generally been reluctant to commit NIAC issues to international law. Additionally, there is a lack of consensus among States as to the law applicable to NIAC. However, NIAC law is changing. It is possible to imagine a future where some States—and perhaps tribunals—recognize rules regulating participation of government forces in NIAC. Although NIAC rules are often developed by analogy from rules of IAC, the more likely source for such a rule would be some derivation of the existing NIAC rule of distinction. Professor Watts suggested, however, that such a rule would be ineffective in addressing the traditional concerns of distinction. The real concern with government forces' participation in NIAC is their conduct rather than their legal status. Ultimately, this exercise requires a choice between conceiving of combatant status as a gateway to protections and obligations and conceiving of status in purely political terms. This forces a more theoretical consideration of *jus in bello* than usual.

Mr. Pomper noted that the rules governing actors in NIAC are less developed than in IAC. Often NIAC rules are drawn from their analogs in IAC and translated into the NIAC context, but this exercise can be difficult. There are identity and status issues at the center of this exercise. Parallels exist between NIAC and IAC, but it is difficult to categorize the actors in NIAC the same way we do in IAC. How this is defined has important implications for life and liberty, and has great operational significance for warfighters. There appears to be growing consensus among the United States and like-minded countries that there are two primary ways an individual becomes liable to attack in a NIAC. The first is if he is a member of an organized armed group; the second is if he is a civilian who directly participates in hostilities, whether or not a member of an organized armed group. An individual who is a member of an organized armed group can be attacked at any time. By contrast, a civilian who directly participates in hostilities loses protection only for the duration of the participation. There also appears to be growing support for the concept that to determine whether there is direct participation in hostilities, the nature of the harm, causation and a nexus to the hostilities must be considered.

Panel III: Means and Methods in NIAC

Lieutenant Colonel George Cadwalader Jr., U.S. Marine Corps, of the International Law Department, moderated this panel, which discussed means and methods in NIAC. The panel consisted of Air Commodore Bill Boothby of the Royal Air Force, Professor Dr. Wolff Heintschel von Heinegg of Europa-Universität Viadrina and Mr. Dick Jackson, the Special Assistant to the U.S. Army Judge Advocate General for Law of War Matters.

Air Commodore Boothby opened the panel by posing the question whether there is a meaningful distinction between the weapons laws that apply during IAC and NIAC. First examining the similarities, he noted that the fundamental principles of superfluous injury/unnecessary suffering and the prohibition of weapons that are indiscriminate by nature apply equally in both types of conflict. AP II applies to both, as do the Chemical Weapons Convention, the Biological Weapons Convention, the Ottawa Convention and the Cluster Munitions Convention. However, there is an issue raised by expanding bullets. While treaty law bans the use of expanding bullets in IAC, it is questionable whether this is customary international law. The Kampala Review Conference for the Rome Statute of the International Criminal Court (ICC) added the offense of employing expanding bullets to those that could be committed in NIAC, but only if they are employed to "uselessly aggravate suffering." Thus, expanding bullets seem to represent a point of distinction between the laws applicable to IAC and NIAC. In the former, the offense is not tied to superfluous injury and unnecessary suffering; in the latter it is. While the general trend has been convergence in the weapons laws of these two classes of conflict, achieving complete convergence would require State action and adjustment of some legal interpretations.

Professor Dr. Heintschel von Heinegg focused on naval means of warfare in NIAC. Until the 1990s there were not many rules in NIAC related to means and methods. The emerging trend is to expand treaty law applicable to NIAC through the terms of the treaty itself, i.e., the treaty provisions state that it applies in NIACs. However, those treaties that do not distinguish between IACs and NIACs have not become customary international law. If there is a merger between the law in IAC and that in NIAC, then it cannot be a one-way street. The law cannot just speak about protections, but must also address privileges, such as targeting. There have been some historical examples of naval components to NIACs, such as during the Spanish Civil War, and the Sri Lanka, Algerian and, more recently, Libyan conflicts. There are no substantive rules of international law prohibiting naval means and methods in NIAC. Within the State's territory, government forces can interfere with international navigation. However, government forces cannot expand this principle to international waters. And, if non-State actors interfere with navigation, the State must provide notice to international shipping.

Mr. Jackson remarked that the trend has been a collapsing of IAC rules into NIAC, driven largely by the warfighter on the ground who does not know when the situation shifts from an IAC to a NIAC. He then discussed perfidy in NIAC. Perfidy violates the principle of distinction. The most important part of perfidy under NIAC is feigning of civilian status. The Military Commissions Act requires a showing of a violation of LOAC; perfidy may be charged as such a violation.

Panel IV: Recent and Ongoing NIACs

This panel, moderated by Naval War College professor Pete Pedrozo, was comprised of Lieutenant General Raymundo Ferrer of the Philippine Armed Forces, Colonel Juan Carlos Gomez of the Colombian Air Force and Captain Rob McLaughlin of the Royal Australian Navy. Its focus was on recent and ongoing NIACs.

General Ferrer focused on the two major insurgent groups in the Philippines: the Maoist group and the Moro group. The Maoist group, consisting of the Communist Party of the Philippines/New People's Army, operates nationwide and is the longest-running Maoist insurgency in the world. The Moro group operates primarily in the southern Philippines, and consists of three major groups: the Moro National Liberation Front, the Moro Islamic Liberation Front and the Abu Sayyaf Group. General Ferrer opined that the NIAC in the Philippines is a cry for human security.

Colonel Gomez discussed the forty-five years of internal conflict in Colombia. He stated there are three groups of illegal armed actors: the Revolutionary Armed Forces of Columbia (FARC), the National Liberation Army (ELN) and paramilitary forces that have become criminal gangs. Colonel Gomez described the difficulty in the new operational environment that consists of human rights law on one side and international humanitarian law on the other, with the government's effort to combat terrorism and organized crime operating, depending on the circumstances, under one or the other of these two norms. Essentially, human rights law provides the framework in territory controlled by the government and international humanitarian law applies where the organized armed groups control. The dichotomy is that under human rights law, where there is typical criminal violence, the use of force is governed by restrained law enforcement standards, including self-defense. Under international humanitarian law, where there is a high level of violence, the concepts of military necessity, military objective, distinction, humanity and proportionality apply. The nature and location of the operation determine whether government forces are operating under law enforcement–type rules of engagement (ROE) or the more robust ROE applicable to traditional military operations.

Captain McLaughlin analyzed Australia's experience in East Timor, which he described as a high-end law enforcement operation, and contrasted it with the Australian experience in Afghanistan, which was a NIAC. He stated that whether a conflict is classified as law enforcement, a NIAC or an IAC is important because under a law enforcement scenario, lethal force can be used for self-defense, but in NIAC and IAC, the LOAC principles govern the use of force. He opined that Afghanistan has clearly been a NIAC since 2005 and that there was little political or strategic risk in classifying it as such, especially since the Taliban are seen to have few redeeming features. However, East Timor was, for political and strategic reasons as much as legal reasons, classified as a law enforcement action, in large part because the intervening force was invited in by Indonesia and shared responsibility for security with Indonesia. The decision on how to characterize a conflict impacts ROE, determining whether there are attack or only self-defense ROE in place with respect to lethal force. While self-defense ROE are the same under both labels, mission accomplishment ROE are where they differ. He indicated that there is little practical difference between NIAC and law enforcement insofar as detention rules are concerned.

Luncheon Address

The Honorable Harold Koh, Legal Adviser of the Department of State, presented a luncheon address entitled "International Law and Armed Conflict in the Obama Administration." Mr. Koh opined that there was an emerging Obama/Clinton doctrine that espoused four principles: (1) principled engagement, (2) diplomacy as an element of smart power, (3) strategic multilateralism and (4) compliance with the rules of domestic and international law.

Mr. Koh stated that the United States is deeply committed to applying all applicable law, including LOAC, in its non-international armed conflict with al Qaeda with respect to both targeting and detention. Under domestic law, the authority to detain stems from the Authorization for Use of Military Force (AUMF), as informed by the laws of war. Common Article 3 and Additional Protocol II to the Geneva Conventions, as well as the Supreme Court of the United States, all contemplate that parties may lawfully detain belligerents to prevent them from returning to the battlefield. Once detained, all persons in U.S. custody must be treated humanely, and the administration has taken a number of steps to ensure that detainees in U.S. custody are treated humanely in accordance with our domestic and international legal obligations. The United States has unequivocally affirmed that it will not engage in torture and has affirmed that current U.S. military practices are consistent with Additional Protocol II to the Geneva Conventions and with Article 75 of Additional Protocol I to the Geneva Conventions, including the rules within these instruments that parallel the International Covenant on Civil and Political Rights.

He further stated that the United States complies with all applicable law in its targeting practices. The United States is in an armed conflict with al Qaeda, the Taliban and associated forces, and may also use force consistent with the inherent right of self-defense. Congress has authorized force through the AUMF. Osama bin Laden, the leader of al Qaeda, clearly had an ongoing operational role and his activities posed an imminent threat against the United States. There can be no question that he was the leader of an enemy force and a legitimate target in our armed conflict with al Qaeda. Moreover, the operation against him was conducted in a manner consistent with LOAC, including with the principles of distinction and proportionality, and in accordance with U.S. domestic law.

Turning to Libya, Mr. Koh stated that there was a call to international action by the Arab League and NATO, and the use of force to protect civilians was authorized by the UN Security Council under Chapter VII of the UN Charter because the situation within Libya threatened international peace and security. U.S. actions were consistent with the War Powers Resolution in these particular circumstances, specifically as follows: (1) the U.S. mission was limited in nature, duration and scope—with the shift to an explicit support role by the U.S. forces as part of a NATO-led multilateral civilian protection operation; (2) the exposure of U.S. forces was limited, involving no U.S. casualties or threat of significant U.S. casualties and no sustained fighting or active exchanges of fire with hostile forces; (3) the risk of escalation was limited, with no U.S. military forces on the ground; and (4) the military means used were limited, the ordnance dropped being a fraction of that used in Kosovo. Mr. Koh posed the question: Did Congress in 1973, when it enacted the War Powers Resolution as an attempt to prevent future Vietnam Wars, intend that it also interrupt a mission—limited in nature, duration and scope—launched to stop the slaughter of innocent civilians, as was the mission in Libya?

Mr. Koh concluded by remarking that the administration has tried to square its emerging national security policies with the need for interoperability with allies and coalition partners who are parties to the ICC and cluster munitions and landmines treaties.

Panel V: Detention in NIAC

This panel was moderated by Lieutenant Colonel Eric Young, JA, U.S. Army, of the International Law Department, and consisted of Brigadier General Thomas Ayres, JA, U.S. Army; Lieutenant Commander Kovit Talasophon of the Royal Thai Navy; Dr. Knut Dörmann, of the International Committee of the Red Cross; and Deputy Assistant Secretary of Defense; Rule of Law and Detainee Policy, William Lietzau.

General Ayres addressed the role of detainee operations in NIAC. He noted that legal authority existed to detain insurgents in a NIAC to keep them out of the fight until the cessation of hostilities. He noted, however, that based upon his experiences in Iraq, there are four types of insurgents: (1) those acting for a criminal purpose, e.g., to steal; (2) those who oppose the presence of coalition forces and attempt to demonstrate to the civilian populace that the occupying force is incapable of keeping civilians safe; (3) those who oppose the government and seek to discredit it; and (4) foreign fighters who may be training to engage in terrorist activities and pose a threat to the national security interest of the United States or other coalition nations.

The first type of insurgent, those with a criminal purpose, would, in almost all phases of the conflict, be turned over to the government of Iraq to be tried in the domestic criminal courts. With regard to the remaining categories of insurgents, the coalition forces' objective was to detain only the worst of the worst, because, for operational reasons and due to "insurgent math," it was impossible to detain all potential "bad actors." The operational realities drove the coalition to evidence-based detention. Moreover, once the UN Security Council resolution providing authority for the presence of coalition forces in Iraq neared expiration, the coalition began transferring detainees to the Iraqi government. In preparation for that transfer, the coalition sought to assist in the maturation of the Iraqi government institutions in their implementation of the rule of law by increasingly complying with Iraqi law and respecting Iraq's criminal law as the basis for detaining insurgents. General Ayres asserted that the coalition's efforts in modeling adherence to a criminal law paradigm to detain insurgents should not be seen as undercutting the international humanitarian law basis for detaining insurgents in a NIAC.

Lieutenant Commander Talasophon reviewed Thailand's experience with detention in what he characterized as "almost a civil war" with communist groups during the Cold War and in border wars with its neighbors. He indicated that there are ongoing hostilities in the southern portions of Thailand between the government and those with political grievances. However, the Thai government has declared that these hostilities are not a NIAC; therefore, they are dealt with through law enforcement operations. Domestic law has been used instead of international humanitarian law, although the government has complied with the spirit of Common Article 3 in conducting the operations. Detention is used to secure evidence and to ensure that the actor does not engage in further violence.

Dr. Dörmann spoke on the legal framework of detention in NIAC. He began with a general observation that the sources of international law pertaining to detention in NIAC consisted of Common Article 3, Articles 4 through 6 of AP II and customary international law. Next, he opined that it is now generally accepted that human rights law applies alongside international humanitarian law in situations of armed conflict, including, despite the view of some important dissenters like the United States, extraterritorially. Dr. Dörmann discussed the rules on treatment in detention, conditions of detention and fair trial rights, but focused his remarks on internment (i.e., non-criminal detention). He indicated that internment cannot be used solely for interrogation purposes; nor can it be used as punishment for past acts. Internment may be resorted to if there are imperative reasons for security to do so, a standard which includes direct participation in hostilities. He stated that the status of those detained should be periodically reviewed to determine whether they are still a security threat. Dr. Dörmann concluded by stating that there were gaps in the law of detention in NIAC and States should meet to discuss the legal framework to fill those gaps.

Mr. Lietzau observed that the United States used to not think about what law applied in NIAC, particularly with regard to those detained during the conflict. In fact, the United States' last experience with long-term detention was of prisoners of war captured during World War II. The law then was clear—enemy prisoners of war could be held until the end of the conflict. But twenty-first-century conflicts have changed. Now the war is not with another State, but with a non-State actor, al Qaeda. In the early period of this new type of war, the United States was accused of holding detainees indefinitely without providing a means of review to determine whether there was sufficient basis for the detention. Today, newly captured individuals are submitted to a Detainee Review Board. The Board, comprised of three field-grade military officers, reviews each individual's detention for both legality and necessity of continued detention. The detainee receives expert assistance from a U.S. officer who is authorized access to all reasonably available information pertaining to that detainee. This review is repeated periodically after the initial hearing, which must take place within sixty days of arrival at the internment facility. Now some argue that the pendulum has swung too far, and that the United States is releasing detainees (some of whom have returned to the fight) too quickly. What is unarguable is that an indefinite detention without some form of process in these new wars will not be stomached.

Panel VI: Enforcement in NIAC

Panel VI, on enforcement in NIAC, was moderated by Colonel Darren Stewart, OBE, British Army, the Director of the Military Department of the International Institute of Humanitarian Law at San Remo, Italy. The panelists were Professor John Cerone, professor of law and Director, Center for International Law & Policy, New England Law | Boston; University of Essex professor Françoise Hampson; and Johns Hopkins University professor Ruth Wedgwood.

Introducing the topic, Colonel Stewart remarked that there is little substantive black letter law applicable to NIAC when compared to the international humanitarian law applicable to IAC. However, while the law in NIAC has gaps, it is applied day to day by practitioners on the ground. The question of enforcement brings the gaps in the law into sharp focus.

Professor Cerone discussed enforcement issues in the context of the then-current situation in Libya. After reviewing the phases of the conflict, he discussed the legal regimes that applied to each phase, as well as how they related to each other. He stated that it is now widely accepted that international human rights law applies simultaneously with humanitarian law in internal armed conflicts. Even those States that object to simultaneous application in international or transnational armed conflicts do not object to the application of international human rights law in internal armed conflicts. He then focused on international criminal law and the Security Council referral of the situation in Libya to the ICC. As Libya is not a party to the ICC Statute, the Court will need to address issues of immunity and *nullum crimen sine lege*. The Court will have to ensure, in particular, that any crimes prosecuted are well established in customary international law. Professor Cerone indicated that twenty years ago it was debatable whether any violations of NIAC law gave rise to individual criminal responsibility in international law. The legal landscape has changed dramatically since that time. Nonetheless, he concluded that it is clear that not all of the war crimes within the subject matter jurisdiction of the ICC have entered the corpus of customary law.

Professor Hampson opined that in the past fifteen years the focus has been on criminal responsibility, with not enough focus on civil responsibility. The advantages of a civil action are that the claim can be brought against a State without the need to identify the actual perpetrators, there is a lower standard of proof than in criminal cases and the victims have more control over the claims. Claims can be brought in the domestic courts of the State where the violation occurred and possibly in the domestic courts of third-party States. Professor Hampson indicated that there is no international means of bringing a claim against a non-State actor, although possibly arbitration could be used on an ad hoc basis. At the international level, the only way to proceed is to bring a claim against a State. Claims could be brought before the International Court of Justice or other human rights bodies. In fact, she stated, the most important feature of the human rights bodies is the right of an individual to file a petition with them.

Professor Wedgwood offered several suggestions for improving the work of the ad hoc war crimes tribunals. First, indictments should be structured to allow a speedy trial. The charges against Milosevic might have been tried in separate parts in Bosnia, Croatia and Kosovo, instead of the four-year trial in the International Criminal Tribunal for the former Yugoslavia (ICTY) during which both the presiding judge and the defendant passed away. Second, international justice should not be segregated by tribunal; she observed that it is unfortunate the ICTY declined to share evidence from Serb military archives with the International Court of Justice in the latter's adjudication of the Srebrenica genocide case. Third, it is important that cases be tried against defendants from all ethnic communities in a civil conflict, so that there is no misplaced imputation of bias. The failure of the Rwanda tribunal to try any cases against members of the Rwandan Patriotic Front and the Tutsi armed forces, instead remitting them to local justice authorities controlled by the Kagame government, was an unfortunate event. Fourth, political organs are not well suited as the locus for war crimes investigations. In particular, the conducting of investigations of war crime allegations by the UN Secretary-General's office or the Human Rights Council may be problematic because of limited fact-finding capacity and their daily immersion in politics.

Closing Address

Professor Emeritus Yoram Dinstein of Tel Aviv University and the U.S. Naval War College's Stockton Professor of International Law during academic years 1999–2000 and 2002–3 delivered the closing address. Professor Dinstein addressed five main areas: the definition of NIAC, thresholds in armed conflicts, *jus in bello*, intervention and interaction.

Professor Dinstein defined a NIAC as a conflict taking place within the borders of a single State, carried out between the central government of that State and organized armed groups, or, there being no effective government, between organized armed groups fighting each other. A NIAC can spill over across the borders and start another NIAC in a second country, as happened in the Great Lakes region of Africa. Still, the idea (endorsed by the Supreme Court of the United States) that a NIAC can be global is oxymoronic.

Next, Professor Dinstein pointed out that there were three thresholds in armed conflicts: two for NIACs and one for IAC, plus a sublevel of sporadic and isolated violence (e.g., riots) that is below the first threshold, and thus law enforcement in nature. The first threshold of NIACs is established by Common Article 3 of the four Geneva Conventions of 1949. This famous provision (which reflects customary international law) does not spell out what conditions have to be met for the first threshold to be crossed. The Appeals Chamber of the ICTY, in the 1995 *Tadić* case added the element that the violence must be "protracted."

The second threshold of NIACs is set up by AP II of 1977, which requires the exercise of control by an organized armed group over a part of the territory, enabling it to carry out sustained and concerted military operations. Professor Dinstein indicated that this requirement makes the distinction between a NIAC and forms of conflict not amounting to a NIAC much clearer: sustained and concerted military operations are the antonym of sporadic and isolated violence. The acid test of control of some territory explains the difference, for instance, between the then-current internal situations in Libya and Syria. In Libya (not counting the foreign intervention by fiat of the Security Council), there was no doubt a NIAC inasmuch as the insurgents exercised control over vast tracts of land. By contrast, the violence in Syria remained below the threshold—notwithstanding its great intensity and the fact that it was protracted—because no part of the territory was under the control of any insurgent organized armed group.

The third threshold means that the armed conflict amounts to an IAC, and this denotes that two or more States are pitted against each other.

Professor Dinstein then focused on the *jus in bello* in NIAC, noting that while there is a very remarkable trend in treaty law of growing convergence between the *jus in bello* applicable in IACs and that in NIAC, there cannot be a full merger of the law in the two types of armed conflict. He indicated that there are at least three insurmountable obstacles to such merger: (a) the domestic law will always consider insurgents to be traitors and therefore they cannot be accorded the status of prisoners of war by the government of the State (absent recognition of belligerency); (b) neutrality is not an issue, as there is only one State embroiled in a NIAC; and (c) the whole body of law relating to belligerent occupation is irrelevant to NIACs since neither the government nor the insurgents can be in belligerent occupation of their own land. There are additional, less compelling problems relating to the legality of certain means and methods of warfare, e.g., the legality of particular weapons and blockades.

The issue of intervention relates to military assistance requested from, or offered by, a foreign country when a NIAC is going on. International law permits foreign countries to extend military assistance to the State combating insurgents. If and when the foreign country does so, the armed conflict remains a NIAC, despite the participation of foreign troops in the hostilities, inasmuch as the foreign troops are not battling another State. However, if the foreign troops are deployed against the government, the armed conflict automatically crosses the third threshold and becomes an IAC. Moreover, even when the foreign troops arrive at the request of the government, consent to their presence can be withdrawn at any time. Once consent is withdrawn by the government, the foreign forces must leave. Failure to do so will result in the situation becoming an IAC.

The last issue Professor Dinstein addressed is interaction. He first indicated that it must be appreciated that an armed conflict can coexist with the law enforcement paradigm. Criminal activities do not cease when an armed conflict (either a NIAC or an IAC) breaks out. Indeed, usually crime rises in wartime, if only because there are numerous new crimes (such as black market activities or trading with the enemy). Ordinary crimes, even in the course of an armed conflict, are governed not by the *jus in bello* but by domestic criminal law, subject to the precepts of international human rights. Second, a NIAC can segue into an IAC; foreign intervention on behalf of insurgents is a prime example. But an IAC can also be the outcome of the implosion of a State torn apart by a NIAC and the continuation of the hostilities between several new sovereign States created on its ruins. Obviously, as far as fighters in the field are concerned, it may not always be easy to detect at what exact point a NIAC has morphed into an IAC (the situation in Bosnia in 1992 showed that lack of clarity in a graphic manner). It is therefore easier to analyze the situation when there has been an intervening period of time; for instance, Eritrea first rebelled successfully against Ethiopia in a NIAC, and then, several years later, started an IAC against the same country. Third, the reverse is also true: IACs can turn into NIACs. Thus, the IAC between the American-led coalition and the Baathist regime in Iraq came to a successful end, and the fighting that continues in Iraq is today no more than a NIAC. Fourth, a NIAC and an IAC can be waged concurrently in the same country. The best illustration is Afghanistan in 2001, where there was a NIAC between the Taliban and the Northern Alliance, and (starting in October of that year) a separate IAC between the United States (supported by its allies) and the Taliban. Fifth, as indicated by General Ferrer with respect to the Philippines, there may even be several unrelated NIACs going on in the same country simultaneously, where different organized armed groups fight the same central government while having diverse—and perhaps clashing—aims. All this can cause confusion, especially since governments are often "in denial," reversing the thresholds. That is to say, when governments are engaged in an IAC, they tend to claim that the armed conflict is no more than a NIAC. When they are caught in a NIAC, they are inclined to maintain that the violence is sporadic and below the NIAC threshold.

Professor Dinstein concluded by recognizing that times are changing and that NIAC law must change with them.

KENNETH WATKIN
2011–12 Charles H. Stockton
Professor of International Law
U.S. Naval War College

ANDREW J. NORRIS
Captain, U.S. Coast Guard
International Law Department
U.S. Naval War College

PART I

OPENING ADDRESS

I

"Small Wars": The Legal Challenges

Kenneth Watkin*

Rear Admiral Christenson, Ladies and Gentlemen.

Let me begin by saying what a pleasure it is to finally be here at the Naval War College delivering opening remarks at the annual international law conference. I say "finally" because as many of you know I took a detour, quite literally. While driving here last June to look for accommodations, I received a phone call asking if I would be a Foreign Observer on the Israeli independent commission investigating the Gaza maritime incident of May 31, 2010. I accepted and the College was very gracious in delaying my start and, I must say, patient in waiting for my return.

I am not going to comment on the commission, in part because its work is still ongoing; however, Part One of its report dealing with the blockade is available on the commission website for those who have an interest in the law governing such operations.[1] I will say, however, that if I thought traveling to the Middle East a year ago would be my last connection with the Naval War College for a while I was completely mistaken. Perhaps it should have come as no surprise given the subject matter of the inquiry, but it seemed everywhere I turned I found myself in touch with someone or a learned publication connected to this College.

The list of former Stockton Professors was itself impressive. They included, most obviously, Mike Schmitt and Wolff Heintschel von Heinegg, who directly assisted the commission, but also inevitably reference had to be made to the

* Stockton Professor, U.S. Naval War College.

influential works of other Stockton Professors, such as Yoram Dinstein[2] and my fellow Canadian Leslie Green.[3] Craig Allen's article "Limits on the Use of Force in Maritime Operations in Support of WMD Counter-Proliferation Initiatives," found in the eighty-first edition of the International Law Studies series[4] (the "Blue Book"), was particularly informative regarding the law on stopping ships on the high seas. Articles such as Professor Allen's highlight the impact that the product of conferences like this can have on real-world international issues.[5]

The connection to the College did not stop there. Wolff Heintschel von Heinegg's contribution on blockade to the *Max Planck Encyclopedia of Public International Law* is world leading.[6] The International Institute of Humanitarian Law's Rules of Engagement Handbook,[7] brought to life under the steady hand of Dennis Mandsager, provided guidance in an area often ignored by international lawyers: the right to individual personal self-defense, as opposed to State self-defense, under international law. In addition, the book *Naval Blockades and Seapower*,[8] edited by two professors from the Naval War College, Bruce A. Elleman and S.C.M. Paine, provided an excellent historical perspective on blockades and maritime interdiction. Finally, NWP 1-14M, *The Commander's Handbook on the Law of Naval Operations*,[9] a product of the International Law Department, served not only as an essential source on the law governing blockades, but also, importantly, as an indication of the views of a specially affected State, like the United States, which then could be compared with the more international flavor of the 1994 *San Remo Manual*.[10] Quite impressive influence by the International Law Department, its alumni and the much broader Naval Warfare College community on an issue arising a world away. I can admit to feeling a considerable amount of humility given the work of my predecessors as I start my sojourn as the Stockton Professor.

However, we are not here to talk about blockade, but rather "non-international armed conflict," although the relative inattention paid to such conflicts by international lawyers until recently reminds me of the reference in the *San Remo Manual* regarding the participants having commenced their discussion of blockade law with the question of whether it was "entirely archaic," with some participants expressing the view it had fallen into "complete desuetude."[11] I personally can confirm that blockades—and blockade law—have not disappeared and it is clear that in looking at both history and the present situation non-international armed conflict has definitely not fallen into disuse.

I want to start with this quote by Colonel Callwell of, at that time, His Britannic Majesty's Forces, defining in 1906 a form of warfare known as "small wars": "campaigns undertaken to suppress rebellion and guerrilla warfare in all parts of the world where organized armies are struggling against opponents who will not meet them in the open field."[12]

Of course, these often are "non-international armed conflicts" by another name. Now in case anyone is wondering why a "Naval" War College is concerning itself with "small wars," one need not look farther than the United States Marine Corps, whose 1940 *Small Wars Manual* was not only the leading text on the subject in its day, but also identified such wars as representing the "normal and frequent operations of the Marine Corps."[13] Little has changed, when one considers that the Vietnam War and the ongoing conflict in Afghanistan qualify in various aspects as "small wars," although they are anything but small. I leave it up to you to consider whether the Navy and Marine Corps involvement in the air and missile strikes at the opening of the Libya operation constituted participation in yet another "small war."

"Small wars" are not new. Unfortunately, neither is the inability of the international community to provide the parties fighting such conflicts the comparatively extensive and clear legal framework that is in existence for State-versus-State conflict. Indeed, both operators and their legal advisors should get uncomfortable when reference has to be made to an international criminal law treaty, the 1998 Rome Statute,[14] for the clearest convention-based listing of the legal norms applicable to such conflict.[15] Indeed, in what is now over a century after Colonel Callwell's definition of "small wars" was presented, it is hard not to use the term "failure"—or at least more positively "limited success," if you are a "glass half full" individual—when considering how well, in terms of consensus and clarity, the articulation of the law of non-international armed conflict has fared.

As most of you are aware a big part of the reason for this "limited success" is that States themselves have been very reluctant, indeed often hostile, to the notion of clarifying this area of the law. Certainly, the unsuccessful efforts of the International Committee of the Red Cross (ICRC) to have the rules of international armed conflict apply equally to non-international ones during the negotiations of the 1949 Geneva Conventions stand out as one of a number of examples of that reluctance. What was left was the important, but exceptionally watered-down, Common Article 3 protections applicable to "conflicts not of an international character."[16] States, including the brand-new States of the post-colonial period, continued to be very concerned that their non-State opponents, existing and potential, would be "legitimized" by their being provided the same rights as States in a treaty regime governing armed conflict.[17] While I understand the *jus ad bellum* branch of international law governing the recourse to war concerns itself with State-versus-State conflict, and considerable effort is made to ensure the law governing the conduct of hostilities, *jus in bello*, applies equally to all participants, State and non-State alike, it is also clear to me one aspect of just war theory, fighting for a State as the "right authority" in order to have legitimacy, hangs like a dark cloud over the attempts to reach consensus on the legal regulation of non-international armed conflict. In particular, it impacts on issues such as status of participants, detention, targeting and direct participation in hostilities (DPH)—the common topics of contemporary media headlines. In addition, given the evident lack of consensus as to what law applies to these "small wars," it has left open a much broader and more vigorous dialogue regarding how and to what degree human rights law governs the use of force, the treatment of detainees and the accountability process in internal conflicts.

Despite claims that international humanitarian law can be applied in its entirety to non-international conflicts, and the policies of various States that seek to do just that, it appears to me that gaps remain. I also sense, at times, an element of fatigue setting in within the legal community regarding these issues. As someone mentioned to me recently as we were talking about an upcoming event, there is a feeling of "not yet another conference on the interface between human rights and humanitarian law." However, it cannot be a fatigue that is forged with a sense of resounding success. One decade into the twenty-first century many countries are still engaged in "small wars," both long- and short-term, and the requirement to resolve these issues remains more important than ever.

I believe there are a number of reasons why this area of the law must be clarified.

First, non-international armed conflict has been and remains the predominant form of warfare. Notwithstanding a growing concern over potential international armed conflicts with certain States flexing newfound economic and military powers, they remain just that, potential conflicts, which, should they arise, would largely be conducted within a comparatively well-developed framework of international law—although, as will be discussed shortly, not one without some disagreement. The same cannot be said for the existing and future "small wars" that will continue to occupy the attention of States, either because they are occurring within their territory or as a result of having deployed expeditionary forces to deal with them. Non-international armed conflict will not disappear in the same way that blockades were believed by some to have fallen into disuse.

The prevalence of non-international armed conflict has also been ensured by an approach that views only State-on-State conflict as "international" in character. However, such "pure" international armed conflicts are by definition increasingly rare. The effect of a determination that a conflict is non-international in character is that participants are then immersed in a legal environment that in many places lacks the clarity of its international counterpart. In an interesting historical note, such determinations can be made virtually overnight. In Afghanistan, as early as June 2002, there were declarations that the then-existing international armed conflict was over.[18] The conflict from that point was to be considered a non-international one. Of note, the U.S. Supreme Court in *Hamdan* subsequently adopted this categorization for the Afghanistan conflict in 2006.[19] One could wonder if the troops on the ground actually noticed the difference. I can tell you there was no change in the operational environment, the threat or the complexity of the operations they were conducting. I doubt the legal advice provided to them changed either. However, such debates regarding "form" often seem to occur without much thought of the resulting legal uncertainty they are imposing on participants. The debate over categorizing conflict does cause me to think at times of Michael Walzer and, if I can paraphrase him, I think it may fairly be said that lawyers do from time to time appear to construct paper worlds which fail at crucial points to correspond to the world in which everyone else lives.[20] It is no wonder that for many practitioners the key focus is on whether there is an "armed conflict" rather than on a struggle over assessing its degree of "international" or "non-international" character.

It is common to look at the Instructions for the Government of Armies of the United States in the Field of 1863, the famous Lieber Code, as a starting point in the effort to codify the rules governing armed conflict. It is quite ironic this effort commenced with a conflict that itself in contemporary terminology would be termed a "conflict not of an international character." Of course, we all know it better as a civil war. After nearly one hundred fifty years of working to regulate such armed conflict it seems the situation has become less clear. Perhaps the reason the Lieber Code managed to even get off the ground was that it was the product of one government rather than an international effort. In this respect the suggestion by John Bellinger, a former Department of State Legal Advisor, in an article on the law about detainee operations in contemporary conflict found in the 2011 *American Journal of International Law*[21] appears to have considerable merit. He suggests that specially affected States, those engaged in detention operations, should get together and work out a recommended common set of legal rules governing such operations given the inability of the international community to do so.[22]

Unfortunately things actually seem to be getting increasingly muddier. It was suggested at a conference I recently attended that because there were no "combatants" in non-international armed conflict there could be no "combatant privilege" for State armed forces. Further, the authority for a State to use deadly force would have to be found in domestic legislation of the State, even if those soldiers were fighting on the other side of the world. While I am at a loss to think of any State practice of prosecuting its own security forces on the basis there was no empowering domestic legislation, it would be interesting to know how many of the States represented in this room with troops serving in Afghanistan have such specific domestic legislation focused on targeting during a non-international armed conflict in a faraway land. I would suggest there is strong argument supporting the existence of a customary norm of providing State security forces a form of "privilege" in respect to the use of force in internal armed conflicts. Perhaps this will be an issue that can be discussed and clarified during this conference.

Second, the lack of clarity regarding the law of non-international armed conflict can have a profound and sometimes negative effect, not only on the victims of conflict, but also on States in terms of whether their actions are viewed as being legitimate. What if there had been a greater international consensus on the substantive law that applied to the detention, treatment, transfer and status review of unprivileged belligerents (if one can use that term in a non-international armed conflict) detained in the post-9/11 period? Would the potential for abuse and allegations of mistreatment have been the same? One cannot help but think that the dialogue would have been much different if there had been greater clarity in the law. An application of the policy of treating captured personnel under prisoner-of-war standards, without providing that status, or as security detainees under Geneva Convention IV could have been a practical, defensible and ultimately helpful approach. However, even now, some ten years after the issue first arose, an internationally agreed framework governing detainees in non-international armed conflict is lacking. That it remains a topic of academic debate at this conference demonstrates the distance that must still be traveled on this issue before "success" can be declared.

Third, I also sense from time to time that there is a belief that the issues applicable to non-international conflict have no real relevance to conflicts between States. Perhaps this is simply a reflection of the lack of interest demonstrated by States themselves in the regulation of non-international armed conflict. However, there can be significant "cross-pollination" of legal issues. For example, a number of issues that arise in the conduct of internal "small wars" are also inherent in an insurgency being carried out during belligerent occupation, which, of course, occurs during international armed conflict. Both occupation and internal conflicts ultimately involve what General Sir Rupert Smith has called a "war amongst the people."[23] In addition, it is highly likely that any future war between States would involve not only clashes between regular military forces but also "irregular forces," "organized armed groups" or even individual civilians acting on the State's behalf. This includes in the cyber realm. Any suggestion that legal issues in non-international armed conflict are not relevant to international conflict would have to address the controversial aspects of Additional Protocol I[24] that appear for nearly thirty-five years to have stood in the way of its universal acceptance and application to international armed conflicts.[25]

Fourth, and finally, the unwillingness of States to engage in clarifying what law applies to non-international armed conflict has in many respects negatively impacted on their ability to influence how that law will be, and is presently being, shaped. As Yoram Dinstein has noted in the most recent edition of his book *The Conduct of Hostilities under the Law of International Armed Conflict*, "[i]nternational law must march in lockstep with the compelling demands of reality."[26] Gaps, both real and perceived, are being filled through means such as unofficial restatements of the law and manuals of rules crafted by various groups of legal "experts." States do send officials in their personal capacity, although they are often outnumbered, and ultimately lack the voice that they would have in official treaty negotiations. The results can be problematic for States. One example is reflected in the ICRC's DPH study.[27] Now, I am critical of a number of aspects of the study;[28] however, at the same time it must be noted that the ICRC courageously took on one of the most perplexing and difficult issues of the contemporary law of armed conflict—one that States appear to have been "unwilling or unable," to use a contemporary phrase, to address.

My goal today is not to dwell on specific details of the DPH study but rather to refer to it as being representative of a trend of suggesting that States should be held to a different and ultimately more onerous standard than their non-State opponents. The study sets out significantly broader parameters for "membership" in regular armed forces, and therefore for the forces' ultimate targetability, than it does for members in the "organized armed groups" against which they are fighting. In effect, it seems to turn the *jus ad bellum* principle of "right authority" on its head. A principle that provided the basis for giving prisoner-of-war status to those fighting for a State, thereby privileging them over their non-State counterparts, now seems to mean, if you accept the thesis, those same State actors, indeed many of you in this auditorium, can be more easily killed than persons performing exactly the same function in an opposing non-State organized armed group. Indeed the non-State counterparts would be protected from being targeted by being considered to be "civilians."

Ultimately, this approach seems to have a "human rights–like" flavor, where it is the State that is always held more responsible and accountable. In a 2010 report to the Human Rights Council, the Special Rapporteur on Extrajudicial, Summary or Arbitrary Executions, when looking at the DPH study, suggested that while some may see an inequity between State forces and non-State actors identified in the study, it is one built into international humanitarian law in order to protect civilians.[29] It is not immediately clear to me that the statistics from the Afghanistan conflict support this approach. Indeed, it is reported that in Afghanistan in 2010, 75 percent of civilian casualties were caused by insurgents.[30] It is difficult to see how making insurgents who have demonstrated little reticence about killing uninvolved civilians more difficult to target than their State counterparts enhances the protection for those civilians. It also points to one of the acknowledged challenges of applying human rights norms to contemporary armed conflict. International humanitarian law has long sought to have equal application to both sides of the conflict, the issue of prisoner-of-war status notwithstanding. Adding new inequity to the existing law is not likely to aid in reaching consensus among such significant stakeholders in international law as States.

It seems to me that approaches which do not rely on broadly accepted international law—such as approximating what any other detainee captured under the existing treaty regime in armed conflict would receive, in deciding on the standards for the treatment of those captured in non-international conflict—or which do not evenly apply the law in respect of targeting to all parties to the conflict, are more likely to create obstacles rather than help resolve these fundamental issues.

At the same time, it is difficult to see how States can complain about new "soft law" and manuals of rules if they do not become more strategically and fully engaged in the processes that are being used to clarify the law. Ultimately, attempts will be made to fill voids with or without State participation, and with good reason. Civilians must be protected from the ravages of war. The question is the degree to which States want to influence that process.

There are important, indeed essential, issues that need to be resolved. Impressive work is being done. One example is the 2006 Institute of International Humanitarian Law *Manual on the Law of Non-International Armed Conflict*[31]—no surprise, again with a link to the Naval War College, its authors being Yoram Dinstein, Mike Schmitt and Charles Garraway. Unfortunately, it is a work that has not received the publicity that it should and the unsettled State of the law demands. As editor of this year's "Blue Book," I will be interested to see how many authors refer to this manual in their scholarly assessments of non-international armed conflict.

Finally, there is this conference, and the inevitable articles in the "Blue Book" that will result. I encourage all of you to participate fully and ask probing questions of the panelists, thereby shaping the discussion. Indeed, you never know. You, yourself, might someday unexpectedly take a detour and become immersed in a complicated legal problem related to a "small war" occurring on the other side of the world. I do know that you will be able to search the product of this conference, and others like it here at the Naval War College, for guidance when dealing with non-international armed conflict—the difficult humanitarian law issue of our time. Thank you.

Notes

1. Jacob Turkel et al., 1 The Public Commission to Examine the Maritime Incident of 31 May 2010 (2011), *available at* http://turkel-committee.gov.il/files/wordocs//8707200211english.pdf.

2. YORAM DINSTEIN, THE CONDUCT OF HOSTILITIES UNDER THE LAW OF INTERNATIONAL ARMED CONFLICT (2d ed. 2010).

3. LESLIE C. GREEN, THE CONTEMPORARY LAW OF ARMED CONFLICT (3d ed. 2008).

4. Craig H. Allen, *Limits on the Use of Force in Maritime Operations in Support of WMD Counter-Proliferation Initiatives*, *in* INTERNATIONAL LAW CHALLENGES: HOMELAND SECURITY AND COMBATING TERRORISM 77 (Thomas McK. Sparks & Glenn M. Sulmasy eds., 2006) (Vol. 81, U.S. Naval War College International Law Studies).

5. *See* GEORGE WALKER, THE TANKER WAR, 1980–88: LAW AND POLICY 389–394 (2000) (Vol. 74, U.S. Naval War College International Law Studies).

6. Wolff Heintschel von Heinegg, *Blockade*, *in* MAX PLANCK ENCYCLOPEDIA OF PUBLIC INTERNATIONAL LAW (Rüdiger Wolfrum ed., 2010); Wolff Heintschel von Heinegg, *Naval Blockade*, *in* INTERNATIONAL LAW ACROSS THE SPECTRUM OF CONFLICT: ESSAYS IN HONOUR OF PROFESSOR L.C. GREEN ON THE OCCASION OF HIS EIGHTIETH BIRTHDAY 203 (Michael N. Schmitt ed., 2000) (Vol. 75, U.S. Naval War College International Law Studies).

7. INTERNATIONAL INSTITUTE OF HUMANITARIAN LAW, SAN REMO HANDBOOK ON RULES OF ENGAGEMENT (2009), *available at* http://www.iihl.org/iihl/Documents/ROE%20handbook%20ENG%20May%202011%20PRINT%20RUN.pdf.

8. NAVAL BLOCKADES AND SEAPOWER: STRATEGIES AND COUNTER-STRATEGIES, 1805–2005 (Bruce A. Elleman and S.C.M. Paine eds., 2006).

9. U.S. Navy, U.S. Marine Corps & U.S. Coast Guard, The Commander's Handbook on the Law of Naval Operations, NWP 1-14M/MCWP 5-12.1/COMDTPUB P5800.7A (2007), *available at* http://www.usnwc.edu/getattachment/a9b8e92d-2c8d-4779-9925-0defea93325c/1-14M_(Jul _2007)_(NWP.

10. SAN REMO MANUAL ON INTERNATIONAL LAW APPLICABLE TO ARMED CONFLICTS AT SEA (Louise Doswald-Beck ed., 1995).

11. *Id.* at 176.

12. C.E. CALLWELL, SMALL WARS: THEIR PRINCIPLES & PRACTICE 21 (3d ed. 1996) (1896).

13. UNITED STATES MARINE CORPS, SMALL WARS MANUAL ¶ 1-1(d) (1940).

14. Rome Statute of the International Criminal Court, July 17, 1998, 2187 U.N.T.S. 90.

15. *See* YORAM DINSTEIN, WAR, AGGRESSION AND SELF-DEFENCE 6 n.11 (4th ed. 2005).

16. Convention for the Amelioration of the Condition of the Wounded and Sick in Armed Forces in the Field art. 3, Aug. 12, 1949, 6 U.S.T. 3114, 75 U.N.T.S. 31; Convention for the Amelioration of the Condition of Wounded, Sick and Shipwrecked Members of Armed Forces at Sea art. 3, Aug. 12, 1949, 6 U.S.T. 3217, 75 U.N.T.S. 85; Convention Relative to the Treatment of Prisoners of War art. 3, Aug. 12, 1949, 6 U.S.T. 3316, 75 U.N.T.S. 135; Convention Relative to the Protection of Civilian Persons in Time of War art. 3, Aug. 12, 1949, 6 U.S.T. 3516, 75 U.N.T.S. 287.

17. *See* COMMENTARY TO GENEVA CONVENTION III RELATIVE TO THE TREATMENT OF PRISONERS OF WAR 32 (Jean S. Pictet ed., 1960), *available at* http://www.cicr.org/ihl.nsf/COM/375-590006?OpenDocument (Pictet outlines the reaction by a number of States regarding a wholesale application of the Conventions to internal conflict as: "It was said that it would cover all forms of insurrections, rebellion, and the break-up of States, and even plain brigandage. Attempts to protect individuals might well prove to be at the expense of the equally legitimate protection of the State. To compel the Government of a State in the throes of internal conflict

to apply to such a conflict the whole of the provisions of a Convention expressly concluded to cover the case of war would mean giving its enemies, who might be no more than a handful of rebels or common brigands, the status of belligerents, and possibly even a certain degree of legal recognition.").

18. *See* Letter from Philip Spoerri, ICRC Legal Adviser, to Mr. Doherty, Clerk of the Committee on International Development of the House of Commons (Nov. 28, 2002), *available at* http://www.publications.parliament.uk/pa/cm200203/cmselect/cmintdev/84/84ap09.htm (where it is stated that "[f]ollowing the convening of the Loya Jirga in Kabul in June 2002 and the subsequent establishment of an Afghan transitional government on 19 June 2002 . . . the ICRC no longer views the ongoing military operations in Afghanistan directed against suspected Taliban or other armed groups as an international armed conflict.").

19. Hamdan v. Rumsfeld, 548 U.S. 557 (2006).

20. MICHAEL WALZER, JUST AND UNJUST WARS xix (2000).

21. John B. Bellinger III & Vijay M. Padmanabhan, *Detention Operations in Contemporary Conflicts: Four Challenges for the Geneva Conventions and Other Existing Law*, 105 AMERICAN JOURNAL OF INTERNATIONAL LAW 201 (2011).

22. *Id.* at 243.

23. RUPERT SMITH, THE UTILITY OF FORCE: THE ART OF WAR IN THE MODERN WORLD 3–4 (2007).

24. Protocol Additional to the Geneva Conventions of 12 August 1949, and Relating to the Protection of Victims of International Armed Conflicts, June 8, 1977, 1125 U.N.T.S. 3.

25. Ronald Reagan, *The U.S. Decision Not to Ratify Protocol I to the Geneva Conventions on the Protection of War Victims: Letter of Transmittal*, 81 AMERICAN JOURNAL OF INTERNATIONAL LAW 910 (1987).

26. DINSTEIN, *supra* note 2, at 297.

27. NILS MELZER, INTERNATIONAL COMMITTEE OF THE RED CROSS, INTERPRETIVE GUIDANCE ON THE NOTION OF DIRECT PARTICIPATION IN HOSTILITIES UNDER INTERNATIONAL HUMANITARIAN LAW (2009).

28. Kenneth W. Watkin, *Opportunity Lost: Organized Armed Groups and the ICRC "Direct Participation in Hostilities" Interpretive Guidance*, 42 NEW YORK UNIVERSITY JOURNAL OF INTERNATIONAL LAW AND POLITICS 641 (2010).

29. *See* Report of the Special Rapporteur on Extrajudicial, Summary or Arbitrary Executions, *Study on Targeted Killings* ¶ 67, Human Rights Council, U.N. Doc. A/HRC/14/24/Add.6 (May 28, 2010) (by Philip Alston), *available at* http://www2.ohchr.org/english/bodies/hrcouncil/docs/14session/A.HRC.14.24.Add6.pdf.

30. *See Afghanistan Civilian Casualties: Year by Year, Month by Month*, THE GUARDIAN, http://www.guardian.co.uk/news/datablog/2010/aug/10/afghanistan-civilian-casualties-statistics (last visited Nov. 9, 2011).

31. MICHAEL N. SCHMITT, CHARLES H.B. GARRAWAY & YORAM DINSTEIN, THE MANUAL ON THE LAW OF NON-INTERNATIONAL ARMED CONFLICT WITH COMMENTARY (2006), *available at* http://www.dur.ac.uk/resources/law/NIACManualIYBHR15th.pdf.

PART II

OVERVIEW: THE LAW IN NON-INTERNATIONAL ARMED CONFLICTS

II

Will-o'-the-Wisp? The Search for Law in Non-International Armed Conflicts

John F. Murphy*

In his remarks as a member of the Types of NIACs and Applicable Law Panel at the Naval War College's International Law Conference on Non-International Armed Conflict in the 21st Century, held from June 21 to 23, 2011, David Graham described the law of non-international armed conflict as being located at the "vanishing point of the law of war."

This is not surprising, because, as Graham further noted, States resist the application of international law to their struggles with rebels. In particular, they resist according status to rebels by applying the law of armed conflict (LOAC) to them. Rather, they prefer to deal with rebels under their own national criminal laws, free from any constraints that might be imposed by the law of armed conflict. For example, Charles Garraway, speaking on the same panel as Graham, pointed out that the United Kingdom never acknowledged "the Troubles" in Northern Ireland as an "armed conflict" to which the law of armed conflict might apply.

From a historical perspective, express treaty law governing non-international armed conflict was formerly virtually non-existent. After the carnage of World War II, and the extreme brutality of the Nazi Germany forces, however, there was a

* Professor of Law, Villanova University School of Law. I want to acknowledge the excellent research assistance of Bernard G. Dennis and Megan L. O'Rourke, both second-year students at the Villanova University School of Law.

marked change of attitude. As reported by Gary D. Solis in his 2010 magisterial treatise:

> The framers of the 1949 Conventions determined that there must be some minimal international humanitarian protections for the victims of internal armed conflicts—conflicts occurring within one state's borders, not involving a second nation. World War II revealed the stark absence of protections for civilians in wartime. To raise new protections would involve a departure from Geneva's previously uninterrupted fixation on conflicts between states and a certain disregard of the long-entrenched act of state doctrine. The international community was unanimous, however, that it could not stand by while depredations such as those committed by the Nazis took place in future conflicts, internal or not. Not even in the United Nations Charter is there a similar effort to regulate intrastate armed force.[1]

The result was Common Article 3 of the 1949 Geneva Conventions.[2] It is the only article in the Geneva Conventions that covers internal armed conflict, and "when common Article 3 applies, *no other part of the 1949 Geneva Conventions applies.*"[3] Common Article 3 provides:

> In the case of armed conflict not of an international character occurring in the territory of one of the High Contracting Parties, each Party to the conflict shall be bound to apply, at a minimum, the following provisions:
>
> (1) Persons taking no active part in the hostilities, including members of armed forces, who have laid down their arms and those placed *hors de combat* by sickness, wounds, detention, or any other cause, shall in all circumstances be treated humanely . . . .

As Solis notes, "There follows a brief list of prohibitions, acknowledged to be incomplete: violence to life and person, in particular murder, mutilation, cruel treatment, and torture; the taking of hostages; humiliating and degrading treatment; and the passing of sentences without previous judgments from regularly constituted courts."[4] The positive obligation that Common Article 3 imposes on States parties to the Geneva Conventions is, in non-international armed conflicts, to treat those who are *hors de combat* (out of the fight) humanely. The drafters of Common Article 3 decided, however, not to elaborate on the meaning of "humane treatment."[5]

The International Committee of the Red Cross's (ICRC's) study of customary international law does provide generalized guidance as to what constitutes humane treatment:

> The actual meaning of "humane treatment" is not spelled out . . . . The requirement . . . is an overarching concept. It is generally understood that the detailed rules found in

> international humanitarian law and human rights law give expression to the meaning of "humane treatment." . . . However, these rules do not necessarily express the full meaning of what is meant by humane treatment, as this notion develops over time under the influence of changes in society.[6]

By its terms, Common Article 3 applies only to non-international armed conflicts. As shall be seen below, however, international and national court decisions have declared that its humanitarian norms are so basic that, today, Common Article 3 extends to international armed conflicts as well.

At this early stage in this essay, it is important to note that the international and national jurisprudence that has declared Common Article 3 extends to international armed conflict illustrates a major difficulty with Common Article 3: because of its sparse wording and inherent ambiguities, Common Article 3 raises more questions than it answers, and, in particular, these include issues of when it applies and whether it can be the basis for criminal prosecutions in international or national tribunals.

Before we turn to some of these issues, we need to note the second primary source of treaty law on non-international armed conflicts, Additional Protocol II to the 1949 Geneva Conventions.[7] Like Additional Protocol I,[8] which concerns international armed conflicts, Additional Protocol II is a supplement to the 1949 Geneva Conventions and does not amend or replace any part of them.[9] Although Additional Protocol II has 166 States parties,[10] a number of major States, including the United States and Israel, for example, are not parties, and it is unclear what provisions, if any, of the Protocol represent customary international law.[11] Moreover, Additional Protocol II is a good example of the unwillingness of States to be governed by international law in their internal conflicts with rebel groups. This is because the "threshold" of applicability of Protocol II to a non-international armed conflict is extremely high. Under Article 1(1), Protocol II only applies to conflicts between the armed forces of a State party "and dissident armed forces or other organized armed groups which, under responsible command, exercise such control over a part of the territory as to enable them to carry out sustained and concerted military operations and to implement this Protocol." Paragraph 2 of Article 1 provides that the Protocol "shall not apply to situations of internal disturbances and tensions, such as riots, isolated and sporadic acts of violence and other acts of a similar nature, as not being armed conflicts."

The result of these explicit limitations is that Additional Protocol II is basically a non-operational treaty. As one commentator has noted, the international criminal tribunals for the former Yugoslavia and for Rwanda

> have produced very little jurisprudence related to Additional Protocol II . . . and no accused has been convicted for a violation of the Protocol. . . . The limited categories of armed conflicts to which Additional Protocol II may be said to apply and doubts as to the extent to which it is now part of customary international law have deterred the Prosecution from entering the realm of Additional Protocol II with much enthusiasm, preferring instead to rely on common Article 3 . . . .[12]

Similarly, George Aldrich, who was the head of the U.S. delegation to the negotiations on the Protocols, has written dismissively: "Protocol II . . . affords very limited protections and has escape clauses designed to make its applicability easily deniable. In the end, the only useful result of Protocol II may be to make it somewhat more likely that [Common] Article 3 . . . may be found applicable in lieu of Protocol II."[13]

I. Filling the Gaps in and Expanding the Coverage of Common Article 3

Jean-Philippe Lavoyer, a former head of the ICRC's Legal Division, has contended that the current law of armed conflict is not the major problem, but rather it is the failure to implement it in good faith.[14] This seems clear, but there are at the least major differences as to interpretation of the existing rules, even among the leading experts of developed Western States, to say nothing of on a worldwide basis. Ideally, these ambiguities would be resolved by international negotiations to revise the existing law. However, as Dr. Lavoyer has noted, the risk of this route is that it might open Pandora's box and result in a much less rather than more satisfactory law of armed conflict.[15]

As to gaps in Common Article 3, it is important to note that neither the Geneva Conventions, including Common Article 3, nor Additional Protocol I contains a definition of an "armed conflict." In contrast, as we have seen, Additional Protocol II, in paragraphs 1 and 2 of Article 1, defines non-international armed conflicts in such a way as to sharply limit the scope of the Protocol. But in 1995, in the *Tadić* Interlocutory Appeal on Jurisdiction,[16] the International Criminal Tribunal for the former Yugoslavia (ICTY) stepped into the breach and addressed the preliminary issue of the existence of an armed conflict in response to a contention by the defendant that there had been no active hostilities in the area of the alleged crimes at the relevant time:

> [W]e find that an armed conflict exists whenever there is a resort to armed force between States or protracted armed violence between governmental authorities and organized armed groups or between such groups within a State. International

> humanitarian law applies from the initiation of such armed conflicts and extends beyond the cessation of hostilities until a general conclusion of peace is reached; or, in the case of internal conflicts, a peaceful settlement is achieved. Until that moment, international humanitarian law continues to apply in the whole territory of the warring States or, in the case of internal conflicts, the whole territory under the control of a party, whether or not actual combat takes place there.[17]

This definition covers both international and non-international conflicts. There is a question whether under it, the U.S. conflict with Al-Qaeda qualifies as an armed conflict. As I suggested in another forum,

> [t]he only time this conflict could have qualified as an international armed conflict would have been when the United States invaded Afghanistan in 2001 and then only to the extent that Al-Qaeda forces were integrated into the Taliban forces, the de facto army of Afghanistan. At present . . . both the Taliban and Al-Qaeda are fighting as insurgents in Afghanistan, and it is arguable that the conflict there now is an internal armed conflict.[18]

By now it is well known that in *Hamdan v. Rumsfeld*[19] the Supreme Court rejected the assertion by the U.S. government that since Al-Qaeda was not a State and had not accepted that it would be governed by the rules set forth in the Geneva Conventions, its affiliates could not invoke their protections. Rather, a plurality of the Court held that the so-called "war on terror" was a non-international armed conflict, and therefore that at a minimum Common Article 3 applies to the conflict with Al-Qaeda. To be sure, this holding has been subject to considerable criticism, best illustrated perhaps by Yoram Dinstein's argument that "from the vantage point of international law . . . a non-international armed conflict cannot possibly assume global proportions."[20] There are supporters of the Court's holding, however, and there is no consensus on this issue.[21]

In light of current developments, the distinction between international and non-international armed conflict may be becoming irrelevant, at least as long as an "armed conflict" is present. As Kenneth Watkin has noted, there is a "trend under humanitarian law to apply the established rules for governing international armed conflict to its non-international counterpart."[22] This trend, however, has not been based on the conclusion of new conventions, or even the revision of old conventions, on the law of armed conflict. Rather, it has been based on international judicial decisions, especially the decision of the ICTY Appeals Chamber in *Prosecutor v. Tadić*, which claimed in 1995 that "it cannot be denied that customary rules have developed to govern internal strife."[23] The Tribunal identified some of these rules as covering

> such areas as protection of civilians from hostilities, in particular from indiscriminate attacks, protection of civilian objects, in particular cultural property, protection of all those who do not (or no longer) take active part in hostilities, as well as prohibition of means of warfare proscribed in international armed conflicts and ban of certain methods of conducting hostilities.[24]

The ICRC has also actively promoted the idea of applying the rules governing international armed conflict to non-international armed conflict through the customary international law process, especially in its two-volume *Customary International Humanitarian Law* study.[25] Customary international law has long played an important role in the development of the law of armed conflict, as illustrated by the Martens Clause, which was named after Frederick de Martens, a leading Russian international lawyer who was a Russian delegate to the Hague Peace Conferences of 1889 and 1907. The Martens Clause first appeared in the preambles of Hague Convention (II) of 1899 and Hague Convention (IV) of 1907 Respecting the Laws and Customs of War on Land.[26] A recent example of the Martens Clause may be found in Article 1(2) of Protocol I of 1977, which reads as follows: "In cases not covered by this Protocol or by other international agreements, civilians and combatants remain under the protection and authority of the principles of international law derived from established custom, from the principles of humanity and from the dictates of public conscience."

It should be noted, however, that the nature of the customary international law process has become increasingly controversial. Patrick Kelly, a leading critic, has suggested that in many—perhaps most—instances of alleged customary international law norms, there may be little clear evidence that the vast majority of States have accepted the norm as a legal obligation.[27] The result is that, according to Kelly, "much of international law is announced in books and articles with little input from nations . . . . Much of CIL [customary international law] is a fiction."[28] It should come as no surprise therefore that the methodology employed by the ICRC in its study of customary international humanitarian law has itself come under attack—most particularly, in the November 3, 2006 joint letter from John Bellinger III, Legal Adviser, U.S. Department of State, and William J. Haynes, General Counsel, U.S. Department of Defense, to Dr. Jakob Kellenberger, the President of the ICRC, setting forth the U.S. government's "initial reactions" to the ICRC's study.[29] The letter states that "based on our review so far, we are concerned about the methodology used to ascertain rules and about whether the authors have proffered sufficient facts and evidence to support those rules." Although noting that "[g]iven the Study's large scope, we have not yet been able to complete a detailed review of its conclusions," the authors go on to state that they thought it would be "constructive to outline some of our basic methodological concerns and, by examining a few of the rules set forth in the Study, to illustrate how these flaws call into question some of the Study's conclusions."[30]

A detailed discussion of the authors' concerns is beyond the scope of this essay. For present purposes it suffices to note that the letter finds fault with both the study's assessment of State practice and its approach to the *opinio juris* requirement. The authors also find fault with the study's formulation of the rules and its commentary. Significantly, the letter finds that these faults contribute to

> two more general errors in the Study that are of particular concern to the United States:
>
> First, the assertion that a significant number of rules contained in the Additional Protocols to the Geneva Conventions have achieved the status of customary international law applicable to all States, including with respect to a significant number of States (including the United States and a number of other States that have been involved in armed conflict since the Protocols entered into force) that have declined to become a party to those Protocols; and
>
> Second, the assertion that certain rules contained in the Geneva Conventions and the Additional Protocols have become binding as a matter of customary international law in internal armed conflict notwithstanding the fact that there is little evidence in support of those propositions.[31]

In closing the letter the authors indicated their "appreciation for the ICRC's continued efforts in this important area, and hope that the material provided in this letter and in the attachment will initiate a constructive, in-depth dialogue with the ICRC and others on the subject."[32]

In July 2007, Jean-Marie Henckaerts responded to the Bellinger/Haynes letter.[33] His response focused largely on methodological issues and, following the structure of the U.S. comments, addressed the following questions:

> 1. What density of practice is required for the formation of customary international law and what types of practice are relevant?
>
> 2. How did the Study assess the existence of *opinio juris*?
>
> 3. What is the weight of the commentaries on the rules?
>
> 4. What are the broader implications of the Study with respect to Additional Protocols I and II and the law on non-international armed conflicts in particular?

Because U.S. comments also addressed four particular rules of the study, Henckaerts's response dealt with the main aspects of those comments as part of the discussion of the methodological issues. The rules included "Rule 31 (protection of humanitarian relief personnel), Rule 45 (prohibition on causing long-term widespread and severe damage to the environment), Rule 78 (prohibition of the use of antipersonnel exploding bullets) and Rule 157 (right to establish universal jurisdiction over war crimes)."[34]

As with respect to the Bellinger/Haynes letter, this is not the time or place to set forth a detailed discussion of Henckaerts's responses to the U.S. concerns. For present purposes, it suffices to note that the ICRC rejects the U.S. contention that there is little evidence to support the assertion that certain rules in the Geneva Conventions and the Additional Protocols have become binding as a matter of customary international law in internal armed conflict. On the contrary, in the ICRC view:

> [T]he conclusion of the Study that many rules contained in the Geneva Conventions and the Additional Protocols have become binding as a matter of customary international law in non-international armed conflict is the result of state practice to this effect. . . .
>
> [D]evelopments of international humanitarian law since the wars in the former Yugoslavia and Rwanda point towards an application of many areas of humanitarian law to non-international armed conflicts. For example, every humanitarian law treaty adopted since 1996 has been made applicable to both international and non-international armed conflicts. . . .
>
> The criminal tribunals and courts set up, first for the former Yugoslavia and Rwanda and later for Sierra Leone, deal exclusively or mostly with violations committed in non-international armed conflicts. Similarly, the investigations and prosecutions currently under way before the International Criminal Court are related to violations committed in situations of internal armed conflict. These developments are also sustained by other practice such as military manuals, national legislation and case-law, official statements and resolutions of international organizations and conferences. In this respect particular care was taken in Volume I to identify specific practice related to non-international armed conflict and, on that basis, to provide a separate analysis of the customary nature of the rules in such conflicts. Finally, where practice was less extensive in non-international armed conflicts, the corresponding rule is acknowledged to be only "arguably" applicable in non-international armed conflicts.
>
> When it comes to "operational practice" related to non-international armed conflicts, there is probably a large mix of official practice supporting the rules and of their outright violation. To suggest, therefore, that there is not enough practice to sustain such a broad conclusion is to confound the value of existing "positive" practice with the many

> violations of the law in non-international armed conflicts. This would mean that we let violators dictate the law or stand in the way of rules emerging. The result would be that a whole range of heinous practices committed in non-international armed conflict would no longer be considered unlawful and that commanders ordering such practices would no longer be responsible for them. This is not what states have wanted. They have wanted the law to apply to non-international armed conflicts and they have wanted commanders to be responsible and accountable.[35]

The Bellinger/Haynes letter, in challenging the ICRC study's assertion that certain rules contained in the Geneva Conventions and the Additional Protocols have become binding as a matter of customary international law in internal armed conflict, claims that "there is little evidence in support of those propositions."[36] The Henckaerts response attempts to provide such evidence. First, it correctly notes that "every humanitarian law treaty adopted since 1996 has been made applicable to both international and non-international armed conflict."[37] But none of these treaties extends any of the provisions of the Geneva Conventions or of the Additional Protocols to non-international armed conflict, so the relevance of this State practice to the issue is questionable at best.

Similarly, it is, of course, correct that the International Criminal Tribunals for the former Yugoslavia and Rwanda, as well as the globally focused International Criminal Court and the hybrid tribunal for Sierra Leone, deal exclusively or mostly with violations committed in non-international armed conflicts. The basic issue faced by these various tribunals is whether the concept of war crimes and grave breaches are applicable in internal as well as international armed conflict. Resolution of this issue in turn depends upon the statutes of the various tribunals and the tribunals' interpretation of their terms.

As Gary Solis has noted, the ICTY Appeals Chamber, in its decision in the *Tadić* case, first answered the basic question in the negative. According to the Appeals Chamber, "[we] must conclude that, in the present state of development of the law, Article 2 of the [ICTY] Statute ["Grave breaches of the Geneva Conventions of 1949"] only applies to offences committed within the context of international armed conflicts."[38] By its decision the Appeals Chamber reversed the Trial Chamber's ruling to the contrary. At the same time, later in its decision, in *dicta,* the Appeals Chamber foreshadowed later change when it stated,

> [W]e have no doubt that they [violations of rules of warfare in international law] entail individual responsibility, regardless of whether they are committed in internal or international armed conflicts. Principles and rules of humanitarian law reflect "elementary considerations of humanity" widely recognized as the mandatory minimum for conduct in armed conflicts of any kind.[39]

As Solis notes, six years later the Appeals Chamber took the step it had foreshadowed in its *dicta* in *Tadić*.[40] It ruled in the *Celebici* case that "to maintain a legal distinction between the two legal regimes and their criminal consequences in respect of similarly egregious acts because of the differences in the nature of the conflicts would ignore the very purpose of the Geneva Conventions."[41]

Many commentators welcomed the *Celebici* ruling. Guénaël Mettraux, for example, opined that "[t]he acknowledgement by the *ad hoc* [Yugoslav and Rwanda] Tribunals that much of the law of international armed conflicts would apply in the context of internal armed conflicts may be one of their most significant jurisprudential achievements, as far as war crimes are concerned."[42] For his part, Theodor Meron emphatically stated, "There is no moral justification, and no truly persuasive legal reason, for treating perpetrators of atrocities in internal conflicts more leniently than those engaged in international wars."[43]

This commentator, however, is concerned that both the Yugoslav and Rwanda tribunals and commentators such as Mettraux and Meron may be setting forth the *de lege ferenda* rather than the *lex lata.* To put it somewhat differently, they may be failing to distinguish between the *is* and the *ought*. There would seem to be compelling reasons for applying much of the law of international armed conflict in the context of non-international armed conflicts, but it is not clear that States, acting through treaties or the customary international law process, have done so. Neither judges on the Yugoslav and Rwanda tribunals nor prominent scholars, despite the important roles they play in the international legal process in general, have been endowed with the capacity to make that extension of the law.

On the other hand, Solis may be on sounder ground when he reports that "[t]he domestic legislation of fifty-four states criminalizes serious violations of LOAC in internal armed conflicts."[44] Such legislation is generally regarded as constituting a form of State practice that may contribute to the formulation of a customary international law norm. Moreover, the binding nature of such legislation in the domestic legal system of the acting State may supply evidence of *opinio juris,* acceptance of the practice as law, the second, and perhaps most important, element of customary international law.[45]

Solis also points to the United Kingdom's *Manual of the Law of Armed Conflict* in support of the proposition that customary international law provides for war crimes and grave breaches in non-international armed conflicts.[46] He quotes the *Manual* as follows:

> Although the treaties governing internal armed conflict contain no grave breach provisions, customary international law recognizes that serious violations of those treaties

> can amount to punishable war crimes. It is now recognized that there is a growing area of conduct that is criminal in both international and internal armed conflict. . . .[47]

Yoram Dinstein has applauded reliance on legislative codes and military manuals as illustrations of State practice: "Irrefutably, legislative codes and military Manuals (i.e., binding instructions to the armed forces) are invaluable sources of genuine State practice."[48] It is noteworthy, however, that Solis cites and quotes only the U.K. *Manual*. It is not clear, therefore, whether the position of the U.K. *Manual* has been adopted in the manuals of other major military powers.

In any event, it is likely that the challenges contained in the Bellinger/Haynes letter to the alleged two general errors in the ICRC study will not be successful. This is because the two positions of the ICRC study are so attractive as *de lege ferenda* that they will eventually be accepted as the *lex lata*. The reality is that Common Article 3 and Protocol II are clearly inadequate to govern non-international armed conflicts, and selective extension of the legal regime governing international armed conflicts to supplement the current law governing non-international armed conflicts makes enormous good sense. Ideally, of course, this extension should be effected by the conclusion of new—or the revision of current—global treaties. But if this method of extension is a mission impossible, as the evidence convincingly demonstrates, then customary international law methodology will have to be employed, even if there is continuing disagreement as to exactly what that methodology entails.

II. Rethinking the Possible Benefits of Additional Protocol II

Perhaps it is time for the United States to reevaluate the possible benefits of becoming a party to Additional Protocol II. As indicated above, the primary criticism of Additional Protocol II has been that its threshold of applicability is too high. It should be noted, however, that when President Ronald Reagan submitted Additional Protocol II to the Senate for its advice and consent to ratification,[49] he did so with a declaration that read: "The United States declares that it will apply this Protocol only to those conflicts covered by Article 3 common to the Geneva Convention of 12 August 1949 and to all such conflicts, and encourages all other States to do likewise." Secretary of State George P. Shultz's Letter of Submittal to President Reagan of December 13, 1986 describes the reasons for the declaration:

> The final text of Protocol II did not meet all the desires of the United States and other western delegations. In particular, the Protocol only applies to internal conflicts in which dissident armed groups are under responsible command and exercise control over such a part of the national territory as to carry out sustained and concerted military operations.

> This is a narrower scope than we would have desired, and has the effect of excluding many internal conflicts in which dissident armed groups occupy no significant territory but conduct sporadic guerrilla operations over a wide area. We are therefore recommending that US ratification be subject to an understanding declaring that the United States will apply the Protocol to all conflicts covered by Article 3 common to the 1949 Conventions (and only such conflicts), which will include all non-international armed conflicts as traditionally defined (but not internal disturbances, riots and sporadic acts of violence). This understanding will also have the effect of treating as non-international these so-called "wars of national liberation" described in Article 1(4) of Protocol I which fail to meet the traditional test of an international conflict.[50]

The approach of the Reagan administration, therefore, would resolve the primary problem of Additional Protocol II by declining to follow the provisions of Article 1(1) of Additional Protocol II that would severely limit its applicability, opting instead to apply its other provisions to all non-international armed conflict covered by Common Article 3. It also would counter the most unacceptable—to the United States—aspect of Additional Protocol I by treating as non-international the "wars of national liberation" that are described and treated in Article 1(4) of Additional Protocol I as international armed conflicts. Such an approach might serve to turn Additional Protocol II from its current status as a basically non-operational treaty to one that could usefully be applied to many of the internal conflicts characteristic of today's armed conflicts, and a treaty that could enhance and strengthen the legal regime governing non-international armed conflicts.

The report of the Department of State on Additional Protocol II, transmitted by President Reagan with the Protocol to the Senate,[51] contains a detailed analysis of the various provisions of the Protocol. In his Letter of Submittal to President Reagan, Secretary of State George Shultz spells out the ways in which the Protocol

> was designed to expand and refine the basic humanitarian provisions contained in Article 3 common to the four 1949 Geneva Conventions with respect to non-international conflicts. While the Protocol does not (and should not) attempt to apply to such conflicts all the protections prescribed by the Conventions for international armed conflicts, such as prisoner-of-war treatment for captured combatants, it does attempt to guarantee that certain fundamental protections be observed, including: (1) humane treatment for detained persons, such as protection from violence, torture, and collective punishment; (2) protection from intentional attack, hostage-taking and acts of terrorism of persons who take no part in hostilities; (3) special protection for children to provide for their safety and education and to preclude their participation in hostilities; (4) fundamental due process for persons against whom sentences are to be passed or penalties executed; (5) protection and appropriate care for the sick and wounded, and medical units which assist them; and (6) protection of the civilian population from military attack, acts of terror, deliberative starvation, and attacks against installations

> containing dangerous forces. In each case, Protocol II expands and makes more specific the basic guarantees of common Article 3 of the 1949 Conventions.[52]

Hence, application of Additional Protocol II to non-international armed conflicts would greatly strengthen the humanitarian protections of Common Article 3, and, as President Reagan suggested in his Letter of Transmittal, "[i]f these fundamental rules were observed, many of the worst human tragedies of current internal armed conflicts could be avoided."[53]

It is worth noting that on March 7, 2011, the Obama administration issued a White House press release in which it indicated its strong support for the ratification of Additional Protocol II and its intention to apply the principles of Article 75 of Protocol I to "any individual it detains in an international armed conflict."[54] In pertinent part, the press release reads as follows:

> **Support for a Strong International Legal Framework**
>
> Because of the vital importance of the rule of law to the effectiveness and legitimacy of our national security policy, the Administration is announcing our support for two important components of the international legal framework that covers armed conflicts: Additional Protocol II and Article 75 of Additional Protocol I to the 1949 Geneva Conventions.
>
> Additional Protocol II, which contains detailed humane treatment standards and fair trial guarantees that apply in the context of non-international armed conflicts, was originally submitted to the Senate for approval by President Reagan in 1987. The Administration urges the Senate to act as soon as practicable on this Protocol, to which 165 States are a party. An extensive interagency review concluded that United States military practice is already consistent with the Protocol's provisions. Joining the treaty would not only assist us in continuing to exercise leadership in the international community in developing the law of armed conflict, but would also allow us to reaffirm our commitment to humane treatment in, and compliance with legal standards for, the conduct of armed conflict.
>
> Article 75 of Additional Protocol I, which sets forth fundamental guarantees for persons in the hands of opposing forces in an international armed conflict, is similarly important to the international legal framework. Although the Administration continues to have significant concerns with Additional Protocol I, Article 75 is a provision of the treaty that is consistent with our current policies and practice and is one that the United States has historically supported.
>
> Our adherence to these principles is also an important safeguard against the mistreatment of captured U.S. military personnel. The U.S. Government will therefore choose

> out of a sense of legal obligation to treat the principles set forth in Article 75 as applicable to any individual it detains in an international armed conflict, and expects all other nations to adhere to these principles as well.[55]

The comments of the Reagan administration and more recently of the Obama administration would seem to belie the dismissive remarks of George Aldrich regarding the value of Additional Protocol II, reported earlier in this essay.[56] In sharp contrast to the Aldrich position, both the Reagan and Obama administrations state forcefully that ratification of Additional Protocol II would greatly expand on and strengthen the humanitarian provisions of Common Article 3 of the Geneva Conventions. President Reagan pointed out that Additional Protocol II "makes clear that any deliberate killing of a noncombatant in the course of a non-international armed conflict is a violation of the laws of war and a crime against humanity, and is therefore also punishable as murder."[57]

In another part of his message President Reagan foreshadows the approach more specifically adopted by the Obama administration with respect to Additional Protocol I. While emphatically rejecting ratification of Additional Protocol I, he stated at the same time a desire to

> devise an alternative reference for the positive provisions of Protocol I that could be of real humanitarian benefit if generally observed by parties to international armed conflicts. We are therefore in the process of consulting with our allies to develop appropriate methods for incorporating these positive provisions into the rules that govern our military operations, and as customary international law. I will advise the Senate of the results of this initiative as soon as it is possible to do so.[58]

It appears that President Reagan never advised the Senate of the results of his administration's initiative. For its part, the Obama administration appears to have acted without consulting allies—although this is not clear—in deciding to treat Article 75 of Additional Protocol I as binding on the United States and choosing to "treat the principles set forth in Article 75 as applicable to any individual it detains in an international armed conflict," and expecting "all other nations to adhere to these principles as well."[59] If this policy is implemented by the Obama administration, this would greatly strengthen the argument that Article 75 is part of customary international law.

As to whether the Senate will finally give its advice and consent to U.S. ratification of Additional Protocol II, it is hard to be optimistic, because the Senate has so many other issues before it that are likely to receive higher priority. But it appears the Reagan and Obama administrations have set forth a convincing case for the Senate's giving its advice and consent to ratification.

U.S. ratification of Additional Protocol II and application of its substantive provisions to any armed conflict covered by Common Article 3 would also make law in non-international armed conflict much less of a will-o'-the-wisp. This would be an important step because, as Eyal Benvenisti has noted in a recent provocative essay,[60] there is currently an emerging struggle between "states engaged in transnational armed conflict [read non-international asymmetric warfare] and third parties—courts, international institutions, NGOs, and civil society—in developing and enforcing the law."[61]

III. Who Shall Determine the Law in Non-International Armed Conflicts?

As noted earlier in this essay, the International Criminal Tribunal for the former Yugoslavia has concluded in its decisions that "customary rules have developed to govern internal strife."[62] For his part, Benvenisti states emphatically that the applicability of international criminal law

> to internal armed conflicts must be attributed to the jurisprudence of the International Criminal Tribunal of the former Yugoslavia ("ICTY"), which has in only a few years of adjudicating war crimes in the former Yugoslavia virtually rewritten the law on internal armed conflicts. By formally asserting the law[']s customary status, the ICTY overcame years of governmental resistance to regulating methods for fighting insurgents.[63]

Benvenisti believes that the increased involvement of various third-party actors, including domestic courts, foreign governments and courts, international organizations and international tribunals, humanitarian NGOs, and domestic and global civil society, in indirect monitoring, lawmaking and enforcement functions constitutes a major challenge to States. As Benvenisti suggests:

> [T]he intensified involvement of third parties creates a new conflict between the conventional armies that fight insurgents or terrorists and seek more discretion and fewer constraints and the third parties who insist on maintaining and even increasing constraints in warfare. We might call it a conflict between the "IHL camp," that emphasizes the humanitarian aim of the *jus in bello*, which they refer to as International Humanitarian Law, and the "LOAC camp," that wishes to point out that the Law of Armed Conflict is primarily designed to regulate the relations between fighting armies and therefore must take military concerns seriously into account. The LOAC camp insists that this "lawfare" is not only hypocritical but also perilous: that the IHL camp is being manipulated by the terrorists, who endanger the population on whose behalf they ostensibly fight by their abuse of civilian immunities. In a sense, and certainly unwillingly, the IHL camp becomes a strategic ally of the terrorists because the terrorists benefit indirectly from whatever constraints the IHL camp would impose.[64]

It is worthwhile quoting Benvenisti's summary of the arguments of the third-party actors at some length, because they couldn't be more in sharp contrast to the arguments advanced by governments, and their supporters, engaged in the asymmetric warfare characteristic of non-international armed conflict:

> In general, third party actors, and certainly third party norm entrepreneurs, suggest that the legal restraints on transnational conflict must treat the stronger party as responsible for positively protecting the population in the theater of operation from harm because the stronger party often exclusively, has effective—even if only virtual—control over the population. In fact, with recourse to new types of weaponry and reconnaissance tools, with 24/7 presence of unmanned aerial vehicles ("UAV") over foreign territory, contemporary armies often have the capacity to control some of the activities of the population on the ground effectively as an occupying power. Such control can perhaps be regarded as virtual occupation. As the law stands, during conventional international armed conflict, obligations to occupied populations are more demanding than those toward foreign civilians in the combat zone.
>
> This last point requires explanation: in symmetric warfare, the attacker's power does not amount to an ability to fully control the lives of the enemy's population. The defending government is still in control and in fact forcefully resists the attacker's effort to gain exclusivity. Lacking such exclusive control, there is no basis to impose an obligation on the attacking army to *ensure* enemy civilians' lives (protecting them, for example, from internal ethnic conflicts). Their army, which is still in control, has the duty to ensure their rights. Instead, before and during the attack, the attacking army owes a duty to *respect* enemy civilians' lives, consisting of the duty to avoid unnecessary harm. In contrast, the same army will assume the duty to *ensure* the rights of enemy civilians when they become subject to its effective control as prisoners of war or "protected persons" in occupied territories. An obligation to ensure the civilians' rights is fundamentally different from an obligation to respect them, applicable to parties to symmetric conflicts. The vertical power relations that exist in transnational asymmetric conflicts, particularly against non-state actors, seem to call for recognizing positive duties towards those civilians, like in an occupation. Such a duty will reflect the nature and scope of the power that the "attacking" army (during an on-going, indefinite "attack") has over the attacked population.
>
> The obligation to protect in transnational asymmetric armed conflict, if recognized, would be quite demanding. It would call for three specific obligations. First, it would require the consideration of alternatives to military action and the determination of whether the decision to use force against legitimate military targets rather than exploring non-forcible, or less-forcible alternatives, was justified under the circumstances. In fact it would imply injecting *jus ad bellum* considerations, or human rights law, into *jus in bello* analysis. Secondly, if there were no available alternatives, a second requirement would demand that the army invest significant resources to minimize harm to

civilians. Finally, the army would be required to conduct a transparent and accountable investigation after the use of force.

A case in point concerns the dispute about targeted killing. This policy treats individuals as military targets per se, given the paucity of conventional non-human military targets of an irregular fighting force. The LOAC camp argues that armies that target individual combatants regard them as legitimate targets in war, as there is no distinction between human and non-human military targets. But the alternative view is sensitive to the fact that the laws regarded the killing of combatants as a legitimate *means* to achieve military goals, rather than a goal in and of itself. As the 1868 St. Petersburg Declaration envisioned, war was not about killing combatants; wars were understood to be fought to achieve non-human military goals and fighting was to be conducted against an abstract, collective enemy. Therefore, it was possible to stipulate that "the only legitimate object which States should endeavour to accomplish during war is to *weaken* the military forces of the enemy; That [*sic*] for this purpose it is sufficient to *disable* the greatest possible number of men." Although war always involved the killing of combatants, killing the adversary was never the goal. Applying this logic to the effort to preempt individuals from engaging in an attack would require a consideration of whether it is possible to *disable* rather than kill them. This explains why the IHL camp insists on pausing to consider alternatives to targeted killing; something that is viewed by the LOAC camp as injecting irrelevant requirements of human rights law into *jus in bello* analysis.

The tension between governments engaged in transnational warfare and third parties can therefore not be starker: whereas governments seek to deny or dilute the applicability of conventional warfare obligations to transnational asymmetric conflicts, third parties insist on their applicability and lean toward imposing even more stringent constraints, which governments regard as impermissibly endangering their troops and irresponsibly immunizing non-state fighters. Only time can tell if and how this tension can be resolved.[65]

In the rest of his article Benvenisti argues that the growing involvement of third parties in the monitoring and assessment of military decisions "raises a third challenge to the legal regulation of warfare: how to regulate the exercise of discretion by the military commander."[66] He suggests that in conventional, symmetric warfare the parties to the conflict are presumed to promote their self-interests and not the interests of the other government involved in the conflict. But with the pressure from third parties to positively protect enemy civilians it has arguably become necessary for governments involved in non-international armed conflicts to consider interests other than their own. He notes that the greatly increased access to information about such conflicts afforded by technical advances in technology and improved intelligence allows third parties to assess the exercise of discretion by the military commander. He adds,

> If we accept that attacking armies in transnational asymmetric conflicts have a "duty to ensure" the lives of civilians in the area they attack then perhaps they are expected to treat all civilians with similar respect (obviously, such blindness would relate only to the human rights of the relevant civilians and not to the national interests of the foreign state). It can be expected, however, that the LOAC camp will resist such a conclusion, stating that there is no moral or legal basis for the obligation to consider other-regarding considerations in the absence of reciprocity and mutuality of obligations, when there is no assurance that others are equally committed to act selflessly.[67]

In the conclusion to his article, Benvenisti states that

> [i]it is beyond the scope of this essay to assess if and how such a cleavage between two visions of the law can be bridged and how the law would look in the future. Much depends on the continued ability of courts, both domestic and international, to assert positions independent of governments and the continued commitment of global civil society to constrain conventional armies. . . . Even the domestic courts of those governments that engage in such conflicts resist the demand to yield authority to the executive. If these attitudes persist, it can be expected that the recourse to third parties as partners in the regulation of transnational armed conflicts will expand.[68]

By way of initial comment on some of the points made by Benvenisti, it should be noted that, although the domestic courts of some governments that engage in non-international asymmetric armed conflict have asserted positions independent of their governments on the regulation of such conflicts,[69] other domestic courts, including those of the United States, have been quite deferential to the executive branch's decisions with respect to the conduct of hostilities in such conflicts.[70] A good recent example of such deference by U.S. courts is the December 7, 2010 decision of the District Court for the District of Columbia dismissing a suit brought to enjoin the targeted killing of U.S. citizen Anwar Al-Aulaqi, who was operating out of Yemen.[71] The court ruled that the plaintiff (Al-Aulaqi's father) did not have standing to bring the suit and that the political question doctrine barred the court from considering the merits of the plaintiff's suit.

In describing the arguments of third-party actors, Benvenisti states that "the legal restraints on transnational conflict must treat the stronger party as responsible for positively protecting the population in the theater of operation from harm because the stronger party often exclusively, has effective—even if only virtual—control over the population."[72] In many cases involving asymmetric non-international armed conflicts, however, the stronger party has no such control over the population. In Afghanistan, for example, the Taliban and Al-Qaeda forces embed themselves among the general population. Moreover, in Afghanistan, it is important to note, the sovereign power is not the U.S. government or coalition forces, but the

Afghan government of President Karzai. Increasingly, the Karzai government has demanded that there be no civilian casualties from drone or airplane attacks, thus denying the coalition forces an important military advantage.

Moreover, to impose an obligation on U.S. and coalition forces, as demanded by some third parties, to *ensure* that there are no civilian casualties in asymmetric non-international armed conflicts would be a dramatic change in the law of armed conflict and would ensure the failure of U.S. and coalition forces in Afghanistan and in other theaters where the Taliban and Al-Qaeda are operating. The reality is that so-called "collateral damage" to civilians is unavoidable in armed conflict, and especially in the asymmetric non-international armed conflict characteristic of today's wars. The current test under the law of armed conflict is whether the collateral damage is expected to be "excessive" in relation to the concrete and direct military advantage anticipated.[73]

In a recent essay, Samuel Estreicher has helpfully emphasized that "[d]angers to civilians during armed conflict are a joint product of both attackers and defenders, and minimization of such harm—presumably the overriding mission of IHL—requires establishing the right incentives for *both* attackers and defenders."[74] Estreicher also quotes the observation of W. Hays Parks in his "classic" article, "Air War and the Law of War," that

> Protocol I constitutes an improvement in the law of war in recognizing that an attacker should, in most cases, give consideration to minimization of collateral civilian casualties. The issue is the degree to which an attacker should assume this responsibility. If the new rules of Protocol I are to have any credibility, the predominant responsibility must remain with the defender, who has control over the civilian population.[75]

Estreicher elaborates on Parks's point by noting that

> [i]t is clear that attackers cannot, because of defender violations, claim excuse for their non-compliance with, say, their duty to "do everything feasible to verify that the objectives to be attacked are neither civilians nor civilian objects" under AP I, Article 57(2)(a)(i). But the feasibility inquiry under Article 57(2)(a)(i), or the proportionality inquiry under Article 57(2)(a)(iii), necessarily requires that account be taken of whether defenders have disguised military operations as civilian operations or have deliberately embedded their military assets in close proximity to civilian areas, all in violation of defender obligations under IHL.[76]

In a subsequent, follow-up essay,[77] Estreicher focuses on the "so-called principle of 'proportionality.'" He explains that he uses

> the qualifying adjective "so-called" because "proportionality" in this context is a misnomer. The actual obligation, as set forth in Articles 51(5)(b) and 57(2)(b) of AP I, speaks in terms of prohibiting (and deferring) attacks expected to cause incidental civilian losses "which would be excessive in relation to the concrete and direct military advantage anticipated." . . . [T]he "excessive loss" formulation is not only truer to the text of AP I but provides a sounder, more principled basis for judging violations than the more elastic, manipulable "proportionality" formulation.[78]

The "excessive loss" formulation is *a fortiori* a more principled basis for judging violations than the requirement reportedly proposed by some third parties that parties to asymmetric warfare "positively protect" enemy civilians.[79] To hold a military commander to such a standard would be grossly dysfunctional, as well as grossly unfair if violations of this standard would subject the military commander to possible criminal or civil penalties. Hence, it is certain that despite pressure that may be brought to bear by third parties to asymmetric armed conflicts, this standard will be rejected by the governments of States that are engaged in such conflicts, including most particularly that of the United States.

IV. Conclusion

The title of this essay states there is a search for law in non-international armed conflicts. Perhaps, however, a more precise way to describe the current situation is as a struggle for law in non-international armed conflicts. As noted by Eyal Benvenisti, this is a struggle between States that are actively involved in non-international armed conflict and a wide array of third-party actors, such as domestic courts, foreign governments and courts, international organizations and international tribunals, humanitarian NGOs, and domestic and global civil society. Some of these third-party actors are promoting an agenda that, if adopted as law, could severely restrict the military capacity of the armed forces of States to deal effectively with Al-Qaeda and other non-State actors employing various strategies to negate the military superiority of the States they are fighting against.

At least to some extent, these third-party actors have been able to be influential because of the inability of States to reform and develop the law applicable to non-international armed conflicts through the conclusion of global treaties that would update the law in such a way as to resolve the tension between humanitarian considerations and the need for military efficiency. The recent efforts of the Obama administration to carry forward the position of the Reagan administration to have the United States finally ratify Additional Protocol II, while issuing a declaration that it will not apply the high threshold requirements of the Protocol and will urge other States parties to follow suit, may be a first step toward overcoming the barriers to expanding and improving the law of non-international armed conflict. Should the United States take this step, and other States follow suit, at a minimum it should allow like-mined States to cooperate to improve the efficiency of efforts to deal with the challenge they face in conducting asymmetric warfare, and could perhaps lead to State practice that evolves eventually into norms of customary international law applicable to non-international armed conflict. Failure of States like the United States and its allies to win this struggle for law in non-international armed conflicts with these third-party actors would have extremely negative effects on their national security.

Notes

1. GARY D. SOLIS, THE LAW OF ARMED CONFLICT: INTERNATIONAL HUMANITARIAN LAW IN WAR 97 (2010).

2. Convention for the Amelioration of the Condition of the Wounded and Sick in Armed Forces in the Field art. 3, Aug. 12, 1949, 6 U.S.T. 3114, 75 U.N.T.S. 31; Convention for the Amelioration of the Condition of Wounded, Sick and Shipwrecked Members of Armed Forces at Sea art. 3, Aug. 12, 1949, 6 U.S.T. 3217, 75 U.N.T.S. 85; Convention Relative to the Treatment of Prisoners of War art. 3, Aug. 12, 1949, 6 U.S.T. 3316, 75 U.N.T.S. 135; Convention Relative to the Protection of Civilian Persons in Time of War art. 3, Aug. 12, 1949, 6 U.S.T. 3516, 75 U.N.T.S. 287.

3. SOLIS, *supra* note 1, at 99 (emphasis in original).

4. *Id.* at 98.

5. In his treatise, *id.*, Solis cites and quotes Jean Pictet's commentary on the Geneva Conventions that it is

> pointless and even dangerous to try to enumerate things with which a human being must be provided [to constitute humane treatment] . . . or to lay down in detail the manner in which one must behave towards him in order to show that one is treating him "humanely" . . . . The details of such treatment may, moreover, vary according to circumstances . . . and to what is feasible.

COMMENTARY TO GENEVA CONVENTION I FOR THE AMELIORATION OF THE CONDITION OF THE WOUNDED AND SICK IN ARMED FORCES IN THE FIELD 53 (Jean S. Pictet ed., 1952).

6. 1 CUSTOMARY INTERNATIONAL HUMANITARIAN LAW Rule 87, at 307–8 (Jean-Marie Henckaerts & Louise Doswald-Beck eds., 2005).

7. Protocol Additional to the Geneva Conventions of 12 August 1949, and Relating to the Protection of Victims of Non-International Armed Conflicts, June 8, 1977, 1125 U.N.T.S. 609, *reprinted in* 16 INTERNATIONAL LEGAL MATERIALS 1422 (1977).

8. Protocol Additional to the Geneva Conventions of 12 August 1949, and Relating to the Protection of Victims of International Armed Conflicts, June 8, 1977, 1125 U.N.T.S. 3 [hereinafter Additional Protocol I].

9. *See* SOLIS, *supra* note 1, at 129.

10. *See* International Humanitarian Law – Treaties & Documents, http://www.icrc.org/ihl.nsf/WebSign?ReadForm&id=475&ps=P (last visited Oct. 16, 2011).

11. For an example of a provision in Additional Protocol II that is almost surely *not* representative of customary international law, see Article 13(3). Paragraph 3 of Article 13 provides

that civilians lose protection from being the object of armed attack, only "for such time as they take a direct part in hostilities." In *The Manual on the Law of Non-International Armed Conflict,* the authors state that

> this limitation is not confirmed by customary international law. Such an approach would create an imbalance between the government's armed forces on the one hand and members of armed groups on the other, inasmuch as the former remains legitimate targets (under international law) throughout the conflict. Moreover, the proposition is impractical to implement on the ground. Ordinary soldiers would be required to make complex and immediate assessments as to whether an individual's participation in hostilities is ongoing, at a time when the facts available are incomplete or unclear.

MICHAEL N. SCHMITT, CHARLES H.B. GARRAWAY & YORAM DINSTEIN, THE MANUAL ON THE LAW OF NON-INTERNATIONAL ARMED CONFLICT WITH COMMENTARY ¶ 1.1.2(4) (2006) [hereinafter NIAC MANUAL].

12. GUÉNAËL METTRAUX, INTERNATIONAL CRIMES AND THE AD HOC TRIBUNALS 144 (2005), cited and quoted in SOLIS, *supra* note 1, at 138–39.

13. George H. Aldrich, *Some Reflections on the Origins of the 1977 Geneva Protocols, in* STUDIES AND ESSAYS ON INTERNATIONAL HUMANITARIAN LAW AND RED CROSS PRINCIPLES IN HONOUR OF JEAN PICTET 135–36 (Christophe Swinarski ed., 1984), cited and quoted in SOLIS, *supra* note 1, at 139.

14. *See* Jean-Philippe Lavoyer, *International Humanitarian Law: Should It Be Reaffirmed, Clarified or Developed?, in* ISSUES IN INTERNATIONAL LAW AND MILITARY OPERATIONS 287 (Richard B. Jaques ed., 2006) (Vol. 80, U.S. Naval War College International Law Studies). For comment on Mr. Lavoyer's article, see John F. Murphy, *Enforcing the Law, in id.* at 311.

15. *See* Lavoyer, *supra* note 14, at 302.

16. Prosecutor v. Tadić, Case No. IT-94-1-l, Decision on Defence Motion for Interlocutory Appeal on Jurisdiction (Int'l Crim. Trib. for the Former Yugoslavia Oct. 2, 1995) [hereinafter *Prosecutor v. Tadić*].

17. *Id.*, ¶ 70.

18. *See* John F. Murphy, *Mission Impossible? International Law and the Changing Character of War, in* INTERNATIONAL LAW AND THE CHANGING CHARACTER OF WAR 13, 19 (Raul A. "Pete" Pedrozo & Daria P. Wollschlaeger eds., 2011) (Vol. 87, U.S. Naval War College International Law Studies).

19. Hamdan v. Rumsfeld, 548 U.S. 557, 630–31 (2006).

20. *See* YORAM DINSTEIN, THE CONDUCT OF HOSTILITIES UNDER THE LAW OF INTERNATIONAL ARMED CONFLICT 56 (2d ed. 2010).

21. For brief discussion of the conflicting views, see Murphy, *supra* note 18, at 17–18.

22. Kenneth Watkin, *21st Century Conflict and International Humanitarian Law: Status Quo or Change?, in* INTERNATIONAL LAW AND ARMED CONFLICT: EXPLORING THE FAULTLINES 273 (Michael N. Schmitt & Jelena Pejic eds., 2007).

23. *Prosecutor v. Tadić, supra* note 16, ¶ 125.

24. *Id.*

25. *See* 1 CUSTOMARY INTERNATIONAL HUMANITARIAN LAW, *supra* note 6, at xxix.

26. Convention No. II with Respect to the Laws and Customs of War on Land, July 29, 1899, 32 Stat. 1803; Convention No. IV Respecting the Laws and Customs of War on Land, Oct. 18, 1907, 36 Stat. 2227.

27. *See* J. Patrick Kelly, *The Twilight of Customary International Law,* 40 VIRGINIA JOURNAL OF INTERNATIONAL LAW 449, 469–75 (2000).

28. *See* J. Patrick Kelly, *International Law and the Shrinking Space for Domestic Politics in Developing Countries, in* LAW AND RIGHTS: GLOBAL PERSPECTIVES ON CONSTITUTIONALISM AND GOVERNANCE 259, 261 (Penelope E. Andrews & Susan Bazilli eds., 2008).

29. *See* Letter from John Bellinger III, Legal Adviser, U.S. Dept. of State, and William J. Haynes, General Counsel, U.S. Dept. of Defense, to Dr. Jakob Kellenberger, President, International Committee of the Red Cross, Regarding Customary International Law Study (Nov. 3, 2006), *reprinted in* 46 INTERNATIONAL LEGAL MATERIALS 514 (2007).

30. *Id.*

31. *Id.* at 516.

32. *Id.*

33. *See* Jean-Marie Henckaerts, *Customary International Humanitarian Law: A Response to US Comments*, 89 INTERNATIONAL REVIEW OF THE RED CROSS 473 (2007), *reprinted in* 46 INTERNATIONAL LEGAL MATERIALS 959 (2007).

34. *Id.* at 474.

35. *Id.* at 485–87.

36. *Supra* note 29.

37. Primary examples of such treaties may be found listed, with citations, in the NIAC MANUAL, *supra* note 11, at 66. They include the 2000 Optional Protocol to the Convention on the Rights of the Child on the Involvement of Children in Armed Conflict; the 1999 Second Protocol to the Hague Convention of 1954 for the Protection of Cultural Property in the Event of Armed Conflict; the 1998 Rome Statute of the International Criminal Court; the 1997 Ottawa Convention on the Prohibition of the Use, Stockpiling, Production and Transfer of Anti-Personnel Mines and on Their Destruction; and the 1996 Amended Protocol II on Prohibitions or Restrictions on the Use of Certain Conventional Weapons Which May Be Deemed to Be Excessively Injurious or to Have Indiscriminate Effects.

38. *Prosecutor v. Tadić*, *supra* note 16, ¶ 84, cited and quoted in SOLIS, *supra* note 1, at 100 n.119.

39. *Prosecutor v. Tadić*, *supra* note 16, ¶ 129, cited and quoted in SOLIS, *supra* note 1, at 100. Solis adds, in footnote 120, quoting the Appeals Chamber's decision in paragraph 30, that the migration of war crimes from international armed conflicts to non-international cannot take place "in the form of a full and mechanical transplant of those rules to internal conflicts [but instead] the general essence of those rules, and not the detailed regulation they may contain, has become applicable to internal conflicts."

40. *See* SOLIS, *supra* note 1, at 100.

41. Prosecutor v. Delalic, IT-96-21-T, Judgment, ¶ 172 (Int'l Crim. Trib. for the Former Yugoslavia Feb. 20, 2001).

42. *See* METTRAUX, *supra* note 12, at 132.

43. Theodor Meron, *International Criminalization of Internal Atrocities,* 89 AMERICAN JOURNAL OF INTERNATIONAL LAW 554, 561 (1995).

44. SOLIS, *supra* note 1, at 101, citing EVE LA HAYE, WAR CRIMES IN INTERNAL ARMED CONFLICTS 170 (2008).

45. For general discussion of the customary international law process, see LORI F. DAMROSCH ET AL., INTERNATIONAL LAW: CASES AND MATERIALS 59–121 (5th ed. 2009).

46. SOLIS, *supra* note 1, at 101.

47. *Id.*, citing in footnote 128, UNITED KINGDOM MINISTRY OF DEFENCE, THE MANUAL OF THE LAW OF ARMED CONFLICT ¶¶ 15.32, 15.32.1 (2004).

48. *See* Yoram Dinstein, *The ICRC Customary International Humanitarian Law Study*, 36 ISRAEL YEARBOOK ON HUMAN RIGHTS 1, 6 (2006).

49. *See* A Message from the President of the United States regarding Protocol II Additional to the 1949 Geneva Conventions, and Relating to the Protection of Victims of Non-International Armed Conflicts, US Government Printing Office, 100th Congress, 1st session, Treaty Doc. 100-2, at iii (1987) [hereinafter Message from the President].

50. Letter of Submittal from Secretary of State George P. Shultz to President Ronald Reagan (May 10, 1988), *reprinted in id.* at vii–viii.

51. *See* Message from the President, *supra* note 49, at 1.

52. *Id.* at vii.

53. *Id.* at iii.

54. White House, Fact Sheet: New Actions on Guantanamo and Detainee Policy 3 (Mar. 7, 2011), http://www.whitehouse.gov/the-press-office/2011/03/07/new-actions-guantanamo-bay-and-detainee-policy [hereinafter Fact Sheet]. It is also worth noting that the same plurality of the Supreme Court that held the "war on terror" to be a non-international armed conflict held that the principles of Article 75 were customary international law. Hamdan v. Rumsfeld, 548 U.S. 557, 633 (2006).

55. Fact Sheet, *supra* note 54, at 3.

56. *See* Aldrich, *supra* note 13 and accompanying text.

57. *Id.*

58. *Id.* at iv.

59. *See* Fact Sheet, *supra* note 54, at 3.

60. Eyal Benvenisti, *The Legal Battle to Define the Law on Transnational Asymmetric Warfare,* 20 DUKE JOURNAL OF COMPARATIVE & INTERNATIONAL LAW 339 (2010).

61. *Id.* at 342.

62. *See supra* note 23 and accompanying text.

63. *See* Benvenisti, *supra* note 60, at 347.

64. *Id.* at 348.

65. *Id.* at 350–52 (emphasis in original) (citations omitted).

66. *Id.* at 353.

67. *Id.* at 356 (citation omitted).

68. *Id.* at 359.

69. The Supreme Court of Israel has been especially active in this respect. *See, e.g.*, HCJ 769/02 Public Committee against Torture in Israel v. Government of Israel (2) PD 459 [2006] (Isr.), *reprinted in* 46 INTERNATIONAL LEGAL MATERIALS 373 (2007), *available at* http://elyon1.court.gov.il/files_eng/02/690/007/a34/02007690.a34.pdf (holding unlawful various coercive tactics for interrogation, while avoiding specifically labeling them "torture"); HCJ 2056/04 Beit Sourik Village Council v. Government of Israel 58(5) PD 807 [2004], *reprinted in* 43 INTERNATIONAL LEGAL MATERIALS 1099 (2004), *available at* http://elyon1.court.gov.il/files_eng/04/560/020/a28/04020560.a28.pdf.

70. To be sure the Supreme Court has handed down several decisions against the U.S. government in cases involving the use of military commissions to prosecute alleged terrorists. *See* Rasul v. Bush, 542 U.S. 466 (2004); Hamdi v. Rumsfeld, 542 U.S. 507 (2004); Hamdan v. Rumsfeld, 548 U.S. 557 (2006); Boumediene v. Bush, 553 U.S. 723 (2008). But the Supreme Court has refrained from sitting in judgment on the executive branch's conduct of military hostilities.

71. Nasser Al-Aulaqi v. Barack H. Obama, Robert M. Gates, and Leon E. Panetta, 727 F. Supp. 2d 1 (2010).

72. *See* Benvenisti, *supra* note 60, at 350.

73. Additional Protocol I, *supra* note 8, arts. 51(5)(b) & 57(2)(b).

74. Samuel Estreicher, *Privileging Asymmetric Warfare? Part I: Defender Duties under International Humanitarian Law*, 11 CHICAGO JOURNAL OF INTERNATIONAL LAW 425, 431 (2011) (emphasis in original).

75. *Id.* at 432 n.20 (emphasis in original). *See also* W. Hays Parks, *Air War and the Law of War*, 32 AIR FORCE LAW REVIEW 1, 153–54 (1990).

76. Estreicher, *supra* note 74, at 435 (citations omitted).

77. *See* Samuel Estreicher, *Privileging Asymmetric Warfare (Part II)?: The "Proportionality" Principle Under International Humanitarian Law*, 12 CHICAGO JOURNAL OF INTERNATIONAL LAW 143, 144 (2011).

78. *Id.* at 146.

79. *See* Benvenisti, *supra* note 60, at 353.

PART III

TYPE OF NON-INTERNATIONAL ARMED CONFLICTS AND THE APPLICABLE LAW

III

Defining Non-International Armed Conflict: A Historically Difficult Task

David E. Graham*

As the initial speaker on the first panel of the Newport conference dealing with non-international armed conflict (NIAC) in the twenty-first century, I was asked to do two things. First, establish the framework for a broad and comprehensive discussion of NIAC by assessing, historically, the way in which the international community has attempted to define this particular form of conflict, to include the issue of whether there now exist various types of NIAC. Second, speak to the U.S. practice with respect to the manner in which the United States has determined whether to designate certain hostilities as NIACs.

In undertaking that mandate, I was reminded of the words of Sir Hersch Lauterpacht: "[I]f international law is, in some ways, at the vanishing point of law, the law of war is, perhaps even more conspicuously, at the vanishing point of international law."[1] And, given the nuances of our current subject matter, I would think it appropriate to add to this statement: "If the law of war is at the vanishing point of international law, then, surely, the law related to non-international armed conflict is at the vanishing point of the law of war."

---

* Colonel, U.S. Army (Ret.); Executive Director, The Judge Advocate General's Legal Center and School, U.S. Army. The author has prepared this article in his personal capacity and does not purport to represent the views of the Department of Defense, the Department of the Army or The Judge Advocate General's Legal Center and School.

My addition to the Lauterpacht quote results from the fact that the matter of what activities do—and do not—constitute a NIAC is an exceptionally contentious one. The criteria to be used in making such a determination enjoy no universal acceptance. Time and again these are said to be "evolving." Increasingly, we are advised that today's NIAC is no longer the NIAC of old. And, by "old," commentators speak in terms of a scant ten years ago. Now, the "traditional" NIAC is said to have been joined by what are referred to as asymmetric "transnational" armed conflicts.[2] So, having set forth these uncertainties surrounding the nature of NIACs, how are we to recognize such a conflict when we see one?

In parsing this puzzle, it is best to cast a large net, beginning with an assessment of the concept of "armed conflict" itself. Having done this, we can then move on to examine the direction in which the international community has moved in its attempt to more closely demarcate the boundaries of what is—and is not—armed conflict of a non-international character.

Let us begin with the fact that, as surprising as it might appear, the law of war, or the law of armed conflict as it is also known, provides no definitive definition of "armed conflict," even though this term is specifically referenced in both Common Article 2 and Common Article 3 of the four 1949 Geneva Conventions, articles that deal with international and non-international armed conflict, respectively.[3] And there exists no agreed test for assessing when certain actions have risen to the level of an "armed conflict."

Having said this, however, it is also true that the International Committee of the Red Cross (ICRC) *Commentary* on these articles (Pictet's *Commentary*) has historically been looked to as the principal source of their interpretation.[4] This *Commentary* references identifiable factors to be considered when making a determination as to whether either an international or non-international armed conflict exists.

The matter of determining the existence of a Common Article 2 international armed conflict is, in fact, a rather straightforward one. The text of Article 2 speaks in terms of "all cases of declared war or of any other armed conflict which may arise between two or more of the High Contracting Parties, even if the state of war is not recognized by one of them." The key here is that the use of force by opposing regular armed forces of two or more States evidences an international armed conflict. The *Commentary* notes in this regard that the reality of the existence of such a conflict is simply not affected by the scope, duration or intensity of the hostilities involved. Instead, the use of the term "armed conflict" in this context was intended to apply to de facto hostilities, no matter their duration or how non-destructive they actually might have been.[5]

Now, having noted that determining the existence of an international armed conflict is not that complex, I would certainly caveat this statement with the observation that this determinative process may become much more problematic in those instances in which a non-international armed conflict might, at some point, become "internationalized." This occurs when one or more external States intervene in such hostilities. Given the focus of this article, however, the debate over the degree of "effective" or "overall" control that a State must exercise over insurgent elements in order for this "internationalization" process to occur will not be addressed.[6] Suffice it to say that the determinative factors related to international armed conflicts contained in Pictet's *Commentary* really do very little to assist in making a judgment as to whether certain actions may—or may not—be designated NIACs. And the ability to make such a determination is, of course, our ultimate goal.

Given this fact, the starting point in assessing the existence of a NIAC must necessarily be Common Article 3: "In the case of armed conflict not of an international character occurring in the territory of one of the High Contracting Parties, each Party to the conflict shall be bound to apply, as a minimum, the following provisions . . . ." The difficulty, historically, in turning to Article 3 has been, of course, that neither the text nor the commentary to this article provides definitive guidance regarding what is meant by the phrase "conflict not of an international character." Pictet, himself, has noted that the negotiators of the 1949 Conventions "deliberately refrained from defining the non-international armed conflicts which were the subject of Common Article 3."[7] Thus, it has never been clear what level of violence must be reached—and how protracted the actions in issue must be—in order for such hostilities to be deemed a non-international armed conflict. Internal situations that have reached a very high level of violence have often been regarded, certainly by the States in which such violence has occurred, as mere banditry—acts which have not achieved the threshold of "armed conflict."[8]

This uncertainty has persisted over the years, notwithstanding the fact that Pictet's *Commentary* offered what he referred to as some "convenient criteria" for determining the existence of a NIAC:

> (1) That the Party in revolt against the *de jure* Government possesses an organized military force, an authority responsible for its acts, acting within a determinate territory and having the means of respecting and ensuring respect for the Convention.
>
> (2) That the legal Government is obliged to have recourse to the regular military forces against insurgents organized as military and in possession of a part of the national territory.
>
> (3) (a) That the *de jure* Government has recognized the insurgents as belligerents; or
>
> (b) that it has claimed for itself the rights of a belligerent; or

> (c) that it has accorded the insurgents recognition as belligerents for the purposes only of the present Convention; or
>
> (d) that the dispute has been admitted to the agenda of the Security Council or the General Assembly of the United Nations as being a threat to international peace, a breach of the peace, or an act of aggression.
>
> (4) (a) That the insurgents have an organization purporting to have the characteristics of a State.
>
> (b) That the insurgent civil authority exercises de facto authority over the population within a determinate portion of the national territory.
>
> (c) That the armed forces act under the direction of an organized authority and are prepared to observe the ordinary laws of war.
>
> (d) That the insurgent civil authority agrees to be bound by the provisions of the Convention.[9]

Despite these criteria, States have, nevertheless, consistently resisted recognition of the existence of an armed conflict within their borders for fear, understandably, of affording some form of de facto status or legitimacy to those responsible for fostering the violence in issue—that is, to those who are engaging in hostile acts in an effort to displace the de jure government. This lack of certainty and lack of consensus regarding the scope of Article 3's applicability has, over the years, led to attempts to better define Common Article 3 conflicts as a means of more effectively triggering the law applicable to them.

Protocols I and II to the 1949 Geneva Conventions

Each of the protocols to the 1949 Geneva Conventions attempted to bring more clarity to activities which were—and were not—to be deemed non-international armed conflicts.[10] The significance of Protocol I to this issue is, of course, its characterization in Article 1(4) of certain essentially non-international, internal conflicts as "international" in character—that is, "armed conflicts in which peoples are fighting against colonial domination [Portugal's colonies in sub-Saharan Africa] and alien occupation [Israel's occupation of territories captured in 1967] and against racist regimes [the then-existing regimes in Rhodesia (now Zimbabwe) and South Africa] in the exercise of their right of self-determination."

While the United States is not a party to Protocol I and is not bound by—and does not accept—Article 1(4) as customary international law, for the purposes of this discussion it must be noted that the ICRC *Commentary* on Protocol I states that the situations specifically set forth in Article 1(4) constitute an "exhaustive list" of those types of internal conflicts that may be viewed as "international" in character.[11] Accordingly, it is apparent that the Protocol has no bearing on internal, non-international conflicts that do not fall within one of these three narrow categories. And, as a practical matter, when has there last been seen an internal conflict that would meet these criteria? In sum, Protocol I really does very little to better enable the international community to define and determine the existence of a NIAC.

Protocol II was, of course, the first attempt to regulate, by treaty, the methods and means of the employment of the use of force in internal armed conflicts. Its purpose was to confirm, clarify and expand upon the minimal protections contained in Common Article 3. The inherent difficulty with Protocol II, given our stated purpose of discerning how to better define and determine the existence of a NIAC, is the fact that this Protocol establishes a much higher threshold of application than does Common Article 3. While Common Article 3 is said to apply to all conflicts "not of an international character," Article 1(1) of Protocol II states that it applies only to armed conflicts

> which take place in the territory of a High Contracting Party between its armed forces and dissident armed forces or other organized armed groups which, under responsible command, exercise such control over a part of its territory as to enable them to carry out sustained and concerted military operations and to implement this Protocol.

This decision by the drafters of Protocol II to define non-international armed conflict, thus triggering the application of the Protocol's provisions on the basis of objective criteria, has, in fact, had the result of substantially narrowing the number of NIACs to which the Protocol might apply. The criteria set forth obviously restrict the Protocol's applicability to those conflicts of a high degree of intensity—essentially classic civil wars. The Protocol has seldom been deemed applicable to the great number of internal armed conflicts that have occurred since its inception, as insurgent groups have rarely, if ever, been able to meet the stringent requirements of Article 1(1).

Moreover, while Article 1(2) goes on to state that the Protocol will not apply to "situations of internal disturbances and tensions, such as riots, isolated and sporadic acts of violence, and other acts of a similar nature, as not being armed conflicts," many cases of internal violence that do not meet the criteria of Article 1(1) are, nevertheless, far more intense in nature than are riots and sporadic violence. As a result, these types of scenarios might legitimately be viewed as non-international armed conflicts to which Common Article 3 should apply. The bottom line is that the criteria contained in Article 1(1) do not greatly assist, as was their intent, in determining the existence of a NIAC. Indeed, it can be argued that the high bar of application established by this provision has served as a further excuse for governments to deny the existence of non-international armed conflicts within their borders.

In summary, then, as a result of Protocols I and II, the Geneva Conventions now recognize and regulate three distinct categories of non-international armed conflict: (1) the very specifically identified and limited internal "wars of national liberation," as defined in Article 1(4) of Protocol I, to which all of the provisions of Protocol I apply; (2) classic "civil wars" as defined in Article 1(1) of Protocol II; and (3) the ambiguously defined Common Article 3 "conflicts not of an international character." Thus, despite the stated intentions of the drafters of the Protocols, it might understandably be argued that we have returned to where we started—an inability to systematically identify, with very few exceptions, when violent activities occurring within States may legitimately be characterized as non-international armed conflicts. If this is the case, where do we next turn?

The 1995 **Tadić** *Jurisdiction Decision*

In October of 1995, the International Criminal Tribunal for the former Yugoslavia (ICTY) issued what has become known as the *Tadić* jurisdiction decision,[12] a decision that many have since contended has considerably influenced the development of the law of armed conflict. This assertion is centered on the argument that the ICTY's statements on when, and in what manner, the basic principles of this body of law should be applied serve as authoritative determinations on such matters. Indeed, some have embraced the Tribunal's pronouncements as an almost instant form of customary law of armed conflict. And, while I am not among those who give such weight to this decision, given our stated purpose, it is useful to examine the definition of "armed conflict" set forth by the ICTY: "An armed conflict exists whenever there is a resort to armed force between States or protracted armed violence between governmental authorities and organized armed groups or between such groups within a State."[13]

The Tribunal thus defined non-international armed conflict as "protracted" armed violence that occurs between governmental authorities and organized armed groups or, significantly, between such armed groups themselves within a State. Important, as well, is the fact that the use of the term "protracted" in the Tribunal's definition of non-international armed conflict can be viewed as meaning that hostilities need not be continuous.

In turn, in interpreting this definition of non-international armed conflict articulated by the *Tadić* Appeals Chamber, the *Tadić* Trial Chamber opined the following:

> The test applied by the Appeals Chamber to the existence of an armed conflict for the purposes of the rules contained in Common Article 3 focuses on two aspects of a conflict; the intensity of the conflict and the organization of the parties to the conflict. In an armed conflict of an internal or mixed character, these closely related criteria are used solely for the purpose, as a minimum, of distinguishing an armed conflict from banditry, unorganized and short-lived insurrections, or terrorist activities, which are not subject to international humanitarian law.[14]

These two aspects of internal armed conflict set forth by the *Tadić* Trial Chamber—the "intensity" of the conflict and the degree of "organization of the parties" involved in the conflict—it might be argued, can now serve as a basis for the recognition of "de facto" non-international armed conflicts, and thus for the application of Common Article 3 to such conflicts. Support for this view can be found in the fact that, in determining the existence of non-international armed conflict within Rwanda, the International Criminal Tribunal for Rwanda employed precisely this approach, noting that in making such a determination, "it is necessary to evaluate both the 'intensity' and 'organization of the parties' to the conflict."[15]

Further endorsement of the reasoning contained in the ICTY's *Tadić* decision is reflected, as well, in the adaptation of the "*Tadić* formula" in the Rome Statute of the International Criminal Court. The second sentence of Article 8(2)(f) of the Statute states that the Statute applies "to armed conflicts that take place in the territory of a State when there is protracted armed conflict between governmental authorities and organized armed groups or between such groups."[16] This adaptation originated in a proposal submitted by Sierra Leone and was accepted in an apparent effort to provide a positive definition of non-international armed conflict.[17]

Given these developments, even absent a detailed examination of the exact meaning of the terms "intensity" of a conflict and "organization of the parties" to a conflict, it is apparent that a legitimate argument can now be made that the *Tadić* formula may well have had the effect of lowering the threshold required for the recognition of a non-international armed conflict. Very importantly, however, it remains to be seen whether future State practice will, in fact, sanction the validity of this approach.

"Global" Non-International Armed Conflicts?

At this juncture, it is essential to recognize that all of the preceding discussion regarding the nature and scope of non-international armed conflict has centered on violence—that is, hostilities—occurring within the boundaries of a State, thus, internal armed conflict. There is good reason for this. This is the geographical context in which NIACs have historically—and legally—been defined. Common Article 3 conflicts "not of an international character" have, since the adoption of the 1949 Geneva Conventions, consistently and uniformly been viewed in this manner. And no State, to include the United States, has ever challenged this interpretation.

So, given this reality, what has recently driven an attempted move away from this historical interpretation of Common Article 3 and non-international armed conflict? The answer resides in the events of 9/11 and the resultant attempts by the Bush administration to exercise the essentially unfettered "wartime" powers of a unitary executive. This resulted in an unprecedented misapplication of international law, in general, and the law of armed conflict, in particular.[18] And, when challenged by this overreach of executive authority, a compliant Congress failed to step forward to exercise its responsibility to rein in an administration running roughshod over the law, particularly that applicable to detainees held in the custody of the U.S. government.

Recognizing this congressional failure, the U.S. Supreme Court had little choice but to act. And, while it can be argued that its intentions were good, the Court's legal reasoning was both faulty and self-serving. In June 2006, the Court issued its *Hamdan* decision.[19] Relevant to the topic at hand, the Court opined that Common Article 3 was, in fact, applicable to a "conflict not of an international character" then being waged between the United States and the terrorist organization Al Qaeda. Its reasoning: the phrase "conflict not of an international character" appears in Common Article 3 simply to evidence a contradistinction to a conflict between nations. "In context," the Court opined, this phrase must bear its literal meaning. And, while acknowledging that "the official commentaries [Pictet's *Commentary*] accompanying Common Article 3 indicate that an important purpose of the provision was to furnish minimal protections to rebels involved in one kind of 'conflict not of an international character,' *i.e.*, a civil war," the Court then proceeded to note that "the commentaries also make clear 'that the scope of the Article must be as wide as possible.'"[20] In referencing this statement, however, the Court intentionally chose to ignore the context in which this comment was made. The *Commentary* text, following the listing of criteria set forth to assist in determining the existence of what clearly can only be viewed as "internal" non-international armed conflicts, reads as follows:

> Does this mean that Article 3 is not applicable in cases where armed strife breaks out *in a country*, but does not fulfil any of the above conditions . . . ? We do not subscribe to this view. We think, on the contrary, that the Article should be applied as widely as possible. There can be no reason against this. For, contrary to what may have been thought, the Article in its reduced form does not in any way limit the right of a State to put down rebellion. Nor does it increase in the slightest the authority of the rebel party.[21]

An objective assessment of Pictet's commentary to Article 3 clearly evidences the fact that the Court either failed to appreciate or deliberately chose to ignore the historical and consistent interpretation of Common Article 3's application to—exclusively—internal armed conflicts occurring within the territorial boundaries of one of the high contracting parties to the 1949 Geneva Conventions. In my view, it was the latter. Unwilling to challenge the President's ill-conceived determination that the United States was engaged in a "global war against terrorism,"[22] the Court, in essence, said: "If you seek to invoke the law of armed conflict to indefinitely incarcerate individuals seized in this 'war,' you must, at the very least, afford such individuals the minimal safeguards provided by this body of law—those of Common Article 3." And, rather than framing such safeguards as customary law of armed conflict provisions (given both the administration's and the Court's disdain for the legitimacy of customary international law), the Court was determined to posture Article 3's requirements as a treaty obligation. Thus, the Court's clearly tortured interpretation of the phrase "conflict not of an international character."

And so was born the misguided notion of the potential existence of non-international armed conflicts capable of spanning State boundaries. Indeed, the *Hamdan* decision has since been cited as definitive proof of this fact, given the Court's recognition of the existence of a "global" NIAC to which Common Article 3 was said to apply.[23] The reality is, of course, that the U.S. Supreme Court does not—and cannot—speak for the international community when it comes to the interpretation of multilateral international agreements. Nevertheless, the Court's attempt to significantly expand the definition and scope of a non-international armed conflict has unquestionably triggered the recent advocacy of the existence of a new form of conflict now said to be in play—that is, "transnational armed conflict."

This term has been used in different ways. One commentator makes use of it to describe a hybrid form of conflict, neither international nor non-international in character, but hostilities that fall somewhere in between and which represent the extraterritorial application of military combat power by the regular armed forces of a State against a transnational non-State entity.[24] Others have identified such conflicts as those that occur between a State and a non-State group (or between non-State groups) on the territory of more than one State, and would characterize these as "armed conflicts of a non-international character." In their view, the geographical element should not serve as the determinative factor in assessing whether a conflict is international in nature. "Internal conflicts are distinguished from international armed conflicts by the parties involved rather than by the territorial scope of the conflict."[25] The most cited examples of what these commentators would adjudge to be "transnational armed conflicts" would appear to be the Israel Defense Forces' incursions into southern Lebanon in 2006 and into Gaza in 2009. While I remain unconvinced of either the existence or the need for creation of this new form of armed conflict, the discussion of such is certain to continue.

So where does this leave us in terms of being able to reasonably identify violence that has risen to the level of a non-international armed conflict? In brief, see Common Article 3, Article 1(4) of Protocol I (which transforms certain NIACs into international armed conflicts), Article 1(1) of Protocol II, and, at least potentially, depending on future State practice, the determinative criteria articulated in the *Tadić* decision.

Identifying Non-International Armed Conflicts: U.S. State Practice

Now to my second assigned mission at the conference: U.S. State practice with respect to the manner in which it determines the existence—or non-existence—of a non-international armed conflict. Here, I am tempted to simply bring this article to a close with the concluding remark "there is none." And while such a premature conclusion is perhaps untenable, I, nevertheless, believe the statement to be an accurate one.

Given the Supreme Court's decision in *Hamdan*, a product of the Bush administration's bastardization of the law of armed conflict, the United States may now feel compelled to at least give lip service to the possibility of affording a slightly broader view of the phrase "conflicts not of an international character." However, I would see the government, having given a nod in this direction, then hastening to note that as the international community has been unable to achieve consensus on an agreed definition of non-international armed conflict, and given that a transition from international to non-international armed conflict is often quite subtle in nature,[26] a decision as to whether any form of violence has—or has not—evolved into a non-international armed conflict is, ultimately, the responsibility of the government faced with the armed threat in issue.

Having taken this position, the United States may well take the view that, in those cases in which it engages in foreign internal defense operations (the provision of U.S. advice and/or assistance to a foreign government faced with an internal threat from a non-State actor), while the decision as to whether this threat does—or does not—constitute a non-international armed conflict might be made jointly by the United States and the host government, the United States would ordinarily defer to the latter's judgment on this matter.[27]

The bottom line is that past practice indicates that the U.S. approach toward the issue of determining whether certain combatant activity is or is not a non-international armed conflict is completely self-serving, as it is for every State. From a purely bureaucratic standpoint, a determination as to whether U.S. military operations taken against an armed non-State actor should be characterized as a non-international armed conflict might be cited as a matter for U.S. interagency coordination. In reality, however, U.S. practice again reflects the fact that in most, if not all, cases, no "official" U.S. government determination is ever made. This was certainly the case in both Iraq and Afghanistan as these conflicts transitioned from international to non-international conflict. Instead, the United States has historically sought to protect its personnel involved in military operations that fall short of international armed conflict—or that might arguably be characterized as non-international armed conflict—and has sought compliance with the basic provisions of the law of armed conflict by its adversaries in such situations by formally stating that, as a matter of policy rather than law: "Members of the DoD Components comply with the Law of War during all armed conflicts, however such conflicts are characterized, and in all other military operations."[28]

I see no reason to expect a change in this U.S. approach toward dealing with the matter of NIAC characterization in the future. The U.S. government will continue to make no "official" determinations regarding whether certain hostilities do or do not constitute non-international armed conflicts. Again, while completely self-serving, it is an approach grounded in practicality and one that has produced a reasonably successful track record thus far.

Notes

1. Hersch Lauterpacht, *The Problem of the Revision of the Law of War*, 29 BRITISH YEARBOOK OF INTERNATIONAL LAW 360, 381–82 (1952).

2. For a discussion of the concept of "transnational" armed conflicts, see Andreas Paulus & Mindia Vashakmadze, *Asymmetric War and the Notion of Armed Conflict—A Tentative Conceptualization,* 91 INTERNATIONAL REVIEW OF THE RED CROSS 95, 110–12 (2009).

3. Convention for the Amelioration of the Condition of the Wounded and Sick in Armed Forces in the Field, Aug. 12, 1949, 6 U.S.T. 3114, 75 U.N.T.S. 31; Convention for the

Amelioration of the Condition of Wounded, Sick and Shipwrecked Members of Armed Forces at Sea, Aug. 12, 1949, 6 U.S.T. 3217, 75 U.N.T.S. 85; Convention Relative to the Treatment of Prisoners of War, Aug. 12, 1949, 6 U.S.T. 3316, 75 U.N.T.S. 135; Convention Relative to the Protection of Civilian Persons in Time of War, Aug. 12, 1949, 6 U.S.T. 3516, 75 U.N.T.S. 287.

4. COMMENTARY TO GENEVA CONVENTION I FOR THE AMELIORATION OF THE CONDITION OF THE WOUNDED AND SICK IN ARMED FORCES IN THE FIELD (Jean S. Pictet ed., 1952) [hereinafter PICTET COMMENTARY].

5. *Id.* at 32.

6. For a discussion of the "internationalization" of a non-international armed conflict, see MICHAEL N. SCHMITT, CHARLES H.B. GARRAWAY & YORAM DINSTEIN, THE MANUAL ON THE LAW OF NON-INTERNATIONAL ARMED CONFLICT WITH COMMENTARY 2 (2006); Legality of the Threat or Use of Nuclear Weapons, Advisory Opinion, 1996 I.C.J. 226, ¶¶ 79 & 82 (July 8); Military and Paramilitary Activities in and against Nicaragua (Nicar. v. U.S.), 1986 I.C.J. 14, ¶ 115 (June 27).

7. JEAN S. PICTET, DEVELOPMENT AND PRINCIPLES OF INTERNATIONAl HUMANITARIAN LAW 47 (1985).

8. For a discussion of State denial of the existence of a non-international armed conflict within its borders, see Anthony Cullen, *Key Developments Affecting the Scope of Internal Armed Conflict in International Humanitarian Law*, 183 MILITARY LAW REVIEW 66, 83–88 (2005).

9. PICTET COMMENTARY, *supra* note 4, at 49–50.

10. Protocol Additional to the Geneva Conventions of 12 August 1949, and Relating to the Protection of Victims of International Armed Conflicts, June 8, 1977, 1125 U.N.T.S. 3; Protocol Additional to the Geneva Conventions of 12 August 1949, and Relating to the Protection of Victims of Non-International Armed Conflicts, June 8, 1977, 1125 U.N.T.S. 609.

11. COMMENTARY ON THE ADDITIONAL PROTOCOLS OF 8 JUNE 1977 TO THE GENEVA CONVENTIONS OF 12 AUGUST 1949 ¶¶ 108–13 (Yves Sandoz, Christophe Swinarski & Bruno Zimmermann eds., 1987).

12. Prosecutor v. Tadić, Case No. IT-94-1-l, Decision on Defence Motion for Interlocutory Appeal on Jurisdiction (Int'l Crim. Trib. for the Former Yugoslavia Oct. 2, 1995).

13. *Id.*, ¶ 70.

14. Prosecutor v. Tadić, Case No. IT-94-1-T, Judgment, ¶ 562 (Int'l Crim. Trib. for the Former Yugoslavia May 7, 1997).

15. Prosecutor v. Akayesu, Case No. ICTR-96-4-T, Judgment, ¶ 620 (Sept. 2, 1998).

16. Rome Statute of the International Criminal Court, July 17, 1998, 2187 U.N.T.S. 90.

17. United Nations Diplomatic Conference of Plenipotentiaries on the Establishment of an International Criminal Court, June 15–July 17, 1998, 35th Meeting of the Committee Whole, ¶ 8, U.N. Doc. A/CONF.183/C.1/SR.35, *available at* http://untreaty.un.org/coddiplomaticconferences/icc-1998/docs/english/vol2/a_conf_183_c1_sr35.pdf.

18. For a detailed discussion of the Bush administration's misapplication of the law of armed conflict to the issue of detainees held by the U.S. government post-9/11, see David E. Graham, *The Dual U.S. Standard for the Treatment and Interrogation of Detainees: Unlawful and Unworkable*, 48 WASHBURN LAW JOURNAL 325 (2009).

19. Hamdan v. Rumsfeld, 548 U.S. 557 (2006).

20. *Id.* at 630–31.

21. PICTET COMMENTARY, *supra* note 4, at 50 (emphasis added).

22. *See, e.g.*, THE WHITE HOUSE, NATIONAL STRATEGY FOR COMBATING TERRORISM 18 (2003), *available at* http://www.comw.org/qdr/fulltext/0302nsct.pdf.

23. Paulus & Vashakmadze, *supra* note 2, at 99.

24. Geoffrey S. Corn, *Hamdan, Lebanon, and the Regulation of Armed Conflict: The Need to Recognize a Hybrid Category of Armed Conflict*, 40 VANDERBILT JOURNAL OF TRANSNATIONAL LAW 295 (2007).

25. Paulus & Vashakmadze, *supra* note 2, at 112.

26. Operation Enduring Freedom in Afghanistan and Operation Iraqi Freedom are classic examples of the subtle nature of such transitions.

27. It can be argued, however, that, in the matter of making a decision as to whether the ongoing conflict in Afghanistan has, over time, transitioned into a non-international armed conflict, the United States has neither deferred to nor acted jointly with the Afghan government in making such a decision.

28. Department of Defense, DoD Directive 2311.01E, DoD Law of War Program ¶ 4.1 (2006), *available at* http://www.dtic.mil/whs/directives/corres/pdf/231101e.pdf.

IV

Self-defense Targeting: Blurring the Line between the *Jus ad Bellum* and the *Jus in Bello*

Geoffrey S. Corn*

I. Introduction

Conflict classification has been and will continue to be one of the most complex issues arising from the intersection of national security policy and international law. From the inception of what the United States dubbed the "Global War on Terror," experts have been debating the meaning of the term "armed conflict," both international and non-international. The proliferation of remotely piloted warfare has only exacerbated the uncertainty associated with the meaning of these terms. In response, the concept of self-defense targeting emerged as an ostensible alternative to determining if and when a national use of armed force qualified as an armed conflict. In essence, this theory averts the need to engage in *jus in bello*[1] classification of counterterror military operations by relying on the overarching *jus ad bellum*[2] legal justification for these operations. Self-defense targeting, or what Professor Kenneth Anderson has called "naked self-defense,"[3] is offered as the U.S. legal framework for employing combat power to destroy or disrupt the capabilities

* Professor of Law, South Texas College of Law, Houston, Texas. Previously Lieutenant Colonel, U.S. Army, and Special Assistant to the U.S. Army Judge Advocate General for Law of War Matters. I would like to thank Nicholas Geohegan and Joel Glover for their excellent contributions in support of completing this article.

of transnational terrorist operatives.[4] This essay will question the validity of substituting *jus ad bellum* principles for those of the *jus in bello*, and why this substitution is a false solution to this extremely complex conflict classification dilemma.

The attack on Osama Bin Laden's (OBL) compound in Pakistan[5] has exposed in stark relief the importance of defining the legal framework applicable to the use of military force as a counterterrorism tool. The initial focus of the public debate generated by the attack was the legitimacy of the U.S. invocation of the inherent right of self-defense to launch a non-consensual operation within the sovereign territory of Pakistan.[6] However, that focus soon shifted to another critical legal question: even assuming the exercise of national self-defense was legitimate, what law regulated the tactical execution of the operation?[7] By virtue of his role as the leader of al Qaeda, was OBL a lawful military objective within the meaning of the law of armed conflict (LOAC),[8] and thereby subject to attack with deadly force as a measure of first resort? Or was he merely an international criminal, subject to a much more limited law enforcement use of force authority? The duality of the *jus belli* issues implicated by the attack generated a two-pronged legal critique: First, did the mission violate the international legal prohibition against use of force (*jus ad bellum*)? Second, did the mission trigger the law of armed conflict, or was the amount of force employed during the mission resulting in OBL's death excessive to that which was necessary to apprehend him? The self-defense targeting theory failed to sufficiently address this duality.

The first prong of this dualistic legal debate touches on an issue that appears well-settled in U.S. practice: the use of military force to attack individuals who are determined to be al Qaeda or Taliban belligerent operatives. The second prong—how such attacks are legally regulated at the tactical execution level—remains a subject of uncertainty. Both Presidents Bush and Obama (with the support of Congress) consistently invoked the inherent right of national self-defense pursuant to Article 51 of the Charter of the United Nations as the legal basis for attacking al Qaeda operatives.[9] However, the Obama administration seems to have superimposed an odd veneer on this authority: the concept of self-defense targeting.[10] Invoking the inherent right of self-defense, this theory suggests that both the resort to armed force *and* the execution of specific operations are regulated by the *jus ad bellum.* In essence, because attacking terrorist targets falls within the scope of international self-defense legal authority, *jus ad bellum* self-defense principles regulate the execution of combat operations used to achieve this self-defense objective, obviating the need to assess whether and what *jus in bello* principles apply to these operations. Thus, so long as the targets fall within the *ad bellum* principles of necessity and proportionality, attacking them is legally permissible.

II. Background

There is nothing unusual about the assertion that the principles of necessity and proportionality regulate combat operations directed against transnational terrorist operatives.[11] What is unusual is the assertion that *jus ad bellum* variants of these principles regulate operational execution.[12] Necessity and proportionality have always been core principles of both branches of the *jus belli*—principles that apply to both the authority to employ military force and the regulation of actual employment. However, in the *jus ad bellum* context, they have never before been viewed as principles to regulate operational and tactical execution.[13] Instead, in that context they frame the legality of national or multinational resort to military force in self-defense. Once the decision is made to employ force pursuant to this authority, the *jus in bello* variant of these principles (necessity of the mission and proportionality of collateral damage) operate to regulate the application of combat power during mission execution (in other words, they provide the foundation for the regulation of the application of combat power in the context of the self-defense-justified mission).

This self-defense targeting paradigm—Professor Kenneth Anderson's "naked self-defense"[14]—is certainly responsive to concerns over the legality of extending counterterror combat operations beyond the geographic limits of Afghanistan (and to an increasingly lesser degree Iraq). However, it does not and cannot become a substitute for defining the rules that regulate the actual execution of such missions. This *ad bellum* targeting theory may in some ways be responsive to the uncertainty related to the legal characterization of the struggle against transnational terrorism, or perhaps more precisely the question of whether an armed conflict can exist within the meaning of international law when States employ armed force to find, fix and destroy terrorist operations in diverse geographic locations.[15] A subcomponent of this question regarding the existence of an armed conflict is, even assuming the answer is yes, does such a conflict follow the enemy wherever on the globe he may be and does it provide for a "springing" of the LOAC authority for brief periods of time wherever he is located?

Since the United States initiated its military response to the terrorist attacks of September 11, 2001, the uncertainty related to the legal nature of this response has been a central theme in policy and academic discourse. Although the answers to these questions seem increasingly settled in U.S. practice (at least in the practical if not legal sense), questions over the legality of killing OBL—or the availability of viable alternatives—have again highlighted the significance of this uncertainty. While the United States seems to have abandoned the assertion that it is in a "war" against terror that spans the entire globe, its continued attack of what can only be understood as targets of opportunity in places like Yemen, Somalia and Pakistan have kept this uncertainty at the forefront of contemporary debate on counter-terror operations.[16]

Various interpretations of what triggers the *jus in bello* emerged following the U.S. military response to the terror attacks of September 11. In general terms, these theories ranged across a spectrum from a strict adherence to the theretofore widely accepted international/internal armed conflict paradigm, to the other extreme, proffered by me and others, that military operations conducted against international terrorist organizations like al Qaeda should be characterized as transnational armed conflicts: non-international armed conflicts of international scope.[17] Within that range were included concepts such as militarized law enforcement and extraterritorial law enforcement (military operations within the framework of human rights principles). All of these approaches shared a common theme: they sought to define the rules of tactical execution applicable to this military response within a framework of established legal norms.[18]

This essay will argue that the concept of self-defense targeting does not and cannot provide a substitute for resolving the debate about *in bello* applicability to transnational counterterror military operations. The reasons for this are multifaceted. First, the *jus ad bellum* has never been understood as a source of operational or tactical regulation nor a substitute for the law providing that regulation.[19] Indeed, one of the central tenets of the *jus belli* has always been the invalidity of reliance on the *jus ad bellum* to define *jus in bello* obligations. Instead, the de facto nature of tactical execution is the principal factor for assessing applicability of the *jus in bello*. Second, because the *jus ad bellum* has never been conceived as a tactical regulatory framework, using it as a substitute for the *jus in bello* injects unacceptable confusion into the planning and execution of combat operations. Finally, while the principles of necessity and proportionality are central to both branches of the *jus belli*, the meaning of these principles is not identical in each branch but, in fact, disparate. As a result, the scope of lawful authority to employ force during mission execution will be subtly but unquestionably degraded if *ad bellum* principles are utilized as a substitute for *in bello* regulation.

A. Transnational Armed Conflict: Genesis and Controversy

Transnational armed conflict as a legal term of art was nonexistent prior to September 11, 2001. Other writings provide extensive explanation of the term's origins and the concept it proposed.[20] In essence, it was a concept intended to bridge the chasm between the two traditionally acknowledged—and ostensibly only—situations triggering the *jus in bello*: international or inter-State armed conflicts and non-international or internal armed conflicts.[21] Adopted in the 1949 revisions to the Geneva Conventions, the concept of armed conflict, and these two categories of armed conflict, manifested an effort to ensure a genuine de facto law-triggering standard.[22] While this did not eliminate all uncertainty as to when the law applies, preventing humanitarian law avoidance through reliance on technical legal concepts such as war was unquestionably the primary motive behind the adoption of the armed conflict law trigger.

This was a profound development in conflict regulation. For the first time in history, a treaty-based legal test dictated applicability of LOAC regulation.[23] Although originally linked only to application of the Geneva Conventions, these triggers rapidly became the standard for applicability of the entire corpus of the LOAC.[24] An entire generation of military and international lawyers learned that armed conflict triggers LOAC application.[25] However, they also learned that there were only two types of armed conflict: international and internal.[26]

This dichotomy was under-inclusive from its inception. The international/internal armed conflict dichotomy was clearly responsive to the law avoidance that occurred during World War II and the law inapplicability during the Spanish Civil War.[27] However, it failed to account for the possibility of extraterritorial armed conflicts between States and non-State belligerents.[28] Although not a common situation in the history of modern warfare, hostilities in such a context were not unknown.[29] Nor did the armed-conflict-law trigger account for the emergence of other external military operations involving minimal hostilities, such as United Nations peacekeeping missions.[30] Understanding the necessity of providing a regulatory framework for such operations, commanders and legal advisors thrust into these zones of uncertainty resorted to policy-based application of *jus in bello* principles, a methodology that proved generally effective in the decade preceding 9/11.[31] However, this approach to filling the regulatory void created by the international/internal dichotomy also averted attention from the underlying issue of regulatory under-inclusiveness.[32]

This under-inclusiveness was fully exposed when the United States initiated its military response to al Qaeda following the terror attacks of September 11.[33] As the United States began to preventively detain captives in that struggle, the implicit invocation of LOAC authority became clear.[34] Use of the designation "unlawful combatant" confirmed this invocation—these terrorist operatives were detained not as criminals awaiting adjudication, but as enemy operatives to prevent their return to hostilities.[35] However, pursuant to the advice provided by his Attorney General, President Bush concluded that LOAC protections were inapplicable to these detainees.[36] The basis for this conclusion was clear: the armed conflict with al Qaeda did not fit within the international/internal armed conflict law-triggering equation.[37] Because al Qaeda was not a State, the conflict could not qualify as international; because al Qaeda operated outside the territory of the United States, the conflict could not qualify as internal.[38]

This determination was problematic on numerous levels, but for military lawyers trained to ensure compliance with LOAC principles during all military operations no matter how they might be legally classified,[39] it was particularly troubling. As I have written previously, the concept of transnational armed conflict evolved to respond to this newly exploited gap in legal protections for individuals subjected to LOAC-based authority.[40] The objectives of the concept were simple: adopt a characterization for the non-international armed conflict with al Qaeda consistent with the non-State but nonetheless international character of the organization; require application of fundamental LOAC principles; and deny al Qaeda any credibility windfall from suggesting the conflict was international within the meaning of the law. In short, it was simply a term to denote a non-international armed conflict (within the meaning of Common Article 3 of the four 1949 Geneva Conventions) of international scope, what others have called an "internationalized non-international armed conflict."[41]

Reaction to the transnational armed conflict concept has ranged the spectrum from rejection[42] to endorsement;[43] however, it is important to note that the underlying objective is also reflected in other conceptions of the legal framework for the military component of counterterror operations. As noted, these include "internationalized" non-international armed conflict and militarized extraterritorial law enforcement.[44] For the United States, this debate was essentially resolved by the Supreme Court's 2006 decision in *Hamdan v. Rumsfeld*.[45] A majority of the Court concluded the term "non-international armed conflict" in Common Article 3 is not restricted to internal armed conflicts, but covers any armed conflict that does not qualify as international within the meaning of Common Article 2.[46] This "contradistinction" interpretation effectively achieved the transnational armed conflict objective: a majority of the Court closed the gap identified (some might say exploited) by the Department of Justice analysis and relied on by President Bush.[47] By concluding that any armed conflict that fails to qualify as "international" within the meaning of the Geneva Conventions is non-international (irrespective of geographic scope) and therefore triggers the baseline humanitarian protections of Common Article 3, the Court created a simple equation: if the government treats the struggle against al Qaeda as an armed conflict, it must be either international or non-international within the meaning of the Geneva Conventions.[48] Thus, it closed the gap in humanitarian law applicability and ensured that future invocations of armed conflict authority must trigger minimum humanitarian obligations.[49]

The *Hamdan* opinion has not, however, eliminated the uncertainty and controversy over the legal characterization of military operations directed against al Qaeda.[50] Experts continue to struggle with this question, and new theories continue to emerge.[51] It remains indisputable, however, that characterizing the contention between al Qaeda and the United States as an armed conflict defies indicators traditionally applied to identify the existence of non-international armed conflicts.[52] Those most notably lacking include a sustained nature of combat operations directed against al Qaeda targets outside the Afghanistan zone of combat[53] (even loosely defined), and the lack of continuous and concerted hostilities by al Qaeda against the United States.[54] This lack of "intensity" and "duration" was in fact central to the conclusion by a working group of the International Law Commission that counterterror operations cannot be properly characterized as armed conflicts, even of the non-international type.[55] Following President Obama's election, expectations were high that the new administration might abandon the armed conflict theory altogether and revert to the international law enforcement approach to dealing with the transnational terrorist threat.[56] Not only were these expectations unfounded; the new administration opened an entirely new front in the legal characterization debate.[57]

B. Self-defense Targeting: A Third Rail?

It did not take long for the Obama administration to demonstrate that it was not about to abandon an armed conflict–based approach to dealing with the al Qaeda threat.[58] To this date, the United States continues to employ combat power against al Qaeda operatives in locations both proximate to and far removed from ongoing hostilities in Afghanistan.[59] These operations involve the employment of deadly force as a measure of first resort, an unavoidable indicator that the United States continues to rely on an armed conflict–based legal framework.[60] The discomfort with such an expansive concept of armed conflict is certainly understandable. What is equally understandable is the pragmatic reality that the nature of these operations makes them inconsistent with peacetime law enforcement legal principles.[61] Nonetheless, the apparent aversion to recognizing some type of "springing" armed conflict paradigm has produced not only opposition, but also a proposal for an alternative legal framework that avoids the need to address the conflict classification dilemma: self-defense targeting.[62]

This alternative methodology is most notably attributed to Professor Kenneth Anderson.[63] In a series of essays, Anderson began to proffer the argument that the *jus ad bellum* provides sufficient—and ostensibly exclusive—legal authority for the regulation of attacks directed against terrorist operatives.[64] This theory has also been embraced by Professor Jordan Paust.[65] Although Paust has consistently rejected characterizing the response to transnational terrorism as an armed conflict[66] (based primarily on a classical interpretation of Common Articles 2 and 3 of the Geneva Conventions),[67] his position has evolved to acknowledge the legitimate use of military force in self-defense against external non-State threats.[68] That response would not qualify as an armed conflict, because it could not fit within the traditionally understood scope of the Geneva Convention law-triggering framework. Instead, the *jus ad bellum* right of self-defense would be the exclusive source of legal authority related to the response.

Professor Anderson characterizes this theory as "naked self-defense."[69] According to Anderson, this term characterizes the legal basis for drone strikes articulated by State Department Legal Advisor Harold Koh: exercise of *jus ad bellum* self-defense does not *ipso facto* trigger the *jus in bello*. As will be explained more fully below, in the same essay Anderson signals a significant revision of this theory—a retreat motivated by his reflection on the inability to effectively define the geographic scope of a transnational non-international armed conflict. What is significant here, however, is that the theory itself presents a complex question: is it possible to employ military force pursuant to a claim of *jus ad bellum* national self-defense without triggering the *jus in bello*? And if the answer is yes, what international legal principles regulate the application of combat power during the execution of such operations?

In this essay, I argue that *jus ad bellum* targeting—or naked self-defense—is a flawed substitute for embracing the alternate (albeit controversial) conclusion that employing combat power in self-defense against transnational non-State operatives must be characterized as armed conflict. In support of this argument, the essay will expose what I believe is the implicit acknowledgment by proponents of self-defense targeting that these operations do indeed trigger the LOAC. I will do this by exploring the nature of two fundamental *jus belli* principles invoked by these proponents: necessity and proportionality.[70] Contrasting the effect of these principles within the self-defense targeting framework with their effect within a *jus in bello* framework will illustrate that self-defense targeting reflects an implicit acknowledgment of *jus in bello* applicability during operational mission execution.

III. The Traditional Distinction between the Jus ad Bellum *and the* Jus in Bello

At the core of the self-defense targeting theory is the assumption that the *jus ad bellum* provides sufficient authority to both *justify* and *regulate* the application of combat power.[71] This assumption ignores an axiom of *jus belli* development: the compartmentalization of the *jus ad bellum* and the *jus in bello*.[72] As Colonel G.I.A.D. Draper noted in 1971, "equal application of the Law governing the conduct of armed conflicts to those illegally resorting to armed forces and those lawfully resorting thereto is accepted as axiomatic in modern International Law."[73] This compartmentalization is the historic response to the practice of defining *jus in bello* obligations by reference to the *jus ad bellum* legality of conflict.[74] As the *jus in bello* evolved to focus on the humanitarian protection of victims of war, to include the armed forces themselves,[75] the practice of denying LOAC applicability based on assertions of conflict illegality became indefensible.[76] Instead, the de facto nature of hostilities would dictate *jus in bello* applicability, and the *jus ad bellum* legal basis for hostilities would be irrelevant to this determination.[77]

This compartmentalization lies at the core of the Geneva Convention law-triggering equation.[78] Adoption of the term "armed conflict" as the primary triggering consideration for *jus in bello* applicability was a deliberate response to the more formalistic *jus in bello* applicability that predated the 1949 revision of the Geneva Conventions.[79] Prior to these revisions, *in bello* applicability often turned on the existence of a state of war in the international legal sense, which in turn led to assertions of inapplicability as the result of assertions of unlawful aggression.[80] Determined to prevent the denial of humanitarian regulation to situations necessitating such regulation—any de facto armed conflict—the 1949 Conventions sought to neutralize the impact of *ad bellum* legality in law applicability analysis.[81]

This effort rapidly became the norm of international law.[82] Armed conflict analysis simply did not include conflict legality considerations.[83] National military manuals, international jurisprudence and expert commentary all reflect this development.[84] This division is today a fundamental LOAC tenet—and is beyond dispute.[85] In fact, for many years the United States has gone even farther, extending application of LOAC principles beyond situations of armed conflict altogether so as to regulate any military operation.[86] This is just another manifestation of the fact that States, or perhaps more importantly the armed forces that do their bidding, view the cause or purported justification for such operations as irrelevant when deciding what rules apply to regulate operational and tactical execution.

This aspect of *ad bellum/in bello* compartmentalization is not called into question by the self-defense targeting concept.[87] Nothing in the assertion that combat operations directed against transnational non-State belligerent groups qualifies as armed conflict suggests the inapplicability of LOAC regulatory norms on the basis of the relative illegitimacy of al Qaeda's efforts to inflict harm on the United States and other victim States (although as noted earlier, this was implicit in the original Bush administration approach to the war on terror).[88] Instead, the self-defense targeting concept reflects an odd inversion of the concern that motivated the armed conflict law trigger. The concept does not assert the illegitimacy of the terrorist cause to deny LOAC principles to operations directed against them.[89] Instead, it relies on the legality of the U.S. cause to dispense with the need for applying LOAC principles to regulate these operations.[90] This might not be explicit, but it is clear that an exclusive focus on *ad bellum* principles indicates that these principles subsume *in bello* conflict regulation norms.[91]

There are two fundamental flaws with this conflation. First, by contradicting the traditional compartmentalization between the two branches of the *jus belli*,[92] it creates a dangerous precedent. Although there is no express resurrection of the just war concept of LOAC applicability, by focusing exclusively on *jus ad bellum* legality and principles, the concept suggests the inapplicability of *jus in bello* regulation as the result of the legality of the U.S. cause. To be clear, I believe U.S. counterterror operations are legally justified actions in self-defense. However, this should not be even implicitly relied on to deny *jus in bello* applicability to operations directed against terrorist opponents, precisely because it may be viewed as suggesting the invalidity of the opponent's cause deprives them of the protections of that law, or that the operations are somehow exempted from LOAC regulation. Second, even discounting this detrimental precedential effect, the conflation of *ad bellum* and *in bello* principles to regulate the execution of operations is extremely troubling.[93] This is because the meaning of these principles is distinct within each branch of the *jus belli*.[94]

Furthermore, because the scope of authority derived from *jus ad bellum* principles purportedly invoked to regulate operational execution is more restrictive than that derived from their *jus in bello* counterparts,[95] this conflation produces a potential windfall for terrorist operatives. Thus, the *ad bellum/in bello* conflation is ironically self-contradictory. In one sense, it suggests the inapplicability of *jus in bello* protections to the illegitimate terrorist enemy because of the legitimacy of the U.S. cause.[96] In another sense, the more restrictive nature of the *jus ad bellum* principles it substitutes for the *jus in bello* variants to regulate operational execution provides the enemy with increased protection from attack.[97] Neither of these consequences is beneficial, nor necessary. Instead, compliance with the traditional *jus ad bellum/jus in bello* compartmentalization methodology averts these consequences and offers a more rational approach to counterterrorism conflict regulation.[98]

IV. Necessity and Proportionality: The Risk of Authority Dilution

The most problematic aspect of the self-defense targeting concept is that it produces a not so subtle substitution of *jus ad bellum* necessity and proportionality for the *jus in bello* variants of these principles.[99] While these principles are fundamental in both branches of the *jus belli*,[100] they are not identical in effect. The *ad bellum* variants are intended to limit State resort to force to a measure of last resort;[101] the *in bello* variants are intended to strike an appropriate balance between the authority to efficiently bring about the submission of an enemy and the humanitarian interest of limiting the inevitable suffering associated with armed conflict.[102]

It is a foundational principle of international law that the *jus ad bellum* restricts resort to force by States to situations of absolute necessity—and necessity justifies only proportional force to return the *status quo ante*.[103] In this sense, national self-defense is strikingly analogous to individual self-defense as a criminal law justification.[104] In both contexts, necessity requires a determination of an imminent threat of unlawful attack, a situation affording no alternative other than self-help measures.[105] Furthermore, even when the justification of self-help is triggered by an imminent threat, both bodies of law strictly limit the amount of force that may be employed to respond to the threat.[106] States, like individuals, may use only that amount of force absolutely necessary to meet the threat and restore the *status quo ante* of security.[107] Using more force than is necessary to subdue the threat is considered excessive, and therefore outside the realm of the legally justified response.[108]

There is no question that these variants of necessity and proportionality are critical to the stability of international relations.[109] The UN Charter reflects an obvious judgment that States are obligated to endeavor to resolve all disputes peacefully, and that resort to force must be conceived as an exceptional measure.[110] A very limited conception of necessity requiring an actual and imminent threat of unlawful aggression serves this purpose by prioritizing alternate dispute resolution modalities over uses of force—the core purpose of the Charter.[111] Even after a justifiable resort to force, the requirement to provide notice to the Security Council[112] reflects this purpose by enhancing the probability of Security Council action to restore international peace and security and thereby nullify the necessity for continued use of force by the State.[113] The *jus ad bellum* proportionality rule also serves this purpose by reducing the risk of uncontrollable escalation.[114] By limiting the justified response to only that amount of force absolutely necessary to reduce the threat, proportionality operates to mitigate the risk of a justified self-defense response morphing into an unjustified use of military force to achieve objectives unrelated to self-defense.[115] As a result, conflagration is limited, thereby enhancing the efficacy of alternate dispute resolution modalities.

These principles make perfect sense when assessing the justification for a national resort to military force outside the umbrella of a Security Council authorization. However, as operational execution parameters, they impose a peacetime self-defense model onto wartime employment of combat power. This is because the *jus in bello* variants of necessity and proportionality have never been understood to function analogously with their peacetime variants.[116] Instead, these principles have unique meaning in the context of armed conflict.[117] As a result, they are simply not interchangeable with the *ad bellum* variants. As a result, the self-defense targeting concept ostensibly regulates the execution of combat operations with norms inconsistent with those historically and logically suited for that purpose.

Jus in bello necessity means something fundamentally different than self-defense necessity.[118] In the context of armed conflict, necessity justifies a much broader exercise of authority—the authority to employ *all* measures not otherwise prohibited by international law to bring about the prompt submission of the enemy.[119] Unlike self-defense necessity, there is no "measure of last resort" aspect to *jus in bello* necessity.[120] Accordingly, armed conflict triggers authority to employ force in a manner that would rarely (if ever) be tolerated in peacetime, even when acting in self-defense.[121]

The most obvious (and relevant for purposes of this essay) illustration of the difference between *ad bellum* and *in bello* necessity is the authority to employ deadly force against an opponent. Like peacetime self-defense, *jus ad bellum* self-defense justifies a State's use of deadly military force only as a measure of last resort.[122] In contrast, *jus in bello* necessity authorizes the use of deadly combat power against an enemy as a measure of first resort. This necessity justification is implemented through the rule of military objective, which establishes who and what qualify as a lawful object of attack.[123] However, once that status is determined, it is the principle of military necessity[124] that justifies employment of deadly combat power against such "targets" as a measure of first resort.[125]

It is clear that this authority in no way requires manifestation of actual threat to the attacking force.[126] Instead, the status of military objective alone results in a presumption of threat that justifies the use of deadly force.[127] This presumption itself indicates the unique function of *in bello* necessity. This central premise of the *jus in bello* was reflected as early as Rousseau's 1762 *Contract social*, in which he noted that "[w]ar is not a relation between man and man, but a relation between State and State in which individuals are enemies only incidentally, not as men, or citizens, but as soldiers."[128]

Because armed conflict involves a contest between armed belligerent *groups*, and not merely *individual actors*, the use of force authority triggered by military necessity is focused on collective rather than individual effect.[129] In other words, unlike a peacetime exercise of necessity (which focuses on neutralizing an individual threat), wartime[130] necessity focuses on bringing about the submission of the enemy in the corporate and not individual sense.[131] This collective vice individual focus of justifiable violence applies at every level of military operations. At the strategic level, nations seek to break the will of an opponent by demonstrating to enemy leadership the futility of resistance; at the operational level, commanders seek to impose their will on forces arrayed against them by the synchronized employment of all combat capabilities.[132] The ideal outcome of such employment is the establishment of full-spectrum dominance, allowing the friendly commander to impose his will on the enemy at the time and place of his choosing.[133] This routinely necessitates use of overwhelming combat power at the decisive point in the battle—use that is often far more robust than may be required to overcome resistance at that specific point.[134] At the tactical level, forces may use mass and shock to paralyze enemy forces, disrupt their ability to maneuver and adjust to the fluidity of the battle, and demoralize individual unit members.[135] All of these effects contribute to "the prompt submission of the enemy."[136]

Employing overwhelming combat power at the decisive place and time of battle (known as the principle of mass in the lexicon of military doctrine)[137] would arguably be inconsistent with *jus ad bellum* necessity.[138] Instead, a commander would be restricted from employing any amount of force beyond what was *actually* necessary to subdue the *individual* object of attack.[139] Thus, the assertion that the *jus ad bellum* suffices to justify necessary measures to subdue an opponent misses the point. The question is not whether the resort to force by the State is necessary—a question that certainly must be answered through the lens of *jus ad bellum* necessity.[140] The question is whether the amount of force then employed by the armed forces of the State to subdue the enemy is justified, a question that must be answered through the lens of a very different conception of necessity.[141]

Even more problematic than the extension of *jus ad bellum* necessity as an operational regulatory norm is the extension of *jus ad bellum* proportionality. Like necessity, proportionality is a core principle of both the *jus ad bellum* and the *jus in bello*.[142] And like necessity, the principle has a significantly different meaning in each branch of the *jus belli*.[143] Conflating these disparate principles into a singular regulatory norm substantially degrades the scope of lawful targeting authority and confuses those charged with executing combat operations.

In the *jus ad bellum*, proportionality really means proportionality. This might seem like an odd statement, but it is critical when comparing the two *jus belli* variants of the principle. Proportionality normally means no more than is absolutely necessary to achieve a valid purpose.[144] It is a concept that is normally linked to a justification of necessity.[145] Similarly, under U.S. criminal law, actions in self-defense are invalid if executed with more force than is necessary to reduce the threat. Use of excessive force in that context, because not strictly necessary, is unjustified.[146] The *jus ad bellum* reflects an analogous conception of proportionality.[147] First, the amount of force a State is permitted to employ in self-defense is strictly limited to that amount necessary to reduce the imminent threat.[148] Second, the source of aggression is the beneficiary of the proportionality constraint.[149] In other words, as in the criminal law context, a State (like an individual) responding to unlawful aggression may be authorized to employ force in self-defense, but is prohibited from responding to the source of aggression with any amount of force in excess of that necessary to reduce that immediate threat.

In contrast, proportionality in the *jus in bello* context *does not* really mean proportionality. Again, this may seem like an odd proposition. Nonetheless, even a cursory review of the *jus in bello* proportionality principle validates this conclusion. First, unlike traditional proportionality, the *jus in bello* variant in no way protects the object of deliberate violence (the lawful target). Instead, the beneficiaries of the protection are the knowing but non-deliberate victims of a deliberate attack—civilians and civilian property in proximity to the lawful target.[150] Protecting these potential victims from what is referred to in colloquial terms as collateral damage and incidental injury reflects a fundamentally different purpose for this proportionality constraint. Unlike in the self-defense context, *jus in bello* proportionality is not directly linked to the necessity of subduing an imminent threat. Instead, the objective of the principle is to protect innocent people and property in the vicinity of a lawful object of attack from the consequences of employing combat power against lawful targets. As for the lawful target itself, the suggestion that an attack might be disproportionate is a legal oxymoron; the status alone justifies that amount of force determined necessary to bring about enemy submission, which justifies use of deadly force as a measure of first resort.[151] The only limitation on that use of force is the prohibition against the use of methods (tactics) or means (weapons) calculated or of a nature to cause superfluous injury or unnecessary suffering. However, this rule is not synonymous with the protections provided by the principle of proportionality, and rarely is considered a limitation on the employment of authorized weapon systems against enemy personnel, facilities or equipment.

Second, beneficiaries of *jus in bello* proportionality (potential victims of collateral damage and incidental injury) are not protected from disproportionate effects, but from excessive effects.[152] An attack is unlawful within the meaning of *jus in bello* proportionality only when the knowing but non-deliberate harm will be *excessive* in relation to the anticipated military advantage. While the principle, like its *ad bellum* counterpart, does trigger a balance of interests, the fulcrum upon which that balance is made is fundamentally different. Excessive is not, nor ever has been, analogous to disproportionate.[153] To begin with, the meaning of the word is far more elusive than that of traditional proportionality. Proportionality connotes something slightly more than necessary to produce an outcome. While this is not a precise concept, it lends itself to objective evaluation. Indeed, juries sitting in judgment of defendants claiming the justification of self-defense routinely critique the amount of force employed by the defendant, asking whether it was more than necessary to respond to the threat.

Excessive, in contrast, connotes a significant imbalance. While the precise meaning of excessive collateral damage or incidental injury remains nearly as elusive today as it was when the concept was incorporated into Additional Protocol I,[154] one thing is clear: it is not analogous to disproportionate harm as the term is used in relation to traditional proportionality analysis. Instead, it means something more analogous to harm so overwhelming that it actually nullifies the legitimacy of attacking an otherwise lawful target. Thus, the *jus in bello* proportionality principle does not obligate commanders to strictly limit the amount of force employed against a lawful target to the absolute minimum necessary to eliminate a threat. Instead, it obligates the commander to cancel an attack only when the anticipated harm to civilians and/or civilian property is so beyond the realm of reason that inflicting that harm, even incidentally, reflects a total disregard for the innocent victims of hostilities.[155] In this sense, it is almost as if the law imputes an illicit state of mind to a commander because of the disregard of the risk of overwhelming harm to the civilian population.[156]

This *jus in bello* variant of proportionality is further distinguished from its *ad bellum* counterpart because of the nature of operational and tactical targeting. In a traditional self-defense context, the employment of force (individually or nationally) is justified for the sole purpose of eliminating the imminent threat. In armed conflict, the potential effect to be achieved by employing combat power against a lawful target often varies depending on mission requirements. Accordingly, elimination of an individual threat is not the unitary objective of force employment. Instead, commanders leverage their combat power to achieve defined effects against the range of enemy targets in the battlespace, effects that collectively facilitate enemy submission.[157] Destruction is obviously one of these effects. However, doctrinal effects also include disruption, degradation, interdiction, suppression and harassment.[158] Each of these effects requires a different type and amount of force to achieve; and each effect therefore implicates a very different proportionality analysis.

This variable nature of justifiable effects in armed conflict—known in operational terms as "effects-based operations"[159]—is a critical factor in applying the *jus in bello* proportionality principle, and finds no analogue in self-defense targeting. Nations employ force to reduce the threat, and only that amount of force required to do so is justified. Accordingly, if disruption alone is sufficient to restore the non-threat environment, the *jus ad bellum* obligates the State to employ force limited in intensity to achieve this effect. However, no analogous minimum necessary force obligation exists pursuant to the *jus in bello* proportionality principle. Instead, each employment of force is operationally connected to the broader overall objective of compelling enemy submission. Thus, disruption and bypass of enemy forces may be a selected course of action at one point in the battle, while total destruction may be selected for a similar enemy force at another point in the battle. Obviously, these different selected effects will drive the amount of force employment required, which will in turn influence the risk of collateral damage and incidental injury. Furthermore, under the *ad bellum* construct, proportionality is traditionally assessed at the strategic (macro) level.[160]

The importance of this aspect of *jus in bello* proportionality is reflected in the requirement that the consequences of force employment be assessed against the overall operational objective, and not the individual tactical objective. A number of States included this macro conception of proportionality in understandings when they ratified Additional Protocol I.[161] The motivation to enter such reservations seems obvious: attribution of the value of employing combat power in armed conflict for purposes of balancing the anticipated effects of that employment against collateral damage and incidental injury must be framed by the broader concept of how it contributes to the legitimate operational objective of compelling enemy submission, not through a micro assessment of whether it is sufficient to achieve any given and isolated tactical objective. This aspect of *jus in bello* proportionality once again reflects the most fundamental difference between the two variants of the principle: the beneficiary of the protection is not the object of attack.

Collectively, all of these considerations indicate that extending *jus ad bellum* proportionality to *jus in bello* decision making produces at worst a significant distortion of legitimate operational authority, and at best confusion as to the scope of targeting authority. Are forces executing *jus ad bellum* self-defense missions obligated to employ minimum force to subdue the object of attack? Is the object of attack protected by the principle? Must proportionality be assessed based on an exclusive consideration of reducing the threat presented by the immediate object of attack, or may the broader impact on enemy forces be considered? These questions are nullified by maintaining the traditional division between *jus ad bellum* authority and *jus in bello* regulation. Pursuant to this division, the nation acts in response to an actual or imminent threat and the armed forces executing operations pursuant to that *justification* employ force in order to bring about the prompt submission of the enemy entity posing the threat. In so doing, they balance the risk of collateral damage and incidental injury to civilians and civilian property in the vicinity of enemy objects of attack. But nothing obligates them to employ the minimum amount of force to achieve each individual tactical objective.

V. If It Ain't Broke Don't Fix It: Jus in Bello *Principles and Tactical Clarity*

As noted earlier in this essay, some commentators continue to assert the inapplicability of *jus in bello* principles to the struggle against transnational terrorism on the basis that this struggle cannot qualify as armed conflict, or that if it does it is geographically restricted to zones of traditional combat operations.[162] Some of these commentators also reject the legitimacy of invoking *jus ad bellum* self-defense to attack terrorists. This rejection at least renders their position logically consistent. The same cannot be said for advocates of self-defense targeting: those who assert the legitimacy of invoking the right of national self-defense to respond to the threat of transnational terrorism, but insist such operations cannot normally qualify as armed conflicts triggering the *jus in bello*.[163] If, as they assert, responding to terrorism with military force is justified pursuant to the *jus ad bellum*, then the use of combat capability to execute such missions is, in the view of this author and others, sufficient to qualify as armed conflict. Why is there such aversion to acknowledging *jus in bello* applicability to military operations executed to achieve these legitimate self-defense objectives? The most obvious answer appears to be the conclusion that these operations, while justified as actions in self-defense, fail to satisfy the internationally accepted elements to qualify as armed conflicts.[164]

This self-defense-without-armed-conflict approach reflects a visceral discomfort with the suggestion that States may properly invoke *jus in bello* authority whenever they choose to employ combat power abroad. Transnational armed conflict opponents argue that since the inception of the "Global War on Terror," unless combat operations fit within the traditional Geneva Convention international/internal armed conflict equation, they cannot be characterized as armed conflicts.[165] Others (including the author) have responded to this argument at length in previous articles.[166] However, what is perplexing is that this argument loses all merit when connected with the self-defense targeting theory. That theory presupposes the use of combat power to defend the nation against an imminent and ongoing threat posed by transnational terrorist operatives.

If this is the basis for refusing to acknowledge the applicability of *jus in bello* regulation, it is the ultimate manifestation of willful blindness. Essentially, self-defense targeting proponents implicitly acknowledge operations conducted under this authority involve armed hostilities against transnational non-State threats. However, they then avoid assessing the nature of these hostilities, and how they implicate *jus in bello* applicability, by substituting *ad bellum* principles to provide a regulatory framework for operational execution.[167]

Professor Kenneth Anderson's latest essay on this subject is particularly insightful on the validity of the self-defense targeting concept.[168] An (or perhaps the) original proponent of self-defense targeting,[169] Anderson candidly acknowledges his reversal on this issue, and that what he calls "naked self-defense" is insufficient to provide comprehensive regulation to transnational counterterror operations.[170] This is an important step in the right direction, for it will better focus debate on the underlying and critical question of whether a nation's resort to force in self-defense against an external non-State opponent can qualify as something other than armed conflict. My response to this question has been consistent: when a State employs combat power in a manner that indicates it has implicitly invoked LOAC principles (by employing deadly force as a measure of first resort), it is engaged in an armed conflict. As a result, it is bound to comply with core LOAC principles.[171] This does not mean that any use of armed forces qualifies as armed conflict. Such a view would certainly be overbroad, and I have argued against this approach consistently in the past. However, when armed forces employed to achieve a national security objective conduct operations pursuant to LOAC-based targeting authority—status-based targeting—that combination of armed forces and engagement authority indicates they are utilizing the "tools" of war, and must respect, at a minimum, the core principles of the "rules" of war.[172]

Irrespective of the relative support for or opposition to this interpretation of LOAC applicability, it remains a critical question that has been obscured by the self-defense targeting alternative. If, as proponents like Professor Paust argue, an exercise of national self-defense against transnational non-State threats is not armed conflict, focus must be redirected to determine the alternative controlling legal framework for regulating the execution of such operations. Can national self-defense be executed with an employment of military (or paramilitary) force falling below the threshold of armed conflict? For example, are there situations where a State when asserting the right of national self-defense is obligated by the *jus ad bellum* proportionality requirement to rely on police powers instead of combat power?

This seems a particularly critical question in an era of transnational non-State threats. Terrorism is obviously first on that list (at least for the United States), but organized criminal syndicates operating across national boundaries, piracy and non-State-generated cyber threats all share similarities with transnational terrorism. All of these threats challenge the national security of multiple States; all of these threats emanate from entities that are rarely organized in traditional military character; all of these threats may compel reliance on military force in response. Yet in the view of many, the lack of organization, territorial control and concerted military-type operations by these threats exclude responses (even with military force) from the category of armed conflict.[173]

Invoking the *jus ad bellum* as a justification to respond to such threats is insufficient to resolve this important question. Instead, resolving this question requires a careful assessment of the nature of the threat, the nature of the requisite response and the very real consequences of subjecting operational execution to either a law enforcement or armed conflict legal framework. Some experts (the author included) continue to believe that LOAC principles provide an effective and operationally logical framework to regulate any combat operation. But as noted above, this view is based on the conclusion that the key trigger for application of these principles is a use of force that reflects reliance on the principle of military objective. In those situations, there is arguably no value—and indeed substantial risk—in attempting to substitute *jus ad bellum* principles to regulate operational execution. However, there are plausible arguments that the nature of some self-defense missions might justify a more restrictive operational framework based on a hybrid of LOAC and law enforcement principles.[174] What seems clear, however, is that even if true, these principles would be applied as the result of the nature of the threat/response continuum, not as an extension of *jus ad bellum* principles to regulate operational execution.

VI. One Step Forward, One Step Back: Are We Missing Something?

The statement by Legal Advisor Koh following the Bin Laden raid addressing U.S. legal authority for the mission and for killing Bin Laden is perhaps as clear an articulation of a legal basis for a military action ever provided by the Department of State.[175] Indeed, the fact that Koh articulated an official U.S. interpretation of both the *jus ad bellum* and *jus in bello* makes his use of a website titled *Opinio Juris*[176] especially significant (as such a statement by a government official in Koh's position is clear evidence of *opinio juris*). Unlike his earlier statement at a meeting of the American Society of International Law,[177] Koh did not restrict his invocation of law to the *jus ad bellum*. Instead, he asserted the U.S. position that the mission was justified pursuant to the inherent right of self-defense, but also that Bin Laden's killing was lawful pursuant to the *jus in bello*. Koh properly noted that as a mission executed in the context of the armed conflict with al Qaeda, the LOAC imposed no obligation on U.S. forces to employ minimum necessary force. Instead, Bin Laden's status as an enemy belligerent justified the use of deadly force as a measure of first resort, and Bin Laden bore the burden of manifesting his surrender in order to terminate that authority. Hence, U.S. forces were in no way obligated to attempt to capture Bin Laden before resorting to deadly force.[178]

A recent statement made by John Brennan, Deputy National Security Advisor for Homeland Security and Counterterrorism, further clarifies the current administration's justification for using deadly force as a first resort against al Qaeda operatives:

> The United States does not view our authority to use military force against al-Qa'ida as being restricted solely to "hot" battlefields like Afghanistan. Because we are engaged in an armed conflict with al-Qa'ida, the United States takes the legal position that . . . we have the authority to take action against al-Qa'ida and its associated forces without doing a separate self-defense analysis each time. . . .
>
> This Administration's counterterrorism efforts outside of Afghanistan and Iraq are focused on those individuals who are a threat to the United States, whose removal would cause a significant—even if only temporary—disruption of the plans and capabilities of al-Qa'ida and its associated forces. Practically speaking, then, the question turns principally on how you define "imminence."
>
> We are finding increasing recognition in the international community that a more flexible understanding of "imminence" may be appropriate when dealing with terrorist groups, in part because threats posed by non-state actors do not present themselves in the ways that evidenced imminence in more traditional conflicts. . . . Over time, an increasing number of our international counterterrorism partners have begun to recognize that the traditional conception of what constitutes an "imminent" attack should be broadened in light of the modern-day capabilities, techniques, and technological innovations of terrorist organizations.[179]

These two articulations of the Obama administration's interpretation of international law reflect an important evolution of the U.S. legal framework for military operations directed against transnational terrorist operatives. They leave virtually no doubt that the United States has embraced the concept of transnational armed conflict, that the nation is engaged in an armed conflict against al Qaeda, that this armed conflict is non-international within the meaning of the *jus in bello* and that it transcends national borders. There is also no doubt that the United States invoked the *jus in bello* as the framework to regulate execution of the Bin Laden mission. Koh's clear emphasis on the *in bello* variants of the principles of distinction and proportionality cannot be read as meaning anything else.

Koh, however, included one qualifier that suggests possible uncertainty. Rejecting the criticism that attacks such as that on Bin Laden are unlawful extrajudicial killings, Koh noted that "a state that is engaged in an armed conflict or in legitimate self-defense is not required to provide targets with legal process before the state may use lethal force."[180] What is perplexing is the "or" in the statement. Koh preserved a division between armed conflict *and* other actions in legitimate self-defense. It is significant that he asserts the right to kill as a measure of first resort in either context (which seems to rebut any inference that he is suggesting some actions in self-defense must be exercised pursuant to a law enforcement legal framework). Why was that "or" necessary? What was Koh suggesting if he was not suggesting a law enforcement limitation to some actions in self-defense?

One possible answer is that Advisor Koh is simply preserving the authority of the United States to act in limited self-defense against an imminent terrorist threat that is not considered associated with al Qaeda or the Taliban. In such situations, the attack would accordingly be unrelated to the existing armed conflict the United States asserts is ongoing with these enemies. If this was the meaning of his use of the "or," it produces little confusion: imminent terrorist threats to the United States may justify military action as an exercise of *jus ad bellum* self-defense, and use of force for such a purpose triggers LOAC applicability. However, distinguishing armed conflict *from* self-defense with an "or" could also be interpreted as an endorsement of self-defense targeting, suggesting that uses of military force are regulated by the *jus in bello* or *jus ad bellum* principles. This is an unnecessary dichotomy, and hopefully one that Advisor Koh did not intend. There is no viable reason to attempt to establish such a distinction; as discussed in this essay, the suggestion that *ad bellum* principles are interchangeable with their *in bello* variants is flawed and operationally confusing.[181]

VII. Conclusion

Transnational non-State threats are not going away any time soon. Indeed, it is likely that identifying a rational and credible legal basis for national response to such threats will continue to vex policymakers and legal advisors in the coming years. These threats will almost certainly lead States to continue to invoke the inherent right of national and/or collective self-defense to justify extraterritorial responses. This legal basis is not, however, an adequate substitute for defining the legal framework to regulate the operational exercise of this self-defense authority. Nonetheless, the advent of the self-defense targeting theory purports to be just that.

The *jus ad bellum* was never conceived as a legal framework to regulate the execution of military operations. Instead, it is analogous to the law that permits individuals to act in self-defense when faced with an imminent threat of death or grievous bodily harm. Like the domestic self-defense concept, *jus ad bellum* self-defense reflects a necessity foundation based on minimizing situations where States resort to force and limiting the risk of conflagration resulting from such resort. Self-defense, as a form of self-help, is intended to be a measure of last resort, and the *jus ad bellum* principles of necessity and proportionality reflect that foundation. In contrast, the *jus in bello* variants of these two principles are based on a fundamentally different foundation: facilitating the prompt submission of operational opponents in the collective—not individual—sense. Accordingly, the scope of permissible violence justified by the *jus in bello* is fundamentally different from that tolerated through the exercise of peacetime self-defense.

Attempting to substitute *jus ad bellum* principles for their *jus in bello* variants is not only confusing; it fundamentally degrades target engagement authority. As discussed in this essay, this degradation is the result of imposing peacetime concepts on wartime operations. It may be conceivable that some actions in self-defense—especially in response to non-State threats—may permit only a law enforcement–type response. For example, if members of Mexican drug cartels began engaging in violence on the U.S. side of the border requiring, in the judgment of the President, some action to neutralize this threat, armed forces might be used to augment law enforcement officers during a mission to capture cartel members for subsequent trial. In such a situation, the use of armed force might be subject to law enforcement–type use of force authority. However, even if such situations are conceptually lodged within the scope of national self-defense authority, this cannot justify the wholesale abandonment of *jus in bello* principles. Instead, the nature of the threat and the authority invoked by the State to respond to that threat must dictate the existence of armed conflict. When States utilize armed forces and grant them the authority to engage opponents pursuant to the LOAC rule of military objective—an invocation revealed by the employment of deadly force as a measure of first resort—it indicates the existence of an armed conflict. It is the *jus in bello*, and not the *jus ad bellum*, that must regulate such operations.

Notes

1. Eyal Benvenisti, *Rethinking the Divide Between* Jus ad Bellum *and* Jus in Bello *in Warfare Against Nonstate Actors*, 34 YALE JOURNAL OF INTERNATIONAL LAW 541 (2009) (defining *jus in bello* as "the law governing the conduct of hostilities").

2. *Id.* (defining *jus ad bellum* as "the law governing resort to force").

3. Kenneth Anderson, *Targeted Killing and Drone Warfare: How We Came to Debate Whether There Is a "Legal Geography of War"* 7 (WCL Research Paper No. 2011-16, 2011), *available at* http://ssrn.com/abstract=1824783.

4. *Id.*

5. Nicholas Schmidle, *Getting Bin Laden: What Happened That Night in Abbottabad*, THE NEW YORKER, Aug. 8, 2011, at 34, *available at* http://www.newyorker.com/reporting/2011/08/08/110808fa_fact_schmidle (detailing the raid into Pakistan executed without the permission or knowledge of the Pakistani government by American forces to kill Osama Bin Laden).

6. *U.S. Attorney General: Bin Laden Raid "Lawful,"* AGENCE FRANCE-PRESSE (May 4, 2011), *available at* http://www.google.com/hostednews/afp/article/ALeqM5gYsheAr3sLXs6ERJ-d6pkkoULHKg?docId=CNG.e73a3d4ada4c822cbcaee9345abb3385.d1 (quoting White House spokesman Jay Carney: there was "no question" the raid was legal and that it was "an act of national self-defense").

7. *The Killing of bin Laden: Was It Legal?*, CNN WORLD (May 4, 2011), http://articles.cnn.com/2011-05-04/world/bin.laden.legal_1_al-qaeda-leader-bin-cia-director-leon-panetta?_s=PM:WORLD (again quoting White House spokesman Jay Carney, "[the raid] was conducted in a manner fully consistent with the laws of war").

8. *U.S. Attorney General: Bin Laden Raid "Lawful," supra* note 6 (discussing the shoot-first-or-capture orders to the SEALs who killed Osama Bin Laden).

9. *See* John O. Brennan, Assistant to the President for Homeland Security and Counterterrorism, Remarks at the Program on Law and Security, Harvard Law School: Strengthening Our Security by Adhering to Our Values and Laws (Sept. 16, 2011), http://www.whitehouse.gov/the-press-office/2011/09/16/remarks-john-o-brennan-strengthening-our-security-adhering-our-values-an. *See also* Attorney General Eric Holder, Remarks at Northwestern University School of Law (Mar. 5, 2012), http://www.justice.gov/iso/opa/ag/speeches/2012/ag-speech-1203051.html; Ryan J. Vogel, *Drone Warfare and the Law of Armed Conflict*, 39 DENVER JOURNAL OF INTERNATIONAL LAW AND POLICY 101, 108 (2010).

10. Vogel, *supra* note 9, at 114.

11. Robert D. Sloane, *The Cost of Conflation: Preserving the Dualism of* Jus ad Bellum *and* Jus in Bello *in the Contemporary Law of War*, 34 YALE JOURNAL OF INTERNATIONAL LAW 47, 67 (2009) (asserting the use of force must be necessary and proportional with respect to both the *jus ad bellum* and the *jus in bello*).

12. Geoffrey S. Corn & Eric T. Jensen, *Transnational Armed Conflict: A "Principled" Approach to the Regulation of Counter-Terror Combat Operations*, 42 ISRAEL LAW REVIEW 46, 78 (2009); Sloane, *supra* note 11, at 69–78.

13. *See generally* Eran Shamir-Borer, *Revisiting Hamdan v. Rumsfeld's Analysis of the Laws of Armed Conflict*, 21 EMORY INTERNATIONAL LAW REVIEW 601 (2007).

14. *See* Anderson, *supra* note 3.

15. *Id.* at 4.

16. Christine Gray, *President Obama's 2010 United States National Security Strategy and International Law on the Use of Force*, 10 CHINESE JOURNAL OF INTERNATIONAL LAW 35, 43 (2011). *See* Headquarters, Department of the Army, FM 3-60, The Targeting Process ¶ 1-14 (2010).

17. *See generally* Geoffrey S. Corn & Eric T. Jensen, *Untying the Gordian Knot: A Proposal for Determining Applicability of the Laws of War to the War on Terror*, 81 TEMPLE LAW REVIEW 787 (2008); Rebecca Ingber, *Untangling Belligerency From Neutrality in the Conflict with Al-Qaeda*, 47 TEXAS INTERNATIONAL LAW JOURNAL 75, 80–81 (2011).

18. Corn & Jensen, *supra* note 17.

19. *See* William H. Taft IV, *Self-Defense and the Oil Platforms Decision*, 29 YALE JOURNAL OF INTERNATIONAL LAW 295, 303–6 (2004). The International Court of Justice considered a case between Iran and the United States, commonly known as *Oil Platforms*, named for Iranian platforms attacked by the United States in retaliation for Iranian strikes on Kuwaiti vessels under U.S. control. *Id.* 296–98. *See also* Oil Platforms (Iran v. U.S.), 2003 I.C.J. 161 (Nov. 6). The Court dismissed the case, but not before spending a substantial amount of time discussing self-defense in the realm of international law. *See generally* Taft, *supra*, at 296–98.

20. *See generally* Geoffrey S. Corn, *Hamdan, Lebanon, and the Regulation of Hostilities: The Need to Recognize a Hybrid Category of Armed Conflict*, 40 VANDERBILT JOURNAL OF TRANSNATIONAL LAW 295 (2007) (a detailed discussion of the term "transnational armed conflict"); Robert J. Delahunty & John C. Yoo, *What Is the Role of International Human Rights Law in the War on Terror?*, 59 DEPAUL LAW REVIEW 803 (2010).

21. Corn, *supra* note 20, at 300–10; Delahunty & Yoo, *supra* note 20, at 825–34.

22. Convention for the Amelioration of the Condition of the Wounded and Sick in Armed Forces in the Field, Aug. 12, 1949, 6 U.S.T. 3114, 75 U.N.T.S. 31 [hereinafter GC I]; Convention for the Amelioration of the Condition of Wounded, Sick and Shipwrecked Members of Armed Forces at Sea, Aug. 12, 1949, 6 U.S.T. 3217, 75 U.N.T.S. 85 [hereinafter GC II]; Convention Relative to the Treatment of Prisoners of War, Aug. 12, 1949, 6 U.S.T. 3316, 75 U.N.T.S. 135 [hereinafter GC III]; Convention Relative to the Protection of Civilian Persons in Time of War, Aug. 12, 1949, 6 U.S.T. 3516, 75 U.N.T.S. 287 [hereinafter GC IV].

23. *See* Fionnuala Ní Aoláin, *Hamdan and Common Article 3: Did the Supreme Court Get It Right?*, 91 MINNESOTA LAW REVIEW 1523, 1525–34 (2007); Corn, *supra* note 20, at 300–301 (discussing the traditional two LOAC triggers used before the concept of transnational conflict emerged).

24. *See* International and Operational Law Department, The Judge Advocate General's Legal Center and School, Department of the Army, Law of War Workshop Deskbook 25–34 (Bill J. Brian et al. eds., 2004); *see also* UNITED KINGDOM MINISTRY OF DEFENCE, THE MANUAL OF THE LAW OF ARMED CONFLICT ¶ 3.1 (2004).

25. *See* COMMENTARY TO GENEVA CONVENTION I FOR THE AMELIORATION OF THE CONDITION OF THE WOUNDED AND SICK IN ARMED FORCES IN THE FIELD 19–23 (Jean S. Pictet ed., 1952). A similar commentary was published for each of the four Geneva Conventions. Because Articles 2 and 3 are identical—or common—to each Convention, however, the commentary for these articles is also identical in each of the four commentaries.

26. *See* Ní Aoláin, *supra* note 23; Corn, *supra* note 20, at 300.

27. Corn, *supra* note 20, at 307.

28. *Id.* at 309.

29. *Id.* at 305 (noting that the conflict between Israel and Hezbollah and the United States' removal of General Noriega did not fall into either category).

30. *Id.* at 300 (explaining that the only two triggers of war as set out by the Geneva Convention–based law-triggering paradigm are international armed conflict between two sovereign nations and non-international armed conflict taking place within the borders of a State that is a party to the conflict).

31. *See* U.S. Department of Defense, Directive 5100.77, DoD Law of War Program (1998) [hereinafter 1998 DoD Law of War Program]. *See also* Corn, *supra* note 20, at 314 ("Fortunately, the policy-based application of the principles of the law to the entire range of combat operations has mitigated this uncertainty and provided a consistent regulatory framework at the operational and tactical level of command."); David E. Graham, *Counterinsurgency, the War on Terror, and the Laws of War: A Response*, 95 VIRGINIA LAW REVIEW IN BRIEF 79, 85–86 (2009) (citing American policy-based approach to law of war applicability and its impact on counterinsurgency operations).

32. *See* Corn, *supra* note 20, at 314.

33. *See* Memorandum from Assistant Attorney General Jay S. Bybee to Counsel to the President Alberto R. Gonzales and General Counsel of the Department of Defense William J. Haynes II, Application of Treaties and Laws to al Qaeda and Taliban Detainees 1 (Jan. 22, 2002), *available at* http://www.gwu.edu/~nsarchiv/NSAEBB/NSAEBB127/02.01.22.pdf [hereinafter Bybee Application of Treaties and Laws Memorandum] (asserting treaties that form the laws of armed conflict do not apply to the conditions of detention and the procedures for trial of captured al Qaeda or Taliban members); *see also* Memorandum from Assistant Attorney General Jay S. Bybee to Counsel to the President Alberto R. Gonzales, Status of Taliban Forces under Article 4 of the Third Geneva Convention 1 (Feb. 7, 2002), *available at* http://www.gwu.edu/~nsarchiv/NSAEBB/NSAEBB127/020207.pdf (asserting captured members of

the Taliban do not meet the requirements under the Geneva Convention Relative to the Treatment of Prisoners of War under Article 4(A)(1), (2) or (3) and thus can be held indefinitely without convening a tribunal); Memorandum from President George W. Bush to Vice President Dick Cheney, Regarding Humane Treatment of al Qaeda and Taliban Detainees 2 (Feb. 7, 2002), *available at* http://www.gwu.edu/~nsarchiv/NSAEBB/NSAEBB127/02.02.07.pdf (adopting the recommendations of Bybee to not apply Article 3 of Geneva Convention III to detained al Qaeda or Taliban members).

34. David Cole, *Out of the Shadows: Preventive Detention, Suspected Terrorists, and War*, 97 CALIFORNIA LAW REVIEW 693, 701 (2009) (discussing the law of war allowance of preventive detention, and the *Hamdi* decision that allowed even U.S. citizens to be preventively detained in some circumstances).

35. *See* Hamdi v. Rumsfeld, 542 U.S. 507 (2009).

36. Hamdan v. Rumsfeld, 548 U.S. 557, 628–30 (2006) (discussing the government's position that Hamdan was not entitled to the full protections of the Geneva Conventions because the conflict did not clearly fit into Article 2 or 3 of the Conventions).

37. *Id.*

38. *Id.*

39. *See generally* Michael F. Lohr & Steve Gallotta, *Legal Support in War: The Role of Military Lawyers*, 4 CHICAGO JOURNAL OF INTERNATIONAL LAW 465 (2003) (discussing the role of the military lawyer in conflicts ranging from declared State-on-State war to the war on terror). *See also* 1998 DoD Law of War Program, *supra* note 31. The exact policy mandate required that the heads of the DoD components "[e]nsure that the members of their Components comply with the law of war during all armed conflicts, however such conflicts are characterized, and with the principles and spirit of the law of war during all other operations." *Id.*, ¶ 5.3.1. *See also* U.S. Department of Defense, Directive 2311.01E, DoD Law of War Program ¶ 4.1 (2006), *available at* http://www.dtic.mil/whs/directives/corres/pdf/231101e.pdf [hereinafter Directive 2311.01E] ("Members of the DoD Components comply with the law of war during all armed conflicts, however such conflicts are characterized, and in all other military operations.").

40. *See generally* Corn, *supra* note 20; Eyal Benvenisti, *The Legal Battle to Define the Law on Transnational Asymmetric Warfare*, 20 DUKE JOURNAL OF COMPARATIVE AND INTERNATIONAL LAW 339, 342 (2010).

41. *See* Hans-Peter Gasser, *Internationalized Non-International Armed Conflicts: Case Studies of Afghanistan, Kampuchea, and Lebanon*, 33 AMERICAN UNIVERSITY LAW REVIEW 145, 147 (1983) (utilizing the term "internationalized non-international armed conflict" to denote an armed conflict between State and non-State forces that transcends national boundaries).

42. Natasha Balendra, *Defining Armed Conflict*, 29 CARDOZO LAW REVIEW 2461, 2512 (2008) (asserting many scholars believe these types of conflicts should be classified as law enforcement operations and conducted accordingly).

43. *See generally* Benvenisti, *supra* note 40 (entire essay discussing "tension between the two conflicting visions on the regulation of transnational armed conflict").

44. *See* Corn & Jensen, *supra* note 12, at 66 (discussing Professor Yoram Dinstein's classification of counterterrorism activities as extraterritorial law enforcement).

45. 548 U.S. 557 (2006).

46. *Id.* at 629–32.

47. *Id.*

48. *Id.*

49. *Id.*

50. *See, e.g.*, Corn & Jensen, *supra* note 12; Michael Greenberger, *You Ain't Seen Nothin' Yet: The Inevitable Post-Hamdan Conflict Between the Supreme Court and the Political Branches*, 66 MARYLAND LAW REVIEW 805, 833–34 (2007).

51. Corn & Jensen, *supra* note 12.

52. Michael W. Lewis, *International Myopia: Hamdan's Shortcut to "Victory,"* 42 UNIVERSITY OF RICHMOND LAW REVIEW 687, 706 (2008) ("[T]he *Hamdan* court defined armed 'conflict not of an international character,' determined the requirements of a regularly constituted court, and decided what judicial guarantees are recognized as indispensable by civilized people in just over five pages . . . without significantly reviewing the drafting history of Common Article 3 and the Additional Protocols, or investigating any state practice outside this country."). *See* Bybee Application of Treaties and Laws Memorandum, *supra* note 33, at 10 (asserting the conflict with al Qaeda does not fit into either of the two traditional categories of armed conflict as established by Articles 2 and 3 of the Geneva Conventions).

53. *See* Vogel, *supra* note 9, at 132 (mentioning that although a majority of the United States' combat operations against al Qaeda are in Afghanistan, it does use drone strikes against al Qaeda operatives in Yemen and Somalia). *See also* Gabor Rona, *Interesting Times for International Humanitarian Law: Challenges from the "War on Terror,"* 27 FLETCHER FORUM OF WORLD AFFAIRS 55, 62 (2003) (mentioning one such attack in Yemen in 2004). *See* International Law Association, Use of Force Committee, Final Report on the Meaning of Armed Conflict in International Law 29–32 (2010), *available at* http://www.ila-hq.org/en/committees/index.cfm/cid/1022 [hereinafter Final Report on the Meaning of Armed Conflict] (discussing the criteria of intensity and territorial scope aspects of classifying hostilities as armed conflict).

54. Final Report on the Meaning of Armed Conflict, *supra* note 53.

55. *Id.* at 30.

56. Jeffrey F. Addicott, *Efficacy of the Obama Policies to Combat Al-Qa'eda, the Taliban, and Associated Forces—the First Year*, 30 PACE LAW REVIEW 340, 353–54 (2010) (mentioning President Obama's campaign desire to dismantle key elements of President Bush's policies on combating terrorism and his actions shortly after entering office attempting to do so).

57. *See* Anderson, *supra* note 3, at 1 (mentioning the Obama administration's expanded use of drone strikes in countries outside of Afghanistan).

58. Tess Bridgeman, *The Law of Neutrality and the Conflict with Al Qaeda*, 85 NEW YORK UNIVERSITY LAW REVIEW 1186, 1191 (2010) (discussing the Obama administration's immediate stance that those taken prisoner in Afghanistan would be detained pursuant to the law of armed conflict). *See also* Robert M. Chesney, *Who May Be Held? Military Detention through the Habeas Lens*, 52 BOSTON COLLEGE LAW REVIEW 769, 830–31 (2011) (discussing the Obama administration's decision early in March 2009 to continue to assert its authority "to detain without charge pursuant to a substantive detention standard not much different from the Combatant Status Review Tribunal (CSRT) standard of the Bush administration").

59. Vogel, *supra* note 9, at 109 (mentioning the United States' use of drone strikes in Pakistan, Somalia and Yemen).

60. Jeff Bovarnick, *A Review of: The War on Terror and the Laws of War: A Military Perspective*, 44 NEW ENGLAND LAW REVIEW 885, 892 (2010) (book review) (citing the use of deadly force as the most basic right under the laws of armed conflict). *See also* Schmidle, *supra* note 5 (noting the "killing as a first resort" mentality was present, because nobody on the mission to kill Osama Bin Laden wanted detainees).

61. Bovarnick, *supra* note 60, at 892 (again noting that the use of deadly force as a first resort in military operations is inconsistent with law enforcement norms).

62. *See generally* Jordan J. Paust, *Self-Defense Targetings of Non-State Actors and Permissibility of U.S. Use of Drones in Pakistan*, 19 JOURNAL OF TRANSNATIONAL LAW AND POLICY 237 (2010) (the entire article discussing this new alterative legal framework).

63. *See* Kenneth Anderson, *Targeted Killing in U.S. Counterterrorism Strategy and Law, in* LEGISLATING THE WAR ON TERROR: AN AGENDA FOR REFORM 346 (Benjamin Wittes ed., 2009). Kenneth Anderson is a professor of law at the Washington College of Law at American University. Professor Anderson is also a visiting fellow at the Hoover Institution on War, Revolution and Peace, Stanford University.

64. *See* Anderson, *supra* note 3, at 15. *See also* Kenneth Anderson, *The Rise of International Criminal Law: Intended and Unintended Consequences*, 20 EUROPEAN JOURNAL OF INTERNATIONAL LAW 331, 354 (2009) ("Although in theory a single adjudicator could hear both the resort to force and conduct questions [*jus ad bellum* and *jus in bello*], and simply maintain perfect independence, in reality the same tribunal—even with separate panels—would tend to conflicts of interest, path dependence between the two *supposedly* independent areas.") (emphasis added).

65. *See* Paust, *supra* note 62, at 262 (justifying the ability of the United States to capture Osama Bin Laden or other members of al Qaeda in Afghanistan or other countries simply because the hostilities with al Qaeda were commenced under a notion of self-defense). *See also* Jordan Paust, *Permissible Self-Defense Targeting and the Death of Bin Laden*, 39 DENVER JOURNAL OF INTERNATIONAL LAW AND POLICY 569 (2011). Professor Paust is the Mike and Teresa Baker Law Center Professor of International Law at the Law Center of the University of Houston.

66. Jordan J. Paust, *War and Enemy Status After 9/11: Attacks on the Laws of War*, 28 YALE JOURNAL OF INTERNATIONAL LAW 325, 326 (2003) ("the United States simply cannot be at war with bin Laden and al Qaeda").

67. *See id. generally.*

68. *See* Paust, *supra* note 62, at 279 ("As this article affirms, self-defense can be permissible against non-state actor armed attacks, and measures of self-defense can occur in the territory of another state without special consent of the other state or imputation of the armed attacks to that state as long as the measures of self-defense are directed against the non-state actors.").

69. *See* Anderson, *supra* note 3, at 7 (labeling the use of force under self-defense that would not be part of an armed conflict "naked self-defense").

70. *See* Paust, *supra* note 62, at 270 (stating reasonable necessity and proportionality are integrated into the law of armed conflict under the Geneva Conventions). *See also* Paust, *supra* note 65, at 572–73 (stating the need to conduct self-defense targeting within the principles of distinction, reasonable necessity and proportionality to protect the general human right to life).

71. *See generally* Paust, *supra* note 65, at 577–78 (discussing generally and specifically how the justification for self-defense targeting of non-State actors determines which targets are allowed to be attacked and where, as long as such decisions are based on necessity and proportionality).

72. *See* Benvenisti, *supra* note 1, at 541 (stating the traditional clear distinction between the *jus ad bellum* and the *jus in bello*).

73. G.I.A.D. Draper, *Ethical and Juridical Status of Constraints in War*, 55 MILITARY LAW REVIEW 169, 174 (1972) (the paper was first presented by Colonel Draper at the Judge Advocate General's School, U.S. Army, Charlottesville, Virginia, on September 10, 1971).

74. *See* Sloane, *supra* note 11, at 48 (discussing the Special Court for Sierra Leone's Appeals Chamber's clearly separating *jus ad bellum* and *jus in bello* by refusing to justify a defendant's actions based on the legitimacy of his right to fight).

75. *Id.* at 65 (discussing the UN Charter's application of *jus in bello* to all belligerents, regardless of their *jus ad bellum* status).

76. *Id.* ("Articles 1 and 2 of the Geneva Conventions of 1949 affirmed that the *jus in bello* codified in those treaties applied in 'all circumstances' and to 'all cases of declared war or of any other armed conflict.'").

77. *Id.*

78. *See* GC I, GC II, GC III, GC IV, all *supra* note 22. *See also* Sloane, *supra* note 11, at 65.

79. *See* COMMENTARY TO GENEVA CONVENTION III RELATIVE TO THE TREATMENT OF PRISONERS OF WAR 22 (Jean S. Pictet ed., 1960) [hereinafter COMMENTARY III].

80. *Id.* at 28–35. *See also* Geoffrey S. Corn, *"Snipers in the Minaret—What Is the Rule?" The Law of War and the Protection of Cultural Property: A Complex Equation*, ARMY LAWYER, July 2005, at 36 (endnote 27 discusses this topic at great length, citing to the *Commentary, supra*).

81. *See* COMMENTARY III, *supra* note 79, at 22.

82. *See* Hamdan v. Rumsfeld, 548 U.S. 557, 628–33 (2006) (finding the classification or description of the conflict between the United States and al Qaeda did not impact the rights detainees were entitled to under the Geneva Conventions). *See also* Sloane, *supra* note 11, at 75 (recognizing Common Article 3 of the Geneva Conventions' application in all cases of armed conflict as "custom," with no mention of *jus ad bellum*) and at 48 (discussing the Special Court for Sierra Leone's Appeals Chamber's clearly separating *jus ad bellum* and *jus in bello* by refusing to justify a defendant's actions because of the legitimacy of his right to fight); Directive 2311.01E, *supra* note 39 (ordering all U.S. armed forces to comply with principles of the law of war during all military operations).

83. *See, e.g.*, Directive 2311.01E, *supra* note 39.

84. *See* Antoine Bouvier, *Assessing the Relationship between* Jus in Bello *and* Jus ad Bellum*: An "Orthodox" View*, 100 AMERICAN SOCIETY OF INTERNATIONAL LAW PROCEEDINGS 109, 110 (2006) ("The idea that both branches [*jus ad bellum* and *jus in bello*] operate autonomously is firmly rooted in (1) the legal literature, (2) State practice, (3) the jurisprudence of national and international courts and (4) several treaties."). *See also* COMMENTARY III, *supra* note 79.

85. Protocol Additional to the Geneva Conventions of 12 August 1949, and Relating to the Protection of Victims of International Armed Conflicts pmbl., June 8, 1977, 1125 U.N.T.S. 3 [hereinafter AP I] ("Reaffirming further that the provisions of the Geneva Conventions of 12 August 1949 and of this Protocol must be fully applied in all circumstances to all persons who are protected by those instruments, without any adverse distinction based on the nature or origin of the armed conflict or on the causes espoused by or attributed to the Parties to the conflict.").

86. *See* Directive 2311.01E, *supra* note 39 (ordering all U.S. armed forces to comply with principles of the law of war (*jus in bello*) during all military operations); *see also* 1998 DoD Law of War Program, *supra* note 31 (the predecessor to DoD Directive 2311.01E, which mandated that heads of Defense components "[e]nsure that the members of their DoD Components comply with the law of war during all armed conflicts, however such conflicts are characterized, and with the principles and spirit of the law of war during all other operations").

Whether this policy directive reflects an emerging principle of customary international law that requires compliance with core LOAC principles during all military operations as a "default" setting is a question beyond the scope of this essay. However, in prior articles this author has asserted that the policy does, at a minimum, suggest that a strict interpretation of the situations that trigger application of these core principles is inconsistent with the underlying objective of the Geneva Conventions to ensure that no military operation falls outside the scope of humanitarian regulation. *See* Corn, *supra* note 20.

87. *See generally* Paust, *supra* note 62 (relying simply on the right of self-defense, not on the illegality of the attack by al Qaeda, to defend the United States' use of drone attacks against non-State actors).

88. *See generally id.* (discussing self-defense targeting in great detail throughout the article).

89. *Id.*

90. *Id.*

91. *Id.*

92. *See* Sloane, *supra* note 11, at 104 (recognizing the traditional separation—that *ad bellum* judgments should not have an impact on *in bello* obligations). *See also* MICHAEL WALZER, JUST AND UNJUST WARS 21 (4th ed. 2006) (referring to *ad bellum* and *in bello* principles as "logically independent").

93. *See* Sloane, *supra* note 11, at 50 (discussing the troubling results of conflating *ad bellum* and *in bello* principles, citing examples such as the 1999 NATO conduct in Serbia and the Bush administration's authorization of torture against detainees).

94. *See* Benvenisti, *supra* note 1, at 541–42 (mentioning the current scholarly distinction between *ad bellum* and *in bello* principles).

95. *Id.* at 546 (discussing the greater impact that *ad bellum* principles have over *in bello* principles in military operations).

96. *See* Sloane, *supra* note 11, at 49–50 (discussing actions in Sierra Leone's civil war, NATO's actions against Serbia and the United States' post-9/11 torture of detainees and the inappropriate attempts of each relevant party to justify its *in bello* conduct with the legitimacy of its *ad bellum* cause).

97. *See* Benvenisti, *supra* note 1, at 546 ("the percolation of *ad bellum* considerations into the *jus in bello* proportionality analysis can prove a rather sophisticated and effective constraint on the stronger regular army").

98. *See* Sloane, *supra* note 11, at 103 (discussing the benefits of having separated *ad bellum* and *in bello* principles: *ad bellum* principles to prohibit the use of force except in self-defense situations and *in bello* principles to include necessity, proportionality and discrimination in conducting armed conflict).

99. *See* Paust, *supra* note 62, at 250 (justifying the United States' use of non-State actor targeting by drones across international borders as a tool in the war against al Qaeda based on the necessity of self-defense).

100. *See* Alexander Orakhelashvili, *Overlap and Convergence: The Interaction between* Jus ad Bellum *and* Jus in Bello, 12 JOURNAL OF CONFLICT & SECURITY LAW 157, 164 (2007) (citing the existence of the concept of necessity in both the *jus ad bellum* and *jus in bello*). *See also* Sloane, *supra* note 11, at 52–53 (discussing both *ad bellum* and *in bello* proportionality) and at 67 ("any use of force must be necessary and proportional relative to both the *jus ad bellum* and the *jus in bello*").

101. *See* Michael Novak, *Just Peace and the Asymmetric Threat: National Self-Defense in Uncharted Waters*, 27 HARVARD JOURNAL OF LAW & PUBLIC POLICY 817, 827 (2004) (including the use of war as a last resort in considerations for *jus ad bellum*).

102. *See id.* (including proportionality and discrimination between combatants and noncombatants as considerations for the *jus in bello*).

103. *See id.* (*ad bellum* principles restrict the use of force to only proportionate means when necessary). *See also* Military and Paramilitary Activities in and against Nicaragua (Nicar. v. U.S.), 1986 I.C.J. 14, ¶ 194 (June 27); Legality of the Threat or Use of Nuclear Weapons, Advisory Opinion, 1996 I.C.J. 226, ¶ 142 (July 8); Oil Platforms (Iran v. U.S.), 2003 I.C.J. 161, ¶ 43

(Nov. 6); Armed Activities on the Territory of the Congo (Dem. Rep. Congo v. Uganda), 2005 I.C.J. 168, ¶ 147 (Dec. 19).

104. DAVID RODIN, WAR AND SELF-DEFENSE 110–11 (2002) (stating it is "universally acknowledged that the right of national-defense is bounded by the same intrinsic limitations as the right of personal self-defense").

105. *See* Shana Wallace, *Beyond Imminence: Evolving International Law and Battered Women's Right to Self-Defense*, 71 UNIVERSITY OF CHICAGO LAW REVIEW 1749, 1766–77 (2004) (comparing the necessity and proportionality requirements of personal and national self-defense).

106. *Id.*

107. *Id.*

108. *Id.*

109. Thomas Yoxall, *Iraq and Article 51: A Correct Use of Limited Authority*, 25 INTERNATIONAL LAWYER 967, 986 (1991) (discussing the UN Charter requirements of necessity and proportionality in the use of force in self-defense).

110. U.N. Charter art. 1.

111. *Id.*

112. *Id.*, art. 51.

113. Scott S. Evans, *International Kidnapping in a Violent World: Where the United States Ought to Draw the Line*, 137 MILITARY LAW REVIEW 187, 240 (1992) (detailing purposes for the Article 51 notification requirement, including creating awareness of the aggression).

114. Brian L. Bengs, *Legal Constraints upon the Use of a Tactical Nuclear Weapon Against the Natanz Nuclear Facility in Iran*, 40 GEORGE WASHINGTON INTERNATIONAL LAW REVIEW 323, 370 (2008) (*ad bellum* proportionality "is intended to prevent a state from overreacting to a situation and escalating the level of conflict").

115. *Id.* This is not to suggest the absence of uncertainty related to the scope of action permitted pursuant to the *jus ad bellum* principle of proportionality. Indeed, this remains an area of significant international legal debate. However, what seems relatively clear is that whatever the permissible scope of action, the objective is strictly limited to reduction of the imminent threat that triggers the right of national or collective self-defense. As Professor David Kretzmer notes in the abstract for his forthcoming analysis of *jus ad bellum* proportionality:

> While force used by a state in self-defence must meet the demands of proportionality there is confusion over the meaning of the term in this, ius ad bellum, context. One source of confusion lies in the existence of two competing tests of proportionality, the "tit for tat" and the "means-end" tests. Since the legality of unilateral use of force by a state depends on the legitimacy of its aim—self-defence against an armed attack—the "means-end" test would seem more appropriate. However, there is no agreement over the legitimate ends of force employed to achieve this aim. Is the defending state limited to halting and repelling the attack that has occurred, or may it protect itself against future attacks by the same enemy? May a state that has been attacked use force in order to deter the attacker from mounting further attacks? The "means-end" test of proportionality rests primarily on the necessity of the means used to achieve legitimate ends. *Disagreements over proportionality are in this context usually really disagreements over those ends.* While the appropriate test in this context is generally the "means-end" test, in some cases, such as use of force in response to a limited armed attack, the "tit for tat" test of proportionality might be more appropriate.

See David Kretzmer, *The Inherent Right of Self-Defence and Proportionality in* Ius ad Bellum, EUROPEAN JOURNAL OF INTERNATIONAL LAW (forthcoming 2012) (emphasis added), *available at* http://papers.ssrn.com/sol3/papers.cfm?abstract_id=2014282; *see also* Taft, *supra* note 19 (criticizing the overly restrictive interpretation of *jus ad bellum* proportionality adopted by the International Court of Justice in the *Oil Platforms* decision).

116. *See* Sloane, *supra* note 11, at 67 ("The *in bello* concepts of necessity and proportionality have *ad bellum* analogues—with quite distinct meanings.").

117. *Id.* at 74 (stating conflating the proportionality of *jus ad bellum* and *jus in bello* would allow a nation's self-serving *ad bellum* reason for engaging in conflict to impact its *in bello* conduct during the hostilities with the ultimate outcome being negative for the soldiers in the field).

118. Michael N. Schmitt, *Clipped Wings: Effective and Legal No-Fly Zone Rules of Engagement*, 20 LOYOLA OF LOS ANGELES INTERNATIONAL AND COMPARATIVE LAW JOURNAL 754 (1998) (stating necessity in reference to self-defense pertains to when force may be resorted to, contrasted to necessity in the *jus in bello* context, which determines how force may be used).

119. *See* Department of the Army, FM 27-10, The Law of Land Warfare ¶ 3(a) (1956); David Kaye, *Khashiyev & Akayeva v. Russia; Isayeva, Yusupova & Basayeva v. Russia; Isayeva v. Russia*, 99 AMERICAN JOURNAL OF INTERNATIONAL LAW 873, 880 (2005) (*jus in bello* necessity's function is to ensure that force is used to obtain a military objective). *See also* Craig J.S. Forrest, *The Doctrine of Military Necessity and the Protection of Cultural Property During Armed Conflicts*, 37 CALIFORNIA WESTERN INTERNATIONAL LAW JOURNAL 177, 181 (2007) (*in bello* necessity forces a party to strike a balance between obtaining military victory and observing the needs of humanity) and 183 (*in bello* necessity allows the pursuit of military objectives, which includes disabling as many enemy combatants as possible, so long as it is done in a manner that minimizes suffering and damage); Department of the Air Force, AFP 110-31, International Law—The Conduct of Armed Conflict and Air Operations 1-5–1-6 (1976) [hereinafter AFP 110-31] ("Military necessity is the principle which justifies measures of regulated force not forbidden by international law which are indispensable for securing the prompt submission of the enemy, with the least possible expenditures of economic and human resources."); William A. Wilcox Jr., *Environmental Protection in Combat*, 17 SOUTHERN ILLINOIS UNIVERSITY LAW JOURNAL 299, 302 (1993) ("The concept of military necessity provides that a combatant is justified in applying any force necessary to secure the complete submission of the enemy as soon as possible—as long as the means are not prohibited by provisions of the laws of war.").

120. *See* Christian Henderson, *The 2010 United States National Security Strategy and the Obama Doctrine of "Necessary Force,"* 15 JOURNAL OF CONFLICT & SECURITY LAW 403, 423 (2010) (identifying that the condition in necessity as it applies to self-defense is that the use of force be used only as a measure of last resort). *See also* Kaye, *supra* note 119, at 880 ("Necessity in the *jus in bello* does not require force to be a last resort.").

121. *See generally* Laurie R. Blank & Benjamin R. Farley, *Characterizing US Operations in Pakistan: Is the United States Engaged in Armed Conflict?*, 34 FORDHAM INTERNATIONAL LAW JOURNAL 151, 187 (2011) (distinguishing between armed conflict, which grants the authority to use force as a first resort, and law enforcement, which only allows force in self-defense).

122. *See* Matthew C. Waxman, *The Structure of Terrorism Threats and the Laws of War*, 20 DUKE JOURNAL OF COMPARATIVE AND INTERNATIONAL LAW 429, 447 (2010) ("*jus ad bellum* is fundamentally about promoting peaceful resolution of conflicts and balancing restraints on aggression with legitimate self-defense").

123. *See* AP I, *supra* note 85, art. 52(2) ("Attacks shall be limited strictly to military objectives. In so far as objects are concerned, military objectives are limited to those objects which by their nature, location, purpose or use make an effective contribution to military action and whose total or partial destruction, capture or neutralization, in the circumstances ruling at the time, offers a definite military advantage.").

124. *See* COMMENTARY ON THE ADDITIONAL PROTOCOLS OF 8 JUNE 1977 TO THE GENEVA CONVENTIONS OF 12 AUGUST 1949, ¶ 1389 (Yves Sandoz, Christophe Swinarski & Bruno Zimmermann eds., 1987) [hereinafter COMMENTARY ON THE ADDITIONAL PROTOCOLS] ("Military necessity means the necessity for measures which are essential to attain the goals of war, and which are lawful in accordance with the laws and customs of war.").

125. As long as the use of force as a first resort comports with military necessity, it is valid in armed conflict. *See* Blank & Farley, *supra* note 121, at 187 (citing the ability to use force as a first resort as the primary distinction between armed conflict and law enforcement).

126. *See* Sean Watts, *Reciprocity and the Law of War*, 50 HARVARD INTERNATIONAL LAW JOURNAL 365, 423 (2009) (discussing the authority to use force against persons and property as an authority under the law of war, outside the scope of self-defense).

127. *See* Nobuo Hayashi, *Requirements of Military Necessity in International Humanitarian Law and International Criminal Law*, 28 BOSTON UNIVERSITY INTERNATIONAL LAW JOURNAL 39, 114 (2010) (noting that a property's "status as a military objective justifies attacks being directed against it").

128. JEAN-JACQUES ROUSSEAU, THE SOCIAL CONTRACT AND DISCOURSES 11 (G.D.H. Cole trans., J. M. Dent & Sons Ltd. 1913) (1762).

129. *See* Nils Melzer, *Keeping the Balance Between Military Necessity and Humanity: A Response to Four Critiques of the ICRC's Interpretive Guidance on the Notion of Direct Participation in Hostilities*, 42 NEW YORK UNIVERSITY JOURNAL OF INTERNATIONAL LAW AND POLITICS 831, 904–5 (2010) ("the principle of military necessity as defined in national military manuals is addressed to governments and senior military commanders and does not intend to restrict the individual soldier's use of force against the enemy").

130. This term is used colloquially to indicate situations of armed conflict that trigger the *jus in bello*.

131. *See* Melzer, *supra* note 129, at 904–5.

132. *See* Headquarters, Department of the Army, FM 100-5, Operations 6-15 (1993) [hereinafter FM 100-5] ("Commanders set favorable terms for battle by synchronizing ground, air, sea, space, and special operations capabilities to strike the enemy simultaneously throughout his tactical and operational depths.").

133. *Id.* at 2-6 ("Army forces in combat seek to impose their will on the enemy.").

134. *See generally id.* at 8-4 (the term "overwhelming combat power" and nearly identical terms are used twenty-two times over the course of the manual).

135. *Id.* ("The attack must be violent and rapid to shock the enemy and to prevent his recovery as forces destroy his defense.").

136. AFP 110-31, *supra* note 119, at 1-5–1-6 (The U.S. Air Force defines military necessity as the "principle which justifies measures of regulated force not forbidden by international law which are indispensable for securing the prompt submission of the enemy, with the least possible expenditures of economic and human resources.").

137. FM 100-5, *supra* note 132, at 2-4 ("Mass the effects of overwhelming combat power at the decisive place and time. Synchronizing all the elements of combat power where they will have decisive effect on an enemy force in a short period of time is to achieve mass.").

138. *See* Sloane, *supra* note 11, at 84 (stating *ad bellum* necessity allows for only the use of force necessary to rebut a current and immediate threat).

139. *Id.*

140. Michael N. Schmitt, *The Resort to Force in International Law: Reflections on Positivist and Contextual Approaches*, 37 AIR FORCE LAW REVIEW 105, 116 (1994) ("*Jus ad bellum* necessity queries whether force was necessary at all.").

141. Jill M. Sheldon, *Nuclear Weapons and the Laws of War: Does Customary International Law Prohibit the Use of Nuclear Weapons in All Circumstances?*, 20 FORDHAM INTERNATIONAL LAW JOURNAL 181, 239 (1996) (discussing how the amount of force that should be used in a conflict is determined by balancing military necessity and humanitarian concerns and by considering if the goal of harming the enemy can be achieved by causing less suffering).

142. *See* Sloane, *supra* note 11, at 52–53 (discussing both *ad bellum* and *in bello* proportionality) and at 67 ("Any use of force must be necessary and proportional relative to both the jus ad bellum and the jus in bello.").

143. *Id.* at 73 (discussing proportionality's "distinct *ad bellum* and *in bello* components").

144. *Just War Theory,* INTERNET ENCYCLOPEDIA OF PHILOSOPHY, http://www.iep.utm.edu/justwar/#H2 (last visited Oct. 10, 2011); *see also* Taft, *supra* note 19, at 305 ("[P]roper assessment of . . . proportionality . . . require[s] looking not only at the immediately preceding armed attack, but also at whether it was part of an ongoing series of attacks, what steps were already taken to deter future attacks, and what force could reasonably be judged to be needed to successfully deter future attacks.").

145. Taft, *supra* note 19, at 303 ("[I]t is generally understood that the defending State's actions must be both 'necessary' and 'proportional.'"). *See also* CHRISTINE GRAY, INTERNATIONAL LAW AND THE USE OF FORCE 150 (3d ed. 2008) ("It is not clear how far the two concepts can operate separately. If a use of force is not necessary, it cannot be proportionate and, if it is not proportionate, it is difficult to see how it can be necessary.").

146. WAYNE R. LAFAVE & AUSTIN W. SCOTT JR., 2 SUBSTANTIVE CRIMINAL LAW § 10.4 (2d ed. 1986) (self-defense justifies only the use of force that is reasonably related to the harm the actor is seeking to avoid).

147. YORAM DINSTEIN, WAR, AGGRESSION, AND SELF-DEFENCE 217 (1988).

148. *Id.*

149. *Id.*

150. *See* AP I, *supra* note 85, art. 51. *See also* YORAM DINSTEIN, THE CONDUCT OF HOSTILITIES UNDER THE LAW OF INTERNATIONAL ARMED CONFLICT 119–25 (2004).

151. *See* AP I, *supra* note 85, art. 52(2). *See also* Blank & Farley, *supra* note 121. Some contemporary scholarship asserts that an implicit proportionality restriction applies to attacks against enemy belligerents as an aspect of the general principle of humanity—an interpretation of the *jus in bello* attenuated from operational logic and one I have addressed previously. *See* Geoffrey S. Corn, *Mixing Apples and Hand Grenades: The Logical Limit of Applying Human Rights Norms to Armed Conflict,* 1 JOURNAL OF INTERNATIONAL HUMANITARIAN LEGAL STUDIES 30 (2010).

152. AP I, *supra* note 85, art. 51.

153. *Definition of Excessive,* MERRIAM-WEBSTER, http://www.merriam-webster.com/dictionary/excessive (last visited Oct. 10, 2011) ("exceeding what is usual, proper, necessary, or normal"); *Definition of Disproportionate,* MERRIAM-WEBSTER, http://www.merriam-webster.com/dictionary/disproportionate (last visited Oct. 10, 2011) ("being out of proportion"). *See also* COMMENTARY ON THE ADDITIONAL PROTOCOLS, *supra* note 124, ¶ 1979.

154. *See* W. Hays Parks, *Air War and the Law of War,* 32 AIR FORCE LAW REVIEW 1, 171–76 (1990) (discussing the use of "excessive" in AP I).

155. AP I, *supra* note 85, art. 57. *See also* COMMENTARY ON THE ADDITIONAL PROTOCOLS, *supra* note 124, ¶¶ 2204–15 (commentary on Additional Protocol I, Article 57(2)(a)(iii)).

156. Geoffrey S. Corn & Gary P. Corn, *The Law of Operational Targeting: Viewing the LOAC Through an Operational Lens,* 47 TEXAS INTERNATIONAL LAW JOURNAL 337, 365 (2012) ("When a commander launches such an attack with awareness that the unintended harm to

civilians will be excessive in relation to the benefit of creating the risk (achieving the military objective), the law essentially imputes to the commander the intent to engage in an indiscriminate attack.").

157. Corn, *supra* note 151, at 37; *see also* Jerrett W. Dunlap Jr., *The Economic Efficiency of the Army's Maneuver Damage Claims Program*, 190/191 MILITARY LAW REVIEW 1, 37 (2006/2007) (discussing training events and the ways in which commanders prepare to accomplish their mission when deployed).

158. Corn & Corn, *supra* note 156, at 362 ("it is clear that the law recognizes that the desired effect of an attack need not be total destruction[;] . . . [f]or example, a doctrinal mission employing indirect fire assets serves the purpose of not only target destruction, but also disruption, harassment, and degradation").

159. Chairman, Joint Chiefs of Staff, JP 3-60, Joint Targeting I-8 (2007), *available at* http://www.bits.de/NRANEU/others/jp-doctrine/jp3_60(07).pdf.

160. While the *Oil Platforms* decision, *supra* note 19, by the International Court of Justice (ICJ) calls this "macro" assessment perspective into question, it is this aspect of the decision that has triggered the most criticism. *See* Taft, *supra* note 19, at 302–3. The ICJ's application of international law moves away from widespread, accepted understanding of self-defense targeting. *Id.* Generally, so long as the actions of one State affect another State, self-defense is warranted. *Id.* Whether the inciting State acted indiscriminately is irrelevant. *Id. See also* Ruth Wedgwood, *The ICJ Advisory Opinion on the Israeli Security Fence and the Limits of Self-Defense*, 99 AMERICAN JOURNAL OF INTERNATIONAL LAW 52, 57 (2005) (addressing the "questionable logic" applied by the ICJ in *Oil Platforms* regarding self-defense).

161. Australia, Belgium, Canada, France, Germany, Italy, the Netherlands, New Zealand, Spain and the United Kingdom all included an understanding in their ratification to AP I that the "military advantage" referenced in Articles 51 and 57 is to be considered as a whole and not examined on an individual attack basis. Protocol Additional to the Geneva Conventions of 12 August 1949, and Relating to the Protection of Victims of International Armed Conflicts (Protocol I), 8 June 1977, INTERNATIONAL COMMITTEE OF THE RED CROSS, http://www.icrc.org/ihl.nsf/WebSign?ReadForm&id=470&ps=P (then follow date of Reservation hyperlink for each country) (last visited Oct. 10, 2011).

162. *See* Mary Ellen O'Connell, *Defining Armed Conflict*, 13 JOURNAL OF CONFLICT & SECURITY LAW 393, 393–95 (2008) (asserting that the United States' armed conflict against terror is limited to Iraq and Afghanistan). *See also* David E. Graham, *The Dual U.S. Standard for the Treatment and Interrogation of Detainees: Unlawful and Unworkable*, 48 WASHBURN LAW JOURNAL 325, 331 (2009) (asserting terrorism and armed conflict are two separate things, governed by their own sets of laws); Rona, *supra* note 53, at 64–65 (stating American targeting of terrorists in Yemen in 2002 was not part of an armed conflict between the United States and terrorism).

163. *See* Paust, *supra* note 62, at 251–52 (supporting the United States' use of force in self-defense outside its own territory even outside the existence of a "relevant international or non-international armed conflict").

164. *See generally* Final Report on the Meaning of Armed Conflict, *supra* note 53, at 10–18 (adopting a definition of armed conflict that requires satisfaction of both organization and intensity of hostilities elements).

165. Rona, *supra* note 53, at 60–65 (analyzing the traits of armed conflict and finding they don't always apply to the war on terror); Mary Ellen O'Connell, *The Legal Case Against the War on Terror*, 36 CASE WESTERN RESERVE JOURNAL OF INTERNATIONAL LAW 349, 352–57 (2004)

(arguing against a global war on terror because it does not meet traditional Geneva ideas of armed conflict).

166. *See generally* Corn, *supra* note 20; Delahunty & Yoo, *supra* note 20; *see also* Blank & Farley, *supra* note 121. *See generally* Balendra, *supra* note 42 (the entire article discussing what constitutes an armed conflict).

167. *See* Paust, *supra* note 62, at 258–60 (stating the United States does not need to be at war with, or involved in an armed conflict with, al Qaeda to use force in self-defense, that use of force outside the scope of an armed conflict would not be governed by *ad bellum* principles).

168. *See generally* Anderson, *supra* note 3.

169. *See generally* Anderson, *supra* note 63.

170. *See* Anderson, *supra* note 3, at 8 ("The invocation of naked self-defense does not lower the standards-of-care conduct in the use of force below what the uniformed military would be required to do in a formal state of armed conflict. Rather, it merely locates them in customary law rather than in the technical law of armed conflict.")

171. Corn & Jensen, *supra* note 12, at 56–57, 75–76; Eric T. Jensen, *Applying a Sovereign Agency Theory of the Law of Armed Conflict*, 12 CHICAGO JOURNAL OF INTERNATIONAL LAW 685, 692–701 (2012).

172. *See generally* Corn & Jensen, *supra* note 17. In this article, the authors address the complex question of distinguishing constabulary uses of military force (for example, deployment of armed forces in the context of a peacekeeping mission) from uses of armed force that trigger LOAC principles. It is suggested that the nature of the use of force authority granted to the forces to execute the mission is a key indicator of the line between armed conflict and other uses of military force falling below that threshold. In so doing, the authors categorically reject the suggestion that any use of armed force abroad triggers LOAC applicability. Instead, analysis of the nature of the mission and the scope of authority employed will drive this determination. The authors recognize this is not a talisman; however, they believe that this approach provides a more operationally realistic method of assessing when compliance with humanitarian constraints is legally obligatory than the elements approach.

173. *See generally* Final Report on the Meaning of Armed Conflict, *supra* note 53.

174. *See, e.g.*, Public Committee against Torture in Israel v. Government of Israel, HCJ 769/02, Judgment (Dec. 13, 2006), 46 INTERNATIONAL LEGAL MATERIALS 373 (2007), *available at* http://elyon1.court.gov.il/files_eng/02/690/007/a34/02007690.a34.pdf. In this case, which concerned the legality of targeted killings, the Israel High Court of Justice ultimately decided that it cannot be determined in advance that every targeted killing is prohibited according to customary international law, but it also cannot be determined in advance that every targeted killing is lawful under customary international law. Each circumstance must be examined on a case-by-case basis.

175. Harold Hongju Koh, *The Lawfulness of the U.S. Operations Against Osama bin Laden*, OPINIO JURIS (May 19, 2011), http://opiniojuris.org/2011/05/19/the-lawfulness-of-the-us-operation-against-osama-bin-laden/ ("[B]in Laden continued to pose an imminent threat to the United States that engaged our right to use force, a threat that materials seized during the raid have only further documented. Under these circumstances, there is no question that he presented a lawful target for the use of lethal force.").

176. *Id.*

177. Harold Hongju Koh, Legal Adviser, U.S. Department of State, Remarks at the Annual Meeting of the American Society of International Law: The Obama Administration and International Law (Mar. 25, 2010), http://www.state.gov/s/l/releases/remarks/139119.htm.

178. Koh, *supra* note 175 ("The laws of armed conflict require acceptance of a genuine offer of surrender that is clearly communicated by the surrendering party and received by the opposing force, under circumstances where it is feasible for the opposing force to accept that offer of surrender. But where that is not the case, those laws authorize use of lethal force against an enemy belligerent, under the circumstances presented here.").

179. Brennan, *supra* note 9.

180. Koh, *supra* note 177.

181. One possible explanation is that Koh may be hinting at a consideration generally overlooked. The fact that the Director of Central Intelligence (and not the Commander of U.S. Special Operations Command) directed the Bin Laden mission is one of the most interesting aspects of the publicly disclosed information about the mission. Concerning the prior widespread reference to a Central Intelligence Agency (CIA) drone operations program, see, e.g., David S. Cloud, *CIA Drones Have a Widened Focus across Pakistan: Since 2008, the Agency Has Been Allowed to Kill Unnamed Suspects*, PITTSBURGH POST-GAZETTE, May 9, 2010, at A6. *See also* Associated Press, *Suspected US Drone Strike Kills 20 in Pakistani Tribal Area, Say Intel Officials*, WATERLOO CHRONICLE, Jan. 17, 2010, at 1; Ken Dilanian, *CIA Drones Joining Fight Inside Yemen*, CHICAGO TRIBUNE, June 15, 2011, at 18. This revelation was not particularly remarkable. However, like the drone program itself, it does raise serious questions related to the legality of employing civilian intelligence personnel to execute missions under the rubric of *jus ad bellum* self-defense. *See* Mary O'Connell, *To Kill or Capture Suspects in the Global War on Terror,* 35 CASE WESTERN RESERVE JOURNAL OF INTERNATIONAL LAW 325, 327–38 (2003) (discussing the legality of CIA operatives using drones to kill suspected al Qaeda operatives in Yemen); Dave Glazier, *Playing by the Rules: Combating al Qaeda Within the Law of War*, 51 WILLIAM AND MARY LAW REVIEW 957, 958 (2009) (stating under certain conditions the military—but not the CIA—can legally kill or detain suspected terrorists under the law of war); Gary Solis, *America's Own Unlawful Combatants*, WASHINGTON POST, Mar. 12, 2010, at A17 (citing the illegality of the CIA's use of drones to kill members of al Qaeda). Perhaps that "or" is a reference to some type of legal division that exists between self-defense operations executed by the armed forces and those executed by the CIA. Is Koh's statement part of an effort to shield the use of CIA operatives from the "lawful belligerent" requirement of the *jus in bello*, and to suggest that CIA operations, while justified pursuant to the *jus ad bellum*, are technically not part of the armed conflict with al Qaeda?

If this is the genesis of Koh's "or," it should be explicitly acknowledged and he should articulate the legal theory for the use of deadly force outside the context of armed conflict. The relative merits of such a theory are well beyond the scope of this essay. However, it is interesting to consider how the U.S. view of war crimes liability for unprivileged belligerents may be influencing this apparent attempt to preserve some *jus ad bellum* targeting carved out from *jus in bello* applicability. It is well known that one of the most contentious offenses in the Military Commission Act of 2006 (as amended) is murder in violation of the law of war. *See* 10 U.S.C. § 950(t)(15) (2009) ("Murder in violation of the law of war. Any person subject to this chapter who intentionally kills one or more persons, including privileged belligerents, in violation of the law of war shall be punished by death or such other punishment as a military commission under this chapter may direct.").

V

War and Peace: Where Is the Divide?

Charles Garraway*

Regarding the rules of warfare, whether we think of Hugo Grotius (*De Jure Belli ac Pacis*),[1] Oppenheim (*International Law: A Treatise*)[2] or Tolstoy (*War and Peace*),[3] we look back at an earlier age. A hundred years ago, there was war and there was peace. Each was clearly identifiable and subject to its own rules. To codify one area, in 1907, the Hague Peace Conference agreed upon a Convention on the Opening of Hostilities (Hague Convention III).[4] For centuries, there had been customary rules dealing with armistices, capitulation, surrender and the restoration of peace. The laws of war were applicable in the period between the opening of hostilities and the restoration of peace.

The middle of the twentieth century began to place this system under strain. States had sought to avoid the application of the laws of war by denying that hostilities amounted to a "war" within the legal definition. The Geneva Conventions of 1949[5] attempted to resolve this problem by changing the application threshold from "war," with its legal technicalities, to "armed conflict," a factual assessment. The spotlight turned from the initial threshold to a new problem. Whereas "war" had always been looked upon as the use of force between States, the nature of armed conflict was different. No longer did States hold a monopoly of violence. The end of colonialism and the Cold War led to war by proxy, often fought between armed groups within a State fighting for control of that State. Sometimes,

* Associate Fellow at Chatham House on the International Security Programme and a Fellow of the Human Rights Centre, University of Essex.

one group represented the recognized government fighting an insurgency; in other cases, the fight was between groups and each might have recognition from States on different sides of the ideological divide. The laws of war, or as they were now known, the laws of armed conflict, were still primarily a matter of treaty law, applicable only to wars between States, now called international armed conflicts. Only limited provisions applied to these new internal armed conflicts, now referred to as non-international armed conflicts. The key issues became, on the one hand, defining the distinction between international and non-international armed conflict and, on the other hand, working on extending the rules applicable to non-international armed conflict.

However, in recent years, the initial threshold of armed conflict has again become relevant. This has been caused to some extent by the success of those who have sought, for humanitarian reasons, to merge the rules relating to international and non-international armed conflict, but also by politicians, who have sought to take advantage of the greater freedom of action normally granted to States in time of war by seeking to apply the laws of war in areas beyond their traditional field. The tensions have led to a debate that has suffered from a seeming inability by different sides to understand where others are coming from. It has become multifaceted and in some cases issues have been lost in confusion over vocabulary. This article will seek to look at how the problems have arisen and whether there is still room for a comprehensive approach that will accommodate to some extent all the competing factions.

In order to find a solution, it is first necessary to identify the problem and how it has arisen. As it has arisen from two separate confrontations, this is more complicated than usual; however, the attempt must be made. First, let us look at the legal arguments that have led to the increasing merger of the law relating to international and non-international armed conflict.

As we have seen, this first arose as an issue after the Second World War. Until that time, the use of violence was seen as the monopoly of States. Similarly, international law involved States and not, for the most part, private individuals. The laws of war therefore dealt with wars between States and what went on within the boundaries of a State was for that State alone and not a matter for the international community. This is to some extent reflected even in the United Nations Charter, where Article 2(7) states:

> Nothing contained in the present Charter shall authorize the United Nations to intervene in matters which are essentially within the domestic jurisdiction of any State or shall require the Members to submit such matters to settlement under the present

> Charter; but this principle shall not prejudice the application of enforcement measures under Chapter VII.[6]

Sovereignty continued to rule but the first chink in the impregnability of the State sovereignty doctrine could be seen here. Even sovereignty could not act as a shield against action by the Security Council, acting on behalf of the international community, when using its powers under Chapter VII of the Charter.

The lessons of the Second World War had shown quite clearly that States could no longer, if they ever could, be trusted entirely to protect their own citizens. The Holocaust was the ultimate betrayal of the duty to protect. While Article 2(7) created a small opportunity for intervention, lawyers were also working to see if the laws protecting peoples could also be strengthened. This work was in two strands. On the one hand, the International Committee of the Red Cross (ICRC), working on revisions of the law protecting victims of war, saw the need to extend that protection down into non-international armed conflicts. At the same time, the United Nations, reluctant as an organization pledged to the abolition of war to involve itself in revision of the laws of war, sought to develop a new branch of international law designed to protect the individual from the powers of the State. Thus human rights law, conceived in the cauldron of two world wars, was developed separately from the laws of war and seen, in essence, as part of the law of peace. It is the separate but contemporaneous development of these two powerful branches of international law that has contributed both to the increased legal protection available to individual victims of armed conflict, and also to a growing overlap between the laws of war and the laws of peace. That overlap has, for the most part, been mutually beneficial, but as the laws of war and human rights law have expanded into each other's "territory," tensions have occurred. These tensions may not be immediately apparent and indeed for many years have lain comparatively unexposed, but recent political events, particularly "9/11" and the subsequent "war on terror," have exposed these tensions to view. Some still refuse to accept that the tensions exist, but I would suggest that if we are to bring these two branches into coexistence, then the tensions must be faced and dealt with.

First we need to see how the tensions have developed.

The ICRC had already been seeking to strengthen the laws relating to victims of armed conflict prior to the Second World War. As a result, it was well placed to make progress in developing "Geneva" law and gained the international community's agreement to the four Geneva Conventions of 1949.[7] These are often seen as the bedrock of modern international humanitarian law, but, again, they approached matters essentially from the viewpoint of the protection of victims. However, the ICRC failed in one of its major objectives. The ICRC had recognized that the nature of warfare was changing and that States no longer had a monopoly on the use of force. As a result, in 1949 it had initially sought to apply the full weight of "Geneva" law, as embodied in the four 1949 Conventions, to non-international armed conflict. The ICRC failed. States were not prepared to go that far in allowing international supervision of their internal affairs. The result was that only one article, common to all four of the 1949 Conventions, was applied to non-international armed conflict. Significantly, the wording of Common Article 3,[8] as it is called, is very similar to the wording used in human rights law. However, the law relating to the conduct of hostilities remained frozen in the form that it had adopted in 1907 in the Regulations Respecting the Laws and Customs of War on Land, annexed to Hague Convention IV.[9] The Regulations had, however, been strengthened by the pronouncement of the Nuremberg Tribunal that they now reflected customary international law and were thus binding on all States.[10]

At the same time, the United Nations was drafting and promulgating the 1948 Universal Declaration of Human Rights.[11] Human rights law, however, initially developed slowly. The two international covenants on economic, social and cultural rights[12] and civil and political rights[13] were not adopted until 1966. In the meantime, Europe had adopted its own Convention for the Protection of Human Rights in 1950, which came into force in 1953.[14] Where this Convention was particularly significant was that it had a judicial enforcement mechanism in the form of the European Court of Human Rights (ECtHR), a Court that has increasingly taken a proactive line in terms of interpreting and enforcing the European Convention.

Although the Universal Declaration was seen as part of the law of peace, the European Convention's terms provided for its continued applicability in times of war. Its derogation clause specifically referred to "war or other public emergency threatening the life of the nation."[15] It was difficult, therefore, to argue that human rights played no part in governing conduct in time of war, at least for European States. Nevertheless, it was generally accepted that in time of "war"—armed conflict between States—it was the laws of war that took priority. The position was less clear in non-international armed conflict, where the law of armed conflict was still only in rudimentary form. While Common Article 3 clearly applied to non-international armed conflict, the application of "Hague" law on the conduct of hostilities was much more problematic. The Hague treaties almost exclusively dealt only with international armed conflict between States and few, if any, commentators were prepared to argue that as a matter of custom, such law extended into non-international armed conflict. States still considered that sovereignty was an overriding consideration and they were not prepared to allow international law to govern how they conducted operations against rebel forces on their own territories. But human rights law was already beginning to do just that.

In 1974, the ICRC again attempted to extend the ambit of the law of armed conflict. It prepared two draft protocols for consideration by States. There were two notable features to these drafts. First, the text was clearly heavily influenced by human rights law. Second, the text not only dealt with "Geneva" law, the traditional area in which the ICRC had operated, but also contained substantial elements of "Hague" law dealing with the conduct of hostilities. The two draft protocols dealt respectively with international armed conflict and non-international armed conflict. These drafts were considered by a diplomatic conference convened by the Swiss government between 1974 and 1977 before two texts were adopted in June 1977.[16] The original draft texts had again sought to bring together the law relating to the two distinct types of conflict, but at the last minute the text of Additional Protocol II relating to non-international armed conflict was substantially trimmed. States again were cautious about allowing too much international control over internal matters. What remained was almost entirely "Geneva" law, expanding the minimal provisions contained in Common Article 3. Furthermore, although Common Article 3 had no "threshold of violence" and thus applied to any "armed conflict not of an international character occurring in the territory of one of the High Contracting Parties,"[17] Additional Protocol II had a much higher threshold, applying only to non-international armed conflicts taking place

> in the territory of a High Contracting Party between its armed forces and dissident armed forces or other organised armed groups which, under responsible command, exercise such control over a part of its territory as to enable them to carry out sustained and concerted military operations and to implement this Protocol.[18]

Thus "Hague" law still was seen as having a minimal impact on non-international armed conflicts.

All this was to change in the 1990s. The conflicts caused by the breakup of the Socialist Federal Republic of Yugoslavia were both bitter and complex. Neighbor was pitted against neighbor and it was often difficult to assess the legal context in which atrocities were being committed. The United Nations Security Council established the International Criminal Tribunal for the former Yugoslavia and passed the problem from the political to the judicial arena.[19]

The Yugoslav Tribunal found itself in something of a quandary. The characterization of the conflicts in the former Yugoslavia was not without considerable doubt. Were they international, that is, between the new States, or internal, between ethnic groups within the new States? Indeed, did the nature of the conflicts change at various points and, if so, when? The rules on the conduct of international hostilities were comparatively clear following the adoption in 1977 of Additional Protocol I to the 1949 Geneva Conventions.[20] Although this treaty did not have the universal acceptance of the Geneva Conventions themselves, its key provisions, including proportionality and precautions in attack, were accepted as custom even by those States who, as a result of objections to other provisions, had not ratified it. But what was the situation in non-international armed conflict? In the early 1990s, even the ICRC had considered that the concept of war crimes in non-international armed conflict did not exist,[21] those being matters within the jurisdiction of the domestic courts as crimes under the States' domestic laws. While this orthodoxy had been turned on its head by the establishment of the International Criminal Tribunal for Rwanda,[22] Rwanda quite clearly being a non-international armed conflict, there remained doubts as to how far the law could extend. As we have seen, treaty law in relation to non-international armed conflict was almost entirely based on "Geneva" law concepts. But here we had conflicts fought with a ferocity that certainly equated to that found in international armed conflicts. To what extent were the participants bound by "Hague" law on the conduct of hostilities?

The Yugoslav Tribunal met this challenge head-on in its first case, that of *Dusko Tadić*.[23] While the Tribunal was not prepared to go as far as some wanted and declare a total assimilation of the law in international and non-international armed conflicts, it stated that "a number of rules and principles . . . have gradually been extended to apply to internal conflicts." However, it put down an important caveat that "this extension has not taken place in the form of a full and mechanical transplant of those rules to internal conflict; rather, the general essence of those rules, and not the detailed regulation they may contain, has become applicable to internal conflicts."[24] While the judgment itself may have been understandably cautious, it opened Pandora's box. Within a very short period, the caveat seemed to have been forgotten.

In 1998, the Statute of the International Criminal Court followed the *Tadić* decision by transposing some of the war crimes applicable in international armed conflict into non-international armed conflict.[25] While most were still of the "Geneva" law type, some were clearly "Hague" law, including pillage and directing attacks against protected persons and objects. The Secretary-General's Bulletin on observance by United Nations forces of international humanitarian law of 6 August 1999[26] drew no distinction between international and non-international armed conflict and the seminal ICRC study *Customary International Humanitarian Law*,[27] while identifying 161 "Rules" of customary international humanitarian law, found that no fewer than 147 applied across the board in both international and non-international armed conflicts.[28] Furthermore, the study drew no distinction between high-intensity non-international armed conflicts, those covered by Additional Protocol II, and those of a lower intensity, subject in treaty law only to the provisions of Common Article 3. The clear conclusion was that, subject to those areas where there were obvious distinctions (e.g., status of prisoners of war), the rules, particularly those relating to the conduct of hostilities, were the same. The unwillingness of States to accept such conclusions in 1949 or more recently in 1977 was thus overcome by a combination of judicial activism and interpretation of customary law.

But if the conduct of hostilities in non-international armed conflicts is now governed by the rules of international humanitarian law, where does that leave human rights law? Under international humanitarian law, it is recognized that in war people die and things get broken. Even a degree of innocent death is acceptable if it is counterbalanced by military advantage. This would seem to fly in the face of human rights law with its more hardened attitude based on the rights of the victim. As international humanitarian law sought wider applicability in non-international armed conflict, it was inevitable that it would collide with human rights law as that too sought to protect the victims of conflicts of all types.

While other bodies have also played a part, the ECtHR has been at the forefront of this confrontation. Cases were referred to the Court arising out of the "Troubles" in Northern Ireland and, as the United Kingdom never acknowledged that these ever reached the level of an "armed conflict," it was no surprise that the Court dealt with the cases purely on the basis of human rights law with no reference to international humanitarian law.[29] Slightly more problematic were cases arising out of the Kurdish insurgency in eastern Turkey. Again, the Court dealt with these entirely on the basis of human rights law, seemingly reluctant even to acknowledge any application of international humanitarian law.[30] The Court was also called upon in cases arising from the Turkish invasion of Cyprus in 1974 and the subsequent occupation, an international armed conflict. The signs of a disagreement between the two bodies of law were apparent when the Court was asked to deal with issues arising from the detention of prisoners of war. These cases were also dealt with solely on the basis of human rights law.[31] In the light of Article 5 of the European Convention for the Protection of Human Rights, which, unlike the International Covenant on Civil and Political Rights, contains an exclusive list of the grounds for deprivation of liberty,[32] it is hard to see how the detention of prisoners of war can be lawful under the European Convention unless a State derogates from the Convention. No State has sought to do so in relation to an armed conflict outside its own territory.

Insofar as the conduct of hostilities is concerned, the Court first became involved in the *Bankovic* case,[33] involving the bombing by NATO forces of a Serbian television station during the Kosovo air campaign, again an international armed conflict. The case was brought by some of those injured in the attack and by families of those killed. Had the Court reached a decision on the merits, a number of crucial questions involving international humanitarian law would seemingly have become relevant. Was the TV station a military objective? If so, how should the anticipated military advantage be assessed and what was the expected incidental loss or damage? How is this balance to be calculated? How does all of this fit with the right to life under human rights law? There was no derogation under Article 15 of the Convention[34] and so to what extent could the Court take into account international humanitarian law at all? Should the Court deal with the matter solely as a human rights issue without any reference to international humanitarian law? Much to the relief of many, but the chagrin of some academics, the Court decided on a preliminary issue that the victims of such an air attack did not fall within the "jurisdiction" of the Court.

However, this was not the end of the matter. This was an international armed conflict and it was clear that NATO had no control over the ground. Furthermore, the territory involved, Serbia, was not within the "*espace juridique*" of the European Convention. The armed conflict in Chechnya provided a different scenario, a non-international armed conflict on the territory of a State party to the Convention. Here the jurisdictional arguments that had prevented the Court from adjudicating the *Bankovic* case did not apply. The Court therefore had to bite the bullet. This conflict involved both land and air operations and it was not long before a case involving the conduct of hostilities came before the Court.

The case involved the bombing from the air of what turned out to be a civilian convoy of vehicles fleeing Grozny.[35] It hinged therefore, in international humanitarian law terms, on the issue of precautions in attack. The Court, however, dealt with it entirely in human rights terms, although international humanitarian law had been discussed in arguments before the Court. As it happens, the facts were such that the same result would probably have been reached under either system of law and the Court used language very similar to that contained in international humanitarian law, particularly Additional Protocol I. However, the Court, on the facts, was able to evade some of the key issues, including that of proportionality. Had the convoy turned out to be a military objective, perhaps because of a number of military vehicles embedded in the convoy, would the issue of proportionality have been dealt with differently under human rights law and the right to life rather than under humanitarian law, where a certain measure of incidental loss and damage is acceptable? The tectonic plates were beginning to rub together.

The legal uncertainty has been accompanied by political events to create "the perfect storm." When the British Prime Minister Harold Macmillan was once asked what he feared most, he is alleged to have replied, "Events, dear boy, events."[36] The 9/11 attacks were certainly such an event. Prior to that date, terrorism was, of course, already a recognized phenomenon; however, it was considered to be on the "peace" side of the line and to be a matter for law enforcement authorities. The series of United Nations conventions on terrorism drafted during the 1970s, '80s and '90s in response largely to acts carried out by Palestinian groups concentrated on international criminal law cooperation.[37] It was acknowledged that terrorism could take place within armed conflict and "acts of terrorism" were specifically prohibited under Additional Protocol II.[38] States, for the most part, sought to differentiate between "terrorism" and armed conflict. On the one hand, Arab groups refused to acknowledge that acts carried out by Palestinian factions were "acts of terrorism" at all, but rather insisted they were legitimate acts of resistance.[39] Conversely, the United Kingdom consistently refused to accept that the campaign by the Irish Republican Army (IRA) and other Republican factions in Northern Ireland amounted to armed conflict. Even the deployment of large numbers of British military forces did not change that position. They were deployed in the capacity of military aid to the civil power,[40] were subject to civilian control and were at all times subject to domestic law. Thus, insofar as the use of force was concerned, they operated in a law enforcement paradigm, not in an armed conflict one. This led to soldiers being investigated for—and even charged with—murder where, under an armed conflict paradigm, their use of force might have been entirely justified.[41] The United Kingdom, when ratifying Additional Protocol I in 1998, made a specific statement of understanding in the following terms: "It is the understanding of the United Kingdom that the term 'armed conflict' of itself and in its context denotes a situation of a kind which is not constituted by the commission of ordinary crimes including acts of terrorism whether concerted or in isolation."[42]

It should be pointed out that the United States seems to have adopted a similar position. As late as April 17, 2000, Madeleine Albright, then Secretary of State, said in a speech to the University of World Economy and Diplomacy at Tashkent in Uzbekistan:

> Terrorism is a criminal act and should be treated accordingly—and that means applying the law fairly and consistently. We have found, through experience around the world, that the best way to defeat terrorist threats is to increase law enforcement capabilities while at the same time promoting democracy and human rights.[43]

The events of 9/11 were to change all that. While the world accepted that the attacks of that day on the Twin Towers and the Pentagon amounted to an "armed attack" sufficient to bring Article 51 of the UN Charter into play,[44] the legal categorization of what happened next was highly controversial. Most accepted that the subsequent attacks on Taliban forces in Afghanistan amounted to an international armed conflict between members of the coalition, most prominently the United States, and Afghanistan; however, that was where consensus seemed to stop. After much internal argument,[45] President Bush decided that there were two separate armed conflicts, one against the Taliban in Afghanistan to which the laws of war applied and another against Al Qaeda, the latter creating a "new paradigm" outside the existing laws of war.[46] The "war on terror" had begun.

I am well aware that the phraseology has now changed. The U.S. administration appears now to have abandoned the concept of a "war on terror" under pressure from the Supreme Court, but the consequences of that initial categorization live with us still. Although the "war" is now stated to be an "overseas contingency operation" against Al Qaeda and affiliated terrorist groups, to some extent nothing has changed. "Al Qaeda and affiliated forces" is a phrase that is remarkably difficult to define to any degree of certainty. Al Qaeda itself has become like a chameleon, changing its shape as circumstances change. It would seem that almost any terrorist group whose aim is to destroy or damage the United States could be brought within the definition on the basis that "my enemy's friend is my enemy." While the current administration does not like it to be stated as bluntly, the United States seems to reserve the right to apply the laws of war to operations against "terrorists"—as defined by the United States—anywhere in the world. The argument is that this is self-defense and the right would only be exercised where the territorial State is unwilling or unable to take action itself. This has applied in both Yemen and Pakistan, though certainly in the case of the former there may have been a degree of consent from the local authorities. It is perhaps ironic that when Israel sought to exercise a similar right in the Entebbe raid, this was condemned by the international community and even by the Secretary-General of the United Nations.[47]

There is no doubt, as we have already seen, that terrorism can take place in armed conflict. What we are now seeing, however, is an increasing tendency to label all dissidents as "terrorists" and, as such, "unlawful combatants" in order to take advantage of the looser controls on the use of force under the laws of armed conflict. Furthermore, the increasing restrictions imposed by human rights law on the right to detain and try individuals under the law enforcement paradigm have increased the temptation to rely on emergency detention provisions, allegedly based on the laws of armed conflict. As we have also seen, the United States appears to assert that in this area at least, the laws of armed conflict displace human rights law so that human rights bodies and even domestic courts have little or no influence.[48]

Faced with this dichotomy, intensive efforts have been made to justify the actions of the two successive administrations. One is reminded of the old Irish story where the lost traveler seeking directions to Mullingar was advised, "If I was you, sir, I would not start from here!" An admission that the original decision, to declare a "war on terror" and invoke the laws of armed conflict as the authority for acts by the President in his capacity as Commander in Chief, was wrong would have incalculable consequences. It could lay the United States open to lawsuits from hundreds, if not thousands, of "victims." It could also have political consequences that would go beyond the issue of terrorism. An attempt, therefore, has been made to alter the direction of travel without making any concessions on the rightness or wrongness of the original course (though comments may be made as to its advisability). In some ways, it is like trying to turn around a supertanker—it cannot simply be thrust into reverse.

Lawyers and scholars in the United States have approached this problem from different angles. Some have castigated the successive administrations for riding roughshod over legal traditions and have effectively demanded that the ship be slammed into reverse.[49] While, in an ideal world, this might be advisable, it is probably impracticable in the political sense. Others have backed the extreme line taken in the early days and see any withdrawal from the original position as a weakening of U.S. resolve and as a triumph for the powers of evil.[50] This does not help the position of the United States in the rest of the world.

A third school is made up of what I will call "the pragmatists." Here are people who recognize the underlying principles of law and are keen to present the United States as a country steeped in the legal tradition and merely seeking to respond to new circumstances within the existing framework of international law. As such, they seek to find innovative ways of justifying U.S. positions without undermining international law as it is understood and accepted by the rest of the world. Examples of this particular school can be found in some of the pronouncements of the Supreme Court, anxious not to appear to impinge upon the President's authority under the separation of powers. The clearest of these is that in *Hamdan* where the Court found that persons held in detention were, at least, subject to the protections given under Common Article 3.[51] This was immediately seized upon by many as a statement by the Court that the "war against Al Qaeda" was a non-international armed conflict.[52] However, with respect, the Court did not answer the fundamental question—whether there was a "war" at all. The Court felt that this fell within the jurisdiction of others to decide and, therefore, for the purposes of its ruling, it accepted that there was such a "war." Others in this volume will deal in greater depth with this and other Supreme Court decisions.[53]

I also place within this school the writings of Professor Geoffrey Corn, also featured in this volume.[54] Professor Corn has long argued most eloquently for a new category of conflict, "transnational armed conflicts," to reflect the nature of a conflict against a non-State actor with global operations and reach.[55] In one way he is right in that few non-international armed conflicts have been confined operationally within the borders of a single State. Most have had a transnational element, even if only by dissidents using a porous border to seek protection. In most of these cases, however, a distinction has been drawn between operations within the territory of the State involved in the non-international armed conflict and those outside. Nobody, for example, among those who argued that Northern Ireland was a non-international armed conflict would have alleged that this gave the United Kingdom the right to strike targets in Boston where IRA leaders were regular speakers at fund-raising rallies, or even in Libya, from where much of the Semtex used by the IRA came and which was a major player in both training and funding.

Professor Corn seems to argue that once military forces are used, it should be the laws of war that apply. This is, of course, in line with accepted Department of Defense policy,[56] but I would suggest is based on a somewhat U.S.-centric view of the use of military force cultured to a considerable extent by the Posse Comitatus Act.[57] Other jurisdictions do not have the same restrictions on the use of military force for domestic law enforcement purposes. As already stated, the United Kingdom for decades relied upon military forces to support the Royal Ulster Constabulary in Northern Ireland, relying completely on a law enforcement paradigm.[58] Although it must be admitted that, to a certain extent, this was a political decision, it does not take away from the fact that the UK armed forces were perfectly capable of acting within the constraints of a law enforcement mode. Indeed, it could be argued that the refusal by the UK government to "escalate" the conflict eventually led to the decision by the IRA leadership to enter into the political arena and seek to obtain its political aims through the ballot box rather than the bullet.

Perhaps a more striking example of this ability of UK armed forces to operate in a law enforcement paradigm can be found in the Iranian Embassy siege of 1980.[59] Terrorists seized the Iranian Embassy in London and took a large number of hostages, including Iranian and British staff. Negotiations with the terrorists were conducted by the Metropolitan Police as the lead agency, but a squadron of Special Air Service (SAS) soldiers was put on immediate standby and deployed to London. Once negotiations broke down and a hostage was killed, the SAS soldiers stormed the building, killing five terrorists, capturing one and rescuing all the surviving hostages. In some ways, this is comparable to the attack on the Bin Laden compound.

Despite the intensity of the siege operation, this was treated throughout as a law enforcement operation. There was an inquest into the deaths of each of those killed—hostages and terrorists alike—and the surviving terrorist was tried (and duly convicted) at the Central Criminal Court in London ("The Old Bailey").

While the deaths of the hostages were clearly unlawful killing, each of the deaths of the terrorists had to be justified under a law enforcement paradigm. It was not sufficient to say, "I saw this guy and I shot him!" The inquest was held in public, but it was hardly difficult in the circumstances to satisfy the coroner that these deaths were lawful. The soldiers involved did not hesitate to fire when appropriate, but at the same time were perfectly capable of restraint when appropriate as well. This controlled use of lethal force is an essential part of training and, even in a situation governed by the laws of armed conflict, would be necessary to reduce the risk of collateral damage. I would therefore challenge those who maintain that the use of military force must inevitably require the application of the laws of armed conflict. Indeed, it could be argued that the use of restrained force, as under the law enforcement paradigm, may be more appropriate in some armed conflict situations where it is difficult to distinguish between fighters and civilians not taking a direct part in hostilities.

I would also note here the attempts by government lawyers, under both the Bush and Obama administrations, to find legal justifications for U.S. actions. It is not the case, despite the views of some right-wing commentators, that the United States does not consider itself bound by international law, or, as John Bolton, the former U.S. ambassador to the United Nations, would see it, there is no law superior to the U.S. Constitution.[60] Successive administrations, while accepting the inadequacies of international law in some respects, have sought to place themselves within the framework of that law. This is particularly true of the excellent lawyers in the State Department. Whether officially or in their private capacities, they have sought to uphold the integrity of international law without seeking to undermine their political masters.

Again an example is to be found with the arguments of Karl Chang on new uses of the principle of neutrality.[61] While there may be disagreement with his attempts to introduce the concept of neutrality into non-international armed conflict, it is at least an acceptance of the need to justify actions under international law. Neutrality has indeed been relevant in the past in high-intensity non-international armed conflict, but this has been linked to another doctrine, recognition of belligerency, which traditionally has internationalized a non-international armed conflict, introducing the legal regime applicable to international armed conflict. This doctrine too appears to be making a comeback in some circles after decades in the legal wilderness.[62]

The danger of all this debate is that developments in international law will be seen to be being driven by the domestic law requirements of a single State. However powerful that State may be, international law remains the "law of nations"—

plural—and while it is inevitable that some States will be more influential than others, one State alone should not be in a position to set the rules for all.

The confusion on the borders between law enforcement and armed conflict can be seen clearly in the events of the Arab Spring in 2011. The first two major States affected were Egypt and Tunisia. In both cases, mass demonstrations toppled the regime in power. In Egypt, the military took over the control of the demonstrations from the police and, indeed, on the fall of the Mubarak regime took over power itself. Despite the deployment of military forces and the existence of what social scientists would undoubtedly describe as a "conflict,"[63] few would argue that the confrontations reached the level necessary to constitute an "armed conflict" sufficient to invoke the laws of armed conflict. The Egyptian military was thus judged in its actions under a law enforcement paradigm.

On the other hand, Libya clearly crossed the threshold of armed conflict even before the NATO operations conducted under the authority of UN Security Council Resolution 1973.[64] But what of Syria and Yemen? At the time of this writing (October 2011), it seems clear that Yemen is, at least, close to a state of civil war, a non-international armed conflict.[65] In Syria also, the intensity of violence would seem to cross the threshold, but the lack of organization of the opposition forces may be considered to rule out the existence of an "armed conflict" due to the difficulty in identifying an opposition "party" to that armed conflict.[66] Certainly, military forces have been deployed within Syria, but does that automatically lead to an "armed conflict" bringing into force the laws of armed conflict? I would argue that the actions of the military forces, in such a context, will be judged under human rights law—crimes against humanity—rather than under the laws of armed conflict as war crimes.

Bahrain also raises similar issues. Military forces have been deployed, including troops from neighboring Saudi Arabia, but I would argue that the situation there has not yet developed into an armed conflict.[67]

But does this matter? Is the distinction a matter of practical importance on the ground or is it simply another example of lawyers debating how many angels can dance on the head of a pin? In my opinion, resolution of this issue is hugely significant, as it illustrates the coming together of the two tectonic plates, the laws of armed conflict and human rights law. Lawyers from each camp claim priority for their legal regime, but can they all be right? A common tendency today is to dismiss the argument by saying that the two systems are "complementary" and, therefore, there is no underlying problem.[68] I would suggest, however, that a closer examination does not support this "complementary" theory.

Insofar as "Geneva" law is concerned, it can be accepted that there is a considerable degree of compatibility. Both systems of law grew from the same root, a need to protect those who were seen as victims. Although "Geneva" law was mainly designed, in the early days, to protect combatants who were placed *hors de combat* and human rights law was designed to protect civilians from the power of States, the underlying principles are similar. While there may be differences of emphasis—and, in places, of detail—these can be overcome and the two legal systems can sit reasonably comfortably together.

"Hague" law on the conduct of hostilities is different in origin. It grew from the acceptance of State entities' right to use violence. While "Hague" law sought to restrain that use of violence, it did not seek to prevent it and, therefore, acknowledged that, in time of war, people (including civilians) will die and things will get broken. It is here that the laws of armed conflict begin to diverge from human rights law, which starts with the rights of the individual and limits the occasions on which States can override those rights. The two systems therefore approach matters from opposite ends of the philosophical spectrum.

Insofar as "Hague" law seeks to limit the conduct of States, again there is a degree of compatibility with human rights law. Thus, many of the "protection" provisions and weaponry restrictions sit happily alongside human rights law. However, it is in the "authorizations" accepted by "Hague" law that the greatest difficulty lies. For centuries it was accepted that the right to use force was an inherent power of sovereignty. Those authorized by the sovereign were immune from prosecution for acts of violence that would be criminal if committed outside the context of war. This became known as "combatant immunity."[69] In return, such belligerents were themselves lawful targets and could be killed without question simply because of their status. The threat they posed was irrelevant. This customary rule became tempered over time by custom itself, which developed the principle of protection, which subsequently developed into "Geneva" treaty law, affording protection to a belligerent who was rendered *hors de combat*; but the underlying principle that a belligerent was a legitimate target was unchallenged.

Belligerents who were captured could be detained until the end of active hostilities.[70] They were not criminals; just as it was accepted that belligerents could be killed because of their status, so they could be detained for the same reason. Again this was mitigated to allow for the early release of those seriously injured,[71] but the general principle remained. Early release was the exception, not the rule.

Human rights law approaches both the use of force and detention from the opposite direction. Use of lethal force is prohibited except in certain specified circumstances.[72] Authority to use force is based on the threat posed by the individual on whom the force is to be used. The right to life is a fundamental right and thus lethal force is obviously a last resort. It may only be resorted to in the most extreme circumstances. These provisions will be well understood by anyone engaged in law enforcement.

Similarly, the right to liberty of the person may only be restricted in specific circumstances.[73] Again, this would be assessed on an individual basis and the assessment would be based on threat. It would not include the mass detention of prisoners of war on the basis of status.

It follows that the tests involved for both use of force and detention are fundamentally different under human rights law and the laws of armed conflict. Let us take the example of Bin Laden, leaving aside for these purposes issues of the *ad bellum* authority for the operation being conducted in Pakistan.

It is the U.S. position that this operation was conducted as part of its ongoing "war" against Al Qaeda, that Osama Bin Laden was a "belligerent" within that armed conflict and therefore a legitimate target.[74] On that basis, under traditional "Hague" rules, lethal force could be used against Bin Laden because of his status. It was not necessary that he pose any threat to the attacking forces at the time that the lethal force was used. Of course, the essential *hors de combat* rules would have applied and, if Bin Laden had sought to surrender, then that surrender should have been accepted. However, the burden was on Bin Laden to display a clear intention to surrender, not on the troops themselves to inquire as to his intentions. There may have been orders to capture Bin Laden, if possible, but this would have been a matter of operational requirements, not international law.

On the other hand, if this was a law enforcement operation conducted under human rights law, then the primary aim of the operation would have to have been to capture Bin Laden. Any use of force would have needed to be directly responsive to the threats posed to the troops on the ground in the circumstances ruling at the time. Any use of lethal force in particular would have needed to be justified specifically on the basis of the threat faced at the moment that the lethal force was used and not simply by the fact that this was Osama Bin Laden. The burden would have been on the troops to justify their use of force, not on Bin Laden himself.

As the example of the Iranian Embassy siege shows, the end results may be little different. In a case where hostages have been killed and there remains a serious risk to other hostages, as well as to the troops themselves, from well-armed terrorists who have wired a building with explosives, little justification is needed for the immediate use of lethal force. However, the aim of the operation is different. Put simply, it is the difference between "kill or capture" and "capture or kill."

While on many occasions, and it may well be that the Bin Laden case is an example, the results may be the same under either a law enforcement or armed conflict operation, there will be others where the results may differ. An example is the *Bankovic* case referred to earlier.[75] In that case, during the Kosovo air campaign,

NATO aircraft attacked the main television station in Belgrade, causing a number of civilian casualties. The families of the deceased and some of the injured initiated proceedings against the European NATO States, alleging breaches of their right to life. As earlier stated, the case fell at the admissibility hurdle when it was ruled that the "victims" did not fall within the jurisdiction of the European States. This meant that the case did not reach the merits stage. Had it done so, the applicants would have argued that the TV station was not a legitimate military objective under the laws of armed conflict, which would have resulted in the ECtHR being faced with the dilemma of deciding whether the loose language of Article 52(2) of Additional Protocol I[76] is consistent with the strict standards on the use of force under human rights law. Furthermore, even if the Court had decided that the TV station was a military objective and therefore liable to attack, the Court might have then had to rule on the issue of proportionality.

In cases involving the right of an individual to be free from torture and cruel or inhumane treatment, the ECtHR has already ruled in deportation cases that a State cannot set against the rights of the applicant the danger that the applicant poses to national security, and thus to the rights of the wider population.[77] With this precedent, it would have been interesting to see how the Court dealt with the balance between the anticipated collateral damage and the anticipated military advantage.

Nor is this a theoretical problem. Cases have been filed with the ECtHR arising from the Russia-Georgia conflict in 2008.[78] It therefore is likely that the Court will have to deal with these issues within the foreseeable future. To date, the Court has shown a marked reluctance to consider the laws of armed conflict, preferring to approach matters from a human rights perspective, occasionally paying lip service to law of armed conflict principles. This can be seen at its most extreme in the Chechnya cases, where the Court held in one case that where there was no derogation the Court was bound to consider matters on the basis of a normal law enforcement paradigm.[79] That case involved air operations, and so it seemed that the Court was taking a purely legalistic approach, refusing to accept the actual facts on the ground. A similar approach to the Russia-Georgia conflict would involve, at best, the interpretation of law of conflict principles through a human rights prism and, at worst, a claim that human rights law trumps the law of armed conflict, even in international armed conflict.

If, as seems likely, we are heading for a clash between the competing philosophies of "Hague" law and human rights law, is there any way of avoiding such a clash while retaining the key principles of each? One way would be to seek to incorporate human rights standards into the laws of armed conflict. The ICRC seems to have encouraged this approach in its *Interpretive Guidance on the Notion of Direct*

Participation in Hostilities under International Humanitarian Law.[80] In one of the more controversial parts of this document, the ICRC states in Part IX:

> In addition to the restraints imposed by international humanitarian law on specific means and methods of warfare and without prejudice to further restrictions that may arise under other applicable branches of international law, the kind and degree of force which is permissible against persons not entitled to protection against direct attack must not exceed what is actually necessary to accomplish a legitimate military purpose in the prevailing circumstances.[81]

Despite its careful wording, this has been seen as incorporating a requirement for a graduated use of force. Indeed, it claims to be an interpretation of a statement by Jean Pictet:

> If we can put a soldier out of action by capturing him, we should not wound him; if we can obtain the same result by wounding him, we must not kill him. If there are two means to achieve the same military advantage, we must choose the one which causes the lesser evil.[82]

While this is entirely consistent with the underlying philosophy of "Geneva" law, it runs counter to the recognized interpretation of "Hague" law in which belligerents are targetable with lethal force at all times because of their status. As such, this part of the *Interpretive Guidance* has been criticized by States, particularly those involved in major operations, as an attempt to rewrite existing law in a manner that, when applied to all forms of armed conflict, would be unrealistic on the ground.

Another possible way forward would depend on an acceptance that the complementary view is not the answer and that there will be circumstances where the two legal systems conflict. In such cases, it will be necessary to decide which legal system should have priority. This would not affect the basic principle that there is sizable overlap, but would seek to make operational the Delphic dictum of the International Court of Justice, when it sought to deal with the relationship between the two bodies of law. It stated:

> As regards the relationship between international humanitarian law and human rights law, there are thus three possible situations: some rights may be exclusively matters of international humanitarian law; others may be exclusively matters of human rights law; yet others may be matters of both these branches of international law. In order to answer the question put to it, the Court will have to take into consideration both these branches of international law, namely human rights law and, as *lex specialis*, international humanitarian law.[83]

But where should the division be? It would seem clear that in international armed conflict, priority should go to the laws of armed conflict. In cases falling short of armed conflict, the laws of armed conflict do not apply at all and so human rights law will govern. However, the situation is not so simple in relation to non-international armed conflict or, within the sphere of international armed conflict, situations of occupation. In each of these situations, as we have seen, the boundaries between law enforcement operations and armed conflict are blurred and difficult to define. The answer may be not to look at the technical classification of the armed conflict but at the level of violence within it. Some non-international armed conflicts are low-level, consisting principally of individual incidents rather than concerted operations. To permit "Hague" law authorizations to apply to such armed conflicts would encourage every despot to declare his internal disturbances to be an armed conflict in order to permit wider powers of detention and use of force. In low-level non-international armed conflicts of this nature, human rights law should take priority when there is a conflict between human rights law and the laws of armed conflict.

Other non-international armed conflicts are of very high intensity, equivalent to that of an international armed conflict. In the past, these often led to "recognition of belligerency" and the application of the law relevant to international armed conflict. However, as "recognition of belligerency" has fallen away in recent decades, the level of intensity to be found has certainly not. The Sri Lankan civil war is a good example.[84] To require militaries to comply with a law enforcement paradigm in relation to the use of force in such circumstances would be close to suicidal. In cases of such intensity, the laws of armed conflict would prevail.

A similar test could be applied to situations of occupation. Where resistance is comparatively low-key and consists primarily of individual attacks, however effective, human rights law would normally have priority. On the other hand, where—as, for example, in Iraq[85]—the resistance was of high intensity, the laws of armed conflict would take priority.

This will not be a complete resolution of the problem in that there will still be "gray" areas where authorities will need to make "good faith" decisions. In fact, this reflects what already happens with respect to rules of engagement. Even in international armed conflict, there will be occasions when, whatever the circumstances under the laws of armed conflict, soldiers have already been restricted in their use of force by rules of engagement that have been imposed for political or other reasons.

However, what is not acceptable is for the current position to continue, where service personnel may find their actions subject to *ex post facto* investigation, an investigation which starts with uncertainty over the underlying legal regime. This is neither fair to the personnel themselves nor conducive to respect for the law. There must be a better way!

Notes

1. HUGO GROTIUS, *DE IURE BELLI AC PACIS LIBRI TRES* (Francis W. Kelsey trans., 1925) (1625). This is only one of the many translations.

2. L. OPPENHEIM, INTERNATIONAL LAW: A TREATISE (1905). The ninth edition was published in 1992.

3. LEO TOLSTOY, WAR AND PEACE (1869).

4. Convention No. III Relative to the Opening of Hostilities, Oct. 18, 1907, 36 Stat. 2259, 2271 T.S. 598.

5. Convention for the Amelioration of the Condition of the Wounded and Sick in Armed Forces in the Field, Aug. 12, 1949, 6 U.S.T. 3114, 75 U.N.T.S. 31; Convention for the Amelioration of the Condition of Wounded, Sick and Shipwrecked Members of Armed Forces at Sea, Aug. 12, 1949, 6 U.S.T. 3217, 75 U.N.T.S. 85; Convention Relative to the Treatment of Prisoners of War, Aug. 12, 1949, 6 U.S.T. 3316, 75 U.N.T.S. 135 [hereinafter GC III]; Convention Relative to the Protection of Civilian Persons in Time of War, Aug. 12, 1949, 6 U.S.T. 3516, 75 U.N.T.S. 287; all *reprinted in* DOCUMENTS ON THE LAWS OF WAR 197, 222, 244, 301, respectively (Adam Roberts & Richard Guelff eds., 3d ed. 2000).

6. U.N. Charter art. 2, para. 7 (Oct. 24, 1945), *reprinted in* BASIC DOCUMENTS IN INTERNATIONAL LAW 2, 4 (Ian Brownlie ed., 5th ed. 2002).

7. *See supra* note 5.

8. Common Article 3 to the four Geneva Conventions of 12 August 1949, *reprinted in* DOCUMENTS ON THE LAWS OF WAR, *supra* note 5, at 198, 223, 245, 302, respectively.

9. Regulations Respecting the Laws and Customs of War on Land, annexed to Convention No. IV Respecting the Laws and Customs of War on Land, Oct. 18, 1907, 205 Consol. T.S. 277, *reprinted in id.* at 73.

10. See extract from the Judgment of the International Military Tribunal at Nuremberg, November 1948, *reprinted in id.* at 78.

11. Universal Declaration of Human Rights, G.A. Res. 217A, at 71, U.N. GAOR, 3d Sess., 1st plen. mtg., U.N. Doc. A/810 (Dec. 10, 1948), *reprinted in* BASIC DOCUMENTS IN INTERNATIONAL LAW, *supra* note 6, at 192.

12. International Covenant on Economic, Social and Cultural Rights, G.A. Res. 2200A (XXI), U.N. Doc. A/6316 (Dec. 16, 1966), 993 U.N.T.S. 3, *reprinted in id.* at 197.

13. International Covenant on Civil and Political Rights, G.A. Res. 2200A (XXI), U.N. Doc. A/6316 (Dec. 16, 1966), 999 U.N.T.S. 171, *reprinted in id.* at 205 [hereinafter ICCPR].

14. European Convention for the Protection of Human Rights and Fundamental Freedoms, Nov. 4, 1950, Europ. T.S. No. 5, 213 U.N.T.S. 222 (entered into force Sept. 3, 1953), *reprinted in id.* at 245 [hereinafter ECHR].

15. *Id.*, art. 15.

16. Protocol Additional to the Geneva Conventions of 12 August 1949, and Relating to the Protection of Victims of International Armed Conflicts, June 8, 1977, 1125 U.N.T.S. 3 [hereinafter AP I]; Protocol Additional to the Geneva Conventions of 12 August 1949, and Relating to the Protection of Victims of Non-International Armed Conflicts, June 8, 1977, 1125 U.N.T.S. 609 [hereinafter AP II]; both *reprinted in* DOCUMENTS ON THE LAWS OF WAR, *supra* note 5, at 422 and 483, respectively.

17. *Supra* note 8.

18. AP II, *supra* note 16, art. 1(1).

19. *See* S.C. Res. 827, U.N. Doc. S/RES/827 (May 25, 1993).

20. *Supra* note 16.

21. *See* Preliminary Remarks on the Setting-Up of an International Tribunal for the Prosecution of Persons Responsible for Serious Violations of International Humanitarian Law Committed in the Territory of the Former Yugoslavia ¶ 4, DDM/JUR/442b (1993), *reprinted in* 2 VIRGINIA MORRIS & MICHAEL P. SCHARF, AN INSIDER'S GUIDE TO THE INTERNATIONAL CRIMINAL TRIBUNAL FOR THE FORMER YUGOSLAVIA 391–92 (1995) ("according to International Humanitarian Law as it stands today, the notion of war crimes is limited to situations of international armed conflict").

22. *See* S.C. Res. 955, U.N. Doc. S/RES/955 (Nov. 8, 1994).

23. Prosecutor v. Tadić, Case No. IT-94-1-l, Decision on Defence Motion for Interlocutory Appeal on Jurisdiction (Int'l Crim. Trib. for the Former Yugoslavia Oct. 2, 1995), *reprinted in* 35 INTERNATIONAL LEGAL MATERIALS 32 (1996).

24. *Id.*, ¶ 126.

25. Rome Statute of the International Criminal Court art. 8.2.(c)–(e), July 17, 1998, 2187 U.N.T.S. 90, *reprinted in* DOCUMENTS ON THE LAWS OF WAR, *supra* note 5, at 671, 678–79.

26. Secretary-General's Bulletin: Observance by United Nations Forces of International Humanitarian Law, U.N. Doc. ST/SGB/1999/13 (Aug. 6, 1999), *reprinted in id.* at 725.

27. CUSTOMARY INTERNATIONAL HUMANITARIAN LAW (2 volumes: Vol. I, Rules; Vol. II, Practice (2 Parts)) (Jean-Marie Henckaerts & Louise Doswald-Beck eds., 2005).

28. *See* Jean-Marie Henckaerts, *The ICRC Study on Customary International Humanitarian Law – An Assessment, in* CUSTOM AS A SOURCE OF INTERNATIONAL HUMANITARIAN LAW 50 (Larry Maybee & Benarji Chakka eds., 2006).

29. *See, e.g.*, McCann v. United Kingdom, 324 Eur. Ct. H.R. (ser. A) 97 (1995).

30. *See, e.g.*, Ergi v. Turkey, 1998-IV Eur. Ct. H.R. 1751, 1777.

31. Cyprus v. Turkey, 35 Eur. Ct. H.R. 967 (2001); Varnava & Others v. Turkey, App. Nos. 16064/90, 16065/90, 16066/90, 16068/90, 16069/90, 16070/90, 16071/90, 16072/90 and 16073/90, Eur. Ct. H.R. (2009), *reprinted in* 49 INTERNATIONAL LEGAL MATERIALS 358 (2010).

32. ECHR, *supra* note 14, art. 5.

33. Bankovic and Others v. Belgium, 2001-XII Eur. Ct. H.R. 333, *reprinted in* 41 INTERNATIONAL LEGAL MATERIALS 517 (2002).

34. *Supra* note 15.

35. Isayeva v. Russia, 41 Eur. Ct. H.R. Rep. 39 (2005).

36. Although the quotation is open to challenge, see Robert Harris, *As Macmillan Never Said*, TELEGRAPH (UNITED KINGDOM) (June 4, 2002), http://www.telegraph.co.uk/comment/personal-view/3577416/As-Macmillan-never-said-thats-enough-quotations.html.

37. *See, e.g.*, Convention for the Suppression of Unlawful Seizure of Aircraft, Dec. 16, 1970, 22 U.S.T. 1641, 860 U.N.T.S. 105.

38. AP II, *supra* note 16, art. 4(2)(d).

39. *See, e.g.*, Arab Convention for the Suppression of Terrorism art. 2(a), Apr. 22, 1998, *available at* http://www.al-bab.com/arab/docs/league/terrorism98.htm.

40. *See* Ministry of Defence, UK Defence: Statistics, 2008, ch. 7, http://www.dasa.mod.uk/modintranet/UKDS/UKDS2008/c7/intro.html.

41. *See, e.g.*, R v. Clegg, [1995] 1 A.C. 482 (H.L.) (appeal taken from N. Ir.).

42. United Kingdom statement (d) on ratification of Additional Protocol I, *reprinted in* DOCUMENTS ON THE LAWS OF WAR, *supra* note 5, at 510.

43. Cited in TOM BINGHAM, THE RULE OF LAW 133 (2010).

44. *See* S.C. Res. 1368, S/RES/1368 (Sept. 12, 2001).

45. *See* Charles Garraway, *Afghanistan and the Nature of Conflict*, *in* THE WAR IN AFGHANISTAN: A LEGAL ANALYSIS 157 (Michael N. Schmitt ed., 2009) (Vol. 85, U.S. Naval War College International Law Studies).

46. Memorandum from George Bush to Vice President et al., Humane Treatment of al Qaeda and Taliban Detainees (Feb. 7, 2002), *reprinted in* THE TORTURE PAPERS: THE ROAD TO ABU GHRAIB 134 (Karen J. Greenberg & Joshua Dratel eds., 2005).

47. *See* Leslie Green, *Rescue at Entebbe*, 6 ISRAEL YEARBOOK ON HUMAN RIGHTS 312, 315 (1976).

48. The United States is engaged in an armed conflict with al Qaida, the Taliban, and their supporters. As part of this conflict, the United States captures and detains enemy combatants, and is entitled under the law of war to hold them until the end of hostilities. The law of war, and not the Covenant, is the applicable legal framework governing these detentions.

Comments by the Government of the United States of America on the Concluding Observations of the Human Rights Committee, U.N. Doc. CCPR/C/USA/CO/3/Rev.1/Add.1, at 2, 3 (Feb. 12, 2008).

49. *See, e.g.*, Mary-Ellen O'Connell, *When Is a War Not a War? The Myth of the Global War on Terror*, 12 ILSA JOURNAL OF INTERNATIONAL & COMPARATIVE LAW 1 (2005).

50. *See, e.g.*, David B. Rivkin Jr. & Lee A. Casey, *Awlaki vs Predator*, WALL STREET JOURNAL (Aug. 13, 2010), http://online.wsj.com/article/SB10001424052748704901104575423253031580156.html.

51. Hamdan v. Rumsfeld, 548 U.S. 557, 628–32 (2006).

52. *See* John Bellinger, *Armed Conflict with Al Qaida: A Response*, OPINIO JURIS (Jan. 16, 2007), http://opiniojuris.org/2007/01/16/armed-conflict-with-al-qaida-a-response/.

53. *See* John F. Murphy, *Will-o'-the-Wisp? The Search for Law in Non-International Armed Conflicts*, which is Chapter I in this volume, at 15; David E. Graham, *Defining Non-International Armed Conflict: A Historically Difficult Task*, which is Chapter III in this volume, at 43; Geoffrey S. Corn, *Self-defense Targeting: Blurring the Line between the* Jus ad Bellum *and the* Jus in Bello, which is Chapter IV in this volume, at 57; Yoram Dinstein, *Concluding Remarks on Non-International Armed Conflicts*, which is Chapter XVII in this volume, at 399.

54. Corn, *supra* note 53.

55. *See, e.g.*, Geoffrey S. Corn, *Making the Case for Conflict Bifurcation in Afghanistan: Transnational Armed Conflict, Al Qaeda, and the Limits of the Associated Militia Concept*, *in* THE WAR IN AFGHANISTAN, *supra* note 45, at 181.

56. *See* Department of Defense, DoD Directive 2311.01E, DoD Law of War Program ¶ 4.1 (2006), *available at* http://www.dtic.mil/whs/directives/corres/pdf/231101e.pdf.

57. Posse Comitatus Act, 18 U.S.C. § 1385 (2006).

58. *See supra* note 40.

59. For an account, see TONY GERAGHTY, WHO DARES WINS: THE STORY OF THE SPECIAL AIR SERVICE 1950–1980 ch. 7 (1980).

60. *See* Wade Mansell & Emily Haslam, *John Bolton and the United States' Retreat from International Law*, 14 SOCIAL LEGAL STUDIES 459 (2005).

61. *See* Karl S. Chang, *Enemy Status and Military Detention in the War Against Al-Qaeda*, 47 TEXAS INTERNATIONAL LAW JOURNAL 1 (2011); Karl S. Chang, *Enemy Status and Military Detention: Neutrality Law and Non-International Armed Conflict, Municipal Neutrality Statutes, the U.N. Charter, and Hostile Intent*, 47 TEXAS INTERNATIONAL LAW JOURNAL 381 (2012).

62. *See* Anthony Cullen, *Key Developments Affecting the Scope of Internal Armed Conflict in International Humanitarian Law*, 183 MILITARY LAW REVIEW 65 (2005).

63. *See, e.g.*, *Egypt Urged to Protect Families of Those Killed in Protests from Intimidation* (Feb. 25, 2011), AMNESTY INTERNATIONAL, http://www.amnesty.org/en/news-and-updates/egypt-urged-protect-families-those-killed-protests-intimidation-2011-02-25 (describing excessive use of force by security forces in response to "some protestors [who] behaved violently, attacking public and private property, associated with repression and corruption, such as police stations and local authorities' buildings, and members of the security forces, using rocks, and in rarer instances petrol bombs").

64. S.C. 1973, U.N. Doc. S/RES/1973 (Mar. 17, 2011).

65. *See* U.N. Human Rights Council, Report of the High Commissioner for Human Rights on the Visit of the Office of the High Commissioner for Human Rights to Yemen, U.N. Doc. A/HRC/18/21 (Sept. 13, 2011).

66. Although the Syrian National Council was formed in October 2011, it remains to be seen whether this is a genuine opposition.

67. *See Bahrain Crackdown on Protests in Manama's Pearl Square*, BBC NEWS (Mar. 16, 2011), http://www.bbc.co.uk/news/world-middle-east-12755852.

68. *See* IHL and Other Legal Regimes, 29 October 2010, http://www.icrc.org/eng/war-and-law/ihl-other-legal-regmies/overview-other-legal-regimes.htm.

69. *See* Geoffrey S. Corn, *Thinking the Unthinkable: Has the Time Come to Offer Combatant Immunity to Non-State Actors?*, 22 STANFORD LAW & POLICY REVIEW 253, 256 (2011).

70. GC III, *supra* note 5, art. 118.

71. *Id.*, art. 109.

72. ICCPR, *supra* note 13, art. 6; ECHR, *supra* note 14, art. 2.

73. ICCPR, *supra* note 13, art. 9; ECHR, *supra* note 14, art. 5.

74. *See* Harold Koh, State Department Legal Adviser, *The Lawfulness of the U.S. Operation Against Osama bin Laden*, OPINIO JURIS (May 19, 2011), http://opiniojuris.org/2011/05/19/the-lawfulness-of-the-us-operation-against-osama-bin-laden/.

75. *Supra* note 33.

76. AP I, *supra* note 16, art. 52(2).

77. *See* Chahal v. United Kingdom, 1996-V Eur. Ct. H.R. 1831.

78. *See* Press Release, European Court of Human Rights, Hearing in the Inter-State Case Georgia v. Russia (II) Concerning the 2008 Armed Conflict between the Two Countries (Sept. 22, 2011) (ECHR 150 (2011)).

79. Isayeva v. Russia, 41 Eur. Ct. H.R. Rep. 39, ¶ 91 (2005).

80. NILS MELZER, INTERNATIONAL COMMITTEE OF THE RED CROSS, INTERPRETIVE GUIDANCE ON THE NOTION OF DIRECT PARTICIPATION IN HOSTILITIES UNDER INTERNATIONAL HUMANITARIAN LAW (2009).

81. *Id.* at 77.

82. JEAN PICTET, DEVELOPMENT AND PRINCIPLES OF INTERNATIONAL HUMANITARIAN LAW 75–76 (1985).

83. Legal Consequences of the Construction of a Wall in the Occupied Palestinian Territory, Advisory Opinion, 2004 I.C.J. 136, ¶ 106 (July 9).

84. The Sri Lankan civil war lasted from 1983 to 2009.

85. For example, the first Battle of Fallujah in April 2004.

PART IV

LEGAL STATUS OF THE ACTORS IN NON-INTERNATIONAL ARMED CONFLICTS

VI

The Status of Opposition Fighters in a Non-International Armed Conflict

Michael N. Schmitt*

The treaty law applicable to the classification of participants in a non-international conflict is limited to Common Article 3 to the 1949 Geneva Conventions[1] and the 1977 Additional Protocol II.[2] The former is generally deemed reflective of customary international law, whereas the latter is not (although certain individual provisions thereof certainly are).[3] Other treaties apply during non-international armed conflicts, but do not bear on the issue of classifying those involved in the conflict.[4]

Common Article 3, which appears in each of the four Geneva Conventions, provides no specific guidance as to who qualifies as a "Party to the conflict," although subsequent case law has clarified that the article encompasses conflict at a certain level of intensity that occurs between a State's armed forces and organized armed groups, or between such groups.[5] Textually, the article merely refers to "persons taking no active part in hostilities," including "members of the armed forces" who are *hors de combat*.[6] The reference is somewhat useful in that it suggests a normative distinction between those who actively participate in a non-international armed conflict and those who do not. Yet, the failure to address party status

* Chair of Public International Law, Durham University Law School, United Kingdom. Professor Schmitt became the Chairman, International Law Department, U.S. Naval War College on October 1, 2011.

directly is unfortunate, for it begs the question of when non-State individuals or groups qualify as a party. Complicating the issue of participant classification is the fact that Common Article 3 makes no mention of the category "civilians."

Additional Protocol II contains slightly more granularity in its provision on the instrument's material field of application. Article 1 extends coverage to "all armed conflicts" between the armed forces of a State party to the Protocol and "dissident armed forces or other organized armed groups which, under responsible command, exercise such control over a part of its territory as to enable them to carry out sustained and concerted military operations and to implement this Protocol."[7] This is a higher threshold of applicability than that of Common Article 3 in two regards.[8] First, it does not include conflicts that are solely between organized armed groups; a State must be involved.[9] Second, the group in opposition to the government must exercise a certain degree of control over territory. The higher thresholds are not dealt with in this chapter, as they bear on the law that applies to a conflict, not on the status of its participants. What is significant with regard to classification of participants, though, are the references to dissident armed forces and organized armed groups.

Additional Protocol II also adopts the notion of "civilian," most notably in Article 13 on the "protection of the civilian population." That article extends "general protection against the dangers arising from military operations" to civilians, and specifically prohibits both attacks against them and any actions intended to terrorize the civilian population, but withdraws said protection "for such time as they take a direct part in hostilities."[10] Unfortunately, Additional Protocol II, in contrast to its international armed conflict counterpart, offers no definition of the term "civilian."[11]

Taking the two treaties together, and in light of Common Article 3's customary status, it can be concluded that two broad categories of non-international armed conflict participants lie in juxtaposition: civilians and organized armed groups. The former can be subdivided into those who directly participate in hostilities and those who do not. Organized armed groups consist of a State's armed forces, dissident armed forces or "other" organized armed groups.

This chapter examines the three types of "opposition fighters"—dissident armed forces, other organized armed groups and civilians directly participating in hostilities. A companion contribution to the volume deals with the status of government fighters. The chapter does not address the criteria for the existence of a non-international armed conflict, the subject of other contributions, except as that topic bears on classification of participants.[12] Accordingly, it does not explore such contentious topics as whether a non-international armed conflict can exist during a belligerent occupation, the legal status of a conflict with transnational terrorists, internationalization of a conflict through intervention of another State or external State control of insurgent groups. Rather, assuming a non-international armed conflict (whatever form it takes), it asks how opposition force participants in the conflict are to be classified.[13]

The significance of classification is limited. For instance, the international armed conflict concept of combatancy and the related notion of belligerent immunity do not exist in non-international armed conflicts.[14] Members of the opposition forces may be prosecuted for any acts that violate domestic law, even if they are not violations of the law of armed conflict (LOAC), as is the case with attacking members of the armed forces.[15] In light of the absence of combatancy in a non-international armed conflict, this chapter has adopted the term "fighters" in lieu of "combatants" to refer to those who participate in the conflict.[16] Similarly, there is no prisoner of war regime in the context of a non-international armed conflict, although, as explained in the chapters on detention, certain basic protections do inure to the benefit of detainees in these conflicts.

The key consequences of classification lie in the law of targeting, for classification determines whether LOAC prohibits an attack on an individual during a non-international armed conflict.[17] To the extent no prohibition exists on attacking persons with a particular classification, harm to an individual within that group plays no role in proportionality calculations (except as military advantage) and need not be considered when determining the precautions that attackers are required to take during attacks to avoid harming civilians.[18] As will become apparent, the targetability of the various categories of opposition fighters is a matter of some contention in LOAC circles.

Before turning to an examination of the various categories of opposition fighters, it should be briefly noted that if the forces of another State intervene on behalf of the opposition, an international armed conflict ensues between that State and the State against whom the pre-existing rebellion is under way; the conflict has been internationalized.[19] Unless the external State exercises a sufficiently high level of control over the opposition forces, a non-international armed conflict continues between those forces and their government.[20] Because the external State's forces are involved in an international armed conflict, their status, which would be that of combatants, is not examined below.[21]

Individuals Who Are Not Members of a "Traditional" Opposition Force

As a general rule, individual criminals and purely criminal groups do not constitute "parties" to a non-international armed conflict, regardless of whether they engage alone in acts of violence against the government (or non-government organized armed groups) or operate in the midst of an ongoing non-international armed conflict. Since they neither are a party nor operate on behalf of one, domestic law and international human rights norms will usually govern actions taken against them.

The official International Committee of the Red Cross (ICRC) commentary on Common Article 3 suggests that the drafters intended to preclude its applicability to common criminality. Early in the drafting process, a proposal to extend the 1949 Geneva Conventions to "all cases of armed conflict which are not of an international character, especially cases of civil war, colonial conflicts, or wars of religion, which may occur in the territory of one or more of the High Contracting Parties"[22] was met with objection on the basis that it might be interpreted as applying to situations involving "no more than a handful of rebels or common brigands."[23] Further concern was expressed about the "risk of ordinary criminals being encouraged to give themselves a semblance of organization as a pretext for claiming the benefit of the Convention, representing their crimes as 'acts of war' in order to escape punishment for them."[24] According to the commentary, numerous delegations concluded that "[t]he expression [not of an international character] was so general, so vague, that . . . it might be taken to cover any act committed by force of arms—any form of anarchy, rebellion, or even plain banditry."[25]

Proponents of the text in question were sensitive to these concerns, responding that "insurgents . . . are not all brigands" and "the behaviour of the insurgents in the field would show whether they were in fact mere felons, or, on the contrary, real combatants who deserved to receive protection under the Conventions."[26] The ICRC's non-binding and non-exclusive list of sample criteria for non-international armed conflicts, by making reference to "the Party in revolt against the de jure Government" and "insurgents," adopts the same position,[27] one likewise strengthened by the ICRC *Commentary*'s use elsewhere of the term "rebel Party."[28]

As these examples illustrate, the law of armed conflict traditionally envisioned non-international armed conflict as consisting of only those activities evidencing some sort of politically motivated challenge to State authorities in order to attain political control and authority or displace those of the government. However, the evolving nature of criminality has brought this traditional understanding into question.

Consider the criminal gangs active in Colombia and Mexico.[29] They field forces today that often outgun the regular armed forces. Unlike brigands, bandits and other criminals who merely take advantage of the instability characterizing armed conflict, these gangs directly challenge State authorities in order to create zones in which they can with impunity pursue their criminal activities. The respective governments must resort to military force to counter the organizations, civilians are placed at great risk from the ensuing hostilities and criminal gangs often control wide swaths of territory.

In other words, these are situations in which criminal gangs are highly organized and conduct hostilities with the government at a level of intensity consistent with the existence of a non-international armed conflict. There is little to distinguish them from the *Commentary*'s description of Common Article 3 non-international armed conflicts as "armed conflicts, with armed forces on either side engaged in hostilities—conflicts, in short, which are in many respects similar to an international war, but take place within the confines of a single country."[30] To the extent that the law of non-international armed conflict frees States to deal militarily with high-order political violence through application of LOAC conduct of hostilities rules, the same rationale would justify application to sufficiently organized and intense criminal activity directed against the State. Such an interpretation would be consistent with the assertion in the commentary on Common Article 3 that "the scope of application of the Article must be as wide as possible."[31] Accordingly, it is at least arguable that in light of the context and nature of the criminal armed activities States face today, imposing a political motivation requirement, in addition to organization and intensity, for qualification as a non-international armed conflict makes little normative or practical sense.

Should members of a criminal group or individual criminals become involved in a non-international armed conflict *on behalf of* one of the parties, they would qualify as members of an organized armed group or direct participants in hostilities, respectively, as those appellations are described below. With regard to groups, their activity in support of the party, considered as a whole, would have to constitute what is in a sense "group participation in hostilities" before qualifying as an organized armed group involved in a non-international armed conflict. Key factors in such an assessment include the nature of the group's activity and its nexus to the conflict. For instance, if a dissident armed force that controls territory allows a criminal group to engage in criminal activities in exchange for conducting attacks on the State's armed forces, guarding its military facilities or providing logistics for its combat operations, the criminal group would be operating on the dissident group's behalf and therefore qualify. By way of contrast, merely paying a "tax" on production or transhipment of drugs to an organized armed group in control of an area, as is the case in Afghanistan with certain narcotics organizations, would not render the criminal group an organized armed group.[32]

Dissident Armed Forces

The most straightforward category of opposition forces is dissident armed forces. As noted, Common Article 3 and Additional Protocol II both utilize the term "armed forces," the former with regard to protections that attach once members thereof are *hors de combat,* the latter in its provision on material field of application. The context of the Common Article 3 reference clearly implies the possibility of "armed forces" on both sides of a non-international armed conflict, since the relevant provision applies to "each Party to the conflict."[33] This interpretation becomes express with Additional Protocol II's reference to "dissident" armed forces.

In the latter instrument, the phrase "dissident armed forces" is used in contradistinction to "other organized armed groups." On this basis, it might be argued that "other organized armed groups" constitutes a separate category from dissident armed forces, a point with which the author disagrees since there is no meaningful difference in the legal regimes governing the detention or targeting of the two categories. However, acknowledging that some commentators distinguish among various members of an "other organized group" with regard to targeting, a point to be discussed, this chapter treats dissident armed forces and other organized armed groups separately for the sake of analysis.

What is clear is that dissident armed forces do not attain civilian status by virtue of their break from the State's regular military. According to the ICRC's 2009 *Interpretive Guidance on the Notion of Direct Participation in Hostilities,*

> Although members of dissident armed forces are no longer members of State armed forces, they do not become civilians merely because they have turned against their government. At least to the extent, and for as long as, they remain organized under the structures of the State armed forces to which they formerly belonged, these structures should continue to determine individual membership in dissident armed forces as well.[34]

While other aspects of the *Interpretive Guidance* proved controversial, this text elicited no serious objection from the international experts participating in the drafting process.[35]

Yet, merely having been members of the armed forces of a State does not suffice to qualify individuals as members of a dissident armed force. Only breakaway units that retain some degree of their original organizational structure qualify.[36] Fighters who are former members of the armed forces but have not remained with their units (such as deserters) are either members of other organized armed groups or civilians directly participating in hostilities.

Near-universal consensus exists that dissident armed forces, like members of the State's armed forces, are targetable at all times under the law of armed conflict. Stated with greater precision, it is not a violation of the law of armed conflict to "attack" them.[37] This is evident from the plain text of Common Article 3(1), which protects persons who are taking no active part in hostilities from acts of violence, including members of the armed forces who have laid down their arms or are *hors de combat*. The only reasonable interpretation of the provision is that those members of the armed forces who are still "in the fight" lack protection from attack under LOAC during a non-international armed conflict. This position comports with the common understanding of the principle of distinction, which requires an attacker to distinguish between combatants and civilians and direct attacks only against the former. The principle is universally accepted as customary law in both international armed conflicts and non-international armed conflicts.[38]

Although the notion of "armed forces" transcends the boundary between international and non-international armed conflict, its precise parameters do not. Plainly, members of the regular armed forces qualify as "armed forces" in a non-international armed conflict, as do members of the regular armed forces in rebellion against the State.[39] The concept of armed forces in international armed conflict includes "militia and volunteer corps forming part of such armed forces."[40] It is reasonable to extend this inclusion into non-international armed conflict such that they would also qualify as part of the State's armed forces, or, if in rebellion, a component of the dissident armed forces.

The case of paramilitary or armed law enforcement agencies involved in a non-international armed conflict is more complicated. As a matter of customary international law in international armed conflict, they may be incorporated into the armed forces, and thereby lose any claim to civilian status.[41] Additional Protocol I adds a further requirement, that incorporation be notified to the other party to the conflict,[42] although by customary law incorporation is solely a factual matter and failure to so notify the enemy does not preclude such groups' treatment as members of the armed forces for purposes of targeting and detention.[43]

The situation in non-international armed conflict differs markedly. In that opposition fighters are in violation of domestic law by virtue of their armed activities, law enforcement agencies necessarily engage in operations against them. Accordingly, in non-international armed conflict there is no logic for incorporation; fighting lawlessness is the very *raison d'être* of law enforcement entities, a task undiminished by the existence of a non-international armed conflict. Thus, even if wholly separate from the military, perhaps even conducting autonomous operations that are not coordinated with those of the armed forces, law enforcement and similar agencies qualify as the armed forces for the purposes of non-international armed conflict classification. The *Commentary* to Additional Protocol II explicitly embraces this interpretation:

> The term "armed forces" of the High Contracting Party should be understood in the broadest sense. In fact, this term was chosen in preference to others suggested such as, for example, "regular armed forces", in order to cover all the armed forces, including those not included in the definition of the army in the national legislation of some countries (national guard, customs, police forces or any other similar force).[44]

To the extent any such groups—or units thereof—act in opposition to the government, they will be considered and treated as "dissident armed forces."

Finally, it is possible for State armed forces to be transformed into opposition organized armed groups once they lose power. This was the situation in Afghanistan upon either adoption of United Nations Security Council Resolution 1386 in December 2001 or the installation of Hamid Karzai as interim president during the June 2002 *loya jirga*.[45] Arguably, it is also the situation of Qaddafi's forces, at least from the perspective of those States, such as the United States, which have recognized the Transitional National Council as the legitimate government of Libya. Whether former military forces qualify as a dissident armed force or "other organized armed group" is unresolved as a matter of law, but this is of little practical significance in light of the position taken in this chapter that dissident armed forces are but a category of organized armed forces.[46]

Other Organized Armed Groups

A second category of opposition forces consists, for the sake of analysis, of "other organized armed groups," an expression drawn from the text of Additional Protocol II. It is well established that the existence of an armed conflict requires the participation of an armed force of some sort. In the context of international armed conflict, this requirement poses little difficulty. Armed forces of one State, which are organized by definition, face those of another. By contrast, the situation is more complex in non-international armed conflict, for armed conflict must be distinguished from "situations of internal disturbances and tensions, such as riots, isolated and sporadic acts of violence or other acts of a similar nature."[47] In *Tadić*, the Appeals Chamber of the International Criminal Tribunal for the former Yugoslavia (ICTY) made such a distinction by defining non-international armed conflict as situations of "protracted armed violence between governmental authorities and organized armed groups or between such groups within a State,"[48] a test combining intensity and organization which has been adopted in the Rome Statute of the International Criminal Court.[49]

Until recently, it was unclear whether organized armed groups other than the dissident armed forces comprise groups who are directly participating in hostilities or constitute a separate category of "non-civilians."[50] Neither Common Article 3 nor Additional Protocol II directly addresses the scope of the concept of civilian. As noted, the former avoids the term altogether, instead simply extending protection to those taking no active part in hostilities, while the latter employs the term without defining it.[51]

The issue of whether members of organized armed groups are civilians or a separate category bears on the conduct of hostilities. In particular, Article 13 of Additional Protocol I, which is generally accepted as reflective of customary international law,[52] provides:

> 2. The civilian population as such, as well as individual civilians, shall not be the object of attack. Acts or threats of violence the primary purpose of which is to spread terror among the civilian population are prohibited.
>
> 3. Civilians shall enjoy the protection afforded by this part, unless and for such time as they take a direct part in hostilities.[53]

So, if the members are civilians, they are only targetable while participating in the hostilities. If not, they may be treated as analogous to members of the armed forces, and thereby remain targetable even when not participating.

The ICRC acknowledged this normative dilemma in its 2005 *Customary International Humanitarian Law* study:

> It can be argued that the terms "dissident armed forces or other organized armed groups . . . under responsible command" in Article 1 of Additional Protocol II inferentially recognise the essential conditions of armed forces, as they apply in international armed conflict . . . , and that it follows that civilians are all persons who are not members of such forces or groups. Subsequent treaties, applicable to non-international armed conflicts, have similarly used the terms civilians and civilian population without defining them.
>
> While State armed forces are not considered civilians, practice is not clear as to whether members of armed opposition groups are civilians subject to Rule 6 on loss of protection from attack in case of direct participation or whether members of such groups are liable to attack as such, independently of the operation of Rule 6 [which deals with the issue of direct participation in hostilities].[54]

This very issue occupied the attention of a group of international experts convened by the ICRC from 2003 to 2008 to consider the notion of direct participation by civilians. Various suggestions were offered, including an approach by which members of an organized armed group might be treated as civilians who were continuously participating in hostilities, and therefore continuously legitimate targets. However, the ICRC worried that the approach would "seriously undermine the conceptual integrity of the categories of persons underlying the principle of distinction, most notably because it would create parties to non-international armed conflicts whose entire armed forces remain part of the civilian population,"[55] a point later acknowledged by the District Court for the District of Columbia in *Gherebi*.[56]

Accordingly, the *Interpretive Guidance* took the reasonable position that "as the wording and logic of Article 3 GC I–IV and Additional Protocol II reveals, civilians, armed forces, and organized armed groups of the parties to the conflict are mutually exclusive categories also in non-international armed conflict."[57] Individuals who are members of organized armed groups are accordingly not civilians.[58] The ICTY embraced this stance in *Galic*.[59] This is an important point, for if members of an organized armed group are not civilians, the LOAC extending protection to civilians is inapplicable to them. For instance, they may be attacked regardless of whether they are directly participating; their vulnerability to attack is status, not activity, based.

Not all groups in a battlespace are "organized armed groups." To qualify, the group in question must be both "organized" and "armed." With regard to the organized criterion, Article 1 of Additional Protocol I refers to a group that is "under responsible command." This phrase is explicatory of the notion of organization. The ICRC commentary to the article explains that

> [t]he existence of a responsible command implies some degree of organization of the insurgent armed group or dissident armed forces, but this does not necessarily mean that there is a hierarchical system of military organization similar to that of regular armed forces. It means an organization capable, on the one hand, of planning and carrying out sustained and concerted military operations, and on the other, of imposing discipline in the name of a de facto authority.[60]

The ICTY dealt with the issue of the threshold level of organization in the case of *Limaj*. In assessing the Kosovo Liberation Army (KLA), the Trial Chamber held that

> *some degree of organisation* by the parties will suffice to establish the existence of an armed conflict. This degree need not be the same as that required for establishing the responsibility of superiors for the acts of their subordinates within the organisation, as

no determination of individual criminal responsibility is intended under this provision of the Statute.[61]

It went on to cite an ICRC document submitted to the Preparatory Commission for the Rome Statute's elements of crimes, which stated that armed conflict "presupposes the existence of hostilities between armed forces organised *to a greater or lesser extent*."[62] Looking to factors like the existence of a general staff and headquarters, designated military zones, adoption of internal regulations, the appointment of a spokesperson, coordinated military actions, recruitment activities, the wear of uniforms and negotiations with the other side,[63] the Chamber concluded that the KLA was an organized armed group,[64] a determination consistent with those in other cases examining the same issue.[65]

Similarly, in the *Haradinaj* case the ICTY surveyed all previous judgments relevant to the issue of organization before concluding that no single factor was necessarily determinative. Rather, the Trial Chamber suggested a holistic approach. Illustrative factors that bore on organization included

> existence of a headquarters; the fact that the group controls a certain territory; the ability of the group to gain access to weapons, other military equipment, recruits and military training; its ability to plan, coordinate and carry out military operations, including troop movements and logistics; its ability to define a unified military strategy and use military tactics; and its ability to speak with one voice and negotiate and conclude agreements such as cease-fire or peace accords.[66]

These cases suggest two indispensable elements of the "organized" criterion. To begin with, the group in question must exhibit a degree of structure. The structure need not be strictly hierarchical or implemented in any formalistic manner, although such factors are highly indicative of the required organizational robustness. For instance, many non-military organized armed groups have flat and decentralized structures. Yet, as has been noted elsewhere, while such organizational models may complicate identification of a group's members, "operations in Afghanistan and Iraq demonstrate that these challenges are not insurmountable."[67] Nor need an organized armed group have explicit ranks, wear distinctive emblems, operate from established bases or recruit in a particular fashion.

That said, a group that is transitory or ad hoc in nature does not qualify; in other words, an organized armed group can never simply consist of those who are engaging in hostilities against the State, *sans plus*. It must be a distinct entity that the other side can label the "enemy" for reasons ranging from the development of field strategy and tactics to the conduct of negotiations. A qualifying group must also be capable of exercising some degree of control over the activities of its members. In particular, it must be sufficiently organized to enforce compliance with LOAC, although failure to actually do so does not bar qualification as an organized armed group.[68]

Additionally, to be "organized," a group must be able to act in a coordinated fashion, albeit not to the extent of the regular armed forces. This requirement implies an ability to plan and execute group activities, collect and share intelligence, communicate among members, deconflict operations and provide logistic support to combat operations. Collective action alone, in the sense of multiple autonomous actions against the State (or another organized armed group), does not suffice; the actions engaged in must evidence a group character.

The organization requirement is especially relevant in three regards. First, there is no non-international armed conflict equivalent of international armed conflict's *levée en masse*.[69] An uprising against the government, no matter how intense, can only constitute a non-international armed conflict once the opposition begins to exhibit some degree of organization. Until then, it is an internal disturbance and thereby excluded from the ambit of non-international armed conflict.

Second, an organized armed group cannot consist solely of those who share the same basis for opposition to the government, for they lack the requisite degree of organization and coordination. As an example, whereas individual terrorist groups in a non-international armed conflict may qualify separately as organized armed groups, it is only once they begin to affiliate and to coordinate their activities that they become a single organized armed group. Consider al Qaeda, an organized armed group consisting of loosely related subgroups. The fact that others may share al Qaeda's ideology or are inspired by the organization does not alone suffice to qualify them as al Qaeda members. Instead, they are either members of a separate organized armed group, civilians directly participating in hostilities or mere violent criminals. Thus, there can, legally, be no such thing as a "war on terrorism" as such, because the generic category of terrorists cannot constitute a single party to an armed conflict. It is only once particular groups are somehow affiliated and plan or coordinate activities in concert that they may be treated as a distinct organized armed group.

Third, cyber attacks have raised the possibility of virtual organization. Online organizations are commonplace in contemporary life. In many cases, the members thereof never physically meet. They may not even know the identities of other members. If a collection of online hackers conducts related operations against a government (assuming such operations rise to the level of armed actions as a matter of law), can it meet the organization criterion? Along similar lines, can persons who conduct kinetic actions as members of a group constituted and coordinating entirely online make up an organized armed group?

Individuals operating autonomously, even if targeting the same State entities, are not an organized armed group. There is no organizational element and their actions lack coordination. A similar conclusion would hold with regard to individuals who operate collectively, but not cooperatively. During the cyber attacks against Georgia in 2008, for example, a website appeared containing hacker tools and a list of Georgian government and civilian targets.[70] Using that site, hundreds of individuals began conducting individual attacks. Again, the absence of organization and of cooperative activities would preclude characterization of the attackers as members of an organized armed group.

On the other hand, a virtual group can have a specific leadership and organizational structure and conduct highly synchronized cyber operations. The only apparent obstacle to qualification as an organized armed group would appear to be the requirement that organizational structure allow for enforcement of LOAC. There is presently no consensus as to whether the difficulty a virtual group would have enforcing LOAC precludes qualification as an organized armed group, such that the virtual members would at most qualify as civilian direct participants.

The second criterion of an organized armed group is that it be "armed." Logically, a group is armed when it has the capacity to carry out "attacks," defined in LOAC as "acts of violence against the adversary, whether in offence or in defence."[71] Such acts must be based on the group's intentions, not those of individual members. This conclusion derives from the fact that while many members of the armed forces have no violent function, the armed forces as a whole are nevertheless "armed" as a matter of LOAC.[72] Conversely, the mere fact that certain members of a group participate in hostilities does not render the group "armed" absent a shared purpose of carrying out the qualifying attacks.

More problematic is a group that does not itself carry out attacks, but performs acts that amount to direct participation in hostilities, such as collecting tactical intelligence for use by other groups in specific attacks. To the extent that acts constituting direct participation render individual civilians subject to attack, it is a reasonable extrapolation to conclude that a group with a purpose of directly participating in the hostilities is "armed." Of course, such groups could only exist in the context of a non-international armed conflict in which another group was conducting attacks, for without attacks there is no armed conflict in the first place.

The one area of potential difficulty with regard to the armed criterion involves groups that engage in cyber operations. By the approach taken above, a group of this kind would have to be mounting operations that rose to the level of a cyber "attack" as a matter of law or otherwise be engaging in cyber activities that amounted, as discussed, to direct participation in either cyber or kinetic attacks. While disagreement exists as to which cyber operations constitute attacks under LOAC,[73] there is consensus that any cyber operation resulting in injury to or death of individuals or damage to or destruction of objects qualifies. There is also agreement that cyber activities that merely cause inconvenience or irritation do not.

Certain organized groups consist of both armed and non-armed wings. This is the case, for instance, with Hamas and Hezbollah. It is generally accepted that when the group in question is composed of subgroups, only those that engage in hostilities qualify as organized armed groups. Individuals who straddle both wings, such as the overall leader, are members of the armed subgroup, notwithstanding their non-hostile roles.

Controversy surrounds one aspect of status as a member of an organized armed group. Specifically, the question is who among the members may be attacked when not directly engaged in hostilities. A restrictive view, represented by the *Interpretive Guidance*, adopts the notion of "continuous combat function" as the key to membership. The term is defined as a "continuous function for the group involving his or her direct participation in hostilities."[74]

Although the question of which acts qualify as "direct participation" is itself somewhat contentious,[75] the issue need not be explored here. Suffice it to say that by the *Guidance* standard only those with a continuous combat function may be treated as members of an organized armed group and therefore attackable at any time during the period of their membership. Absent such a function, individuals affiliated with the group are to be treated as civilians who can only be attacked for such time as they participate in the hostilities.[76]

In justification, the *Interpretive Guidance* correctly notes the difficulty during a non-international armed conflict of distinguishing civilians from members of organized armed groups, and points to the fact that membership in an organized armed group is seldom formalized, "other than taking up a certain function for the group."[77] Groups may not wear uniforms, operate from fixed bases or fight employing classic military tactics and they are often organized informally and operate clandestinely. Complicating matters is the reality that civilians in the battlespace may carry weapons for their own protection. Therefore the requirement of continuous combat function, by setting a high bar for membership, appears to afford the civilian population enhanced protection from mistaken attacks.

These concerns are valid, but, for both practical and normative reasons, overstated. In fact, organized armed groups often have a membership structure based on more than mere function. Members frequently wear uniforms or other distinguishing garb and may operate from fixed bases, especially when in control of territory or operating from remote locations.[78] For example, the Red Army, Hamas, Hezbollah, FARC, Tamil Tigers and KLA were often distinguishable from the civilian population and operated in a manner not unlike the regular armed forces.

Membership may also be confirmed by intelligence ranging from human sources and communications intercepts to captured documents and interrogation of captured fighters. So, from a practical perspective, it is frequently a relatively simple matter to discriminate between civilians and members of organized armed groups. When it is not, the law itself takes account of the uncertainty. Article 50.1 of Additional Protocol I, a provision generally deemed reflective of customary international law in both international armed conflicts and non-international armed conflicts,[79] provides that "[i]n case of doubt whether a person is a civilian, that person shall be considered to be a civilian."

The result of the continuous combat function criterion is therefore inequity in the law. By the proposed standard, direct attack on a member of an organized armed group without a continuous combat function is prohibited (indeed, such an attack would be a war crime since the individual qualifies as a civilian), but a member of the State's armed forces who performs no combat-related duties may be attacked at any time. This is a rather curious result in light of the fact that the organized armed group lacks any domestic or international legal basis for participation in the conflict in the first place. The standard badly skews the balance between military necessity and humanitarian considerations that undergirds all of LOAC.[80]

A more reasoned approach, and one that better comports with the underlying logic of the distinction between civilians and organized armed groups, is to simply treat insurgent fighters and members of the armed forces equally. By it, members of organized armed groups may be attacked so long as they remain active members of the group, regardless of their function. It makes no more sense to treat an individual who joins a group that has the express purpose of conducting hostilities as a civilian than it would to differentiate between the various members of the regular armed forces. After all, and as noted in the *Interpretive Guidance* itself (albeit in the context of international armed conflict),

> it would contradict the logic of the principle of distinction to place irregular armed forces under the more protective legal regime afforded to the civilian population merely because they fail to distinguish themselves from that population, to carry their arms openly, or to conduct their operations in accordance with the laws and customs of war. Therefore, even under the terms of the Hague Regulations and the Geneva Conventions, all armed actors showing a sufficient degree of military organization and belonging to a party to the conflict must be regarded as part of the armed forces of that party.[81]

A final issue with regard to organized armed groups in non-international armed conflicts involves mixed conflicts, that is, conflicts with both international and non-international components. The *Interpretive Guidance* raises this prospect in its assertion that "organized armed groups operating within the broader context of an international armed conflict without belonging to a party to that conflict could still be regarded as parties to a separate non-international armed conflict."[82] A group belongs to a party when at least a de facto relationship exists between the group and the party to the international armed conflict. Mere tacit agreement suffices so long as it is clear for which side the group is fighting.[83] The basis for the position is straightforward—since only States may be party to an international armed conflict, a non-State group would have to be affiliated with a State to qualify as a party. By contrast, non-international armed conflict necessarily involves at least one party that is not a State or otherwise an extension thereof.

The prospect of groups appearing in the battlespace that do not belong to any of the parties to an international armed conflict is far from hypothetical. For instance, during the international armed conflict phases in Afghanistan and Iraq, coalition troops regularly faced forces that were not allied with the Taliban or the Baathist regimes. In particular, certain Shia militia groups in Iraq opposed both the coalition forces and those of the Iraqi government in the hope of eventually seizing power themselves.

From a practical perspective, an approach that automatically renders hostilities with a non-affiliated organized armed group as a separate non-international armed conflict is problematic in that it requires application of separate bodies of law to colocated hostilities. Therefore, an argument can be made that it is preferable to ask whether there is an unambiguous nexus between the actions of the group in question and the international armed conflict.[84] If so, the law applicable in international armed conflict would continue to govern hostilities with the group. If not, the group would qualify as an organized armed group in a non-international armed conflict.

Regardless of one's position on this specific issue, there are undoubtedly situations in which international and non-international conflicts coexist.[85] For instance, a non-international armed conflict may survive in a situation where an international armed conflict breaks out. In Afghanistan, non-international armed conflict between the Taliban-led Afghan government and the Northern Alliance was under way at the time coalition forces began operations in 2001. Until the coalition exercised "overall control" of Northern Alliance operations, that conflict continued alongside the international armed conflict between the coalition States and Afghanistan.[86]

Despite the complexity of classifying conflict, it is important to emphasize the fact that classification of participants in such conflicts tracks the criteria normally applied in the two types of conflicts. The fact that an international armed conflict is ongoing in the same battlespace and at the same time as a non-international armed conflict has no bearing on qualification of any groups involved in the latter as "organized armed groups."

Civilians Who Directly Participate in Hostilities

The final category of fighters in armed opposition to the government comprises individuals who are members of neither dissident armed forces nor any other organized groups. Their activities alone cannot constitute a non-international armed conflict, for such a conflict cannot exist without an organized armed group on at least one side. Thus, the category of directly participating civilians only has meaning in the context of an ongoing non-international armed conflict.

Individuals "who directly participate in hostilities on a merely spontaneous, sporadic or unorganized basis" make up the category.[87] Examples include those who engage in individual acts for pay (e.g., a fee for emplacement of improvised explosive devices (IEDs)) or for other reasons unrelated to group affiliation, as well as groups of individuals who take part in the hostilities without prior organization and coordination (as in a mob that attacks a military facility). By the *Interpretive Guidance*'s approach, the category would extend to those members of an armed group who do not have a continuous combat function, but which at times take up arms or engage in other acts amounting to direct participation.

The topic of direct participation in hostilities has been the subject of extensive and lively discourse in the literature and need only be summarized here.[88] It is an important debate, for, unlike members of the dissident armed forces and other organized armed groups, direct participants may only be attacked while they engage in acts of participation. As noted in Additional Protocol II, Article 13.3, civilians enjoy protection from attack, "unless and *for such time as they take a direct part in hostilities.*" Resultantly, the options for targeting them are dramatically reduced.

With regard to the concept of direct participation, two questions are key: (1) what acts qualify a civilian as a direct participant in hostilities; and (2) when is he or she participating? The *Interpretive Guidance* proffers three cumulative "constitutive elements" of acts that constitute direct participation.

> 1. The act must be likely to adversely affect the military operations or military capacity of a party to an armed conflict or, alternatively, to inflict death, injury, or destruction on persons or objects protected against direct attack (threshold of harm), and
>
> 2. There must be a direct causal link between the act and the harm likely to result either from that act, or from a coordinated military operation of which that act constitutes an integral part (direct causation), and

3. The act must be specifically designed to directly cause the required threshold of harm in support of a party to the conflict and to the detriment of another (belligerent nexus).[89]

These criteria generally capture the essence of direct participation, although there is some disagreement with the standards around the margins.[90] For instance, the first criterion could be expanded to encompass acts that enhance one's own military capacity, rather than merely negatively affecting the enemy. Further, the causal link as explained in the *Guidance* is overly restrictive.[91] As an example, it excludes assembly of an improvised explosive device on the basis that such participation is *in*direct.[92] This assertion flies in the face of common sense; no State that engages in combat could reasonably accept it. The *Guidance* also labels voluntary human shielding as indirect, a position that is likewise highly questionable.[93] Despite such concerns, the three elements fairly capture what is generally understood to be direct participation—acts that militarily affect the parties in a fairly direct manner and that are related to the ongoing armed conflict.

Much more problematic is the question of when may direct participation be said to be happening, for a civilian only loses immunity from attack during that period. At issue is the "for such time" verbiage in the direct participation norm, which is properly characterized as customary in nature.[94]

The *Interpretive Guidance* asserts that "measures preparatory to the execution of a specific act of direct participation in hostilities, as well as the deployment to and the return from the location of its execution, constitute an integral part of the act."[95] However, many of the experts involved in the project of developing the *Guidance* argued for a broader interpretation of "preparatory," such that the period of participation should extend as far before and after a hostile action as a causal connection existed.[96] As an example, the broader approach would include assembling an IED and perhaps even acquiring the necessary materials.

There was also significant objection to the *Interpretive Guidance*'s assertion that individuals who participate in hostilities on a recurrent basis regain protection from attack between their operations, losing it again only upon launching the next attack. This dynamic has become known as the "revolving door," which the *Guidance* somewhat curiously suggests is an "integral part, not a malfunction of IHL."[97]

The approach flies in the face of military common sense and accordingly represents a distortion of LOAC's military advantage/humanitarian considerations balance. This is especially so in the context of irregular warfare, where clandestine activities by insurgent groups are common. Again, consider the case of an IED attack. If the insurgent is discovered deploying to the attack location, implanting the IED or returning from the operation, the attack will likely be foiled since IED attacks are usually only successful when the devices can be laid secretly. As a result, the best option for countering future attacks is through heuristic intelligence analysis, which would reveal patterns of IED-implanting activities that allow for pinpointing those involved through human and technical intelligence. Yet by the *Interpretive Guidance* position, they could not be attacked until launching the next operation, an unacceptable result militarily.

The only viable approach is one in which a civilian who directly participates in hostilities on a recurring basis remains targetable until he or she opts out of the hostilities in an unambiguous manner. There is, of course, a risk that a direct participant might actually have decided to cease all hostile activities without the knowledge of the forces he or she has been attacking. But it is more sensible to have the participant, who enjoyed no right to participate in the first place, bear the risk of mistake rather than his or her former victims. The requirement to presume civilian status in the event of reasonable doubt further mitigates this risk.

Conclusions

In a non-international armed conflict, opposition fighters can be divided into two categories—members of an organized armed group and civilian direct participants in hostilities. The former category includes dissident armed forces and other groups that are both "organized" and "armed." The argument that a member of an organized armed group must be treated as a civilian if he or she does not have a continuous combat function in the group was rejected as both impractical and contrary to the logic of the law.

The result of this binary classification is that there is no LOAC prohibition on attacking members of organized armed groups at any time, just as there is no international law prohibition on attacking members of the government's forces.[98] Only when dealing with a fighter who is unaffiliated with a group, and who is therefore a civilian temporarily deprived of protection as such, does a temporal limitation arise. This approach accords neatly with the foundational premise of the law of armed conflict—that the law must balance military necessity and humanitarian considerations. Further parsing of the prevailing binary classification or otherwise complicating it will only serve to confuse matters in what is perhaps the most confusing genre of conflict—that which is non-international.

Notes

1. Convention for the Amelioration of the Condition of the Wounded and Sick in Armed Forces in the Field art. 3, Aug. 12, 1949, 6 U.S.T. 3114, 75 U.N.T.S. 31; Convention for

the Amelioration of the Condition of Wounded, Sick and Shipwrecked Members of Armed Forces at Sea art. 3, Aug. 12, 1949, 6 U.S.T. 3217, 75 U.N.T.S. 85; Convention Relative to the Treatment of Prisoners of War art. 3, Aug. 12, 1949, 6 U.S.T. 3316, 75 U.N.T.S. 135 [hereinafter GC III]; Convention Relative to the Protection of Civilian Persons in Time of War art. 3, Aug. 12, 1949, 6 U.S.T. 3516, 75 U.N.T.S. 287 [hereinafter Common Article 3].

2. Protocol Additional to the Geneva Conventions of 12 August 1949, and Relating to the Protection of Victims of Non-International Armed Conflicts, June 8, 1977, 1125 U.N.T.S. 609 [hereinafter AP II].

3. Legality of the Threat or Use of Nuclear Weapons, Advisory Opinion, 1996 I.C.J. 226, ¶¶ 79 & 82 (July 8); Military and Paramilitary Activities in and against Nicaragua (Nicar. v. U.S.), 1986 I.C.J. 54, ¶ 218 (June 27) [hereinafter *Nicaragua*]. It is generally acknowledged that certain Additional Protocol II provisions, such as that prohibiting attacks on civilians (Article 13.2), are reflective of customary international law.

4. Examples include the Statute of the International Criminal Court, the Ottawa Convention on the Prohibition of Anti-personnel Mines, the Convention on Certain Conventional Weapons as amended, the Chemical Weapons Convention, the Hague Convention for the Protection of Cultural Property and its Second Protocol and the Convention on Cluster Munitions.

5. Prosecutor v. Tadić, Case No. IT-94-1, Appeals Chamber Decision on the Defence Motion for Interlocutory Appeal on Jurisdiction, ¶ 70 (Int'l Crim. Trib. for the Former Yugoslavia Oct. 2, 1995) [hereinafter *Tadić*]; Prosecutor v. Limaj, Case No. IT-03-66-T, Judgment, ¶ 90 (Int'l Crim. Trib. for the Former Yugoslavia Nov. 30, 2005) [hereinafter *Limaj*]; Prosecutor v. Milošević, Case No. IT-02-54-T, Decision on Motion for Judgment of Acquittal, ¶ 16 (Int'l Crim. Trib. for the Former Yugoslavia June 16, 2004) [hereinafter *Milošević*]. The test was adopted in the Statute of the International Criminal Court. Rome Statute of the International Criminal Court art. 8(2)(f), July 17, 1998, 2187 U.N.T.S. 90 [hereinafter Rome Statute].

6. Common Article 3.1, *supra* note 1.

7. AP II, *supra* note 2, art. 1.1.

8. On the distinction between the thresholds, see Charles Lysaght, *The Scope of Protocol II and Its Relation to Common Article 3 of the Geneva Conventions of 1949 and Other Human Rights Instruments*, 33 AMERICAN UNIVERSITY LAW REVIEW 9 (1983); Sylvie Junod, *Additional Protocol II: History and Scope*, 33 AMERICAN UNIVERSITY LAW REVIEW 29 (1983).

9. The drafters of the Protocol considered including the situation of a conflict between organized armed groups without the involvement of a State, but decided against doing so on the basis that the scenario was largely theoretical. COMMENTARY ON THE ADDITIONAL PROTOCOLS OF 8 JUNE 1977 TO THE GENEVA CONVENTIONS OF 12 AUGUST 1949 ¶ 4461 (Yves Sandoz, Christophe Swinarski & Bruno Zimmermann eds., 1987) [hereinafter AP COMMENTARY].

10. AP II, *supra* note 2, art. 13.3.

11. The 1977 Additional Protocol I defines civilians in the negative, as those individuals who "do not belong to one of the categories of persons referred to in Article 4(A)(1), (2), (3) and (6) of the Third Convention and in Article 43 of this Protocol." The former sets forth categories of persons entitled to prisoner of war status, whereas the latter defines the term "armed forces." Protocol Additional to the Geneva Conventions of 12 August 1949, and Relating to the Protection of Victims of International Armed Conflicts art. 50.1, June 8, 1977, 1125 U.N.T.S. 3 [hereinafter AP I]. The drafters of Additional Protocol II originally intended to include a definition of the term, but the proposals were dropped in order to shorten the text. See discussion in 1 CUSTOMARY INTERNATIONAL HUMANITARIAN LAW 19 (Jean-Marie Henckaerts & Louise Doswald-Beck eds., 2005) [hereinafter CIHL]. One possible distinction would be the treatment of law enforcement personnel. In an international armed conflict, they are civilians

unless incorporated into the armed forces. In a non-international armed conflict, it is conceivable that they would assume the status of "fighters," who do not enjoy the same protections under international humanitarian law as civilians.

12. For an excellent examination of the subject, see Jelena Pejic, *Status of Armed Conflicts, in* PERSPECTIVES ON THE ICRC STUDY ON CUSTOMARY INTERNATIONAL LAW 77 (Elizabeth Wilmshurst & Susan Breau eds., 2007); *see also* GARY D. SOLIS, THE LAW OF ARMED CONFLICT ch. 5 (2010).

13. On non-international armed conflicts generally, see ANTHONY CULLEN, THE CONCEPT OF NON-INTERNATIONAL ARMED CONFLICT IN INTERNATIONAL HUMANITARIAN LAW (2010); LINDSAY MOIR, THE LAW OF INTERNAL ARMED CONFLICT (2002); EVE LA HAYE, WAR CRIMES IN INTERNAL ARMED CONFLICTS (2008); Dieter Fleck, *The Law of Non-International Armed Conflict, in* THE HANDBOOK OF INTERNATIONAL HUMANITARIAN LAW (Dieter Fleck ed., 2d ed. 2008); MICHAEL N. SCHMITT, CHARLES H.B. GARRAWAY & YORAM DINSTEIN, THE MANUAL ON THE LAW OF NON-INTERNATIONAL ARMED CONFLICT WITH COMMENTARY ¶ 1.1.2 (2006) [hereinafter NIAC Manual]; A.P.V. ROGERS, LAW ON THE BATTLEFIELD ch. 9 (2d ed. 2004); UNITED KINGDOM MINISTRY OF DEFENCE, THE MANUAL OF THE LAW OF ARMED CONFLICT ch. 15 (2004) [hereinafter UK Manual].

14. See, e.g., the discussion in *Al-Marri v. Pucciarelli*, 534 F.3d 213, 233 (4th Cir. S.C. 2008); INTERNATIONAL COMMITTEE OF THE RED CROSS, OFFICIAL STATEMENT: THE RELEVANCE OF IHL IN THE CONTEXT OF TERRORISM 1, 3 (Feb. 21, 2005), http://www.icrc.org/Web/Eng/siteeng0.nsf/htmlall/terrorismihl-210705. For international armed conflict, Additional Protocol I provides that "[m]embers of the armed forces . . . are combatants, that is to say, they have the right to participate directly in hostilities." AP I, *supra* note 11, art. 43.2.

15. Of course, they may also be prosecuted for any war crimes they commit. The point is that international law does not shield fighters from domestic prosecution for acts during a non-international armed conflict that are "immunized" in international armed conflict. For a discussion of the distinction and its rationale, see Waldemar Solf, *The Status of Combatants in Non-International Armed Conflicts under Domestic Law and Transnational Practice*, 33 AMERICAN UNIVERSITY LAW REVIEW 53, 57–61 (1983).

16. Note that the term "combatant" is occasionally used in the context of non-international armed conflict. *See, e.g.*, Respect for Human Rights in Armed Conflicts, G.A. Res. 2676 (XXV), pmbl. & ¶ 5, U.N. Doc. A/8052 (Dec. 9, 1970); Cairo Declaration, §§ 68–69, *available at* http://unpan1.un.org/intradoc/groups/public/documents/CAFRAD/UNPAN002865.pdf, and Cairo Plan of Action, § 82, *available at* http://www.iss.co.za/af/regorg/unity_to_union/pdfs/au/afreurplan00.pdf, both adopted at the Africa-Europe Summit held under the aegis of the Organization of African Unity and the European Union, April 3–4, 2000; Rome Statute, *supra* note 5, art. 8(2)(e)(ix). However, as noted in the *Customary International Humanitarian Law* study commentary, "this designation is only used in its generic meaning and indicates that these persons do not enjoy the protection against attack accorded to civilians, but this does not imply a right to combatant status or prisoner-of-war status, as applicable in international armed conflicts." CIHL, *supra* note 11, at 12. To avoid confusion, the authors of the *NIAC Manual* adopted the term "fighters" to refer to those who engaged in hostilities during a non-international armed conflict. NIAC Manual, *supra* note 13, ¶ 1.1.2.

17. For a study which deals extensively with the relationship between targeting and status, see NILS MELZER, TARGETED KILLING IN INTERNATIONAL LAW (2008).

18. AP I, *supra* note 11, arts. 51.5(b) & 57 (international armed conflict). The rule of proportionality and the requirement to take precautions in attack are generally deemed reflective

of customary law in non-international armed conflict. CIHL, *supra* note 11, chs. 4 & 5; NIAC Manual, *supra* note 13, ¶¶ 2.1.1.4 & 2.1.2.

19. The classic work on the subject is Hans-Peter Gasser, *Internationalized Non-International Armed Conflicts: Case Studies of Afghanistan, Kampuchea, and Lebanon*, 33 AMERICAN UNIVERSITY LAW REVIEW 145 (1983).

20. This was the situation in the *Nicaragua* case, where the International Court of Justice found U.S. activities against Nicaragua to be governed by the law of international armed conflict, but held that the hostilities between the Nicaraguan armed forces and the contra rebels remained a non-international armed conflict. *Nicaragua*, *supra* note 3, ¶ 219.

21. A separate issue is external control of guerrilla forces. At a certain point, sufficient control is exercised to render what would otherwise be a non-international armed conflict international in character. On this issue, see the *Tadić* Appeals Judgment, which sets forth the "overall control" test. Prosecutor v. Tadić, Case No. IT-94-1-A, Appeals Chamber Judgment, ¶ 137 (Int'l Crim. Trib. for the Former Yugoslavia July 15, 1999). This test was adopted with approval by the International Criminal Court Pretrial Chamber in *Prosecutor v. Lubanga*, Case. No. ICC-01/04-01/06, Decision on Confirmation of Charges, ¶ 211 (Jan. 29, 2007) [hereinafter *Lubanga*].

22. COMMENTARY TO GENEVA CONVENTION III RELATIVE TO THE TREATMENT OF PRISONERS OF WAR 30 (Jean S. Pictet ed., 1960) [hereinafter GC-III COMMENTARY]; COMMENTARY TO GENEVA CONVENTION IV RELATIVE TO THE PROTECTION OF CIVILIAN PERSONS IN TIME OF WAR 31 (Jean S. Pictet ed., 1958) [hereinafter GC-IV COMMENTARY].

23. GC-IV COMMENTARY, *supra* note 22, at 31

24. GC-III COMMENTARY, *supra* note 22, at 32.

25. GC-IV COMMENTARY, *supra* note 22, at 35. The *Commentary* to the Second Convention uses the term "brigandage." COMMENTARY TO GENEVA CONVENTION II FOR THE AMELIORATION OF THE CONDITION OF WOUNDED, SICK AND SHIPWRECKED MEMBERS OF ARMED FORCES AT SEA 32 (Jean S. Pictet ed., 1960).

26. GC-III COMMENTARY, *supra* note 22, at 32.

27. *See, e.g.*, GC-IV COMMENTARY, *supra* note 22, at 35, 36.

28. *See, e.g.*, *id.* at 34.

29. On the Mexican case, see Carina Bergal, *The Mexican Drug War: The Case for a Non-International Armed Conflict Classification*, 34 FORDHAM INTERNATIONAL LAW JOURNAL 1042 (2011), although the author does not fully address the points raised herein.

30. GC-IV COMMENTARY, *supra* note 22, at 36.

31. GC-III COMMENTARY, *supra* note 22, at 36.

32. See discussion in Michael N. Schmitt, *Targeting Narcoinsurgents in Afghanistan: The Limits of International Humanitarian Law*, 12 YEARBOOK OF INTERNATIONAL HUMANITARIAN LAW 301 (2009).

33. Common Article 3, *supra* note 1.

34. NILS MELZER, INTERNATIONAL COMMITTEE OF THE RED CROSS, INTERPRETIVE GUIDANCE ON THE NOTION OF DIRECT PARTICIPATION IN HOSTILITIES UNDER INTERNATIONAL HUMANITARIAN LAW 32 (2009) [hereinafter IG].

35. The project involved a group of international experts convened on multiple occasions between 2003 and 2008 to consider direct participation in hostilities by civilians; the ultimate product reflects the views of the ICRC informed by that process. The author was a member of the group.

36. IG, *supra* note 34, at 32.

37. Of course, as discussed above, in the absence of combatant immunity, attacks on members of the armed forces can be criminalized in domestic law.

38. AP I, *supra* note 11, arts. 48 & 51; CIHL, *supra* note 11, Rule 6; U.S. Navy, U.S. Marine Corps & U.S. Coast Guard, The Commander's Handbook on the Law of Naval Operations, NWP 1-14M/MCWP 5-12.1/COMDTPUB P5800.7A, ¶ 8.1 (2007).

39. The Additional Protocol II *Commentary* specifically references situations "where there is a rebellion by part of the government army." AP COMMENTARY, *supra* note 9, ¶ 4460.

40. GC III, *supra* note 1, art. 4A(1)

41. CIHL, *supra* note 11, at 16–17.

42. AP I, *supra* note 11, art. 43.3.

43. CIHL, *supra* note 11, at 17.

44. AP COMMENTARY, *supra* note 9, ¶ 4462.

45. Resolution 1386 authorized the International Security Assistance Force to aid the interim Afghan government in maintaining security. S.C. Res. 1386, U.N. Doc. S/RES/1386 (Dec. 20, 2001). There is a degree of disagreement over precisely when to mark the establishment of the new Afghan government, such that the Taliban became an opposition force.

46. The legal issue is whether the (former) Libyan military can qualify as a dissident armed force given the fact that its units were never part of the opposition forces, which now constitute the State's armed forces.

47. AP II, *supra* note 2, art. 1.2; Rome Statute, *supra* note 5, arts. 8(2)(d) & 8(2)(f).

48. *Tadić*, *supra* note 5, ¶ 70.

49. Rome Statute, *supra* note 5, art. 8(2)(f).

50. The uncertainty was acknowledged by the ICRC in the CIHL study, *supra* note 11, at 19, and the IG, *supra* note 34, at 21.

51. AP II, *supra* note 2, art. 13.

52. On the customary law status, see, e.g., CIHL, *supra* note 11, Rule 6; NIAC Manual, *supra* note 13, ch. 2.

53. AP II, *supra* note 2, art. 13.2–3.

54. CIHL, *supra* note 11, at 19.

55. IG, *supra* note 34, at 28.

56. The court noted that "it would be odd for the drafters of Additional Protocol II to devote a portion of the convention to protecting a discrete group of individuals labeled 'civilians' if every member of the enemy in a non-international armed conflict is a civilian." Gherebi v. Obama, 609 F. Supp. 2d 43, 66 (D.D.C. 2009).

57. IG, *supra* note 34, at 28. In this sentence, the expression "armed forces" applies to the State's armed forces. Dissident armed forces would be included in the category of organized armed groups.

58. This interpretation was adopted in *Gherebi*, *supra* note 56, at 65.

59. Prosecutor v. Galic, Case No. IT-98-29-T, Judgment, ¶ 47 (Int'l Crim. Trib. for the Former Yugoslavia Dec. 5, 2003) ("For the purpose of the protection of victims of armed conflict, the term 'civilian' is defined negatively as anyone who is not a member of the armed forces or of an organized military group belonging to a party to the conflict."). *See also* Prosecutor v. Blaskic, Case No. IT-95-14-T, Judgment, ¶ 180 (Int'l Crim. Trib. for the Former Yugoslavia Mar. 3, 2000) ("Civilians within the meaning of Article 3 are persons who are not, or no longer, members of the armed forces."); Hamlily v. Obama, 616 F. Supp. 2d 63, 73–74 (D.D.C. 2009) ("The clear implication of Part IV, then, is that Additional Protocol II recognizes a class of individuals who are separate and apart from the 'civilian population'—i.e., members of enemy armed groups.").

60. AP COMMENTARY, *supra* note 9, ¶ 4663.

61. *Limaj*, *supra* note 5, ¶ 89 (emphasis added).

62. *Id.*, citing International Committee of the Red Cross, Working Paper, June 29, 1999, *available at* http://www.iccnow.org/documents/ICRCWorkPaperArticle8Para2e.pdf (submitted by the ICRC as a reference document to assist the Preparatory Commission in its work to establish the elements of crimes for the International Criminal Court) (emphasis added).

63. *Id.*, ¶¶ 90–134.

64. *Id.*, ¶ 134.

65. *See, e.g.*, *Milošević*, *supra* note 5, ¶¶ 16–25.

66. Prosecutor v. Haradinaj, Case No. IT-04-84-T, Judgment, ¶ 60 (Int'l Crim. Trib. for the Former Yugoslavia Apr. 3, 2008), surveying Prosecutor v. Tadić, Case No. IT-94-1-T, Judgment (Int'l Crim. Trib. for the Former Yugoslavia May 7, 1997); Prosecutor v. Mucić et al., Case No. IT-96-21-T, Judgment (Nov. 16, 1998); *Milošević*, *supra* note 5; Prosecutor v. Halilović, Case No. IT-01-48-T, Judgment (Int'l Crim. Trib. for the Former Yugoslavia Nov. 16, 2005); *Limaj*, *supra* note 5; Prosecutor v. Hadžihasanović, Case No. IT-01-47-T, Judgment (Int'l Crim. Trib. for the Former Yugoslavia Mar. 15, 2006); Prosecutor v. Maštić, Case No. IT-95-11-T, Judgment (Int'l Crim. Trib. for the Former Yugoslavia June 12, 2007); Prosecutor v. Mrksić, Case No. IT-95-13/1-T, Judgment (Sept. 27, 2007).

67. Kenneth H. Watkin, *Opportunity Lost: Organized Armed Groups and the ICRC "Direct Participation in Hostilities" Interpretive Guidance*, 42 NEW YORK UNIVERSITY JOURNAL OF INTERNATIONAL LAW AND POLITICS 641 (2010).

68. *See* AP II, *supra* note 2, art. 1.1; AP COMMENTARY, *supra* note 9, ¶ 4470. It is important to recognize that there is no requirement that the group actually enforce compliance, but only that it be sufficiently organized to be able to do so. Since organization is a requirement for Common Article 3 conflicts, it is reasonable to apply it to such conflicts in addition to those meeting the AP II thresholds.

69. A *levée en masse* consists of inhabitants of a non-occupied territory who rise up and spontaneously resist invading forces without having had time to organize themselves into regular armed units. GC III, *supra* note 1, art. 4A(6).

70. The conflict was an international armed conflict between Georgia and Russia, although the example is one that could apply equally in a non-international armed conflict. On the cyber aspects of this conflict, see ENEKEN TIKK, KADRI KASKA & LIIS VIHUL, INTERNATIONAL CYBER INCIDENTS: LEGAL CONSIDERATIONS (2010).

71. AP I, *supra* note 11, art. 49. On the notion of attack in the cyber context, *contrast* Knut Dörmann, *Applicability of Additional Protocols to Computer Network Attack*, paper delivered at the International Expert Conference on Computer Network Attacks and the Applicability of International Humanitarian Law, Stockholm, November 17–19, 2004, http://www.icrc.org/web/eng/siteeng0.nsf/htmlall/68lg92?opendocument, *with* Michael N. Schmitt, *Wired Warfare: Computer Network Attack and Jus in Bello*, 84 INTERNATIONAL REVIEW OF THE RED CROSS 365 (2002).

72. Analogously, Additional Protocol I (*supra* note 11), Article 43.2 categorizes "members of the armed forces" as "combatants . . . [who] have the right to participate directly in hostilities," not as individuals who do so participate. The group's activities matter, not those of select members.

73. *Contrast* Dörmann, *supra* note 71, *with* Schmitt, *supra* note 71. Note that the reference here is to an attack under the *jus in bello*, not an "armed attack" under the *jus ad bellum*.

74. IG, *supra* note 34, at 33.

75. *See generally* Michael N. Schmitt, *Deconstructing Direct Participation in Hostilities: The Constitutive Elements*, 42 NEW YORK UNIVERSITY JOURNAL OF INTERNATIONAL LAW AND POLITICS 697 (2010); Nils Melzer, *Keeping the Balance between Military Necessity and Humanity: A Response to Four Critiques of the ICRC's Interpretive Guidance on the Notion of Direct Participation*

in Hostilities, 42 NEW YORK UNIVERSITY JOURNAL OF INTERNATIONAL LAW AND POLITICS 831 (2010).

76. The *Interpretive Guidance* provides that

> [i]ndividuals who continuously accompany or support an organized armed group, but whose function does not involve direct participation in hostilities, are not members of that group within the meaning of IHL. Instead, they remain civilians assuming support functions, similar to private contractors and civilian employees accompanying State armed forces.

IG, *supra* note 34, at 34.

77. *Id.* at 32–33.

78. For a discussion of the extent to which organized armed groups take on such characteristics, see Watkin, *supra* note 67, at 674–82.

79. *See* CIHL, *supra* note 11, at 23–24. The application of the rule has been subject to important qualifications. *See, e.g.*, UK Statement upon Ratification, ¶ (h), Jan. 28, 1998, *available at* http://www.icrc.org/ihl.nsf/NORM/0A9E03F0F2EE757CC1256402003FB6D2?OpenDocument (noting the obligation of a commander to protect his or her forces); UK Manual, *supra* note 13, ¶ 5.3.4. *See also* HARVARD PROGRAM ON HUMANITARIAN POLICY AND CONFLICT RESEARCH, COMMENTARY ON THE HPCR MANUAL ON INTERNATIONAL LAW APPLICABLE TO AIR AND MISSILE WARFARE, commentary to Rule 12(a) (2010).

80. *See* Michael N. Schmitt, *Military Necessity and Humanity in International Humanitarian Law: Preserving the Delicate Balance*, 50 VIRGINIA JOURNAL OF INTERNATIONAL LAW 795 (2010).

81. IG, *supra* note 34, at 22.

82. *Id.* at 24. The position was based on the ICRC's commentary to Article 4 of the Third Geneva Convention, which provides that "[r]esistance movements must be fighting on behalf of a 'Party to the conflict' in the sense of Article 2, otherwise the provisions of Article 3 relating to non-international conflicts are applicable, since such militias and volunteer corps are not entitled to style themselves a 'Party to the conflict.'" GC-III COMMENTARY, *supra* note 22, at 57. It should be noted, though, that the drafters of the Convention saw Article 3 conflicts exclusively in the guise of hostilities conducted against a force's own government. There is no hint that the ICRC envisaged hostilities against the military forces of States with which the force's own government was fighting as a non-international armed conflict. On the contrary, the commentary is crafted in terms of the "Party in revolt against the de jure Government," "rebellion" and "rebel Party." *Id.* at 36.

83. See IG, *supra* note 34, at 23, which defines "belongs" by reference to the GC-III COMMENTARY, *supra* note 22, at 57. This concept should not be confused with the notion of "belonging to" in the context of external involvement in a non-international armed conflict at a level which internationalizes the conflict. In such cases, the issue is "overall control" of the group (see *Tadić*, *supra* note 21), described by the International Criminal Court in *Lubanga* as "a role in organising, co-ordinating, or planning the military actions of the military group." *Lubanga*, *supra* note 21, ¶ 211.

84. An example might be armed opposition to an occupation, not in support of the government which has been occupied, but rather in order to expel the occupiers and assume control over the territory in question.

85. Yoram Dinstein labels these conflicts "horizontally mixed." YORAM DINSTEIN, THE CONDUCT OF HOSTILITIES UNDER THE LAW OF INTERNATIONAL ARMED CONFLICT 14–15 (2004). *See also* Christopher Greenwood, *International Law and the "War Against Terror,"* 78 INTERNATIONAL AFFAIRS 301, 309 (2002); *Lubanga*, *supra* note 21, ¶¶ 210–14.

86. On overall control, see *Tadić*, *supra* note 21.

87. IG, *supra* note 34, at 25.

88. The most significant debate was published in volume 42:3 (2010) of the *New York University Journal of International Law and Politics.*

89. IG, *supra* note 34, at 46.

90. *See, e.g.*, Schmitt, *supra* note 75.

91. "[D]irect causation should be understood as meaning that the harm in question must be brought about in one causal step" and "it is not sufficient that the act and its consequences be connected through an uninterrupted causal chain of events." IG, *supra* note 34, at 53–54.

92. *Id.* at 54.

93. *Id.* at 56. On human shields, see Michael N. Schmitt, *Human Shields in International Humanitarian Law*, 47 COLUMBIA JOURNAL OF TRANSNATIONAL LAW 292 (2009), *reprinted in* 38 ISRAEL YEARBOOK ON HUMAN RIGHTS 17 (2008).

94. This point was affirmed by the Israeli Supreme Court in *Public Committee against Torture in Israel v. Government of Israel* ¶ 38, HCJ 769/02, Judgment (Dec. 13, 2006), 46 INTERNATIONAL LEGAL MATERIALS 373 (2007), *available at* http://elyon1.court.gov.il/files_eng/02/690/007/a34/02007690.a34.pdf.

95. IG, *supra* note 34, at 65. The interpretation is based on AP COMMENTARY, *supra* note 9, ¶¶ 1943–44, 4789.

96. *See, e.g.*, Yoram Dinstein, *Distinction and the Loss of Civilian Protection in International Armed Conflict, in* INTERNATIONAL LAW AND MILITARY OPERATIONS 183, 189–90 (Michael D. Carsten ed., 2008) (Vol. 84, U.S. Naval War College International Law Studies), *reprinted in* 38 ISRAEL YEARBOOK ON HUMAN RIGHTS 1 (2008). *See also* Kenneth H. Watkin, *Controlling the Use of Force: A Role for Human Rights Norms in Contemporary Armed Conflict*, 98 AMERICAN JOURNAL OF INTERNATIONAL LAW 1, 17 (2004).

97. IG, *supra* note 34, at 70.

98. With the obvious exception of those who are *hors de combat.*

VII

Present and Future Conceptions of the Status of Government Forces in Non-International Armed Conflict

Sean Watts*

Introduction

It seems there are two types of international lawyers—those who view apparent legal voids as vacuums to be filled by international law and those who view legal voids as barriers to the operation of international law. Voids, and for that matter ambiguity, provoke different reactions from different international lawyers. How an international lawyer or tribunal regards an apparent legal void may be, to borrow a poker term, one of the great international law "tells." In addition to providing doctrinal or descriptive clarity, resolutions of voids usually expose a lawyer's level of confidence in the international legal system as well as his or her outlook on the propriety of sovereignty-based regulation.

Disagreement over the significance of international legal voids is not merely academic. To the contrary, debate over perceived or real legal voids between international law interpretive camps quickly brings questions of abstract legal theory into the practical worlds of international policy and practice. Even the hardened international-rule skeptic must see that States' conceptions of international law translate almost directly into policy.[1] With respect to the international law of war,

* Associate Professor, Creighton University Law School; Reserve Instructor, Department of Law, United States Military Academy.

such interpretations can produce widespread life-or-death consequences and, with the rebirth of international criminal law, severe criminal sanctions.

Legal voids exist and operate nowhere more clearly and widely in international law than in the laws of war applicable to non-international armed conflicts (NIACs), understood classically as civil wars.[2] In purely quantitative terms, the positive law of NIAC pales in comparison to the law-of-war provisions applicable to conflicts between States.[3] For example, the 1949 Geneva Conventions, including their 1977 updates, contain well over five hundred substantive articles applicable to international armed conflict (IAC)[4] yet fewer than thirty applicable to NIAC. There is thus no small irony in the fact that the modern law of war actually traces its beginning to a document created to regulate conduct in a civil war.[5] Yet ever since, States have rejected invitations and proposals to level the positive legal gap between IAC and NIAC. The result has been what some regard as glaring legal voids regarding the latter.[6]

Status of government actors in NIAC provides an intriguing and specific example of just such a void. Whereas the protections and obligations of the law of IAC are premised almost entirely on the status of affected persons, the law of NIAC spurns such classifications, as well as the IAC taxonomy of status-based protection generally. International lawyers have long regarded status of persons as largely irrelevant to NIAC.[7] Yet modern forms of conflict and State responses may soon place pressure on the NIAC status void. Increasing media attention, growing international oversight and progressively heightening sensitivity to the suffering produced by NIAC conspire to match the legal protective regime of NIAC with that of IAC, including perhaps the latter's use of status.

Status in IAC describes a number of circumstances and legal relationships (e.g., wounded, wounded at sea, prisoner-of-war, or civilian status). This chapter focuses on the use of status to determine lawfulness of participation in hostilities, or what is sometimes referred to in IAC as combatant status.[8] In particular, this chapter explores the extent to which the international law of NIAC regulates the status of persons who participate in hostilities on behalf of the State.

This chapter begins by addressing the descriptive question whether the international law of NIAC speaks to government forces' status at all. An analytical section accompanies, offering explanations of the likely influences behind the state of the law. A predictive effort follows, addressed to the question whether the law is settled or instead likely to change. This section identifies a number of pressures conspiring to fill the NIAC status void. An argument in favor of imposing status-like limitations on government forces in NIAC is derived from the law-of-war principle of distinction, and then rebutted by logical, structural and operational arguments. The chapter concludes by addressing a series of considerations related to the chapter's opening generalization about international legal voids as an opportunity to reflect more deliberately on an appropriate interpretive approach to the law of NIAC.

The International Legal Status of Government Forces in NIAC

The law of war is riddled with categories—categories of conflicts,[9] categories of weapons,[10] categories of persons. With respect to persons, the primary byproduct of these categories is an elaborate system of status for individuals participating, or caught up, in armed conflict. Principled application of the law requires a deep understanding of how the law of war employs status.[11] Just as the law of war confers status to implement its humanitarian goals, the law's denial of status often produces disappointing or even inhumane results. Frequently, the complexities and nuances of status seem to frustrate alignment of legally correct outcomes with intuitively moral or normatively desirable outcomes. A great many of the present and past errors in the application of the law of war are attributable either to failure to understand how status attaches and operates in armed conflict or simply to unwillingness to accept the practical consequences of correct status determinations.[12]

In war between States, status plays out primarily in the allocation of the protections and obligations of the law of war. Nearly every important protection of the law of IAC requires a predicate determination of the status of persons seeking protection.[13] A prominent commentator observed with respect to IAC, "Every person in enemy hands must have some status under international law . . . ; nobody in enemy hands can be outside the law."[14] In most cases, protection from intentional targeting requires the status of civilian,[15] that of wounded person[16] or, generally, that of *hors de combat.* Persons qualifying for wounded or civilian status receive protection from attack "unless and for such time as they take direct part in hostilities."[17] To benefit from the most elaborate law-of-war treatment obligations, persons in the hands of an adversary must qualify for wounded and sick,[18] prisoner-of-war[19] or protected-person status.[20] The 1949 Geneva Convention on Civilians includes subcategories of civilian, including the "populations of countries in conflict,"[21] "national[s] of neutral state[s]"[22] and "interned protected persons."[23] The law further classifies members of the armed forces into subcategories of combatant and non-combatant.[24]

In addition to allocating protection, the law of war uses status to deny protection and treatment obligations. Designation as a spy, mercenary, or, somewhat more controversially, an unprivileged belligerent, unlawful combatant, saboteur or guerilla can greatly reduce or alter a person's protection or treatment under the law of war.[25] Status has been the focus of not only operational, humanitarian and academic attention but also some of the most significant criminal litigation to enforce the law of war.[26]

The law of NIAC, however, stands generally as an exception to law-of-war reliance on status. Whereas the legal regime applicable to IAC is replete with categories of status, no such system or taxonomy operates in the law of NIAC. The traditional response to the question whether international law regulates status in NIAC has been a confident no.[27] While Additional Protocol II of 1977, the most developed treaty law applicable in NIAC, speaks in terms of a "civilian population," it offers neither qualifying criteria nor any definition of the term "civilian."[28] Perhaps more significantly, the Protocol offers no counterpart to civilian status such as the Additional Protocol I status of combatant.[29]

To the uninitiated, the most noticeable legal void of NIAC might be the absence of prisoner-of-war status. Along with protection of the wounded and sick, prisoner-of-war status has long been one of the consummate law-of-war topics.[30] Few of the major law-of-war treaties addressed to the protection of victims of armed conflict have failed to address prisoners of war. While treatment provisions and living conditions of the captured garner the lion's share of popular attention, the most important aspect of prisoner-of-war protection has been immunity from prosecution for lawful hostile acts—so-called combatant immunity. Combatant immunity protects most prisoners of war from prosecution by their captors for mere participation in hostilities.[31] Thus, nearly all law-of-war prosecutions of prisoners of war have concerned the manner in which they conducted hostilities rather than the fact of their participation in war or their otherwise lawful, warlike acts.

Fighters[32] captured in NIAC do not share the status, immunity or regime of treatment obligations afforded to their IAC counterparts.[33] Despite development of a separate protocol dedicated to developing humanitarian protection in NIAC, the law of war affords no prisoner-of-war status in NIAC.[34] States' desire to avoid attachment of status in NIAC is perhaps apparent in the Additional Protocol II label for the captured, "[p]ersons whose liberty has been restricted."[35] This is a strained label, even by international legal standards; it is likely States wished to avoid any implications of status or legitimacy arising from use of a term of art to describe detention in NIAC. The international law of NIAC affords captured fighters treatment obligations no different from those applicable to the general, non-hostile population.[36] Neither efforts to comply with criteria of conduct or appearance nor any offer of reciprocal observance of the law can compel recognition of prisoner-of-war status by a captor during NIAC.[37] Instead, opposition fighters captured in NIAC, no matter their appearances or conduct, are likely to be regarded as mere criminals, fully subject to the domestic penal regime of the territorial State.[38] The nearest comment Additional Protocol II offers on the topic of combatant immunity is Article 6(5).[39] However, this provision merely charges States to "endeavor" to grant amnesty to fighters. Amnesty is by no means an international legal obligation in NIAC. Domestic law represents the far more relevant legal source for both treatment obligations and immunities if any arising from participation in NIAC. The law of NIAC is nearly silent.

The NIAC status void is even more pronounced with respect to the status of government actors in NIAC. Investigation reveals no treatment in relevant treaty law, nor any significant international custom or usage on the topic. The well-known criteria used to evaluate combatant status in IAC appear nowhere in the positive law of NIAC.[40] And while some States' military manuals address NIAC, none of those reviewed acknowledges international legal input to government forces' status.[41] Instead, most emphasize that the existing law of NIAC has no effect on the legal status of the parties to the conflict.[42] Finally, there is there no evidence of internationally based prosecutions of government actors for their mere participation in NIAC or based on the nature or composition of such forces.

States thus appear to be free from international regulation of the status or nature of government actors they employ against rebels in NIAC. Although States have created rules regulating the conduct of their forces in NIAC, no positive international rules limit the nature of persons or organizations governments may employ in NIAC. Nor does the law of NIAC provide any general status for such forces. In fact, government forces' status in NIAC generally can be said to constitute one of the remaining voids of the international laws of war. Three explanations for this void seem apparent: one practical, a second probable and a third speculative but possible.

The most practical explanation may be that there has simply been little need. Government actors involved in NIAC have not looked to international law for the legitimacy of their participation or for their legal mandate to carry out acts that are essentially internal or non-international in character. Actions taken to defend the State from internal threats lie at the heart of sovereignty. Even the highly internationalized collective security system of the United Nations includes a barrier to outside intervention in internal conflicts.[43] The nature and status of government forces used in NIAC has been an area dominated by municipal law. Responses to insurgency or rebellion, though typically of greater intensity than routine crime, remain essentially law enforcement operations.[44]

There are lively debates concerning domestic legal status and participation in hostilities—none more timely and relevant than the U.S. Title 10–Title 50 division of national security authority.[45] Conceptions of U.S. domestic law might well restrict authority to engage in combat to the armed forces as organized under Title 10 of the United States Code. Although likely envisioned in extraterritorial contexts, debate also swirls around permissible roles for private security contractors (PSCs) in armed conflict. Episodes such as the Blackwater Nisoor Square shootings[46] and other examples of excessive use of force by PSCs have fostered efforts to restrain them from direct participation in hostilities.[47] Proposals to limit PSC activities appear to have gained momentum, notwithstanding the considerable economies that have developed around that corner of the military-industrial complex. Clearly, States may resort to domestic law to limit the activities of their agents in armed conflict. The question remains apart, however, from whether they have resorted or will resort to international law to do the same.

To be certain, government actors may very well find themselves called to task for the international legality of specific conduct and means and methods used in combat.[48] International criminal tribunals of the late twentieth and early twenty-first centuries have developed the NIAC *jus in bello* through extensive cases. Yet the legality of their mere participation in NIAC itself has not been addressed in any forum applying international law.

A related factor contradicting indications of international legal treatment of status may be that States have tended to use forces practically appropriate to the task, that is, armed forces. When the activities of opposition fighters reach a scale or level of intensity sufficient to cross the threshold from mere banditry or riot into armed conflict, resort by the government to the armed forces of the State becomes an obvious, often necessary response. Indeed, forcing the State to resort to armed forces is often regarded as a condition precedent to classifying a situation as armed conflict in the first place.[49]

By contrast, the prevailing view of the law of IAC seems to limit the types of forces States may employ as direct participants in hostilities while preserving the protections of the combatant class, most obviously prisoner-of-war status.[50] To expect prisoner-of-war status for their forces upon capture, it is generally agreed that States must employ regular armed forces or their equivalent in direct hostilities.[51] If this view is correct and if one extends it by custom to NIAC then it's likely the case, as the late Louis Henkin might say, that most States are in compliance, most of the time.[52] Thus the problem, if there is one at all, may frequently be preempted by supposed compliance.

A second, highly probable explanation for why international law does not explicitly regulate status of government actors in NIAC concerns States' general attitudes toward the relationship between international law and NIAC. States have steadfastly resisted creating parity between the law of IAC and that of NIAC. It is likely the absence of international law is simply a byproduct of States' general reluctance to commit to positive rules in NIAC. The reasons for this reluctance are by now well known. Fear of conferring legitimacy on rebels, concerns over failure of reciprocal observance,[53] fear of limiting operational freedom of action and fear of erecting obstacles to domestic prosecutions of persons who take up arms against the State have all driven States to resist expanding the law of NIAC to match that of IAC. States simply do not view opposition fighters in NIAC as legal equals.

Equality of status between sanctioned combatants has long been bedrock of the international law of IAC. Indeed, equality before the law has been a distinguishing feature of the *jus in bello*, setting it apart from its law-of-war counterpart, the *jus ad bellum*. Yet no "equal application" principle operates in the present law of NIAC.[54] Indeed, States conditioned their consent to what little positive law of NIAC exists on an explicit guarantee that legal status would form no part of the law.[55] The concluding clause of Common Article 3 of the 1949 Geneva Convention provides, "The application of the preceding provisions shall not affect the legal status of the Parties to the conflict."[56]

The point is made again when one looks to the law of IAC. Even in its current, highly developed state, the law of IAC does not fully regulate the status of government forces. The concept of combatant status has ancient law-of-war roots.[57] Yet the positive law does not directly address or commit to this area. The Third Geneva Convention does not address combatant status, or immunity for that matter, at all—surprising, perhaps, for a prisoner-of-war convention comprising over 130 articles.

Building on the Third Convention, Additional Protocol I of 1977 states that combatants "have the right to participate directly in hostilities" and is likely reflective of custom. Yet this commitment represents only a partial comment on the issue of combatant status. For instance, the relevant article does not affirmatively indicate whether combatants' right to participate in hostilities is exclusive. Thus it is unclear whether international law actually proscribes or even regulates participation in hostilities by persons not qualifying as combatants. Most law-of-war experts might posit that the right is exclusive to combatants but the soundest view is that international law is merely silent on the matter of privilege with respect to civilians. The matter is not committed to international law whatsoever. It is left to State prerogative and hence to municipal law. Additional Protocol I, Article 51(3), which merely outlines the targeting consequences of civilian participation, is the most the law of IAC offers on the topic.[58]

Commentary indicates the Additional Protocol I drafters intended to codify and clarify international custom on the point of combatant privilege.[59] Still, experts debate what exactly that article and the law of IAC do for combatants in terms of authority. Some describe international law of armed conflict (LOAC) as a source of authority to participate in hostilities—a combatant's privilege.[60] Others disagree, characterizing the article as merely immunity—insulation from prosecution—rather than an affirmative grant of authority, a right or permission.[61] The better phrasing may be that the article merely prohibits prosecutions rather than constitutes affirmative authority or positive sanction. Notwithstanding contrary interpretations by the 2009 United States Congress and the mid-twentieth-century U.S. Supreme Court, the majority view is that the law of IAC does not concern itself with the question of criminal consequences for mere direct participation in hostilities.[62] The best view is that IAC regulates combatant status only as an instrumentality—a means to effecting other ends, such as treatment upon capture or for purposes of contrast with persons protected from attack.

The point for purposes of this chapter is that States' apparent reluctance to commit combatant status fully to international law in IAC makes the prospect that they would do so in NIAC extremely unlikely. Nothing even approaching the partial coverage offered by Additional Protocol I appears in Additional Protocol II. Nor do any of the usual indicators of customary norms, such as military manuals or statements of *opinio juris*, indicate any State commitment of combatant status in NIAC to international law.

A final and possible reason for NIAC's void concerning government actor legal status is lack of consensus. The details of how to treat NIAC have long split the authors of international law.[63] Balancing the competing interests of humanity and respect for sovereignty has bogged down nearly every law-of-war treaty diplomatic conference. But this balance has been particularly elusive with respect to NIAC. Both Common Article 3 to the 1949 Conventions and Additional Protocol II proved to be especially contentious on topics as fundamental as the definition of military objective.[64] Each instrument generated highly divisive factions at its respective diplomatic conference.[65]

For example, the 1949 Geneva Conventions diplomatic conference generated a lengthy report on the scope of NIAC.[66] Consensus that the Conventions would only operate in conflicts analogous to classic civil war required fifteen weeks of work and twenty-three meetings on NIAC.[67] Later, at the diplomatic conference that produced the 1977 Additional Protocols, the scope of covered NIAC again proved contentious. Somewhat surprisingly, the majority of delegations appeared more concerned with contracting LOAC rather than expanding it to cover the entire range of NIAC.[68] These delegations scored a partial victory in the comparatively stingy application provisions of Protocol II. It is generally agreed that Protocol II applies to a narrower class of conflicts than its 1949 counterpart, Common Article 3.[69] Thus, while there may well be a faction of States who, given the opportunity, would consent to international regulation of government forces' status in NIAC, they seem not to have garnered sufficient support at major treaty conferences.[70]

In the final analysis it is overwhelmingly apparent that States have not made any clear commitment of the issue of government forces' status in NIAC to international law. Considerations including lack of necessity, general reluctance to yield sovereignty over internal affairs and lack of consensus have all contributed to the NIAC legal void. Yet given evolving notions of the formation of international law, including the law of war, the staying power of this void may be in doubt.

Pressures on the Existing NIAC Framework

A host of developments call into question whether government actor status in NIAC will remain unregulated by international law. First, if, as argued above,[71] States have previously evaded international regulation of the status of their forces in NIAC because they have largely conformed to what some regard as limits applicable in IAC, this may not hold true much longer. It seems the threats posed by modern insurgencies and hostile non-State actors are steadily provoking more comprehensive responses from States than previously. Leveraging technology, social media and increasingly open borders, States appear to resort to a broader spectrum of national power to counter today's non-State actors. Modern strategy and tactics feature informational and economic elements of State power almost as prominently as more traditional military and diplomatic elements in countering current threats.[72]

Although intelligence work has always played an important part in armed conflict, modern NIAC appears to place even greater emphasis on intelligence gathering. Insurgencies and terrorist groups have frustrated many traditional intelligence collection practices by operating as diffuse networks rather than as rigid "command and control" organizations. To counter these adaptations, national intelligence assets outside the Department of Defense appear to provide not just strategic and operational assessments but also tactical-level intelligence used in small-unit engagements. Civilian intelligence assets appear to provide tactical operators detailed, constantly updated information on enemy locations and activities far more analogous to that provided by reconnaissance spotters and scouts than to the templated, prepackaged and static information previously provided.[73]

The involvement of intelligence community actors in the recent operation against Osama bin Laden provoked not only questions concerning the lawfulness of the operation but interest in the status of the various actors and agencies involved. Reports indicate that in addition to special operations members, Central Intelligence Agency personnel were deeply involved in preparations for and conduct of the raid.[74] Defending the operation on *PBS Newshour*, the Director of the Central Intelligence Agency explained the mission as a so-called "'title 50' operation, which is a covert operation."[75] Elaborating, the Director explained that he commanded the mission but that "the real commander" was the Commander of Joint Special Operations Command, a component of the armed forces.[76] Although his motives for the characterization were unclear, it would not be unreasonable to detect some effort to fend off allegations that civilian participation in a military operation would have been illegal. Although agency lawyers might have later advised him otherwise, particularly given the non-international nature of the conflict with al-Qaeda,[77] the Director's response reveals at least intuitive or implied concern for the impact participation in hostilities might have on the status of his personnel.

Similar intermingling of the missions and assets of the military and civilian intelligence communities is apparent in the growing use of aerial drones.[78] Initially conceived as intelligence-gathering platforms, drones are now capable of carrying out highly lethal and destructive kinetic attacks.[79] Reports indicate the U.S. armed forces are not the sole operators of the nation's arsenal of lethal drones.[80] Intelligence organizations such as the Central Intelligence Agency own and "pilot" drones capable of attack operations, providing a compelling example of blurred lines between intelligence activities and conduct of hostilities. Moreover, the United States no longer holds a monopoly on lethal drone technology, if indeed it ever held one. States such as Israel, China and France are reported to possess lethal drones, broadening the scope of involved international actors.[81] Although perhaps only now in its infancy, drone use has already provoked intense legal debate. The majority of debate currently concerns authority for States to use lethal force outside the traditional confines of battlefields.[82] Yet strains of debate concerning the authority of non-military personnel to participate in hostilities are gaining momentum.[83]

Further intermingling of government civilian and military communities is envisioned in emerging mid- and postwar nation-building doctrine. An outgrowth of admitted failures in the Iraq and Afghanistan conflicts, stability operations seek to build government capacity either to hasten or to sustain transitions from war to peace.[84] Stability operations emphasize "soft power" such as education, agricultural, economic and humanitarian assistance to address the deeper causes of armed conflict. Consistent with popular notions of the "three-block war," stability operations may occur at the same time as, and very near, active hostilities.[85] In 2005, stability operations received a high-powered endorsement in the form of a Department of Defense directive.[86] The directive instructed all U.S. commanders to give stability operations "priority comparable to combat operations."[87] Yet the centerpiece of military stability operations doctrine is the conviction that the armed forces must perform only a supporting role. Stability operations envision heavy, often lead-agency roles for civilian governmental organizations such as the U.S. Department of State, Department of Justice and the U.S. Agency for International Development.[88] While actual civilian agency participation has lagged behind expectations, stability operations that intermingle civilian and military missions, particularly in complex or dynamic security environments, seem on the rise and likely to blur notions of participation in hostilities.[89]

A final emerging field of warfare also illustrates the intermingling of agencies provoked by modern armed conflict. States increasingly recognize cyberspace as a critical domain of national security.[90] Few steeped in this evolving form of conflict are unfamiliar with stories of empty legal formalism with respect to personnel involved in cyber operations. Informal discussions of practices associated with State involvement in cyber operations frequently recall stories of the uniformed service member who clicks "Send" at the conclusion of a cyber operation otherwise prepared, designed, scouted and executed exclusively by civilian personnel. Although off-the-record and susceptible to exaggeration, no doubt, the anecdote may be indicative of both the extent of civilian participation in U.S. cyber operations up to and likely including the moment of attack, and ingrained or intuitive notions of what constitutes lawful civilian participation in hostilities.[91]

Second, as the armed conflict in Libya showed, a stronger international spotlight shines on NIAC than previously. The legal character of the Libyan conflict is complex. It is clear that by February 2011, hostilities rose beyond mere riot and crossed the threshold for armed conflict, resulting in a NIAC for legal purposes. Yet not long afterward, international intervention on behalf of the rebels in mid-March likely converted portions of the conflict into IAC for the legal purposes of participating States.[92] Whether the situation devolved into two separate conflicts, an IAC between Libya and the NATO States conducting attacks on one hand, and a NIAC between the Libyan government and the rebels on the other, is debatable.[93] The better view acknowledges each as a separate conflict, notwithstanding practical complications. Either way, media and social networking made the details of government reactions to civil disturbances and especially the rebel armed groups instantly public.[94] Even the academic legal community responded, producing near-instantaneous analysis and reactions to the conflict.[95] The information age appears to have ended the era when States could rely upon the internal nature of NIAC to shield the nature of their responses from public attention. One wonders whether the same can long be said with respect to international legal attention.

Third, and finally, the rise of so-called transnational armed conflict may bring pressure on the government forces status void. "Transnational armed conflict" typically describes armed conflict between a State and non-State actors not confined to the State's own territory.[96] U.S. operations against al-Qaeda since 2001 are often cited as an example of transnational armed conflict given their extension beyond the sites of the original 2001 attacks to at least four continents. Although of limited legal recognition and acceptance among law-of-war experts, transnational armed conflicts remain related to NIAC in their likely scope of international regulation. At present they remain, in the most important respect for purposes of conflict classification, non-international. That is, despite crossing international borders, transnational armed conflicts still do not pit two States directly against one another.

Yet the broader geographic and political scope of transnational armed conflicts may render increased input from international law attractive to important international legal personalities. Transnational armed conflict greatly strains traditional territorial or politically based claims of exclusive sovereign prerogative on the part of the government under attack. Classic, non-extraterritorial NIAC has relied greatly on traditional notions of territorial sovereignty to fend off international regulation. With their associated cross-border incursions and movements, transnational armed conflicts unmoor NIAC from many of its traditional claims to general freedom from international regulation. To be sure, the soundest approach looks for such regulation from the traditional sources of international law—the agreements and binding practices of States. But from a normative perspective, rights of non-intervention in internal affairs[97] and insulation from international legal meddling seem significantly weaker in transnational armed conflict.

The emerging forms of warfare showcased above reinforce the point. To return to cyber operations, it appears nearly impossible to conduct an effective, networked cyber attack within the territory of one State.[98] For instance, although of uncertain origin, the denial of service attacks suffered by Estonia in 2007 are estimated to have transited servers and networks located in as many as 178 countries.[99] Cyber attacks are likely to appear attractive to non-State actors challenging better-resourced government opponents in NIAC.[100] Cyber warfare offers insurgents anonymity, economy and access to destructive potential often difficult to acquire with respect to kinetic means.[101] To the extent cyber operations can be expected as a feature of NIAC, these conflicts will continue to involve transnational elements, such as attacks either originating from the territory of third-party States or at least transiting servers therein. Government responses to insurgent cyber attacks may be less than discriminating given the difficulties of cyber attribution. One can easily foresee false positives leading governments in NIAC to unwittingly attack assets of neutral third-party States. The temptation to resort to international law of war to regulate such events, to the extent they are not already regulated in the *jus ad bellum* and law of State responsibility, may be great.

Ultimately, the effect of each of these phenomena of modern armed conflict—mixing of traditional missions, increasingly available information on how States conduct NIAC and the enlarged geographic scope of NIAC—is likely to be heightened scrutiny of State responses to NIAC. If, as the prior section asserted, State responses have largely conformed to tradition, modern conflict's demand for interagency responses will likely involve actors not traditionally associated with direct participation in NIAC. If States could formerly rely on the fog of war and geographic borders to obscure the details of how and with whom they carried out military operations, the networked world will certainly make their practices and tactics apparent and subject to scrutiny. And if the previously internal nature of NIAC permitted States to defend claims of sovereign prerogative, the increasingly transnational nature of NIAC will surely increase pressure to internationalize the applicable legal regime, perhaps even with respect to status.

Re-examining Status in NIAC

The extent to which one concludes the international law of NIAC regulates the status and composition of government forces may be a function of the level of legal generality at which one operates. As demonstrated above, the positivist claim to international regulation of the topic is weak. Certainly, no specific treaty provisions address the subject directly. Nor does one find extensive signs of State consent to international regulation of the topic through recitation of custom or litigation generally. Yet drawing back to the level of principles, one might find evidence to undermine the voids previously described. Paired with looser interpretive practices, such as giving tangible effect to the perceived objects and purposes of such legal norms, a colorable case for limits on government forces in NIAC emerges.[102] This section examines briefly the case for principle-derived international law limits on State participation in NIAC similar to the status-based limits found in IAC.

The principle of distinction has been called "the grandfather of all principles" of the law of armed conflict.[103] Enumerated alternately as "distinction"[104] or "discrimination,"[105] in both practice and custom warriors have long recognized the principle. Distinction's first clear codification appeared in one of the founding documents of the law of armed conflict. The U.S. Lieber Instructions, drafted in 1863, state:

> [A]s civilization has advanced during the last centuries, so has likewise steadily advanced, especially in war on land, the distinction between the private individual belonging to a hostile country and the hostile country itself, with its men in arms. The principle has been more and more acknowledged that the unarmed citizen is to be spared in person, property, and honor as much as the exigencies of war will admit.[106]

The modern international law of armed conflict expresses the principle similarly in Additional Protocol I, Article 48, titled appropriately "The Basic Rule."[107] Most frequently, distinction operates on the targeting practices of combatants, restricting lawful attacks to legitimate military objectives and enemy combatants and fighters.[108] Distinction forbids attacks on civilians not participating directly in hostilities and on civilian objects.[109] The principle also forbids attacks producing effects that cannot be contained or limited to their intended targets.[110]

Beyond limiting attacks and their effects to lawful targets, distinction also comprises combatants' duty to distinguish *themselves* from civilians. Located among the Additional Protocol I provisions related to prisoner-of-war and combatant statuses, Article 44 requires that combatants "distinguish themselves from the civilian population while they are engaged in an attack or in a military operation preparatory to an attack."[111] Historically, combatants have satisfied this aspect of distinction by setting themselves apart from civilians both spatially and in appearance. Uniforms and the practice of carrying arms openly, combined with tactics involving tight formations and relatively confined battlefields, formerly made distinction a relatively simple matter. Recognizing modern practices of militia and other organized resistance movements in twentieth-century warfare, however, Article 44 permits combatants to derogate from distinguishing themselves in the traditional manner in some instances. Under Article 44, in occupied territory and wars of national liberation, unconventional combatants need merely carry arms openly during and in preparation for attacks.[112] Relaxing the uniform and insignia aspects of the distinction requirement, Article 44 proved one of the most contentious provisions of Protocol I.[113] Yet the general duty for participants in hostilities to distinguish themselves clearly during combat persists.

Addressed more squarely to targeting operations than status, Additional Protocol I, Article 58 outlines precautions against attacks and reinforces the second aspect of the principle of distinction.[114] Article 58 generally requires that parties remove or separate civilians located in their own territories from likely military objectives. Commentary to the rule clarifies its intent also to prevent construction of military buildings near civilian populations and objects.[115] The rule's relationship to distinction lies in its facilitation of attackers' efforts to observe the principle themselves. In some sense, Article 58 responds to critiques that the targeting provisions of Additional Protocol I focus too narrowly on attackers.[116] Law-of-war experts have observed that in many targeting scenarios, the defender or object of attack is better positioned to limit civilian casualties and collateral damage to civilian objects.[117] Though perhaps not to the entire satisfaction of Protocol I critics, Article 58 remedies a portion of the supposed misallocation of the distinction burden.

Carried to its logical conclusion, the above conception of distinction, in both IAC and NIAC,[118] can be understood to carry an implicit limitation on the categories of government actors authorized to take part in hostilities. In NIAC, government use of agencies or actors indistinguishable from the civilian population or from government agencies not participating directly in hostilities frustrates insurgents' efforts to observe the principle of distinction in their attacks. For instance, co-location of an interagency intelligence analysis cell with other civilian agency assets not engaged in a NIAC effort might frustrate discriminate attacks on the former. More important, widespread use of personnel from civilian government agencies to conduct hostilities in NIAC could easily induce insurgent forces to regard all civilian government personnel as hostile, even those not actually taking direct part in attacks.

As critics of Additional Protocol I observe, the defender, in this case the *de jure* government is usually better positioned to prevent harm to civilians. Either by clearly identifying persons taking direct part in hostilities on behalf of the government or by restricting such activities to members of the armed forces, the government could greatly aid efforts to ensure discriminate attacks. Under the proposed principle-based rule, any contrary course of action would be characterized as inconsistent with the principle of distinction or at least inconsistent with its object and purpose.

Such a rule might easily translate into a status-like conception for NIAC. Although NIAC generally rejects the use of status to apportion authority and protection, a distinction-derived rule limiting participation in hostilities to members of the government armed forces might operate similarly to a status-based rule. In practical terms, the rule would create two categories of persons in NIAC: those whose direct participation does not frustrate the principle of distinction and those whose direct participation in hostilities violates the principle. Such bifurcations are entirely parallel to the status-based legal regime of IAC in important respects, lacking only the familiar taxonomy of combatant and civilian.

Finally, in addition to the rule's logical connection to the most important principle of the law of war, proponents might point to recent trends toward parity between the international law of IAC and that of NIAC. The very late twentieth and early twenty-first centuries have seen an expansion of international instruments applicable in NIAC as well as extensions of existing IAC treaties into NIAC. Major treaties expanded to cover NIAC include the 1954 Hague Cultural Property Convention;[119] the1980 Convention on Conventional Weapons, including its five protocols;[120] the 1997 Ottawa Landmines Convention;[121] the 1993 Chemical Weapons Convention;[122] and the 2008 Convention on Cluster Munitions.[123] Additionally, 118 States have ratified the Rome Statute of the International Criminal

Court, which includes a highly developed article of war crimes in NIAC.[124] Beyond application of the technical provisions of these treaties, such expansions might signal an important erosion of State hostility toward international regulation of the conduct of hostilities in NIAC.

In sum, attractive logical, humanitarian and even mildly positivist cases might be made for status-like limits on government forces participating in NIAC. For purposes of argument, this section imagines a distinction-derived rule that would, as some consider is the case in IAC, limit direct participation in hostilities in NIAC to armed forces or militia similarly organized and belonging to a party to the conflict.[125] In fact, a recent book dedicated to the topic of combatant status in NIAC asserts as much, arguing, "By definition, any person who participates in an internal armed conflict who is not a member of the states' armed forces is an 'unlawful' combatant—that is, a person who is not immunized for their warlike acts."[126] Despite apparent humanitarian payouts, the imagined rule runs afoul of important structural and technical facets of the law of war. Logical, structural and practical reasons counsel against recognition of the rule as *lex lata* and perhaps even as *lex ferenda*.

First among logical objections, the distinction-derived rule proves too much. The logic of the proposed rule would extend to practically absurd conclusions. For example, the appearances of some non-military government actors in NIAC would not frustrate the principle of distinction. Many States' domestic security forces would appear to most observers as combatants. Few, if any, NIAC fighters could claim to have been misled by the uniforms, armaments and even vehicles used by such actors despite their non-military character. Yet because they are not actually armed forces or, alternatively, not subject to a system of command and internal discipline they would be excluded from conducting hostilities under the supposed rule. The same might easily be said of private security contractors employed by States in NIAC. For all the complexities PSCs have introduced to the modern battlefield, confusion with innocent civilians is not typically among them.[127]

Additionally, a blanket rule limiting government conduct of hostilities in NIAC to members of the armed forces would extend beyond situations that implicate the appearance of the hostile actor at all. So-called over-the-horizon or non-line-of-sight attacks seem not to provoke concern that the attacker distinguish him- or herself through visual means. In this respect, there is great danger that the distinction-derived rule would operate too broadly in a logical sense. That is, application of a rule requiring the wearing or display of distinctive insignia or uniforms applied to over-the-horizon warfare fails to serve the rule's intended purpose of facilitating the defender's efforts to distinguish attackers from innocent, non-hostile parties. Limiting the conduct of attacks to members of the armed forces in such circumstances amounts at least to empty formalism—and at worst to absurdity—harmful to the reputation and perceived legitimacy of the law of war.

As related above, the material field of application of a number of important international law-of-war instruments has recently been expanded to NIAC. By their terms, these treaties formerly regulated only IAC. Previously, their extension to NIAC could only be achieved by proof of customary status—a technique fraught with ambiguity and subject to vexing caveat. It may be, as previously observed, that these expansions reflect a reduction of State hostility to international regulation of NIAC. Yet closer examination suggests evidence of a more restrained enthusiasm for international regulation of NIAC.

With the notable exception of the Rome Statute, each of the treaties recently expanded to cover NIAC concerns means and methods of warfare. They are primarily weapons treaties consistent with the Hague tradition of the law of war.[128] Weapons treaties have long been an exception to the use of status to apportion protection in IAC. In contrast to the instruments of the so-called Geneva or "respect and protect" tradition, weapons treaties associated with the Hague tradition have operated universally, benefiting both combatants and civilians, though typically in a collateral sense with respect to the latter. Weapons treaties usually do not concern interpersonal interactions or the control of individuals and have not been a source of protected or privileged status under the law of war. None of the expanded treaties introduces to NIAC a new or protected status. While certainly humanitarian advances and arguably a boon to the prospect of international regulation of NIAC, the recent expansions actually reflect no alternation whatsoever to the general dearth of status-based regulation in NIAC. The larger significance of these expansions may not be general State willingness to submit to international regulation of NIAC, but rather recognition of the near-perfect alignment of concern for unnecessary suffering produced by certain classes of weapons in both IAC and NIAC.

By contrast, the Rome Statute's significant NIAC jurisdictional grant to the International Criminal Court (ICC) spans both traditions of the law of war. The NIAC-relevant portions of the Rome Statute undoubtedly represent a significant concession to the international legal system. And other international tribunals share the ICC's broad authority with respect to conduct in NIAC.[129] Yet the extent to which the mandates of these tribunals reflect willingness to commit NIAC to the international legal system should not be overstated. First, it should be remembered that the jurisdiction of the ICC, through the principle of complementarity, takes a backseat to domestic proceedings.[130] States willing and able to hear claims arising from participation in NIAC in their own courts preempt ICC jurisdiction. Complementarity stands as a powerful bar to international intrusion into NIAC.

Second, the most legally significant outcomes of the decisions at the International Criminal Tribunal for the former Yugoslavia (ICTY) have been achieved only through controversially broad outlooks on the scope of customary law applicable to NIAC. None is better illustrative than the ICTY decision in *Prosecutor v. Tadić*, in which the Appeals Chamber observed that the distinction between IAC and NIAC had lost much of its value and weight.[131] The Tribunal's observation is only defensible under the least rigorous conceptions of customary international law. Applied to the nationals of minor powers, involved in unquestionably inhumane conduct, the Appeals Chamber's observation attracted only minor protest. One wonders whether applied to agents of more influential international actors, and to less obviously atrocious circumstances, the Chamber's bold pronouncement would have weathered as well.

Third, and most important, it should be understood that criminal tribunals deal with conduct, as distinct from status. For the tribunals, status is examined solely for the purposes of evaluating jurisdiction or determining whether charged conduct satisfies the elements of an enumerated offense. For instance, a tribunal vested with jurisdiction to hear grave breaches of the Third Geneva Convention must determine whether any alleged victims held the status of prisoner of war as understood by that Convention.[132] Similarly, grave breaches of the Fourth Convention require that purported victims be protected persons as defined by Article 4 of that Convention.[133] Criminal tribunals do not resolve questions of status for their own sake or for such inherently political purposes as determining the legitimacy of participation itself. None of the tribunals has litigated status as such or at least in the sense applied by this chapter. Despite a rich jurisprudence concerning NIAC, no international case has examined status of any fighter with respect to lawfulness of mere participation. Claims advancing a distinction-derived rule on government participation in hostilities in NIAC likely confuse conduct with status.

The preceding argument illustrates a critical point, namely, the function of status. Status is instrumental; it is an intermediary for larger, more meaningful legal outcomes. Under the laws of war, status confers protection, treatment, obligations and, in the case of combatants, a limited form of immunity from prosecution. While protection from hostilities, treatment standards upon capture and other obligations concerning handling of captured combatants share an essentially humanitarian impetus, immunity remains an end distinct from the humanitarian status-derived ends. Immunity is quintessentially political. Immunity from prosecution for participation in hostilities and the derivative rule limiting the classes of persons who may claim immunity lie at the heart of sovereignty. If status is conceived as a gateway to immunity, then it is true that in NIAC "status is the prize for which fighting is waged."[134] The suggestion, such as that advanced by the distinction-derived rule on government forces in NIAC that States would surrender the ultimate prize of revolutionary war to the international legal system, is severely at odds with both the historical experience of NIAC, and their clearest self-interest. In terms of logical argument, conceiving status in NIAC as a means to lawful participation begs the question of the conflict itself. Only if status is conceived as an instrumentality to purely humanitarian ends can it be fairly said to operate at all with respect to government forces in NIAC.

From a still wider perspective, it is difficult to reconcile serious claims of IAC-NIAC parity with the positivist record.[135] As emphasized above, States have consistently, by compelling majorities, rebuffed invitations to drop the IAC-NIAC distinction in law-of-war treaties.[136] Even where States have consented to overlapping norms, they have made critical caveats. The Martens clause made an early appearance in the Hague Conventions and has reappeared in nearly every major law-of-war instrument since. An eponymous homage to an influential Russian diplomat, the clause first resolved an impasse of the treatment of resistance fighters during belligerent occupation by referring to the common law of war and to more general norms of humanitarian treatment.[137] Since then, the clause has served the function in treaties of holding a place for the customary law of war, and also as a sort of residual clause for the operation of peacetime humanitarian norms.

While the clause appears in the NIAC-specific Additional Protocol II of 1977, it bears crucial alterations to its traditional form.[138] The Protocol II iteration excludes reference to "law of nations"/"international law" and "established custom."[139] Also omitted is the traditional reference to "usages established among civilized peoples."[140] Academic commentary to Additional Protocol II indicates these were deliberate omissions, intended to honor States' historical reluctance to commit NIAC to international law.[141] As is plain, each omission shares with the others reference to the international legal system. A clearer desire to keep international norms at bay in NIAC is difficult to conjure. That States would in the modern period of positive law-of-war development require alterations to such a widely accepted and fundamental precept of the law of IAC certainly bears witness to the persistence of the IAC-NIAC divide.

To be sure, some IAC norms transpose easily to NIAC. International tribunals and respected non-governmental and academic studies have made compelling cases to close the substantive legal gap between the two recognized conflict types.[142] For instance, minimal treatment standards for persons in custody applicable in IAC present few, if any, NIAC-specific obstacles to military or political necessity. But even if many IAC norms transpose easily, status does not appear to be one of them. Although a certain parity between treatment obligations and protections in IAC and NIAC can be conceded, it is worth noting that status has not made the leap between two conflict types. Conferral of status, even as a humanitarian instrumentality, has proved the point where State willingness to level the law of IAC and that of NIAC ends. The issue remains of sufficient political importance to NIAC to withstand even the considerable aforementioned pressures on the existing NIAC status void.

Finally, and aside from descriptive debates, calls for leveling the international law of NIAC with that of IAC fail to make the normative case that international law is the best answer to perceived problems in NIAC. Typically claims that IAC norms have migrated to NIAC appeal to strong humanitarian logic. How could persons, especially victims of hostilities, be less deserving of protection simply by virtue of conflict classification? While compelling on some levels, these claims fail to appreciate the entire calculus of commitment of an issue to the international legal system. Commitments to international law reflect not only normatively desirable outcomes, but also the judgment of States that such outcomes are best achieved collectively rather than independently. No single theory of international law prescribes a comprehensive formula for such determinations. States appear to make such determinations on an ad hoc basis, balancing multiple and dynamic variables.

Since the late nineteenth century, States have judged international law as a good fit for international armed conflict largely by virtue of the identities of the actors. Coincidence of interests and guarantees of reciprocity continue to inform the international bargains struck through treaties. By definition, the parties to NIAC upset the logic of this prescription. Assumptions concerning capacity and willingness to observe internationally based legal obligations do not migrate from IAC to NIAC as easily as rules themselves. Moreover, domestic legal systems' implementations of international law are often imperfect. Legal nuances are often lost in translation, frustrating expectations of uniformity and universality. Hard-won bargains at diplomatic conferences may be selectively or not at all implemented. Considering the inherently internal, sovereign nature of issues in NIAC, the likelihood that international norms would be implemented to the credit of international law legitimacy seems dim. Finally, modern perceptions of the laws of war themselves may be part of the problem. Characterizations of the law of war as exclusively humanitarian mislead and present an incomplete picture of its true object and purpose.[143] While many of the humanitarian aspects of the law of IAC have proved well disposed to migration to NIAC, the use of status generally, and particularly to apportion political outcomes such as immunity, appears to be the current limit of State willingness to submit to IAC-NIAC legal parity.

Conclusion

As the chapter's opening assertion, a gross generalization to be sure, suggests, international lawyers' reactions to purported voids in international law coverage vary greatly according to interpretive preferences and general outlooks on international law. Whatever one's interpretive bent, it seems undeniable that positive voids in international law no longer mean what they used to. Substantive gaps in treaty coverage seem to represent neither the end of descriptive debate, nor the beginning of the end, but only perhaps the end of the beginning of such discussions.[144] In addition to the possibilities of international custom, theories accepting a proliferation of "international lawmakers" now include suggestions that non-State actors might form international law, greatly increasing the likelihood that perceived voids will be filled to the satisfaction of interpretivist schools of thought.[145] The signs are all around that if the NIAC status void is to remain in effect it will have to be defended rather than assumed.

With respect to the status of government forces in NIAC a distinction-derived rule limiting government forces' participation in hostilities explored in this chapter is more than a rhetorical straw man. Accepting evolution in NIAC, the prospect of international regulation appears highly possible. In addition to changes in international law interpretive theory, evolutions in State military doctrine applicable to NIAC and increased popular attention to how NIAC is waged by States provide fertile ground for transplanting IAC norms into NIAC.

Despite their shortcomings, *jus in bello* treaties have been highly successful at humanizing IAC. The desire to import such success to NIAC is both laudable and understandable. Yet voids are not in all cases invitations to interpretive gap-filling. Voids are, as in the case of status in NIAC, often reflections of States' general outlook on the propriety and likely efficacy of international regulation. To preserve the legitimacy of the law of war generally, a sound and principled methodology is needed to regulate the migration of norms from IAC to NIAC.

It may be fair to say the *jus in bello* is under-theorized and thus not up to the task. Compared to domestic legal regimes, international law generally and even its legal sibling the *jus ad bellum*, the law governing the conduct of hostilities lacks a deliberate and well-defended interpretive theory. One finds far greater attention to compliance theory in *jus ad bellum* than *jus in bello*.[146] That law-of-war specialists haven't paid particular attention to interpretive theory is to some extent forgivable. The pressing practicalities of its relevance, the life-and-death implications of its operation, and the still unsorted doctrinal and descriptive challenges are enough to occupy a career. However, in addition to the possibility of resolving a pressing doctrinal question, the NIAC status void may offer an opportunity to spark more deliberate discussion of interpretive theory in the *jus in bello*.

The temptation to address voids from a purely humanitarian perspective can be great. Yet purely moral reasoning fails to account for the current positive disparities between the law of IAC and that of NIAC. Ultimately, deliberate and principled interpretive efforts, such as this chapter has endeavored to provide, present the more promising course, unveiling areas of potential progress, while sustaining the underlying logic and nature of the current international legal system.

Notes

1. Professor Hart described "rule-scepticism" as "the claim that talk of rules is a myth, cloaking the truth that law consists simply of the decisions of courts and the prediction of them." H.L.A. HART, THE CONCEPT OF LAW 133 (1961).

2. This article uses the term "non-international armed conflict" to describe hostilities between a State and an organized armed group not formally affiliated with a State. Significant debate has developed over the scope of conflicts included in the term "NIAC." Classically, conceptions of the regulation of such conflicts have been confined to the territory of a single State. *See* Memorandum from John C. Yoo & Robert Delahunty to William J. Haynes II, General Counsel, Department of Defense, Re: Application of Treaties and Laws to al Qaeda and Taliban Detainees (Jan. 9, 2002), *reprinted in* THE TORTURE PAPERS: THE ROAD TO ABU GHRAIB 37, 44 (Karen J. Greenberg & Joshua Dratel eds., 2005) (rejecting application of Common Article 3 of the 1949 Geneva Conventions to cross-border conflicts with non-State actors) [hereinafter THE TORTURE PAPERS]. Controversy notwithstanding, there is strong support for the notion that when they adopted the term NIAC, States meant to refer only to civil wars in the classic sense. *See* ANTHONY CULLEN, THE CONCEPT OF NON-INTERNATIONAL ARMED CONFLICT IN INTERNATIONAL HUMANITARIAN LAW 41–49 (2010). Recently, scholars have called for legal recognition of a class of conflict between State actors and non-State actors that crosses international borders, such as the United States' conflict with al-Qaeda. *See* Geoffrey S. Corn & Eric Talbot Jensen, *Untying the Gordian Knot: A Proposal for Determining Applicability of the Laws of War to the War on Terror*, 81 TEMPLE LAW REVIEW 787 (2008) (advocating recognition and application of the law of war to "transnational armed conflict").

3. The 1949 Geneva Conventions, synonymous for many with the law of war, include over four hundred provisions addressed specifically to international armed conflict and only one addressed to non-international armed conflict. Convention for the Amelioration of the Condition of the Wounded and Sick in Armed Forces in the Field art. 3, Aug. 12, 1949, 6 U.S.T. 3114, 75 U.N.T.S. 31 [hereinafter 1949 Geneva Convention I]; Convention for the Amelioration of the Condition of Wounded, Sick and Shipwrecked Members of Armed Forces at Sea art. 3, Aug. 12, 1949, 6 U.S.T. 3217, 75 U.N.T.S. 85; Convention Relative to the Treatment of Prisoners of War art. 3, Aug. 12, 1949, 6 U.S.T. 3316, 75 U.N.T.S. 135 [hereinafter 1949 Geneva Convention III]; Convention Relative to the Protection of Civilian Persons in Time of War art. 3, Aug. 12, 1949, 6 U.S.T. 3516, 75 U.N.T.S. 287 [hereinafter 1949 Geneva Convention IV].

4. The most widely accepted treaty-based definition of international armed conflict is found in Common Article 2 of each of the four 1949 Geneva Conventions. Additional Protocol I to the Conventions controversially expanded the scope of material application of the Geneva

tradition to so-called wars against "colonial domination and alien occupation and against racist regimes . . . ." Protocol Additional to the Geneva Conventions of 12 August 1949, and Relating to the Protection of Victims of International Armed Conflicts art. 1(4), June 8, 1977, 1125 U.N.T.S. 3 [hereinafter Additional Protocol I]. States parties to Additional Protocol I have interpreted the phrase narrowly, however, greatly limiting the practical effect of the expansion. *See* GARY D. SOLIS, THE LAW OF ARMED CONFLICT: INTERNATIONAL HUMANITARIAN LAW IN WAR 123–25 (2010).

5. *See* U.S. Department of War, Instructions for the Government of Armies of the United States in the Field, General Orders No. 100, Apr. 24, 1863 [hereinafter Lieber Code], *reprinted in* THE LAWS OF ARMED CONFLICTS 3 (Dietrich Schindler & Jiri Toman eds., 4th ed. 2004) [hereinafter Schindler & Toman]. Originally issued as military policy, the Instructions—or Lieber Code, as it is now widely known—inspired States not only to codify the customs of warfare but also to commit these rules to international, rather than domestic, law. *See* Jordan J. Paust, *Dr. Francis Lieber and the Lieber Code*, 95 AMERICAN SOCIETY OF INTERNATIONAL LAW PROCEEDINGS 112 (2001); Richard R. Baxter, *The First Modern Codification of the Law of War*, 3 INTERNATIONAL REVIEW OF THE RED CROSS 171 (1963).

6. *See, e.g.*, Georges Abi-Saab, *Non International Armed Conflicts*, *in* INTERNATIONAL DIMENSIONS OF HUMANITARIAN LAW 217, 218–25 (UNESCO ed., 1988) (noting absence of provisions dealing with attacks on civilians in Article 3 of the 1949 Geneva Conventions); Michael Bothe, *Article 3 and Protocol II: Case Studies of Nigeria and El Salvador*, 31 AMERICAN UNIVERSITY LAW REVIEW 899 (1982) (illustrating legal gaps through case studies and arguing Protocol II did not go far enough toward advancing humanitarian causes in NIAC).

7. HILAIRE MCCOUBREY & NIGEL D. WHITE, INTERNATIONAL LAW AND ARMED CONFLICT 323 (1992) (observing that "[r]eferences to 'prisoner of war' status would be legally and politically inappropriate in a context of non-international armed conflict").

8. Combatant status is also used with reference to persons lawfully targetable under the law of IAC. *See* Additional Protocol I, *supra* note 4, art. 50.

9. *See* 1949 Geneva Convention I, *supra* note 3, art. 2. So-called Common Article 2, as it appears identically in each of the four 1949 Geneva Conventions, identifies the category of conflict to which the Conventions apply. *See* David E. Graham, *Defining Non-International Armed Conflict: A Historically Difficult Task*, which is Chapter III in this volume, at 43; Charles Garraway, *War and Peace: Where Is the Divide?*, which is Chapter V in this volume, at 93; Geoffrey S. Corn, *Self-defense Targeting: Blurring the Line between the* Jus ad Bellum *and the* Jus in Bello, which is Chapter IV in this volume, at 57.

10. *See* Convention on Prohibitions or Restrictions on the Use of Certain Conventional Weapons Which May Be Deemed to Be Excessively Injurious or to Have Indiscriminate Effects, Oct. 10, 1980, 1342 U.N.T.S. 137 (identifying prohibited categories of weapons and weapons generating additional obligations through five separate protocols, including weapons with undetectable fragments, mines and booby traps, incendiary weapons, blinding lasers, and explosive remnants of war) [hereinafter Conventional Weapons Convention].

11. *See* Paul Kantwill & Sean Watts, *Hostile Protected Persons or "Extra-Conventional Persons,"* 28 FORDHAM INTERNATIONAL LAW JOURNAL 681 (2005).

12. *See, e.g.*, Prosecutor v. Tadić, Case No. IT-94-1-A, Judgment, ¶¶ 164–71 (Int'l Crim. Trib. for the Former Yugoslavia July 15, 1999) (reversing, unfortunately, a Trial Chamber's highly informed and principled application of protected-person status under the Fourth Geneva Convention) [hereinafter *Prosecutor v. Tadić*].

13. The most significant exception to the status-dependent international law of war is the category of rules limiting weapons and means of warfare, the so-called Hague tradition. *See infra* text accompanying note 128.

14. COMMENTARY IV GENEVA CONVENTION RELATIVE TO THE PROTECTION OF CIVILIAN PERSONS IN TIME OF WAR 51 (Jean S. Pictet ed., 1958) [hereinafter GENEVA CONVENTION IV COMMENTARY].

15. *See* Additional Protocol I, *supra* note 4, arts. 48–71.

16. *See* 1949 Geneva Convention I, *supra* note 3, arts. 12–13 (outlining, respectively, protections owed to the wounded and qualification criteria for the status of wounded).

17. Additional Protocol I, *supra* note 4, art. 51(3). A recent symposium offers a helpful cross-section of views on the meaning of this phrase. Forum, *Direct Participation in Hostilities: Perspectives on the ICRC Interpretive Guidance*, 42 NEW YORK UNIVERSITY JOURNAL OF INTERNATIONAL LAW AND POLITICS 637 (2010). Article 13 of Additional Protocol II applicable to NIAC replicates Article 51(3), although without an accompanying definition of the term "[c]ivilians." Protocol Additional to the Geneva Conventions of 12 August 1949, and Relating to the Protection of Victims of Non-International Armed Conflicts art. 5, June 8, 1977, 1125 U.N.T.S. 609 [hereinafter Additional Protocol II].

18. *See* 1949 Geneva Convention I, *supra* note 3, art. 13.

19. *See* 1949 Geneva Convention III, *supra* note 3, art. 4. *See also* YORAM DINSTEIN, THE CONDUCT OF HOSTILITIES UNDER THE LAW OF INTERNATIONAL ARMED CONFLICT 39–51 (2d ed. 2010) (providing a clear application of the prisoner-of-war qualification criteria); Memorandum from Alberto R. Gonzales, Counsel to the President, Office of Counsel to the President, to George W. Bush, President of the United States, Decision re Application of the Geneva Convention on Prisoners of War to the Conflict with Al Qaeda and the Taliban (Jan. 25, 2002), *reprinted in* THE TORTURE PAPERS, *supra* note 2, at 118, 121 (offering a controversial application of the prisoner-of-war criteria). Reinforcing the importance of prisoner-of-war status, the Third Geneva Convention requires detaining powers convene "competent tribunals" to determine the proper status of detainees potentially eligible for protection under the Convention. *See* 1949 Geneva Convention III, *supra*, art. 55.

20. *See* 1949 Geneva Convention IV, *supra* note 3, art. 4. *See also* Derek Jinks, *The Declining Significance of P.O.W. Status*, 45 HARVARD INTERNATIONAL LAW JOURNAL 367 (2004) (explaining the nature of the Fourth Convention's protective regime); Knut Dörmann, *The Legal Situation of "Unlawful/Unprivileged Combatants,"* 85 INTERNATIONAL REVIEW OF THE RED CROSS 45 (2003) (explaining clearly the application of qualifying criteria for Fourth Convention protected persons status).

21. 1949 Geneva Convention IV, *supra* note 3, art. 13. The "whole of the populations of the countries in conflict" receives the protections of Part II of the Fourth Convention. *Id.* Part II protects access to medical treatment as well as shelter from the effects of hostilities through hospital and safety zones. *Id.*, arts. 14–26.

22. *Id.*, art. 4. The Fourth Convention leaves protection of nationals of neutral States largely to the diplomatic system. *See* GENEVA CONVENTION IV COMMENTARY, *supra* note 14, at 48.

23. 1949 Geneva Convention IV, *supra* note 3, arts. 78–79. The Fourth Convention prescribes a detailed regime of treatment obligations for interned protected persons in Part IV. *Id.*, arts. 79–141.

24. Regulations Respecting the Laws and Customs of War on Land art. 3, annexed to Convention No. IV Respecting the Laws and Customs of War on Land, Oct. 18, 1907, 36 Stat. 2277, 1 Bevans 631 (distinguishing, within the armed forces, combatants from non-combatants such as chaplains and medical personnel) [hereinafter 1907 Hague Convention IV].

25. *See* Additional Protocol I, *supra* note 4, arts. 46–47; Richard R. Baxter, *So-Called "Unprivileged Belligerency": Spies, Guerrillas, and Saboteurs*, 28 BRITISH YEARBOOK OF INTERNATIONAL LAW 323 (1951). The status of unprivileged belligerent or unlawful combatant has provoked significant legal debate. A strong textual case can be made that no such separate, treaty-based status exists. *See* Mark Maxwell & Sean Watts, *Unlawful Enemy Combatant: Status, Theory of Culpability, or Neither?*, JOURNAL OF INTERNATIONAL CRIMINAL JUSTICE 19 (2007) (concluding U.S. use of the term "unlawful enemy combatant" reflects legal convenience more than objective assessment of the existing laws and customs of war); Dörmann, *supra* note 20, at 46–47 (emphasizing that neither term appears in the 1949 Geneva Conventions). *But see* DINSTEIN, *supra* note 19, at 33–36 (defending, in one of the most respected texts on the *jus in bello*, recognition of the class of unlawful combatant).

26. *See, e.g.*, *Prosecutor v. Tadić*, *supra* note 12, ¶¶ 164–69 (announcing surprising legal findings on Fourth Geneva Convention protected-person status).

27. *See* UNITED KINGDOM MINISTRY OF DEFENCE, THE MANUAL OF THE LAW OF ARMED CONFLICT ¶ 15.6.1 (2004) (stating, "The law relating to internal armed conflict does not deal specifically with combatant status or membership of the armed forces") [hereinafter UK LOAC MANUAL]; SOLIS, *supra* note 4, at 191 (observing, "[T]here are no 'combatants,' lawful or otherwise, in Common Article 3 conflicts").

28. Additional Protocol II, *supra* note 17, art. 5.

29. *See* Additional Protocol I, *supra* note 4 , art. 43(2) (stating, "Members of the armed forces of a Party to a conflict . . . are combatants, that is to say, they have the right to participate directly in hostilities") (parenthetical omitted).

30. Codified protection of prisoners and the status of prisoner of war date back to some of the earliest multilateral law-of-war instruments. *See* Lieber Code, *supra* note 5, arts. 53–56; PROJECT OF AN INTERNATIONAL DECLARATION CONCERNING THE LAWS AND CUSTOMS OF WAR arts. 23–34 (Aug. 27, 1874), *available at* http://www.icrc.org/ihl.nsf/INTRO/135?OpenDocument; Institute of International Law, *Oxford Manual 1880: The Laws of War on Land*, *reprinted in* Schindler & Toman, *supra* note 5, at 29, arts. 61–72; Hague Convention (II) Respecting the Laws and Customs of War on Land with Annex of Regulations arts. 4–20, July 29, 1899, 32 Stat. 1803 1 Bevans 247 [hereinafter 1899 Hague Convention II].

31. Not all prisoners of war enjoy combatant immunity. For instance, while "war correspondents, supply contractors, and members of labor units" who accompany the armed forces qualify for prisoner-of-war status, few if any detaining powers would be likely to afford combatant immunity in the event they took a direct part in hostilities. 1949 Geneva Convention III, *supra* note 3, art. 4.A(4) This view accords with the inclusion of these groups in the law-of-war definition of civilian. *See* Additional Protocol I, *supra* note 4, art. 50.

32. Writers have adopted the term "fighters" to describe persons taking direct part in NIAC hostilities, whether government or rebel. *See, e.g.*, MICHAEL N. SCHMITT, CHARLES H.B. GARRAWAY & YORAM DINSTEIN, THE MANUAL ON THE LAW OF NON-INTERNATIONAL ARMED CONFLICT WITH COMMENTARY ¶ 1.1.2 (2006) [hereinafter NIAC MANUAL]; I CUSTOMARY INTERNATIONAL HUMANITARIAN LAW rule 6 (Jean-Marie Henckaerts & Louise Doswald-Beck eds., 2005) (omitting entirely reference to non-international armed conflict in rules governing "Combatants and Prisoners-of-War") [hereinafter CUSTOMARY INTERNATIONAL HUMANITARIAN LAW].

33. *See* NIAC MANUAL, *supra* note 32, ¶ 3.6 (outlining minimal protections afforded to "[p]ersons whose liberty has been restricted"); UK LOAC MANUAL, *supra* note 27, ¶ 15.6.3; Michael N. Schmitt, *The Status of Opposition Fighters in a Non-International Armed Conflict*, which is Chapter VI in this volume, at 119.

34. *See* UK LOAC MANUAL, *supra* note 27, ¶¶ 15.34–15.56 (reviewing rules added to the law of NIAC by Protocol II without mention of prisoner-of-war status).

35. Additional Protocol II, *supra* note 17, art. 5. Article 6 echoes this reluctance, referring to "those deprived of their liberty for reasons related to the armed conflict." *Id.*, art. 6.

36. *See* 1949 Geneva Convention III, *supra* note 3, art. 3; Additional Protocol II, *supra* note 17, art. 5. An increasing number of international lawyers view international human rights law (IHRL) as applicable or at least complementary to the law of war. *See* RENE PROVOST, INTERNATIONAL HUMAN RIGHTS AND HUMANITARIAN LAW (2002); Franoçise J. Hampson, *The Relationship between International Humanitarian Law and Human Rights Law from the Perspective of a Human Rights Treaty Body*, 90 INTERNATIONAL REVIEW OF THE RED CROSS 549 (2008); Cordula Droege, *Elective Affinities? Human Rights and Humanitarian Law*, 90 INTERNATIONAL REVIEW OF THE RED CROSS 501 (2008); Dietrich Schindler, *Human Rights and Humanitarian Law*, 31 AMERICAN UNIVERSITY LAW REVIEW 935 (1982). Particularly given the territorial nature of NIAC, many would regard IHRL as a source of treatment obligations in NIAC. Nonetheless, this chapter focuses exclusively on protections derived from the law of war.

37. By comparison, in IAC armed groups not part of States' regular armed forces can gain prisoner-of-war status for their members by complying with criteria enumerated in the Third Geneva Convention: belonging to a party, submitting to a command hierarchy, bearing arms openly, wearing distinctive insignia and observing the laws of war. *See* 1949 Geneva Convention III, *supra* note 3, art. 4.A(2).

38. *See* EVE LA HAYE, WAR CRIMES IN INTERNAL ARMED CONFLICTS ch. 5, 256–70 (2008) (outlining domestic prosecutions arising from NIACs); NIAC MANUAL, *supra* note 32, ¶ 3.7 (outlining due process obligations applicable to domestic prosecution for "crime[s] related to the hostilities"); THE HANDBOOK OF INTERNATIONAL HUMANITARIAN LAW ¶ 1202.3 (Dieter Fleck ed., 2008) (noting States' interest in prosecution of insurgents' acts of murder and destruction in NIAC) [hereinafter HANDBOOK OF INTERNATIONAL HUMANITARIAN LAW].

39. Additional Protocol II, *supra* note 17, art. 6(5). Commentary interprets the clause as intended to promote general reconciliation rather than to recognize or effectuate any right to immunity or amnesty held by captured fighters. COMMENTARY ON THE ADDITIONAL PROTOCOLS OF 8 JUNE 1977 TO THE GENEVA CONVENTIONS OF 12 AUGUST 1949, at 1402 (Yves Sandoz, Christophe Swinarski & Bruno Zimmermann eds., 1987) [hereinafter COMMENTARY ON THE ADDITIONAL PROTOCOLS].

40. The most widely applicable standard for combatant status is found among select provisions of the Third Geneva Convention's categories of prisoner of war. In an ironic twist, the LOAC definition of civilian identifies four categories of prisoner of war as constituting the combatant class in IAC. *See* Additional Protocol I, *supra* note 4, art. 50. For its States parties, Additional Protocol I refines in Articles 43 and 44 the criteria for combatant status. Combatant status under Protocol I is commonly understood to require only affiliation with an armed force or group which employs a system of discipline enforcing compliance with LOAC and carrying one's arms openly in attack. *See id.* The Protocol's elimination of the criterion of distinctive insignia or a uniform has been widely criticized. *See* Douglas Feith, *Law in the Service of Terror—The Strange Case of Additional Protocol I*, 1 THE NATIONAL INTEREST 36 (1985); Guy B. Roberts, *The New Rules for Waging War: The Case Against Ratification of Additional Protocol I*, 26 VIRGINIA JOURNAL OF INTERNATIONAL LAW 109 (1985); Abraham Sofaer, *Terrorism and the Law*, 64 FOREIGN AFFAIRS 901 (1986). Although a persistent objector to some of Additional Protocol I, the United States regards significant portions of the Protocol as reflective of customary law. *See* Memorandum from W. Hayes Parks et al. to Mr. John H. McNeill, Assistant General Counsel, Office of the Secretary of Defense, 1977 Protocols Additional to the Geneva Conventions:

Customary International Law Implications (May 9, 1986), *reprinted in* THE JUDGE ADVOCATE GENERAL'S LEGAL CENTER & SCHOOL, LAW OF WAR DOCUMENTARY SUPPLEMENT 388, 389 (Sean Watts ed., 2006); Michael J. Matheson, *Remarks in Session One: The United States Position on the Relation of Customary International Law to the 1977 Protocols Additional to the 1949 Geneva Conventions*, 2 AMERICAN UNIVERSITY JOURNAL OF INTERNATIONAL LAW & POLICY 419, 425 (1987).

41. UK LOAC MANUAL, *supra* note 27, ch. 15; OFFICE OF THE JUDGE ADVOCATE GENERAL, CHIEF OF DEFENCE STAFF, JOINT DOCTRINE MANUAL, LAW OF ARMED CONFLICT AT THE OPERATIONAL AND TACTICAL LEVELS ch. 17 (2001) [hereinafter CANADIAN LOAC MANUAL]. The German law of armed conflict manual does not treat NIAC in detail. *See* FEDERAL MINISTRY OF DEFENCE, FEDERAL REPUBLIC OF GERMANY, *HUMANITÄRES VÖLKERRECHT IN BEWAFFNETEN KONFLIKTEN – HANDBUCH* ¶¶ 210–11 (1992). The manual simply instructs German armed forces to apply "fundamental humanitarian provisions of international law embodied in the four 1949 Geneva Conventions (Common Art. 3), the 1954 Cultural Property Convention (Art. 19) and the 1977 Additional Protocol II" to NIAC. *Id.*, ¶ 211. Comments by a prominent German legal expert note that the International Criminal Tribunal for the former Yugoslavia interpreted this paragraph as a statement equating the law of IAC and NIAC. Wolff Heintschel von Heinegg, *The German Manual*, *in* INTERNATIONAL PEACE RESEARCH INSTITUTE, FORUM FOR INTERNATIONAL CRIMINAL AND HUMANITARIAN LAW, NATIONAL MILITARY MANUALS ON THE LAW OF ARMED CONFLICT 112 (Nobuo Hayashi ed., 2d ed. 2010), *available at* http://www.fichl.org/publication-series (citing International Criminal Tribunal for the former Yugoslavia, *Tadic Jurisdiction Decision* ¶ 118). The UK *Manual on the Law of Armed Conflict* includes an interesting historical notation regarding French practice in Algeria. While French forces unsurprisingly tried and executed Algerian rebels without according prisoner-of-war status, the French also expected opposition fighters to accord prisoner-of-war status to captured French soldiers. UK LOAC MANUAL, *supra*, ¶ 15.4.1 n.21. The current U.S. law-of-war manual includes only a single paragraph on "civil war," the bulk of which merely reprints Common Article 3 of the 1949 Geneva Conventions. Department of the Army, FM 27-10, The Law of Land Warfare ¶ 11 (1956). A closely held draft of a new U.S. manual is currently under review by executive branch agencies.

42. UK LOAC MANUAL, *supra* note 27, ¶ 15.6.1; CANADIAN LOAC MANUAL, *supra* note 41, ¶ 1706.1.

43. U.N. Charter art. 2(7). Article 2(7) states, "Nothing in the present Charter shall authorize the United Nations to intervene in matters which are essentially within the domestic jurisdiction of any state. . . ." *Id.*

44. *See* UK LOAC MANUAL, *supra* note 27, ¶ 15.6.1.

45. A prominent law-of-war handbook asserts, "All states have legal frameworks which privilege their own police and armed forces as against insurgents who oppose them." HANDBOOK OF INTERNATIONAL HUMANITARIAN LAW, *supra* note 38, ¶ 1202.2. Title 10 of the United States Code provides legal authority for and organizes the U.S. armed forces. Title 50 organizes employees of U.S. federal intelligence agencies. Recent operations, particularly those carried out against global terrorist networks, have blurred the lines of authority between Title 10 and Title 50 agencies. Debate has also developed over other agencies' participation in national security activities, such as the U.S. Drug Enforcement Agency's work in counterterrorism operations. *See* Johnny Dwyer, *The DEA's Terrorist Hunters: Overreaching Their Authority?*, TIME.COM (Aug. 8, 2011), http://www.time.com/time/world/article/0,8599,2087220,00.html.

46. *See* James Glanz & Alissa J. Rubin, *From Errand to Fatal Shot to Hail of Fire to 17 Deaths*, NEW YORK TIMES, Oct. 3, 2007 at A1.

47. *See* Moshe Schwartz, Congressional Research Service, *The Department of Defense's Use of Private Security Contractors in Afghanistan and Iraq: Background, Analysis, and Options for Congress* (2011).

48. Several international criminal tribunals wield jurisdiction over the conduct of NIAC. *See e.g.*, Rome Statute of the International Criminal Court art. 8(2)(c)–(f), July 17, 1998, 2187 U.N.T.S. 90 (amended Jan. 16, 2002) [hereinafter Rome Statute].

49. *See* GENEVA CONVENTION IV COMMENTARY, *supra* note 14, at 35.

50. *See* J. Ricou Heaton, *Civilians at War: Reexamining the Status of Civilians Accompanying the Armed Forces*, 57 AIR FORCE LAW REVIEW 155 (2005); Michael N. Schmitt, *Wired Warfare: Computer Network Attack and the* Jus in Bello, *in* COMPUTER NETWORK ATTACK AND INTERNATIONAL LAW 187, 198 (Michael N. Schmitt & Brian T. O'Donnell eds., 2002) (Vol. 76, U.S. Naval War College International Law Studies). *But see* Sean Watts, *Combatant Status and Computer Network Attack*, 50 VIRGINIA JOURNAL OF INTERNATIONAL LAW 392 (2009) (arguing that perceived limits on types of persons and agencies States may employ in computer network attack are overstated).

51. *See* W. Hays Parks, *Special Forces' Wear of Non-Standard Uniforms*, 4 CHICAGO JOURNAL OF INTERNATIONAL LAW 493, 508–11 (2003) (discussing the criteria for prisoner-of-war status and distinguishing entitlement to or loss of status from criminality).

52. LOUIS HENKIN, HOW NATIONS BEHAVE 253 (1968) (observing that "most states obey most law most of the time").

53. *See* Sean Watts, *Reciprocity and the Law of War*, 50 HARVARD INTERNATIONAL LAW JOURNAL 365 (2009).

54. Adam Roberts, *The Equal Application of the Laws of War: A Principle under Pressure*, 90 INTERNATIONAL REVIEW OF THE RED CROSS 931 (2008).

55. *See* GENEVA CONVENTION IV COMMENTARY, *supra* note 14, at 6–7. Jean Pictet observes, "Without [the guarantee] neither Article 3, nor any other Article in its place, would ever have been adopted." *Id.* at 44.

56. *See* 1949 Geneva Convention IV, *supra* note 3, art. 3.

57. *See* Waldemar Solf, *The Status of Combatants in Non-International Armed Conflicts under Domestic Law and Transnational Practice*, 33 AMERICAN UNIVERSITY LAW REVIEW 53, 57–58 (1983) (tracing recognition of combatant status to Belli, Grotius, Pufendorf and Vattel).

58. Additional Protocol I, *supra* note 4, art. 51(3). Article 51(3) states, "Civilians shall enjoy the protection afforded by this section, unless and for such time as they take a direct part in hostilities."

59. COMMENTARY ON THE ADDITIONAL PROTOCOLS, *supra* note 39, at 514.

60. *See* DINSTEIN, *supra* note 19, at 33 (noting lawful combatants' "license to kill").

61. Early commentators viewed skeptically claims that international law could authorize or "give positive sanction to" States to do anything. 2 JOHN WESTLAKE, INTERNATIONAL LAW 52 (1907) (explaining that rules of war "are always restrictive, never permissive"). *See also* Roberts, *supra* note 54, at 935 (rejecting that international law grants belligerents the "right" to participate in hostilities); Baxter, *supra* note 25, at 323–324 (arguing, with characteristic prescience, a similar point prior to the codification of Additional Protocol I).

62. Ex parte Quirin, 317 U.S. 1, 30–31 (1942) (finding in international laws of war support for the concept of unlawful combatancy); Military Commissions Act of 2009, 10 U.S.C. § 950t(15) (2009) (defining, for purposes of U.S. military commissions, the crime of murder in violation of the law of war, including the otherwise lawful killing of a "privileged belligerent").

63. *See* George J. Andreopoulos, *The Age of National Liberation Movements*, *in* THE LAWS OF WAR: CONSTRAINTS ON WARFARE IN THE WESTERN WORLD 191 (Michael Howard, George J. Andreopoulos & Mark R. Shulman eds., 1994). Andreopoulos observes, "The overt politicization of the symbols of recognition, whether dealing with rebellion, insurgency, or belligerency, led to the disappearance of the concern with correlating status with facts. . . ." *Id.* at 193.

64. On June 6, 1977, the fifty-second plenary meeting of States rejected a committee proposal to include reference to, and definitions of, military objectives into what became Article 13 of Protocol II. IV OFFICIAL RECORDS OF THE DIPLOMATIC CONFERENCE ON THE REAFFIRMATION AND DEVELOPMENT OF INTERNATIONAL HUMANITARIAN LAW APPLICABLE IN ARMED CONFLICTS, GENEVA 1974–1977, at 71 (1978). Consequently, Additional Protocol II includes no provision on military objective.

65. *See, e.g.*, II-B FINAL RECORD OF THE DIPLOMATIC CONFERENCE OF GENEVA OF 1949, at 9–15 (William S. Hein & Co. 2004) (1949) [hereinafter 1949 GENEVA CONFERENCE FINAL RECORD]; VII OFFICIAL RECORDS OF THE DIPLOMATIC CONFERENCE ON THE REAFFIRMATION AND DEVELOPMENT OF INTERNATIONAL HUMANITARIAN LAW APPLICABLE IN ARMED CONFLICTS, GENEVA 1974–1977, at 60–65 (1978) (summarizing States' divergent views on the scope of draft Protocol II expressed in Plenary Session).

66. II-B 1949 GENEVA CONFERENCE FINAL RECORD, *supra* note 65, at 129.

67. CULLEN, *supra* note 2, at 41–42.

68. *Id.* at 98, 101.

69. *See* COMMENTARY ON THE ADDITIONAL PROTOCOLS, *supra* note 39, at 1350 (noting that the material application of Protocol II does not affect that of Common Article 3). The Protocol's requirement that opposition groups control territory and its exclusion of conflicts solely between such groups excludes armed conflicts that Common Article 3 would cover. Additional Protocol II, *supra* note 17, art. 1.

70. At the diplomatic conference that produced the Additional Protocols, Norway failed in its attempt to persuade States to drop the distinction between IAC and NIAC. *See* Hans Peter Gasser, *International Non-International Armed Conflicts: Case Studies of Afghanistan, Kampuchea, and Lebanon*, 31 AMERICAN UNIVERSITY LAW REVIEW 911, 912 (1982) (citing 5 DIPLOMATIC CONFERENCE ON THE REAFFIRMATION AND DEVELOPMENT OF INTERNATIONAL HUMANITARIAN LAW APPLICABLE IN ARMED CONFLICTS, OFFICIAL RECORDS, SUMMARY RECORD 91–99 CDDH/SR.10 (1978)).

71. See discussion supported by notes 49–52.

72. HEADQUARTERS, DEPARTMENT OF THE ARMY & HEADQUARTERS, MARINE CORPS COMBAT DEVELOPMENT COMMAND, FM 3-24/MCWP 3-33.5, COUNTERINSURGENCY ¶ 1-2 (2006). The Field Manual notes, "*Counterinsurgency* is military, paramilitary, political, economic, psychological, and civic actions taken by a government to defeat insurgency" (citing Joint Chiefs of Staff, Joint Publication 1-02, Department of Defense Dictionary of Military and Associated Terms 82 (Aug. 15, 2011)) (emphasis in original).

73. *See* Nicholas Schmidle, *Getting Bin Laden*, NEWYORKER.COM (Aug. 8, 2011), http://www.newyorker.com/reporting/2011/08/08/110808fa_fact_schmidle?currentPage=all.

74. *See id.*

75. *CIA Chief Panetta: Obama Made "Gutsy" Decision on Bin Laden Raid*, PBS NEWSHOUR, May 3, 2011, http://www.pbs.org/newshour/bb/terrorism/jan-june11/panetta_05-03.html.

76. *Id.*

77. *See* Hamdan v. Rumsfeld, 548 U.S. 557, 630–31 (2006) (holding that U.S. operations against al-Qaeda constituted NIAC for purposes of application of Common Article 3 of the 1949 Geneva Conventions).

78. Scott Shane, *C.I.A. Is Disputed on Civilian Toll in Drone Strikes*, NEW YORK TIMES, Aug. 12, 2011, at A1, *available at* http://www.nytimes.com/2011/08/12/world/asia/12drones.html?_r=1&pagewanted=print (relating U.S. rebuttals to allegations of widespread civilian casualties in CIA drone strikes in Pakistan); Charli Carpenter & Lina Shaikhouni, *Don't Fear the Reaper*, FOREIGN POLICY (June 7, 2011), http://www.foreignpolicy.com/articles/2011/06/07/dont_fear_the_reaper (noting that a CIA-led drone attack in Pakistan "arguably violates the rules on lawful combat in the Geneva Conventions").

79. Peter Bergen & Katherine Tiedemann, *The Year of the Drone: An Analysis of U.S. Drone Strikes in Pakistan, 2004–2010*, NEW AMERICA FOUNDATION (Feb. 24, 2010), http://counterterrorism.newamerica.net/sites/newamerica.net/files/policydocs/bergentiedemann2.pdf.

80. *See* Schmidle, *supra* note 73 (relating President Barack Obama's expansion of the CIA.'s classified drone program); Charlie Savage, *U.N. Official Set to Ask U.S. to End C.I.A. Drone Strikes*, NYTIMES.COM (May 27, 2010), http://www.nytimes.com/2010/05/28/world/asia/28drones.html.

81. J.R. Wilson, *UAVs: A Worldwide Roundup, More and More Countries Are Developing or Cooperating on UAVs as Their Numbers and Versatility Grow*, AEROSPACE AMERICA (June 2003), *available at* http://www.aiaa.org/aerospace/Article.cfm?issuetocid=365. Israel used UAVs in the 2006 conflict in Lebanon. *See* Larry Dickerson, *New Respect for UAVs*, AVIATION WEEK & SPACE TECHNOLOGY, Jan. 26, 2009, at 94. UAVs were also used in 2008 between Russia and Georgia in the South Ossetia region. *Id.*

82. *See* Amitai Etzioni, *Unmanned Aircraft Systems: The Moral and Legal Case*, JOINT FORCE QUARTERLY, May 2010, at 66, *available at* http://www.ndu.edu/press/lib/images/jfq-57/etzioni.pdf; Kenneth Anderson, *Predators over Pakistan*, THE WEEKLY STANDARD, Mar. 8, 2010, at 24 (defending the Obama administration's global use of CIA. and military drone strikes against terrorists); Mary Ellen O'Connell, *Flying Blind: U.S. Combat Drones Operate Outside International Law*, AMERICA (Mar. 15, 2010), http://www.americamagazine.org/content/article.cfm?article_id=12179.

83. *See* Savage, *supra* note 80 (noting that Philip Alston as United Nations author of a report on U.S. drone practices agreed that it is "not per se illegal" for CIA. operatives to fire drone missiles); Report of the Special Rapporteur on Extrajudicial, Summary or Arbitrary Executions, *Study on Targeted Killings*, ¶¶ 70–71, Human Rights Council, U.N. Doc. A/HRC/14/24/Add.6 (May 28, 2010) (by Philip Alston), *available at* www2.ohchr.org/english/bodies/hrcouncil/docs/14session/A.HRC.14.24.Add6.pdf (noting illegality of civilian participation in hostilities is not addressed by IHL, merely consequences for purposes of targeting and lack of immunity). Matt Cover, *House Committee Questions Legality of Drone Strikes against Terrorists*, CNS NEWS (Apr. 28, 2010), http://www.cnsnews.com/node/64916 (featuring statements by Professor O'Connell that a drone strike is only legal when used by military personnel in a combat situation where there is an ongoing armed conflict in which the United States is engaged and Professor Glazier, in contrast, stating that the "United States was engaged in an armed conflict with al Qaeda terrorists around the world" and "international legal principles . . . justified the use of drones to kill terrorists in Afghanistan, Iraq and beyond").

84. DEPARTMENT OF THE ARMY, FM 3-07, STABILITY OPERATIONS ¶¶ 1-11–1-13 (2008) [hereinafter FM 3-07 STABILITY OPERATIONS].

85. General Charles Krulak coined the term "three-block war" to describe complex conflicts calling on armed forces to perform a range of missions simultaneously. General Charles C. Krulak,

The Strategic Corporal: Leadership in the Three Block War, MARINES MAGAZINE, Jan. 1999, at 28. Krulak imagined soldiers in a single urban area engaged in high-intensity combat on one block, conducting humanitarian operations on the next, and separating warring factions on a third. *Id.*

86. Department of Defense, DoD Directive 3000.05, Military Support for Stability, Security, Transition, and Reconstruction (SSTR) Operations (2005).

87. *Id.*

88. FM 3-07 STABILITY OPERATIONS, *supra* note 84, app. A.

89. *See* NATHAN HODGE, ARMED HUMANITARIANS (2011) (describing recent U.S. experience with nation-building and challenges faced by military leaders adapting to the new mission set).

90. DEPARTMENT OF DEFENSE, DEPARTMENT OF DEFENSE STRATEGY FOR OPERATING IN CYBERSPACE 5 (2011). The *Strategy* identifies "treat[ing] cyberspace as an operational domain to organize, train and equip so that DoD can take full advantage of cyberspace's potential." *Id. See also* DEPARTMENT OF DEFENSE, QUADRENNIAL DEFENSE REVIEW 37 (2010) (which observes, "Although it is a man-made domain, cyberspace is now as relevant a domain for DoD activities as the naturally occurring domains of land, sea, air, and space"); SECRETARY OF STATE FOR THE HOME DEPARTMENT, CONTEST: THE UNITED KINGDOM'S STRATEGY FOR COUNTERING TERRORISM 41 (2011) (predicting increases in terrorists' use of cyber attack and directing counterterrorism assets to integrate responses into planning).

91. The extent and nature of civilian participation in cyber operations, including attack, are difficult to discern. States guard their cyber practices and capabilities closely. Some reliable indications exist, however, that support the conclusion that the United States uses civilians in aspects of cyber operations approaching or even constituting attack. *See* Watts, *supra* note 50, at 407–10 (concluding from public statements and executive branch budget requests that civilians likely play significant roles in U.S. cyber operations).

92. *See* Hadeel al-Shalchi & Ryan Lucas, *Qaddafi Defiant in the Face of Allied Strikes*, THE CHRISTIAN SCIENCE MONITOR (Mar. 19, 2011), http://www.csmonitor.com/World/Middle-East/2011/0319/Qaddafi-defiant-in-the-face-of-allied-strikes; Hadeel al-Shalchi & Ryan Lucas, *Allies Pound Libya*, CHICAGO SUN-TIMES, Mar. 20, 2011, at 3 (relating British, French and U.S. strikes against government forces in Libya).

93. Authors have written on the topic of conflict characterization and conflict parsing in particular. *See* Carina Bergal, *The Mexican Drug War: The Case for Non-International Armed Conflict Classification*, 34 FORDHAM INTERNATIONAL LAW JOURNAL 1042 (2011); Corn & Jensen, *supra* note 2.

94. *See* Paul Schemm & Zeina Karam, *Gadhafi Drives Rebels from One of Last Strongholds*, CHICAGO SUN-TIMES, Mar. 14, 2011, at 16; Donald Macintyre, *Gaddafi's Iron Fist Won't Help Him Keep a Grip on a Divided Nation*, THE INDEPENDENT, Mar. 12, 2011, at 24; Paul Schemm & Maggie Michael, *Gadhafi Escalates War on Rebels*, CHICAGO SUN-TIMES, Mar. 7, 2011, at 4; David D. Kirkpatrick & Kareem Fahim, *Khadafy Forces Hit Key City, Lose Port; Residents Describe Massacre by Army*, BOSTON GLOBE, Mar. 6, 2011, at 1; Leila Fadel & Anthony Faiola, *Khadafy's Forces Assault Rebels, Protestors*, BOSTON GLOBE, Mar. 5, 2011, at 3 (reporting firing on demonstrators); Jason Koutsoukis, *Gaddafi's Forces Unleashed on Rebels*, SYDNEY MORNING HERALD, Mar. 3, 2011, at 1 (reporting alleged government use of mercenaries); Maggie Michael & Paul Schemm, *Gadhafi Forces Strike Back*, CHICAGO SUN-TIMES, Feb. 25, 2011, at 25.

95. Michael N. Schmitt, *Wings Over Libya: The No-Fly Zone in Legal Perspective*, 36 YALE INTERNATIONAL LAW JOURNAL ONLINE 45 (2011), *available at* http://www.yjil.org/online/volume-36-spring-2011/wings-over-libya-the-no-fly-zone-in-legal-perspective; Michael W. Lewis,

How Should the Conflict in Libya Be Categorized?, OPINIO JURIS (Mar. 30, 2011), http://opiniojuris.org/2011/03/30/how-should-the-conflict-in-libya-be-categorized/; Kenneth Anderson, *Humanitarian Intervention in Libya*, OPINIO JURIS (Mar. 7, 2011), http://opiniojuris.org/2011/03/07/humanitarian-intervention-in-libya-follow-up-post/; Patrick O'Donnell, *Humanitarian (i.e., military and/or otherwise) Intervention in Libya?*, RATIO JURIS (Feb. 24, 2011), http://ratiojuris.blogspot.com/2011/02/humanitarian-ie-military-and-otherwise.html (summarizing early blog posts concerning the Libyan situation).

96. *See* Tamas Hoffman, *Squaring the Circle? – International Humanitarian Law and Transnational Armed Conflicts*, *in* RULES AND INSTITUTIONS OF INTERNATIONAL HUMANITARIAN LAW PUT TO THE TEST OF RECENT ARMED CONFLICTS 217 (Michael J. Matheson & Djamchid Momtaz eds., 2010); Geoffrey S. Corn, *Transnational Armed Conflict: A "Principled" Approach to the Regulation of Counter-Terror Combat Operations*, 42 ISRAEL LAW REVIEW 46 (2009); Andreas Paulus & Mindia Vashakmadze, *Asymmetrical War and the Notion of Armed Conflict – A Tentative Conceptualization*, 91 INTERNATIONAL REVIEW OF THE RED CROSS 95 (2009); Marco Sassoli, *Transnational Armed Groups and International Humanitarian Law*, Program on Humanitarian Policy and Conflict Research, Harvard University, Occasional Paper Series No. 6 (Winter 2006), *available at* http://www.hpcrresearch.org/sites/default/files/publications/OccasionalPaper6.pdf (expressing skepticism at the application of the law of war to what are in the author's opinion legally novel groups).

97. *See* U.N. Charter art. 2(7). Part of the Charter's international security regime, Article 2(7) states, "Nothing in the present Charter shall authorize the United Nations to intervene in matters which are essentially within the domestic jurisdiction of any state. . . ." *Id.*

98. The term "networked cyber attack" is intended to distinguish attacks using the Internet or other electronic communications as a means of delivery of malware from attacks delivered manually or from the physical location of the target computer. The latter would be quite possible to conduct within the territorial boundaries of a single State—for instance, as part of a NIAC.

99. Charles Clover, *Kremlin-backed Group Behind Estonia Cyber Blitz*, FINANCIAL TIMES (Mar. 11, 2009), http://www.ft.com/cms/s/0/57536d5a-0ddc-11de-8ea3-0000779fd2ac.html.

100. *See* Alan Travis, *Counter-Terrorism Strategy Driven by "Cyberjihad" Threat*, THE GUARDIAN (London), July 12, 2011, *available at* http://www.guardian.co.uk//politics/2011/jul/12/counter-terrorism-strategy-cyberjihad-threat/print?mobile-redirect=false.

101. *See* Rain Ottis, *From Pitchforks to Laptops: Volunteers in Cyber Conflicts*, *in* CONFERENCE ON CYBER CONFLICT, PROCEEDINGS 2010, at 97 (Christian Czosseck & Karlis Podins eds., 2010); TECHNOLOGY, POLICY, LAW, AND ETHICS REGARDING U.S. ACQUISITION AND USE OF CYBER-ATTACK CAPABILITIES 2-2 (William A. Owens, Kenneth W. Dam & Herbert S. Lin eds., 2009).

102. Resort to the object and purpose of international law norms is widely accepted as a means of resolving ambiguity, particularly among continental European international lawyers and jurists. The term appears in the widely ratified Convention on Treaties. Vienna Convention on the Law of Treaties art. 31, May 23, 1969, 1155 U.N.T.S. 331.

103. *See* INTERNATIONAL AND OPERATIONAL LAW DEPARTMENT, THE JUDGE ADVOCATE GENERAL'S SCHOOL, U.S. ARMY, LAW OF WAR HANDBOOK 166 (2004).

104. A.P.V. ROGERS, LAW OF THE BATTLEFIELD 7 (1996).

105. W. Hays Parks, *Air War and the Law of War*, 32 AIR FORCE LAW REVIEW 1, 4 (1990).

106. Lieber Code, *supra* note 5, art. 22. The nearly contemporaneous St. Petersburg Declaration of 1868 stated similarly, "[T]he only legitimate object which States should endeavor to accomplish during war is to weaken the military forces of the enemy." Declaration Renouncing the Use, in Time of War, of Explosive Projectiles under 400 Grammes Weight, Dec. 11, 1868, 138 Consol. T.S. 297, *reprinted in* Schindler & Toman, *supra* note 5, at 91, 92.

107. "In order to ensure respect and protection of the civilian population and civilian objects, the Parties to the conflict shall at all times distinguish between the civilian population and combatants and between civilian objects and military objectives and accordingly shall direct their operations only against military objectives." Additional Protocol I, *supra* note 4, art. 48.

108. Protocol I employs two prongs in the targeting aspect of distinction. First, combatants must direct their weapons only against specific military objectives. *Id.*, arts. 51(4)(a), 52(2). Second, targeting distinction requires that combatants not employ weapons that are inherently incapable of distinguishing between enemy combatants and civilians. *Id.*, art. 51(4)(b).

109. *See id.*, arts. 51(3) and 52.

110. *Id.*, art. 51(4).

111. *Id.*, art. 44(3).

112. *Id.*

113. *See* COMMENTARY ON THE ADDITIONAL PROTOCOLS, *supra* note 39, ¶ 1684. The *Commentary* notes that fifty speakers addressed Article 44 in debate and introduced thirteen amendments to the original proposal. *Id.* The United States does not consider Article 44(3) reflective of customary international law and specifically objects to it. *See* Matheson, *supra* note 40, at 419.

114. Additional Protocol I, *supra* note 4, art. 58.

115. COMMENTARY ON THE ADDITIONAL PROTOCOLS, *supra* note 39, ¶ 2244.

116. *See* Parks, *supra* note 105, at 112. Parks observes,

> Any claim of "humanitarian gain" is offset by the fact that the provisions contained in Protocol I shift the responsibility for the protection of the civilian population away from the host nation (which has custody over its civilian population, and which traditionally has borne the principal responsibility for the safety of the civilian population) almost exclusively onto an attacker.

Id.

117. *Id.*

118. States did not fully incorporate the Additional Protocol I expressions of distinction into the NIAC targeting provisions of Additional Protocol II. Protocol II protects the civilian population from "the dangers arising from military operations." Additional Protocol II, *supra* note 17, art. 13(1). The same article observes, "The civilian population as such, as well as individual civilians, shall not be the object of attack." *Id.*, art. 13(2). The article forbids attacks intended to terrorize the civilian population. *Id.* And finally, Additional Protocol II reproduces the Protocol I rule protecting civilians from intentional targeting "unless and for such time as they take a direct part in hostilities." *Id.*, art. 13(3). An influential manual on the law of armed conflict applicable to NIAC concludes, "Today, it is indisputable that the principle of distinction is customary international law for both international and non-international armed conflict." NIAC MANUAL, *supra* note 32, ¶ 1.2.2. Similarly, an ICRC-sponsored study of customary international law concludes distinction is a norm of customary international law in both IAC and NIAC. CUSTOMARY INTERNATIONAL HUMANITARIAN LAW, *supra* note 32, at 3.

119. Second Protocol to the Hague Convention of 1954 for the Protection of Cultural Property in the Event of Armed Conflict art. 22, Mar. 26, 1999, 2253 U.N.T.S. 212 [hereinafter 1999 Second Protocol to 1954 Hague Convention]. The base 1954 Hague Convention applies to international armed conflict and occupation. Convention for the Protection of Cultural Property in the Event of Armed Conflict art. 18, May 14, 1954, 249 U.N.T.S. 240. The 1999 Second Protocol expands application to "conflict not of an international character, occurring within the territory of one of the Parties." 1999 Second Protocol to 1954 Hague Convention, *supra*, art. 22.

120. Conventional Weapons Convention, *supra* note 10. In 2001, States parties amended the scope of material application of the Convention. Previously the Convention only applied to international armed conflict. Currently the scope of application reads:

> 1. This Convention and its annexed Protocols shall apply in the situations referred to in Article 2 common to the Geneva Conventions of 12 August 1949 for the Protection of War Victims, including any situation described in paragraph 4 of Article I of Additional Protocol I to these Conventions.
>
> 2. This Convention and its annexed Protocols shall also apply, in addition to situations referred to in paragraph 1 of this Article, to situations referred to in Article 3 common to the Geneva Conventions of 12 August 1949. This Convention and its annexed Protocols shall not apply to situations of internal disturbances and tensions, such as riots, isolated and sporadic acts of violence, and other acts of a similar nature, as not being armed conflicts.
>
> 3. In case of armed conflicts not of an international character occurring in the territory of one of the High Contracting Parties, each party to the conflict shall be bound to apply the prohibitions and restrictions of this Convention and its annexed Protocols.
>
> 4. Nothing in this Convention or its annexed Protocols shall be invoked for the purpose of affecting the sovereignty of a State or the responsibility of the Government, by all legitimate means, to maintain or re-establish law and order in the State or to defend the national unity and territorial integrity of the State.
>
> 5. Nothing in this Convention or its annexed Protocols shall be invoked as a justification for intervening, directly or indirectly, for any reason whatever, in the armed conflict or in the internal or external affairs of the High Contracting Party in the territory of which that conflict occurs.
>
> 6. The application of the provisions of this Convention and its annexed Protocols to parties to a conflict which are not High Contracting Parties that have accepted this Convention or its annexed Protocols, shall not change their legal status or the legal status of a disputed territory, either explicitly or implicitly.
>
> 7. The provisions of Paragraphs 2–6 of this Article shall not prejudice additional Protocols adopted after 1 January 2002, which may apply, exclude or modify the scope of their application in relation to this Article.

Id., art. 1.

121. Convention on the Prohibition of the Use, Stockpiling, Production and Transfer of Anti-Personnel Mines and on Their Destruction art. I.1(a), Sept. 18, 1997, 2056 U.N.T.S. 211.

122. Convention on the Prohibition of the Development, Production, Stockpiling and Use of Chemical Weapons and on Their Destruction art. I.1(b), Jan. 13, 1993, 1974 U.N.T.S. 45.

123. Convention on Cluster Munitions art. 1, May 30, 2008, 48 INTERNATIONAL LEGAL MATERIALS 357 (2008) (stating, "Each State Party undertakes never under any circumstances to use cluster munitions").

124. Rome Statute, *supra* note 48, art. 8(2)(c)–(f).

125. The criteria here referenced are derived from the Third Geneva Convention, Article 4, and are supposed by many to constitute criteria for privileged participation in hostilities. They include belonging to a party, being commanded by a person responsible for his subordinates, having a fixed distinctive sign, carrying arms openly and conducting operations in accordance with the law of war. 1949 Geneva Convention III, *supra* note 3, art. 4.

126. EMILY CRAWFORD, THE TREATMENT OF COMBATANTS AND INSURGENTS UNDER THE LAW OF ARMED CONFLICT 68 (2010).

127. Private security contractors may have been, however, intermingled with the civilian population inconsistent with the object of Additional Protocol I, Article 58 or a customary rule to similar effect.

128. WILLIAM H. BOOTHBY, WEAPONS AND THE LAW OF ARMED CONFLICT 2 (2008).

129. *See* Statute of the International Criminal Tribunal for the former Yugoslavia art. 3, amended Sept. 2009, *available at* http://www.icty.org/x/file/Legal%20Library/Statute/statute_sept09_en.pdf (criminalizing violations of the customs of war, including those applicable in NIAC); Statute of the International Criminal Tribunal for Rwanda art. 4, S.C. Res. 955, U.N. Doc. S/RES/955 (Nov. 8, 1994) (criminalizing violations of Common Article 3 of the 1949 Geneva Conventions and Protocol II).

130. Rome Statute, *supra* note 48, art. 17(1)(a).

131. *Prosecutor v. Tadić*, *supra* note 12, ¶ 97.

132. 1949 Geneva Convention III, *supra* note 3, art. 130.

133. 1949 Geneva Convention IV, *supra* note 3, art. 147.

134. CULLEN, *supra* note 2, at 56 (quoting Eldon Van C. Greenberg, *Law and the Conduct of the Algerian Revolution*, 11 HARVARD INTERNATIONAL LAW JOURNAL 37, 70–71 (1970)). In full, Greenberg's maxim addresses "revolutionary war." *Id.*

135. *See, e.g.*, *Prosecutor v. Tadić*, *supra* note 12, ¶¶ 97–98 (observing the distinction between law of IAC and that of NIAC as irrelevant).

136. The International Committee of the Red Cross prepared the first draft of what would become the 1949 Geneva Conventions. The most ambitious passage of the draft would have applied the Conventions to all conflicts. Article 2 of the Stockholm Draft would have made the Conventions applicable in their entirety not only to armed conflict and belligerent occupation between States parties, but also to "armed conflict not of an international character which may occur in the territory of one or more of the High Contracting Parties." Draft Convention for the Protection of Civilian Persons in Time of War, 1949, *reprinted in* I 1949 GENEVA CONFERENCE FINAL RECORD, *supra* note 65, at 113. States rejected the proposal. II-B 1949 GENEVA CONFERENCE FINAL RECORD, *supra*, at 41–43. Among other conceptual concerns, States noted that applying the Civilians Convention to insurgents would be problematic because the Convention relied on enemy nationality to define the civilian protected-person class. *Id.* at 41.

137. *See* DOCUMENTS ON THE LAWS OF WAR 9 (Adam Roberts & Richard Guelff eds., 3d ed. 2000) (citing Ministère des Affaires Étrangères, Report of the Second Subcommission in the official report, *Conférence Internationale de la Paix, La Haye, 18 Mai–29 Juillet 1899,* at 49–51 (Imprimerie Nationale, The Hague, 1899); WILLIAM I. HULL, THE TWO HAGUE CONFERENCES AND THEIR CONTRIBUTIONS TO INTERNATIONAL LAW 215–20 (1908)).

138. *See* CRAWFORD, *supra* note 126, at 29.

139. The references to "international law," to "the law of nations" and to "established custom" appear, respectively, in the Hague and Additional Protocol I versions of the Martens clause. 1899 Hague Convention II, *supra* note 30, pmbl.; 1907 Hague Convention IV, *supra* note 24, pmbl.; Additional Protocol I, *supra* note 4, art. 1(2).

140. The reference to "usages established among civilized peoples" appears in the 1899/1907 Hague expression of the clause, as well as the 1949 Geneva Convention expression. 1899 Hague Convention II, *supra* note 30, pmbl.; 1907 Hague Convention IV, *supra* note 24, pmbl.; 1949 Genva Convention IV, *supra* note 3, art. 158.

141. MICHAEL BOTHE ET AL., NEW RULES FOR VICTIMS OF ARMED CONFLICTS: COMMENTARY ON THE TWO 1977 PROTOCOLS ADDITIONAL TO THE GENEVA CONVENTIONS OF 1949, at 620 (1982).

142. *See* NIAC MANUAL, *supra* note 32; CUSTOMARY INTERNATIONAL HUMANITARIAN LAW, *supra* note 32; Eric Talbot Jensen, *Applying a Sovereign Agency Theory of the Law of Armed Conflict*, 12 CHICAGO JOURNAL OF INTERNATIONAL LAW 685 (2012).

143. *See* DINSTEIN, *supra* note 19, at 13, 16–20.

144. Describing British efforts to defeat Germany in North Africa, Winston Churchill is credited with the phrase, "Now this is not the end. It is not even the beginning of the end. But it is, perhaps, the end of the beginning." The Churchill Society, http://www.churchill-society-london.org.uk/EndoBegn.html (quoting Winston Churchill, *The End of the Beginning*, The Lord Mayor's Luncheon, Mansion House (Nov. 10, 1942)).

145. Anthea Roberts & Sandesh Sivakumaran, *Hybrid Sources of Law: Armed Groups and the Creation of International Law*, 37 YALE JOURNAL OF INTERNATIONAL LAW 107 (2011).

146. *See* Kal Raustiala & Anne-Marie Slaughter, *International Law, International Relations and Compliance*, *in* THE HANDBOOK OF INTERNATIONAL RELATIONS (Walter Carlsnaes, Thomas Risse & Beth A. Simmons eds., 2002); Michael W. Doyle & Geoffrey S. Carlson, *Silence of the Laws? Conceptions of International Relations and International Law in Hobbes, Kant, and Locke*, 46 COLUMBIA JOURNAL OF TRANSNATIONAL LAW 648 (2008); Eric A. Posner & Alan O. Sykes, *An Economic Analysis of State and Individual Responsibility under International Law*, 9 AMERICAN LAW & ECONOMICS REVIEW 72 (2007).

VIII

Toward a Limited Consensus on the Loss of Civilian Immunity in Non-International Armed Conflict: Making Progress through Practice

Stephen Pomper*

I. Introduction and Overview

A quick glance at the Geneva Conventions and their Additional Protocols is sufficient to reveal that the treaty rules governing the conduct of parties to a non-international armed conflict (NIAC) are less developed than those governing parties engaged in international armed conflicts (IACs). The total number of treaty provisions governing the latter outstrips the number governing the former by many dozens. While there is a range of historical and political reasons for this, there is also a core practical question that appears to have hampered the development of the law of armed conflict (LOAC) with respect to NIACs: How do we identify the specific actors to whom the rules in this area would apply?

Finding a satisfying answer to this question—which in a variety of ways requires us to translate from familiar concepts and categories in the world of international

* This article closely derives from a presentation given at the U.S. Naval War College on June 21, 2011 when the author was serving as the Assistant Legal Adviser for Political-Military Affairs at the U.S. Department of State. This article (like that presentation) was prepared in his personal capacity and does not necessarily represent the official views of the Department of State or the U.S. government.

armed conflict into the world of non-international armed conflict—is both very difficult and critically important. It is very difficult because in NIAC the amorphous, clandestine nature of the organizations with which we are dealing—and the often mercurial nature of the relationship between individuals and these organizations—challenges the instinctive desire that lawyers have to draw tight parallels between the clearly defined actors with which we are used to dealing in IAC (including uniformed soldiers fighting on behalf of often declared enemies with legal personality and right authority) and the murkier ones that we are required to deal with in NIAC. The parallels are there but frequently they are not as tidy as we want them to be, and operators will tell us that if we define categories too rigidly, we will impede their ability to meet the threat they are facing. Yet, if they are too loosely drawn, then there is a risk of sanctioning deprivations of life and liberty that will be criticized as illegitimate and arbitrary.

Unsurprisingly, efforts to develop a clearer answer to this question have been at the center of some very important legal conversations in recent years. In Guantanamo habeas litigation, the U.S. government has been required to articulate in numerous pleadings how to assess whether someone is "part of" al Qaeda, the Taliban or associated forces, and the U.S. federal courts (in particular the District of Columbia (D.C.) Circuit) have built up some jurisprudence in this area. There have also been efforts to synthesize expert opinion—notably, if not fully successfully, in the International Committee of the Red Cross's (ICRC's) *Interpretive Guidance*[1] that was released in 2009. Finally, and most significantly for purposes of the emergence of shared international norms, States have been talking to each other about their experience, some of which is of course shared experience, in places like Afghanistan, Iraq and Libya.

This article will touch briefly on the ways in which the conversation about when an individual loses protection from attack through membership in an organized armed group (and related questions of what it means to take direct part in hostilities) have developed in the course of the last several years. In so doing, it will underscore that the development of the law in this area remains for the time being largely in the hands of States, and, in particular, their executive branches. It will also give a sense of where like-minded States with which the U.S. government works particularly closely have reached consensus in this area, as well as identify some areas where there remains a range of views. To keep the scope of this exercise manageable, the paper will keep a narrow focus on the threshold for membership in organized armed groups and direct participation in hostilities on the non-State side of a NIAC. It will not address a number of important related questions that also have a bearing on the question of when individuals lose immunity from being made the object of attack in non-international armed conflict, including questions about the point at which armed violence can be deemed an armed conflict, the level of cohesion that is required in order to deem an organization an "organized armed group," the circumstances under which an organized armed group can be said to be engaged in armed conflict, the geographic scope of armed conflict and the circumstances in which legal rules outside the law of armed conflict may be relevant.

II. Guantanamo Litigation

When in June 2008 the Supreme Court decided in the *Boumediene* case[2] that Guantanamo detainees would have an opportunity to challenge the legality of their detention in U.S. federal court, without addressing the standard for who could be detained, it left the lower courts poised to engage in a sustained lawmaking exercise with potentially significant implications for the question of who forms part of a non-State organized armed group (like al Qaeda, the Taliban or their associated forces) that is engaged in an armed conflict against a State.

The issue came pointedly to a head when, shortly after the present administration came into office, Judge Bates asked the government to file a brief in the *Hamlily* case[3] describing its detention authority under the 2001 Authorization for the Use of Military Force (AUMF).[4]

The U.S. government complied by filing its brief of March 13, 2009, which argued that (i) when giving content to the broad language of the AUMF the U.S. government, consistent with the Supreme Court's 2004 *Hamdi* decision,[5] would look to the principles of the law of armed conflict, and (ii) because of the lack of codification in the law of armed conflict relating to non-State actors it would sometimes be necessary to draw analogies to the international laws of war applicable to international armed conflicts between States. The brief then asserted (in relevant part) that when viewed through this lens the U.S. government had the authority in the present conflict to hold individuals who were "part of" or "substantially supported" al Qaeda, the Taliban or associated forces, but left to be explored in future cases what the precise contours of those terms would be.

As of mid-2011, two years (and roughly fifty trial court and appellate decisions) later, what do we see? As concerns the topic of this article, one thing that appears to have emerged is an increasingly clear picture that the courts are unlikely to become the laboratory in which the metes and bounds of armed group membership are worked out. Initially, the district courts sought to draw parallels between armed groups and traditional armed forces in wrestling with the question of how LOAC ought to apply. Notably, the 2009 *Hamlily* (Judge Bates)[6] and *Gherebi* (Judge Walton)[7] opinions took the view that although it was possible to reach the conclusion that LOAC permitted the detention of certain individuals working within the al Qaeda structure based on status, it was necessary that they be part of the command structure in order for this to be the case. There was arguably some distance between these two opinions on the question of whether the command structure must be within the military wing of the armed group, and how the issue of "support" should be addressed for purposes of determining status (either treating it as contributing to membership analysis or treating it as irrelevant), but they were operating very much within the LOAC framework, as were later trial court opinions that may have varied in their interpretation of LOAC but essentially accepted it as the analytic framework.

This has decidedly not, however, been the case at the appellate court level, where relevant decisions are marked in part by the following characteristics: First, while the law has not been entirely settled yet, at least one panel has, in the *Bihani* case, overtly dismissed the importance of international law in interpretation of the AUMF in an opinion that, although effectively overruled by an en banc decision that described this feature of the panel decision as dictum, marks a disinclination to use the international law of armed conflict as a tool with which to excavate the meaning of the AUMF.[8] Second, although the appellate court continues to offer its views about what sorts of fact patterns would suffice in its views to establish detention authority for purposes of the AUMF, commentators have noted (correctly in my view) that the Circuit Court's approach to the definition of who may be detained has been far less important to the outcome of cases than its focus on evidentiary issues. Professor Stephen Vladeck noted in May 2010 that although he found the D.C. Circuit caselaw governing the scope of the government's detention power to be troubling, in his view "[it] has not yet had a meaningful impact on any individual cases. In marked contrast is the D.C. Circuit's jurisprudence concerning the government's burden of proof in post-*Boumediene* habeas cases, and how that burden should affect district court assessments of the facts of individual detainees' claims."[9] Third, as the D.C. Circuit has increasingly focused on what is required for the government to meet its evidentiary burden, its rulings in this area have had the effect of creating a substantial zone of deference for executive branch judgment. In the *al-Adahi* decision,[10] the Circuit Court rejected trial court views that items of evidence must rise or fall on their own, instead requiring that they be looked at as a mosaic in which suspicious data points are taken as corroborating each other even if not fully proven on their independent merits. And although "preponderance of the evidence" continues to be the governing standard, some Circuit judges have suggested that a lower standard might be appropriate.[11]

If the D.C. Circuit's caselaw indicates a disinclination on its part to decide detention decisions based on a fine parsing of LOAC, and therefore to become a significant engine driving refinements to the U.S. perspective on that body of law, then it is hardly clear that the Supreme Court will be any more eager to wander into these thickets. To be sure, in the past, the Supreme Court has very much been the final word on the extension of key rights and privileges to Guantanamo (as was the case in *Rasul* (2004),[12] *Hamdan* (2006)[13] and *Boumediene* (2008)). There is reason, however, to believe that the Court may not wade in so dramatically on the issues being addressed in the present litigation. The composition of the Court has changed since the pathbreaking decisions of 2004–8 (including through the addition of Justice Kagan, who, because of her involvement as Solicitor General, may be recused from a number of cases that would present the Court with core detainee status questions) and so have the atmospherics. Criticism of review procedures and treatment issues—issues that may have helped draw the Court's attention in the past—have largely been addressed over the past few years through a combination of judicial decisions (in particular the confirmation that Common Article 3 applies to al Qaeda detainees in the *Hamdan* decision, and the extension of habeas to Guantanamo in the *Boumediene* decision) and executive acts (including the treatment guarantees offered under Executive Order 13,491).[14] Whether a set of facts or an issue of law might arise that the Court considers in need of its review remains to be seen, but it would not be surprising if in light of the above the Court were to continue to maintain its posture of reserve.

It bears mention that the judicial review of Guantanamo detainees has occurred in the detention context, and that there are questions about whether issues relating to targeting in the context of an armed conflict would even be justiciable. Even if they were, however, the courts seem to have placed their decisions in a framework where it appears that they are essentially creating a broad zone of deference for the exercise of reasonable military judgment. In its current form, it is somewhat difficult to draw from the caselaw more than broad guidance about the boundaries of that zone, and there is a great deal that is left unsaid about the specific factors that a specific decision maker in a specific set of circumstances should weigh in taking a targeting decision. For at least the time being, then, the core issues remain very much for the executive branch to work through.

III. Experts' Processes (the ICRC Report)

If the D.C. Circuit has created a de facto zone of deference around military decision making, the same cannot so readily be said of the ICRC's *Interpretive Guidance on the Notion of Direct Participation in Hostilities*. Because the report has been much discussed, it will be addressed here only briefly with the following few observations.

By way of background, in 2003, the ICRC (together with the Asser Institute) mounted an effort to provide guidance on the question of when civilians lose their immunity from attack in both international and non-international armed conflict. They convened an experts group to study the question and produce a report. The process was guided by, among others, Nils Melzer, who has done his own scholarly work on the issue of targeted killings. Among the main findings in the report were that individuals who perform a "continuous combat function"—i.e., a role that involves direct participation in hostilities on a persistent, non-sporadic and non-spontaneous basis—on behalf of the military wing of an organized armed group that is party to a conflict become targetable on the basis of their status as "members" of the organized armed group until their status changes. With regard to direct participation in hostilities, the report also found that three components must be present in order for an action to constitute direct participation in hostilities: a threshold of harm must be met; there must be causation; and there must be a "belligerent nexus"—i.e., a sufficient connection between the action and the armed conflict. Each one of these criteria was explored at some length, and the report set forth lists of activities that would, or would not, satisfy the criteria as conceived by the report.[15]

The ICRC effort produced a report that, although a contribution to the literature in this area, has generated a fair amount of criticism, and has not become the gold standard that might originally have been hoped for. There were some major issues over content. As has been much discussed, the report included a section arguing that there was a legal foundation for the principle that militaries must use the least harmful means in addressing legal targets, which generated great concern among certain prominent experts who participated in the process, who believed that it lacked a basis in law or practice, and was not consistent with what had been discussed in the drafting process. From the operational perspective, the feedback was that the report was too rigid and complex, and did not give an accurate picture of State practice or (in some respects) of a practice to which States could realistically aspire. Many of the experts who had participated in the ICRC process declined to be named in the report, and the U.S. government in its habeas filings made clear that it did not regard the study as an authoritative statement of the law. In the final analysis, it appeared that the "experts' process" through which the product developed could not substitute for the difficult, painstaking and necessary process of allowing States to develop the law in areas such as this.

Nevertheless, notwithstanding the issues that have been raised with respect to the ICRC report, we should not lose sight of two very important contributions that it made—one substantive and one procedural. Substantively, it is critical to recognize that the study is in some ways pathbreaking in the level of recognition that it gives to the concept that individuals who become members of organized armed groups lose their civilian status and, while members, can be targeted on the basis of their status alone for the duration of a NIAC. Moreover, procedurally, the report has helped to catalyze important discussion among the U.S. government and its partners about the topics that are addressed in the report. The emerging spectrum of views on this subject is addressed in the following section.

IV. State Practice

When the ICRC report emerged, one reaction that at least some of its readership offered was that it would take some time for States to digest its contents and provide some feedback on where it tracked—and did not track—State practice. As noted above, this process has in fact been under way and, based on conversations with interlocutors in a number of partner governments, it is possible to offer a general assessment of the spectrum within which the views of the United States and a number of its closest partners fall. These observations draw from personal and professional exchanges over the past several years, but are relayed in the author's personal capacity.[16]

A. Overarching Considerations

There is a strong consensus that the point of departure for any analysis of when civilians become liable to attack under LOAC is the customary principle of distinction. Consistent with this principle, both Additional Protocol I[17] (in Article 51(3)) and Additional Protocol II[18] (in Article 13(3)) provide that in armed conflict civilians enjoy protections from being made the object of attack "unless and for such time as they take a direct part in hostilities."[19] Moreover, with respect to NIAC, the commentary on Article 13(3) additionally explains that "[*t*]*hose who belong to armed forces or to organized armed groups may be attacked at any time.* If a civilian participates directly in hostilities, it is clear that he will not enjoy any protection against attacks for as long as his participation lasts."[20]

Taken together, the Additional Protocols and the quoted passage from their commentary suggest that in armed conflict the following individuals (in addition to the members of regular armed forces who are liable to attack) relinquish their protection under international humanitarian law from being made the object of attack: (i) individuals who become members of organized armed groups (i.e., those referred to in the first sentence of the above-quoted passage from the Article 13(3) commentary) and (ii) civilians who are taking direct part in hostilities without belonging to an armed force or organized armed group (i.e., those referred to in the second sentence of the above-quoted passage).[21] Taking into account that current treaty law does not provide specific guidance on what it means to be a member of an organized armed group, or to take direct part in hostilities, the following principles emerge from Article 51(3) of Additional Protocol I and Article 13(3) of Additional Protocol II, and are supported by their Commentaries:

- A critical difference between individuals who lose their protection from attack because of their membership in an organized armed group and individuals who lose such protection as a result of direct participation in hostilities without belonging to an organized armed group is that an individual who loses protection because of membership in an organized armed group may be attacked "at any time." Because his or her membership deprives him or her of protection, such an individual does not then need to be actually involved in particular hostilities to be lawfully attacked at any point in time.[22] By contrast, a civilian who is not a member of an organized armed group and is taking direct part in hostilities loses protection from attack only "for as long as his participation lasts."
- The determination whether an individual is a member (or ceases to be a member) of an organized armed group or is taking direct part in hostilities should be taken by the decisionmaker based on information reasonably available to him or her at the time and taking into account the considerations set forth below.
- Individuals making targeting decisions based on a determination that an individual is a member in an organized armed group, or is taking direct part in hostilities, may not act in the absence of sufficient confidence in the information establishing the factual basis for the determination.[23] When there is insufficient confidence in the information, the determination should not be made unless and until such time as sufficient information to make a reasonable determination has been identified. Depending on the facts, deferral of one determination (e.g., that an individual is a member of an organized armed group) need not foreclose the other (e.g., that an individual is directly participating in hostilities).

B. Membership in Organized Armed Groups

As to whether an individual has become a member of an organized armed group and therefore is liable to attack at any time, there is a range of views among the United States and its partners on the precise "test" that should be applied to determine membership. Some partners appear to believe that the test for membership must be based fundamentally on the function performed by the individual in question. But there is also a view that, because of the clandestine and decentralized nature of certain organized armed groups, it may be difficult to discern a command structure that is clearly analogous to the structures that would be found in State militaries, and that it is accordingly important to be cautious about focusing too stringently on functions that can be analogized to those performed in a traditional command structure. Notwithstanding this spectrum of views about how to define the membership test, there is a shared sense that the following factors may bear on such a determination, with the precise weight given to any of these factors dependent on, among other things, the test that is applied:

- The extent to which an individual performs a function on behalf of an organized armed group that is both analogous to a function traditionally performed by a member of a State military who is liable to attack and that is performed within the command structure of the organization (i.e., the individual is either carrying out or giving orders to perform such a function).[24] Examples of activities that would likely qualify include those that would constitute combat, combat support and combat service support functions if performed for a regularly constituted armed force and carrying arms openly, exercising command over the group or one of its units, or conducting planning related to the conduct of hostilities.[25]
- The frequency of the individual's preparation, command or execution of operations amounting to direct participation in hostilities and the intensity of the damage or harm likely to be inflicted by such participation.
- Other similar factors determined in the reasonable military judgment of the decisionmaker to demonstrate an individual's integration into the organized armed group, such as the adoption of a rank, title or style of communication; the taking of an oath of loyalty; or the wearing of a uniform or other clothing, adornments or body markings that mark out members in the group—in each case in a context and manner indicating that these acts of identification reliably connote meaningful assimilation into the group.[26]

Relevant factors in determining that an individual has ceased to be a member of an organized armed group include the amount of time that has passed since that individual has taken relevant action on behalf of the group in question, and whether he or she affirmatively has disassociated himself or herself from the organized armed group. Decisionmakers should base these determinations on the standard of reasonableness in the prevailing circumstances.

C. Direct Participation in Hostilities

With respect to determining what it means to take "direct part in hostilities," as a threshold matter there seems to be a common view that direct participation in hostilities stands in contrast to support by a general population to a nation's war effort. Civilians who are contributing to a nation's war effort accordingly do not by dint of this alone lose their protection. Any determination that a civilian is taking part in hostilities (and thus loses immunity from being made the object of attack) will be highly situational and needs to be made by a decisionmaker taking the following considerations into account:

- Nature of the harm: Is the individual's activity directed at (i) adversely affecting one party's military capacity or operations or enhancing the capacity/operations of the other, or (ii) killing, injuring or damaging civilian objects or persons?
- Causation/integration between action and harm: Is there a sufficiently direct causal link between the individual's relevant act and the relevant harm, or does the act otherwise form an integral part of coordinated action resulting in that harm? (Although it is not enough that the act merely occurs during hostilities, there is no requirement that the act be only a single causal step removed from the harm.)
- Nexus to hostilities: Is the individual's activity linked to an ongoing armed conflict and is it intended either to disadvantage one party, or advance the interests of an opposing party, in that conflict?

The period during which an individual can be deemed to be directly participating in hostilities is generally viewed to include the period during which that individual is deploying to and returning from the hostile act, but there is a range of views about whether the acquisition of specific materials necessary for an attack might under certain circumstances be considered part of the deployment period, and whether the period in which an individual goes into hiding following an attack might under certain circumstances be considered part of the return. There is also a range of views about whether each of the foregoing three factors must be present in order to make a determination that an individual is directly participating in hostilities (or whether a "totality of the circumstances" approach should govern), and about whether certain types of activities must be excluded from the definition of direct participation in hostilities (e.g., financial support). Moreover, there is a range of views concerning the relevance of geographic and temporal proximity of an individual's actions to particular hostile acts in ongoing hostilities.

At some point, as noted above, the frequency or intensity of an individual's direct participation may establish that the individual is a functional member of an organized armed group, and there is also a perspective that persistent direct participation in hostilities may establish the individual in question to be continuously liable to attack for the period of persistent activity even if it is insufficient to establish functional membership.[27] Accordingly, where an individual takes direct part in hostilities, it is important to determine whether the nature and frequency of the direct participation is such that the loss of protection lasts only for the duration of specific acts, or is sufficiently persistent that the individual is liable for attack for a wider period, including the periods between the specific acts.

V. Conclusion

The above description of views suggests in some ways a clustering by the U.S. government and its partners around certain views that are put forward in the ICRC study on direct participation in hostilities. There is increasing convergence, for example, around the notion that there are two roads to loss of immunity—membership and direct participation in hostilities. Among the considerations that bear on membership, there is growing consensus that functional factors echoing some of the factors from the ICRC's "continuous combat function test" are at least relevant. Moreover, the factors that a number of States look at in assessing whether an action constitutes direct participation in hostilities parallel, to some extent, the three factors that were captured in the ICRC study.

There are, of course, important differences between what is described in this article and what is described in the ICRC study. The tests and factors described here, reflecting States' operational experience, are less rigidly constructed. They do not have the complexity of the tests and factors articulated in the ICRC document. And there is no reference to the ICRC's suggested rule that parties must use the "least harmful means" for subduing opponents as described in Section IX of the *Interpretative Guidance*—a test for which it is difficult to detect much, if any, support among the United States and like-minded partners.

But, as noted above, it is increasingly clear that it will be State practice—rather than international expert groups or the courts of any one country—that will drive the development of a common view within the international community. We are already seeing the outline of a limited consensus emerging, and, as we move forward, we may well see an increasing level of accord among certain like-minded States on the question of how individuals lose immunity from being made the object of attack in the context of non-international armed conflicts.

Notes

1. NILS MELZER, INTERNATIONAL COMMITTEE OF THE RED CROSS, INTERPRETIVE GUIDANCE ON THE NOTION OF DIRECT PARTICIPATION IN HOSTILITIES UNDER INTERNATIONAL HUMANITARIAN LAW 32 (2009), *available at* http://www.icrc.org/eng/assets/files/other/icrc_002_0990.pdf [hereinafter INTERPRETIVE GUIDANCE].
2. Boumediene v. Bush, 553 U.S. 723 (2008).
3. Hamlily v. Obama, 616 F. Supp. 2d 63 (D.D.C. 2009).
4. Pub. L. No. 107-40, 115 Stat. 224 (2001), codified at 50 U.S.C. § 1541 note (Supp. V 2005).
5. Hamdi v. Rumsfeld, 542 U.S. 507 (2004).
6. Hamlily, 616 F. Supp. 2d at 63.
7. Gherebi v. Obama, 609 F. Supp. 2d 43 (D.D.C. 2009).

8. Al-Bihani v. Obama, 590 F.3d 866, 871 (D.C. Cir. 2010), cert. denied, 131 S. Ct. 1814 (2011). Notably, a different panel of the D.C. Circuit looking at the *al Warafi* case suggested somewhat greater receptivity to applying the law of armed conflict when, in remanding the case to the district court, it asked the lower court to "address whether Al Warafi was permanently and exclusively medical personnel within the meaning of Article 24 of the First Geneva Convention . . . , assuming arguendo [its] applicability." Al Warafi v. Obama, 409 F. App'x 360, 361 (D.C. Cir. 2011).

9. Stephen I. Vladeck, *National Security Policy and the Role of Lawyering: Guantanamo and Beyond: The D.C. Circuit after* Boumediene, 41 SETON HALL LAW REVIEW 1451, 1466 (2011), *available at* http://papers.ssrn.com/sol3/papers.cfm?abstract_id=1838402##.

10. Al-Adahi v. Obama, 613 F.3d 1102 (D.C. Cir. 2010).

11. The panel in the *Almerfedi* decision (which reversed a district court's decision to grant the habeas petition based on evidence that the detainee had spent a few months at the guesthouse of an al Qaeda-associated organization in Pakistan and had traveled in an eastward direction within Iran (i.e., toward Afghanistan and away from Europe) carrying several thousand dollars) appeared to suggest that a "minimum threshold of persuasiveness" or "credible evidence" standard for an initial showing, which could be rebutted by petitioner, might be sufficient under the Supreme Court's *Hamdi* ruling. Almerfedi v. Obama, 654 F.3d 1, 9–10 (D.C. Cir. 2011).

12. Rasul v. Bush, 542 U.S. 466 (2004).

13. Hamdan v. Rumsfeld, 548 U.S. 557 (2006).

14. Exec. Order No. 13,491, 74 Fed. Reg. 4893 (Jan. 22, 2009).

15. INTERPRETIVE GUIDANCE, *supra* note 1, at 22–26, 48–64.

16. As indicated above, there are multiple issues not addressed here that may have a bearing on the lawfulness of targeting operations, including the threshold at which armed violence can be deemed an "armed conflict," the level of cohesion that is required in order to deem an organization an "organized armed group," the circumstances under which an organized armed group can be said to be engaged in armed conflict, the geographic scope of armed conflicts and the circumstances in which legal rules outside the law of armed conflict may be relevant.

17. Protocol Additional to the Geneva Conventions of 12 August 1949, and Relating to the Protection of Victims of International Armed Conflicts, June 8, 1977, 1125 U.N.T.S. 3.

18. Protocol Additional to the Geneva Conventions of 12 August 1949, and Relating to the Protection of Victims of Non-International Armed Conflicts, June 8, 1977, 1125 U.N.T.S. 609.

19. The United States is not a party to either of the Additional Protocols (and has expressed continuing significant concerns about Additional Protocol I), but it draws guidance where appropriate from relevant provisions of both instruments. *See* Gregory Nickels, U.S. Senior Advisor to the 65th General Assembly, Statement on Agenda Item 82: Status of the Protocols Additional to the Geneva Conventions of 1949 and Relating to the Protection of Victims of Armed Conflicts, in the 6th Committee (Oct. 18, 2010), *available at* http://usun.state.gov/briefing/statements/2010/149784.htm. The United States has affirmed its intention to proceed toward the ratification of Additional Protocol II. *See* White House, Fact Sheet: New Actions on Guantanamo and Detainee Policy 3 (Mar. 7, 2011), http://www.whitehouse.gov/the-press-office/2011/03/07/new-actions-guantanamo-bay-and-detainee-policy.

20. COMMENTARY ON THE ADDITIONAL PROTOCOLS OF 8 JUNE 1977 TO THE GENEVA CONVENTIONS OF 12 AUGUST 1949 ¶ 4789 (Yves Sandoz, Christophe Swinarski & Bruno Zimmermann eds., 1987) (emphasis added).

21. The question of whether an individual is liable to attack for either reason is separate from the question of whether that individual should benefit from combatant immunity, and also the

question of whether an individual may be detained (as the scope of detention authorities in armed conflict is different from the scope of targeting authorities).

22. As discussed below, there is a range of views on whether individuals who pass the membership threshold lose their civilian status (and are therefore unprivileged belligerents) or remain civilians but are deemed to be continuously taking a direct part in hostilities and accordingly continuously lose their protections from being made the object of attack.

23. There is a range of views about the specific level of doubt that would preclude action from being taken.

24. There is a range of views with respect to the significance of combat support and combat service support in assessing membership.

25. There is a range of views with respect to the significance of combat support and combat service support in assessing membership.

26. There is a range of views about the extent to which indications of formal membership (such as swearing an oath of loyalty) may be considered.

27. Under this view, factors relevant to whether an individual ceases to be liable to attack because of direct participation in hostilities include (but are not limited to) the amount of time that has passed since the last relevant act, and whether there are concrete and verifiable facts or persuasive indicia that the individual has affirmatively foresworn taking a direct part in hostilities.

PART V

MEANS AND METHODS IN NON-INTERNATIONAL ARMED CONFLICTS

IX

Differences in the Law of Weaponry When Applied to Non-International Armed Conflicts

William H. Boothby*

Introduction

It is sensible to pose the question whether there is a meaningful distinction between the weapons law that applies during international armed conflict and that which governs hostilities during a non-international armed conflict. After all, philosophically, it could be argued that there is no rational basis for such a distinction. Why, the rhetorical question would go, should it be legitimate to expose individuals during a civil war to injuring mechanisms that have been found to be unacceptable for employment during wars between States?[1] If this is seen as a plea that the law applicable in these classes of conflict be merged, that is not the purpose of this article. Rather, the intent in what follows is to consider whether there are in fact such differences in the law as it is, to identify the precise extent of any such divergences and to ask whether they make sense.

* Air Commodore, Royal Air Force. The views expressed in this article represent the views of the author in his personal capacity and are not intended to reflect the views of the Royal Air Force, the United Kingdom Ministry of Defence or the United Kingdom government.

Fundamental Principles and the Conventional Weapons Convention

So, is there still a meaningful weapons law distinction between non-international armed conflict and international armed conflict? Well, the fundamental principles prohibiting weapons that are of a nature to cause superfluous injury or unnecessary suffering[2] and weapons that are indiscriminate by nature[3] apply equally in both types of conflict. For the seventy-five States[4] that have ratified the 2001 extension in scope of the Conventional Weapons Convention (CCW),[5] the Convention's scope and thus that of its protocols extend to both types of conflict.

Amended Protocol II (AP II)[6] to the CCW always did, of course, apply to both categories of conflict.[7] Equally, the Chemical Weapons Convention,[8] the Biological Weapons Convention,[9] the Ottawa Convention[10] and the Cluster Munitions Convention[11] were all drafted as arms control treaties in that they prohibited a range of activities that went significantly beyond mere use of the relevant weapons. Thus, by prohibiting possession of such weapons and by including undertakings to never under any circumstances assist, encourage or induce in any way anybody to engage in any activity prohibited to a State party,[12] the use of these weapons was effectively prohibited in non-international as well as in international armed conflicts.

Expanding Bullets

It is not, however, correct to say that the whole of the rest of weapons law applies equally to both classes of armed conflict—indeed in certain important details that is not currently the case. Expanding bullets pose particular and complex issues in this regard. Let us therefore at this point consider that specific munition and the particular issues that have been brought into sharp focus as a result of a recent international conference.

The Kampala Review Conference for the Rome Statute of the International Criminal Court adopted on June 10, 2010, by consensus, Resolution 5, which amended Article 8(2)(e) of the Statute. It achieved this by inserting additional offenses under the heading of "other serious violations of the laws and customs applicable in armed conflicts not of an international character, within the established framework of international law."[13] Those additional offenses are the following:

(xiii) Employing poison or poisoned weapons;

(xiv) Employing asphyxiating, poisonous or other gases, and all analogous liquids, materials or devices;

(xv) Employing bullets which expand or flatten easily in the human body, such as bullets with a hard envelope which does not entirely cover the core or is pierced with incisions.[14]

The reference to "the established framework of international law" makes it clear that the States that adopted this provision by consensus were asserting that the listed activities, when conducted in the course and context of an armed conflict not of an international character, constitute activities that, in their view, are offenses only if they were committed in such a way as is prohibited by the existing framework. The significance of that implicit assertion, of course, is that, so far as those States are concerned, these activities constitute offenses irrespective of whether the perpetrator's State has ratified this addition to the Rome Statute, if the activities themselves breach international law and amount to war crimes.[15] There would not appear to be any controversy about that assertion as it applies to the poison, poisoned weapons, asphyxiating and poisonous gas, and analogous liquids, materials or devices provisions. International law already prohibits the use of such weapons by any State in both international and non-international armed conflicts[16] and we can safely also conclude that the use of those weapons in such conflicts is an offense under customary international law.[17]

However, the position in relation to expanding bullets is rather more complex. In negotiating the third Hague Declaration of 1899,[18] the plenipotentiaries agreed "[t]o abstain from the use of bullets which expand or flatten easily in the human body, such as bullets with a hard envelope which does not entirely cover the core or is pierced with incisions."[19] When negotiated, the Declaration was subject to a general participation clause such that it only applied to a war between States party and ceased to apply if a non-party State joined the conflict.[20]

Hays Parks has made the point that militaries of all nations used only full-metal-jacketed bullets before and after the adoption of the Declaration, mainly because they were the only ones that would function reliably when fired from military weapons.[21] He therefore speculates whether compliance was due to law of war considerations or military reliability concerns.

But there is a wider matter to consider here. Christopher Greenwood has reportedly expressed doubts that the 1899 Declaration was customary law. He considered the matter in relation to the distinction principle. He was contemplating the type of expanding ammunition that may be more accurate or less likely to ricochet or over-penetrate than full-metal-jacketed ammunition, thus reducing the risks to innocent civilians during urban or counterterrorist operations. In such circumstances, he wondered whether some increased potential for injury to the combatant or terrorist target would necessarily amount to superfluous injury. The thought he was putting forward was that the protection of civilians under the principle of distinction in those circumstances might outweigh considerations of additional injury to the targeted individual.[22]

To take this analysis one stage further, in particular military circumstances expanding bullets may be the weapon of choice, for example, in order to stop a terrorist from detonating a bomb or abducting a hostage or in other similar circumstances.[23]

Expanding Bullets under Customary Law

However, the International Committee of the Red Cross (ICRC), in its *Customary International Humanitarian Law* study, finds the following rule: "The use of bullets which expand or flatten easily in the human body is prohibited."[24]

The ICRC study asserts that this customary rule applies in both international and non-international armed conflicts.[25] One difficulty with the ICRC's formulation is that the phrase "bullets which expand" can be interpreted in a number of ways. It could mean "bullets which are designed, or designed or adapted, in order to expand," or "bullets which in the normal or intended circumstances of their use will normally or inevitably expand" or even "bullets which are capable of expanding." While there is no doubt that there is a rule of customary law in relation to expanding bullets, one may doubt that that rule has been correctly formulated in the ICRC study. On balance, it would seem most likely that any such rule would be based on the design purpose and intent of the weapon, rather than on how it might behave in unspecified but perhaps particular circumstances. In short, the design purpose is to be preferred to the effects as the basis for any customary rule, which should also, the author would suggest, be linked to the superfluous injury/unnecessary suffering principle in its application in both categories of conflict.

Interestingly, the ICRC study acknowledges that several States have decided to use such ammunition in domestic law enforcement operations.[26] Kenneth Watkin, in a 2006 article, indicates that rather more States have done this than the word "several" would indicate.[27] The ICRC asserts, however, in the customary law study that the use of such ammunition by police forces occurs in situations other than armed conflict and that the bullets are fired from firearms which deposit less energy than a rifle bullet.[28]

The purpose, of course, for using such bullets in domestic law enforcement will usually be to stop the individual quickly and before he has the opportunity to act in a potentially extremely damaging way. The range and circumstances of use of the weapon by law enforcement officers may or may not be different from the circumstances in which members of the armed forces would be inclined to use such weapons. There is also, of course, the point that, for a number of countries, the weapons and ammunition used by members of the armed forces are likely to be substantially the same as those used by the internal security or police force. The ICRC has, in its customary law study, frequently argued that rules that apply in international armed conflict in the field of weapons law also apply in non-international armed conflict because the weapons used by the armed forces are the same in both types of conflict.[29] While that may not necessarily be a particularly convincing argument, nevertheless it would seem illogical to take that line and then, in the next breath, as it were, to suggest that different rules on expanding bullets apply as between police forces and armed forces units, recognizing as one must that in many States the weapons used, and sometimes even the users, are the same.

Expanding Bullets at the Kampala Conference

When the Kampala Conference delegates adopted the additions to Article 8 that we have been discussing, they inserted into the Resolution the following important preambular paragraph:

> *Considering* that the crime referred to in article 8, paragraph 2(e)(xv) (employing bullets which expand or flatten easily in the human body), is also a serious violation of the laws applicable in armed conflict not of an international character, and *understanding* that the crime is committed only if the perpetrator employs the bullets to uselessly aggravate suffering or the wounding effect upon the target of such bullets, as reflected in customary international law . . . .[30]

When we seek to interpret this paragraph, we should start by noting in a positive sense that it usefully suggests that the offense is only committed in non-international armed conflicts if the bullets are used "to uselessly aggravate." The implication is, therefore, that if there is military utility attached to the additional injury or suffering—for example, in the sense discussed earlier—then the offense will not have been committed. The important question to consider is whether this implication is made legally effective by the language of the preamble and of the relevant element of crime. Of course, if this preambular language and the element of crime are interpreted by the Court as restricting the circumstances in which the use of such ammunition constitutes an offense under the Rome Statute, this would be of fundamental importance. In order to determine whether the preambular language and the element of crime are legally effective in this sense, we must therefore consider first the law which the Court is obliged to apply and thereafter the legal significance of the elements of crimes.

Applicable Law under the Rome Statute

The Rome Statute prescribes the law that the International Criminal Court (ICC) shall apply in the following terms:

> (a) In the first place, this Statute, Elements of Crimes and its Rules of Procedure and Evidence;
>
> (b) In the second place, where appropriate, applicable treaties and the principles and rules of international law, including the established principles of the international law of armed conflict;
>
> (c) Failing that, general principles of law derived by the Court from national laws of legal systems of the world including, as appropriate, the national laws of the States that would normally exercise jurisdiction over the crime, provided that those principles are not inconsistent with this Statute and with international law and internationally recognized norms and standards.[31]

The effect of this language is that the Court is obliged to take into account the elements of the crime of using expanding bullets in a non-international armed conflict when interpreting that offense for the purposes of proceedings before the Court. Because of the effect of Article 9 of the Statute, however, the Court is not specifically required to apply the elements, merely to take them into account.[32]

The elements of the war crime of employing prohibited bullets are prescribed in paragraph 3 of Annex II to the Resolution of the Kampala Conference and, so far as relevant, include the following: "The perpetrator was aware that the nature of the bullets was such that their employment would uselessly aggravate suffering or the wounding effect."[33]

This language, which a judge of the ICC considering a prosecution for such an offense would be obliged to take into account, makes it clear that the offense is only made out if the person concerned knew that the employment of the ammunition would uselessly aggravate suffering or wounds. Such aggravation is not useless if there is a corresponding military purpose for it. This would be the case, for example, if expanding ammunition is used to target a hostage taker, hijacker or suicide bomber in circumstances where the resulting instant disabling of the targeted individual is essential to protect civilians.

Putting that aspect to one side for a moment, a careful analysis of the preambular words may be interpreted by some as implying that the use of such bullets in all circumstances in the context of a non-international armed conflict breaches international law. Such an interpretation may suggest the Kampala delegates intended that while the prohibition applies in all circumstances during non-international armed conflicts, the preambular caveat only apply to the offense provision. However, such a conclusion applies in the light of the more fundamental concerns discussed above.

Significance of the Kampala Preamble and Associated Element of the Crime
Paragraph 3 of the elements of the crime in relation to expanding bullets is therefore of vital importance. It should indeed be borne in mind that established human rights norms may be breached if, in circumstances other than armed conflict, the use of high-velocity ammunition would be less discriminating than expanding bullets, e.g., because of greater over-penetration or ricochet risks that needlessly put civilians in the vicinity at enhanced risk.[34]

Equally, the customary principle of distinction arguably comes into play in the manner referred to earlier and as noted by Christopher Greenwood. Indeed, it is difficult to believe that customary international law should be regarded as prohibiting a weapon that is more likely to be effective in protecting the innocent in circumstances of acute danger than less apparently legally controversial high-velocity ammunition.

Returning to the broader theme of this article, the main point to note is that expanding bullets seem to represent a limited point of distinction between the law applicable in international and non-international armed conflicts. In international armed conflict the offense under the Rome Statute is also tied to superfluous injury and unnecessary suffering by the application of a similar element of crime to that appearing in the annex to the Kampala Resolution. However, the treaty prohibition, which, as we have seen, applies only in the case of international armed conflicts, make no such reference to superfluous injury or unnecessary suffering.[35] Equally, it remains to be seen what approach the ICC will adopt in interpreting the Resolution, in particular with respect to the words of the preamble and of the element of the crime. While the 1969 Vienna Convention's rules on interpretation of treaties[36] would suggest the need to interpret the main body of the Resolution by reference to the preambular words as text adopted by the participants at the Conference, there can be no certainty that a Court, confronted by proceedings under the Statute for an offense alleged to have been committed in a non-international armed conflict, will do so.[37]

Extension of the Scope of the Conventional Weapons Convention

The CCW provides another point of difference between the law applicable in international and that in non-international armed conflicts that, although fairly obvious, is nevertheless worthy of mention—namely, that the CCW protocols (other than AP II) apply equally to both classes of conflict only for States that have ratified the relevant protocol and the 2001 extension of scope. For the States that have not ratified the scope extension, protocols to which that State is party will continue only to apply in international armed conflicts. This has the equally obvious result that fewer States are bound by those rules with respect to non-international armed conflict, which may, but will not necessarily, have the effect that the achievement of a customary rule based on the language of a particular protocol may happen more quickly in respect to international than non-international armed conflict. This would clearly suggest that the ICRC should have been rather more hesitant when finding customary weapons law rules applying in non-international armed conflict based on the relatively recently adopted CCW protocols and on the CCW extension of scope.

The Natural Environment

Something should be said about the natural environment. Under the Convention on the Prohibition of Military or Any Other Hostile Use of Environmental Modification Techniques (ENMOD),[38] States party undertake not to engage in military or any other hostile use of environmental modification techniques having widespread, long-lasting or severe effects as the means of destruction, damage or injury to any other State party.[39] If the technique is not employed by a State party or if the destruction, damage or injury is not applied to another State party, it is at face value hard to see how this provision is engaged. Accordingly, this would seem to be another treaty provision that applies in armed conflicts between States but not in an armed conflict that is internal to a single State.

While the ENMOD was concerned with the use of the environment as a weapon, the focus of Articles 35 and 55 of 1977 Additional Protocol I (AP I)[40] was on collateral damage to the environment resulting from an attack directed at some other objective. These articles apply to weapons and means of warfare and, thus, are also provisions that form part of the law of weaponry. It is well understood that these provisions are one of the reasons for the U.S. decision not to ratify the treaty.[41]

Putting that to one side, the fact remains that for States that are party to AP I, the treaty rules apply only in an international armed conflict. The ICRC in Rule 43 of its *Customary International Humanitarian Law* study suggests that there are rules that protect the environment as a matter of customary law and that these rules apply in international and in non-international armed conflict.[42] In the same rule the ICRC finds an additional sub-rule requiring that methods and means of warfare must be employed with due regard for the protection and preservation of the natural environment. The rule goes on to require that in the conduct of military operations, all feasible precautions must be taken to avoid and, in any event, to minimize incidental damage to the environment.[43] The ICRC adds as a further element to the rule that a party to the conflict is not absolved from taking such precautions by lack of scientific certainty as to the environmental effects of certain military operations. In the associated commentary, however, the editors conclude that while State practice supports the conclusion that these are customary rules applicable in international armed conflicts, their status as customary rules in non-international armed conflicts is "arguable." So, while it is clear that there is a difference in the application of the treaty rules, the position at customary law is the subject of some controversy.

Weapons Procurement and Expanding Bullets

Given budgetary constraints on weapons procurement by States, it is foreseeable that weapons procured for law enforcement purposes will increasingly be made available for use by armed forces personnel, such use being not necessarily restricted to a law enforcement context. The author acknowledges that the customary nature of the expanding bullets prohibition was readily and widely accepted until relatively recently. However, the advent in more recent years of certain responses to asymmetric inferiority, such as aircraft hijacking, suicide bombing, hostage taking or command detonation of devices directed at civilian infrastructure targets, is liable to render expanding ammunition the weapon of choice for police or armed forces personnel seeking to respond effectively to such challenges. Such asymmetric activity may be criminal in nature, or it may foreseeably be employed by or at the direction of a party to an armed conflict, for example, a State, in furtherance of its strategic war aims. It seems most unlikely, however, that a less effective response than expanding ammunition will be employed by States simply because the particular context may be regarded as hostilities associated with an international armed conflict. Equally, it is inconceivable that the authorities will pause in what is likely to be an urgent, highly charged and dangerous situation in order to debate the existence and status of any associated armed conflict and, thus, the nature of the applicable rule.

If States in any significant number do retain expanding ammunition for use in the context of international armed conflict in the sense discussed in the preceding paragraphs, or indeed if such use occurs on any regular basis, the continued existence of the customary rule will become, at the very least, questionable and, perhaps, unsustainable. States party to the 1899 Declaration would, of course, remain bound thereby. Arguably, however, practice of States party to the Declaration that is contrary to its provisions would be rather potent evidence that the treaty is being overtaken by events, a circumstance not unknown in the law of weaponry.[44]

Do These Differences Make Sense?

Now that we have established that differences in the law applicable in our two classes of conflict exist, the final question to pose is whether such differences make sense. Here we return to the issue posed at the beginning of this short piece. Should, indeed, the law that is designed to limit the sufferings of combatants and to seek to ensure that the law of distinction is properly complied with differ between conflicts confined to a State and conflicts not so confined? But perhaps that is the wrong question. Alternative, and perhaps altogether more revealing, questions are these:

- How long will it be before all States party to the CCW ratify the 2001 scope extension?
- How long before the thinking that underpins ENMOD is seen by States to be equally applicable when the conflict occurs within the boundaries of a single nation?
- How long before the points we have discussed in relation to expanding bullets are seen to have resonance in international and non-international armed conflict, not just in relation to the Rome Statute offenses?
- And how long before States that accept the environmental rules in AP I do so with regard to both classes of conflict?

States are and will remain in charge of the process of creating international law and it is States that therefore will determine the answers to these questions. Legal developments in recent years as noted above suggest that the process of legal convergence is under way. It will, however, be for individual States to decide whether to regard that process as complete.

In conclusion, while the general trend seems to be toward convergence, achieving complete convergence would require a collective willingness among States and the limited adjustment of some detailed legal interpretations. It remains to be seen whether States see this as a priority and whether State practice develops so as to bring about complete convergence.

Notes

1. Indeed, elementary considerations of humanity and common sense make it preposterous that the use by States of weapons prohibited in armed conflicts between themselves be allowed when States try to put down rebellion by their own nationals on their own territory. What is inhumane, and consequently proscribed, in international wars, cannot but be inhumane and inadmissible in civil strife . . . .

Prosecutor v. Tadić, Case No. IT-94-1-l, Decision on Defence Motion for Interlocutory Appeal on Jurisdiction, ¶ 119 (Int'l Crim. Trib. for the Former Yugoslavia Oct. 2, 1995).

2. Protocol Additional to the Geneva Conventions of 12 August 1949, and Relating to the Protection of Victims of International Armed Conflicts art. 35.2, June 8, 1977, 1125 U.N.T.S. 3 [hereinafter AP I] ("It is prohibited to employ weapons, projectiles and material and methods of warfare of a nature to cause superfluous injury or unnecessary suffering"). This is a rule of customary law which therefore binds all States and which the International Committee of the Red Cross customary law study found to apply in both international and non-international armed conflicts. 1 CUSTOMARY INTERNATIONAL HUMANITARIAN LAW, Rule 70 at 237 (Jean-Marie Henckaerts & Louise Doswald-Beck eds., 2005) [hereinafter ICRC Study]. Under the rule, the legitimacy of a weapon must be determined by comparing the nature and scale of the generic military advantage to be anticipated from the use of the weapon in the applications for which it is designed to be used with the pattern of injury and suffering associated with the normal, intended use of the weapon. *See further* William J. Fenrick, *The Conventional Weapons Convention: A Modest but Useful Treaty*, 279 INTERNATIONAL REVIEW OF THE RED CROSS 498, 500 (1990); W. Hays Parks, *Means and Methods of Warfare*, 38 GEORGE WASHINGTON INTERNATIONAL LAW REVIEW 511, 517 n.25 (2006); WILLIAM H. BOOTHBY, WEAPONS AND THE LAW OF ARMED CONFLICT 55–68 (2009).

3. The prohibition of indiscriminate attacks is restated in Article 51(4) of Additional Protocol I. The innovation of that provision was to spell out what indiscriminate attacks are, namely:

> (a) those which are not directed at a specific military objective;
>
> (b) those which employ a method or means of combat which cannot be directed at a specific military objective; or
>
> (c) those which employ a method or means of combat the effects of which cannot be limited as required by [the] Protocol; and consequently, in each such case, are of a nature to strike military objectives and civilians or civilian objects without distinction.

AP I, *supra* note 2.

This rule is also reflective of customary law and was found by the ICRC study to apply in both international and non-international armed conflicts. *See* ICRC Study, *supra* note 2, Rule 71 at 244. It is really paragraphs (b) and (c) in the treaty text that provide the rule as it applies in weapons law.

4. ICRC Treaty Database, http://www.icrc.org/IHL.nsf/(SPF)/party_main_treaties/$File/IHL_and_other_related_Treaties.pdf (last visited March 22, 2012).

5. Convention on Prohibitions or Restrictions on the Use of Certain Conventional Weapons Which May Be Deemed to Be Excessively Injurious or to Have Indiscriminate Effects, Oct. 10, 1980, 1342 U.N.T.S. 137. The Convention, on adoption, applied to international armed conflicts covered by Common Article 2 to the 1949 Geneva Conventions. By virtue of an extension in scope agreed to at the 2001 CCW Review Conference, the Convention and its protocols now apply, for the States that ratify the extension, to the non-international armed conflicts referred to in Common Article 3 to the 1949 Conventions.

6. Amended Protocol on Prohibitions or Restrictions on the Use of Mines, Booby-Traps and Other Devices (Amended Protocol II), May 3, 1996, S. Treaty Doc. No. 105-1 (1997). *See* Alicia H. Petrarca, *An Impetus of Human Wreckage?: The 1996 Amended Landmines Protocol*, 27 CALIFORNIA WESTERN INTERNATIONAL LAW JOURNAL 205 (1996).

7. Protocol Additional to the Geneva Conventions of 12 August 1949, and Relating to the Protection of Victims of Non-International Armed Conflicts art. 1(2), June 8, 1977, 1125 U.N.T.S. 609.

8. Convention on the Prohibition of the Development, Production, Stockpiling and Use of Chemical Weapons and on Their Destruction, Jan. 13, 1993, 1974 U.N.T.S. 45 [hereinafter Chemical Weapons Convention].

9. Convention on the Prohibition of the Development, Production, and Stockpiling of Bacterial (Biological) and Toxin Weapons and on Their Destruction, Apr. 10, 1972, 26 U.S.T. 583, 1015 U.N.T.S. 163.

10. Convention on the Prohibition of the Use, Stockpiling, Production and Transfer of Anti-Personnel Mines and on Their Destruction, Sept. 18, 1997, 2056 U.N.T.S. 211 [hereinafter Ottawa Convention].

11. Convention on Cluster Munitions, Dec. 3, 2008, 48 INTERNATIONAL LEGAL MATERIALS 357 (2008).

12. *See, e.g.*, Ottawa Convention, *supra* note 10, art. 1(1)(c).

13. Rome Statute of the International Criminal Court art. 8(2)(e), July 17, 1998, 2187 U.N.T.S. 90 [hereinafter Rome Statute].

14. Review Conference of the Rome Statute of the International Criminal Court, Kampala, Uganda, May 31–June 11, 2010, Amendments to Article 8 of the Rome Statute, RC/Res.5, Annex I (June 16, 2010), available at http://www.icc-cpi.int/iccdocs/asp_docs/Resolutions/RC-Res.5-ENG.pdf [hereinafter Article 8 Amendments].

15. The author is grateful to Professor Charles Garraway, a member of the UK delegation to the Rome Diplomatic Conference, for his clarification of this issue.

16. ICRC Study, *supra* note 2, Rule 72 at 251, Rule 74 at 259.

17. However, riot control agents are prohibited as a method of warfare, but their use remains lawful when, during an armed conflict, international or otherwise, they are not being used as a method of warfare. Chemical Weapons Convention, *supra* note 8, art. 5.

18. Hague Declaration (IV, 3) Concerning Expanding Bullets, July 29, 1899, 1 AMERICAN JOURNAL OF INTERNATIONAL LAW (Supp.) 157, 157–59 (1907) [hereinafter Expanding Bullets Declaration].

19. *See id.*, first operative paragraph.

20. The second and third operative paragraphs of the Expanding Bullets Declaration, *id.*, provide: "The present Declaration is only binding for the contracting Powers in the case of a war between two or more of them. It shall cease to be binding from the time when, in a war between the contracting Powers, one of the belligerents is joined by a non-contracting power."

21. W. Hays Parks, *Conventional Weapons and Weapons Reviews*, 8 YEARBOOK OF INTERNATIONAL HUMANITARIAN LAW 55, 69 (2005).

22. Comments attributed to Professor Greenwood during a keynote speech at Legal Aspects of Current Regulations, Third International Workshop on Wound Ballistics (Mar. 28–29, 2001), reported by Parks, *id.* at 89–90 n.23.

23. BOOTHBY, *supra* note 2, at 147 n.4.

24. ICRC Study, *supra* note 2, Rule 77 at 268.

25. *Id.*

26. *Id.* at 270.

27. Kenneth Watkin, *Chemical Agents and Expanding Bullets: Limited Law Enforcement Exceptions or Unwarranted Handcuffs?*, 36 ISRAEL YEARBOOK ON HUMAN RIGHTS 43, 52 (2006).

28. ICRC Study, *supra* note 2, at 270. It is worth noting that the UK's *Manual of the Law of Armed Conflict* does not list expanding bullets among the weapons prohibited in non-international armed conflicts, although weapons of a nature to cause superfluous injury or unnecessary suffering are so listed. UNITED KINGDOM MINISTRY OF DEFENCE, THE MANUAL OF THE LAW OF ARMED CONFLICT ¶ 15.28 (2004). *See also* BOOTHBY, *supra* note 2, at 147 n.4.

29. ICRC Study, *supra* note 2, at 246, 2nd paragraph under "Non-international armed conflicts."

30. Article 8 Amendments, *supra* note 14, preambular para. 9.

31. Rome Statute, *supra* note 13, art. 21(1).

32. Article 9 provides that the elements "shall assist the court" in interpreting the crimes in the Statute. This seems to have been intended by those who negotiated the treaty as qualifying the Article 21 requirement to apply, *inter alia*, the elements. The effect on international law of these two provisions will be determined by applying the Article 31, Vienna Convention interpretation rules. Vienna Convention on the Law of Treaties, May 23, 1969, 1155 U.N.T.S. 331 [hereinafter Vienna Convention].

It seems to the author that it will, in practice, be for the judges of the Court to decide whether the Article 21 requirement to apply and the Article 9 assertion that the elements shall assist produce an ambiguity of meaning or a clarity that the elements are non-binding or, indeed, a clarity that they are binding. The interpretation reflected in this article is coherent with that understood during the negotiations and the author is grateful to Professor Garraway for clarifying these matters.

33. Article 8 Amendments, *supra* note 14, Annex II.

34. An analogy may be drawn with the European Court of Human Rights decision in *Güleç v. Turkey*. The Court said:

> The Court, like the Commission, accepts that the use of force may be justified in the present case under paragraph 2 (c) of Article 2 [of the European Convention], but it goes without saying that a balance must be struck between the aim pursued and the means employed to achieve it. The gendarmes used a very powerful weapon because they apparently did not have truncheons, riot shields, water cannon, rubber bullets or tear gas. The lack of such equipment is all the more incomprehensible and unacceptable because the province of Şırnak, as the Government pointed out, is in a region in which a state of emergency has been declared, where at the material time disorder could have been expected.

Güleç v. Turkey, 1998-IV Eur. Ct. H.R. ¶ 71.

There seem to be two important aspects to this case. The first was the use of one type of weapon because the alternative, impliedly preferable, weapon was not available. It seems that it was the potential lethality of the weapon that was used that was a crucial consideration. The final cited sentence suggests, furthermore, that riot control equipment should have been made available as the authorities should have understood the nature of domestic emergencies in Şırnak. It may, however have been equally appropriate to provide *both* types of weapon there because of a history of armed clashes in that area.

35. Paragraph 3 of the elements of the war crime of employing prohibited bullets contrary to Article 8(2)(b)(xix) of the Rome Statute is as follows: "The perpetrator was aware that the nature of the bullets was such that their employment would uselessly aggravate suffering or the wounding effect." International Criminal Court, Elements of Crimes, U.N. Doc. ICC-ASP/1/3 (Sept. 9, 2002).

36. Vienna Convention, *supra* note 32, art. 31(1)–(2).

37. The argument against referring to the preamble for interpretative purposes would assert that Article 31 of the Rome Statute exhaustively lists the law to be applied by the Court, absent ambiguity, and that there is no such ambiguity in the expanding bullets provision in the Kampala Resolution.

38. Convention on the Prohibition of Military or Any Other Hostile Use of Environmental Modification Techniques, May 18, 1977, 31 U.S.T. 333, 1108 U.N.T.S. 151.

39. *Id.*, art. 1(1).

40. *Supra* note 2.

41. *See, e.g.*, Memorandum from W. Hayes Parks, Michael F. Lohr, Dennis Yoder & William Yoder for Mr. John H. McNeill, Assistant General Counsel (International), Office of the Secretary of Defense, 1977 Protocols Additional to the Geneva Conventions: Customary International Law Implications (May 8, 1986); Michael J. Matheson, *The United States Position on the Relation of Customary International Law to the 1977 Protocols Additional to the 1949 Geneva Conventions*, 2 AMERICAN UNIVERSITY JOURNAL OF INTERNATIONAL LAW AND POLICY 419 (1987).

42. ICRC Study, *supra* note 2, Rule 43 at 143. The rule asserts, non-controversially, that the general principles on the conduct of hostilities apply to the natural environment, but then states:

> A. No part of the natural environment may be attacked, unless it is a military objective; B. Destruction of any part of the natural environment is prohibited, unless required by imperative military necessity; C. Launching an attack against a military objective which may be expected to cause incidental damage to the environment which would be excessive in relation to the concrete and direct military advantage anticipated is prohibited.

These suggested rules seem to go somewhat beyond the rules in AP I. It may be argued that there is not yet sufficient depth and generality of State practice to support all of the sub-rules as drafted.

43. *Id.*, Rule 44 at 147.

44. For an example of a treaty whose operative provision was overtaken by events consider the 1868 St. Petersburg Declaration. Declaration Renouncing the Use, in Time of War, of Explosive Projectiles Under 400 Grammes Weight, Dec. 11, 1868, 138 Consol. T.S. 297.

X

Methods and Means of Naval Warfare in Non-International Armed Conflicts

Wolff Heintschel von Heinegg*

Introduction

The law of naval warfare is part of the larger body of law applicable to international armed conflicts.[1] Accordingly, it applies to an armed conflict between two or more States, including conflicts involving State-sponsored forces.[2] Whether the law of naval warfare also applies to situations of non-international armed conflicts is a contentious issue. Therefore, the distinction between international and non-international armed conflicts is important when it comes to the applicability of the law of naval warfare to a particular armed conflict.

Unfortunately, the distinction between international and non-international armed conflicts is less clear than it seems at first glance. On the one hand, the "facts on the ground" may make it difficult to draw the line of demarcation between the two.[3] Additionally, international scholars have taken quite different positions. For some, the distinctive criterion is the identity of the parties to the conflict, with the issue being whether or not those parties qualify as States under public international law.[4] For others, it is not the identity of the parties alone, but also the geography of an armed conflict; they are prepared to apply the law applicable to international armed conflict to any case in which armed conflict "crosses the borders of the state,"[5] even if one of the parties is a non-State actor.[6] Still others believe that the distinction has become irrelevant, because, they maintain, the formerly

* Professor of Public Law, Europa-Universität Viadrina, Frankfurt (Oder), Germany.

separate bodies of law have merged into a single body of law applying equally to both international and non-international armed conflict.[7]

With regard to the alleged merger, it is acknowledged that there has been a remarkable development of the law of non-international armed conflict during the last decade. Some treaties no longer distinguish between international and non-international armed conflicts.[8] The concept of war crimes, until recently strictly limited to international armed conflicts, has been introduced into the law of non-international armed conflict.[9] Still, it is doubtful whether that development justifies the conclusion that the two bodies of law have merged. First, those treaties that do not distinguish between international and non-international armed conflict have not become customary international law. Second, one of the prime references relied upon by the International Criminal Tribunal for the former Yugoslavia when addressing international and non-international armed conflict issues, the German *Humanitarian Law in Armed Conflicts Manual*, is under revision. The first edition did not distinguish between the two; however, the forthcoming second edition will contain a separate section on non-international armed conflicts. Third, those who advocate a merger focus on the obligations and prohibitions imposed upon the parties to the conflict. In other words, they maintain that in both international and non-international armed conflict the parties are increasingly bound by the same rules, while ignoring the fact that the law of international armed conflict offers belligerents certain rights, especially vis-à-vis the nationals of other States (neutrals). This especially holds true for the law of naval warfare, which provides for prize measures, blockade and various maritime zones. It is doubtful that the proponents of merger would be prepared to accept the exercise of the full spectrum of belligerent rights during a non-international armed conflict, even if exercised only by the State actor.

Those who focus on the identity of the parties to the conflict to determine the nature of the conflict are correct insofar as a non-international armed conflict presupposes that at least one party to the armed conflict is a non-State actor. This does not mean, however, that geography is irrelevant. To the contrary, according to Common Article 3, which appears in each of 1949 Geneva Conventions, the armed conflict must occur "in the territory of one of the High Contracting Parties."[10] Article 1(1) of 1977 Additional Protocol II applies to "all armed conflicts which take place in the territory of a High Contracting Party."[11] Hence, it cannot be denied that non-international armed conflict is characterized by a territorial element.

Those who take the position that an international armed conflict comes into existence as soon as there is a trans-border element seem to base that position on a literal reading of the provisions of Common Article 3 and Additional Protocol II. However, mere "spillover effects" into the territory of another State do not necessarily change the character of a non-international armed conflict into that of an international armed conflict as long as the governments concerned refrain from hostilities against each other.[12]

Differences of opinion on how to characterize a conflict increase if the situation under scrutiny does not easily fit into one of the traditional categories, as, for instance, the armed conflicts in Gaza and in Afghanistan/Pakistan. Very often the different approaches to distinguishing international from non-international armed conflicts seem to be guided by desired result rather than by a sober analysis of customary international law. Although the different characterization approaches are interesting, this article is not designed to provide further criteria of distinction nor to add yet another category of armed conflict to the existing categories of international and non-international. It starts, therefore, with the premise that the law of international armed conflict applies

- "whenever there is a resort to armed force between States";[13]
- if the non-State actors in a non-international armed conflict obtain recognition of belligerency by the government;[14] or
- for States parties to Additional Protocol I,[15] if the conditions of Article 1(4) are fulfilled.

In those armed conflicts the law of naval warfare undoubtedly applies, at least insofar as measures taken by the State party to the conflict are concerned. The non-State party to the conflict may also apply methods and means of naval warfare against its State enemy. However, the non-State actor may not interfere with neutral shipping unless the neutral State has—either explicitly or implicitly—recognized it as a belligerent.

A non-international armed conflict exists whenever there is "protracted armed violence between governmental authorities and organized armed groups or between such groups within a State."[16] The focus of the present article is on the question of whether, and to what extent, the parties to a non-international armed conflict are entitled to exercise belligerent rights under the law of naval warfare. The first part gives a short overview of nations' practice involving the use of methods and means of naval warfare during non-international armed conflicts. The second part addresses the question of a geographical limitation of the hostilities. The third part deals with the conduct of hostilities and the fourth part discusses measures taken by the parties to the conflict that interfere with the shipping and/or aviation of other States. It will be shown that the law of naval warfare can be applied to non-international armed conflicts, albeit partly modified, between the parties to the conflict. If, however, the parties interfere with the shipping and/or aviation of other States beyond the outer limit of the State party's territorial sea or contiguous zone, an additional legal basis for the measures in question must be found.

Part I. Practice

A. American Civil War

The blockade during the American Civil War is an important example of applying the law of naval warfare to a non-international armed conflict. It must be borne in mind, however, that the declaration of the blockade by President Abraham Lincoln was considered as recognition of belligerency,[17] thus triggering the applicability of the law of blockade and of the law of naval warfare. Moreover, the British government had proclaimed its neutrality, thus also recognizing a state of belligerency between the United States and the Confederate States.[18] Accordingly, the blockade of the American Civil War serves as a precedent only in a limited manner for the general applicability either of the law of blockade or of the law of naval warfare to non-international armed conflicts. Nevertheless, it needs to be emphasized that, although recognition of belligerency has occurred only infrequently in recent State practice, it continues to exist as a legal concept.[19] Moreover, as illustrated by the blockade of the Confederate States, recognition of belligerency may be explicit or implicit.

B. Spanish Civil War

During the Spanish Civil War (1936–39) a number of merchant vessels of various nationalities supplying the government forces were attacked by aircraft and submarines. The identity of the State or group to which the attacking aircraft and submarines belonged is uncertain; however, it is clear that it was not a party to the conflict.[20] In response, nine States, including the United Kingdom and France, concluded the 1937 Nyon agreements[21] and decided on collective measures against submarines, surface vessels and aircraft that were, or that were suspected of being, engaged in unlawful attacks against merchant vessels. For the purposes of the present paper, the treatment of those attacks as "acts of piracy" is unimportant. It should be noted, however, that the parties to the Nyon Arrangement in the preamble emphasized that they were not "in any way admitting the right of either party to the conflict in Spain to exercise belligerent rights or to interfere with merchant ships on the high seas even if the laws of warfare at sea are observed." Therefore, it is probably correct to state that "despite the scale of hostilities involved and the degree of international intervention on both sides . . . , no European state conceded to any party to the conflict any right to interfere with neutral shipping."[22]

C. Algeria

Both prior to and during the conflict between France and Algerian groups seeking independence, France instituted an extensive maritime control zone in the Mediterranean. Acting under a decree of March 17, 1956,[23] the French Navy intercepted more than 2,500 ships per year[24] in an effort to prevent the flow of arms to rebels in Algeria.[25] According to Articles 4 and 5 of that decree, vessels of less than one hundred tons were liable to visit and search inside the "customs zone" that extended fifty kilometers off the Algerian coast.[26] After 1958, vessels of more than one hundred tons were also subjected to visit and search. Whereas most of the measures were taken within fifty kilometers of the Algerian coast, a number of vessels were visited well beyond the "customs zone."[27] Vessels were diverted when boarding was impossible due to adverse weather conditions or the nature of the cargo, including cargo consisting of arms and explosives. In the latter case, the cargo was confiscated unless it was determined that the arms and/or explosives were not to be used in a manner that constituted a danger to French forces in Algeria.[28] In most instances, the ships were released. The French measures that met sharp protests of the affected flag States were justified by reference to the rights of self-defense and self-preservation.[29]

D. Sri Lanka

The armed conflict in Sri Lanka (1983–2009) was characterized by a considerable naval element. The "Sea Tigers"—the naval wing, which was established in 1984, of the Tamil Tigers—proved to be a serious threat to government forces. According to unconfirmed reports, the Sea Tigers deployed small suicide boats and fast patrol boats that sank twenty-nine government fast patrol boats and attacked naval bases of the Sri Lankan Navy. The Sea Tigers did not limit their operations to enemy forces, but also interfered with innocent shipping in the Indian Ocean. As a result, on May 14, 2007, the Indian Navy announced that it would increase its presence in the Palk Strait and deploy unmanned aerial vehicles in the region.[30]

In December 2004, demands were made in India to neutralize the Sea Tigers because they had become a "credible third naval force in the southern part of South Asia."[31] In 1984 and again in 2009, the Sri Lankan government forces were alleged to have established naval blockades against parts of the coastline controlled by the Tamil Tigers. However, those references to naval blockade are misleading. The measures taken by the government forces in 1984 were indeed aimed at preventing entry and exit to and from the coastal area, but their main purpose was to prevent the Tamil Tigers from receiving both training and equipment from the southern Indian state of Tamil Nadu. Additionally, the maritime interdiction operations occurred within the Sri Lankan territorial sea and contiguous zone, and were directed against vessels suspected of being engaged in smuggling weapons or supplies to the Tamil Tigers. The Sri Lankan government did not assert the right to interfere with all neutral vessels encountered in high seas areas.[32] The so-called "blockade" of the Mullaitivu coast in 2009 was part of a major military operation against the headquarters of the Sea Tigers that eventually resulted in its neutralization. Again, the Sri Lankan armed forces did not claim any right to interfere with neutral shipping.

E. Gaza

On August 13, 2008, the Shipping Authority at the Israeli Ministry of Transport published a Notice to Mariners calling upon shipping to refrain from entering the territorial waters off the Gaza coast.[33] That measure was considered inadequate, and was followed on January 3, 2009 by a Minister of Defense–ordered naval blockade of the coast of the Gaza Strip that extended to a maximum distance of twenty nautical miles from the coast. The Notice to Mariners advising of the establishment of the blockade provided: "All mariners are advised that as of 03 January 2009, 1700 UTC, Gaza maritime area is closed to all maritime traffic and is under blockade imposed by Israeli Navy until further notice. Maritime Gaza area is enclosed by the following coordinates. . . ."[34] The notice was published on the websites of the Israel Defense Force, the Shipping and Ports Authority and the Ministry of Transport, and on several standard international channels, such as NAVTEX, an international satellite network that collects and distributes notices to vessels worldwide. Moreover, this notice was broadcast twice a day on the emergency channel for maritime communications to vessels that sailed within three hundred kilometers of the Israeli coast. On May 31, 2010, the so-called "Gaza flotilla," including the *Mavi Marmara*, was intercepted.[35]

F. Libya

The 2011 conflict in Libya was a "mixed" conflict. On one hand, it was a non-international armed conflict between the government forces loyal to Gaddafi and the rebels. On the other hand, it was an international armed conflict between Libya and the international alliance that exercised certain belligerent rights on the basis of UN Security Council Resolution 1973.[36] For the purposes of this article, it is irrelevant whether the measures taken by the alliance were in compliance with the terms of the resolution. During the conflict, NATO warships intercepted several boats operated by Gaddafi forces that were laying anti-shipping mines outside the harbor of Misurata, a city that was dependent for much of its food and supplies on the sea link with the rebel capital Benghazi. British Brigadier Rob Weighill, director of NATO operations in Libya, condemned the minelaying by stating: "We have just seen Gaddafi forces floating anti-ship mines outside Misurata harbour today. It again shows his complete disregard for international law and his willingness to attack humanitarian delivery efforts."[37]

Part II. Region of Operations

A. Internal Waters and Territorial Sea

As non-international armed conflicts occur *within* a State,[38] the parties to the conflict are not prohibited from conducting hostilities in that State's internal waters and territorial sea, as those are defined by the law of the sea. As long as the parties to the conflict do not interfere with the navigation of other States, they may apply methods and means of naval warfare against their adversary in those sea areas.

At the same time, however, other States continue to enjoy the right of innocent passage. There is no indication in either treaty law or State practice that the right of innocent passage is automatically suspended at the commencement of a non-international armed conflict. Rather, the general rules continue to apply. The coastal State, under Article 25(3) of the 1982 United Nations Convention on the Law of the Sea (LOS Convention),[39] may in certain circumstances temporarily suspend innocent passage in specified parts of its territorial sea. To be effective, the suspension must be "duly published."

The reference to "weapons exercises" in Article 25(3) as a basis for suspending the right of innocent passage is not the exclusive circumstance in which suspension may occur. The article goes on to indicate that suspension may occur when "essential for the protection of its [the coastal State's] security." In determining whether such suspension is essential, the coastal State enjoys a wide margin of discretion.[40] The existence of a non-international armed conflict certainly constitutes a threat to the coastal State's security; hence, the authorities of the coastal State are entitled to suspend the right of innocent passage in order to prevent foreign shipping from navigating in close vicinity to the conflict area. In view of a lack of conclusive State practice, it is unclear whether innocent passage may be suspended in the entire territorial sea. While suspension in a State's entire territorial sea would appear to be inconsistent with Article 25(3)'s "in specified areas," the circumstances of a given non-international armed conflict may be such that the government considers it necessary to close the entire territorial sea to foreign navigation. If, however, the armed hostilities are limited to a certain region, it would be difficult for the government to justify a suspension of the right of innocent passage in coastal sea areas remote from the area of operations.

The non-State party to a non-international armed conflict is not entitled to suspend or otherwise interfere with the right of innocent passage. This clearly follows from the wording of Article 25(3) ("The *coastal State* may . . .").[41] If the non-State party nevertheless takes measures affecting foreign shipping, the authorities of the coastal State under Article 24(2) must "give appropriate publicity to any danger to navigation, of which it has knowledge, within its territorial sea."[42] The government is not obligated to actively take measures with a view to protecting foreign navigation against interference by the non-State party to the conflict.

B. International Straits and Archipelagic Sea Lanes

Neither the government nor, *a fortiori*, the non-State party to a non-international armed conflict is entitled to interfere with the rights of transit passage and of archipelagic sea lanes passage within international straits and archipelagic waters. Even during an international armed conflict the belligerents are obliged to preserve those passage rights.[43] There is no indication in State practice that the existence of a non-international armed conflict would entitle the government to adopt laws and regulations relating to passage that are in excess of that permissible under the law of the sea. In particular, there may be no suspension of transit passage even if the exercise of navigation or overflight were dangerous to the transiting vessel or aircraft. As is the case with dangers to navigation within the territorial sea, the authorities of the States bordering an international strait and the archipelagic State are obliged to give "appropriate publicity to any danger to navigation or overflight."[44] And, again, the government is not obliged to take active measures against the non-State party to the conflict in order to protect international navigation and aviation.

C. Sea Areas beyond the Territorial Sea

The government of the State concerned is entitled to exercise maritime interdiction/interception operations within its contiguous zone if the conditions of Article 33[45] of the LOS Convention are met. Hence, the "special naval surveillance zone" established and enforced by Sri Lankan government forces in 1984 and the measures taken against foreign vessels that were engaged in smuggling weapons and supplies to the Tamil Tigers were "justified under ordinary customs and policing powers available within 24 nautical miles of Sri Lanka's baselines."[46]

State practice seems to provide sufficient evidence that there is no rule of customary international law prohibiting the parties to a non-international armed conflict from engaging in hostilities against each other in high seas areas. As in an international armed conflict, there is, however, a positive obligation to pay due regard for the rights enjoyed by other States.[47] Moreover, the parties are prohibited from damaging submarine cables and pipelines that do not exclusively serve either party to the conflict.[48]

Hostile actions taken within the exclusive economic zone or on the continental shelf of another State during a non-international conflict are more questionable.

While the law of international armed conflict contains no prohibition on conducting hostilities in those areas,[49] it is doubtful whether this also holds true for non-international armed conflicts. In view of a lack of conclusive practice, it is not possible to reach a clear conclusion on that issue. It is, however, safe to state that measures taken by a non-State party to a non-international armed conflict within the exclusive economic zone or on the continental shelf of another State will, in all likelihood, not be tolerated by that State. This certainly will be the case if either party to the conflict decides to lay naval mines in those areas. If such minelaying occurs, the coastal State is entitled to remove or otherwise neutralize the mines.

Part III. Conduct of Naval Hostilities

This section addresses only relations between the parties to a non-international armed conflict, and not their relations with non-parties. Its object is to determine which rules of the law of naval warfare are applicable in a non-international armed conflict by focusing on the rules and principles applicable to the methods and means of naval warfare.

A. Entitlement

Under the law of international armed conflict, only warships are entitled to exercise belligerent rights.[50] This rule goes back to the prohibition of privateering under the 1856 Paris Declaration.[51] Warships are those vessels that meet the criteria set forth in Articles 2–5 of the 1907 Hague Convention VII,[52] Article 8(2) of the 1958 High Seas Convention[53] and Article 29 of the LOS Convention.[54] Limitations on the exercise of belligerent rights are most important with regard to interference with neutral navigation and aviation; thus, neutral vessels and aircraft must accede to such interference only if the measures are taken by warships.

No such limitation applies to non-international armed conflicts vis-à-vis the parties.[55] It follows from the object and purpose of the rule limiting the exercise of belligerent rights under the law of naval warfare—i.e., the transparent entitlement of the warship—that the non-State actor will obviously not have ships that meet the criteria for classification as a warship since one of the criteria is that it be a State vessel. The government forces may make use of any vessel or aircraft, including, for example, those used for law enforcement and customs enforcement, in the conduct of hostilities. This may not be the case, however, if the government takes measures against foreign shipping. I will return to that issue.[56]

B. Lawful Targets

Under the international law of non-international armed conflict, members of the regular armed forces, dissident armed forces and an organized armed group formed by the non-State party to a non-international armed conflict are lawful targets.[57] The International Committee of the Red Cross's (ICRC's) *Interpretive Guidance on the Notion of Direct Participation in Hostilities under International Humanitarian Law* provides that members of organized armed groups "consist only of individuals whose continuous function is to take a direct part in hostilities ('continuous combat function')."[58] The *Interpretive Guidance* provides that "continuous combat function" "requires lasting integration into an organized armed group acting as the armed forces of a non-State party to an armed conflict."[59] Persons that accompany or support an organized armed group but "who assume exclusively political, administrative or other non-combat functions" are civilians who have "protection against direct attack unless and for such time as they directly participate in hostilities."[60] Members of the regular armed forces, however, regardless of the function they serve[61] are not considered to be civilians and are subject to direct attack. This introduction of a double standard is not practicable in the context of armed conflicts. It would have been preferable had the *Interpretive Guidance* accepted the conclusion of the ICRC's *Customary International Humanitarian Law* study which rightly states, "Such imbalance would not exist if members of organized armed groups were, due to their membership, either considered to be continuously taking a direct part in the hostilities or not considered to be civilians."[62]

In the context of the Libyan conflict, the Libyan rebels were lawful targets at that point when the rebellion against the Gaddafi government passed the threshold to become a non-international armed conflict. They were not protected under Security Council Resolution 1973, which afforded protection to civilians, but not to members of organized armed groups. Civilians, more generally under the law of non-international armed conflict, are not subject to direct attack unless (and for such time as) they take a direct part in hostilities.[63] Thus, civilians, who would otherwise have been entitled to protection, who directly participated in the hostilities by attacking either the Gaddafi or the rebel forces became lawful targets during their period of participation as well.

When it comes to objects—which are, of course, the focus of naval operations—it is generally agreed that the definition set forth in Article 52(2) of Additional Protocol I is customary in character and thus applies to both international and non-international armed conflicts.[64] All objects that have an "intrinsic military significance" are to be considered lawful military objectives "by nature."[65] Hence, the military equipment, such as fast patrol boats and ammunition depots, or military headquarters of either party may be attacked at all times. For instance, the vessels used by the Sea Tigers for naval operations, as well as their stronghold in Mullaitivu, were lawful targets. The same holds true for the military equipment of the Sri Lankan government forces.[66] All other objects, although of a civilian nature, may become lawful military objectives by either their use, purpose or location.

It follows from the foregoing that civilians and civilian objects may not be directly attacked.[67] Moreover, the parties to a non-international armed conflict are obliged to always distinguish between members of armed forces or organized armed groups and civilians, and between military objectives and civilian objects.[68] Civilians are those who are neither members of an organized armed group nor directly participating in the hostilities.[69] Civilian objects are objects that do not constitute a military objective under the customary international law definition.[70]

In a non-international armed conflict, it may be difficult to clearly establish whether an individual is a member of an organized armed group or a civilian or whether an object constitutes a military objective or a civilian object. For instance, the parties are under no obligation to use vehicles that are marked or otherwise clearly identifiable as military in nature. This does not render the rules on lawful targets and the principle of distinction obsolete; it simply increases the difficulty in applying them.

C. Use of Naval Mines

As was seen in the Libyan conflict, the use of naval mines by the forces loyal to Gaddafi was condemned as being in "complete disregard for international law."[71] That statement, however, referred to interference with "humanitarian delivery efforts"; Resolution 1973 required Libyan authorities to "take all measures to protect civilians and meet their basic needs, and to ensure the rapid and unimpeded passage of humanitarian assistance."[72] In the absence of Resolution 1973, it would have been difficult to condemn the laying of naval mines as a violation of international law or of the law of non-international armed conflict had Libyan authorities publicized their employment. The mines were laid within the Libyan territorial sea and their purpose seems to have been to prevent supplies from reaching Misurata via the sea. Such conduct does not violate the law applicable to non-international armed conflict. Moreover, it would be difficult to conclude that the laying of naval mines violated the prohibition of indiscriminate attacks or any specific prohibition under the law applicable to such weapons or their use.

The fact that the mines were laid within the Libyan territorial sea is not alone sufficient to determine that the establishment of the minefield accorded with the applicable international law, however. A minefield certainly impedes upon the right of innocent passage. As was seen earlier, any suspension of the right of innocent passage requires prior notification, e.g., by issuing a Notice to Mariners.[73]

Libyan authorities neither publicly announced the laying of mines nor issued a warning to international shipping. Even if the mines were not directed against the effort to deliver humanitarian supplies, but were employed merely as a method of naval warfare applied against the rebels, the minelaying was still unlawful because it was conducted in disregard of the right of innocent passage of other States.

The law of non-international armed conflict does not prohibit the laying of naval mines in the internal waters or in the territorial sea of the State. The law recognizes that naval mines serve legitimate purposes, to include area denial, coastal defense and maintaining and enforcing a blockade.[74] Of course, indiscriminate attacks, i.e., "attacks that are not specifically directed" against lawful targets,[75] the use of weapons that are indiscriminate by nature[76] and the indiscriminate use of weapons[77] are prohibited both in international and in non-international armed conflict. The fact that naval mines may equally hazard military objectives and civilian objects is not sufficient in itself to conclude that the laying of mines is in violation of any of these prohibitions. Moreover, the law of naval mine warfare contains a specific rule on indiscriminate attacks, by explicitly prohibiting the use of "free-floating mines, unless they are directed against a military objective and they become harmless within an hour after loss of control over them."[78]

If Misurata had constituted a rebel stronghold, it would have been lawful to cut it off from outside resupply. However, the laying of naval mines by the Gaddafi forces was illegal because it occurred in disregard of the obligation to take all feasible precautions for the safety of peaceful shipping[79] (the failure to provide notification to the international community) and of the obligation to provide for humanitarian relief consignments. With regard to relief consignments, the parties to an armed conflict are obliged to provide for their free passage if the civilian population is "inadequately provided with food and other objects essential for its survival."[80] While this obligation originated in the law of blockade it is, I would assert, customary in character as a specification of the principle of humanity.

In conclusion, the use of naval mines in non-international armed conflict neither is expressly prohibited nor *ab initio* violates the principle of distinction or the rules of the law of non-international armed conflict prohibiting indiscriminate attacks. It must be borne in mind, however, that this is true only if naval mines are laid within the internal waters or, subject to prior notification, the territorial sea of the State. In sea areas beyond the outer limit of the territorial sea, naval mines may be used by the parties to a non-international armed conflict only if they are directed against a military objective.

D. The Natural Environment

The *Customary International Humanitarian Law* study states that "[i]t can be argued that the obligation to pay due regard to the environment [in international armed conflicts] also applies in non-international armed conflict if there are effects in another State."[81] Although the arguments are based on the law of peace, i.e., international environmental law, this may be a correct statement of the law because there is no rule of general international law that would absolve a State of its obligations vis-à-vis other States under either general international law or international environmental law merely because that State has become a party to a non-international armed conflict.

Unfortunately, the study fails to be sufficiently clear as to who is bound by the obligation to pay due regard. The commentary only refers to obligations of States; it does not clarify whether non-State actors are also bound by it. The failure to indicate that non-State actors are bound may be correct, because there are good reasons to assume that the obligations under international environmental law exclusively apply to States as subjects of international law.

Far more interesting than the reference to the obligation to pay due regard to the natural environment beyond the territory of the State is the following conclusion by the ICRC:

> [T]here are indications that this customary rule [i.e., the duty to pay due regard] may also apply to parties' behaviour within the State where the armed conflict is taking place. Some support for drafting a treaty rule for this purpose existed during the negotiation of Additional Protocol II. It was not adopted then, but the general acceptance of the applicability of international humanitarian law to non-international armed conflicts has considerably strengthened since 1977. In addition, many environmental law treaties apply to a State's behaviour within its own territory. There is also a certain amount of State practice indicating the obligation to protect the environment that applies also to non-international armed conflicts, including military manuals, official statements and the many submissions by States to the International Court of Justice in the *Nuclear Weapons case* to the effect that the environment must be protected for the benefit of all.[82]

It is to be noted that this statement is characterized by cautious formulations—"indications," "may also apply," "some support," "certain amount of State practice"—that indicate that the authors of the study are less than convinced of the correctness of their assumptions. In any event, those formulations do not distract from the suggestion that the authors were guided by their political and ecological aspirations, rather than by a sound analysis of State practice. State practice during non-international armed conflicts does not provide sufficient evidence to determine that the parties to the conflict are obliged to take into consideration—or to pay due regard to—the natural environment of the State in which the conflict is occurring.

It should also be noted that there still is no generally accepted definition of the term "natural environment."[83] But even if there were agreement that, for example, certain sea areas or marine living resources constitute "natural environment," this would not have an impact on the lawfulness of naval operations during a non-international armed conflict that have, or may have, detrimental effects on the marine environment of the State concerned.

Part IV. Interference with the Navigation of Other States

The law of non-international armed conflict contains no prohibitions going beyond those applying to land or air operations with regard to naval operations of the parties that occur within the internal waters and the territorial sea of the State party to the conflict so long as they do not interfere with the navigation of other States.

State practice during the Spanish Civil War and the Algerian conflict seems to provide convincing evidence that the parties to a non-international armed conflict are not allowed to interfere with the navigation of other States in sea areas beyond the outer limit of the territorial sea (unless such measures are lawful under the law of the sea or general international law). This finding is certainly correct as concerns measures taken by non-State actors. As regards interference by government forces one author has taken the position that

> the right of states to implement measures against neutral vessels in NIACs is thus at best an unsettled question. The most one can say is that in higher-intensity conflicts states have sometimes acknowledged or acquiesced in blockades targeting non-state actors. . . . However, in equally violent conflicts such a right has sometimes not been recognised and attempts to assert rights of blockade or similar measures have been protested (for instance, the Spanish Civil War and the Algerian rebellion). Where such measures are protested as contrary to international law those protests must weigh against the conclusion that there is *opinio juris* supporting the rule of custom invoked. On the basis of relevant state practice one can at most hazard a suggestion that irrespective of the precise classification of a conflict, states are likely to tolerate the assertion of a blockade only in cases of higher-intensity conflicts on a par with the traditional understanding of war.[84]

A. Neutral Vessels and Aircraft as Lawful Targets

It must be emphasized that the doubts expressed with regard to the authority of the State party to a non-international armed conflict to interfere with neutral vessels and aircraft have only concerned measures short of attack, i.e., visit, search and capture, and blockade. To date there has been no study addressing the question of whether foreign vessels and aircraft may qualify as lawful targets under the law of non-international armed conflict.

If the definition of lawful military objectives in an international armed conflict also applies in non-international armed conflict,[85] there is no convincing reason that would justify its limitation to vessels and aircraft of the nationality of the State concerned. Accordingly, any vessel, regardless of the flag it is flying, and any aircraft, wherever registered, used by an organized armed group in the course of a non-international armed conflict for military purposes constitute lawful military objectives by either their nature or use. If, for instance, another State comes to the assistance of the government forces, the warships and military aircraft deployed by that State will qualify as lawful military objectives by their nature. If the government of the State party makes use of vessels operated by a private military/security company that flies the flag of another State, that vessel will be a lawful target by reason of its use. In such cases, it does not make a difference whether the vessel or aircraft is encountered in the territorial sea or national airspace or in sea areas beyond the outer limit of the territorial sea or in international airspace. It is unimaginable that the parties to a non-international armed conflict will refrain from attacking such vessels or aircraft simply because they have departed the territorial sea or national airspace. It is equally unimaginable that other States will protest attacks on such vessels and aircraft on the sole basis of the attacks' occurring on the high seas or in international airspace.

The correctness of these findings cannot be questioned even in view of the practice of States during the Spanish Civil War, during which the parties to the 1937 Nyon agreement were not prepared to recognize a right of the parties to that armed conflict "to exercise belligerent rights or to interfere with merchant ships on the high sea even if the laws of warfare at sea are observed."[86] The fact that those States were not prepared to recognize the exercise of belligerent rights, including attacks on neutral merchant vessels qualifying as lawful targets, does not mean that the law of non-international armed conflict is the same today. While the law as it stood in 1937 may have contained a prohibition preventing the parties to a non-international armed conflict from exercising belligerent rights on the high seas, this is no longer the case under the contemporary law of non-international armed conflict. The customary definition of lawful military objectives contains no exceptions for objects that have the nationality of foreign States.

B. Visit, Search and Capture

The interceptions of foreign vessels conducted by the French Navy during the Algerian conflict met strong resistance from affected flag States. France, however, was less than impressed and continued to intercept foreign merchant vessels for years. O'Connell rightly observes that since the nineteenth century there had not

> been such an extensive invasion—for security reasons—of the principle of the freedom of the seas as in the case of the Algerian operation. The large number of ships affected, and the large number of countries which became diplomatically involved, would have led one to imagine that more attention would have been paid to this situation. Since only a few ships had their cargoes removed, and those ships were clearly engaged in the smuggling of arms into Algeria, the operation did not seriously affect the navigation of the high sea, and this, together with the political situation prevailing, would seem to explain the reticence on the part of flag States of the ships affected with respect to demands of the French government. The fact that France was able for so long and in so extensive a manner to exercise naval power on the high seas on the ground of self-defence causes one to ponder on the extent to which a conservative appreciation of international law has a role in defence planning.[87]

There is also the question of the Israeli blockade of Gaza. As will be discussed in Part IV.C, it is the view of this author that the conflict should be classified as an international armed conflict. However, it is also useful to consider what the legal position would have been if it were considered to be non-international in nature, as it is by some scholars.

Beginning in 2008, and continuing until the establishment of the blockade of the Gaza Strip on January 3, 2009, Israel exercised the right of visit and search in order to prevent the flow of arms into the Gaza Strip. The few measures taken against foreign vessels that were suspected, upon reasonable grounds, of being engaged in the transportation of arms destined for Hamas did not give rise to strong protests. Either the flag States implicitly recognized Israel's security interests or they simply did not want to admit that ships flying their flags had been engaged in the smuggling of arms and ammunition. Whatever the rationale, there is a clear parallel to the Algerian operation insofar as security interests and the right of self-defense may serve as a justification for interference with foreign shipping by the State party to a non-international armed conflict.

Both the Algerian and Gaza conflicts seem to justify the conclusion that the State party to a non-international armed conflict—*not* the non-State actor—is entitled to intercept foreign vessels on the high seas if the following conditions are met:

(1) vital security interests of the State are at stake;

(2) there are reasonable grounds for believing that the foreign vessels are engaged in activities jeopardizing those security interests (e.g., by supplying the non-State party with arms); and

(3) the measures are undertaken in close proximity to the conflict area.

It must be emphasized that the recognition of the right of interception (visit, search and capture) does not imply recognition of the right to exercise measures short of attack under prize law. Prize law *stricto sensu* only applies in international armed conflicts. Rather, the legal basis is found in the right of self-defense or in the customary right of self-preservation in order to protect the territorial and political integrity of the State. This right is equally exercisable in an international or non-international armed conflict. The finding by the International Court of Justice in the *Wall* advisory opinion that the right of self-defense does not apply if there is no trans-border element[88] has no basis in State practice.

C. Blockade: The Gaza Case

1. General Considerations

Unaddressed thus far is the question of whether the parties to a non-international armed conflict are entitled to establish and enforce a naval or aerial blockade.

Blockades are, by necessity, established in international waters or international airspace, apply to all vessels or aircraft regardless of their nationality,[89] and are distinguished from more limited actions such as measures undertaken with the objective of preventing exit from or entry into a given part of the coast or a port controlled by the other party to a non-international armed conflict. These latter measures do not qualify as a blockade under the law of armed conflict as long as they are limited to the territorial sea of the State, or are not applied against foreign vessels or aircraft.

As noted previously in the context of the American Civil War, it may be the declaration of a blockade by the government as an implicit recognition of belligerency of the non-State party to the conflict that triggers the applicability of the law of international armed conflict and, thus, of the law of naval warfare.[90]

If, however, the declaration of blockade cannot be understood as an implicit recognition of belligerency—either because the concept is no longer recognized as being part of the *lex lata* or because the circumstances surrounding the declaration do not justify a conclusion to that effect—it is doubtful whether the State party to a non-international armed conflict is entitled to establish and enforce a blockade. One author who classifies the conflict between Israel and Hamas as a non-international armed conflict has come to the conclusion that in view of the sporadic, on-again, off-again nature of the hostilities, "Israel had no right to impose a blockade on the Gaza Strip and its enforcement of that unlawful blockade against the flotilla . . . was an act incurring state responsibility."[91] According to that author's view, "there is no consistent state practice and *opinio juris* suggesting blockade is available outside an [international armed conflict]."[92] While that writer's opinion of the legality of the Israeli blockade is not shared by this author, it is a correct statement of the contemporary law that, absent recognition of belligerency, the parties to a non-international armed conflict are not entitled to establish and enforce a naval or aerial blockade against foreign vessels or aircraft.

2. The Gaza Case

The legal classification of the Gaza conflict is a contested issue. Those international lawyers who deal with the subject in a serious manner[93] and hold that Israel's blockade of the Gaza Strip is illegal arrive at that conclusion because they characterize the conflict as a non-international armed conflict.[94] Even if that characterization is correct, their finding that the blockade is therefore unlawful does not necessarily follow, because recognition of belligerency continues to be a valid concept. The mere fact that a given rule or concept of international law has not been made use of for an extended period does not mean that the rule or concept has become void by reason of desuetude.[95] There is no evidence that States, by refraining from recognizing a status of belligerency, have abolished that concept for good. Rather, States are unwilling to bring into operation the legal consequences that flow from a recognition of belligerency, but by the very study of the consequences they acknowledge that the concept is alive and well.

However, while this author accepts that others have reached a contrary position, the Gaza conflict cannot be classified as a non-international armed conflict. There are convincing reasons to conclude that it is an international armed conflict in view of the continuing belligerent occupation.[96] The Supreme Court of Israel does not share this opinion, because, according to the Court, Israel, since the 2005 disengagement, no longer exercises effective control over the Gaza Strip.[97] The Court, however, takes the position that international humanitarian law applies to an armed conflict between Israel and terrorist organizations not merely in an area that is subject to occupation, but "in any case of an armed conflict of an international character—in other words, one that crosses the borders of the state —whether or not the place in which the armed conflict occurs is subject to a belligerent occupation."[98] Thus the Court reaches the same conclusion, albeit by a different route than belligerent occupation.

The Turkel Commission, which was established by the Israeli government to examine the circumstances surrounding the boarding of the *Mavi Marmara* on May 31, 2010, concurred with the Supreme Court that the conflict in the Gaza Strip is "international in character."[99] Additionally, the Commission took into consideration (1) the degree of de facto control that Hamas exercises over the Gaza Strip, (2) the significant security threat that Hamas presents, and (3) Hamas's attempts to import weapons, ammunition and other military supplies by sea. The Commission then concluded that it "would have considered applying the rules governing the imposition and enforcement of a naval blockade even if the conflict between Israel and the Gaza Strip had been classified as a non-international armed conflict."[100]

The Palmer Report, which was prepared by the panel appointed by the UN Secretary-General to examine the boarding of the *Mavi Marmara*, also concluded that the conflict was international in nature, stating:

> The Panel considers the conflict should be treated as an international one for the purposes of the law of blockade. This takes foremost into account Israel's right to self-defence against armed attacks from outside its territory. In this context, the debate on Gaza's status, in particular its relationship to Israel, should not obscure the realities. The law does not operate in a political vacuum, and it is implausible to deny that the nature of the armed violence between Israel and Hamas goes beyond purely domestic matters. In fact, it has all the trappings of an international armed conflict.[101]

The findings of the Turkel Commission and the Secretary-General's panel lend further support to the government of Israel's determination that it was entitled to establish the naval blockade.

A naval blockade is a lawful method of naval warfare.[102] As such, it overrides the peacetime right of all States to freely navigate in the high seas areas covered by the blockade.[103] The blockading power is not only entitled to prevent vessels from either entering or leaving the blockaded area, but, in fact, has an obligation to achieve that goal by ensuring the blockade is effective.[104] The blockading power must use whatever means it has available to prevent entry and exit of all vessels; if it fails to do so the blockade becomes ineffective and legally void. In other words, if the blockading power permits some vessels to cross the blockade, while denying that ability to other vessels, it is not effectively enforcing the blockade. In the absence of an effective blockade, any interference with the navigational rights of vessels would be unlawful. Hence, if the Israeli government wishes to maintain the naval blockade of Gaza, it has no choice but to prevent all vessels from either entering or leaving the blockaded area.

Under the international law of naval blockade, all vessels, irrespective of the flag they fly, must be prevented from entering or leaving the blockaded area. In this instance, if they breach the blockade by crossing the blockade line twenty nautical miles off the Gaza coastline, or if they attempt to breach the blockade, they are liable to capture or to any other measure taken by blockading units to prevent a continuation of their voyage.[105]

On some occasions it may be difficult to establish an attempt to breach the blockade. That is not the case with the "Gaza flotilla." The organizers had expressly stated their intent to breach the blockade and the vessels' approach to the blockaded area constituted an attempted breach of blockade. Given the expressed intent and the approach of the vessels, the Israeli Defense Force units did not need to wait to act until the vessels were either close to the blockade line or crossing it. Rather, they were entitled to take the necessary measures at a considerable distance because the attempt to breach the blockade was obvious.[106]

Vessels either breaching or attempting to breach a naval blockade must comply with all legitimate orders by the blockading power. If summoned to stop they may not continue their voyage nor attempt to escape. They are obligated to let a boarding team on the vessel and to allow the team to take control of the ship. Any act of escape or resistance may be overcome by the use of proportionate force, including, if necessary, the use of deadly force.[107]

Humanitarian considerations play a role in determining the lawfulness of a blockade. A naval blockade is unlawful if "the damage to the civilian population is, or may be expected to be, excessive in relation to the concrete and direct military advantage anticipated from the blockade."[108] "Excessive" does not mean "extensive." Applied to the blockade of the Gaza Strip, there can be no doubt that it has resulted in inconveniences for the civilian population, but certainly not in excessive damage. In this context it is important to note that the military advantage gained, i.e., the prevention of the flow of arms and the entry of terrorists, is quite substantial.

Moreover, the blockading power is obliged to provide for relief consignments if the civilian population of the blockaded area is no longer adequately provided with goods essential for its survival, i.e., with food, water and medical supplies.[109] The "Gaza flotilla" was allegedly on a purely humanitarian mission to provide the civilian population in Gaza with such essential goods. It is immaterial whether this was true, whether the cargoes indeed consisted of essential goods only or whether the flotilla was only pursuing political and provocative goals. Even if the flotilla had been on a purely humanitarian mission it would have had no right to approach the Gaza coastline. Rather, the blockading power could prescribe "the technical arrangements, including search, under which the relief consignments are permitted."[110] It is important to note that, in 2010, the Israeli government was prepared to allow the shipment of the flotilla's cargo to Gaza under the condition that it was unloaded in an Israeli port and its distribution entrusted to the United Nations. That proposal was well in accordance with the applicable law. The mere claim of pursuing humanitarian goals or to be a humanitarian organization does not give rise to a right to breach a blockade. Any refusal to accept reasonable technical arrangements offered by the blockading power and any continuation of the voyage without complying with the legitimate orders of the blockading power will entitle the latter to take appropriate and proportionate measures, including the use of force, to prevent the vessels from entering the blockaded area.

Conclusion

It has been shown that the parties to a non-international armed conflict are not obliged to confine the armed hostilities to the land territory of the State and that they may make use of recognized methods and means of naval warfare. As long as the measures they take against each other have no detrimental impact on international navigation and aviation there are no considerable legal obstacles.

While there seems to be widespread agreement that neither party to a non-international armed conflict is entitled to interfere with foreign shipping and aviation in sea areas beyond the outer limit of the territorial sea, the State party to a non-international armed conflict continues to enjoy the right to enforce its domestic law under the law of the sea. Moreover, it would be difficult to maintain that the definition of lawful military objectives that undoubtedly applies in non-international armed conflicts ceases to be valid merely by reason of the geographical position of the target. Hence, foreign vessels and aircraft that contribute to the enemy's military action by, for example, providing targeting data are lawful targets even if they are located on the high seas or in international airspace.

As regards measures short of attack, i.e., visit, search and capture, States seem to be prepared to tolerate such measures if taken by the State party to a non-international armed conflict, if vital security interests are at stake and if the interception measures are taken in the vicinity of the coast. Similar considerations may apply if the State party decides to establish and enforce a naval blockade.

Notes

1. SAN REMO MANUAL ON INTERNATIONAL LAW APPLICABLE TO ARMED CONFLICTS AT SEA 73 (Louise Doswald-Beck ed., 1995) ("although the provisions of this Manual are primarily meant to apply to international armed conflicts at sea, this has intentionally not been expressly

indicated . . . in order not to dissuade the implementation of these rules in non-international armed conflicts involving naval operations").

2. YORAM DINSTEIN, THE CONDUCT OF HOSTILITIES UNDER THE LAW OF INTERNATIONAL ARMED CONFLICT 26–28 (2d ed. 2010). For the latter aspect, see Prosecutor v. Tadić, Case No. IT-94-1, Appeals Chamber Decision on the Defence Motion for Interlocutory Appeal on Jurisdiction, ¶ 70 (Int'l Crim. Trib. for the Former Yugoslavia Oct. 2, 1995) [hereinafter *Tadić*].

3. For an analysis of such "amorphous situations," see DINSTEIN, *supra* note 2, at 26.

4. *See, e.g.*, NOAM LUBELL, EXTRATERRITORIAL USE OF FORCE AGAINST NON-STATE ACTORS 103 (2010); Douglas Guilfoyle, *The* Mavi Marmara *Incident and Blockade in Armed Conflict*, 81 BRITISH YEARBOOK OF INTERNATIONAL LAW 171, 186–87 (2011).

5. Public Committee against Torture in Israel v. Government of Israel, HCJ 769/02, Judgment (Dec. 13, 2006), 46 INTERNATIONAL LEGAL MATERIALS 373 (2007), *available at* http://elyon1.court.gov.il/files_eng/02/690/007/a34/02007690.a34.pdf [hereinafter *Public Committee against Torture*].

6. This position is taken by Cassese, who maintains that "an armed conflict which takes place between an Occupying Power and rebel or insurgent groups . . . in an occupied territory amounts to an international armed conflict." ANTONIO CASSESE, INTERNATIONAL LAW 420 (2d ed. 2005).

7. This is the position taken in the German military manual. FEDERAL MINISTRY OF DEFENCE (Germany), HUMANITARIAN LAW IN ARMED CONFLICTS MANUAL (1992). However, in the forthcoming edition of the manual, there will be a separate section dealing with the law of non-international armed conflict.

8. *See, e.g.*, Amendment to the Convention on Prohibitions or Restrictions on the Use of Certain Conventional Weapons Which May Be Deemed to Be Excessively Injurious or to Have Indiscriminate Effects, Doc. No. CCW/CONF/II/2 (Dec. 21, 2001).

9. *See* Rome Statute of the International Criminal Court art. 8(2)(c), July 17, 1998, 2187 U.N.T.S. 90. Additionally, in 1993 the International Committee of the Red Cross stated that "according to humanitarian law as it stands today, the notion of war crimes is limited to situations of international armed conflict." Some Preliminary Remarks by the International Committee of the Red Cross on the Setting up of an International Tribunal (Feb. 22, 1993), *reprinted in* 2 VIRGINIA MORRIS & MICHAEL P. SCHARF, AN INSIDER'S GUIDE TO THE INTERNATIONAL CRIMINAL TRIBUNAL FOR THE FORMER YUGOSLAVIA 391, 392 (1995).

10. Convention for the Amelioration of the Condition of the Wounded and Sick in Armed Forces in the Field art. 3, Aug. 12, 1949, 6 U.S.T. 3114, 75 U.N.T.S. 31; Convention for the Amelioration of the Condition of Wounded, Sick and Shipwrecked Members of Armed Forces at Sea art. 3, Aug. 12, 1949, 6 U.S.T. 3217, 75 U.N.T.S. 85; Convention Relative to the Treatment of Prisoners of War art. 3, Aug. 12, 1949, 6 U.S.T. 3316, 75 U.N.T.S. 135; Convention Relative to the Protection of Civilian Persons in Time of War art. 3, Aug. 12, 1949, 6 U.S.T. 3516, 75 U.N.T.S. 287.

11. Protocol Additional to the Geneva Conventions of 12 August 1949, and Relating to the Protection of Victims of Non-International Armed Conflicts, June 8, 1977, 1125 U.N.T.S. 609.

12. DINSTEIN, *supra* note 2, at 27.

13. *Tadić*, *supra* note 2.

14. DINSTEIN, *supra* note 2, at 28.

15. Protocol Additional to the Geneva Conventions of 12 August 1949, and Relating to the Protection of Victims of International Armed Conflicts, June 8, 1977, 1125 U.N.T.S. 3.

16. *Tadić*, *supra* note 2. *See also* MICHAEL N. SCHMITT, CHARLES H.B. GARRAWAY & YORAM DINSTEIN, THE MANUAL ON THE LAW OF NON-INTERNATIONAL ARMED CONFLICT WITH

COMMENTARY ¶ 1.1.1 (2006) [hereinafter NIAC MANUAL] ("Non-international armed conflicts are armed confrontations occurring within the territory of a single State and in which the armed forces of no other State are engaged against the central government.").

17. *See* LESLIE C. GREEN, THE CONTEMPORARY LAW OF ARMED CONFLICT 343 n.1 (2000).

18. *Id.*

19. Admittedly, scholars disagree on whether recognition of belligerency is still a valid legal concept. For an analysis, see Yair M. Lootsteen, *The Concept of Belligerency in International Law*, 166 MILITARY LAW REVIEW 109 (2000).

20. Norman J. Padelford, *International Law and the Spanish Civil War*, 31 AMERICAN JOURNAL OF INTERNATIONAL LAW 226 (1937); George A. Finch, *Piracy in the Mediterranean*, 31 AMERICAN JOURNAL OF INTERNATIONAL LAW 659 (1937).

21. Nyon Arrangement, Sept. 14, 1937, 181 L.N.T.S. 135; Agreement Supplementary to the Nyon Arrangement, Sept. 17, 1937, 181 L.N.T.S. 149. For the text of the agreements and an analysis by L.F.E. Goldie, see *1937 Geneva Agreement Supplementary to the Nyon Arrangement*, *in* THE LAW OF NAVAL WARFARE 487–502 (Natalino Ronzitti ed.,1988).

22. Guilfoyle, *supra* note 4, at 192.

23. Décret 56/274, Journal Officiel (Mar. 17, 1956), at 2665.

24. The exact figures are unclear. Some report that 4,775 ships were searched in the first year alone. *See* ROBIN R. CHURCHILL & ALAN V. LOWE, THE LAW OF THE SEA 217 (3d ed. 1999).

25. Laurent Lucchini, *Actes de Contrainte Exercés par la France en Haute Mer au Cours des Opérations en Algérie*, 1966 ANNUAIRE FRANÇAIS DE DROIT INTERNATIONAL 803. *See also* D.P. O'Connell, *International Law and Contemporary Naval Operations*, 44 BRITISH YEARBOOK OF INTERNATIONAL LAW 19, 36–39 (1970).

26. Note that the distance was 50 kilometers, not 50 nautical miles.

27. The German *Bilbao* and the Bulgarian *Chipka* were visited in the English Channel, the German *Las Palmas* twenty-two nautical miles south of Cape Vicent and the German *Archsum* fifty-four nautical miles east of Gibraltar.

28. *See* ROLF OTTMÜLLER, DIE ANWENDUNG VON SEEKRIEGSRECHT IN MILITÄRISCHEN KONFLIKTEN SEIT 1945, at 137 (1978).

29. O'Connell, *supra* note 25, at 37–39.

30. *Wary of Sea Tigers, India tightens security*, REDIFF INDIA ABROAD (May 14, 2007), http://www.rediff.com/news/2007/may/14ltte.htm.

31. *India Must Neutralise Sea Tigers*, THE HINDU (Dec. 12, 2004), http://www.hindu.com/2004/12/12/stories/2004121206020400.htm.

32. Guilfoyle, *supra* note 4, at 193.

33. Notice to Mariners No. 6/2008 (Aug. 13, 2008), http://en.mot.gov.il/index.php?option=com_content&view=article&id=74:no62008&catid=17:noticetomariners&Itemid=12.

34. Notice to Mariners No. 1/2009 Blockade of Gaza Strip (Jan. 6, 2009), http://199.203.58.11/EN/index.php?option=com_content&view=article&id=124:no12009&catid=17:noticetomariners&Itemid=12.

35. For the facts of what has become known as the "flotilla incident," see U.N. Secretary-General's Panel of Inquiry, *Report on the 31 May 2010 Flotilla Incident*, ¶¶ 83–93 (July 2011) (Geoffrey Palmer et al.), *available at* http://www.un.org/News/dh/infocus/middle_east/Gaza_Flotilla_Panel_Report.pdf [hereinafter Palmer Report].

36. S.C. Res. 1973, U.N. Doc. S/RES/1973 (Mar. 17, 2011).

37. *Libya: Nato intercepts boats laying mines outside Misurata*, THE TELEGRAPH (United Kingdom) (Apr. 29, 2011), http://www.telegraph.co.uk/news/worldnews/africaandindianocean/libya/8483805/Libya-Nato-intercepts-boats-laying-mines-outside-Misurata.html.

38. *See supra* note 16 and text accompanying notes 12, 16.

39. United Nations Convention on the Law of the Sea, Dec. 10, 1982, 1833 U.N.T.S. 397 [hereinafter LOS Convention].

40. CHURCHILL & LOWE, *supra* note 24, at 87–88, 90.

41. Emphasis added.

42. CHURCHILL & LOWE, *supra* note 24, at 100.

43. SAN REMO MANUAL, *supra* note 1, ¶ 27. *See also* U.S. Navy, U.S. Marine Corps & U.S. Coast Guard, The Commander's Handbook on the Law of Naval Operations ¶ 9.2.3, NWP 1-14M/MCWP 5-12.1/COMDTPUB P5800.7A (2007), *available at* http://www.usnwc.edu/getattachment/a9b8e92d-2c8d-4779-9925-0defea93325c/1-14M_(Jul_2007)_(NWP [hereinafter Commander's Handbook].

44. LOS Convention, *supra* note 39, arts. 44, 54.

45. To "prevent infringement of customs, fiscal, immigration or sanitary laws within its territory or territorial seas" or to "punish infringement of . . . [those] laws and regulations committed within its territory or territorial seas."

46. Guilfoyle, *supra* note 4, at 193.

47. SAN REMO MANUAL, *supra* note 1, ¶ 36.

48. *Id.*, ¶ 37.

49. *Id.*, ¶¶ 34, 35.

50. *Id.*, ¶ 13.21.

51. Declaration Respecting Maritime Law, Apr. 16, 1856, 115 C.T.S. 1, *reprinted in* THE LAWS OF ARMED CONFLICTS 1056 (Dietrich Schindler & Jiri Toman eds., 4th ed. 2004).

52. Convention Relating to the Conversion of Merchant Ships into War-Ships, Oct. 18, 1907, 205 Consol. T.S. 319, *reprinted in id.* at 1066.

53. Convention on the High Seas, Apr. 29, 1958, 13 U.S.T. 2312, 450 U.N.T.S. 82.

54. *See* Commander's Handbook, *supra* note 43, ¶ 2.2.2.

55. PROGRAM ON HUMANITARIAN POLICY AND CONFLICT RESEARCH, MANUAL ON INTERNATIONAL LAWS APPLICABLE TO AIR AND MISSILE WARFARE ¶ 17(a) (2009), *available at* http://ihlresearch.org/amw/HPCR%20Manual.pdf ("Only military aircraft, including UCAVs, are entitled to engage in attacks."). The commentary indicates, "Rule 17 (a) does not apply in non-international armed conflict. States are more likely to employ law-enforcement and other State aircraft during these conflicts. It is not in contravention with the law of international armed if such aircraft conduct combat functions." *Id.* at 101.

There is a very limited exception in those instances when the States parties to a non-international armed conflict are undertaking prize measures against enemy merchant vessels or civilian aircraft. In those cases, only warships may exercise belligerent rights.

56. *See infra* Part IV.

57. *See* NIAC MANUAL, *supra* note 16, ¶¶ 1.1.2, 2.1.1. Although members of the State's armed forces are lawful targets under the law of non-international armed conflict, members of the dissident armed forces or an organized armed group who target them do not have combatant immunity and are subject to prosecution under the State's domestic criminal law.

58. NILS MELZER, INTERNATIONAL COMMITTEE OF THE RED CROSS, INTERPRETIVE GUIDANCE ON THE NOTION OF DIRECT PARTICIPATION IN HOSTILITIES UNDER INTERNATIONAL HUMANITARIAN LAW 27 (2009).

59. *Id.* at 34.

60. *Id.*

61. Except for medical and religious personnel, who may not be targeted unless they take an active part in hostilities. NIAC MANUAL, *supra* note 16, ¶ 1.1.2.

62. 1 CUSTOMARY INTERNATIONAL HUMANITARIAN LAW 21 (Jean-Marie Henckaerts & Louise Doswald-Beck eds., 2005) [hereinafter CIHL].

63. NIAC MANUAL, *supra* note 16, ¶¶ 2.1.1.1, 2.1.1.2.

64. *Id.*, ¶ 1.1.4. *See also* CIHL, *supra* note 62, at 30–31.

65. *See* NIAC MANUAL, *supra* note 16, ¶ 1.1.4.3.

66. Such attacks are lawful under the international law of non-international armed conflict, but, as with attacks on members of the armed forces, those who carry out the attacks are subject to prosecution under the State's domestic law. *See supra* note 57.

67. NIAC MANUAL, *supra* note 16, ¶ 2.1.1.1; CIHL, *supra* note 62, at 5–8, 32–34.

68. *See* NIAC MANUAL, *supra* note 16, ¶ 1.2.2.

69. *Id.*, ¶ 1.1.3; CIHL, *supra* note 62, at 19.

70. *See* NIAC MANUAL, *supra* note 16, ¶ 1.1.5.

71. *See supra* Part I.F.

72. S.C. Res. 1973, *supra* note 36, ¶ 6.

73. LOS Convention, *supra* note 39, art. 25(3).

74. *See* Commander's Handbook, *supra* note 43, ¶ 9.2. *See also* HOWARD S. LEVIE, MINE WARFARE AT SEA (1992); Wolff Heintschel von Heinegg, *The International Law of Mine Warfare at Sea*, 23 ISRAEL YEARBOOK ON HUMAN RIGHTS 53 (1993).

75. *See* NIAC MANUAL, *supra* note 16, ¶ 2.1.1.3.

76. *Id.*, ¶ 2.2.1.1.

77. *Id.*, ¶ 2.2.1.2.

78. SAN REMO MANUAL, *supra* note 1, ¶ 82.

79. *See* Heintschel von Heinegg, *supra* note 74, at 62.

80. SAN REMO MANUAL, *supra* note 1, ¶ 103. *See also* Guilfoyle, *supra* note 4, at 198–200.

81. CIHL, *supra* note 62, at 148.

82. *Id.* at 149.

83. Some prefer a comprehensive approach and tend to equate the natural environment with an "ecosystem." Accordingly, components of the natural environment, such as flora, fauna, the lithosphere or the atmosphere, would only be covered by the term if they interact in a way that they may be considered part of an interdependent and mutually influencing system of diverse components of the natural environment. In contrast, others are prepared to consider components of the natural environment to be specially protected by the law of armed conflict, irrespective of their interdependence with other components. The only common denominator is that the term "natural environment" does not cover man-made components of the environment.

84. Guilfoyle, *supra* note 4, at 193–94.

85. *See supra* text accompanying notes 64–66.

86. Nyon Arrangement, *supra* note 21, pmbl.

87. O'Connell, *supra* note 25, at 38–39.

88. Legal Consequences of the Construction of a Wall in the Occupied Palestinian Territory, Advisory Opinion, 2004 I.C.J. 136, ¶ 139 (July 9) ("The Court also notes that Israel exercises control in the Occupied Palestinian Territory and that . . . the threat which it regards as justifying the construction of the wall originates within, and not outside, that territory. The situation is thus different from that contemplated by Security Council resolutions 1368 (2001) and 1373 (2001) . . . . Consequently, the Court concludes that Article 51 of the Charter has no relevance in this case.").

89. *See* Wolff Heintschel von Heinegg, *Blockade*, *in* MAX PLANCK ENCYCLOPEDIA OF PUBLIC INTERNATIONAL LAW (Rüdiger Wolfrum ed , 2010), http://www.mpepil.com/subscriber _article?script =yes&id=/epil/entries/law-9780199231690-e252&recno=3&author=Heintschel von Heinegg Wolff.

90. *See supra* Part I.A.

91. Guilfoyle, *supra* note 4, at 217.

92. *Id.*

93. It is interesting to note that a 2009 report submitted to the Human Rights Council does not contain a legal analysis under the law of naval blockade. *See* U.N. Human Rights Council, Human Rights in Palestine and Other Occupied Arab Territories, Report of the United Nations Fact-Finding Mission on the Gaza Conflict, U.N. Doc. A/HRC/12/48 (Sept. 25, 2009) (Richard Goldstone).

94. Guilfoyle, *supra* note 4, at 178–91.

95. For the concept of desuetude, see, e.g., Michael J. Glennon, *How International Law Dies*, 93 GEORGETOWN LAW JOURNAL 939 (2005).

96. *See* YORAM DINSTEIN, THE INTERNATIONAL LAW OF BELLIGERENT OCCUPATION 276–83 (2009).

97. *See* HCJ 9132/07 Al-Bassiouni v. Prime Minister ¶ 12 [Jan. 30, 2008] (unpublished), *available at* http://www.mfa.gov.il/NR/rdonlyres/938CCD2E-89C7-4E77-B071-56772DFF79CC/0/HCJGazaelectricity.pdf.

98. *Public Committee against Torture*, *supra* note 5.

99. Jacob Turkel et al., 1 The Public Commission to Examine the Maritime Incident of 31 May 2010, ¶ 41 (2011), *available at* http://turkel-committee.gov.il/files/wordocs//8707200211english.pdf.

100. *Id.*, ¶ 44.

101. Palmer Report, *supra* note 35, ¶ 73.

102. SAN REMO MANUAL, *supra* note 1, ¶¶ 93–104; Commander's Handbook, *supra* note 43, ¶ 7.7.

103. For the relationship between the law of the sea and the law of naval warfare, see Wolff Heintschel von Heinegg, *The United Nations Convention on the Law of the Sea and Maritime Security Operations*, 48 GERMAN YEARBOOK OF INTERNATIONAL LAW 151 (2005).

104. Declaration Respecting Maritime Law, *supra* note 51, ¶ 4; Declaration Concerning the Laws of Naval War art. 2, Feb. 26, 1909, 208 Consol. T.S. 338, *reprinted in* THE LAWS OF ARMED CONFLICTS, *supra* note 51, at 1113 (never in force); SAN REMO MANUAL, *supra* note 1, ¶ 95; Commander's Handbook, *supra* note 43, ¶ 7.7.2.3.

105. SAN REMO MANUAL, *supra* note 1, ¶¶ 67(a), 98, 146(f). *See also* Declaration Concerning the Laws of Naval War, *supra* note 105, art. 20; Heintschel von Heinegg, *supra* note 89, ¶¶ 41–48.

106. The boarding of the *Mavi Marmara* and the other vessels in the flotilla occurred approximately 72 nautical miles at sea. Palmer Report, *supra* note 35, ¶ 1.

107. SAN REMO MANUAL, *supra* note 1, ¶¶ 67(a), 146(f); Commander's Handbook, *supra* note 43, ¶ 7.10.

108. SAN REMO MANUAL, *supra* note 1, ¶ 102(b).

109. *Id.*, ¶ 103; Heintschel von Heinegg, *supra* note 89, ¶¶ 49–52.

110. SAN REMO MANUAL, *supra* note 1, ¶ 103(b); Heintschel von Heinegg, *supra* note 90, ¶¶ 50–51.

XI

Perfidy in Non-International Armed Conflicts

Richard B. Jackson*

Introduction

Perfidy is a grave breach, or serious crime, under the law of war. It is generally defined as "acts inviting the confidence of an adversary to lead him to believe that he is entitled to, or is obliged to accord, protection under the rules of international law applicable in armed conflict, with intent to betray that confidence."[1] Examples include using the white flag to lure an enemy into the open, or feigning incapacitation by wounds or sickness; the most egregious violations include using protected status, as a civilian or a medical professional, to treacherously kill or wound an enemy.

In the current and recent conflicts in Iraq, Afghanistan, Somalia and Pakistan, all of which are non-international armed conflicts of varying degrees of intensity, actions that would be described as perfidy if they had occurred in an international armed conflict are rampant. On January 19, 2011, for example, Iraqi insurgents used an ambulance bomb to attack an Iraqi police station in Diyala province, killing five and wounding seventy-six individuals, the majority of whom were civilians.[2] On the afternoon of July 5, 2011, a suicide bomber, disguised as a civilian, detonated a truckload of explosives near a municipal building in Taji, Iraq; as

* Colonel, U.S. Army (Ret.); Special Assistant to the Judge Advocate General of the Army for Law of War Matters. The views and opinions expressed are those of the author alone and not necessarily those of the U.S. government or the U.S. Army.

friends and neighbors, including young children, rushed to help the injured, a second suicide bomber attacked from among the crowd.[3] In Afghanistan, on April 7, 2011, a suicide bomber used an ambulance to infiltrate a police checkpoint and then detonated his bomb, killing six.[4] In Somalia, Al-Shabaab, an Al Qaeda–affiliated group fighting the fledgling Somali government, has trained women to be suicide bombers, so they can launch their attacks while appearing to be innocent civilian females, dressed in traditional Moslem garb.[5] And Pakistani insurgents have employed similar asymmetric tactics. On May 13, 2011, just days after the death of Bin Laden, the Pakistani Taliban returned to the practice of launching suicide attacks from among the civilian populace.[6]

The question to be addressed is whether the war crime of perfidy exists in the law of war pertaining to non-international armed conflicts. Or phrased in another manner, is it appropriate to apply this term outside of international armed conflict, where the rules are defined by treaty and customary international law? The *Manual on the Law of Non-International Armed Conflict* suggests that at least some of the conduct defined as perfidy when occurring during an international armed conflict is also perfidious when occurring during non-international armed conflicts.[7] What are its parameters and how many of the concepts from international armed conflict are to be incorporated into the law of non-international armed conflicts?

An answer to these questions requires an examination of the Additional Protocol I (AP I) definition of perfidy in international armed conflict and its antecedents, an analysis of the existing treaty law of non-international armed conflict (Additional Protocol II (AP II))[8] and an extrapolation of the principles established in AP I for international armed conflicts into the law for non-international armed conflicts. Although many of the specific provisions of AP I were not included in AP II, Additional Protocol II includes the same general protections as AP I, which suggests that the more specific provisions of AP I that give form and substance to the general protections can be used to enforce compliance with those general protections in non-international armed conflict, as a matter of customary international law. As Bothe, Partsch and Solf suggest in their seminal work on the protocols, "The concept of general protection . . . is broad enough to cover protections which flow as necessary inferences from other provisions of Protocol II."[9] The basic principle of distinction and the protective principle of the law of armed conflict (also referred to as international humanitarian law) logically lead to the incorporation of the prohibition on perfidy, by inference, into the law applicable to non-international armed conflict. In addition, the near-universal condemnation of perfidious attacks and current State practice in those conflicts, the practice of some international criminal tribunals, the practices adopted by States fighting these conflicts and recent U.S. military commission cases provide substantial support for application of a rule against perfidy in non-international armed conflicts in order to provide a sanction for the perfidious use of internationally recognized emblems and protected statuses.

Protection of the civilian populace is essential in these complex conflicts. As the U.S. Army and Marine Corps' *Counterinsurgency Manual* indicates, the protection of civilians is the paramount requirement of the State in a non-international armed conflict: "The cornerstone of any COIN [counterinsurgency] effort is establishing security for the civilian populace."[10] The prosecution of perfidy, as a serious crime or grave breach under the law of war, is required to protect the civilian population and respect humanitarian efforts in this prevalent form of conflict, whether labeled "transnational" or "intra-State non-international armed conflict."

The law that applies to the conduct of armed forces in a non-international armed conflict is derived from treaty law and customary international law. However, the customary international law status of perfidy in non-international conflict is difficult to establish under the current U.S. view of customary international law.[11] There is little or no evidence of perfidy violations being prosecuted under international law in non-international armed conflicts, nor is there clear *opinio juris* by States on this matter. Emerging customary international law must be inferred, therefore, from the principles of the law of armed conflict supported by evidence provided by jurists, official statements, statutes, the works of eminent writers and evidence of State practice.[12]

Treaty Provisions

General Principles

Treaty provisions adopting perfidy as a crime in non-international armed conflict are nearly non-existent.[13] The law of armed conflict provisions from which a rule against perfidy may be derived, however, are clearly enunciated in Additional Protocol II. The United States has signed AP II and three presidents have recommended it be ratified by the Senate under the U.S. advice and consent constitutional process.[14] At a minimum, U.S. forces are bound not to act contrary to the purpose and intent of the treaty.[15] President Reagan, in transmitting the treaty to the Senate for advice and consent, noted the importance of the humanitarian provisions of AP II, focusing on the provisions designed to protect those who are *hors de combat* from intentional killing:

> The United States has traditionally been in the forefront of efforts to codify and improve the international rules of humanitarian law in armed conflict, with the objective of giving the greatest possible protection to victims of such conflicts, consistent with

> legitimate military requirements. The agreement I am transmitting today is, with certain exceptions,[16] a positive step toward this goal. Its ratification by the United States will assist us in continuing to exercise leadership in the international community in these matters. . . . Protocol II to the 1949 Geneva Conventions is essentially an expansion of the fundamental humanitarian provisions contained in the 1949 Geneva Conventions with respect to non-international armed conflicts, including humane treatment and basic due process for detained persons, protection of the wounded, sick, and medical units, and protection of noncombatants from attack and deliberate starvation. If these fundamental rules were observed, many of the worst human tragedies of current internal armed conflicts could be avoided. . . . This Protocol makes clear that any deliberate killing of a noncombatant in the course of a non-international armed conflict is a violation of the laws of war and a crime against humanity, and is therefore punishable as murder.[17]

In addition, various U.S. officials have signaled the intent of the United States government to comply with provisions of the treaty, including the protection of civilians and the prevention of intentional killing or serious bodily harm of those that are protected under the humanitarian provisions of the law of war.[18] In his discussion of President Reagan's intent to ratify AP II, Judge Abraham Sofaer, the Department of State Legal Advisor in 1987, expressed the desire of the U.S. government to "guarantee that certain fundamental protections be observed," including "protection from intentional attack, hostage taking, and acts of terrorism [against] persons who take no active part in hostilities," "protection and appropriate care for the sick and wounded, and medical units which assist them" and "protection of the civilian population from military attack [and] acts of terror."[19]

Additional Protocol II contains several provisions that articulate general principles of the law of armed conflict that are relevant to the crime of perfidy. Article 4 provides for humane treatment for those no longer taking a direct part in hostilities; Article 7 protects the wounded and sick; and Articles 9 through 12 provide protection to medical personnel, units, transports, and functions, via the internationally recognized red cross, red crescent and red lion emblems.[20] Article 12 concludes that the emblems "shall not be used improperly." Article 13 provides that civilians "shall not be the object of attack . . . unless and for such time as they take a direct part in hostilities." Article 16 provides protection to cultural objects and places of worship. Relief societies, marked with the aforementioned emblems, are also allowed to "offer their services" to perform their traditional functions in relation to the victims of armed conflict under Article 18, so long as they provide services of an "exclusively humanitarian and impartial nature." All of these provisions provide for the general protections that are enforced through the prohibition of the grave breach of perfidy.

Origins of the Prohibition of Perfidy

The origins of the prohibition of perfidy are found in the early law of war treatises and treaties of the nineteenth and early twentieth centuries. In his 1810 *Treatise on the Law of War*, Van Bynkershoek wrote that he believed that fraud and deceit were lawful and essential stratagems of war: "For my part, I think that every species of deceit is lawful, perfidy only excepted. . . ."[21] He decried as an example of perfidious conduct the offer of a Dutch sea captain of passage to the governor of the Canary Islands, whom, when the governor accepted, the captain made a prisoner for ransom. Van Bynkershoek likened this to an act of perfidy: "precisely the same as going to an enemy under the protected flag of truce, with an intention to seize upon the first favourable opportunity to take away his life."[22]

Francis Lieber, who gathered in his Lieber Code much of the law of nations from the same Napoleonic period, noted:

> Art. 16. Military necessity does not admit of cruelty—that is, the infliction of suffering for the sake of suffering or revenge, nor of maiming or wounding except in fight. . . . It admits of deception, but disclaims acts of perfidy; and, in general, military necessity does not include any act of hostility which makes the return to peace unnecessarily difficult.
>
> Art. 65. The use of the enemy's national standard, flag, or other emblem of nationality, for the purpose of deceiving the enemy in battle, is an act of perfidy by which they lose all claim to the protection of the laws of war.
>
> Art. 101. While deception in war is admitted as a just and necessary means of hostility, and is consistent with honorable warfare, the common law of war allows even capital punishment for clandestine or treacherous attempts to injure an enemy, because they are so dangerous, and it is so difficult to guard against them.
>
> Art. 117. It is justly considered an act of bad faith, of infamy or fiendishness, to deceive the enemy by flags of protection [including flags of truce and hospital designation].[23]

Finally, Lieber provided that these "rules of war" are appropriate for a civil war, without reference to the legitimacy of the "rebels," as "humanity induces the adoption of rules of regular war toward the rebels, whether the adoption is partial or entire, [while] it does in no way whatever imply a partial or complete acknowledgement of their government."[24] In its earliest form of codification, the law of war provided for the grave breach of perfidy, even in non-international armed conflict.

The 1907 Hague Regulations codified, in a broadly adopted treaty, the concept of perfidy.[25] Article 23(b) provided that it was "especially forbidden" to "kill or wound treacherously individuals belonging to the hostile nation or army" and Article 23(f) prohibited "improper use of a flag of truce, of the national flag or of the military insignia and uniform of the enemy, as well as the distinctive badges of the Geneva Convention."[26] Although the Hague Regulations applied between States parties, the famous "Martens clause" in Article 2 arguably extends many of these rules to other forms of warfare in stating that "the inhabitants and the belligerents remain under the protections of and the rule of the principles of the law of nations, as they result from the usages established among civilized peoples, from the laws of humanity, and the dictates of the public conscience."

In Spaight's 1911 seminal *War Rights on Land*, he noted the application of the rule against perfidy to a broad range of conduct. Quoting Hall, Oppenheim and Bluntschli, Spaight found that use of an enemy uniform, insignia or flag is permitted "up to the commencement of actual fighting."[27] Spaight also provided numerous examples of strict and less strict interpretations of this provision from the U.S. Civil War, the Franco-Prussian War, the Crimean War and the Boer War.[28] As a clear case of "treacherous attempts to kill or wound," he cited the use of civilian clothes by belligerent troops of the Japanese in the Russo-Japanese War.[29] And, as an example of the perfidious use of a protected emblem, Spaight cited both the "treacherous overt act—if, for instance, by making a sudden attempt [under a white flag], he kills the enemy commander"[30]—and the "treacherous simulation of sickness or wounds" in the Russo-Japanese War.[31] These examples, applied in international (Franco-Prussian and Crimean Wars) and non-international (Boer and U.S. Civil Wars) armed conflicts, validate the strength, breadth and application of the prohibition on perfidious conduct across the spectrum of conflict.

Application of the Rules against Perfidy

Skorzeny Case

As evidenced by documents and treatises antecedent to the Second World War, perfidy was a crime that included treacherous use of the enemy uniform. A significant case that arose during the prosecutions before the International Military Tribunals illuminated the difference between the ruse of infiltration using the enemy uniform, and the "improper use" of the enemy uniform to kill or wound in violation of Article 23(f) of the Hague Regulations. Colonel Otto Skorzeny, the celebrated German commando who had rescued Mussolini from Italian partisans, was prosecuted, along with nine of his soldiers, for the "improper use of American uniforms by entering into combat disguised therewith and treacherously firing upon and killing members of the armed forces of the US."[32] The trial produced testimony that Skorzeny's commandos, who were charged with seizing bridges and road intersections in advance of the Battle of the Bulge, were instructed to use American uniforms to infiltrate the lines, but to avoid fighting in enemy uniforms. At trial, no evidence of U.S. soldiers being killed or wounded by Germans fighting in American uniforms was produced, so all the accused were acquitted.[33] Since the published report contains only the findings of the court, without explanation, the "Notes on the Case," prepared by the War Crimes Commission, provide the only rationale for the decision. They explain the decision by noting the lack of treacherous killing or wounding, as well as citing the U.S. Rules of Land Warfare of October 1940, which permitted the use of enemy uniforms and insignia as a ruse, but prohibited their use during combat, requiring that they be discarded before opening fire upon the enemy.[34] While the prohibition on use of enemy uniforms in combat has survived, even into non-international armed conflict,[35] the modern grave breach of perfidy has not included the misuse of enemy uniforms.[36]

Perfidy during the Cold War: Special Operations Forces

In a 2003 article, W. Hays Parks described numerous examples of the use of civilian clothing in special operations missions that ranged from clandestine direct action missions to special reconnaissance missions deep within enemy-held territory.[37] Several reported cases of soldiers wearing civilian clothes while on a mission to attack civilian objects arose from the conflict between Indonesia and Malaysia in the 1960s. A Malaysian case, *Krofan and Another*, arising from the international armed conflict between Malaysia and Indonesia over the status of Singapore (then a part of Malaysia) and other nearby territories, illustrates the use of civilian clothes as a violation of the law of war.[38] While the case turns on the issue of the lack of status of the Indonesian soldiers as prisoners of war due to their mission of sabotage, the Singapore court decried the tactic of wearing civilian clothes because of its tendency to endanger civilians: "Both [spies and saboteurs] seek to harm the enemy by clandestine means by carrying out their hostile operations in circumstances which render it difficult to distinguish them from civilians."[39]

Parks also cites several examples of Soviet Spetsnaz (Special Operations) Forces and Israeli commandos using civilian clothes to infiltrate and capture or kill enemy forces.[40] None of these cases resulted in charges of perfidy, however, as they rested on claims of "unlawful belligerency" and the crimes of espionage or sabotage under domestic statutes, rather than law of war violations. Parks cautioned military forces to avoid perfidy, which he said was synonymous with "treacherous wounding" under the Hague Regulations,[41] and noted that the principle of distinction is "at the heart of the balance" between lawful military operations and perfidy. Finally, he concluded that the drafters of the 1977 Protocols decided to criminalize use of civilian clothing "in the most egregious circumstances, such as terrorism and treacherous use of civilian clothing."[42]

A Modern Definition of Perfidy: Additional Protocol I

While it may be difficult to trace the precise application of the "treacherous killing or wounding" provisions of Article 23 from the Hague Regulations to the present, Additional Protocol I, which unified the Hague and Geneva traditions of the law of war, specifically addresses the definition of perfidy in international armed conflict:

> It is prohibited to kill, injure, or capture an adversary by resort to perfidy. Acts inviting the confidence of an adversary to lead him to believe he is entitled to, or is obliged to accord, protection under the rules of international law applicable in armed conflict, with intent to betray that confidence, shall constitute perfidy. The following are examples of perfidy:
>
> (a) the feigning of an intent to negotiate under a flag of truce or of a surrender;
>
> (b) the feigning of an incapacitation by wounds or sickness;
>
> (c) the feigning of civilian, non-combatant status; and
>
> (d) the feigning of protected status by the use of signs, emblems or uniforms of the United Nations or of neutral or other States not Parties to the conflict.[43]

Article 37 goes on to distinguish "ruses of war," or acts "intended to mislead an adversary . . . which are not perfidious because they do not invite the confidence of an adversary with respect to protection under the law." A distinction between these concepts is essential to understanding perfidy. As Oppenheim notes, "whenever a belligerent has expressly or tacitly engaged, and is therefore bound by a moral obligation to speak truth to an enemy, it is perfidy to betray his confidence, because it constitutes a breach of good faith."[44]

While the prohibitions on perfidy contained in AP I are broad, the grave breaches that are prohibited are narrowly defined. First, grave breaches are limited to those violations of the law of war that are "committed willfully" (incorporating a *mens rea* element) and cause "death or serious injury to body or health."[45] And the specific provisions of perfidy that constitute grave breaches only include misuse of internationally protected emblems, outlined in Articles 37 and 38, that result in death or serious bodily harm.[46] So, while perfidy may be more broadly construed to include a number of "breaches of faith" on the international armed conflict battlefield, the violations of the law of war that are designated as "grave breaches," with the requirement to "prosecute or extradite" perpetrators,[47] are few.

Perfidy in Non-International Armed Conflict

So what elements of perfidy, as described in Protocol I, can be extrapolated to non-international armed conflict? The *Manual on the Law of Non-International Armed Conflict* (*NIAC Manual*) describes perfidy in non-international armed conflict rather broadly. It prohibits "[d]isplaying the white flag falsely, or pretending to surrender, be wounded, or otherwise have a protected status . . . if the intent in doing so is to kill or wound an adversary."[48] How much of this definition fits the standard established by Bothe, Partsch and Solf: "The concept of general protection . . . is broad enough to cover protections which flow as necessary inferences from other provisions of Protocol II"?[49] In other words, do the general principles adopted in AP II support a customary international law application of the specific provisions that prohibit that same conduct in international armed conflict? Are the provisions of this proposed rule consistent with the protective principle and the principle of distinction? And how many of these rules have been adopted in practice?

The Principles of Additional Protocol II and Their Connection to Perfidy

The principle of distinction is clearly enunciated in Protocol II, the treaty governing non-international armed conflicts that cross certain thresholds, and customary international law. Article 13 provides that civilians are to be protected "against the dangers arising from military operations . . . unless and for such time as they take a direct part in hostilities."[50] The principle of distinction (also characterized as "discrimination") is also enshrined in treaty law applicable to non-international armed conflict in protocols of the Certain Conventional Weapons Convention.[51] For example, Article 3(8) of the Amended Mines Protocol II, which by its provisions applies to Common Article 3 conflicts, requires distinction between military objectives and civilians or civilian objects.[52] Finally, distinction is clearly recognized in customary international law as applying in non-international armed conflicts.[53] For example, the International Criminal Tribunal for the former Yugoslavia (ICTY) noted in the *Kupreskic* case, "The protection of civilians in armed conflict, whether international or internal [non-international], is the bedrock of modern humanitarian law."[54]

Article 13 of AP II sets forth a general "protective principle"[55] to protect the civilian population and individual civilians from the dangers of military operations. As the International Committee of the Red Cross's *Commentary* notes, the protection extended to civilians in Article 13 reflects the more detailed protections of Article 51 of Additional Protocol I[56]—in particular the principle of distinction in Article 51(4), which defines "indiscriminate attacks" as those attacks which "are of a nature to strike military objectives (including combatants) and civilians or civilian objects without distinction."[57] The *Commentary* goes on to explain that States are required to formulate rules that give form and substance to the principle of distinction:

> This radical simplification does not reduce the degree of protection which was initially envisaged, for despite its brevity, Article 13 reflects the most fundamental rules. How to implement them is the responsibility of the parties, and this means that the safety measures they are obliged to take under the rule on protection will have to be developed so as to best suit each situation, the infrastructure available and the means at their disposal.[58]

Other provisions of Additional Protocol II emphasize the principles that are reinforced by the prohibition on perfidy, thereby strengthening the argument that forbidding perfidy is an essential tool for States as "measures they are obliged to take" to emphasize these protective principles. The "fundamental guarantees" of Article 4 prohibit murder and other violence to life and health, as well as the giving of "order[s] that there shall be no survivors,"[59] a ban reflecting the "no quarter" provision of the Hague Regulations.[60] These prohibitions reinforce the requirement to protect the lives of those that are *hors de combat*, which is so fundamental to the basic guarantees in Common Article 3.[61] Additional Protocol II emphasizes the importance of extending that protection principle to abolish the feigning of "protected person status" to gain an advantage on an enemy; failure to respect those prohibitions on perfidy will encourage enemy soldiers to ignore the protective principle and murder soldiers and civilians, alike, who are *hors de combat*, or no longer taking an active or direct part in hostilities.

Additional Protocol II also extends the protections outlined in AP I to distinctive emblems and medical personnel and units, key targets for protection that are shielded by enforcement of perfidy provisions. Article 12 of AP II clearly protects distinctive emblems, which should be "respected in all circumstances" and never "used improperly." Both of these provisions require the rule against perfidy as an enforcement mechanism to be adopted by States. Finally, medical personnel are to be "respected and protected" under Article 9, and medical units and transports should be "respected and protected at all times and shall not be the object of attack," under Article 11 of AP II. Without the rules against perfidy to guarantee their status and punish offenders, States lack the enforcement mechanism necessary to guarantee these key protective principles.

Capture as Perfidy?

Perfidy in the form of misuse of a protected emblem to *capture* an enemy in non-international armed conflict has not become customary international law. As the commentary in the *NIAC Manual* points out, "The reference to capture does not appear in the original 1899 and 1907 Hague Regulations, Article 23(b), prohibition and is not binding on non-contracting Parties to Additional Protocol I."[62] In addition, as noted above, the grave breach provision of Article 85 of AP I applies only to acts causing "death or serious injury." The International Committee of the Red Cross's *Customary International Law Study* notes that "killing or wounding an adversary by resort to perfidy" is a serious crime, even in non-international armed conflict.[63] In the *Dusko Tadić* case, the ICTY noted that serious crimes, even in non-international armed conflict, not only must "constitute a breach of a rule protecting important values," which the rule against perfidy certainly protects, but also "must involve grave consequences for the victim."[64] Finally, Article 8.2(e)(ix) of the Statute of the International Criminal Court (ICC) only applies perfidy to non-international armed conflict in the case of killing and wounding of an adversary.[65]

State practice supports the view that misuse of protected emblems that is not the proximate cause of death or serious injury is proscribed, even in non-international armed conflict, but it is not considered to be as serious as the crime of perfidy. An example can be found in the dramatic rescue operation conducted by Colombian military forces to free Colombian and U.S. hostages from the Revolutionary Armed Forces of Colombia (FARC).[66] The Colombia military infiltrated the radio net used by the guerrillas and fooled the FARC into believing that the Venezuelan government had provided "humanitarian airlift" to remove the hostages and several guerrillas who were guarding them to a more secure location. Despite the oversight of senior officials in the Colombian government, who instructed the members of the rescue team to avoid the misuse of protected emblems (and had them removed from the aircraft), one of the team members wore a shirt with the red cross emblem clearly visible. Though the Colombian military explained that the misuse of the emblem was unintended, it was roundly criticized in the press for this mistake. While the misuse of the emblem, if intentional, may have violated the prohibition on misuse in Article 12, AP II, the elements of the grave breach of perfidy require more than capture; they require "kill[ing] or wound[ing] treacherously," in the words of the Hague Rules. In the end, cries of "perfidy" were muted, presumably because there is no consensus in the international community about the validity of characterizing the conduct as perfidious when the misuse of the emblem is used to capture, rather than kill.[67]

Law Enforcement Tactics

States involved in non-international armed conflicts, particularly those characterized as "counterinsurgencies" by the government forces, often adopt law enforcement tactics, which can blur the distinction between government forces and the civilian populace. Members of civilian law enforcement agencies routinely wear civilian clothing and agents in some law enforcement agencies never wear uniforms.[68] A close working relationship between the military and civilian law enforcement can be a critical component in counterinsurgency operations.[69] This may include clandestine operations conducted in civilian clothing by law enforcement and military authorities, particularly with respect to surveillance and other intelligence collection operations. An informant or ordinary civilian may be reluctant to be seen speaking with uniformed law enforcement or military personnel, for example. There is no prohibition on "spying" by government forces in non-international armed conflict, as espionage is generally recognized as a domestic law violation, not a violation of international law,[70] and representatives of the host nation or supporting foreign forces cannot commit "espionage" against organized armed groups in an internal armed conflict. As Parks notes in his 2003 article, "A 'double standard' exists within the law of war for regular forces of a recognized government vis-à-vis unauthorized combatant acts by private individuals or non-State actors." In non-international armed conflict, therefore, government forces (including both law enforcement agents and military personnel acting under the color of the law of the host nation) can often be expected to don civilian clothes when gathering information or providing support to civilian authorities. While this would not constitute perfidy, there is a fine line between representing the government in the performance of quasi–law enforcement functions and "feigning civilian status," thereby putting civilians at risk, in an attempt to gain an advantage in attacking insurgent forces.

Feigning Civilian Status

The critical focus of perfidy, in the area of feigning civilian status, is on the principle of "distinction," which protects civilians from combatants (including those classified as "unlawful combatants" and "unprivileged belligerents") on the international and non-international battlefield. Feigning civilian status to gain advantage over an enemy in an attack is an act of perfidy that goes to the very heart of the protective principle and, as such, its designation as a crime in non-international armed conflicts. In *Tadić*, the very first ICTY case, the Tribunal recognized the importance of perfidy as a crime under customary international law:

> State practice shows that general principles of customary international law have evolved with regard to internal armed conflict also in areas relating to methods of warfare. In addition to what has been stated above, with regard to the ban on attacks on civilians in the theatre of hostilities, mention can be made of the prohibition of perfidy.

> Thus, for instance, in a case brought before Nigerian courts, the Supreme Court of Nigeria held that rebels must not feign civilian status while engaging in military operations (citation omitted).[71]

It is important to note that Additional Protocol I's deviation from this principle in Articles 1(4) and 44(3), which collectively expand the notion of international armed conflict to the traditional non-international armed conflicts of "national liberation" and allow members of organized armed groups to claim "combatant" status merely by carrying their arms openly, was critical to the U.S. rejection of the Protocol. In expressing the Reagan administration's concern regarding Protocol I, Judge Sofaer, the then Department of State Legal Adviser, decried the failure of Articles 1(4) and 44(3) to protect civilians, stating that these provisions, when taken together, allow terrorists in wars of "national liberation" to avoid being charged with perfidy when hiding among the civilian population until the moment of attack, even though thereby putting the civilian populace and the principle of distinction at risk.[72] This deviation from the general prohibition of feigning civilian status to gain a military advantage only applies to international armed conflicts of "national liberation"; organized armed groups in non-international armed conflict are not permitted to launch attacks from the civilian populace.

Jawad and *al-Nashiri* Cases

Two U.S. military commission cases illustrate the current U.S. practice with respect to perfidy and the offense of launching an attack while feigning civilian status. Mohammed Jawad was a young Afghan who was alleged to have thrown a hand grenade into a vehicle in which two American service members and their Afghan interpreter were riding. He was charged with three specifications of attempted murder in violation of the law of war and three specifications of intentionally inflicting serious bodily injury. The government alleged that Jawad was concealing the grenade while dressed in civilian clothes and that he launched his attack from a crowd of civilians in the streets of Kabul. In support of the charges, the government argued that by his conduct, "the accused unlawfully engaged in combat by fighting outside of responsible command, by fighting without wearing a distinctive emblem, by failing to carry his arms openly, and by flaunting the laws and customs of war by feigning to be a non-combatant."[73]

The second case involves Abd al-Rahim Hussayn Muhammad al-Nashiri, alleged to be the bomber of *USS Cole* and the attempted bomber of *USS The Sullivans*, who has been charged with perfidy and attempted murder as follows:

> Charge I: Violation of 10 U.S.C. § 950t(17), Using Treachery or Perfidy
> Specification: In that Abd al Rahim Hussayn Muhammad al NASHIRI . . . , an alien unprivileged enemy belligerent subject to trial by military commission, did, in or around Aden, Yemen, on or about 12 October 2000, in the context of and associated with hostilities, invite the confidence and belief of one or more persons onboard USS COLE (DDG 67), including but not limited to then FN Raymond Mooney, USN, that two men dressed in civilian clothing, waving at the crewmembers onboard USS COLE (DDG 67), and operating a civilian boat, were entitled to protection under the law of war, and intending to betray that confidence and belief, did thereafter make use of that confidence and belief to detonate explosives hidden on said civilian boat alongside USS COLE (DDG 67), killing 17 Sailors of the United States Navy . . . and injuring one or more persons, all crewmembers onboard USS COLE (DDG 67). . . .
>
> Charge III: Violation of 10 U.S.C. § 950t(28), Attempted Murder in Violation of the Law of War
> Specification 1: In that Abd al Rahim Hussayn Muhammad al NASHIRI . . . did, . . . with the specific intent to commit Murder in Violation of the Law of War, attempt to intentionally and unlawfully kill one or more persons onboard USS THE SULLIVANS (DDG 68), in violation of the law of war, to wit: by committing an act of perfidy . . . and to effect the commission of Murder in Violation of the Law of War, the two suicide bombers dressed in civilian clothes. . . .[74]

Both these cases illustrate the view of the United States that the wearing of civilian clothes to perfidiously gain an advantage over an opponent when launching an attack is a crime when it occurs during an international armed conflict. As of the date of this writing, only in the *Jawad* case has there been a ruling regarding the offense of perfidy. In that case, Judge Henley ruled that the government could attempt to prove at trial that the attempted murder of the U.S. service members was perfidious conduct that violated the law of war.[75]

Government Forces in Non-International Armed Conflict

Foreign forces supporting the sovereign government and government forces in a non-international armed conflict have a hybrid mission, partly based on armed conflict and partly based on law enforcement concerns. The law of armed conflict is invoked because the normal domestic (law enforcement) authorities are overwhelmed by organized armed groups, who threaten the very existence of the State. In recommending some criteria for application of Common Article 3, Pictet noted that a key element in distinguishing "a genuine armed conflict from a mere act of banditry or an unorganized or short-lived insurrection" was whether the legal government "is obliged to have recourse to regular military forces against insurgents organized as military and in possession of a part of the national territory."[76] But the national security risks entailed in a non-international armed conflict do not require abandonment of societal norms intended to provide minimal protections to the populace. As Pictet notes in commenting on the minimum standards of Common Article 3:

> It merely demands respect for certain rules, which were already recognized as essential in all civilized countries, and enacted in the municipal law of the States in question, long before the Convention was signed. What Government would dare to claim before the world, in a case of civil disturbances which could justly be described as mere acts of banditry, that, Article 3 not being applicable, it was entitled to leave the wounded uncared for, to inflict torture and mutilations and to take hostages? However useful, therefore, the various conditions [of Common Article 3] may be, they are not indispensable, since no Government can object to respecting, in its dealings with internal enemies, whatever the nature of the conflict between it and them, a few essential rules which it in fact respects daily, under its own laws, even when dealing with common criminals.[77]

As the U.S. Army and Marine Corps' *Counterinsurgency Manual* indicates, COIN forces are constantly moving through the spectrum of conflict, at one moment involved in a pitched battle with organized armed groups and in the next (or in the next village) supporting host nation law enforcement personnel in conducting civil security operations, under the rubric of "stability operations."[78] But the *raison d'être* of COIN is the same for both aspects of the counterinsurgency fight, which is "efforts to secure the safety and support of the local populace."[79] Whether it is law enforcement efforts to "protect and serve" (as many local police forces demonstrate by the motto displayed on their police cars) or military forces intent on securing the "safety and support of the local populace"[80] by applying the law of armed conflict through the protective principle discussed above, both have the same objective. For example, most military forces operating in a COIN environment apply self-defense rules of engagement, which in application differ little from law enforcement rules for the use of force.[81] Law enforcement agencies within the United States invariably conduct their "takedowns" of criminals in uniforms emblazoned with the logos of their agencies (the Federal Bureau of Investigation or Drug Enforcement Administration, for example). While such tactics protect the agents by preventing confusing law enforcement agents with criminal gangs and by asserting the lawful power of the government to conduct arrest, search or seizure, they also protect innocent civilian bystanders by isolating the activity from the civilian populace. The tactical distinctions between COIN operations in non-international armed conflicts conducted for law enforcement purposes and those operations conducted with a military purpose fade away when the commander's intent to avoid civilian casualties is factored into the equation.[82]

U.S. Experience in Afghanistan

Twice in the last year, U.S. forces in Afghanistan have applied the protective principle and this approach to perfidy to actions by U.S. forces in the current non-international armed conflict in Afghanistan. The first instance involved the wearing of civilian clothes by members of the U.S. armed forces working in support of Afghan civil authorities, such as in the "Afghan Hands" program, where military members work outside of NATO facilities within the Afghan community performing duties that are not directly combat related. A U.S. Forces–Afghanistan (USFOR-A) position paper analyzed the impact of military personnel wearing civilian clothes and concluded, "The LOW [law of war] does not require U.S. military personnel to wear uniforms if they are not performing a combat-related operation or attempting to deceive the enemy for a military advantage (i.e., perfidy)."[83] The rationale for this approach, at least in part, was to "clearly and identifiably distinguish[] combatants from the civilian population," to avoid civilian exposure to combat operations and the "corresponding risk of harm."[84] The paper noted, "Winning the hearts and minds of the civilian population is a must in a counterinsurgency (COIN) fight and thus protection of the civilian population must be a priority."[85] The paper quoted from a 2003 paper by Major William Ferrell III: "[O]nce combatants begin distinguishing themselves as civilians, or failing to distinguish themselves from civilians to gain an advantage over the enemy, civilians will become suspect and ultimately targets."[86] The USFOR-A paper concludes that the wearing of civilian clothes in offensive operations is a potential law of war violation (perfidy) and counsels against such practice, as "this violates the basic principle of distinction."[87] In a related issue, the USFOR-A Staff Judge Advocate issued an "Information Paper" on May 12, 2011 on the carrying of weapons. The paper opens with the classic military "bottom line up front":

> The rules governing how weapons are carried find their origin in the law of war, specifically the tenet of distinction. The standard for US military members, while in Afghanistan, is to carry their weapons openly. Service members in the CENTCOM Area of Operations (AOR) must wear their weapons openly at all times. *Service members may not conceal their weapons with a perfidious intent.*[88]

The paper goes on to conclude, "A military member may not conceal his weapon with an intent to deceive people into believing he does not have a weapon or to make them believe he is a noncombatant [which the paper calls a "perfidious intent"]."[89] Current State practice, at least by U.S. forces in Afghanistan, reinforces the existence of the concept of perfidy in non-international armed conflict.

Conclusion

A colleague remarked after the Naval War College presentation on perfidy in non-international armed conflict that he "now understood [my] worldview—you believe that all the rules of international armed conflict should be followed, as a matter of law, in non-international armed conflict." I respectfully disagree with that conclusion.[90] But there is much to be said for an approach that applies general protective principles derived from Additional Protocol II as Bothe, Partsch and Solf suggest in their comparison of Article 51of AP I and Article 13 of AP II:

> Article 13 of Protocol II restates the provisions of the first three paragraphs of Art. 51 of Protocol I. It declares that civilians shall enjoy general protection against the dangers arising from military operations. . . . The Article does not, however, explicitly provide protection against indiscriminate or disproportionate attacks, nor does it prohibit explicitly the use of civilians to shield military operations. Moreover, it omits any direct reference to a prohibition against direct attacks or disproportionate collateral damage with respect to civilian objects. . . . Some of the specific protection thus omitted may, however, be inferred from the general protection provided in para.1, but the construction of balanced protection for civilians from the abbreviated Art. 13 places a heavy burden on the term "general protection."[91]

They also suggest that the crime of perfidy can be extrapolated from the basic principles recognized in Common Article 3 and Additional Protocol I, which provide protection from harm for those that are *hors de combat* (fighters who have been wounded or surrendered on the battlefield), civilians who are not directly participating in hostilities, those who are providing basic humanitarian services on the battlefield (protected by the red cross, red crescent and red crystal emblems) and those who have displayed the white flag of surrender.

As evidenced by treatises, the *Customary International Humanitarian Law* study, the findings of international tribunals prosecuting war criminals and State practice, customary international law provides that perfidy is a violation of the law of war in non-international armed conflict. In her excellent work, *War Crimes in Internal Armed Conflicts*, Eve La Haye notes that the amount of State practice and *opinio juris* on the protective principle of distinction "fulfils the criteria of an extensive and virtually uniform practice, coupled with the belief that this principle is legally obligatory."[92] A.P.V. Rogers, in *Law on the Battlefield*, concludes that perfidy consists of conduct that results in killing or wounding an adversary through "treachery," including "killing by feigning civilian status" or *hors de combat* status, or "improper use of the flag of truce, the red-cross or red-crescent emblems, or the flag or military insignia or uniform of the enemy."[93] The ICC Statute makes "[k]illing or wounding treacherously a combatant adversary" an "other serious violation[] of the laws and customs applicable in armed conflicts not of an international character."[94] And the jurisprudence, cited above, both domestic and international, supports this view of perfidy as a crime in non-international armed conflict.[95]

Finally, State practice has developed not only to prohibit feigning of civilian status in non-international armed conflict, as evidenced by the *Jawad* and *al-Nashiri* cases, but also to affirmatively prevent violations of this provision by military forces supporting government efforts in non-international armed conflict.

Notes

1. Protocol Additional to the Geneva Conventions of 12 August 1949, and Relating to the Protection of Victims of International Armed Conflicts art. 37(1), June 8, 1977, 1125 U.N.T.S. 3 [hereinafter AP I].

2. John Leland, *Bomber Uses Ambulance to Hit Iraqi Police Headquarters*, NEW YORK TIMES, Jan. 20, 2011, at A10.

3. Yasir Ghazi & Tim Arango, *Explosion in Iraq Draws Victims for a Second Blast*, NEW YORK TIMES, July 6, 2011, at A10.

4. *Six Die as Afghan Ambulance Bomb Targets Police*, HINDUSTAN TIMES (Apr. 7, 2011), http://www.hindustantimes.com/world-news/afghanistan/Six-die-as-Afghan-ambulance-bomb-targets-police/Article1-682425.aspx.

5. *See, e.g.*, Abdi Guled & Ibrahim Muhamed, *Suicide Bomber Kills 3 Somali Ministers*, REUTERS, Dec. 3, 2009, http://www.reuters.com/article/2009/12/03/us-somalia-conflict-idUSTRE5B217Y20091203.

6. *See, e.g.*, Declan Walsh, *Pakistani Suicide Bombers Kill 80 as Taliban Seek Revenge for Bin Laden*, GUARDIAN (May 13, 2011), http://www.guardian.co.uk/world/2011/may/13/suicide-bombing-revenge-osama. *See also* Anwar Shakir, *UN Halts Aid Distribution After Female Suicide Bomber Kills 46 in Pakistan*, BLOOMBERG (Dec. 27, 2010), http://www.bloomberg.com/news/2010-12-25/pakistan-blast-kills-38-people-edhi-ambulance-service-spokesman-reports.html.

7. MICHAEL N. SCHMITT, CHARLES H.B. GARRAWAY & YORAM DINSTEIN, THE MANUAL ON THE LAW OF NON-INTERNATIONAL ARMED CONFLICT WITH COMMENTARY ¶ 2.3.6 (2006) [hereinafter NIAC MANUAL].

8. Protocol Additional to the Geneva Conventions of 12 August 1949, and Relating to the Protection of Victims of Non-International Armed Conflicts, June 8, 1977, 1125 U.N.T.S. 609 [hereinafter AP II].

9. MICHAEL BOTHE, KARL J. PARTSCH & WALDEMAR A. SOLF, NEW RULES FOR VICTIMS OF ARMED CONFLICTS 677 (1982).

10. Headquarters, Department of the Army & Headquarters, Marine Corps Combat Development Command, FM 3-24/MCWP 3-33.5, Counterinsurgency (2006), *available at* http://www.scribd.com/doc/9137276/US-Army-Field-Manual-FM-324-Counterinsurgency [hereinafter Counterinsurgency Manual].

11. *See* John B. Bellinger & William J. Haynes, *A U.S. Government Response to the International Committee of the Red Cross's Customary International Humanitarian Law Study*, 89 INTERNATIONAL REVIEW OF THE RED CROSS 443 (2007). In criticizing the *Customary International Humanitarian Law* study's methodology, Bellinger and Haynes emphasized that a general and consistent practice of States, combined with evidence of compliance by States out of a sense of legal obligation, or *opinio juris*, was required for the development of customary international law. *See also* North Sea Continental Shelf (F.R.G. v. Den., F.R.G. v. Neth.), 1969 I.C.J. 3, ¶ 43 (Feb. 20) ("State practice, including that of States whose interests are specially affected, should have been both extensive and virtually uniform in the sense of the provision invoked; and should moreover have occurred in such a way as to show a general recognition that a rule of law or legal obligation is involved.").

12. Statute of the International Court of Justice art. 38(1)(d), 33 U.N.T.S. 993.

13. *See infra* text accompanying note 65 for a discussion of the one treaty provision addressing perfidy in non-international armed conflict.

14. *See* Message from the President of the United States Transmitting the Protocol II Additional to the Geneva Conventions of 12 August 1949, and Relating to the Protection of Victims of Non-International Armed Conflicts, Concluded at Geneva on June 10, 1977, S. Treaty Doc. No. 100-2 (1987) (Jan. 29, 1987) [hereinafter Message from the President]. *See also* Message from the President of the United States Transmitting the Hague Convention for the Protection of Cultural Property in the Event of Armed Conflict and, for Accession, the Hague Protocol, S. Treaty Doc. No. 106-1 (Jan. 6, 1999); White House, Fact Sheet: New Actions on Guantanamo and Detainee Policy 3 (Mar. 7, 2011), http://www.whitehouse.gov/the-press-office/2011/03/07/new-actions-guantanamo-bay-and-detainee-policy (reaffirming President Obama's commitment to the ratification of AP II).

15. Vienna Convention on the Law of Treaties art. 18, May 23, 1969, 1155 U.N.T.S. 331.

16. This caveat refers to the reservations or understandings proposed by President Reagan, the principal one being an extension of AP II to all Common Article 3 conflicts, thus expanding the scope of the Protocol. Message from the President, *supra* note 14, at viii.

17. *Id.* at iii.

18. Michael J. Matheson, *The United States Position on the Relation of Customary International Law to the 1977 Protocols Additional to the 1949 Geneva Conventions*, 2 AMERICAN UNIVERSITY JOURNAL OF INTERNATIONAL LAW AND POLICY 419, 425 (1987); Abraham Sofaer, *The Position of the United States on Current Law of War Agreements*, *supra*, at 460.

19. Sofaer, *supra* note 18, at 461.

20. Additional Protocol III adopts the red crystal emblem as the fourth internationally recognized emblem. Protocol Additional to the Geneva Conventions of 12 August 1949, and Relating to the Adoption of an Additional Distinctive Emblem, Dec. 8, 2005, 2404 U.N.T.S. 261 (2006).

21. CORNELIUS VAN BYNKERSHOEK, TREATISE ON THE LAW OF WAR 3 (1810).

22. *Id.* at 15.

23. U.S. Department of War, Instructions for the Government of Armies of the United States in the Field, General Orders No. 100, Apr. 24, 1863, *reprinted in* THE LAWS OF ARMED CONFLICTS: A COLLECTION OF CONVENTIONS, RESOLUTIONS AND OTHER DOCUMENTS 3

(Dietrich Schindler & Jiri Toman eds., 4th ed. 2004), *available at* http://www.icrc.org/ihl.nsf/FULL/110?OpenDocument.

24. *Id.*, art. 152.

25. Regulations Respecting the Laws and Customs of War on Land, annexed to Convention No. IV Respecting the Laws and Customs of War on Land, Oct. 18, 1907, 36 Stat. 2227 [hereinafter Hague Regulations].

26. *Id.*

27. J.M. SPAIGHT, WAR RIGHTS ON LAND 105 (1911).

28. *Id.* at 104–9.

29. *Id.* at 110.

30. *Id.* at 220.

31. *Id.* at 434.

32. Trial of Otto Skorzeny and Others, 9 Law Reports of Trials of War Criminals 90 (1949).

33. *Id.* at 91.

34. *Id.* at 93.

35. *See* NIAC MANUAL, *supra* note 7, at 42. However, at the Naval War College conference from which the articles in this volume derive, the authors of the *Manual*, when questioned, expressed uncertainty concerning the validity of this provision.

36. Compare Articles 37 and 39 of AP I, which prohibit perfidy and use of the "uniforms of adverse parties," respectively, without making the latter a grave breach, with Article 85. The author is using the term "grave breach" to distinguish those offenses that must be criminally prohibited and prosecuted under the law of war from other violations, which the parties are obligated to take measures to suppress. *See, e.g.*, Convention Relative to the Protection of Civilian Persons in Time of War art. 146, Aug. 12, 1949, 6 U.S.T. 3516, 75 U.N.T.S. 287 [hereinafter GC IV]; *see also* War Crimes Act, 18 U.S.C. § 2441 (1996) (making the enumerated grave breaches federal crimes and defining "grave breaches" of Common Article 3). Other "measures necessary" may include making such conduct criminal, administrative action, training or other corrective action, as appropriate.

37. W. Hays Parks, *Special Forces' Wear of Non-standard Uniforms*, 4 CHICAGO JOURNAL OF INTERNATIONAL LAW 493 (2003).

38. Krofan v. Public Prosecutor, 1 MALAYAN LAW JOURNAL 133 (1967), *available at* http://www.icrc.org/ihl-nat.nsf/46707c419d6bdfa24125673e00508145/0711dbb7117f01a4c1256ae8003f8cde!OpenDocument.

39. *Id. See also* Mohamed Ali v. Public Prosecutor, [1969] 1 A.C. 430, *available at* http://www.icrc.org/ihl-nat.nsf/39a82e2ca42b52974125673e00508144/383128666c8ab799c1256a1e00366ad3!OpenDocument. In a similar case to *Krofan*, the Judicial Committee of the Privy Council in its decision emphasized the importance of distinction: "International law, however, recognises the necessity of distinguishing between belligerents and peaceful inhabitants. 'The separation of armies and peaceful inhabitants' wrote Spaight in *War Rights on Land* at p. 37, 'is perhaps the greatest triumph of international law. Its effect in mitigating the evils of war has been incalculable.'"

40. Parks, *supra* note 37, at 557–59.

41. *Id.* at 521.

42. *Id.* at 523.

43. AP I, *supra* note 1, art. 37.

44. 2 LASSA F.L. OPPENHEIM, A TREATISE: DISPUTES, WAR AND NEUTRALITY 430 (H. Lauterpacht ed., 7th ed. 1952), *quoted in* Parks, *supra* note 37, at 521.

45. AP I, *supra* note 1, art. 85.

46. *Id.*

47. GC IV, *supra* note 36, art. 146.
48. NIAC MANUAL, *supra* note 7, at 43.
49. BOTHE, PARTSCH & SOLF, *supra* note 9, at 677.
50. AP II, *supra* note 8, art. 13.
51. Convention on Prohibitions or Restrictions on the Use of Certain Conventional Weapons Which May Be Deemed to Be Excessively Injurious or to Have Indiscriminate Effects, Oct. 10, 1980, 1342 U.N.T.S. 137.
52. Amended Protocol on Prohibitions or Restrictions on the Use of Mines, Booby-traps and Other Devices, May 3, 1996, S. Treaty Doc. No. 105-1 (1997). Similar treaty-based distinction requirements, specifically applicable in non-international armed conflict, can be found in the Incendiary Weapons Protocol (Protocol III) to the Conventional Weapons Convention and the Second Protocol to the 1954 Hague Cultural Property Convention. Protocol on Prohibitions or Restrictions on the Use of Incendiary Weapons art. 2, Oct. 10, 1980, 1342 U.N.T.S. 171 & Second Protocol to the Hague Convention of 1954 for the Protection of Cultural Property in the Event of Armed Conflict, Mar. 26, 1999, 2253 U.N.T.S. 172, respectively.
53. 1 CUSTOMARY INTERNATIONAL HUMANITARIAN LAW 26–28 (Jean-Marie Henckaerts & Louise Doswald-Beck eds., 2005). The study provides persuasive evidence of the existence of a "protective principle" of distinction in non-international armed conflict in the commentary to Rule 7, which provides that "[t]he parties to the conflict must at all times distinguish between civilian objects and military objectives." *Id.* at 25.
54. Prosecutor v. Kupreskic, Case No. IT-95-16-T, Judgment, ¶ 521 (Int'l Crim. Trib. for the Former Yugoslavia Jan. 14, 2000), *available at* http://www.icty.org/x/cases/kupreskic/tjug/en/kup-tj000114e.pdf.
55. BOTHE, PARTSCH & SOLF, *supra* note 9, at 676.
56. *See* COMMENTARY ON THE ADDITIONAL PROTOCOLS OF 8 JUNE 1977 TO THE GENEVA CONVENTIONS OF 12 AUGUST 1949, ¶ 4762 (Yves Sandoz, Christophe Swinarski & Bruno Zimmermann eds., 1987), *available at* http://www.icrc.org/ihl.nsf/COM/475-760019?OpenDocument [hereinafter COMMENTARY ON THE ADDITIONAL PROTOCOLS].
57. AP I, *supra* note 1, art. 51.
58. COMMENTARY ON THE ADDITIONAL PROTOCOLS, *supra* note 56, ¶ 4764.
59. AP II, *supra* note 8, art. 4.
60. Hague Regulations, *supra* note 25, art. 23(d).
61. *See, e.g.*, GC IV, *supra* note 36, art. 3. Common Article 3 is given more form and substance in Articles 4–6 of AP II, but its basic intent, to protect "[p]ersons taking no active part in the hostilities, including members of the armed forces who have laid down their arms and those placed *hors de combat* by sickness, wounds, detention, or any other cause," is the bedrock value of the law of war that extends into non-international armed conflict.
62. NIAC MANUAL, *supra* note 7, ¶ 2.3.6.2.
63. 1 CUSTOMARY INTERNATIONAL HUMANITARIAN LAW, *supra* note 53, at 599.
64. Prosecutor v. Tadić, Decision on Defence Motion for Interlocutory Appeal on Jurisdiction, Case No. IT-94-1-l, ¶ 94 (Int'l Crim. Trib. for the Former Yugoslavia Oct. 2, 1995), *available at* http://www.icty.org/x/cases/tadic/acdec/en/51002.htm [hereinafter *Tadić*].
65. Rome Statute of the International Criminal Court, July 17, 1998, 2187 U.N.T.S. 90 [hereinafter Rome Statute]. *But see also* 10 U.S.C. § 950t(17) (2006):

> USING TREACHERY OR PERFIDY.—Any person subject to this chapter who, after inviting the confidence or belief of one or more persons that they were entitled to, or obliged to accord, protection under the law of war, intentionally makes use of that confidence or belief in killing, injuring, *or capturing* such person or persons shall be

punished, if death results to one or more of the victims, by death or such other punishment as a military commission under this chapter may direct, and, if death does not result to any of the victims, by such punishment, other than death, as a military commission under this chapter may direct. (emphasis added)

66. *See generally* Maureen Orth, *Operation Checkmate: Inside Colombia's Hostage War*, VANITY FAIR, Nov. 2008, *available at* http://www.vanityfair.com/politics/features/2008/11/hostages200811. Some of the information concerning this operation was obtained by the author directly from Colombian officials in briefings conducted in Colombia and the United States.

67. *Compare id.* ("the . . . soldier . . . was wearing a Red Cross bib, which was against the rules of the Geneva Conventions"), *with* John C. Dehn, *Permissible Perfidy?*, 6 JOURNAL OF INTERNATIONAL CRIMINAL JUSTICE 627, 653 (2008) ("the most satisfactory explanation for the lack of any condemnation of this perfidious capture by the [International Committee of the Red Cross] might be that the scope of the perfidy prohibition applicable in non-international armed conflict is subject to question"). Even the FARC's lawyer, Rodolfo Rios, deemed the operation "almost perfect," despite this "transgression." Orth, *supra* note 66.

68. For example, special agents of the Federal Bureau of Investigation do not wear uniforms except during arrests or tactical assaults. The U.S. Secret Service has a uniformed division, but its other agents wear civilian attire. Similarly, during the 1948–60 Malayan Emergency, British Colonial Special Branch officers wore civilian or *Min Yuen* clothing during efforts to locate guerrilla groups, often through mail drops, to persuade them to surrender, while so-called "pseudo-gangs," attired in clothing like that of the Mau Mau, proved effective in a variety of ways during the non-international armed conflict in Kenya. FRANK KITSON, BUNCH OF FIVE 33–41, 168 (1977).

69. Counterinsurgency Manual, *supra* note 10, at 2-1 ("The integration of civilian and military efforts is crucial to successful COIN operations.").

70. Richard R. Baxter, *So-Called "Unprivileged Belligerency": Spies, Guerrillas, and Saboteurs*, 28 BRITISH YEARBOOK OF INTERNATIONAL LAW 323, 327 (1951).

71. *Tadić*, *supra* note 64, ¶ 125.

72. Sofaer, *supra* note 18, at 467.

73. Government's Response to the Defense Motion to Dismiss for Failure to State an Offense and for Lack of Subject Matter Jurisdiction under R.M.C. 907, at 6, United States v. Jawad (Military Commission Guantanamo Bay, Cuba, June 3, 2008), *available at* http://www.mc.mil/Portals/0/pdfs/Jawad%20(AE083%20-%20D007)%20Gov%20Resp%20to%20Def%20Mot.pdf.

74. United States v. Al-Nashiri, Charge Sheet, *available at* http://www.mc.mil/Portals/0/pdfs/Al%20Nashiri%20II%20(Referred%20Charges).pdf (last visited Feb. 7, 2012).

75. United States v. Jawad, Ruling on Defense Motion to Dismiss (Sept. 24, 2008) (motion to dismiss on grounds of lack of subject matter jurisdiction), *available at* http://www.mc.mil/CASES/MilitaryCommissions.aspx (follow Mohammed Jawad hyperlink under "Cases"). Trial was never held in this case, however. Jawad was repatriated to Afghanistan, after charges were dismissed without prejudice, following a successful habeas corpus petition.

76. COMMENTARY TO GENEVA CONVENTION I FOR THE AMELIORATION OF THE CONDITION OF THE WOUNDED AND SICK IN ARMED FORCES IN THE FIELD 49–50 (Jean S. Pictet ed., 1952).

77. *Id.* at 50. This comment, of course, raises the question of the applicability of human rights norms in non-international armed conflict, a fascinating topic that is beyond the scope of this paper.

78. Counterinsurgency Manual, *supra* note 10, at 1-1–1-19.

79. *Id.* at x.

80. *Id.*

81. *Compare generally* the discussion of "imminence," under the Standing Rules of Engagement in INTERNATIONAL AND OPERATIONAL LAW DEPARTMENT, THE JUDGE ADVOCATE GENERAL'S LEGAL CENTER AND SCHOOL, OPERATIONAL LAW HANDBOOK 73–102 (2011), *with* the discussion of "rules for use of force" in CENTER FOR LAW AND MILITARY OPERATIONS, THE JUDGE ADVOCATE GENERAL'S LEGAL CENTER AND SCHOOL, DOMESTIC OPERATIONAL LAW HANDBOOK 175–91 (2011).

82. *See, e.g.*, Headquarters, International Security Assistance Force, Tactical Directive (July 6, 2009), *available at* http://www.nato.int/isaf/docu/official_texts/Tactical_Directive_090706 .pdf.

83. U.S. Forces–Afghanistan, Position Paper, US Military Forces' Wear of Military Uniforms in Afghanistan 8 (Mar. 28, 2011) (on file with author).

84. *Id.* at 3.

85. *Id.*

86. William H. Ferrell III, *No Shirt, No Shoes, No Status: Uniforms, Distinction, and Special Operations in International Armed Conflict*, 178 MILITARY LAW REVIEW 94, 121 (2003).

87. U.S. Forces–Afghanistan, Position Paper, *supra* note 83, at 5.

88. U.S. Forces–Afghanistan, Information Paper, Carrying of Weapons 1 (May 12, 2011) (emphasis added) (on file with author).

89. *Id.* at 2.

90. I would suggest, however, that the U.S. *policy* view is to apply the law of international armed conflict "during all armed conflicts, however such conflicts are characterized, and in all other military operations." *See* Department of Defense, DoD Directive 2311.01E, DoD Law of War Program ¶ 4.1 (2006), *available at* http://www.dtic.mil/whs/directives/corres/pdf/231101e .pdf. "Law of War" is defined as "[t]hat part of international law that regulates the conduct of armed hostilities . . . [and] encompasses all international law for the conduct of hostilities binding on the United States or its individual citizens, including treaties and international agreements to which the United States is a party, and applicable customary international law." *Id.*, ¶ 3.1. "It is DoD policy that . . . [t]he law of war obligations of the United States are observed and enforced by the DoD Components and DoD contractors assigned to or accompanying deployed Armed Forces." *Id.*, ¶ 4.2.

91. BOTHE, PARTSCH & SOLF, *supra* note 9, at 676.

92. EVE LA HAYE, WAR CRIMES IN INTERNAL ARMED CONFLICTS 67 (2008).

93. A.P.V. ROGERS, LAW ON THE BATTLEFIELD 225 (2004) (citing the Hague Regulations, *supra* note 25, art. 23). There was discussion during the conference about whether "perfidy" or "treacherous wounding" includes improper use of enemy military emblems, insignia, flags or uniforms during combat in a non-international armed conflict. The authors of the *NIAC Manual*, Professors Schmitt, Garraway and Dinstein, acknowledged they were wrong in including this provision in the *Manual*. *Compare* Article 2.3.5 ("it is forbidden to make use of enemy military emblems, insignia, flags or uniforms during combat"), *with* 2.3.6 ("[d]isplaying the white flag falsely, or pretending to surrender, be wounded or otherwise have a protected status is forbidden if the intent in doing so is to kill or wound an adversary") of the NIAC MANUAL, *supra* note 7, at 42–43.

94. Rome Statute, *supra* note 65, art. 8(2)(e)(ix).

95. *See supra* text accompanying notes 71–75.

PART VI

RECENT AND ONGOING NON-INTERNATIONAL ARMED CONFLICTS

XII

Non-International Armed Conflicts in the Philippines

Raymundo B. Ferrer and Randolph G. Cabangbang*

Many U.S. soldiers serving in Joint Special Task Force–Philippines, with extensive experience in Afghanistan, Iraq and other theaters of war, have repeatedly described the non-international armed conflicts (NIACs) in Mindanao as particularly complex. In an area where there is a strong gun culture, where local residents are part-time insurgents and where kinship ties serve as force multipliers, how indeed do we distinguish civilians from armed insurgents?

This article discusses NIACs in the Philippines and briefly notes the challenges they pose to the security sector in applying the rules of international humanitarian law (IHL). To provide a basic framework in understanding the nature of conflict in the Philippines, we begin with an organizational-level analysis of the NIACs. However, it must be noted that on the ground, from the individual and operational levels of analysis, it is not so neatly delineated. For example, organizational identities in southern Mindanao, unlike in the West, are highly temporal and fluid. Civilians can be recruited to work seasonally for an insurgent group and then quickly and seamlessly resume their civilian lives after operations are completed. Added to this complexity are the changing organizational labels civilians effortlessly assume without much question. Some civilians may work for one insurgent group that has

* General Raymundo B. Ferrer, Armed Forces of the Philippines, and Lieutenant Colonel Randolph G. Cabangbang (INF), Philippine Army.

an outstanding peace agreement with the government and then on the same day join a command structure of a known terrorist group. Then they very quickly switch to supporting relatives and kin who belong to a group currently in peace negotiations with the government.

Organizations in the Philippines revolve around personalities rather than positions.[1] While the Armed Forces of the Philippines (AFP) strives for interoperability among its branches and with its allies, in Mindanao is an enemy for whom interoperability seems like second nature. The NIACs in the Philippines are largely a homegrown phenomenon with some components heavily influenced by foreign elements. Conflicts rooted in ideologies outside the Philippines have been co-opted to provide a philosophical justification to a grassroots-driven insurgency. This article will primarily focus on two major NIACs facing the Philippines. For convenience, they will be referred to as the two "Ms": the Maoist group and the Moro group. Their origins will be traced and a description provided of their basic strategies and structures.

The Communist Party of the Philippines (CPP) and its armed wing, the New People's Army (NPA), use Maoist ideology to justify the armed struggle against the government. The CPP is considered the biggest threat to the security of the Philippines.[2] Its scope is nationwide. While strongest in the northern region of the Philippines, the Maoist group also has a presence in northern and eastern Mindanao. It tends to target farmers in the rural areas, workers in the mining industry, teachers, youth, women's groups and many other segments of the working-class population that are vulnerable to the persuasion of the Maoist ideology for recruitment. The Moro group, on the other hand, limits itself to the southern Philippines. Like the CPP-NPA, it is also homegrown—a secessionist movement that has been fighting for independence for more than a hundred years. Islamic ideology inspires its members to fight for self-determination and recognition of their ethnic identity.

The Maoist and Moro groups both exploit conditions of poverty and marginalization in marshalling their armed struggle against the government. According to the Asian Development Bank, in 2008 about twenty-six million Filipinos out of a total population of ninety-two million lived below the Asian poverty line.[3] In other words, they lived on about US$1.35 per day. The poorest of the poor live in Muslim Mindanao. The Muslim poor are particularly marginalized from mainstream Filipino society and this fuels much of their grievance against the Philippine government. While the Maoist group targets people through their occupation, the Moro group appeals to ethnicity and shared history in its recruitment efforts.

The Maoist Movement

The communist insurgency—the longest-running Maoist insurgency in the world—is waged by the CPP and the NPA. In August 2002 the United States designated the NPA as a foreign terrorist organization. Not long after, in November 2005, so did the European Union.[4] The CPP-NPA—together with its legal arm, the National Democratic Front of the Philippines (NDFP)[5]—seeks to overthrow the Philippine government.

The CPP was established in 1968 as part of a larger sociological wave that was then taking the world by storm—the rise of student activism in the 1960s and 1970s. Many scholars argue, however, that the roots of the organization could be traced back to the Hukbalahap—a contraction of the Filipino term *Hukbong Bayan Laban sa mga Hapon*, which means "People's Army against the Japanese."[6] Also known as the Huks, these fighters mobilized against Japanese occupation. The Huks were largely farmers from central Luzon, and were estimated by one source to have about fifteen to twenty thousand active members and fifty thousand members in reserve in the early 1940s. After World War II, the Huks moved on to wage a guerrilla war against the government of the newly independent Philippines.[7] By the early 1960s, the Huk campaign began to wane and the Sino-Soviet split at that time further fractured the group. The CPP established itself as separate from the Soviet-style Huk organization and in 1969 renamed the remnants of the Huks the New People's Army. The current strength of the NPA is estimated to be around 4,200.

The Maoist group believes that the power of the gun is necessary to protect ordinary citizens from human rights abuses perpetuated by the government and local politicians. The NPA envisions a protracted people's war, ideally, that would bring about the downfall of the status quo and the replacement of the Philippine government by a socialist State. The *modus operandi* of the NPA involves the targeting of foreign investors and businesses for extortion, or what it euphemistically terms "revolutionary taxes." The ultimate goal is to drive these investors out of the Philippines and to bankrupt the economy. The NPA also assassinates individuals such as politicians, members of the media and other personalities who, it deems, stand in the way of its attaining its objectives.

It is observed that the general trend of the rise and fall of the CPP-NPA membership coincides with the level of violence associated with each presidential administration. During the Marcos era (1965 to 1986), rampant human rights abuses fueled the rise of membership in the CPP-NPA. Followers of Marx and Mao in Philippine colleges and universities formed student organizations that protested the plight of farmers in the countryside and the urban poor. Anti-government activism was fashionable back in the 1970s. College students then did not carry cell phones. Instead, they carried a small red book which they used as a reference when they gathered together to talk about the ideology of Mao Tse-tung and a classless society.

In 1972, Marcos declared martial law and for the next thirteen years under his dictatorial regime the CPP attracted many recruits. That trend shifted in 1986 when Corazon "Cory" Aquino, the mother of the current president, Benigno "Noynoy" Aquino, came to power. She became the first woman president through the seminal People's Power movement in 1986 that was largely propelled by the outpouring of outrage against Marcos over the assassination three years earlier of her husband, Ninoy.[8] Early in Cory's term (1986 to 1992), a ceasefire with the NPA was declared, political prisoners were released and peace talks with the CPP-NPA-NDFP were initiated. When the talks collapsed in 1987, the NPA returned to arms. The situation worsened when security forces violently dispersed and killed some peasants rallying for land reform one year after Cory assumed power. Acting under the advice of the United States, Cory launched a total war against the NPA.

Sustained military offensives successfully reduced the communist forces from 25,200 in 1987 to 14,800 in 1991. A two-pronged strategy was used that could be described in current counterinsurgency parlance as hard power, or military offensive, combined with soft power, or socioeconomic development. In addition to the government actions, there were also brutal purges within the Maoist group that further demoralized its rank and file.[9] Following the attacks of September 11, 2001, the NPA declared an all-out war against the central government, believing it to be controlled by the United States as part of its global war on terror. Although the NPA is unlikely to win a military victory against government forces, its presence persists in the countryside where poverty, injustice and the lack of social services provide conditions for marshaling people's grievances against the government.

The Moro Front—Three Forms of Struggle

In addition to fueling the CPP insurgency, the oppressive rule of former President Marcos's martial law in the 1970s triggered the Moro outcry against the central government, which they believed to be the cause of Moro suffering. As with the CPP-NPA, the perception of marginalization drives the underlying anger that fuels the Moro armed struggle. In contrast to the CPP-NPA, the secessionist Moro insurgency largely limits its armed struggle to the southern portion of the country, where the majority of Muslim Filipinos reside. For three centuries under Spanish rule and nearly fifty years of U.S. dominance in the Philippines, the Moros were never conquered as a group. Today, they feel that they have to live under the

Filipino Christian rule of the central government and abide by its non-Islamic way of governance.

Philippine Muslim academic Macapado Muslim neatly summarized six key elements in the Moro grievance: economic marginalization and destitution, political domination, physical insecurity, threatened Moro and Islamic identity, a perception that government is the principal culprit and a perception of hopelessness under the present order of things.[10] Indeed, on the matter of economic marginalization and destitution, the regions where most Muslims reside in Mindanao still remain among the poorest regions in the Philippines. Unemployment, illiteracy and poverty rates are highest in Muslim Mindanao.[11] In terms of political representation in the government, Muslims in Mindanao still feel that they do not have a voice in the central government.[12] And while tremendous gains have been made over the past several years to reduce the extremist hold in the various islands in Mindanao, physical security for the residents has still not reached an acceptable level. There is more to be done in order to encourage business investments in Mindanao and change the perception of rampant lawlessness in the islands.

Secessionist Moro groups have been insisting on the notion of a Moro and Islamic identity as justification for their right to have some form of self-determination. One of these groups, the Moro Islamic Liberation Front (MILF), was seeking independence for southern Mindanao, but a Supreme Court decision held that a draft settlement with the government that would have given the MILF control over large areas of Mindanao was unconstitutional. Now under the peace process it is pursuing with the central government, the MILF is asking to become a sub-state of the Philippines in which the political structure would be similar to the federal system of the United States.[13]

The fifth and sixth elements are also related to the Moro identity—namely, the perception of the inability of the central government to understand Muslim Mindanao and the general apathy of most politicians in the north toward matters concerning the south. Marginalization of the south has always been an effective rallying cry for those who seek to manipulate Moro grievances to gain support for ultimately extremist causes. The perception of the hopelessness of the status quo is partly driving the moral justification for an armed struggle in southern Mindanao. The current Philippine president is trusted, however, by many Muslims and the attempt by the central government in Manila to extend various social services into the far reaches of Mindanao is slowly defeating the perception of hopelessness in many Muslim sectors in the southern Philippines.

These six elements of Muslim grievances have been used in one form or another in the rhetoric of many insurgent groups. There are three major Moro insurgent groups engaged in violence in the southern Philippines. These are the Moro National Liberation Front (MNLF), the notorious Abu Sayyaf Group (ASG) and the MILF.[14] As defined by IHL,[15] only the MILF among these three can truly be considered as engaged in a NIAC—it has a clear leadership and an organizational structure to implement whatever agreements it may forge with the State, as well as an armed force that it can use to pursue its belligerent agenda. The MNLF, on the other hand, signed a Final Peace Agreement with the government in 1996,[16] although it argues that such has not been fully implemented. For its part, the ASG lacks command and control and in many ways, like the MNLF, no longer possesses a formidable armed capability. The MILF remains as the largest fighting force with an agenda of carving a distinct territory for itself in the southern Philippines.

The MNLF and the Origins of the MILF

Around the same time the CPP-NPA was formed, Nur Misuari, who was very much influenced by Maoist ideology, founded the MNLF in 1972 and started an underground youth movement in Mindanao. His goal was to free Muslims from what he described as the terror, oppression and tyranny of Filipino colonialism, and to secure a free and independent State for the Bangsamoro.[17] *Bangsa* means "country" or "nation." *Moro* is derived from the term early Spanish colonizers used to refer to the Moors and has over time become the collective word used for all the various Muslim ethnic groups in Mindanao. Muslims in Mindanao turned this pejorative term into a badge of honor. *Bangsamoro* means "Moro Nation." When Nur Misuari declared jihad against the Philippine government in 1972, the MNLF led the armed resistance of all Muslims in Mindanao against martial law. The MNLF became the organizational vehicle that symbolized the Moro cause of thirteen disparate Islamized ethno-linguistic groups in Mindanao; their aim was and is the establishment of an independent Moro nation.

Four years of bloody war in Mindanao prompted the Organization of Islamic Cooperation[18] to pressure the MNLF to accept some form of political autonomy in lieu of secession and independence. The MNLF signed the Tripoli Agreement in 1976,[19] but frustrations over its implementation a year later led Misuari to revert to armed struggle, while his Vice Chairman, Salamat Hashim, broke away from the MNLF to establish the MILF as the second Moro secessionist group in 1984. The MNLF-MILF split was largely based on differences in political strategy and ideological orientation. The MILF could be described as Islamic revivalist, while the MNLF is more secular-nationalist. Hashim of the MILF wanted to push the peace process under the Tripoli Agreement; this commitment to peace negotiations remains one of the defining points of the MILF. The MNLF, however, believes the use of force—the same type of armed struggle in which the Maoists of the NPA engage—is necessary to the achievement of peace in the southern Philippines.

The MILF wants to govern the Moro homeland under the ideals of Islam and Shari'ah law. Religion is central to the workings of the MILF, as can be seen in the active involvement of ulama, or Islamic scholars, in the leadership and internal organization of the group. The MNLF, on the other hand, largely concerns itself with fighting for independence. The leadership style of the MILF is consultative with a central committee that drives the organization's agenda, while the MNLF has centralized decision making that revolves around the group's leader. In addition, the MILF is mostly dominated by the Maguindanaos from central Mindanao, while the MNLF is largely composed of ethnic Tausugs, the warrior class, from the Sulu Archipelago. Traditionally, these two Muslim tribes could not stand each other.

The rise of the MILF coincided with Misuari's declining influence. The MNLF became increasingly fragmented in 1982 and ceased to be a formidable fighting force after signing the Final Peace Agreement. Some of the MNLF rebels were integrated into the armed forces and national police, and some joined various livelihood programs to help them reintegrate into society. Many of the livelihood programs were successfully sponsored by the United States Agency for International Development and the United Nations Development Program. Fisheries, seaweed farming and various other livelihood programs benefited many former MNLF rebels in the Sulu Archipelago.

The MILF Today

The twelve-thousand-strong MILF is the largest Muslim guerrilla group today and the most potent security threat in Mindanao. It is mainly based in central Mindanao, although it has a presence in Palawan, Basilan and other islands in the Sulu Archipelago. Since 1997, it has been pursuing what many describe as an on-and-off peace negotiation with the government. During this period, however, several breakaway groups have continued to engage government forces in armed conflict. To date, about 120,000 people have been killed and about two million people displaced from their homes as a result of MILF-led encounters with government forces.

The latest major conflict was in 2008 when the government of the Philippines initialed the Memorandum of Agreement on the Ancestral Domain (MOA-AD) that gave the MILF its own distinct territory, with a governing body called the Bangsamoro Juridical Entity.[20] Before the agreement could be signed, however, certain non-Muslim leaders in central Mindanao received a copy of the embargoed MOA-AD and began a campaign to undo the agreement, claiming that part of the territory covered by the MOA-AD included areas that were never under Muslim leadership. A Christian Vice Governor of a Mindanao province declared that if the MOA-AD was signed there would be bloodshed. Other non-Muslim leaders in other parts of Mindanao filed a separate petition asking the government not to sign the agreement.

The non-Muslim groups were able to bring enough political pressure to prompt the Supreme Court to issue a temporary restraining order preventing signature of the agreement. When the signing ceremony of the MOA-AD was aborted, MILF renegade commanders went on a rampage and attacked villages in northern and central Mindanao.[21] Hundreds died and about 390,000 people were displaced in what is considered to be a NIAC. The Supreme Court eventually declared the MOA-AD to be unconstitutional and Philippine military forces engaged the three renegade MILF commanders. One of those commanders, Ameril Umra Kato, broke away from the MILF and recently spoke of taking up arms if the current government of the Philippines–MILF peace process fails again or is endlessly delayed.

The MILF leaders put forth significant effort to bring an international audience into the peace negotiations. An International Monitoring Team, composed of representatives from Malaysia, Brunei, Libya, Japan, Norway and the European Union, oversees the 2001 ceasefire agreement between the MILF and the government of the Philippines. With international monitoring, over seventy agreements have been reached between the MILF and the Philippine government since 1997.

Alliance with the Abu Sayyaf Group

One Moro group without any form of ceasefire agreement with the government is the ASG. Although the conflict with the ASG now consists of isolated and sporadic acts of violence and thus does not meet the threshold requirement of a "protracted armed conflict" against an "organized armed group" to be classified as a NIAC,[22] the ASG does have tactical alliances with the MILF and in the conflict's early years it could be argued that it was a NIAC.

The inspiration for the al Qaeda–linked ASG came from radical Islamism—notably the jihad against the Soviet invasion of Afghanistan. Around the time that the MNLF was engaged in peace negotiations with the Philippine government in the late 1980s/early 1990s, an underground movement of disenchanted youth began to be mobilized by a charismatic preacher in Basilan, Abdurajak Abubakar Janjalani. He wanted an independent State for the Muslims in Mindanao. Academics continue to debate whether Janjalani participated in the fighting against the Soviets during the Afghanistan war. Regardless of whether he did or did not participate, the primary driving force behind the ASG's formation was the perception by many idealistic Muslim youth that the MNLF had engaged in a jihadist war that it failed to complete. The disenchanted Muslim youth felt that the older cadres had abandoned the spirit of the Bangsamoro's 1970s struggle against the government. They felt the MNLF leaders had betrayed their cause and acquiesced to the Philippine government when it entered into peace negotiations.

Janjalani formally founded the ASG in 1992 and justified his jihad-based violence on the following arguments: (1) the Philippine government with the help of its Christian allies, notably the United States, severely oppressed the Bangsamoro people; (2) this oppression occurred because of the unwelcome intrusion of Christians into the Muslim homeland; (3) to defeat this oppression, the struggle for the cause of Allah must be waged against the Christian invaders; and (4) it was the personal obligation of every Muslim to carry out this jihad and failure to do so would be a sin against Allah.

Obviously, many of the ideals espoused by the group overlap with those of the MILF; thus, the movement of members between these groups tends to be seamless. Additionally, many of the members of the two groups are related through blood ties.

Driven by its secessionist and extreme Islamic ideology, the ASG quickly became internationalized with the involvement of the Jemaah Islamiyah,[23] whose goal is to establish a Muslim caliphate throughout Southeast Asia. With the death of Janjalani and the demise of several key ASG leaders, the ASG's jihadist ideological fervor has died down, particularly among the rank and file. Many argue that the ASG has now been reduced to a criminal band.[24] Kidnapping has always been a consistent staple for the ASG to raise funds, prompting many observers to argue that Janjalani's jihad has become a cloak to justify the criminality of the ASG. While the long-time ASG members remain loyal to the original cause that led to the organization's establishment, the financial pressures, lack of loyalty among the rank and file and the U.S.-backed military offensives against the ASG have degraded the once notorious Moro fighters into a bunch of thugs.

Challenges in Applying the Rules of IHL

IHL rules, for humanitarian reasons, seek to limit the harmful effects of wars and armed conflicts on non-participants. While these rules do not prevent the use of force by the State, IHL restricts the means and methods that may be employed. Memorandum Order 9, issued on August 7, 1998, directed Philippine security forces to implement the Comprehensive Agreement on Respect for Human Rights and the International Humanitarian Law (CARHRIHL) that was signed by the NDFP and the Philippine government five months earlier in The Hague.[25] Prior to the issuance of the order, the issue of human rights protection and the application of IHL rules were not clearly spelled out to the parties to the ongoing NIAC.

For over forty years, the two concurrent NIACs in the southern Philippines have extracted an exorbitant toll in the number of lives lost, damage to property, expenditure of government resources and economic opportunities lost due to the prolonged conflicts. The social cost of the conflict in terms of damaged social cohesion and the diaspora of Muslims in Mindanao is arguably much greater. During the early years of the conflict, there were indeed IHL violations committed by the major players—government forces, Moro rebels and communist insurgents. Most of the abuses blamed on the government forces happened during the martial law years from 1972 to 1981. Reports on the protracted conflicts, however, make it appear that there were widespread and continuing violations of human rights.[26]

In fact, during the early years of the Moro secessionist and the Maoist communist insurgencies, NIAC rules were not at all clear to State security forces. The Cold War period was characterized by wars of national liberation or internal wars. The four 1949 Geneva Conventions were a product of World War II and, except for Common Article 3, applied only to international armed conflict. Additional Protocols I and II to the 1949 conventions, the latter of which applies to non-international armed conflicts, were not agreed to until 1977. These rules would emerge after both the NPA and the MNLF had initiated hostilities with the State military forces.

The AFP has been involved in internal security operations since martial law was declared by President Marcos in September 1972. Since then, the AFP and the Philippine National Police have been performing both law enforcement and combat operations against insurgent groups. For lack of an understood legal framework, human rights law and IHL rules were confusing when applied to these two types of missions.

The nature of the NIAC in the Philippines today and the operational strategies employed by insurgent groups pose serious challenges to adherence to IHL. Discussed below are some of these challenges.

Principle of Distinction

The principle of distinction requires that combatants be distinguished from noncombatants in carrying out military operations and that only the former may be the direct object of attack. This principle has, at times, been difficult to implement. The often-used phrase to describe the dilemma faced by the AFP is "a farmer by day and a guerrilla by night." This phrase is literally true in the case of NPA militia members, who can be both farmers and fighters. Even though IHL permits these farmer/fighters to be targeted at all times, since they are members of an organized armed group performing a continuous combat function, this is extremely difficult in practice, because their failure to distinguish themselves from the civilian population makes the issue of identification a difficult one.

Another issue is that the NPA routinely engages in conduct that would be perfidious in international armed conflict. Regular communist guerrillas usually carry guns similar to those issued to the State security forces. Disguised in regulation government uniforms and bearing arms, the insurgents deceive civilians enough to avoid detection and get inside police stations or military detachments to successfully conduct raids.

In addition, the NPA routinely uses unarmed civilians as couriers and messengers, as an early warning system and as bearers of logistics for their fighters. Although this is not a distinction issue, when arrested they simply deny their participation in NPA activities. In most cases such arrests are carried out by government forces based only on intelligence information. While no arrest is made until the intelligence information has been corroborated by informants or captured enemy personnel, courts hold this is insufficient to gain a conviction without accompanying physical evidence that, in most cases, cannot be supplied. The result is a cycle of arrest followed by release and return to participation in NPA operations.

In their operations, communist guerrillas are known to mingle with civilians. They move around villages, engaging in propaganda work and soliciting foodstuffs. When government troops come upon them in the villages, civilians can get caught in the crossfire. Also, within NPA camps, civilians, who are generally relatives of the rebels, are utilized as cooks, for various errands in support of the NPA or as lookouts. While these camps are situated well away from civilian villages and can be targeted without risk to the inhabitants of those villages, endangering the civilians within the camps can be characterized as a human rights issue for the NPA's propagandists to exploit.

For the members of the MILF, on the other hand, their camps are also their communities. It is not uncommon for MILF villages to be fortified with trenches, firing positions, outposts, guard posts and other defense structures. Usually, Muslims build a mosque or madrasah within their camps around which, because of the communal nature of their society, houses are clustered. During ceasefires, the MILF members have their families staying in the camps to farm and do other chores.

The AFP does not have precision-guided munitions in its inventory. While the munitions employed by the AFP are sufficiently discriminate to meet the requirements of the law of armed conflict, civilian objects are sometimes hit by the AFP's bombs or artillery rounds. In order to minimize these occurrences, the AFP has established a rule of engagement (ROE) whereby a forward air controller or a forward observer is required to be present before engaging a target with indirect fire.

Most MILF members are part-time farmers and part-time fighters. During engagements with military forces, they shift easily from civilian status to fighters. The MILF also has women members who serve as auxiliaries and are employed to carry the ammunition, food and medical supplies. Because of these circumstances, military operations frequently result in internal displacements, especially to the families of MILF members. It is required, therefore, that before offensives, evacuation areas be coordinated with the local government to ensure the safety of the internally displaced persons (IDPs), many of whom are family members of the MILF active fighters. This humanitarian consideration can work to the advantage of the MILF members. Food and medical supplies distributed to the IDPs have been known to end up with the MILF fighters, legitimately raising the need to control the distribution of relief goods to ensure they are not passed on by the IDPs to the MILF combatants.

Principle of Proportionality and Limitations on the Use of Means and Methods of Combat

This principle is generally addressed in AFP ROEs issued by higher authorities to operational commanders. It is, for example, generally prohibited to use artillery or bombs to attack NPA camps unless the camp is well fortified, since the NPA uses only light weapons,[27] and since the use of higher-order weapons has the potential to cause excessive fear among civilians living nearby.

In the case of the MILF, which has well-fortified camps in or around its communities, it is sometimes necessary to use artillery or bombs to neutralize these strongholds. Care is taken during the early stages of the hostilities, however, to avoid targeting the center of the camp, where the houses are clustered, on the assumption that these could still be occupied by civilian family members.

Children Involved in Armed Conflict

Both the Maoist group and the MILF use children as child soldiers. There have been many incidents when our troops have captured child soldiers, both male and female.

Landmines

Landmines of various types continue to be used by all rebel groups—NPA, MILF, MNLF, ASG. Some are used in accordance with IHL; some are not. In the period 2000–2006, total reported casualties (killed and wounded) from landmines and improvised explosive devices were 362, of which 299 were soldiers and policemen, while 63 were civilians, some of them children. The NPA commonly uses improvised command-detonated anti-personnel mines and anti-vehicle mines. In recent years it has extensively used improvised claymore mines in command-detonated mode, using scrap metal in lieu of steel balls. Because of CARHRIHL, the CPP-NPA-NDFP made certain commitments which were generally consistent with IHL rules on the use of landmines.

Unexploded Ordnance and Explosive Remnants of War

Unexploded ordnance (UXO) or explosive remnants of war (ERW) left in the battlefield pose danger to IDPs returning to their homes and farms in conflict-affected areas. As a result, during the cessation of hostilities, the AFP is undertaking an extra effort to recover these UXOs and ERW.[28]

Proliferation of Small Arms and Light Weapons

Small arms and light weapons proliferate in the Philippines, complicating the armed conflicts, particularly in the southern Philippines. There are an estimated one million licensed firearms in the country and more than two million illegally acquired firearms in Mindanao alone.[29] The proliferation of small arms and light weapons contributes to the formation of private armed groups and warlordism, as well as the frequency and intensity of lawlessness and clan wars in Mindanao.

Addressing NIACs in the Southern Philippines

There are parallel peace tracks currently under way in connection with the non-international armed conflicts in the southern Philippines under which the Philippine government is pursuing peace negotiations with both the CPP-NPA and the MILF.

Today's environment is one in which localized conflicts have become increasingly intertwined with the social values of a larger international audience, bringing about the downfall of institutions and governments. Small grassroots movements and extremist cells throughout the world have capitalized on social media networks to gain sympathy from an international audience all too willing to impose its moral values and judgments on the legitimacy of armed conflicts. In the case of the Philippines, however, one could argue that these two NIACs, with long roots in the past, largely remain outside the reach of an increasingly globalized world. These NIACs appear to be propagated in the hearts and minds of people who simply refuse to let go of the past.

Yet there is hope for a future generation in which the fatigue of war and the rhetoric of grievance no longer inspire the same intense anger. Experience in working with various communities has demonstrated that promoting peace is another way to defeat the enemy. We have learned that people will behave according to the way they are viewed—if treated as an enemy, then they will become one; if treated as partners they will respond in kind. With all their complexities, the non-international armed conflicts in the Philippines could be viewed simply as a cry for human security—the need to lead a dignified way of life where the basic necessities of survival become a fundamental right for each and every individual. If that need can be met, peace may follow.

Notes

1. BrandLab, The Mindanao-Sulu Power Game: An Ethnography of Emergent Players—Final Report (2011) (on file with authors). This is a commissioned research report recently completed for a restricted audience.

2. Deputy Chief of Staff for Intelligence, J2, Armed Forces of the Philippines, First Semester 2011 Intelligence Report (2011). This restricted source is also used for figures on enemy strength and operational strategies employed by armed threat groups that are cited elsewhere in this paper.

3. Ifzal Ali, *Launch of Key Indicators 2008: Introducing the Asian Poverty Line* (Aug. 27, 2008), http://beta.adb.org/news/podcasts/launch-key-indicators-2008-introducing-asian-poverty-line?page=5.

4. *See NPA transforms into a terrorist group, says AFP*, BALITA.PH, http://balita.ph/2010/03/28/npa-transforms-into-terrorist-group-says-afp/ (Mar. 28, 2010).

5. The NDFP serves as the umbrella for various mass organizations of Maoist persuasion.

6. *The Huk Rebellion in the Philippines 1946–1954*, ONWAR.COM, http://www.onwar.com/aced/data/papa/philippines1946.htm (last visited Oct. 26, 2011).

7. For a history of the Huk rebellion, see RONALD E. DOLAN, PHILIPPINES: A COUNTRY STUDY (1991), *available at* http://countrystudies.us/philippines/ (then follow "The Huk Rebellion" hyperlink). For a history of both the Huk campaign against the Japanese occupation and the Huk rebellion, see LAWRENCE M. GREENBURG, U.S. ARMY CENTER OF MILITARY HISTORY, THE HUKBALAHAP INSURRECTION: A CASE STUDY OF A SUCCESSFUL ANTI-INSURGENCY OPERATION IN THE PHILIPPINES, 1946–1955 (1987), *available at* http://www.history.army.mil/books/coldwar/huk/huk-fm.htm.

8. Ninoy, or Senator Benigno Aquino Jr., was recognized as the staunchest critic of the Marcos regime. He was assassinated on August 21, 1983.

9. *See* Patricio N. Abinales, *Shifting tactics: Notes on civil society politics and the power of the local in the Philippines*, 25 TAMBARA 73–96 (2008).

10. MACAPADO A. MUSLIM, THE MORO ARMED STRUGGLE IN THE PHILIPPINES: THE NONVIOLENT AUTONOMY ALTERNATIVE (1994).

11. *See* HUMAN DEVELOPMENT NETWORK, PHILIPPINE HUMAN DEVELOPMENT REPORT 2005: PEACE, HUMAN SECURITY AND HUMAN DEVELOPMENT IN THE PHILIPPINES (2d ed. 2005).

12. Positive changes may yet emerge to improve political participation in the ongoing peace process and the political will of the current president to address the Moro problem.

13. The sub-state proposal of the MILF is also proving to be a thorny issue that has yet to be resolved by the ongoing talks between the government of the Philippines–MILF peace panels.

See Carolyn O. Arguillas, *"Heaven and Earth," says MILF on GPH proposal; "Not too far apart," says GPH*, MINDANEWS.COM (Aug. 24, 2011), http://www.mindanews.com/top-stories/2011/08/24/"heaven-and-earth"-says-milf-on-gph-proposal-"not-too-far-apart"-says-gph/.

14. In 1984, the MILF spun off from its founding organization, the MNLF.

15. See the Rome Statute of the International Criminal Court, which defines non-international armed conflicts as "armed conflicts that take place in the territory of a State when there is protracted armed conflict between governmental authorities and organized armed groups or between such groups." Rome Statute of the International Criminal Court art. 8(2)(f), July 17, 1998, 2187 U.N.T.S. 90 [hereinafter Rome Statute].

16. Available at http://bangsamoromnlf.blogspot.com/2011/03/mnlf-philippines-final-peace-agreement.html.

17. *See* THOMAS M. MCKENNA, MUSLIM RULERS AND REBELS: EVERYDAY POLITICS AND ARMED SEPARATISM IN THE SOUTHERN PHILIPPINES 164 (1998).

18. Formerly the Organization of the Islamic Conference, the Organization of Islamic Cooperation (OIC) was established in 1969 and now consists of fifty-seven member States. The OIC describes itself as "the collective voice of the Muslim world and ensuring [*sic*] to safeguard and protect the interests of the Muslim world in the spirit of promoting international peace and harmony among various peoples of the world." *About OIC*, ORGANIZATION OF ISLAMIC COOPERATION, http://www.oic-oci.org/home.asp (last visited Oct. 26, 2011). The OIC mediated talks in 1975 and 1976 that led to the Tripoli Agreement, *infra* note 19.

19. Available at http://bangsamoromnlf.blogspot.com/2011/03/mnlf-philippines-tripoli-agreement-of.html.

20. For a discussion of the proposed Bangsamoro Juridical Entity, see Datu Michael O. Mastura, *A Time for Reckoning for the Bangsamoro Struggle*, 24 TAMBARA 91 (2008).

21. Data used in this section come from a paper commissioned by the Government of the Philippines–UN Act for Peace Programme on the issue of internally displaced persons in selected areas of Mindanao. The program was implemented by the Mindanao Economic Development Council and the Autonomous Region in Muslim Mindanao in 2010 to provide an overview and analysis of the IDP situation in these selected areas to contribute to a better understanding and awareness of its complexity and to generate policy recommendations that will guide future actions and programs for the internally displaced.

22. Rome Statute, *supra* note 15.

23. Jemaah Islamiyah has been designated a foreign terrorist organization by the U.S. Department of State.

24. The perception of the ASG's transition from revolutionary to criminality is noted by community residents on Jolo and Basilan islands, where ASG presence had been and continues to be strongest. *See* GAIL T. ILAGAN, THE MINDANAO RESILIENT COMMUNITIES PROJECT REPORT 42–47 (2011).

25. Implementation of the CARHRIHL would only be activated in 2004 with the formation of the government of the Philippines–National Democratic Front Joint Monitoring Committee. In December 2005, the NDFP Human Rights Monitoring Committee published a primer on the CARHRIHL that summarizes the points of the agreement. NDFP Human Rights Monitoring Committee, Primer on the CARHRIHL (2005), *available at* http://www.scribd.com/doc/19432075/Primer-on-the-Carhrihl-by-the-NDFP. The CARHRIHL itself is available at http://peacebuilderscommunity.org/documents/CARHRIHL.pdf (last visited Oct. 26, 2011).

26. In the southern Philippines the conflicts were made more complicated by the proliferation of arms. Also, civilian armed groups and vigilante groups are utilized to serve the personal interests of political warlords. *See* SOLIMAN M. SANTOS JR. & PAZ VERDADES M. SANTOS,

PRIMED AND PURPOSEFUL: ARMED GROUPS AND HUMAN SECURITY EFFORTS IN THE PHILIPPINES 231–54 (2010), *available at* http://www.humansecuritygateway.com/documents/SAS_ArmedGroups_HumanSecurityEfforts_Philippines.pdf.

27. The NPA only has a few mortars and usually uses light machine guns to defend its positions.

28. *See* SOLIMAN M. SANTOS, PRIMER ON LANDMINES ISSUE AND BILL IN THE PHILIPPINES 28–30 (2d ed. 2010).

29. *See* SANTOS & SANTOS, *supra* note 26.

XIII

Twenty-First-Century Challenges: The Use of Military Forces to Combat Criminal Threats

Juan Carlos Gomez*

I can't change the direction of the wind, but I can adjust my sails to always reach my destination.[1]

Introduction

Globalization confronts governments with new threats. Moisés Naim, editor of *Foreign Policy*, described these threats as follows:

> The illegal trade in drugs, arms, intellectual property, people, and money is booming. Like the war on terrorism, the fight to control these illicit markets pits governments against agile, stateless, and resourceful networks empowered by globalization. Governments will continue to lose these wars until they adopt new strategies to deal with a larger, unprecedented struggle that now shapes the world as much as confrontations between nation-states once did.[2]

The use of military forces by democratic States in the fight against these criminal threats is viable and necessary; however, it is important to know when and how military forces may be used legitimately. To do so, it is necessary to understand the transformation of the threat—armed groups, which once challenged governments

* Colonel, Colombian Air Force.

over ideology, now seek financial gain for themselves. While allegedly espousing ideological politics at both ends of the political spectrum (extreme left and right), these groups have created sinister alliances that ignore geographic and political boundaries.[3] This transformation challenges State security and puts the institutional structures of democratic States at risk.

In confronting this new reality, military forces must adapt if they are to effectively neutralize this merger of criminal gangs and terrorist groups. The theories and concepts that guided the State-on-State battlefields of the nineteenth and twentieth centuries, where the opposing belligerents could distinguish their enemy and when guerrilla warfare was conducted in isolated areas far from population centers, will be inadequate to address the new challenge of the criminal terrorist.[4] Rather, new theories and guidance must be developed if military forces are to be successfully employed in this new form of conflict.

Similarly, military forces must develop an understanding of the law that will apply when combating these criminal/terrorist groups. That law will come from human rights law (HRL)[5] and international humanitarian law (IHL),[6] which in "classic" international law are referred to as "the law of peace" and the "law of war," respectively. The determination of when each will apply presents new challenges for military forces that have traditionally focused on the law applicable to international armed conflict.

This article will explore these issues from a Colombian perspective, a country which has been engaged for decades in an armed struggle with insurgent groups and now also with criminal groups using terrorist tactics for economic gain through the drug trade.[7]

The Legal Framework for the Use of Force

Human rights law transformed traditional Westphalian sovereignty by providing that international law can extend into a State and regulate the relationship between an individual citizen and the government. In its specifics, HRL addresses many aspects of an individual's relationship with the government, such as participation in the political process. However, it is HRL's regulation of an individual's encounters with law enforcement agents and the courts that is the most relevant when considering actions that are taken against the criminal terrorist. These norms are designed to protect the citizen from unlawful government actions, while at the same time providing law enforcement agencies the ability to protect citizens from criminal actions and for the judicial system to punish those who do commit crimes.

On the other hand, international humanitarian law permits the use of force to restore peace in international and non-international conflicts, while at the same time minimizing unnecessary suffering to civilians and damage to civilian objects. IHL has evolved since its inception, particularly in the post–World War II era, with the four 1949 Geneva Conventions, the two 1977 Additional Protocols and numerous conventions regulating the use of some weapons and outlawing others. One feature of this evolution has been the expansion of IHL from its application solely to international armed conflict to non-international or internal armed conflict. It is this law that regulates Colombian military forces in the conduct of military operations against the well-organized, well-equipped narco-trafficking groups operating within Colombia.

Human Rights or International Humanitarian Law—Which Governs?

Unfortunately, what seems to be the clear delineation between HRL ("law of peace") and IHL ("law of war") becomes gray in internal conflicts arising from the new threats that confront governments. Traditionally, counternarcotic efforts were law enforcement in nature, even in a country such as the United States which declared a "war on drugs." As such, HRL was the component of international law that applied to those efforts. The illegal armed groups operating within Colombia, however, clearly fulfill the definition of an "organized armed group," which, when combined with the level of violence in which they engage, permits the use of force under the IHL applicable to non-international armed conflicts to be applied against them. That the motive for the use of violence is now economic versus political makes no difference. However, while the right to use military force against these groups is clear, the ability to do so is difficult because they camouflage themselves within the civilian population. There the application of force against them is even more difficult than it was when they operated in isolated jungle-covered areas of the country.

In using force in this new battlefield, mistakes have been made by the armed forces. This has strained the credibility of Colombian government institutions responsible for the conduct of military operations and led to criminal prosecutions of those involved. While it remains clear that the level of threat continues to require the involvement of Colombian military forces[8] applying offensive and lethal force, it is equally clear that every reasonable precaution must be taken to ensure that the use of that force is directed only against legitimate military objectives in accordance with IHL.

We Fight among the People

> [I]ncreasingly we conduct operations amongst the people. The people in the cities, towns, streets and their houses—all the people, anywhere—can be on the battlefield. Military engagements can take place against formed and recognizable groups of enemies moving amongst civilians, against enemies disguised as civilians, and unintentionally and intentionally against civilians.[9]

The *Fuerzas Armadas Revolucionarias de Colombia* (FARC), the principal criminal terrorist group, and the other narco-trafficking groups generally do not possess the capability to engage in conventional armed confrontations with Colombia's military forces. Today, the armed and criminal groups move and act among the people, obtaining benefits from a portion of the citizenry both voluntarily and through extortion.

The brutality of the criminal terrorist groups is unquestioned. They are not supported by most of the population, but this does not necessarily result in support for the government forces who act to protect the public. To the contrary, each mistake or illegal or illegitimate act by a public official damages the people's confidence in the government.[10] The cumulative consequence of these allegations of misconduct is to turn public opinion against the government and those whose responsibility it is to protect them. In effect, the protectors of society become the abusers of society. Public opinion is turned against the government and law enforcement agencies and military forces.

Because law enforcement agencies are often incapable of effectively addressing the threat of the criminal terrorist groups, military forces are often called on to operate in this new environment among the people. Military forces must redesign their doctrine to confront the new threats. In today's war there is no victory, no capitulation by a defeated enemy. As Rupert Smith indicates, "[O]ur operations have become increasingly timeless; they go on and on."[11] The use of military force alone cannot eliminate the threat posed by these groups; it can only contribute positively or negatively to the ultimate outcome. The illegal armed groups do not seek a military victory; they are interested only in creating chaos and provoking overreaction by military forces with the objective of causing a loss of support for the government, thereby perpetuating never-ending conflicts.

The defeat of illegal and criminal armed gangs will not be accomplished through military force. Rather, States must employ methods to dismantle them that comply with the law and bring individual members to courts for prosecution. This will require the cooperation of the citizenry of the country. To gain that cooperation, the population can never be confused with the enemy and the criminals. If it is, the population will become the enemy.

Strategies must be developed to obtain the population's support for the State's efforts to combat the criminal gangs. These strategies must be designed not just to end citizens' complicity with the gangs. They must also end the belief that the population can be neutral in the conflict. What is required is a supportive and cooperative population that assists national institutional authorities in their efforts. In other words, an environment must be created in which each individual citizen feels secure in denouncing the criminal gangs and assisting in the elimination of the support structures for criminal activities. While military and police forces must play an important role in establishing this environment, individual members of society will also have a role to play.

A temporary presence of government forces is insufficient to establish this environment. In areas that organized armed groups have controlled, the citizens will not provide the necessary support if they believe police and military forces will soon withdraw, thus allowing the criminal groups to return. As a result, the new strategy must envision a permanent presence and an assurance to the population that the government forces will be there as long as is necessary.

The use of military force is not always the best option to deal with the activities of the illegal and criminal groups. If mistakes, either intentional or unintentional, are made in attempts to neutralize the threat and innocent members of the population become victims, this is exactly what criminal gangs desire. This delegitimizes the State and its democratic institutions. If military force is necessary it must be used carefully and in full compliance with the law. However, in many instances the more appropriate response is law enforcement actions designed to arrest and prosecute individual group members.

It has been observed that "the British Army was the Irish Republican Army's best recruiter. By targeting Catholic civilians and arbitrarily arresting and killing suspected I.R.A. members, the British angered many young men who turned to the I.R.A. as their only hope for survival; it was also a way to get revenge."[12] This history lesson is also important in the Colombian context. Noncompliance with the rule of law can lead—and has led—some to join the FARC and other criminal groups; can cause a delegitimization of the government, the armed forces and police; and can result in an increase in the number of disciplinary and judicial cases against officials involved in unlawful acts.

New Missions for the Armed Forces

Colombia is not the only country in the Western Hemisphere that uses its military forces within its borders in missions other than national defense of the nation.

El Salvador's President Mauricio Funes, immediately upon assuming office in 2009, ordered military forces to participate in combating the *mara salvatrucha* gang.[13] El Salvadoran military forces continue to be employed in that role.[14] In Brazil, military forces contribute to the law enforcement efforts of the police against the criminal and narco-traffic bands in the favelas.[15] The same use of military forces can be observed in Mexico, where President Felipe Calderon in 2006 declared "war against the narco-traffickers," a "war" engaged in by the federal police, the army and the navy.[16] To a lesser degree, Guatemala, Paraguay and Peru are also using their military forces to address security-related issues within their borders.

Adaptation to the New Operational Environment

As was indicated previously, criminal activity would ideally be dealt with exclusively as a law enforcement matter that could be addressed by law enforcement agencies. Unfortunately, the capabilities and economic capacity of the illegal armed groups and the organized crime organizations are such that they are beyond the ability of law enforcement agencies, acting alone, to address. In these circumstances, governments may legitimately call upon military forces to maintain social order and address the threat created by these groups and organizations. Military forces must adapt, however, to these new missions and operational environment if they are going to effectively and efficiently neutralize the threats they have been called on to address; failure to do so will result in loss of support from the government and citizens.

Particularly over the last eight years, Colombian military forces and law enforcement agencies have been successful in reducing the threat posed by criminal organizations and illegal armed groups. Several have been defeated, and the capabilities of those that remain have been greatly reduced. In addition, the level of violence within the country has greatly decreased. In many areas, the threat has been reduced to the point that military forces no longer need to be used in a traditional military capacity. In those areas, criminal activity, including terrorist acts, can now be dealt with as a law enforcement matter. The rule of law has been reestablished and a security environment established where HRL—not IHL—is applied by military forces performing law enforcement functions. In these areas, illegal armed groups and criminal organizations do not control portions of the territory, although they continue to operate within them. In response to pressure brought by military forces and law enforcement agencies in these areas, the illegal armed groups and criminal organizations simply move their areas of operations to less controlled areas; this is what is known as the "bubble effect."

In those places in Colombia where the FARC still possesses a viable military capability, Colombian military forces employ the use of force in accordance with IHL to combat it. Offensive operations, in the classic sense, remain an option in isolated areas away from population centers. However, when operations are conducted among the people, care must be taken in the application of force. Unnecessarily causing harm to civilians or their property can create greater long-term issues than the immediate military advantage gained. While IHL remains the governing law, the use of force must be more restrictively applied as a last resort and should only be used when necessary in legitimate defense of the military force and when there is no other alternative to accomplish the assigned mission.

The criminal organizations now operating in Colombia, whose motives are economic instead of political, are not interested in a negotiated settlement that would provide them a place in the political process. While they speak of a desire to negotiate, they do so only to obtain immediate benefits and perpetuate the conflict. They look to intervention by churches, politicians, social leaders and international organizations weary of the long conflict. The criminal groups not only subsist among the people; they use the population for their benefit.

The questions that must be answered are how military forces are to be used in a role far different from their principal purpose of maintaining national security against external threats, and how combating criminal activity can be successively accomplished while at the same time retaining that most important attribute of national and international legitimacy.

Knowing the Threat

Knowing and understanding the type of threat to be confronted is of fundamental importance. Real-time intelligence information on the criminal organization's objective, capabilities and membership is essential to formulating strategy and courses of action.

Participation of Military Lawyers

The complexity of international and domestic law and the expectation in Western democracies that the government and military forces will conduct themselves in accordance with the law require that military lawyers be involved in all aspects of military operations, from their planning and execution to post-execution evaluation and analysis.[17] These military lawyers must have the knowledge and experience to be credible with the commanders they advise. The value of such participation by military lawyers has been demonstrated in Colombia.

Rules for the Use of Force

There must be clear, understandable rules provided to military forces on the circumstances under which force may be used and the type and degree of that force.

This is dependent on the mission assigned to the forces. In Colombia, two differently colored cards are used. A blue card is used when the military unit is engaged in a law enforcement mission. The rules on the blue card are based on HRL. They provide for the use of force only when no other option is available to accomplish the mission and in self-defense of the person and others. The red card is used in operations against military objectives. These cards are based on IHL and permit the offensive use of force, including lethal force if demanded by military necessity.

Coordination with the Judicial Branch of Government

The military forces must coordinate their efforts with the judicial branch and the federal police. In the case of Colombia, this is the Office of the Attorney General and the National Police, and subordinate organizations. Each military operation undertaken as a law enforcement mission is undertaken in conjunction with law enforcement agencies so that effective criminal prosecutions can take place. These normally occur in the new operating area among the people, where adherence to HRL is critical.

Investigation of Allegations of Misconduct by Military Members and Public Officials

Allegations of criminal misconduct by law enforcement agents and members of the military are inevitable when operating in the middle of the population. These must be openly and effectively investigated. When allegations are substantiated criminal prosecutions must be initiated. When investigations don't support the allegations, the results must be publicly shared, including the factual details of the incident or event in question. Thorough, complete and transparent investigations are necessary to maintain public support. The worst strategy is government silence, which permits the media and others to speculate or to tell their versions of what they believed happened.

Truth Is Paramount

Mistakes and errors have been made and will be made by military members and law enforcement agents, even when actions are taken in good faith. When these occur, they must be truthfully revealed and explained. Too often, innocent mistakes have been covered up with falsehoods. Actions taken in good faith but with unexpected results can be accepted; falsehoods and cover-ups cannot.[18] As with failures to effectively investigate allegations of misconduct, falsehoods and cover-ups lead to a loss of public support.

Institutional Loyalty

When a military member or law enforcement agent engages in criminal conduct, the institution concerned, whether it is the armed forces or federal police, must provide that individual the rights provided by domestic law, but must not be seen as defending the conduct in question. Loyalty must be given to the institution as a whole, not to the individual member. Regrettably, in Colombia there have been instances when military members or law enforcement agents have used their position of authority to commit crimes. When they go unpunished, there are political, legal and economic costs to the government and institution concerned, and credibility and public support suffer.

Tactical Operations Can Impact National Strategy

Throughout history, conflict has been analyzed at three levels: strategic, operational and tactical. The national strategic level involves development of national policy and objectives, and the use of resources to accomplish those objectives. At the operational level, campaigns and major operations are planned, conducted and sustained to accomplish strategic objectives. At the tactical level, military missions are planned and executed to accomplish military objectives. Today, those levels are closer together than at any time in the past. Technological advances, social networks and an almost instantaneous communications capability allow what is occurring at the tactical level to be made known literally around the world. Because tactical situations can, and often do, have effects at the strategic level in terms of public perceptions and opinion—both negative and positive—it is essential that commanders at the strategic and operational levels be in communication with, and in control of, military units operating at the tactical level. They must have the capacity to react and adapt to the circumstances as they occur on the ground.

Political and Judicial Concerns Arising from the New Operating Environment

The risk of legal action being taken against them is the greatest concern of military members and law enforcement agents operating in the new environment. In Colombia, the potential of criminal and disciplinary investigations being initiated has reduced morale among members and agents. It has caused some to decide in certain circumstances that it is safer not to act, as taking action might subject them to an investigation. Another concern is that making allegations of criminal conduct against public officials and administrative demands of the government is both politically and financially profitable.

Beyond the impact on the individual who is the subject of the allegation, allegations of misconduct damage the credibility of the government. When the allegations have a basis in fact, action to investigate and hold persons accountable is required. Responses to false allegations must publicly identify the allegations as false, and action must be taken against those who make such allegations when they violate Colombian criminal law. Care must be taken in doing so, however; nothing can damage the credibility and reputation of the institution concerned more than to find an allegation is unsupported on the basis of an inadequate or incomplete investigation when the allegation is, in fact, true. False allegations must be vigorously refuted; a failure to do so is nearly the same as accepting the allegation as true.

The inevitable result of the use of military force, whether in international or non-international armed conflict, is that innocent persons will be killed and injured and civilian property will be damaged and destroyed. When this occurs, the government must be prepared to accept responsibility and compensate those who suffered losses. To fail to do so harms morale among civilians and can turn them into supporters of the armed groups combating the government.

In Colombia, there are both non-judicial and judicial processes to evaluate claims for damages caused by military forces and to promptly provide adequate compensation to those harmed. This not only has the benefit of promoting goodwill, but also reduces the likelihood that allegations of criminal misconduct will be brought against the military members causing the harm.

Final Reflections

Naim, in his "The Five Wars of Globalization" article, concludes:

> These five wars stretch and even render obsolete many of the existing institutions, legal frameworks, military doctrines and law enforcement techniques on which governments have relied for years. Analysts need to rethink the concept of war "fronts" defined by geography and the definition of "combatants" according to the Geneva Convention. The functions of intelligence agents, soldiers, police officers, or immigration officers need rethinking and adaption to the new realities.[19]

Facing the reality that threats to national security today are more likely to arise from within rather than from outside, as Naim suggested in 2003, governments, including that of Colombia, have rethought how to employ their military forces to confront these new threats. Colombia's experience has demonstrated that while military forces can be used lawfully in the fight against these internal threats to security and democratic stability, they must adopt new strategies and doctrine to effectively combat these threats that are largely centered in the population. A failure to do so has the potential to more severely damage the State—and State institutions—than does the threat against which military forces are employed.

If military forces are used in a law enforcement capacity to deal with criminal conduct, the law that governs will be HRL. It requires more restrained use of force than is provided under IHL. While military forces can operate effectively under both regimes, the Colombian experience demonstrates that it is essential that military forces understand the law under which they are operating on missions to which they are assigned. Misapprehension of the legal regime can result in excessive use of force, increased risk to military personnel and mission failure.

Democratic societies in the twenty-first century enjoy the benefits and freedoms provided by HRL, and demand that their governments provide them the rights and guarantees set forth in the various human rights instruments. Colombia is no exception. The Colombian population appreciates the threat posed by the criminal gangs, but expects that the government's response and the actions of law enforcement organizations and military forces will be fully consistent with that law. It will not tolerate excesses.

The privilege to govern and have the monopoly on the lawful use of force within a society obligates those who have that privilege to use force in full compliance with the law, whether it be HRL or IHL, and to adhere to the highest ethical and moral values. The wind has blown and societies have changed. Now governments must adjust their sails and respond to internal threats within the framework of the law; their societies expect nothing less.

Notes

1. Jimmy Dean, LIFE QUOTES, http://www.sanjuan.edu/webpages/bgrueneberger/files/Senior%20Grad%20Speech%20Life%20Quotes.pdf (last visited Apr. 10, 2012).

2. Moisés Naim, *The Five Wars of Globalization,* FOREIGN POLICY, Jan.–Feb. 2003, at 29, 29.

3. *See, e.g.*, Steven W. Casteel, Assistant Administrator for Intelligence, U.S. Drug Enforcement Administration, Statement before the Senate Committee on the Judiciary: Narco-Terrorism: International Drug Trafficking and Terrorism—a Dangerous Mix (May 20, 2003), *available at* http://www.justice.gov/dea/ongoing/narco-terrorism_story052003.html ("Globalization has dramatically changed the face of both legitimate and illegitimate enterprise. Criminals, by exploiting advances in technology, finance, communications, and transportation in pursuit of their illegal endeavors, have become criminal entrepreneurs. Perhaps the most alarming aspect of this 'entrepreneurial' style of crime is the intricate manner in which drugs and terrorism may be intermingled. Not only is the proliferation of illegal drugs perceived as a danger, but the proceeds from the sale of drugs provides a ready source of funding for other criminal activities, including terrorism.")

4. RUPERT SMITH, THE UTILITY OF FORCE: THE ART OF WAR IN THE MODERN WORLD 5 (2006) ("It is now time to recognize that a paradigm shift in war has undoubtedly occurred: from armies with comparable forces doing battle on a field to strategic confrontation between a range

of combatants, not all of which are armies, and using different types of weapons, often improvised. The old paradigm was that of interstate industrial war. The new one is the paradigm of war amongst the people . . . .").

5. Human rights law is found in both customary international law and treaty law. *See, e.g.*, Universal Declaration of Human Rights, G.A. Res. 217A, at 71, U.N. GAOR, 3d Sess., 1st plen. mtg., U.N. Doc. A/810 (Dec. 10, 1948); International Covenant on Civil and Political Rights arts. 4, 8, G.A. Res. 2200A (XXI), U.N. Doc. A/6316 (Dec. 16, 1966), 999 U.N.T.S. 171; American Convention on Human Rights, Nov. 22, 1969, 1144 U.N.T.S. 123.

6. As with human rights law, international humanitarian law is found in both customary and treaty law. *See, e.g.*, Convention for the Amelioration of the Condition of the Wounded and Sick in Armed Forces in the Field, Aug. 12, 1949, 6 U.S.T. 3114, 75 U.N.T.S. 31; Convention for the Amelioration of the Condition of Wounded, Sick and Shipwrecked Members of Armed Forces at Sea, Aug. 12, 1949, 6 U.S.T. 3217, 75 U.N.T.S. 85; Convention Relative to the Treatment of Prisoners of War, Aug. 12, 1949, 6 U.S.T. 3316, 75 U.N.T.S. 135; Convention Relative to the Protection of Civilian Persons in Time of War, Aug. 12, 1949, 6 U.S.T. 3516, 75 U.N.T.S. 287. Of particular relevance in each of these Conventions to the internal (or non-international) conflict in Colombia is what is referred to as "Common Article 3." The provisions of that article apply "in the case of armed conflict not of an international character occurring in the territory of one of the High Contracting Parties."

Other treaties applicable in internal conflict include the Convention on Prohibitions or Restrictions on the Use of Certain Conventional Weapons Which May Be Deemed to Be Excessively Injurious or to Have Indiscriminate Effects, Oct. 10, 1980, 1342 U.N.T.S. 137, *reprinted in* 19 INTERNATIONAL LEGAL MATERIALS 1523 (1980). Amended Article 1 to the Convention made all of its protocols applicable in internal conflicts. *See also* Convention on the Prohibition of the Use, Stockpiling, Production and Transfer of Anti-Personnel Mines and on Their Destruction, Sept. 18, 1997, 2056 U.N.T.S. 211, *reprinted in* 36 INTERNATIONAL LEGAL MATERIALS 1507 (1997); Convention on Cluster Munitions, Dec. 3, 2008, 48 INTERNATIONAL LEGAL MATERIALS 357 (2008). *See also* CUSTOMARY INTERNATIONAL HUMANITARIAN LAW (2 volumes: Vol. I, Rules; Vol. II, Practice (2 Parts)) (Jean-Marie Henckaerts & Louise Doswald-Beck eds., 2005).

7. Casteel, *supra* note 3 (stating that three terrorist organizations in Colombia, all with links to the drug trade, were responsible for about 3,500 murders in 2002).

8. Under the Colombian constitutional scheme, the "Military Force" is composed of the Army, Navy and Air Force and what is referred to as the "Public Force" includes the three military services and the National Police.

9. SMITH, *supra* note 4, at 281 (Smith describes war among the people as being the dominant form of war since the end of the Cold War).

10. In a January 2011 interview with former President Alvaro Uribe, he emphasized to the author the importance of dismantling the criminal groups through lawful actions, using the courts for prosecutions whenever possible.

11. SMITH, *supra* note 4, at 291.

12. *Central Intelligence Assassins*, THE TEMPLE NEWS (Nov. 14, 2002), http://temple-news.com/2002/11/14/central-intelligence-assassins/.

13. *Maras* is the term used to label the El Salvadoran youth gangs. The *mara salvatrucha* originated in Los Angeles in the 1980s when young El Salvadoran immigrants, armed with machetes, guns and guerrilla combat training gained during El Salvador's civil war, united and became one of the city's most violent gangs. Using the expedited removal procedures of the Immigration and Nationality Act resulted in large numbers of gang members being deported to El Salvador throughout the 1990s, where they continued their gang activities. El Salvadoran youth, already

desensitized to violence by the civil war, were easy recruits. One author commented, "For all intents and purposes, deportation from the United States merely provided MS-13 [*mara salvatrucha*] with an effective means for transnational expansion—an expansion that would allow the gang to become more organized, powerful, and violent." Kelly Padgett Lineberger, *The United States–El Salvador Extradition Treaty: A Dated Obstacle in the Transnational War Against* Mara Salvatrucha *(MS-13)*, 44 VANDERBILT JOURNAL OF TRANSNATIONAL LAW 187, 194 (2011).

14. Alex Renderos, *Salvadoran Leader Names Newly Retired General to Top Police Post; The Selection Comes after a Similar Security Appointment, and Stirs Fear of Militarization*, LOS ANGELES TIMES, Jan. 26, 2012, at A3.

15. *See, e.g.*, *Open for Business: The Pacification of Brazil's Favelas*, KNOWLEDGE WHARTON, Jan. 3, 2012, http://knowledge.wharton.upenn.edu/article.cfm?articleid=2910.

16. Stephen Sackur, *"No alternative" to Mexico's drug war—says Calderon*, BBC, Oct. 27, 2010, http://news.bbc.co.uk/2/hi/programmes/hardtalk/9130155.stm.

17. *See* Protocol Additional to the Geneva Conventions of 12 August 1949, and Relating to the Protection of Victims of International Armed Conflicts art. 82, June 8, 1977, 1125 U.N.T.S. 3 ("[States] . . . shall ensure that legal advisers are available to advise military commanders at the appropriate level on the application of the [Geneva] Conventions and this Protocol . . . ."). The Colombian Air Force incorporated military lawyers into the planning and execution process in 2001; the other services followed suit. Their participation occurs on a daily basis.

18. During the period of his presidency, Alvaro Uribe stated, "History can forgive an error, but never the lies or half-truths."

19. Naim, *supra* note 2, at 36.

XIV

An Australian Perspective on Non-International Armed Conflict: Afghanistan and East Timor

Rob McLaughlin*

Introduction

Over the course of the last three decades, Australia has committed forces to a wide range of operations that have, collectively, involved the Australian Defence Force (ADF) in its most sustained period of high operational tempo since the Vietnam War. The operations include the first Gulf War, in 1990–91, and the second Gulf War, in 2003 (both international armed conflicts (IACs)); belligerent participation in non-international armed conflicts (NIACs) in Iraq post-2003 and Afghanistan (at least since 2005); and participation in a range of peace operations of widely varied political, physical and legal risk, including transitional administrations in Cambodia and East Timor, sanctions enforcement in the North Arabian Gulf, and stabilization and mitigation operations in Somalia, Rwanda, East Timor, Bougainville and the Solomon Islands. As each operation has unfolded, Australia has learned (or in some cases, relearned) both practical and theoretical lessons in operational law. In many cases, these lessons have been identified and contextualized within a relatively defined (albeit fluid) operational legal paradigm

* Associate Professor of Law, Australian National University; Captain, Royal Australian Navy. The views expressed in this article are my own and should not necessarily be attributed to the Royal Australian Navy, Australian Defence Force or government of Australia.

in that experience with IAC, and non–law of armed conflict (LOAC)–governed peace operations, has tended to be relatively linear and coherently incremental.

With NIACs, however, the trajectory has not always been as logical or smooth. I believe that there are three reasons for this differing path. I shall not examine them in any detail, but it is nevertheless useful to set them out up front for they provide a contextual backdrop to the focus of this study. First, as opposed to IAC and peace operations generally, there was—and remains—much less clarity about what law applies in NIAC. Ongoing debates as to the application of human rights law in armed conflict (which are almost universally conducted by reference to NIAC-based examples)[1] and the lively and contentious discussion surrounding the application of IAC blockade law to what some characterize as a NIAC situation between Israel and Hamas in the Gaza Strip[2] are but two examples that illustrate this point.[3] Indeed the fundamental task of distinguishing the NIAC threshold from its "upper" and "lower" neighbor legal paradigms (IAC and less-than-NIAC law enforcement in situations of civil disturbance) similarly remains a highly contested and politically laden debate. There is little doubt that the relative "scarcity" and "opacity" of NIAC LOAC is one reason why NIAC LOAC is the primary battleground in the current push to harmonize IAC and NIAC LOAC by asserting that most (if not all) of the IAC rules are equally applicable in NIAC, and to humanize LOAC by reinterpreting its scope of application and the substance of many of its constituent concepts in the light of human rights law. The result is that NIAC LOAC is being squeezed between (or indeed, colonized by) its better defined and more fully enumerated paradigmatic neighbors, which in turn creates the perception—if not the actuality—of greater fluidity and indeterminacy than in other elements of operations law.

The second reason, which emanates from the first, is that the existence of a NIAC remains a highly political assessment, whereas the existence of an IAC is generally (or at least relatively when compared to NIAC) easy to establish with a degree of logic and certainty. This is most evident at the lower NIAC threshold, between non-NIAC situations of civil disturbance and NIAC itself. The very large space for political influence in a NIAC characterization decision (much larger than in the equivalent IAC conflict characterization space) has meant that in addition to the application of NIAC LOAC being dogged by a higher degree of substantive uncertainty and opacity than either IAC LOAC or peace operations law, it has also remained a much more politically nuanced and contested body of law at even the initial point of characterization. Perhaps the most striking illustration is the long British reluctance to characterize "the Troubles" in Northern Ireland as anything other than a less-than-NIAC law enforcement situation.[4]

The third reason—certainly evident, in my view, in Australian practice, but common across many partner operating States—is that when Australia has committed forces to IAC situations, it has almost universally been as a belligerent: Iraq/Kuwait, 1990–91; Afghanistan, 2001; Iraq, 2003. However, when Australia has committed forces into NIAC situations, it has almost universally been as a non-belligerent stabilization or mitigation force. There was clearly a NIAC under way in Somalia in 1992, but Australia's force was not a party to it; rather, it was part of a stabilization/mitigation mission and did not exercise the full suite of LOAC powers that would have been available to it, *de jure*, if it had been a party to the NIAC. Accordingly, the force was authorized to use lethal force in self-defense, but not to conduct lethal targeting operations under the auspices of LOAC.[5] In Cambodia and Rwanda it was similarly so. In East Timor, although there is debate as to whether there was a NIAC (or even an IAC) afoot in 1999–2001, Australian forces were not a party to any armed conflict and thus could not avail themselves of the sharper end of LOAC authorizations *de jure*. Thus, until Australia substantially re-engaged in Afghanistan in 2005 as a belligerent party in what was by then clearly a NIAC, Australia had to some extent been able to bypass the complexities of NIAC LOAC. While the ADF often deployed into NIAC contexts, those forces were not parties to the NIAC and operated under the "routine" peace operations legal paradigm.

Aim

My aim in this short study is to ask how, from a legal perspective, Australia has approached the issue of "NIAC." I will seek to achieve this by examining four discrete issues: conflict characterization, characterization of the opposing force, rules of engagement (ROE) and treatment of captured/detained personnel. The methodology I have adopted is to examine each of these issues through a broadly comparative prism—a comparison between a high-level non-NIAC operation (East Timor, 1999–2001) and a NIAC operation (Afghanistan, ongoing since 2005). The purpose behind adopting this methodology is to provide a framework for establishing an alternative against which NIAC practice can be compared. It also provides a means of illustrating the degree to which this practice is either consistent or different across the lower threshold of NIAC, that is, between less-than-NIAC "peace" operations (law enforcement operations or stabilization/mitigation operations), and NIAC operations themselves. The reasons Australia has taken different characterization paths, and the consequences of these choices, are, I believe, central to understanding any "Australian approach to NIAC." My underlying premise, as will quickly become evident, is that any legal understanding of NIAC and of the threshold between NIAC and less than NIAC is beholden to non-legal influences to a much greater degree than in clear law enforcement or clear IAC contexts.

Characterization of the Conflict: Afghanistan vs. East Timor

Characterization of the conflict situation is fundamental to Australia's approach to almost every other element of operational authority. Although this issue is less significant for some other States, the choice to characterize a conflict as a NIAC or as "law enforcement," or to characterize Australian involvement in a NIAC as belligerency or as law enforcement or stabilization/mitigation partnership, results in a vital use-of-force caveat for the ADF. This caveat is, in essence, that where Australia is not a belligerent party to an armed conflict, Australian forces cannot (in general) use lethal force in circumstances other than in individual and unit self-defense (usually including defense of others). Furthermore, use of force where the Australian force is not a belligerent is governed entirely by the "routine" elements of Australian domestic criminal law.[6] There is, consequently, no legally available option for Australian forces to access any of the lethal LOAC authorizations when Australia is not a belligerent party to the NIAC. When Australia is a belligerent party to the NIAC, and lethal force is used in alleged accordance with NIAC LOAC (for example, to target a fighter member of an organized armed group (OAG)), then the applicable law shifts, and brings into play Division 268 of the Commonwealth Criminal Code (which domesticates the 1998 Rome Statute of the International Criminal Court offenses into Australian law).[7]

Afghanistan, at least since Australian forces re-engaged militarily in 2005, is a NIAC and Australia is clearly a belligerent party to that NIAC. East Timor in 1999–2001 was, however, consciously characterized as a "law enforcement" or stabilization operation, even though the issue of characterization as a NIAC (or IAC) was considered. What may have influenced these two legal/policy characterization decisions along very different paths? Certainly, the "facts on the ground" were not radically different when rationalized against a relative scale. The Afghanistan context is current and well known and requires little recap; however, it is perhaps worthwhile briefly reviewing, for comparative purposes, the less current East Timor context. In relation to intensity, there were/are proportionally high casualty rates in both conflict contexts. In East Timor, tens (by some counts hundreds) of thousands had died under Indonesian occupation, and the consequent insurgency, since 1975.[8] At the point of intervention in 1999, there were wide-scale destruction of infrastructure and massive displacement of the population. On September 20, 1999, as the United Nations Security Council–sanctioned International Force East

Timor (INTERFET) commenced deployment, few buildings in Dili were undamaged and all but three of East Timor's main population centers had been either completely destroyed (two towns) or 70 percent burnt down or leveled (four towns).[9] Population displacement was on a massive scale: as recorded subsequently in an ADF "lessons learnt" study: "A preliminary UN inter-agency assessment of the situation issued on 27 September 1999 estimated that of a total pre-ballot population of 890,000, over 500,000 had been displaced by violence, including 150,000 to West Timor [Indonesian territory]."[10]

In terms of organization, in East Timor there were legacy militias and insurgency groupings (which had been fighting Indonesian occupation since 1975), as well as newer militias of both pro-integrationist and independence sympathies. The political context was complicated by external actors (such as Portugal (the former colonial power), Australia, Indonesia and the UN) and militia sponsors (including, it now seems well established, elements within the Indonesian military). The comparison with Afghanistan's political and conflict situation (complicated by the engagement of Pakistan, United States, NATO, UN, and warlord, trans-border militia, and transnational terrorist group interests) is—when scaled—readily evident. The situation in East Timor 1999–2001 could arguably be said to have met both the *Tadić* "intensity of the conflict and organization of the parties to the conflict" elements[11] as readily as the situation in Afghanistan currently does.

However, despite such contextual similarities in terms of the "facts on the ground" of which LOAC takes cognizance, the strategic contexts in which the East Timor and Afghanistan conflict characterization decisions were made were radically different. This clearly played into the fundamentally different characterization decisions Australia arrived at in relation to these two conflict contexts. In Afghanistan, the "other" was the unloved Taliban and its widely detested partner Al Qaeda—both routinely described through militarized rhetoric emphasizing organization, capacity, universal aims, threat level and reach. As Australia's then Prime Minister, John Howard, said of the attacks of September 11, 2001 and those who sponsored and sheltered the perpetrators:

> [I]t is the product of evil minds and it is the product of an attitude of a group of people who in every sense [e]voke those very evocative words of Winston Churchill when he said that those responsible for the Nazi occupation of Europe should be regarded in their brutish hour of triumph as the moral outcasts of mankind.[12]

In announcing the deployment of forces to Afghanistan, Prime Minister Howard was explicit as to the readily condemnable nature of the "other": "Well we certainly don't have any concern about being involved in action against those people who were responsible for the terrorist attack."[13] Indeed, Australia had by this stage invoked the ANZUS Treaty,[14] indicating that the Afghanistan conflict context had been informed by a significant legal act which was more armed conflict focused than not.[15] This militarized (as opposed to law enforcement terminology based) characterization of the conflict remains the case. As Minister for Defence Stephen Smith observed in March 2011, "[o]ur fundamental goal is to prevent Afghanistan from again being used by terrorists to plan and train for attacks on innocent civilians, including Australians in our own region and beyond."[16]

Thus in relation to Afghanistan, defining the context as a NIAC and engaging as a belligerent within it heralded few prospects of causing a damaging rift with an important neighbor or influential member of the international community, or of subscribing to a highly legally contested or politically risky characterization of the "other." In many ways, there was little political or strategic risk to balance against the political and strategic gain of characterizing the situation as a NIAC and of Australian engagement within it being as a belligerent party.

But the strategic context in which the East Timor conflict characterization decision was made was very different indeed. Certainly, if one looks only to the "facts on the ground" there had been a NIAC (or IAC?) during the period of Indonesian occupation. It may even have been an Additional Protocol I Article 1(4) conflict.[17] But for Australia, this was a difficult issue: Australia was one of the few States that had recognized the Indonesian annexation.[18] Even when the conflict morphed in 1999–2001 into something like a NIAC with integrationist militia as the "other," the conflict characterization settled upon appears to have been that there was no NIAC afoot. During INTERFET (an Australian-commanded "green helmet" force), Australia certainly had greater "national" scope to characterize the conflict as a NIAC than in the later UN Transitional Administration in East Timor (UNTAET) "blue helmet" period, but chose not to do so. This decision was maintained even as INTERFET deployed ashore in Dili, where the pro-integrationist militias were burning, looting, killing and terrorizing, and were doing so with the tacit support, if not backing, of some members of the Indonesian military.[19]

These militias were certainly potentially characterizable as an organized armed group in a NIAC context if we apply our Afghanistan-based conception of "organized armed group." But in 1999, the recent (and ongoing) "civilians taking a direct part in hostilities" debate was in the future; thus the assessment was made against the slim—and relatively unnuanced—black letter law criteria recognizable in Additional Protocol I, Additional Protocol II[20] and Common Article 3 to the 1949 Geneva Conventions,[21] and their associated commentaries.

But there were also other vital factors that militated against such characterization. The first was the fact that INTERFET was present in East Timor partly on the basis of an Indonesian invitation.[22] The second was that security was envisaged to be a combined INTERFET/Indonesian responsibility during the transition phase, thus requiring INTERFET to cooperate with Indonesian forces until they withdrew (although in reality this did not turn out to be a long phase, as Indonesian forces rapidly departed). Finally, regardless of whether there was a NIAC afoot, the Security Council and Australia (as the lead troop-contributing nation (TCN) for INTERFET, and also furnishing its commander) consciously determined that the UN-sanctioned force was not involved in a NIAC. This was not a universal view. The International Committee of the Red Cross (ICRC) had indicated to Australia that "militia members detained for acts of violence against INTERFET members were entitled to prisoner of war status. The ICRC's reasoning was that if it were accepted that the militia were at least controlled by the Indonesian armed forces then clashes between militia and INTERFET would constitute armed conflict."[23]

The Australian view was that LOAC did not apply *de jure*, and the situation was one of law enforcement/stabilization. Thus even if the Fourth Geneva Convention (GC IV)[24] was used as a template for managing the situation, this was clearly contemplated as resting upon a policy basis, for quite apart from whether the situation was even an armed conflict at all, GC IV of course applies *de jure* to IACs, not NIACs. However, one revealing element in this decision-making process is instructive as to the sorts of concerns that can inform conflict characterization decisions at the lower threshold (that is, NIAC, or less-than-NIAC law enforcement/stabilization) in that the issue of reciprocity was clearly in mind. For some of those analyzing the context there was certainly a concern that if Australia found that GC IV applied *de jure*, it may "have the legal consequence either of rendering ADF personnel 'lawful' targets, making Australia party to any conflict, or bringing into effect the other Geneva Conventions of 1949."[25] Ultimately, the settled view taken was that

> the Convention [GC IV] would not make Australian troops a party to a conflict who could then be targeted "as of right by other parties to the conflict. . . ." If the Fourth Convention applied and armed elements attacked Australian troops this would be illegal unless it was part of an organised armed force with a responsible command structure.[25]

Clearly, the reciprocity issue—that is, if the East Timor context had been characterized as a NIAC (or IAC) it would have raised the specter of the UN-sanctioned force being subject to legitimate LOAC targeting—was an overt concern, and thus a factor which played into the conflict characterization decision with respect to East Timor.

Characterization of the Opposing Force

In many ways, the "legal" characterization given to the "other" (the adversary) in a conflict situation (be it NIAC or less than NIAC) necessarily follows from the broader conflict characterization decision. However, it is nevertheless worth observing that—arguably, in Australian experience at least—the legal characterization accorded this "other" has two major implications for operations. The first is defining the line in NIAC between targetable fighter activity and merely criminal activity, given that all violent action by an OAG in a NIAC is fundamentally characterizable as criminal activity *ab initio*. This is an issue that does not arise when the overall conflict characterization is less-than-NIAC status, thus requiring that all "militia" or "armed gang" violence be met with a law enforcement, as opposed to a LOAC-based, response. The second implication concerns the rhetorical treatment of the "other." This factor, while not strictly legal, requires brief examination as it appears to reflect a fundamentally political/legal appreciation of the situation, as opposed to one based purely in "the facts on the ground."

Organized Armed Groups in Non-International Armed Conflict

This study is not the venue for revisiting the battlelines in the ongoing debate on direct participation in hostilities and the ICRC's *Interpretive Guidance*.[27] It is sufficient for our purposes to simply recall that the argument is, in essence, about what activity and which actors are within the targetable envelope (in the LOAC sense of authorization to proactively seek out and kill without having to limit lethal force to situations of self-defense), and what and who are outside that envelope for LOAC purposes. It is therefore sufficient to simply note that a fundamental point of divergence centers around what constitutes an OAG, and, more importantly, what activity/which actors associated with that OAG are targetable in the LOAC sense. The directly relevant question, however, is whether this heralds any significant operational implications.

In Afghanistan, where Australia considers itself to be a belligerent party to a NIAC, the main "other" is defined in terms of an OAG. This characterization, however, is not a simple matter, and as is the case for many States engaged in Afghanistan (and previously Iraq), this concept of OAG has actually evolved as an applied operational and ROE concept in tandem with its evolution as a legal concept. As a consequence, there was a period of working through and settling the parameters of the concept in terms of TCN law and policy at the very time it was also being used to support lethal effects in the field. This evolution of a critical legal and operational concept for NIAC, through the crucible of current operations, has not been without problems. The foremost of these has been that while Australia has been working out what it means when it refers to an OAG, other States have also been doing this and conclusions do differ.

Two examples may serve to illustrate this conundrum. The first is the furor that erupted within the International Security Assistance Force (ISAF) over "targeting drug barons," a debate that is readily traced through the newspapers of many ISAF TCNs. As the *New York Times* reported:

> United States military commanders have told Congress that they are convinced that the policy is legal under the military's rules of engagement and international law. They also said the move is an essential part of their new plan to disrupt the flow of drug money that is helping finance the Taliban insurgency. . . .
>
> The Senate report's disclosure of a hit list for drug traffickers may lead to criticism in the United States over the expansion of the military's mission, and NATO allies have already raised questions about the strategy of killing individuals who are not traditional military targets.[28]

This policy shift caused significant concern among a number of ISAF partner TCNs. As reported in the UK newspaper *The Guardian*,

> Previous missions have been held up by Nato lawyers arguing over whether an operation was primarily a counter-narcotics/policing mission or a counter-terrorism/military mission. European allies have strongly resisted the push to using military assets for counter-narcotics missions.
>
> The new American policy is the outcome of heated debates between the US and many of its European allies in Afghanistan who have long viewed the country's booming narcotics industry as a policing problem, not a military one.[29]

The Canadian view, expressing the compromise that ultimately appears to have been reached in the policy debate, was reported to be as follows:

> Some commanders opposed targeting the drug trade because it is against international law to use military force against civilian targets—even if they are criminals.
>
> NATO secretary general Jaap de [Hoop] Scheffer says the debate is over and there is full agreement within the alliance to go after Afghanistan's illegal drug industry.
>
> Mr MacKay says Canadian troops will attack drug lords and opium traffickers where there is proof of a direct link to the Taliban insurgency.[30]

This formulation of the test as being "proof of a direct link to the Taliban insurgency" still allowed for different national interpretations as to what "legal approach" would be utilized by each individual TCN (law enforcement or LOAC-based targeting). It also explicitly recognized that individual TCNs will employ a variety of criteria (on occasion inconsistent as between those TCNs) for establishing the nexus required to bring drug trafficking (a criminal activity) within the OAG targetable envelope (a LOAC concern). This is generally achieved, it appears, via the legal paths of personal linkages to fighter OAG roles, or the adequacy and directness of the linkage between financing activities and fighting activities. The Canadian formulation of the legal position is thus indicative of the routine need to utilize a degree of constructive ambiguity when publicizing the resolution to contentious legal/policy debates in the context of multinational operations—that is, the words used to explain the resolution must still permit of individual TCN interpretive wriggle room.

The second example relates to the attachment of military members from one TCN to units from another TCN, where those two States may adopt slightly different views on what and who is within—and without—the OAG targetable envelope. For example, when Australia sent Gunners to join a UK artillery regiment on deployment to Afghanistan,[31] it was vital that Australia and the United Kingdom looked very closely at each other's concept of OAG. The legal risk inherent in any such attachment, while remote, is nevertheless present. If, for example, the attached (fully briefed) Australian Gunners under UK command engaged a target who was within the targetable OAG envelope under the UK approach (and thus a completely legitimate target for the UK), but outside the targetable OAG envelope under the Australian approach (and thus perhaps not a legitimate military target under the Australian interpretation), then the Gunners may have opened the door to claims that they stood in legal danger under Australian law. Such risks are often easily mitigated through briefings, caveats, and operational command and control arrangements, but when the risk is linked to a fluid and highly contested legal concept—such as the legitimate envelope of targetable activities and members within OAGs in NIAC—risk mitigation becomes significantly more difficult. In such a case, the first step is to identify the very possibility of different interpretations. The next step is to identify whether those interpretive differences actually herald any substantive differences in what/who may be targeted. For the sake of a clear appreciation of potential TCN domestic legal consequences, this step in operational legal risk management should never be glossed over.

In Afghanistan, the characterization of the "other" as an OAG in the LOAC sense is intimately reflected in the rhetoric employed to describe that "other." The Taliban/Al Qaeda adversary is described as a determined, capable, organized military foe, and the campaign as punctuated by "fighting seasons." In March 2011, the Australian Minister for Defence, for example, indicated that

> [t]here are signs that the international community's recent troop surge, combined now with a strong military and political strategy, has reversed the Taliban's momentum. This progress is incremental and hard-won, but it is apparent. . . .
>
> But I do urge caution. United States Defense Intelligence Agency head, General Ron Burgess, has cautioned that "the security situation remains fragile and heavily dependent on ISAF support" and that the Taliban "remains resilient and will be able to threaten US and international goals in Afghanistan through 2011."
>
> We must expect pushback from the Taliban, particularly in areas recently claimed by ISAF and Afghan troops, when this year's fighting season commences in April or May. We do need to steel ourselves for a tough fighting season.[32]

The rhetoric and concepts associated with a military, as opposed to merely criminal, adversary are well evident: planning, campaigns, the holding of territory, the high level of security threat, coordination, political purpose and so on. In this way, the political/legal rhetoric used to describe the "other" is clearly and fundamentally beholden to the earlier decisions to characterize the conflict as a NIAC, to characterize Australia's involvement in that NIAC as that of a belligerent party and to consequently describe the "other"—the adversary in the NIAC—in terms of an OAG.

"Criminal Gangs" in Less-Than-NIAC Situations

In East Timor, the decision to operate in a "law enforcement" mode, and to avoid characterizing the conflict as a NIAC (or, if a NIAC was afoot, then to characterize Australia as a non-party to it) predetermined the characterization decision as to the "other." As there was no NIAC for INTERFET, there was no targetable "other" in the LOAC sense. Thus the "other" was legally characterizable as a simple criminal, with none of the complications inherent in the LOAC concept of OAG at play. This simplifies the legal regime applicable to dealing with this "other" in that because they are mere criminals, and there is no scope for the application of LOAC targeting authorizations, each criminal and each act of criminal violence can only be dealt with in the law enforcement context of detention, arrest, search and seizure, and use of lethal force only in self-defense. This political/legal decision as to conflict characterization, and its consequent characterization of the "other," thus requires that this adversary is described in terms of criminality, that is, not in de facto military terms. During the height of the crisis in East Timor, for example, one member of the Australian Parliament indicated that "we know what has happened, according to newspaper reports, because of the open communications that took place between elements of the Indonesian military and some of their militia thugs in East Timor."[33] Similarly, the then Australian Foreign Minister was adamant that "[t]he United Nations, Australia and the international community as a whole will not, of course, be bullied by thugs. We will not be bullied out of this United Nations process and we will not be bullied into abandoning the United Nations supervised ballot in East Timor."[34]

He went on to affirm that

> I think it is fair to say that the international community, on balance, thought that the situation would be pretty bad after the announcement of the result, but I do not think the international community quite expected—and Kofi Annan has made this point in the last week or two—the rampant destruction that took place during that period. I do not think the international community, in the end, concluded that people could ever behave that badly.[35]

He continued, "[W]e hope in any case, with the insertion of the multinational force and with the move towards the United Nations taking over control of East Timor, that we will see the rather rapid dissolution of the militias."[36]

The rhetoric of "pure" criminality—thuggery, bad behavior, transience, private ends, lack of coordination, cowardice in the face of a concerted police and military response—is clearly evident, as is the complete absence of any militarized rhetoric in describing this adversary.

Rules of Engagement Issues

The fact that East Timor was characterized as a less-than-NIAC law enforcement and stabilization context, whereas Afghanistan is a NIAC, obviously held significant consequences for ROE. Each characterization decision, however, brings with it a series of unique complications that must be reflected in ROE.

For Afghanistan, ROE are clearly LOAC based and authorize the proactive targeting of certain individuals with lethal force, not being limited to self-defense. This is complicated, however, by the fact that LOAC lends itself to a broad range of interpretive differences between States—much more so than the core legal elements of less-than-NIAC law enforcement and stabilization/mitigation operations. It also necessitates that a whole range of LOAC rules that are applicable only on a patchwork basis (such as those relating to anti-personnel land mines, cluster munitions, riot control agents, explosive remnants of war, etc.) need to be managed and de-conflicted among multiple operational partners. In law enforcement–based operations, most of these LOAC elements are not applicable *de jure*; thus the complexity of managing this patchwork of obligations is to some degree mitigated.

A brief examination of four peculiarly NIAC-related ROE issues that Australia has faced in this context may serve to illustrate this situation. First, as noted previously, the issue of applying—through ROE—concurrently evolving law with respect to determining (as a national legal position) who is within and who is outside the OAG targetable envelope is problematic. This holds direct implications—and potential criminal consequences—for each TCN's forces when conducting combined operations, or while on attachments with units from other TCNs—such as the Australian Gunners deployed with UK artillery regiments or Australian staff officers deployed into U.S.-commanded/controlled combined air operations centers.[37]

Second, one complication of the fact that Australia has characterized the conflict in Afghanistan as a NIAC and Australia as a belligerent party to that NIAC is that Australian ROE had to be drafted with a close eye on the equivalent belligerency-based NATO ROE. This creates a need to explain, "nationalize" and de-conflict some critical items of terminology. One of the more significant is that NATO ROE use the concepts of "hostile act" and "hostile intent" in a radically different way from Australian ROE doctrine and practice. In NATO ROE doctrine, these concepts can be used as components of LOAC-based attack rules,[38] for example, to create ROE that require restraint from attack (in situations where, under LOAC, attack would be lawful) unless the adversary force demonstrates hostile intent toward an own-force element (such as positioning to attack it) or carries out a hostile act against an own-force element (such as attacking it). An example of this form of NATO usage is rule of engagement 421. That rule states: "Attack against *any forces or any targets* demonstrating hostile intent (not constituting an imminent attack) against NATO forces is authorised."[39]

In Australian ROE doctrine and practice, the concepts of hostile act and hostile intent are generally employed in relation to individual and unit self-defense as ROE shorthand for the domestic criminal law requirements of necessity, imminence and reasonableness of use of force in individual self-defense. This is also the manner in which these two concepts are utilized in the International Institute of Humanitarian Law's *Rules of Engagement Handbook*.[40]

The third example of an ROE implication of a NIAC conflict characterization decision is that Australia must apply a whole range of more stringent rules and processes to many enabling capabilities. In NIAC, it really matters what, precisely, the civilian contractor operator of an unmanned aerial vehicle is doing. Certain actions will not place that civilian in the position of becoming a direct participant in hostilities (and thus subject to the temporary or longer-term loss of the civilian protections that attend this change in "status"), whereas certain other acts will do so. In law enforcement/stabilization operations, it does not matter nearly so much who the operator is; the operator's status is incontrovertibly not that of a direct participant in hostilities because there are, in a LOAC sense, no hostilities in which to participate.

Finally, one very interesting ROE issue which has emerged in some civilian casualty incident inquiry reports that Australia and many other TCNs publicly release from time to time is the very fluidity and uncertainty that often surround the status characterization of the person killed. This has meant that assertions of justification are often two-pronged. When explaining a use of lethal force in a NIAC context, it is not unusual for military personnel to report it as a consequence of self-defense *and* the result of a reasonably held belief—in the circumstances prevailing at the time—that the "target" was a fighter member of an OAG. This paradigm mixing is not merely an Australian legal oddity. As Constantin von der Groben observed in relation to the German prosecutor's investigation into the Kunduz tanker incident in Afghanistan in 2009 (a scenario involving uncertainty as to the precise legal paradigm against which to assess the conduct),

> [t]he ambiguity in the facts follows an ambiguity in the applicable laws. The problem with the airstrike is that it was unclear whether it had been performed as part of a non-international armed conflict in Afghanistan or just as part of a stabilization mission below the threshold of "armed conflict."[41]

The consequence was that until the prosecutor settled the issue, there was uncertainty as to whether the deaths inflicted stood to be assessed against general German criminal law (self-defense) or separate LOAC-based German criminal law (targeting). Similarly, the U.S. government—as a consequence of the initially confused manner in which the Osama bin Laden "kill/capture" mission was presented to the public[42]—has also faced this "killing a legitimate target" versus "killed in self-defense when he moved to attack one of those sent to arrest him" justificatory conundrum. This difficulty in paradigmatic justification rarely arises in the context of IAC (other than in situations of occupation), where the reason cited for killing those in enemy uniform is generally precisely that they were targetable enemy combatants, and thus legitimate targets under LOAC. Self-defense does not generally arise in terms of primary legal justifications, even though, of course, it is routine that military personnel of each party to the IAC will kill those of the adversary at a time when both are engaged in what their own domestic law would recognize as an *in extremis* situation where self-defense was naturally available as a justification or excuse. Nor does this dualist justification present as necessary (or indeed legally possible) in less-than-NIAC law enforcement contexts, where status is irrelevant because all are "civilians"; thus, the available justification for use of lethal force is self-defense and LOAC-based targeting authorizations are not legally available.

One example of this paradigm mixing may be found in a publicly released ADF Inquiry Officer Report, "Possible Civilian Casualties Resulting from Clearance of a Compound at [Redacted], Afghanistan, on 2 Apr 09."[43] In this report, the inquiry officer determined that the Australian force element entered a compound where an insurgent leader was identified as being present and in the clearance process shot and killed a number of men whom they believed to be in firing positions and to be directly participating in hostilities. But the precise explanation for each death is said to be "self-defense," although this is buttressed with assertions of belief as to the direct-participation-in-hostilities status of those killed. In my view, this is a potentially substantive legal issue precisely because Australian criminal law requires different standards of assessment for killings in self-defense, as distinct from killings in the context of NIAC of civilians taking a direct part in hostilities and/or fighter members of an OAG. Under LOAC, it is clear that "defense" against an "attack" is bound by the same LOAC rules as attack.[44] This logically means, for example, that a soldier cannot use CS gas "in self-defense" against an attack by fighter members of the adversary OAG, as use of such riot control agents against the LOAC-targetable enemy would likely breach Article 1(5) of the Chemical Weapons Convention.[45] It would also mean that the death, injury and destruction caused in the "defensive" action would be assessable against the unique and highly contextual LOAC conception of proportionality.[46] But "self-defense" in Australian criminal law[47] is not bound by the same limitations or assessment criteria. There is no legal prohibition on use of a chemical spray (Mace, for example) in self-defense and LOAC "proportionality" is not the same as the criminal law self-defense requirements expressed in elements such as "reasonableness," "imminence" and "necessity." In my own view, the concept of a "TIC" (troops in contact) action against civilians taking a direct part in hostilities/OAG fighters in NIAC contexts has complicated this issue by perhaps inadvertently dressing what is fundamentally a LOAC situation of attack and response in the legal rhetoric of urgent self-defense. I do believe that this is a sleeper problem with potentially serious legal consequences that may be deleterious for operational confidence if a claim of "self-defense" (as opposed to a LOAC justification) is tested in a domestic court that may take little—or worse, incorrect but precedent setting—cognizance of the armed conflict context and the alternative assessment criteria that LOAC provides.

Less-Than-NIAC ROE—East Timor

In East Timor, the decision to characterize the conflict as a less-than-NIAC law enforcement/stabilization operation created a different set of ROE issues. The first, and most significant, was the manner by which ROE delineate use-of-force options as between self-defense (where lethal force is permitted) and, separately, mission accomplishment (where, for Australia at any rate, lethal force is not permitted). Working through this issue via the mechanism of ROE is important, but not simple. INTERFET ROE contained a rule apparently authorizing use of force, including lethal force, for mission accomplishment. In NIAC contexts, such a rule is, of course, the norm, as it lays the general authorization for use of lethal force outside self-defense, allowing further rules to then detail when and how this lethal force may be employed—targeting, status and identification rules, for example. But in less-than-NIAC law enforcement operations, Australian criminal law does not generally countenance use of lethal force other than in self-defense, which was the subject of a separate series of rules in the UNTAET ROE. In fact, the Australian commander of INTERFET actually restricted use of lethal force to situations of self-defense only, thus, in effect, reading down the mission accomplishment rule.[48] In my view, it was both operationally sound and legally necessary to read the INTERFET mission accomplishment rule down in this manner.

The second ROE issue in this context—one which is not an issue where the conflict is characterized as a NIAC—is lingering uncertainty as to what, precisely, is permissible in terms of use of lethal force when a United Nations Security Council Chapter VII "all necessary means" authorization is to be applied in a less-than-NIAC context. That is, does this authorization provide a non-LOAC-based permission to use lethal force for mission accomplishment where there is no issue of self-defense in play? This is a highly complicated question that can only be analyzed through an ecumenical approach taking both international and specific TCN domestic law into account. In my view—and I will readily admit it is a contested view—there is no recognition in Australian law (nor in international law, I would also submit) of a "third" paradigm permitting use of lethal force in pursuance of a Security Council mandate, outside of self-defense, in the absence of armed conflict. That is, regardless of a Chapter VII "all necessary means" authorization, if the conflict has not been characterized as an armed conflict, then there is no authority to use lethal force for any reason outside self-defense.[49] Therefore, it is not possible to justify an ROE permitting use of lethal force in (non-self-defense based) mission accomplishment situations on the basis of an "all necessary means" authorization.

In East Timor, upon transition to UNTAET and UN ROE, this situation became even more opaque. The April 28, 2000 UN ROE stated that "UNTAET military personnel are required to comply with International Law, including the Law of Armed Conflict . . . and to apply the ROE in accordance with those laws."[50] The ROE then detailed "Level of Force" rules that permitted use of lethal force in self-defense, but also in a series of what would otherwise be better understood as mission accomplishment–based actions. These rules included authorizations to use lethal force against any party who limited or intended to limit UNTAET freedom of movement, and against any armed party that attempted to prevent UNTAET personnel from discharging their duty.[51] The issue of what, precisely, the UN means when it says "self-defense" in the context of UN operations, and, indeed, whether "self-defense of the mandate" is self-defense as understood in many domestic legal systems at all, is, I believe, a well obfuscated and often avoided operational question.[52] However, given the Australian characterization of the context as less-than-NIAC law enforcement, any mission accomplishment ROE that allowed use of lethal force outside of self-defense had to be assessed against the standard of general Australian criminal law (as that is the standard against which a soldier who used lethal force would be assessed), not the Australian domestication of LOAC into Australian law. Thus these rules—although they were UN ROE—could not, as a matter of Australian law, be applied by Australian forces as drafted, although it is equally clear that other TCNs could apply these rules to their fullest extent and still remain in compliance with their own domestic law.

This general issue discloses a third ROE challenge inherent in deciding to adopt a less-than-NIAC law enforcement characterization—force protection. In the East Timor context, this conundrum came to the fore when militia elements recommenced cross-border raiding activity, killed a number of UNTAET Peacekeeping Force (PKF) members and retreated back into West Timor (Indonesian territory) for sanctuary. To deal with this, the ROE were amended to provide an "expanded" definition of hostile act/hostile intent which provided that militia identified as being armed and moving in a tactical manner could in certain situations be engaged with lethal force "in self-defense." The ROE achieved this by determining that the PKF could legitimately characterize such conduct as constituting an imminent threat.[53]

The ROE issue that arises, however, is that the consciously considered decision to characterize a conflict situation as less-than-NIAC law enforcement when a NIAC characterization possibility exists carries with it some legal risk. This results when the bounds of self-defense—as the only available lawful justification for use of lethal force—have to be stretched within the law enforcement paradigm to allow an adequate response to a developing threat.

Treatment of Captured/Detained Personnel

In many respects, despite the highly political and strategically sensitive nature of detainee issues in military operations, for Australia this field of endeavor actually discloses very little difference between implementation in NIAC and that in less-than-NIAC law enforcement/stabilization operations. This admittedly contentious assertion can be illustrated via a brief examination of the fundamental principles—distilled from public statements and experience, and uncluttered by context-specific legal terminology—applied in detainee operations in East Timor and Afghanistan.

In East Timor, where the structures, institutions, and agents of law and order had entirely dissolved, they had to be rebuilt from scratch, first on an interim basis by INTERFET, and then on a more enduring basis by UNTAET, prior to full East Timorese independence in May 2002. To cover the gap, Australia established a Detainee Management Unit (DMU), which comprised an independent military judge, counsel for detainees, a prosecutor and a detention visitor who maintained an independent check on detention processes and conditions.[54] The DMU was mandated to review ongoing detention, not to try offenses. The ultimate aim was simply to ensure that only those against whom there was a reasonable case of future prosecution for a serious offense (under the transitional justice system then being reconstructed) remained in detention. The fundamental principles governing detention arrangements during INTERFET are arguably distillable as follows:

1. Ensuring a process that allowed for quick initial removal from the streets of people posing security/stability risks.

2. Ensuring protection of the relevant human rights for detainees.

3. Using local criminal or security law as the reason/basis for detention, both as a recognition of the primary sovereignty at play within the territory, and as a means of developing and promoting capacity within that sovereignty.

4. Using analogous elements of LOAC, on a policy as opposed to *de jure* basis, to inform detention operations.

5. Having in place systems of guarantees for fundamental human rights as to treatment and legal processes post-handover into the developing East Timor criminal justice system.

In Afghanistan, when Australia redeployed to Uruzgan Province as a partner with Dutch forces, the detainee management arrangements reflected the fact that Australia had negotiated a memorandum of understanding (MOU) with the Dutch government, under which Dutch forces took full responsibility for the detention and handover of all Australian-apprehended detainees. The Dutch had separately negotiated an MOU with the government of Afghanistan that addressed handover and ongoing monitoring arrangements for all detainees (including Australian-"sourced" detainees) who were handed over to Afghan authorities in line with ISAF arrangements with the government of Afghanistan. On August 1, 2010, as the Dutch force redeployed out of Uruzgan, Australia took full responsibility for its detainees, and, as a consequence, negotiated MOUs with Afghanistan and the United States on handover and monitoring arrangements.[55] Despite the very different conflict context—a NIAC in which Australia is a belligerent party—there is arguably little substantial difference between the fundamental principles governing the Australian approach to detention operations in East Timor under INTERFET and UNTAET, and those governing detention operations in Afghanistan. That is, regardless of the context and the legal paraphernalia that attends it—be it NIAC or less-than-NIAC conflict—the fundamental principles governing detention operations are almost indistinguishable. The quotes beneath each adapted principle distilled from the INTERFET detention operations are taken from the Australian Minister for Defence's December 14, 2010 detainee management arrangements statement and his March 23, 2011 Detainee Arrangements Briefing Paper, and serve to illustrate the virtually unchanged nature of detentions between INTERFET and Afghanistan:

1. Ensuring a process that allows for quick initial removal from the battlespace of people posing security/stability risks.

   "The first priority is the critical need to remove insurgents from the battlefield, where they endanger Australian, International Security Assistance Force and Afghan lives."[56]

2. Ensuring protection of the relevant human rights for detainees.

   "The second priority is the need to ensure humane treatment of detainees, consistent with Australian values and our legal obligations."[57]

3. Using local criminal or security law as the reason/basis for detention, both as a recognition of the primary sovereignty at play within the territory and as a means of developing and promoting capacity within that sovereignty.

"Once initial screening is complete, detainees are transferred either to Afghan or United States custody, or released if there is insufficient evidence to justify ongoing detention."[58]

4. Using elements of LOAC, on a policy basis as opposed to *de jure*, to inform detention operations.

   In comparing detention operations across NIAC and less-than-NIAC contexts, I believe that this "principle" provides the most interesting and sensitive measurement as to the degree to which the two regimes for detention are now almost indistinguishable. As the Minister for Defence observed, "[t]he detainee management framework draws on applicable international standards and advice from international organizations. It is *consistent with* [that is, not based on] the Laws of Armed Conflict and the Geneva Conventions."[59]

   As will be evident, NIAC LOAC was *not* described as the governing law for NIAC detention operations, but rather as simply an informing paradigm. Furthermore, I would hazard to argue that this is not merely an Australian development—UK cases (in the UK Court of Appeal and House of Lords/UK Supreme Court, and before the European Court of Human Rights), such as *Al Jedda*,[60] *Al-Skeini*[61] and *Maya Evans*,[62] also indicate this trend toward assessing detention operations in NIAC through a law enforcement and human rights–governed prism, as opposed to as a primarily LOAC-governed issue.

5. Having in place systems of guarantees for fundamental human rights as to treatment and legal processes post-handover into the developing Afghan criminal justice system.

   As the Minister for Defence stated: "A detainee monitoring team of Australian officials monitors detainees' welfare and conditions while they are in US or Afghan custody, until they are released or sentenced. The monitoring team visit detainees shortly after transfer and around every four weeks after the initial visits."[63]

   This makes clear the scope of and arrangements for this post-handover monitoring are not merely presentational, but are designed to be effective and remedial: "This monitoring is underpinned by formal arrangements with Afghanistan and the US, which include assurances on the humane

> treatment of detainees and free access by Australian officials and human rights organisations."[64]

Indeed, this deep concern with post-handover monitoring, even where the handover has been to proper representatives of the territorial sovereignty—a fundamentally human rights–based as opposed to LOAC-based concern—is reflected in the recognition, but general dismissal, of the logistical difficulties involved in "the current requirement for an initial detainee monitoring visit to occur within 72 hours after a detainee is transferred from the Australian Initial Screening Area to US or Afghan custody."[65] A policy decision to retain this requirement, because it is practically important, regardless of the significant logistical problems it can pose, is indicative of this concern.

It thus seems reasonably safe to assert, I would argue, that the fundamental principles governing detention operations in East Timor and Afghanistan—one a less-than-NIAC context and the other clearly a NIAC LOAC–governed context—are hardly distinguishable. From a purist legal perspective, this may be sound or unsound, laudable or regrettable. But that is not the point. The practical point is that this is how operational practice is evolving, and that—in line with the humanize and harmonize agenda which is seeing NIAC squeezed between colonizing tendencies from below (human rights) and above (IAC LOAC)—there has been little objection to this evolution. Indeed, apart from the detailed requirements of prisoner of war status, processes and regulation that apply in IAC, it is fast becoming arguable that detention operations in armed conflict have now been almost completely colonized by the human rights paradigm and law enforcement sensibilities.

Conclusion

The Australian experience, I believe, clearly illustrates that in potential NIAC contexts, conflict characterization decisions—from which almost all other subordinate operational legal issues will take their lead—are subject to a mixed legal/policy approach. And from this initial stepping-off point, core subsidiary operations law decisions, such as characterization of the adversary, and ROE, will take their divergent leads. I accept that this is a potentially contentious conclusion for LOAC purists who will insist that characterization decisions are only about "the facts on the ground." The rationale for the purist view is well expressed in Pictet's most humanitarian explanation of this seemingly clear and simple principle: "A wounded soldier is not more deserving, or less deserving, of medical treatment according to whether his Government does, or does not, recognize the existence of a state of war."[66]

I respectfully disagree that the characterization obligation, when dealing with the threshold between NIAC and less-than-NIAC conflict contexts, is capable of being read in such a purist, black letter law manner. The purist admonition to rely on "facts" has always been a call to an objective test using a narrow range of fairly self-evident indicators. But the jurisdictional "facts" that inhabit the threshold between NIAC and less-than-NIAC conflict contexts are significantly less objective than in prospective IAC situations, quite apart from lingering legal uncertainties as to how NIAC relates to IAC or "internationalized internal armed conflict" occurring in the same battlespace. The "facts" relevant to determining on which side of the law enforcement/NIAC threshold a situation falls involve assessing highly flexible concepts such as violence, banditry, terrorism and threat. As Geoffrey Best observes of this conundrum for the negotiators of the Geneva Conventions, "[t]hey had known what an international war was, but how were they to know a non-international armed conflict when they saw one? How were they to tell it from mob violence, riots, and banditry? . . . These were not silly or necessarily non-humanitarian questions."[67]

Genuflection to the objective finality of the "facts" has never been, and still is not, the full picture in characterization at the less-than-NIAC civil disturbance/NIAC threshold. I believe that this assessment is readily evidenced in the Australian experience of East Timor and Afghanistan—two conflict contexts in which the "Australian approach to NIAC" (to the extent that a distinct approach could be said to exist) has been played out down very different paths. In both contexts, the decision as to conflict characterization as NIAC or less-than-NIAC civil disturbance was not only intensely political, but also subject to a high degree of reverberation in that each decision clearly indicates that subordinate issues—such as whether to make lethal targeting authorizations available to the country's forces or not—can influence the preliminary conflict characterization decision.

Notes

1. Cordula Droege, *The Interplay between International Humanitarian Law and International Human Rights Law in Situations of Armed Conflict*, 40 ISRAEL LAW REVIEW 310 (2007).

2. See, e.g., the differing conclusions in Report of the Secretary-General's Panel of Inquiry on the 31 May 2010 Flotilla Incident ¶¶ 69–81 (2011), *available at* http://unispal.un.org/pdfs/GazaFlotillaPanelReport.pdf; Jacob Turkel et al., 1 The Public Commission to Examine the Maritime Incident of 31 May 2010, ¶¶ 13–112 (2011), *available at* http://turkel-committee.gov.il/files/wordocs//8707200211english.pdf; Turkish National Commission of Inquiry, Report on the Israeli Attack on the Humanitarian Aid Convoy to Gaza on 31 May 2010, at 60–99 (2011), *available at* http://gazaflotilla.delegitimize.com/wp-content/uploads/2011/02/official-turkish-inquiry.pdf.

3. For example, on Afghanistan 2001–11 see generally Rogier Bartels, *Timelines, Borderlines and Conflicts: The Historical Evolution of the Legal Divide between International and Non-International Armed Conflicts*, 91 INTERNATIONAL REVIEW OF THE RED CROSS 35 (2009); James G. Stewart, *Towards a Single Definition of Armed Conflict in International Humanitarian Law: A Critique of Internationalised Armed Conflict*, 85 INTERNATIONAL REVIEW OF THE RED CROSS 313 (2003); Dawn Steinhoff, *Talking to the Enemy: State Legitimacy Concerns with Engaging Non-State Armed Groups*, 45 TEXAS INTERNATIONAL LAW JOURNAL 297 (2009); Annyssa Bellal, Gilles Giaca & Stuart Casey-Maslen, *International Law and Armed Non-State Actors in Afghanistan*, 93 INTERNATIONAL REVIEW OF THE RED CROSS 1, 5–7 (2011).

4. This labeling was maintained even though the proposed solution was cast in terms of language more traditionally associated with NIAC contexts—"self-determination," "political settlement" and so on. *See* Mr. Prime Minister John Major, Ireland (Joint Declaration), Dec. 15, 1993, 234 PARL. DEB., H.C. (6th ser.) (1993) 1071–82 (U.K.), *available at* http://www.publications.parliament.uk/pa/cm199394/cmhansrd/1993-12-15/Debate-1.html. The United Kingdom maintained this discipline in characterizing the situation throughout the entire operation in Northern Ireland, including through peaks of violence such as in 1970–71, when (for example) the Joint Security Committee was concerned to ensure "balanced reporting" of what was "a near-war situation." *See generally* Conclusions of a Meeting of the Joint Security Committee Held on Thursday 4 February 1971 in Stormont Castle at 1130 AM, *available at* http://cain.ulst.ac.uk/proni/1971/proni_HA-32-3-5_1971-02-04.pdf (last visited Nov. 21, 2011). *See also* Prime Minister's Meeting with Home Secretary – Wednesday 4 February 1970, ¶¶ 1, 12, *available at* http://cain.ulst.ac.uk/proni/1970/proni_CAB-9-G-91-2_1970-02-04.pdf (last visited Nov. 21, 2011). Both provide examples of the UK government's stress upon a law enforcement approach to the situation.

5. *See generally United Nations Operation in Somalia (UNOSOM) 1992*, AUSTRALIAN WAR MEMORIAL, http://www.awm.gov.au/units/unit_20244.asp (last visited Nov. 21, 2011) ("The Australians were based in Baidoa Humanitarian Relief Sector, west of Mogadishu. The Australian contingent in Baidoa had four main roles: maintain a secure environment in Baidoa; maintain a presence in the surrounding countryside; protect aid convoys; and assist in the equitable distribution of aid.").

6. *See, e.g.*, *Criminal Code Act 1995* (Cth) s 10.4 (Austl.) ("self-defence"), *available at* http://www.comlaw.gov.au/Details/ (then follow Key Resources hyperlink; then follow Criminal Code Act 1995 hyperlink).

7. *Id.*, div 268.

8. *See, e.g.*, JOHN MARTINKUS, A DIRTY LITTLE WAR xv (2001).

9. AUSTRALIAN DEFENCE FORCE MILITARY LAW CENTRE, LAW AND MILITARY OPERATIONS IN EAST TIMOR SEPT 1999–FEB 2000: LESSONS LEARNT FOR LEGAL OFFICERS 12 (2000) [hereinafter EAST TIMOR LESSONS LEARNT].

10. *Id. See also* Report of the Security Council Mission to Jakarta and Dili, 8 to 12 September 1999, ¶¶ 7, 11, 14–26, U.N. Doc. S/1999/976 (Sept. 14, 1999), *available at* http://daccess-dds-ny.un.org/doc/UNDOC/GEN/N99/262/20/PDF/N9926220.pdf?OpenElement.

11. Prosecutor v. Tadić, Case No. IT-94-1-T, Judgment, ¶ 562 (Int'l Crim. Trib. for the Former Yugoslavia May 7, 1997), *available at* http://www.icty.org/x/cases/tadic/tjug/en/tad-tsj70507JT2-e.pdf.

12. Cth, Parliamentary Debates, House of Representatives, 17 September 2001, 30739 (John Howard, Prime Minister) (Austl.).

13. Press Conference on U.S.-Led Response, Prime Minister John Howard (Oct. 4, 2001), transcript *available at* http://www.patriotresource.com/wtc/intl/oct/0104/australia.html.

14. Security Treaty between Australia, New Zealand, and the United States of America, Sept. 1, 1951, 3 U.S.T. 3420, 131 U.N.T.S. 83, *available at* http://www.austlii.edu.au/au/other/dfat/treaties/1952/2.html.

15. Press Statement, Prime Minister John Howard, Howard Government Invokes ANZUS Treaty (Sept. 14, 2001), *available at* http://australianpolitics.com/news/2001/01-09-14c.shtml. Prime Minister Howard spoke of the Al Qaeda/Taliban attacks on the United States as "an open assault upon its territorial integrity," clearly indicating a militarized/armed conflict–based appreciation of the conflict context, as opposed to viewing it as a law enforcement challenge. Cth, Parliamentary Debates, House of Representatives, 27 September 2001, 31684 (John Howard, Prime Minister) (Austl.).

16. Stephen Smith, Minister for Defence, Paper on Afghanistan (Mar. 23, 2011), *available at* http://www.minister.defence.gov.au/2011/03/23/minister-for-defence-paper-presented-by-the-minister-for-defence-stephen-smith-on-afghanistan/ [hereinafter Paper on Afghanistan (Mar. 23, 2011)].

17. Protocol Additional to the Geneva Conventions of 12 August 1949, and Relating to the Protection of Victims of International Armed Conflicts, June 8, 1977, 1125 U.N.T.S. 3 [hereinafter AP I].

18. *See, e.g.*, East Timor (Port. v Austl.), 1995 I.C.J. 90 ¶¶ 16–17 (June 30), *available at* http://www.icj-cij.org/docket/files/84/6949.pdf.

19. *See, e.g.*, Michael Kelly et al., *Legal Aspects of Australia's Involvement in the International Force for East Timor*, 83 INTERNATIONAL REVIEW OF THE RED CROSS 101 (2001) ("The Security Council mission reported that the violence in East Timor after the ballot could not have occurred without the involvement of large elements of the Indonesian military and police, concluding that the Indonesian authorities were either unwilling or unable to provide an environment for the peaceful implementation of the 5 May agreements."). The then Australian Foreign Minister, Alexander Downer, was explicit on this point: "We have made the point that there are clearly links between members of the [Indonesian military] and the militias, and that is not a matter that is debated any longer even by the [Indonesian military] itself or by the Indonesian government." Cth, Parliamentary Debates, House of Representatives, 20 September 1999, 9927 (Alexander Downer, Minister for Foreign Affairs) (Austl.).

20. Protocol Additional to the Geneva Conventions of 12 August 1949, and Relating to the Protection of Victims of Non-International Armed Conflicts, June 8, 1977, 1125 U.N.T.S. 609.

21. Convention for the Amelioration of the Condition of the Wounded and Sick in Armed Forces in the Field art. 3, Aug. 12, 1949, 6 U.S.T. 3114, 75 U.N.T.S. 31; Convention for the Amelioration of the Condition of Wounded, Sick and Shipwrecked Members of Armed Forces at Sea art. 3, Aug. 12, 1949, 6 U.S.T. 3217, 75 U.N.T.S. 85; Convention Relative to the Treatment of Prisoners of War art. 3, Aug. 12, 1949, 6 U.S.T. 3316, 75 U.N.T.S. 135; Convention Relative to the Protection of Civilian Persons in Time of War art. 3, Aug. 12, 1949, 6 U.S.T. 3516, 75 U.N.T.S. 287 [hereinafter GC IV].

22. *See* S.C. Res. 1264, pmbl., ¶¶ 4, 5, U.N. Doc. S/RES/1264 (Sept. 15, 1999) ("Welcoming the statement by the President of Indonesia on 12 September 1999 in which he expressed *the readiness of Indonesia to accept an international peacekeeping force* through the United Nations in East Timor"; "4. Welcomes the *expressed commitment of the Government of Indonesia to cooperate with the multinational force* in all aspects of the implementation of its mandate and looks forward to *close coordination* between the multinational force and the Government of Indonesia; 5. Underlines the *Government of Indonesia's continuing responsibility* under the Agreements of 5 May 1999, taking into account the mandate of the multinational force set out in paragraph 3 above,

to maintain peace and security in East Timor in the interim phase between the conclusion of the popular consultation and the start of the implementation of its result and to guarantee the security of the personnel and premises of UNAMET.") (emphasis added).

23. EAST TIMOR LESSONS LEARNT, *supra* note 9, at 23.

24. GC IV, *supra* note 21.

25. *Id.*, Annex E: Defence Legal Office Policy Statement on the Application of the Fourth Geneva Convention of 1949 to Possible Deployment of the ADF to East Timor (Sept. 3, 1999).

26. *Id.*, ¶¶ 13–14.

27. NILS MELZER, INTERNATIONAL COMMITTEE OF THE RED CROSS, INTERPRETIVE GUIDANCE ON THE NOTION OF DIRECT PARTICIPATION IN HOSTILITIES UNDER INTERNATIONAL HUMANITARIAN LAW (2009), *available at* http://www.icrc.org/eng/assets/files/other/icrc_002_0990.pdf.

28. James Risen, *U.S. to Hunt Down Afghan Drug Lords Tied to Taliban*, NEW YORK TIMES (Aug. 9, 2009), http://www.nytimes.com/2009/08/10/world/asia/10afghan.html.

29. Richard Norton-Taylor & Jon Boone, *US puts Afghan drug lords on hit list to disrupt Taliban finances*, THE GUARDIAN (UNITED KINGDOM), Aug. 10, 2009, International, at 17, *available at* http://www.guardian.co.uk/world/2009/aug/10/us-policy-drugs-afghanistan-taliban.

30. Dan Karpenchuk, *NATO troops to go after Afghan drug lords*, ABC NEWS (Feb. 7, 2009), http://www.abc.net.au/news/2009-02-07/nato-troops-to-go-after-afghan-drug-lords/286182.

31. Press Statement, Joel Fitzgibbon, Minister for Defence, Australian Artillerymen Deploy to Afghanistan in Support of UK Operations (Mar. 13, 2008), *available at* http://defence.gov.au/minister/70tpl.cfm?CurrentId=7498.

32. Cth, Parliamentary Debates, House of Representatives, 23 March 2011, 2969 (Stephen Smith, Minister for Defence) (Austl.).

33. Cth, Parliamentary Debates, House of Representatives, 22 September 1999, 10279 (Michael Danby) (Austl.).

34. Cth, Parliamentary Debates, House of Representatives, 30 June 1999, 7929 (Alexander Downer, Minister for Foreign Affairs) (Austl.).

35. Cth, Parliamentary Debates, House of Representatives, 20 September 1999, 9926 (Alexander Downer, Minister for Foreign Affairs) (Austl.).

36. Cth, Parliamentary Debates, House of Representatives, 20 September 1999, 9928 (Alexander Downer, Minister for Foreign Affairs) (Austl.).

37. *See* Australian Government, Department of Defence, Fact Sheet: Australia's Commitment in Afghanistan, http://www.defence.gov.au/op/afghanistan/info/factsheet.htm (last visited Nov. 21, 2011). *See also* Stephen Smith, Minister for Defence, Paper on Afghanistan (May 12, 2011), *available at* http://www.minister.defence.gov.au/2011/05/12/paper-by-presented-by-minister-for-defence-stephen-smith-on-afghanistan/ [hereinafter Paper on Afghanistan (May 12, 2011)].

38. See, for example, the definitions and brief outlines of Rule 421 and Series 41 in the *NATO Legal Deskbook*. SHERROD L. BUMGARDNER ET AL., NATO LEGAL DESKBOOK 255–56 (2d ed. 2010), *available at* https://transnet.act.nato.int/WISE/Library/Legal/LEGALDESKB/file/_WFS/LEGAL%20DESKBOOK%20FIN%20AL%20version%20-%2022%20SEPT%202010.pdf.

39. *Id.* at 256 (emphasis added). The employment of "forces" and "targets" as the descriptors of the subjects of the rule clearly links this conception of hostile intent to LOAC-based status and authorizations, not those relevant to hostile intent in the context of individual or unit self-defense in domestic criminal law.

40. DENNIS MANDSAGER ET AL., INTERNATIONAL INSTITUTE OF HUMANITARIAN LAW, SAN REMO HANDBOOK ON RULES OF ENGAGEMENT 3–4, 22–25, 82 (2009), *available at* http://www.iihl.org/iihl/Documents/ROE%20handbook%20ENG%20May%202011%20PRINT%20RUN.pdf.

41. Constantin von der Groben, *Criminal Responsibility of German Soldiers in Afghanistan: The Case of Colonel Klein*, 11 GERMAN LAW JOURNAL 469, 475 (2010).

42. *See, e.g.*, James J. Zogby, *A Bungled PR Job Keeps the Bin Laden Controversy Alive*, AL ARABIYA NEWS (May 25, 2011), http://english.alarabiya.net/views/2011/05/08/148269.html?PHPSESSID=7dhvn5ksaknr1t13vphk32l9k0.

43. *Available at* http://www.defence.gov.au/coi/reports/IOReport20090402Slipper.pdf. See the bivalence inherent in a combined reading of paragraphs 9, 12–13, 18, 22–23, 25–27 and 31–32.

44. AP I, *supra* note 17, art. 49(1) ("Attacks means acts of violence against the adversary, whether in offence or defence.").

45. Convention on the Prohibition of the Development, Production, Stockpiling and Use of Chemical Weapons and on Their Destruction art. I(5), Jan. 13, 1993, 1974 U.N.T.S. 45 ("Each State Party undertakes not to use riot control agents as a method of warfare.").

46. *See* AP I, *supra* note 17, arts. 51–52, 57.

47. *Criminal Code Act 1995*, *supra* note 6, s 10.4(2) ("A person carries out conduct in self-defence if and only if he or she believes the conduct is necessary: (a) to defend himself or herself or another person . . . and the conduct is a reasonable response in the circumstances as he or she perceives them.").

48. EAST TIMOR LESSONS LEARNT, *supra* note 9, at 38.

49. My view on this issue is more fully described in Rob McLaughlin, *The Legal Regime Applicable to Use of Lethal Force When Operating under a United Nations Security Council Chapter VII Mandate Authorising "All Necessary Means,"* 12 JOURNAL OF CONFLICT AND SECURITY LAW 389 (2007).

50. UN ROE for the Military Component of the United Nations Mission in East Timor (UNTAET) (MPS/3633) ¶ 7(b) (Apr. 28, 2000), *reprinted in* Australian Defence Force, Military Law Centre, Law and Military Operations in East Timor (UNTAET) Feb 2000–May 2002, Annexure X (2002).

51. *Id.*, ¶ 7(b), Rules 1.9 and 1.10.

52. *See generally* TREVOR FINDLAY, THE USE OF FORCE IN UN PEACE OPERATIONS (2002).

53. Australian Defence Force, Military Law Centre, Law and Military Operations in East Timor (UNTAET) Feb 2000–May 2002, 23 (2002); Dale Stephens, *Military Involvement in Law Enforcement*, 92 INTERNATIONAL REVIEW OF THE RED CROSS 453, 462–63 (2010).

54. *See* Kelly et al., *supra* note 19.

55. Press Statement, Stephen Smith, Minister for Defence, Detainee Management in Afghanistan (Dec. 14, 2010), http://www.defence.gov.au/minister/Smithtpl.cfm?CurrentId=11212 [hereinafter Detainee Management in Afghanistan].

56. Paper on Afghanistan (Mar. 23, 2011), *supra* note 16.

57. *Id.*

58. Detainee Management in Afghanistan, *supra* note 55.

59. Paper on Afghanistan (Mar. 23, 2011), *supra* note 16 (my comment and emphasis added).

60. R (on the application of Al-Jedda) v. Secretary of State for Defence, [2007] UKHL 58; Al-Jedda v. United Kingdom, 27021/08 Eur. Ct. H.R. (2011), *available at* http://www.bailii.org/eu/cases/ECHR/2011/1092.html.

61. Al-Skeini and Others v. Secretary of State for Defence, [2007] UKHL 26; Al-Skeini and Others v. United Kingdom, 55721/07 Eur. Ct. H.R. (2011), *available at* http://www.bailii.org/eu/cases/ECHR/2011/1093.html.

62. The Queen (on the application of Maya Evans) v. Secretary of State for Defence, [2010] EWHC 1445 (Admin).

63. Paper on Afghanistan (Mar. 23, 2011), *supra* note 16.

64. *Id.*

65. Paper on Afghanistan (May 12, 2011), *supra* note 37 ("In the period 1 August 2010 to 8 May 2011, Australia apprehended 590 detainees. Of these, 81 have been transferred to Afghan authorities and 40 to US authorities. The remainder have been released following initial screening.").

66. COMMENTARY TO GENEVA CONVENTION I FOR THE AMELIORATION OF THE CONDITION OF WOUNDED AND SICK IN ARMED FORCES IN THE FIELD 29 (Jean Pictet ed., 1952).

67. GEOFFREY BEST, WAR AND LAW SINCE 1945, at 174 (1994).

PART VII

DETENTION IN NON-INTERNATIONAL ARMED CONFLICTS

XV

Detention of Terrorists in the Twenty-first Century

William K. Lietzau*

I. Introduction

Of all the instruments of power that may be employed to further national interests, none yields collateral consequences that are more difficult to predict than the unleashing of military force. And with respect to the past decade's use of that instrument, no consequence has engendered more debate, confusion or passion than U.S. detention policy. This article attempts to clarify the reasons for the controversy surrounding the policy—explaining it primarily as a function of the nature of twenty-first-century warfare, as opposed to competing political or ideological perspectives, as many claim. It then proffers a vision for moving past the controversy.

At first, few recognized the juridical stressors associated with a twenty-first-century armed conflict steeped in terrorism; most simply looked to old laws to address this new type of conflict. In this context a rift began to form and grew ever wider with the years of conflict.[1] Today, even many nations willing to share with the United States the burdens of armed conflict have expressed significant discomfort with U.S. legal endeavors related to detention.[2] This dissonance and the

---

* Deputy Assistant Secretary of Defense, Rule of Law and Detainee Policy. This article is adapted from a speech given at Harvard University Law School in February 2011 at a conference titled "Understanding Detention and Predicting Prosecutions: Legal Challenges and Legislative Options Ten Years After 9/11." The views in this article are those of the author and do not necessarily reflect the views of the Department of Defense or the United States government.

disquiet among our allies have impeded the United States' implementation of its plans, diminished its effectiveness in fighting terrorism and stymied the important work that must be done to establish an effective legal regime for the longer conflict ahead. It is not much of a stretch to assert that the manner in which the United States and its allies take up these challenges may very well reflect the most enduring impact of the 9/11 attacks. Indeed, history teaches that changes in the law often rank among the most noteworthy consequences of war. The goal, then, should be first to diagnose correctly the problem confronting the United States and then to identify the prescription that will yield a principled, credible and sustainable detention policy.

The thesis is simple. Authority to detain and regulation of the conditions of detention in the context of armed conflict derive most appropriately from the law of war. As such, the general rules should be uncontroversial—armies have captured and detained enemy fighters for years. But today's war is different: the enemy is not a State, its fighters are not lawful combatants and the end of this conflict is not easily discerned. Extant law of war was not written for today's conflict, and an analysis of it therefore exposes gaps that offend our twenty-first-century sensibilities. Foremost among the lacunae is the absence of appropriate processes for determining who can and should be detained and for how long. The solution, then, is found in today's efforts to identify the process that best ensures that we detain only those we lawfully can detain and, even then, only those whose threat is so substantial that it can be mitigated only by detention.

II. Identifying the Paradigm

The most fundamental component of controversy associated with the post-9/11 armed conflict is the confluence of legal regimes available to guide detentions. Soon after 9/11, President George W. Bush made clear that he viewed al Qaeda's attack as an act of war,[3] the response to which would include military force.[4] What became known as the "global war on terror" had begun. When President Barack H. Obama took office, he distanced himself from some of the more controversial policies of his predecessor, and he discarded from the conflict's lexicon the terms "global" and "terror." But he did not abandon the legal framework of armed conflict. President Obama, with deliberate clarity, still used the vocabulary of war when describing the conflict with al Qaeda,[5] including in his Nobel Peace Prize acceptance speech, where he explained why peace-loving nations sometimes have a duty to engage in armed conflict.[6] Fundamental to understanding U.S. detention policy over the past decade is the comprehension that authority for detention flows from the nature of warfare and the law of war that regulates it.

As such, one would anticipate that anyone captured during an armed conflict would be dealt with as a prisoner of war, without substantial debate. For centuries, armies have captured and detained enemy fighters; few, if any, anticipated the dissension that would accompany the practice today. Indeed, on 9/11, the office held by this author (Detainee Policy) did not exist; basic humanitarian norms associated with wartime detention were well understood by the United States' highly trained armed forces and a deputy assistant secretary–level position to oversee detention policy would have seemed like substantial overkill.

There are several explanations for the adverse global reaction to such a fundamental and heretofore uncontroversial component of warfighting, but the primary one is that the very status of this conflict as a "war" has been an issue of debate. The clarion call to war discussed above has not always been discernible amid the cacophony of other instruments at work—most notably, that of law enforcement. In addition to his call to arms, President Bush's first post-9/11 speech included the promise that terrorists would be brought to justice.[7] President Obama's 2009 Archives speech similarly suggested a preference for criminal judicial processes.[8] Indeed, prior to 9/11, law enforcement had traditionally been the tool of choice for addressing terrorism, both domestically and in the international realm.[9] Many continue to adhere to the view that law enforcement is the "right" paradigm for the conflict today.[10]

This article takes the view that, both in 2001 and today, war was and is the correct paradigm to apply in characterizing the conflict itself and in addressing the issue of detention. On September 12, 2001, the United Nations Security Council passed a resolution expressly recognizing the United States' right to self-defense.[11] Days later, the North Atlantic Treaty Organization (NATO) took the unprecedented step of passing a collective defense resolution, citing Article 5 of the NATO Charter.[12] ANZUS and Rio Pact nations passed similar resolutions,[13] and the U.S. Congress, on September 13, enacted a joint resolution authorizing the President to use "all necessary and appropriate force against those involved in the terrorist attacks of 9/11."[14] In the early days after 9/11, there seemed to be an almost universal recognition that the felling of New York's tallest buildings and a section of the nation's military headquarters had ignited an armed conflict in the truest sense. But acceptance of that paradigm waned as the population at Guantanamo grew.

Indeed, criticism of the "war" paradigm emerged in 2002 as a collateral ramification of criticism of wartime detention policies. First came the Bush administration's decision that captured combatants would not be considered prisoners of war.[15] The apparent limitless geographic reach of the United States' war-making authorities ("global"), as well as the absence of a clear delineation of the enemy ("terror"), caused substantial concern in the international community that the rule of law itself was at risk. And yet, although there are substantial flaws in the syllogism that leads from discomfort with current policies to denial of the existence of a war, the suggestion that this can be treated as a law enforcement problem is not without sound precedent.

First, there is the simple fact that the citizenry of the United States have not been witness to long-term law of war detention of enemy prisoners since World War II. Both the Korean and Vietnam wars involved prisoners detained by our local allies. Prisoners of war were held for only brief periods of time in the first Gulf War, and detention periods were even shorter in the more limited conflicts that punctuated the interludes.

More important, prior to 9/11 the principal means for dealing with terrorist attacks—at least those without a clear State sponsor—was that of law enforcement. In 1988, 259 people aboard the plane and 11 on the ground were killed in the bombing of Pan American Flight 103.[16] The first Bush administration treated the problem of apprehending suspects as one of diplomacy and extradition;[17] it was clearly a law enforcement matter. In the 1993 World Trade Center bombing, six people were killed and more than one thousand injured.[18] Law enforcement officials conducted an extensive investigation, resulting ultimately in the apprehension, extradition, trial and conviction in U.S. District Court of most of the suspects in the bombing, including Sheik Omar Abdel Rahman.[19] Again, we observe an unquestionably law enforcement response.

The 1998 embassy bombings in Nairobi, Kenya and Dar es Salaam, Tanzania claimed the lives of twelve Americans and more than two hundred Kenyans and Tanzanians.[20] The United States conducted a one-strike military response,[21] and issued indictments against fifteen individuals, four of whom were apprehended by foreign governments, extradited to the United States, and tried and convicted in U.S. District Court.[22] Despite the mixed military and law enforcement response, law enforcement efforts appear to have been both primary and sustained, while the military component was less significant and transitory.[23]

In recent years, international efforts to address the law as it relates to terrorism have yielded a number of international agreements relevant to countering the terrorist threat. As with domestic legislation, however, these conventions also reflect a predisposition toward law enforcement. The United States responded to the attack on the Khobar Towers complex housing U.S. military personnel in Saudi Arabia both by launching a law enforcement investigation and by commencing an international initiative that ultimately resulted in the negotiation and entry into force of the Terrorist Bombing Convention.[24] Through the United Nations, the United States has attempted to shore up weaknesses in the law enforcement model through treaties establishing a regime of *aut dedere aut punire* (extradite or prosecute) for terrorism offenses.[25] Other examples of the campaign to reinforce the law enforcement archetype in countering transnational armed groups include U.S. support for the Terrorist Financing Convention and efforts toward a Nuclear Terrorism Convention.[26]

Internationally, other countries traditionally rely on law enforcement to combat terrorism as well. Numerous countries, including Canada, France, Germany, Israel, Colombia, Russia and the United Kingdom, have established programs to combat terrorism that, while markedly different in organization and process, share striking similarities: each vests primary responsibility for response to terrorist incidents in a designated central authority, typically its national or local police; each embraces a national counterterrorism policy involving a variety of strategies, including intelligence collection, police presence and various physical security measures; and each primarily relies on its general criminal laws to prosecute terrorists, although most also have specific terrorism-related laws that allow for special investigation or prosecution modalities and increased penalties. Taken together, these components evidence an across-the-board, unambiguous reliance on the law enforcement paradigm in countering terrorism.[27] The respective British and Spanish responses to terrorist-sponsored suicide bombings in the London subway and Madrid's rail system confirmed Europe's staunch reliance on the law enforcement model to fight terrorism.[28] And India's response to the Mumbai attack is indicative of the paradigm's favored status even in conflict-torn South Asia. In the same vein, the United States' choice of fora in which to prosecute persons accused in the first few years after 9/11 was limited solely to the federal criminal court system.[29]

The fact that law enforcement was used in the past is not a compelling argument for its post-9/11 prevalence, however. The predominant global perspective immediately after 9/11 appears to have manifested itself as an acknowledgment that law enforcement had failed. Generally, civilizations prefer to live in peace, addressing minor, disruptive violence with law enforcement tools designed for a peaceful state of existence. But no one was interested in status quo after 9/11. Al Qaeda had been at war with the United States for years, but its attack of 2001 changed the way that conflict was viewed by others.

One could explain the United States' relatively unique post-9/11 shift as a function of its relatively unique victimization at the time. But such a reading of history would miss the mark. The United States still approaches terrorism as a law enforcement matter; it is the distinct conflict with al Qaeda that is viewed differently. In the fall of 2001, the United States went to war with al Qaeda, a transnational terrorist organization with global reach, and its territorial sponsors, the Taliban. In hindsight, having substantially degraded the organization and collected massive amounts of intelligence revealing al Qaeda's objectives and capabilities, it can be seen that only the massive effort that amounted to an armed conflict could have brought down Osama bin Laden.

III. Identifying the Problem

Acknowledging the confluence of legal regimes, we turn to the law governing armed conflict, the *lex specialis*, which recognizes that in time of war there has been a disruption of the peacetime legal regime.[30] Because warfare is not new to human experience, and the capture of enemy forces is certainly not unfamiliar to warfare, one would expect that traditional detention modalities might naturally prevail without fanfare. But al Qaeda's war with the United States and its allies continues to challenge both the initial choice-of-law question and the limits of the constitutive tenets of the relevant bodies of law—tenets that largely defined international and domestic orders throughout the last half of the twentieth century. Soon after the United States put boots on the ground in Afghanistan, it became apparent that many of the most familiar *jus in bello* precepts were simply inapplicable to, or inadequate for, armed conflict of this type—armed conflict with a transnational non-State organization employing terrorism as its *modus operandi*.

A graphic may assist in understanding and explaining the legal regimes in play with respect to terrorist detention. This chart, artificial in that it does not exist in any positive statement of international law, is nonetheless useful in reflecting the disparate nature of applicable legal regimes that attend the detention of terrorists.

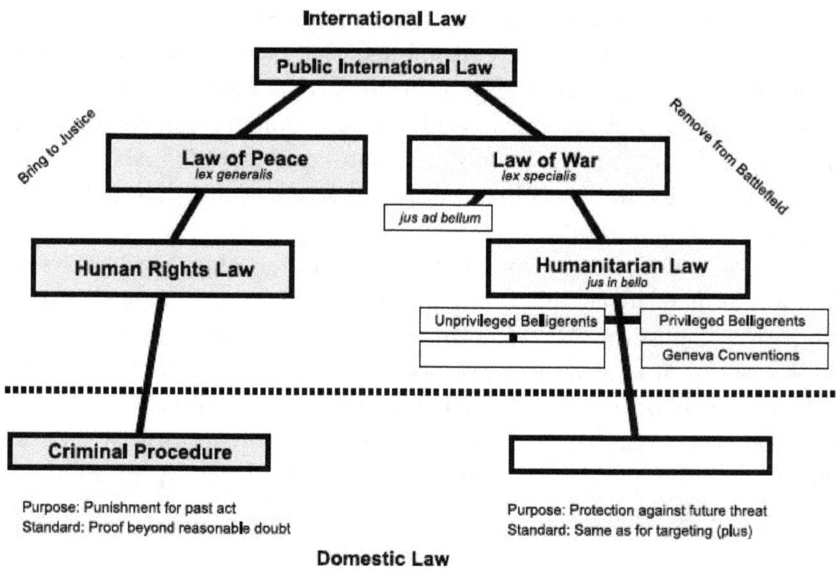

The left side of the chart depicts the *lex generalis* of a peacetime society, labeled "law of peace." On the right side is the *lex specialis* of the law of war. As one continues down the left side, human rights law is identified as most relevant to detention issues. And, more important, crossing the line into domestic implementation of international norms, criminal procedure is depicted as the body of law that provided authority for terrorist criminal detention throughout most of the twentieth century. It represents the body of law applicable to any criminal trial (whether by federal court or military commission). It is the body of law to which habeas judges naturally first looked in their initial Guantanamo cases, and it is the only body of law on this chart that is constituent in the curriculum of every American law student. Even a law student who elects to study international law is more likely to focus on *lex generalis* than its less frequently utile wartime counterpart. Moreover, at least in previous generations, *jus in bello* was likely to get short shrift relative to its more engaging counterpart, *jus ad bellum*. That is changing, but the point is that throughout most of the past decade, lawyers both in the United States and abroad intuitively devolved to the criminal law model when seeking lawful justification for the detention of terrorists.

Conversely, in the days following the establishment of the Guantanamo detention facility, very few even seemed to be aware that a wartime model for terrorist detention existed. Historically, the United States has not used the law of war model for the detention of terrorists; the law enforcement model was the focus of counterterrorism policies for the better part of the last half century.[31] Few looked to the law of armed conflict. And, as the empty boxes more significantly designate, even were one to consult that body of law, one would find a paucity of domestic implementing legislation associated with the authority to detain. Indeed, even a direct application of Geneva law yields no applicable positive authority to capture and detain. Authority to capture is inferred, and while the Third Convention recognizes the propriety of internment for prisoners of war in international armed conflict,[32] such positive authority is absent for non-international armed conflict.

Finally, and most relevant to the international lawyer, a review of the law of war standards applicable to this particular conflict reveals significant omissions. Geneva law, especially as it pertains to detention, is focused on the treatment of prisoners of war—a category principally constituted by members of the armed forces of a State that is party to the Conventions, in conflict with another State party to the Conventions.[33] Rules applicable to a conflict "not of an international character,"[34] if that even accurately describes a conflict halfway around the world in which the United States is joined by the armed forces of more than forty other countries, are scant to say the least.[35]

At its essence, the United States' first and most essential armed conflict at present is that against al Qaeda, a transnational armed group in which none of the members qualify for prisoner of war status.[36] Thus, it is no surprise that few turned to the law of war as the appropriate paradigm for the post-9/11 detention of terrorists. And, even if the polity were completely immersed in the finer points of *jus in bello,* we would find little positive authority or guidance for the detention of an enemy that does not qualify for prisoner of war protections under even the most expansive reading of the Third Geneva Convention, yet is indisputably the primary adversary in the conflict.[37] There are no "privileged belligerents" among those whom the United States opposes.

Because of these unique circumstances, criticism of U.S. detention policies—memorialized in iconic photographs from the early days of Guantanamo Bay—was initially embodied in a claim that the United States was "violating" the Geneva Conventions.[38] These claims morphed into the slightly more defensible assertion that this "global war on terror" was not even a war because the law of war did not extend to this type of undefined conflict. Indeed, President Bush's moniker fueled recrimination as the geographically unbounded nature of the term "global war on terror" disquieted those already uncomfortable with U.S. assertions of *jus ad bellum* authority to use the military instrument.[39] That the target of the application of force was a common noun—terror—only further distanced the endeavor from more traditional armed conflict.[40]

Nevertheless, we have had two U.S. presidents—separated by wide ideological differences—similarly conclude that U.S. national security interests necessitate an armed conflict with a transnational armed terrorist organization.[41] To jump then to the conclusion that a radically different—and inherently unsuitable—peacetime detention paradigm will work to bridge *jus in bello*'s gaps, although conceptually attractive to a litigious society happily governed by the rule of law, is simply not sustainable.

Proof of this is found in the Obama administration's attempt to close Guantanamo Bay and its focused effort to scrutinize thoroughly the case of each Guantanamo detainee. The U.S. government made every effort to diminish the population of detainees at Guantanamo by identifying criminals for prosecution, as well as candidates for release or transfer to another country.[42] And yet, despite these truly unprecedented efforts, the senior-most members of the President's national security team determined *unanimously* that at least forty-eight detainees could be neither prosecuted nor transferred.[43] As President Obama described them in his Archives speech, "[t]hese are people who, in effect, remain at war with the United States."[44]

Some who cling to the polemic of past years may claim that the lot of these forty-eight detainees is simply a function of evidence so tainted by misdirected interrogation techniques that a successful prosecution option was rendered impossible. But such an argument fails to further the effort to solve this complex problem, and it fails to recognize the radically different purposes and circumstances that attend the two disparate detention paradigms.

Looking to the legal regime associated with criminal procedure, the starting point is liberty. In the United States, citizens walk freely in the streets unless arrested based on a police officer's probable cause belief that a crime has been committed and the individual to be detained committed it.[45] Within forty-eight hours, the arresting officer must convince an independent magistrate of that probable cause;[46] to avoid release on bail pending disposition of charges, a convincing case of dangerousness or flight risk must be made,[47] a lawyer must be provided,[48] *Miranda* rights must be read[49] and a speedy trial clock begins to tick.[50] In order to convict a pretrial detainee of the underlying offense that led to his or her detention, a prosecutor must prove to a jury beyond a reasonable doubt every element of an offense for which the individual is charged.[51] Once this occurs, the sentencing authority can decide whether to set the individual free, or whether further detention (incarceration) of the individual is warranted. This is what human rights law provides in the United States. Our domestic implementation is far more refined and nuanced than the antecedent human rights law.

But in war, the starting point is radically different. A member of the enemy force in armed conflict is free only to the extent that he or she can avoid death or capture by the adversary. To a U.S. soldier, the enemy's starting point may be as a target. Under the law of war, combatants may be lawfully shot dead simply for being a member of the enemy force—there is no requirement for proof beyond a reasonable doubt that some past offense was committed.[52]

In certain circumstances, that target might, as a discretionary matter, be captured rather than killed.[53] Were that to occur, it would make no sense suddenly to "turn off" the wartime paradigm and switch to that of law enforcement, providing all the process associated with criminal procedure. To do so would be the equivalent of telling the nineteen-year-old recruit, "You have legal authority to kill another human being, but if you capture him instead, you had better collect enough evidence to prove him guilty of a crime in a courtroom." Making it more complex to capture a person in combat by adding additional obligations could incentivize killing—ironically and perversely—in the name of human rights.[54]

One might conclude that the answer is simply applying the law of war, but that in turn provides very little regulation and permits indefinite detention with no readily foreseeable end. Unlike the State-on-State conflict for which the 1949

Geneva Conventions were written, in the current conflict, combatants are more difficult to recognize and the "end" of hostilities is anything but easily identified or predicted. At the end of World War II, more than four hundred thousand enemy soldiers were incarcerated within the continental United States in a state of indefinite detention, yet all knew that the war and their concomitant detention would end upon surrender. Enemy soldiers at that time, mostly conscripted, could be released to return to their former lives. The end of today's conflict, however, will be far more difficult to identify, both in timing and in circumstance. And instead of conscripts, al Qaeda is manned by a highly committed volunteer force. When does this conflict end? When all senior al Qaeda leaders are killed or surrender?

The Geneva Conventions, written more than a half century ago, simply were not designed for the present conflict. And even if they had been, the past sixty years have witnessed countless enhancements to criminal procedure on the human rights side of the chart, but almost no refinements to the law of war side.[55] Were we to reconfigure the law of war to address today's conflict, we would condition the date and time of release of the detainees on some criteria other than the "end of hostilities." We would be forced to come to grips with some sort of individualized assessment as to when hostilities have ended for each individual detainee.

This body of law associated with the conduct of warfare is naturally far less developed than that attending law enforcement. Its constituting documents were drafted in the 1940s, before the nature of the present conflict was even envisaged. It is natural that jurists would initially look to the far more refined and nuanced criminal procedure to address issues of detention. Indeed, some who have grasped the paradigmatic disparity have claimed that the fact that the law of war does not more fully address relevant detention issues means that human rights norms must apply as a matter of law.

But the dearth of applicable guidance does *not* necessarily militate in favor of shifting to *lex generalis*; the normative gaps are not related to the authority to detain itself. No one questions kinetic targeting authority in non-international armed conflict, and a corollary must be that such authority subsumes the authority to capture and detain. Human rights law applicable to detention is clearly oriented toward the steady-state peacetime regime internal to a State's borders. To apply these rules to overseas wartime circumstances is the equivalent of applying a highway speed limit to an aircraft. That there is no agreed speed limit for aircraft is certainly not a cogent argument to demand application of automobile limits; the circumstances are plainly different.

The fact is, however, that human rights norms are far more relevant to wartime detention than is the speed limit analogy above—but not as a legal requirement. Regardless of whether there exists an applicable regulatory scheme, we have learned that our more refined twenty-first-century sensibilities would accord a detainee far more process than would have been deemed sufficient in another era. Even if appropriate norms had not evolved in favor of process—and they have—unique aspects of this conflict, likely lack of certainty with respect to the status of persons captured and ambiguity attending the end of the hostilities in which they are taking part, all point to the need for a process to provide the missing clarity. For those who believe such a process should be dictated as a matter of law, one would have to conclude that the law of war itself is in need of attention.

The complexity at the joinder of detention policy and law is self-evident as a function of political history. But before leaving the subject a few more observations are apropos It is worth noting that the controversy is most fundamentally premised on this dissonance in the available legal regimes and not in the political policy differences that have, unfortunately, captured headlines for the better part of a decade. In today's counterterrorism conflict, the United States is dealing with persons who are, at once, members of the enemy force in war *and* criminals involved in heinous acts of terrorism. The underlying basis for detention is substantially—but subtly—different for each regime. The law enforcement model is oriented toward punishment for a *prior* crime; the law of war model serves to protect against a *future* threat. Under the law of war, the newly minted recruit is legally just as deserving of capture and detention as is the experienced war criminal. But only the latter may be worthy of prosecution. One paradigm results in *punishment* and then only after the adjudication of *proof beyond a reasonable doubt* of culpability for *past acts*. The other detains as a *protective measure* after a showing of *future threat*, most likely imputed from affiliation.

This confluence of applicable bases for detention and attendant legal paradigms is the primary complicating factor in twenty-first-century detention policy. It resounds in the application of old laws to new wars—the counterterrorism conflict that pits the United States against an enemy dedicated to killing its citizens and eradicating the American way of life, an enemy whose members, if captured in a traditional State-on-State conflict, would be characterized as prisoners of war. The detention authority derives from their status as belligerents—the same status that would have justified targeting them for kinetic strike had they not been fortunate enough to have been captured in the alternative. Each is held because of the threat he poses if released, not as punishment for anything he may have done. Although this amounts to the principal point of confusion in recent years, U.S. detention policy is further complicated by the multiplicity of conflicts in which it is presently engaged.

The war against al Qaeda is not the only one by which the detention landscape of the past decade has been colored. Further complicating the scene are the counterinsurgency that we would like to believe is at its denouement in Iraq and the non-international armed conflict in Afghanistan that is conceived of differently by the more than forty allies who battle at the side of the United States. Even Additional Protocol II,[56] were it applicable, would offer a paucity of guidance for regulating detention in non-international armed conflict.

More important, the existence of a non-international armed conflict may itself be a matter of controversy. Very few countries have or will concede that their internal security issues amount to internal armed conflicts. To do so is to call into question the very ability of an executive to govern his or her nation. And the end-state goal of any counterinsurgency is transition to the *lex generalis*, or law of peace, which provides for detention of terrorist insurgents only as a matter of law enforcement. In States like Iraq the executive is unlikely ever to concede there to be a conflict that would justify law of war detention. If al Qaeda were based in New Mexico, the Federal Bureau of Investigation most likely would be handling detention policy as a law enforcement matter. Foreign armed forces normally are deemed to be engaged in armed conflict or occupation only if acting outside of the parameters of the domestic laws and consent of the host State.

Further, the nature of counterinsurgency is such that success means ultimately winning the hearts and minds of insurgent sympathizers because, unlike the expulsion of foreign attackers, the end state of any successful suppression of insurgency involves peaceful coexistence with the previous adversary. As a consequence, for any number of reasons, it is most useful to shift as quickly as possible to a law enforcement regime that treats insurgent combatants as criminals to be dealt with by a peacetime criminal justice system.

This was reflected by U.S. policy toward, and eventually the legal authorities associated with, the conflict in Iraq. As a general rule, capture and detention that took place during the latter portion of the U.S. presence in Iraq was conducted under a warrant-based program that accorded fully with Iraqi domestic law. Similarly, current initiatives in Afghanistan are taking the conflict, perhaps inextricably, in the direction of a law enforcement paradigm that may or may not serve counterinsurgency interests depending on how it is implemented—a challenge commanders must resolve on the ground. But for purposes of this discussion, the point is that the movement toward law enforcement operations is a function of the peculiarities of the military mission; it is not required by the rule of law even though it has the unfortunate collateral effect of furthering the confusion associated with the disparate legal regimes.

If Iraq sits on the law enforcement side of the chart depicting the various paradigms for the detention of terrorists, with Guantanamo firmly occupying the position on the law of war side (except for the individual cases of criminals who may be brought to justice through criminal proceedings), then Afghanistan sits between the two. Law of war authorities are presently employed to capture terrorists, but ultimately the peacetime society for which Afghans yearn will need to rely on the law enforcement model.

And, as a final complicating factor supplementing those mentioned above—the historic preference for addressing terrorism through the law enforcement paradigm, gaps in the law of war and the unique mandates of counterinsurgency—it cannot be forgotten that the world's perceptions of these evolving policies have been immeasurably impacted by Abu Ghraib and the inevitable association of the reprehensible crimes that took place there with the detention of terrorists at Guantanamo and with every other aspect of U.S. detention policy. This is truly an instance of bad facts putting the United States at risk for bad law. The President's actions in clearly prohibiting certain inappropriate interrogation practices[57] and affirming a commitment to transparency[58] in detention operations are steps in the right direction. International lawyers must be careful not to confuse these matters, which need attention in every armed conflict, with the more recondite developments that characterize twenty-first-century armed conflict with transnational terrorist organizations.

IV. Identifying the Solution

If the taint associated with U.S. detention policy were merely an issue of previous missteps or failed policies, it could have been corrected long ago. But too many have sought a quick answer, either by misapplying the law of war or inappropriately looking to a peacetime legal regime to justify all detention practices—filling regulatory gaps with an entirely different body of law that was drafted for radically different circumstances. If war is the correct paradigm, but extant law of war does not fit the current conflict, it follows that the law of war should be adjusted to fit present circumstances.

An adjustment to the law may follow logically, but it is not necessarily the only solution. Some would argue that international "law" is not always needed if sufficient principles exist to guide nations into morally responsible behavior that appropriately balances military and humanitarian interests. This article takes no position on the advisability of changing the law of war. Instead, it assumes that regardless of the future legal requirements, the first step is to identify and implement policies that fit the current circumstances and, assuming a law-making exercise or development of custom could follow, can usefully inform that future.

The starting point for this discussion is a speech by President Obama in May of 2009 regarding detention policies in the most controversial location—Guantanamo Bay. The fundamental theme of the President's remarks was his affirmation that U.S. detention policies are, and will be, guided by the rule of law and American values. He asserted the importance of American leadership in the international community and in the development of principled legal authorities to guide the evolution of international law.

Applying American values to the new circumstances of twenty-first-century armed conflict, law of war detention is a valid and morally necessary component of the warfighting effort. That authority cannot be encumbered by a requirement to detain only when a criminal case for past acts can be proven. On the other hand, indefinite detention cannot proceed with the simplicity that accompanies the detention of conventional prisoners of war. This conflict suffers from lack of clarity regarding both the "who" and "when" for long-term detention. That weakness, then, is best rectified by the establishment of a clear process from which both the government and the detainee can benefit.

This understanding is not completely new. In prior years Combatant Status Review Tribunals have been used to assess the basis of Guantanamo detentions case by case and Administrative Review Boards have been used to assess the continuing necessity of detention on the basis of threat. Both processes had weaknesses, and as a consequence, both have been discarded, the gap having been partially filled with habeas litigation and Periodic Review Boards. Similarly, experience has led to significant developments that have radically improved the review processes for both Iraq and Afghanistan.

Today, newly captured individuals are submitted to a Detainee Review Board. The Board, comprised of three field-grade military officers, reviews each individual's detention for both legality and necessity of continued detention. The detainee receives expert assistance from a U.S. officer who is authorized access to all reasonably available information pertaining to that detainee. This review is repeated periodically after the initial hearing, which must take place within sixty days of arrival at the internment facility. Similar improvements are forthcoming in Guantanamo. The President's 2009 executive order[59] lays out an even more robust process oriented toward assessing the continued threat of those detained at Guantanamo who already have received access to habeas review in federal courts.

Although some may prefer the certainty associated with a legally imposed review requirement, today the United States benefits from the ability to address the issue as a policy matter—learning from experience that never could have been accurately predicted. Experience is necessary because it is so important to preserve the requisite yet delicate equipoise between military necessity and humanitarian interests. Skewing that equipoise undermines the entire purpose of the law of war. International humanitarian law serves humanitarian interests only if adhered to, and only if adherence serves humanitarian goals. Failing to detain and detaining for too short or too long a period miss both the humanitarian and military necessity marks. The correct process can guide us to those objectives, however.

The fact that the subject of U.S. detention policy has provided fodder for so much discussion among lawyers, policymakers and the public, as well as active involvement by the White House, the courts and Congress, is testament to its continued timeliness and paramount importance. The legal/policy regime that emerges from this era will likely forever alter the way nation-States apply the rule of law in combating external or transnational terrorist threats. If properly nuanced, this framework could effectively maximize the likelihood of success in combating terrorism, while preserving and protecting the human rights and civil liberties that define civilized society.

Sadly, to some, the fits and starts that have thus far characterized this regime's birth and infancy portend neither counterterrorism success nor preservation of civil liberties. U.S. policy with respect to the detention of terrorists has been confused for nearly a decade. It has resulted in criticism from adversaries and allies alike. It has been the focus of heated debate within the national polity. And it was one of the first matters on which President Obama took action after his inauguration. But for these very reasons, there may be hope.

The last ten years have not only provided the clarity of hindsight to identify the need for change; they have provided the benefit of time and impetus for the pendulum to swing in both directions. The United States has been accused of holding innocents in legal black holes[60] and of prematurely releasing terrorists so they can return again to attack us.[61] It has been accused both of abusing detainees and of coddling them.

Optimism should not derive from a new discovery, or a political cure easily administered after an election shifts the polity in one direction or the other. But, at its heart, this is not a political issue; it is one benefitted by years of experience in trying to find the right answer. Oliver Wendell Holmes once said, "[T]he life of the law has not been logic; [but] experience."[62] International lawyers need not only the creativity, energy and persistence that have so well served this nation as it tackled problems in the past—and all of those are needed; also needed is the kind of wisdom that in some cases derives from experience alone. After nearly a decade of trial and error, as the beneficiary of that experience that reaches beyond the limits of human logic, the United States is now better situated than ever to get this right.

V. Conclusion

Anyone who claims the detainee policy problem to be easy does not understand it. Past policies have not always served U.S. interests, but the problem is not a binary one, where one failed solution isolates its antithesis as "the" right answer. But there are principles, honed in the crucible of the last decade, to which one can look for guidance. Twenty-first-century sensibilities will not stomach indefinite detention without process. But if the military instrument is used as a function of armed conflict, kinetic targeting authorities cannot and should not be disconnected from detention authorities. Countries that defer to a requirement for criminal proof in making targeting decisions in war are unlikely to be on the winning side.

The war against al Qaeda and its affiliates is not yet at an end, and it cannot be allowed to proceed without a principled, sustainable and credible detention policy, one that will serve as an example for the international community as well. In September 2010, President Jakob Kellenberger of the International Committee of the Red Cross delivered a speech in Geneva in which he announced an initiative to update the Geneva Conventions.[63] The law of war is indeed in transition—perhaps even to a degree evoking the era of post-Westphalian peace[64] or the order emerging from the chaos of World War II.[65] It goes without saying that lawyers should consciously and conscientiously seek to impact this change.

A failure to participate thoughtfully and deliberately in fashioning the legal norms that are being developed—norms that will guide the global community for the next century—would constitute a missed opportunity of substantial moment. As former British Defence Minister John Reid asserted in April of 2006,

> we owe it to ourselves, to our people, to our forces, and to the cause of international order to constantly reappraise and update the relationship between our underlying values, the legal instruments which apply them to the world of conflict, and the historical circumstances in which they are to be applied or "we risk continuing to fight a 21st century conflict with 20th century rules."[66]

The terrorist attacks of 9/11 thrust the United States into a crisis of historic proportion. In such crises, leaders seize on international lawyers to analyze courses of action with a view to determining their legality. Lawyers are charged to identify, apply and distinguish norms relevant to the situation. Such norms are frequently of long-standing pedigree, their principles having been established in code and treaty and evolved over decades through critical assessment and practical application.

On rare occasions, however, the international lawyer's skill must be exercised not only in the interpretation and application of extant law, but also in the conception and establishment of new law. And, on yet rarer occasions—watersheds of history—national and global interests rise or fall on the establishment of that new normative construct, rendering the legal exercise in itself the object of national strategy and perhaps even an imperative component of international order. At these seminal divides, lawyers must be poised not only to advise on what may be legally permissible, but also to envision what is legally necessary and desirable, both in the day at hand and in the new epoch. Now is such a watershed moment.

Notes

1. *See, e.g.*, STEPHEN M. DUNCAN, A WAR OF A DIFFERENT KIND: MILITARY FORCE AND AMERICA'S SEARCH FOR HOMELAND SECURITY 170–172 (2004). *See generally* Note, *Responding to Terrorism, Crime, Punishment, and War*, 115 HARVARD LAW REVIEW 1217, 1235–37 (2002); William K. Lietzau, *Old Laws, New Wars:* Jus ad Bellum *in an Age of Terrorism*, 2004 MAX PLANCK YEARBOOK OF UNITED NATIONS LAW (Max Planck Institute for Comparative Public Law and International Law) 383; William K. Lietzau, *The Role of Military Force in Foreign Relations, Humanitarian Intervention and the Security Council*, 64/2 ZEITSCHRIFT FÜR AUSLÄNDISCHES ÖFFENTLICHES RECHT UND VÖLKERRECHT (Heidelberg Journal of International Law) 281 (2004).

2. *See, e.g.*, Letter from Brad Davis, Executive Director, Asia Division, Human Rights Watch, to the Secretary General of the North Atlantic Treaty Organization (NATO), Nov. 28, 2006, *available at* http://hrw.org/english/docs/2006/11/28/afghan14684_txt.htm (asserting that substantial disagreements among members of NATO regarding detention policies in Afghanistan are the consequence of the United States' failure to comply with international legal standards).

3. *See, e.g.*, George W. Bush, Public Address (Sept. 11, 2001), http://articles .cnn.com/2001-09-11/us/bush.speech.text_1_attacks-deadly-terrorist-acts-despicable-acts?_s=PM:US; George W. Bush, Address to Joint Session of Congress (Sept. 20, 2001), http://articles .cnn.com/2001-09-20/us/gen.bush.transcript_1_joint-session-national-anthem-citizens?_s=PM:US.

4. *See, e.g.*, George W. Bush, Remarks by the President at the California Business Association Breakfast (Oct. 17, 2001), http://georgewbush-whitehouse.archives.gov/news/releases/2001/10/20011017-15.html.

5. Barack Obama, Remarks by the President on National Security (May 21, 2009), http://www.whitehouse.gov/the_press_office/Remarks-by-the-President-On-National-Security-5-21-09.

6. Barack Obama, Remarks by the President at the Acceptance of the Nobel Peace Prize, (Dec. 10, 2009), http://www.whitehouse.gov/the-press-office/remarks-president-acceptance-nobel-peace-prize.

7. Bush, Public Address, *supra* note 3.

8. Obama, *supra* note 5.

9. For example, the Clinton administration relied primarily on law enforcement tools to combat terrorism throughout the 1990s, including in its response to the 1993 World Trade Center bombing by terrorists.

10. Mary Ellen O'Connell, *When Is a War Not a War? The Myth of the Global War on Terror*, 12 ILSA JOURNAL OF INTERNATIONAL & COMPARATIVE LAW 535 (2005).

11. Press Release, United Nations Security Council, Security Council Condemns in Strongest Terms Terrorist Attacks on United States, U.N. Press Release SC/7143 (Sept. 12, 2001), *available at* http://www.un.org/News/Press/docs/2001/SC7143.doc.htm. *See also* Press Release, United Nations Security Council, Security Council Unanimously Adopts Wide-Ranging

Anti-Terrorism Resolution, U.N. Press Release SC/7158 (Sept. 28, 2001), *available at* http://www.un.org/ News/Press/docs/2001/sc7158.doc.htm; G.A. Res. 56/1, ¶¶ 3–4, U.N. Doc. A/RES/56/1 (Sept. 12, 2001), *available at* http://www.un.org/documents/ga/docs/56/agresolution.htm.

12. Lord Robertson, NATO Secretary General, Statement by NATO Secretary General (Oct. 2, 2001), *available at* http://www.nato.int/docu/speech/2001/s011002a.htm.

13. Press Release, Office of the Press Secretary, Statement by the Press Secretary re: The Anzus Treaty (Sept. 14, 2001), *available at* http://avalon.law.yale.edu/sept11/press_sec_003.asp; Terrorist Threat to the Americas, OAS Resolution, OAS Doc. OEA/Ser.F/II.24, RC.24/RES.1/01 (2001), *reprinted in* 40 INTERNATIONAL LEGAL MATERIALS 1273 (2001); *see also Declaration of Solidarity from the House of the Americas,* OAS Doc. OEA/Ser.F/II.23, RC.23/DEC.1/01 (2001).

14. Authorization for Use of Military Force, Pub. L. No. 107-40, 115 Stat. 224 (2001) (codified at 50 U.S.C. § 1541 note).

15. *See* Memorandum from George Bush to Vice President et al., Humane Treatment of Taliban and al Qaeda Detainees, Feb. 7, 2002, *available at* www.pegc.us/archive/White_House/bush_memo_20020207_ed.pdf.

16. *U.S. Issues Warning on Terrorist Attacks; State Department's Concern Partly Based on Seizure of Explosives, Arrests in Spain,* LOS ANGELES TIMES, Dec. 15, 1989, at 2.

17. *See* Nejla Sammakia, *Libya Starts Parliamentary Process That Could Give Gadhafi Way Out,* ASSOCIATED PRESS, May 8, 1992, *available at* 1992 WL 5296910 (reporting that the UN had instituted sanctions on Libya that would continue until two Libyan suspects in the Pan Am bombing were turned over to either the United States or the United Kingdom).

18. *Death Toll From Bomb Rises to 6; Searchers Sifting the Wreckage at World Trade Center Uncover the Body of a Missing Man,* ORLANDO SENTINEL, Mar. 16, 1993.

19. *See* Larry Neumeister, *Verdict: Sheik, All Co-defendants Guilty in Terror Trial,* ASSOCIATED PRESS, Oct. 2, 1995, *available at* 1995 WL 4408662.

20. *See* President William Clinton, Remarks at the Ceremony Honoring the Men and Women Who Lost Their Lives in the Bombings of the Embassies in Kenya and Tanzania, Andrews Air Force Base, Maryland, The White House, Office of the Press Secretary (Aug. 13, 1998) ("The 12 Americans and the 245 Kenyans and Tanzanians were taken from us in a violent moment by those who traffic in terror and rejoice in the agony of their victims. We pledge here today that neither time, nor distance can bend or break our resolve to bring to justice those who have committed these unspeakable acts of cowardice and horror. We will not rest. We will never retreat from this mission.").

21. *See* John Diamond, *Strikes Only Partly Successful, Reports Suggest,* AP ONLINE, Aug. 21, 1998, *available at* 1998 WL 6711944.

22. *See* U.S. Department of State, Office of the Spokesman, *Fact Sheet, Steps Taken to Serve Justice in the Bombings of U.S. Embassies in Kenya and Tanzania* (Aug. 4, 1999), http://www.state.gov/www/regions/africa/fs_anniv_steps.html. *See also* Greg B. Smith, *Osama's Tech-Thug Pal: Bombings Planner in Jail, Report Says,* DAILY NEWS (New York), Mar. 18, 2002, at 9.

23. One aspect of the law enforcement model for addressing the terrorist threat involves immigration controls and enforcement. This area of law is particularly relevant when addressing questions associated with enemy combatants who may be U.S. citizens, are captured outside a traditional battlefield, or are detained in circumstances not clearly related to an armed conflict. Though significant, concerns raised by these circumstances and concerns associated with the employment of immigration law tools are beyond the purview of this article. Similarly, this article does not discuss areas of potential congressional prerogative as they relate to presidential authority when engaging in a military response. For a discussion of these matters, see generally

STEVEN DYCUS, ARTHUR BERNEY, WILLIAM BANKS & PETER RAVEN-HANSEN, NATIONAL SECURITY LAW (2002).

24. International Convention for the Suppression of Terrorist Bombings, Dec. 15, 1997, 2149 U.N.T.S. 256.

25. *Id.*, art. 4 ("Each State Party shall likewise take such measures as may be necessary to establish its jurisdiction over the offences set forth in article 2 in cases where the alleged offender is present in its territory and it does not extradite that person to any of the States Parties which have established their jurisdiction in accordance with paragraph 1 or 2 of the present article."); *id.*, art. 8 (Providing that States in whose territory a person is present who has committed or is alleged to have committed an offense under the Convention agree to investigate his involvement in the offense, and, if appropriate, take such person into custody for the purpose of prosecution or extradition. If a State does not extradite the person, it is obliged, without exception whatsoever, to prosecute him.).

26. International Convention for the Suppression of the Financing of Terrorism art. 10(1), Dec. 9, 1999, 2178 U.N.T.S. 229.

27. *See generally* U.S. GENERAL ACCOUNTING OFFICE, GAO/NSIAD-00-8, COMBATING TERRORISM: HOW FIVE FOREIGN COUNTRIES ARE ORGANIZED TO COMBAT TERRORISM (2000). *See also* Russian Federal Law No. 35-FZ of Mar. 6, 2006, On Counteraction of Terrorism, Adopted by the State Duma on February 26, 2006, Endorsed by the Federation Council on March 1, 2006 (Establishing the "fundamental principles of counteraction against terrorism, the legal and organizational basics of preventing terrorism and struggling against it, of reducing to minimum and (or) liquidating the consequences of manifestations thereof, as well as the legal and organisational basics of using the Armed Forces of the Russian Federation in struggling against terrorism.").

28. *British Police Hunt for Subway Bombing Ringleaders*, VOICE OF AMERICA NEWS, Aug. 1, 2005, http://www.voanews.com/burmese/archive/2005-08/2005-08-01-voa1.cfm (reporting that British law enforcement was searching for the suspected ringleaders who had provided support to the July subway bombings in London, which killed fifty-six persons on July 7. Three alleged bombers were in British custody at the time; a fourth was arrested in Italy and was fighting extradition); Kevin Sullivan & Karla Adam, *Trial Opens in London Transit Bombing Plot; Good Fortune Spared Travelers Two Weeks After Attacks That Killed 52, Jury Is Told*, WASHINGTON POST, Jan. 16, 2007, at A12; Elaine Sciolino, *10 Bombs Shatter Trains in Madrid, Killing 192*, NEW YORK TIMES, Mar. 12, 2004, at A1 (reporting on Spain's massive manhunt for perpetrators of the deadly March 1, 2004 attack that left 192 dead and more than 1,400 injured).

29. *Criminal Terrorism Enforcement in the United States during the Five Years Since the 9/11/01 Attacks,* http://trac.syr.edu/tracreports/terrorism/169/ (From September 11, 2001 through May 2006, federal investigative agencies referred for prosecution 1,391 individuals whom the Justice Department classified as international terrorists. Prosecutions were filed against 335 of these individuals, 213 were convicted (by trial or plea) and 123 were sentenced to prison.). *See also* Phil Hirschkorn, *Jury Spares 9/11 Plotter Moussaoui,* CNN JUSTICE (May 3, 2006), http://articles.cnn.com/2006-05-03/justice/moussaoui.verdict_1_zacarias-moussaoui-frenchman-of-moroccan-heritage-penalty-phase?_s=PM:LAW (reporting that a federal jury had sentenced al Qaeda terrorist Zacarias Moussaoui to life in prison for his role in the September 11, 2001, attacks on the United States.).

30. A brief comment on terminology is appropriate. This article uses the terms "law of war," "international law of armed conflict," "laws and customs of war," and "international humanitarian law" as synonymous. While international lawyers most frequently claim them to be so, the terms often embody subtle distinctions worthy of note. Most publications refer to the law of war

and international law of armed conflict as having the same meaning. One could say that the latter term is broader in that it captures the concept of internal armed conflict as well. In the case of both terms, they are sometimes used to refer to both *jus ad bellum* and *jus in bello*, and sometimes to refer only to *jus in bello*. The term "international humanitarian law" is not normally used by the United States, because to do so is said to encourage a failure to distinguish adequately between the law of war and human rights law. Indeed, the terminology is frequently misused. The International Committee of the Red Cross (ICRC), however, which together with European countries prefers the term "international humanitarian law," has asserted it to be synonymous with the international law of armed conflict, which both the ICRC and European countries concede is distinct from human rights law. Treating it as a synonym, however, can be misleading. For example, the International Criminal Court's jurisdiction is said to encompass international humanitarian law. However, that treaty, in addition to addressing war crimes (*jus in bello*) and aggression (*jus ad bellum*) also subsumes crimes against humanity and genocide within its subject matter jurisdiction, both of which can be committed in periods of peace and war. Both of these arenas of criminality can be said to have evolved out of the law of war, but while the term "international humanitarian law" is deemed unproblematic when referring to them collectively, the term "law of war" might be seen as inapplicable to crimes against humanity and crimes of genocide committed during peacetime.

31. *See supra* text accompanying notes 16–23. In addition to the embassy bombings, there are numerous examples of past U.S. law enforcement responses to terrorist acts. The first Bush administration treated the problem of apprehending suspects after the 1998 bombing of Pan American Flight 103 as one of diplomacy and extradition, clearly a law enforcement matter. *See* Sammakia, *supra* note 17. After the 1993 World Trade Center bombing, law enforcement tools were employed to investigate, apprehend, extradite, try and convict the perpetrators of the bombing. *See* Neumeister, *supra* note 19.

32. Convention Relative to the Treatment of Prisoners of War art. 21, Aug. 12, 1949, 6 U.S.T. 3316, 3318, 75 U.N.T.S. 135, 136 [hereinafter GC III].

33. A. Prisoners of war, in the sense of the present Convention, are persons belonging to one of the following categories, who have fallen into the power of the enemy:

(1) Members of the armed forces of a Party to the conflict, as well as members of militias or volunteer corps forming part of such armed forces.

(2) Members of other militias and members of other volunteer corps, including those of organized resistance movements, belonging to a Party to the conflict and operating in or outside their own territory, even if this territory is occupied, provided that such militias or volunteer corps, including such organized resistance movements, fulfil the following conditions:

(a) that of being commanded by a person responsible for his subordinates;

(b) that of having a fixed distinctive sign recognizable at a distance;

(c) that of carrying arms openly;

(d) that of conducting their operations in accordance with the laws and customs of war.

(3) Members of regular armed forces who profess allegiance to a government or an authority not recognized by the Detaining Power.

(4) Persons who accompany the armed forces without actually being members thereof, such as civilian members of military aircraft crews, war correspondents, supply contractors, members of labour units or of services responsible for the welfare of the armed forces, provided that they have received authorization, from the

armed forces which they accompany, who shall provide them for that purpose with an identity card similar to the annexed model.

(5) Members of crews, including masters, pilots and apprentices, of the merchant marine and the crews of civil aircraft of the Parties to the conflict, who do not benefit by more favourable treatment under any other provisions of international law.

(6) Inhabitants of a non-occupied territory, who on the approach of the enemy spontaneously take up arms to resist the invading forces, without having had time to form themselves into regular armed units, provided they carry arms openly and respect the laws and customs of war.

B. The following shall likewise be treated as prisoners of war under the present Convention:

(1) Persons belonging, or having belonged, to the armed forces of the occupied country, if the occupying Power considers it necessary by reason of such allegiance to intern them, even though it has originally liberated them while hostilities were going on outside the territory it occupies, in particular where such persons have made an unsuccessful attempt to rejoin the armed forces to which they belong and which are engaged in combat, or where they fail to comply with a summons made to them with a view to internment.

(2) The persons belonging to one of the categories enumerated in the present Article, who have been received by neutral or non-belligerent Powers on their territory and whom these Powers are required to intern under international law, without prejudice to any more favourable treatment which these Powers may choose to give and with the exception of Articles 8, 10, 15, 30, fifth paragraph, 58–67, 92, 126 and, where diplomatic relations exist between the Parties to the conflict and the neutral or non-belligerent Power concerned, those Articles concerning the Protecting Power. Where such diplomatic relations exist, the Parties to a conflict on whom these persons depend shall be allowed to perform towards them the functions of a Protecting Power as provided in the present Convention, without prejudice to the functions which these Parties normally exercise in conformity with diplomatic and consular usage and treaties.

Id., art. 4.

34. *Id.*, art. 3.

35. "Conflicts not of an international character" (or "non-international armed conflicts") are governed only by Common Article 3 of the Geneva Conventions, custom, and, to those that are party, the second Additional Protocol to the Geneva Conventions (Protocol II). The United States signed Protocol II and submitted it to the Senate for advice and consent in 1987, where it remains before Senate subcommittees. Many have asserted that certain provisions in Protocol II have achieved the status of custom. In particular, Articles 4–6, outlining fundamental guarantees for detainees, protections and process requirements for prosecutions, are typically regarded in the international community as reflecting custom. *See* Protocol Additional to the Geneva Conventions of 12 August 1949, and Relating to the Protection of Victims of Non-International Armed Conflicts, June 8, 1977, 1125 U.N.T.S. 609, *reprinted in* 16 INTERNATIONAL LEGAL MATERIALS 1442 (1977) [hereinafter Additional Protocol II].

36. A combatant must meet the criteria outlined in GC III, *supra* note 32, Article 4 in order to be designated as a prisoner of war. *See supra* note 33. Al Qaeda is not a State party to the Convention and its members do not meet the criteria for militias and volunteer corps as described in Article 4(A)(2).

37. GC III, *supra* note 32, art. 4(A).

38. *See, e.g.*, Roy Gutman, Christopher Dickey & Sami Yousafzai, *Guantanamo Justice?*, NEWSWEEK, July 8, 2002, at 34.

39. It is worth noting that AUMF did not impose geographic or temporal limitations on the President's use of force. Instead it provides the President authority to use force against specific targets—those "nations, groups, or persons" that the President determines "planned, authorized, committed, or aided" the terrorist attacks on 9/11, as well as those who "harbored such organizations or persons." AUMF, *supra* note 14. *See also* MOHAMMED-MAHMOUD OULD MOHAMEDOU, NON-LINEARITY OF ENGAGEMENT, TRANSNATIONAL ARMED GROUPS, INTERNATIONAL LAW AND THE CONFLICT BETWEEN AL QAEDA AND THE UNITED STATES (2005), *available at* http://www.hpcrresearch.org/sites/default/files/publications/Non-Linearity_of_Engagement.pdf (discussing the evolutionary nature of warfare as it relates to transnational groups like al Qaeda).

40. However, while the government described the conflict as a "war on terror," it clearly did not intend to engage in conflict with all terrorists anywhere in the world. Instead, the government conducted a war against the armed groups responsible for the attacks of 9/11 (al Qaeda, the Taliban and their associates), as prescribed by the AUMF, and mostly within the territory of Afghanistan.

41. *See supra* text accompanying notes 3–6.

42. U.S. DEPARTMENT OF JUSTICE ET AL., FINAL REPORT OF THE GUANTANAMO REVIEW TASK FORCE (2010), *available at* http://www.justice.gov/ag/guantanamo-review-final-report.pdf.

43. *Id.*

44. Obama, *supra* note 5.

45. Terry v. Ohio, 392 U.S. 1 (1968).

46. County of Riverside v. McLaughlin, 500 U.S. 44 (1991).

47. Bail Reform Act of 1984, 18 U.S.C. §§ 3141–3156 (2006).

48. Gideon v. Wainwright, 372 U.S. 335 (1963).

49. Miranda v. Arizona, 384 U.S. 436 (1966); Dickerson v. U.S., 530 U.S. 428 (2000).

50. U.S. CONST. amend. VI (1791); Barker v. Wingo, 407 U.S. 514 (1972).

51. In re Winship, 397 U.S. 358, 361 (1970).

52. *See* Yoram Dinstein, *The System of Groups in International Humanitarian Law*, *in* INTERNATIONAL HUMANITARIAN LAW FACING NEW CHALLENGES: SYMPOSIUM IN HONOUR OF KNUT IPSEN 145, 148 (Wolff Heintschel von Heinegg & Volker Epping eds., 2007) ("As far as ordinary combatants are concerned, it must be perceived that they are running a *risque du métier*. They can be attacked (and killed) wherever they are, in and out of uniform: even when they are not on active duty. There is no prohibition either of opening fire on retreating troops (who have not surrendered) or of targeting individual combatants."). *See also* MICHAEL WALZER, JUST AND UNJUST WARS 143 (4th ed. 2006).

53. Unless the target is *hors de combat*, the law of war never requires taking less than lethal force against a lawful target. However, if a target might just as easily be captured and detained, commanders may elect in certain circumstances a non-lethal course of action to preserve intelligence collection.

54. *See* Editorial, *What to do with terror suspects?*, WASHINGTON POST, July 4, 2011, at A10, *available at* http://www.washingtonpost.com/opinions/what-to-do-with-terror-suspects/2011/07/01/gHQAduqEyH_story.html.

55. There are some exceptions to this dearth of new rules in the law of war, including the adoption of international agreements related to specific weapons and the development of the

1977 Protocols (I and II) Additional to the Geneva Conventions of 1949. The United States is not party to either of the Additional Protocols. Although the government has consistently supported joining Protocol II, it has been very critical of some provisions of Additional Protocol I since its creation.

56. Additional Protocol II, *supra* note 35.

57. Exec. Order No. 13,491, 74 Fed. Reg. 4893 (Jan. 22, 2009).

58. Obama, *supra* note 5.

59. *Supra* note 57.

60. *See, e.g.*, Richard J. Wilson, *United States Detainees at Guantanamo Bay: The Inter-American Commission on Human Rights Responds to a "Legal Black Hole,"* 10 HUMAN RIGHTS BRIEF 2 (2003).

61. *See, e.g.*, The Editors, *Stop Releasing Terrorists*, NATIONAL REVIEW ONLINE, Dec. 29, 2009, http://www.nationalreview.com/articles/228875/stop-releasing-terrorists/editors.

62. *Lecture 1—Early Forms of Liability, in* OLIVER WENDELL HOLMES, THE COMMON LAW (1881).

63. Jakob Kellenberger, President of the International Committee of the Red Cross, Address at Ceremony to celebrate the 60th anniversary of the Geneva Conventions: Sixty years of the Geneva Conventions: learning from the past to better face the future (Dec. 8, 2009), *available at* http://www.icrc.org/eng/resources/documents/statement/geneva-conventions-statement-president-120809.htm.

64. Peace Treaty between the Holy Roman Emperor and the King of France and Their Respective Allies, Oct. 24, 1648, *available at* http://www.yale.edu/lawweb/avalon/westphal.htm. Ending the Eighty Years' War between Spain and the Dutch, and the German phase of the Thirty Years' War, the Peace of Westphalia recognized the full territorial sovereignty of the member states of the Holy Roman Empire, rendering the princes of the empire absolute sovereigns in their own dominions. *See* Encyclopaedia Britannica, 2002.

65. In 1945, World War II drawing to an end, representatives of fifty countries met in San Francisco at the United Nations Conference on International Organization to draw up the United Nations Charter. Those delegates deliberated on the basis of proposals worked out by the representatives of China, the Soviet Union, the United Kingdom and the United States at Dumbarton Oaks, United States in August–October 1944. The Charter was signed on June 26, 1945 by the representatives of the fifty countries. Poland, which was not represented at the Conference, later signed the Charter and became one of the original fifty-one member States. The United Nations officially came into existence on October 24, 1945, when the Charter had been ratified by China, France, the Soviet Union, the United Kingdom and the United States and by a majority of other signatories. *See* The United Nations, About the United Nations/History, http://www.un.org/aboutun/history.htm (last visited Oct. 26, 2011). The creation of the United Nations is widely recognized as one of the most important events of the post–World War II period. That the delegates were influenced substantially by the war is reflected in the preamble to the United Nations Charter, which provides, "We the people of the United Nations determined to save succeeding generations from the scourge of war, which twice in our lifetime has brought untold sorrow to mankind . . . ." U.N. Charter pmbl. The fundamental purpose of the Charter is the maintenance of international peace and security. *Id.*, art. 1, para. 1. *See* RUTH B. RUSSELL, A HISTORY OF THE UNITED NATIONS, THE ROLE OF THE UNITED STATES 1940–1945, at 964 (providing an in-depth description of the formation of the Charter).

66. John Reid, United Kingdom Secretary of State for Defence, Address at the Royal United Services Institute for Defence and Security Studies: 20th-Century Rules, 21st-Century Conflict (Apr. 3, 2006).

XVI

Detention in Non-International Armed Conflicts

Knut Dörmann*

Introduction

The question of detention in non-international armed conflicts (NIACs) has made it to the forefront of the international legal and operational debate. This is particularly due to the fact that most of current armed conflicts are of a non-international character and that they lead to important numbers of persons being deprived of their liberty. When assessing the legal and operational challenges posed in such situations, it is important to bear in mind that NIACs may take different forms, ranging from classical civil war situations with armed violence essentially occurring within the confines of one single territory between government armed forces and dissident armed forces or other organized armed opposition groups, to NIACs spilling over to neighboring countries, and to armed conflict situations in which multinational forces intervene on the side of a host government against organized armed opposition groups. The debate, therefore, needs to focus on common features to all types of NIACs, as well as on where distinctions need possibly to be made. For example, with regard to a NIAC, when multinational forces intervene on the side of a host government, questions arise as to how to deal

---

* Head, Legal Division, International Committee of the Red Cross (ICRC). Special thanks are due to Jelena Pejic, Legal Advisor, Legal Division, ICRC, for her substantive contribution to this article. Thanks are also due to Helena Sunnegardh, Legal Attaché, Legal Division, ICRC, for her assistance.

with the relationship between the third States and the host government, bearing in mind that they may be subject to different domestic and international legal obligations.

This contribution cannot attempt to look at all the challenges that arise; it can only give a snapshot of them. As will be shown, a more in-depth discussion is required in the years to come. The article will focus on two main issues. It will first address the applicable legal framework to detention in NIAC and, in particular, the interplay between international humanitarian law (IHL) and international human rights law; and second, present the International Committee of the Red Cross's (ICRC's) analysis of the need to strengthen the law in light of humanitarian problems observed in its field operations and the related normative weaknesses. The concluding remarks will then summarize how the international community has responded to the ICRC's analysis.

Before addressing these two issues, some observations on the sources of law applicable in NIAC should be made to set the frame.

The main sources of treaty IHL governing NIAC are Article 3 common to the four Geneva Conventions of 1949[1] (generally considered to reflect customary law[2]), which specifically refers among others to persons in detention,[3] and the 1977 Additional Protocol II to the Geneva Conventions, relating to the protection of victims of non-international armed conflicts,[4] when applicable—namely, Articles 4–6, which specifically relate to persons deprived of liberty.[5] The development of customary international law has complemented treaty law.[6] Due to the paucity of treaty rules, customary IHL plays a more significant role in NIAC than in international armed conflicts (IACs). Still, the question remains whether IHL needs to be further strengthened, taking into account the challenges posed by current forms of NIAC. In particular it needs to be assessed whether existing protections are strong enough in such situations.

IHL is not the only legal framework relevant in NIACs. It is generally accepted, despite the views of a few important dissenters, including the United States,[7] that human rights law applies alongside IHL in armed conflicts, and that it also applies extraterritorially.[8] What is not settled is the precise interplay of the two branches of international law in situations of armed conflict and the extent of the extraterritorial application of human rights law.

It is widely accepted that IHL is the *lex specialis* in IAC (in the field of detention of persons in particular through the detailed regulation on prisoners of war, namely, in the Third Geneva Convention,[9] and internment of persons protected by the Fourth Geneva Convention[10]). However, the interplay is more complex in NIAC for at least two reasons.

First, while it is clear that States' human rights obligations continue in NIAC, determining the interplay of a State's IHL and human rights treaty obligations remains a difficult endeavor. One reason is that—contrary to IHL applicable in IACs—IHL in NIACs is more rudimentary, and thus gives less rise to conflicts between norms that would generally be addressed through application of the *lex specialis* rule. It is also not sufficient to state in general terms that human rights law continues to apply in armed conflict without elaborating on what this means in practice.[11] Situations of armed conflict are different from times of peace. This explains why some IHL and human rights rules differ in content, and thus produce conflicting results when applied to the same situation. The norms of these two bodies of law reflect the different reality for which each body was primarily developed. One example relates to the rules applicable to the use of force: the IHL rules on the conduct of hostilities differ from those that would apply in law enforcement situations.[12] Differences exist as well in the field of detention. The most evident difference between IHL and human rights standards concerns the rules governing procedural safeguards for security detention.[13]

Second, the obligations of the State party under human rights law treaties are not legally shared by the non-State party to an armed conflict.[14] In addition, in many cases these obligations could not be practically carried out by the non-State party because it cannot perform government-like functions on which the implementation of human rights norms is based. IHL is the only branch of international law aimed at the protection of persons that clearly binds both State and non-State parties in armed conflict. Common Article 3 of the four Geneva Conventions, for example, is very clear on that, as it refers to "each Party to the conflict." Based on that, IHL is also the only legal regime binding non-State organized armed groups fighting against each other. It thus remains an indispensable legal framework for these situations.[15]

Bearing in mind these factors, the relationship between IHL and human rights norms in a NIAC, and the respective legal obligations for parties to a NIAC must be determined on a case-by-case basis.

IHL Rules Applicable to Detention in NIAC

Deprivation of liberty is an inevitable and lawful occurrence in armed conflict, including in NIAC. The fundamental obligation underpinning any form of detention in armed conflict is to treat persons deprived of liberty humanely.[16] Other, more specific IHL rules give effect to this obligation and complement it. The different rules on detention (most of which overlap with human rights law) may be broadly divided into four groups: rules on the treatment of detainees in the narrow sense, rules on material conditions of detention, fair trial rights and procedural safeguards in internment.

In the following discussion these rules will be briefly presented and compared to similar or equivalent human rights norms, and the question of whether they remain appropriate and sufficient in contemporary armed conflicts will be addressed.

Rules on the Treatment of Detainees in the Narrow Sense

Rules on the treatment of detainees in the narrow sense aim to protect the physical and mental integrity and well-being of persons deprived of liberty for whatever reason. They comprise, most importantly, the prohibition of murder, torture and other forms of cruel, inhuman or degrading treatment, mutilation, and medical or scientific experiments, as well as other forms of violence to life and health, which includes prohibitions of sexual violence and rape.[17] All of the acts mentioned are prohibited under both IHL and human rights law.[18]

It may be concluded that in this area the normative framework posed by IHL is strong enough. When humanitarian problems arise in contemporary armed conflicts it is due not to lack of norms, but to lack of compliance with and enforcement of these rules.

To the extent that the transfer of detainees may lead to violations of the right to life or of the prohibition of torture and other forms of ill-treatment, this aspect may also be categorized as belonging to the treatment of detainees in the narrow sense.

The transfer of detainees raises significant legal and practical problems in current armed conflicts. The transfer of persons between States has been one of the recurring practices in armed conflicts over the past several years, particularly in situations where multinational forces transfer persons to a "host" State, to their country of origin or to a third State. Generally, there is cause for concern from a humanitarian standpoint whenever there is a risk that a transferred person may be subject to serious violations of IHL upon transfer to the receiving State. The ICRC's view is that the principle of *non-refoulement* must be observed whenever a person might be transferred from one authority to another and when there is a risk that a transferred detainee might be subject to torture and other forms of ill-treatment, arbitrary deprivation of life (which includes the imposition of the death penalty after an unfair trial), enforced disappearance, and persecution.[19] The ICRC works constantly with detaining authorities in various operational contexts to ensure that the principle is adhered to in practice.

There are no explicit IHL rules in treaty law applicable to NIAC dealing with transfers of detainees. However, it may be argued that it would contravene the explicit prohibitions of Common Article 3 to the four Geneva Conventions if a party to a NIAC transferred an individual under its control or authority to another party while there are substantial grounds to believe that the person would be tortured or otherwise ill-treated or arbitrarily deprived of life.[20] Such a rule exists more explicitly in IHL applicable in IAC. The rules relating to the transfer responsibilities of a detaining authority in an IAC go even further for specific categories of persons. They establish specific post-transfer responsibilities for the transferring State in case the receiving State does not comply with the provisions of the Third Geneva Convention[21] or the Fourth Geneva Convention.[22]

It is the ICRC's view that in light of the lack of specificity in NIAC treaty law and the problems observed in a variety of conflict situations throughout the world, it should be considered whether the existing legal framework could be strengthened by identifying specific rules dealing with responsibilities in cases of transfer in NIACs. It would be crucial to provide more legal guidance to detaining authorities. The lack of legal provisions in IHL governing NIACs suggests that it would be highly advisable to provide a set of workable substantive and procedural rules that would both guide the actions of States and non-State organized armed groups and protect the rights of affected persons. Current practice, in which more and more NIACs involve coalitions of States fighting one or more non-State organized armed groups in a "host" country, indicates that uncertainty about how to organize a lawful transfer regime, including with regard to post-transfer responsibilities, is likely to increase, rather than decrease; thus a need to further reflect on the possibility of strengthening the legal framework. The underlying principles of IHL rules applicable in IAC should serve as a starting point.[23]

Rules on Material Conditions of Detention

The purpose of the rules on material conditions of detention is to ensure that detaining authorities adequately provide for detainees' physical and psychological needs, which include food, accommodation, health, hygiene, contacts with the outside world, religious observance and others.[24] Treaty and customary IHL provide a substantial catalogue of standards that pertain first and foremost to conditions of detention in IAC.[25] They also provide less detailed standards that apply in NIAC,[26] as do "soft law" human rights instruments.[27] A common catalogue of norms could be derived from both bodies of law.[28]

In the absence of specific treaty law for NIAC other than what is contained in Additional Protocol II to the Geneva Conventions, this common catalogue can provide important guidance. A normative strengthening in the ICRC's view is nevertheless desirable to better address the humanitarian problems observed by ICRC delegates in places of detention worldwide. They relate particularly to lack of adequate food, water, accommodation and access to medical care; no contact with families and the outside world; failure to separate appropriately (adults from children, those charged with criminal offenses from security detainees, etc.); failure to register detainees; and overcrowding.

When looking at the rules on material conditions of detention it seems important to also analyze the needs of particularly vulnerable groups (namely, women, children, the disabled and the elderly). The situation of women, for instance, requires special attention. When women are detained in the same prison as men, their access to fresh air may be compromised if the courtyard is communal, since mixing with men would put them at risk of abuse and may not be permitted for cultural reasons. Likewise, women often remain locked in their cells if prison corridors are open to both sexes. Female detainees have specific health and hygiene needs. Pregnant women and nursing mothers require dietary supplements and appropriate pre- and postnatal care so that they and their babies remain in good health.[29]

Children in detention also require specific protection and care. Prison conditions and facilities are not always adapted to their needs and vulnerabilities, especially in terms of protection against inhumane or degrading disciplinary measures. In addition, in numerous situations, these children are deprived of access to appropriate schooling or vocational training. They may also suffer from a lack of sufficient recreational and physical activity. They rarely enjoy adequate communication with the outside world, including with their parents, which may seriously affect their emotional development.[30]

Most of these concerns, which include the needs of other categories of persons, such as the elderly and the disabled, are not sufficiently addressed under current IHL governing NIAC. Common Article 3 to the Geneva Conventions does not provide special protection to particularly vulnerable persons in detention, and Additional Protocol II to the Geneva Conventions only obliges the parties to NIACs to separate detained women and men "within the limits of their capabilities."[31] Similarly, under customary law, detained children must be held in quarters separate from those of adults, except when they are accommodated with their family.[32] Besides these rules, the law applicable to NIACs does not provide further specific protection and thus, it is submitted, requires supplementing.

Fair Trial Rights

Persons detained on suspicion of having committed a criminal offense are entitled to a number of fair trial rights. The list of fair trial rights is almost identical under IHL and human rights law. While Common Article 3 to the Geneva Conventions does not provide a list of judicial guarantees, it is now generally accepted that Article 75(4) of Additional Protocol I to the Geneva Conventions[33]—which was drafted based on the corresponding provisions of the International Covenant on Civil and Political Rights (ICCPR)[34]—reflects customary law applicable in all types of armed conflict.[35] Article 75(4), in fact, encapsulates all of Article 6(5) of Additional Protocol II, which supplements Common Article 3 in NIAC. IHL reinforces human rights law in that it allows no derogation from fair trial rights in situations of armed conflict.[36]

In light of the preceding, it would appear that the existing legal framework is robust enough to address the protection needs of persons suspected of having committed a criminal offense. If humanitarian problems arise nevertheless, it is generally due not to a lack of rules, but rather to a lack of implementation or lack of respect for existing rules.

Procedural Safeguards in Internment

The question of procedural safeguards in internment is probably the key issue in terms of legal and practical challenges with regard to detention in NIAC, in particular in "multinational" NIACs.[37]

Internment may be defined as the non-criminal detention of a person based on the serious threat that his or her activity poses to the security of the detaining authority in an armed conflict. The area of procedural safeguards in internment is probably the principal area in which differences emerge in IHL applicable to international and non-international armed conflicts, as well as between IHL and human rights law, and where gaps in IHL governing NIAC may be observed.[38]

Outside armed conflict, non-criminal (i.e., administrative) detention should be very exceptional.[39] In the vast majority of cases, deprivation of liberty happens when a person is suspected of having committed a criminal offense. The rationale under human rights law is the assumption that the courts of a State are functioning, that its judicial system is capable of absorbing whatever number of persons may be arrested at any given time, that legal counsel is available, that law enforcement officials have the capacity to perform their tasks, etc. The reality in situations of armed conflict is, however, different. As a consequence, IHL provides for different rules.[40] While these latter rules are quite detailed in addressing internment in IAC, IHL treaties do not contain rules on procedural safeguards for persons interned in NIAC. They imply, however, that persons would be interned in NIACs. Additional Protocol II explicitly mentions internment in Articles 5 and 6(5). It thus confirms that it is a form of deprivation of liberty inherent to NIAC. At the same time, the Protocol does not list internment grounds or process rights.

In a traditional NIAC occurring in the territory of a single State between government armed forces and one or more non-State organized armed groups, domestic law, informed by the State's human rights obligations and IHL, constitutes the legal framework regulating the deprivation of liberty of members of such non-State armed groups by the State.[41] What does this mean in terms of State obligations? That question is subject to diverging opinions.

According to some views domestic law does not permit non-criminal detention in armed conflict without derogation from obligations under applicable human rights law treaties. Under the ICCPR this would apply even if the State provided judicial review as required under Article 9(4).[42]

Others suggest that derogation would be necessary if the State suspended the right to habeas corpus and provided only administrative review of internment in a NIAC (as would be sufficient in IAC).[43]

According to still other views, the right to habeas corpus is not subject to derogation.[44] Such an approach, which is perfectly valid and necessary in peacetime, seems difficult to reconcile, it is submitted, with the law or the reality of armed conflict, in particular in situations in which a NIAC involves multinational forces fighting abroad alongside a host government and these forces undertake internment.[45]

In NIACs involving States fighting outside their own territories alongside of the host State's armed forces in the latter's territory, identification of the legal framework governing internment is even more complex than in those instances where the NIAC involves only government forces engaging organized armed groups in its territory. There are two examples of such NIACs. The first example is a "multinational NIAC," in which multinational armed forces are fighting alongside the armed forces of a "host" State in its territory against one or more organized armed groups (for example, the situation as it prevailed in Afghanistan after the confirmation of the Karzai government by the Loya Jirga in 2002, which turned the initial IAC into a NIAC). The second is a NIAC in which United Nations forces or forces acting under the aegis of a regional organization are sent to help stabilize a "host" government involved in hostilities against one or more organized armed groups in its territory. The United Nations Organization Stabilization Mission in the Democratic Republic of the Congo and the African Union Mission in Somalia are examples.

Uncertainty surrounding States' human rights obligations in these two NIAC scenarios arise. These exist for internment in general, but are also particularly acute in the field of procedural safeguards. Five such general issues of uncertainty have been identified by Jelena Pejic;[46] these illustrate the complexity:

First, as has been pointed out, a few States still reject the notion of application of human rights law in armed conflict as such.

Second, State members of a multinational force, whether acting under UN auspices or otherwise, may not be bound by the same human rights treaties, including the ICCPR, and may therefore have different legal obligations.

Third, the exact extent of the extraterritorial reach of human rights law remains unclear. The International Court of Justice and the UN Human Rights Committee[47] have opined that States continue to be bound by their human rights obligations when they act abroad. However, their pronouncements, especially those by the International Court of Justice, have not yet settled all the legal, political and practical issues that arise.[48] The concrete implications of the statements must be assessed on a case-by-case basis; this is certainly necessary for internment carried out by multinational forces abroad.

Fourth, and somewhat linked to the preceding points and assuming the applicability of human rights law, a legal issue that has not been addressed by any judicial or other body is whether States must derogate from their human rights obligation to protect personal liberty in order to detain persons abroad without providing habeas corpus review. It seems obvious that if the application of human rights law is to be adapted to battlefield reality—that is, situations in which it may not be feasible to provide judicial review of the lawfulness of internment in thousands or tens of thousands of cases—it would appear that a derogation would be necessary. If this is the case, the next issue that needs to be resolved is which State involved in a NIAC should derogate, the one actually holding the detainees or the host State. In practice, no State of a multinational force has ever made a derogation.

Fifth, what is the legal effect of a bilateral treaty adopted between a detaining State and a host State, or of a Chapter VII[49] UN Security Council resolution authorizing internment by a multinational force, in particular when it comes to determining the extent of procedural safeguards to be granted? For example, can a bilateral treaty override the respective States' human rights obligations and provide a legal basis for internment without judicial review, particularly when there has been no derogation from their human rights obligations? It would seem that such a treaty cannot set aside otherwise applicable human rights obligations.

As regards Security Council authority, the issue arose in the international debate as to whether a Chapter VII resolution authorizing a multinational force to "use all necessary means" to fulfill its mandate may be read as permitting internment. Views remain divided.[50] On the one hand, there is good reason to believe that it may (if the mission can use force against persons—the traditional understanding of the formulation "use all necessary means"—then it must logically be allowed to also intern persons). On the other hand, there are also compelling arguments against such a position (the clause is not specific enough to comply with the principle of legality). In any case, such a general clause referring only to "all necessary means" does not help in determining the applicable procedural safeguards in the absence of further details in the resolution.[51]

In light of this reality, the ICRC has been particularly active in its legal/policy thinking and, based on that, in its operational dialogue with States.

In light of the lack of IHL treaty rules on procedural safeguards in NIAC (and, to a certain extent, the still rudimentary nature of the process due to civilians interned in IAC), the ICRC developed institutional guidelines in 2005 entitled "Procedural Principles and Safeguards for Internment/Administrative Detention in Armed Conflict and Other Situations of Violence."[52] The rules derive from an IHL framework, bearing in mind relevant human rights law, and are complemented by policy considerations. They are meant to be implemented in a manner that takes into account the specific situation at hand. The ICRC relies on these guidelines in its operational dialogue with States, multinational forces and other actors.

Two aspects addressed in the institutional guidelines deserve to be specifically mentioned since they are at the heart of any internment system and are the issues most extensively debated internationally and domestically: the grounds justifying internment and the internment review process. Both are related to the principle of legality that must be respected when a State resorts to internment.[53]

Grounds for Internment

International humanitarian law applicable in NIAC does not specify grounds for internment. In its institutional guidelines and operational dialogue, the ICRC relied on "imperative reasons of security" as the minimum legal standard that should inform internment decisions in all situations of violence, including NIAC. This standard is derived from what is accepted in IAC and is deemed appropriate in NIAC. This policy choice takes into account and highlights the exceptional nature of internment. In addition, the standard is already in wide use.[54] The ICRC believes that this standard is also well adapted to the situation of multinational NIAC, in which foreign forces are detaining non-nationals in the territory of a host State. Due to the similarities with internment in occupation situations, in that both occur abroad, the wording chosen is based on the internment standard applicable in occupied territories under the Fourth Geneva Convention. The ICRC believes that the proposed standard strikes a workable balance between the need to protect personal liberty and the detaining authority's need to protect against activity that is seriously prejudicial to its security.

The "imperative reasons of security standard" is high. It must be carefully evaluated in relation to each person detained as to whether it has been met. It should be uncontroversial that direct participation in hostilities[55] is an activity that would meet the "imperative reasons of security standard." While direct participation in hostilities is a notion that is particularly relevant when it comes to the use of force in armed conflict, as it defines the circumstances under which civilians lose their protection from direct attacks, it seems obvious that the same persons engaging in such activity may *a priori* also be subject to internment. This is dependent, of course, on what direct participation in hostilities encompasses in terms of an individual's conduct. The ICRC has issued its interpretive recommendations on that issue, certain aspects of which are the subject of controversial debate.[56] This article is not the place to elaborate on the substance of the recommendations or the reaction they received. It suffices to say that some of the wide interpretations defended by others would seem quite problematic from a targeting perspective, as would reconciling them with the "imperative reasons of security standard" applicable to internment.

As posted in the ICRC guidelines on procedural principles and safeguards,[57] internment may not be resorted to for the sole purpose of interrogation or intelligence gathering unless the person in question is deemed to represent a serious security threat based on his or her own activity.[58] Similarly, internment may not be used in order to punish a person for past activity.

Internment Review Process

In terms of process, the ICRC's institutional guidelines state, *inter alia,* that a person must be informed promptly in a language he or she understands of the reasons for internment. This must be done in order to enable the internee to exercise his or her right to challenge the lawfulness of the internment with the least possible delay before an independent and impartial body. The right to be informed is specifically recognized for IAC in Article 75(3) of Additional Protocol I, and while not explicitly provided for in NIAC, it can be seen as an element of the obligation of humane treatment applicable to internment in all situations of armed conflict.[59]

An internee has the right to challenge the lawfulness of his or her internment with the least possible delay before an independent and impartial body. In practice, exercising this right in an effective way will require the fulfillment of several procedural and practical steps, including providing internees with sufficient evidence supporting the allegations against them, ensuring that procedures are in place to enable internees to seek and obtain additional evidence and making sure that internees understand the various stages of the internment review process and the process as a whole.[60] In the case that the internment review is administrative in nature and not judicial, it is essential to ensure the independence and impartiality of the review body.[61]

The ICRC's institutional guidelines provide that an internee has the right to automatic, periodic review of the lawfulness of continued internment. Such review requires the detaining authority to ascertain whether the "imperative reasons of security standard" continues to be met, and to order release of the internee if that is not the case. The safeguards that apply to initial review are also to be applied to each periodic review.[62]

The fact that the ICRC felt obligated to produce guidelines based on law *and policy* indicates the need for a discussion of whether IHL applicable in NIAC also must be strengthened. IHL treaty law simply does not spell out procedural safeguards for persons interned in a NIAC.

Conclusion

As has been detailed, there is an important body of law governing detention in NIAC. This body of law is sometimes based on a complex interplay between IHL and human rights law. Still, it is submitted, there are a number of normative gaps or areas in which IHL needs to be further strengthened in order to respond to humanitarian problems posed by detention in NIAC. This is one of the conclusions of a two-year internal study conducted by the ICRC on the need to strengthen the legal protection for victims of armed conflicts.[63] Strengthening the law may mean reaffirmation of existing law in situations where it is not properly implemented and its clarification or development when it does not sufficiently meet the needs of the victims of armed conflict.

The objectives of the ICRC study were to better identify and understand the humanitarian problems arising out of current armed conflicts, and to analyze existing treaty and customary rules of IHL with a view to determining whether this legal framework offers adequate answers to these humanitarian problems or if further development of the law may be needed. With respect to most of the questions examined, the ICRC study showed that IHL, in its current state, provides a suitable legal framework for regulating the conduct of parties to armed conflicts. In almost all cases what is required to improve the victims' situation is stricter compliance with that framework, rather than adoption of new rules. If all parties concerned fully respected IHL, most current humanitarian issues would not exist. If attempts were undertaken to strengthen IHL, these should, therefore, build on the existing legal framework. However, the ICRC study also showed that IHL, in its current state, was not adequate in every respect and should be further developed in some areas. In addition to the issue of persons deprived of their liberty in NIAC, the ICRC identified three other areas where the law should be strengthened: international mechanisms for monitoring compliance with IHL and reparation for victims of violations, the protection of the natural environment in armed conflict and the protection of internally displaced persons in armed conflict. After finalization of the internal study the ICRC consulted States with a view to discovering to what extent the study's conclusions were broadly shared and to assess the possibility of strengthening legal protection for victims of armed conflicts in these areas.[64]

In summary, States who participated in a first round of bilateral consultations confirmed the main conclusion of the ICRC's study, that IHL remains as relevant today as ever before to ensuring protection to all victims of armed conflict. These States agreed that in most cases greater compliance with the existing legal framework is the best way to address the needs of victims. As a consequence, the adequacy of existing rules of IHL was strongly reaffirmed. The States consulted also broadly agreed on the analysis of the humanitarian concerns set out in the study; their views on how to address these concerns in legal terms varied, however, and therefore the best way to proceed remains open for discussion. States were not necessarily convinced that a treaty-making process was required. All options must be studied, including the preparation of soft-law instruments, the identification of best practices and the facilitation of expert processes aimed at clarifying existing rules. The consultation also showed that States were not entirely convinced that the law needed reinforcement in all the areas identified by the ICRC. They also indicated that it would not be realistic to work simultaneously on all four areas. Most States stressed that future discussions should focus in the near term on two areas: protection for persons deprived of liberty and mechanisms for monitoring compliance with IHL.

The ICRC submitted a report with the substantive findings and the results of the consultation with States to the 31st International Conference of the Red Cross and Red Crescent in November 2011.[65] It also proposed a draft resolution with a view to obtaining agreement of the members of the Conference (i.e., all States parties to the Geneva Conventions, all national Red Cross and Red Crescent Societies, the International Federation of Red Cross and Red Crescent Societies and the ICRC) for the way forward. The International Conference adopted resolution 1[66] by consensus, confirming the two priority areas for future work: protection for persons deprived of liberty and mechanisms for monitoring compliance with IHL. The main elements of the resolution relevant for this contribution on detention in NIAC state:

> The 31st International Conference of the Red Cross and Red Crescent, . . .
>
> *mindful of* the need to strengthen international humanitarian law, in particular through its reaffirmation in situations when it is not properly implemented and its clarification or development when it does not sufficiently meet the needs of the victims of armed conflict,[67] . . .

> 2. *acknowledges* that the report [submitted by the ICRC to the International Conference] identifies serious humanitarian concerns and challenges that need to be addressed, in particular those related to the protection of persons deprived of their liberty in relation to armed conflict . . . and that, on the basis of the consultations, the report calls for concrete and coordinated action to address these concerns;
>
> 3. *recognizes* the importance of analyzing the humanitarian concerns and military considerations related to the deprivation of liberty in relation to armed conflict with the aim, *inter alia*, of ensuring humane treatment, adequate conditions of detention, taking into account age, gender, disabilities and other factors that can increase vulnerability, and the requisite procedural and legal safeguards for persons detained, interned or transferred in relation to armed conflict;
>
> 4. *recognizes* . . . that further research, consultation and discussion are needed to assess the most appropriate way to ensure that international humanitarian law remains practical and relevant in providing legal protection to all persons deprived of their liberty in relation to armed conflict; . . .
>
> 6. *invites* the ICRC to pursue further research, consultation and discussion in cooperation with States and, if appropriate, other relevant actors, including international and regional organisations, to identify and propose a range of options and its recommendations to: i) ensure that international humanitarian law remains practical and relevant in providing legal protection to all persons deprived of their liberty in relation to armed conflict; . . . and *encourages* all members of the International Conference, including National Societies, to participate in this work while recognizing the primary role of States in the development of international humanitarian law; . . .
>
> 8. *invites* the ICRC to provide information on the progress of its work at regular intervals to all members of the International Conference and to submit a report on this work, with a range of options, to the 32nd International Conference of the Red Cross and Red Crescent, for its consideration and appropriate action.

Through this resolution the International Conference recognized the need to further assess how best to address the situation of persons deprived of liberty in NIAC. It gave a particular focus to ensuring humane treatment; adequate conditions of detention, taking into account age, gender, disabilities and other factors that can increase vulnerability; and the requisite procedural and legal safeguards for persons detained, interned or transferred during armed conflict. The ICRC will respond to the invitation expressed by the International Conference and continue further research, consultation and discussion in cooperation with States in that particular domain in order to identify and propose a range of options and its recommendations. In light of the many questions addressed in this article, work in this area will be important—but also challenging.

Notes

1. Convention for the Amelioration of the Condition of the Wounded and Sick in Armed Forces in the Field art. 3, Aug. 12, 1949, 6 U.S.T. 3114, 75 U.N.T.S. 31; Convention for the Amelioration of the Condition of Wounded, Sick and Shipwrecked Members of Armed Forces at Sea art. 3, Aug. 12, 1949, 6 U.S.T. 3217, 75 U.N.T.S. 85; Convention Relative to the Treatment of Prisoners of War art. 3, Aug. 12, 1949, 6 U.S.T. 3316, 75 U.N.T.S. 135 [hereinafter GC III]; Convention Relative to the Protection of Civilian Persons in Time of War art. 3, Aug. 12, 1949, 6 U.S.T. 3516, 75 U.N.T.S. 287 [hereinafter GC IV] [hereinafter, collectively, Common Article 3].

2. 1 CUSTOMARY INTERNATIONAL HUMANITARIAN LAW xxx, xliv–xlv (Jean-Marie Henckaerts & Louise Doswald-Beck eds., 2005) [hereinafter CUSTOMARY LAW STUDY]. *See also* Military and Paramilitary Activities in and against Nicaragua (Nicar. v. U.S.), 1986 I.C.J. 54, ¶ 218 (June 27) (holding that Common Article 3 reflected "elementary considerations of humanity" constituting a "minimum yardstick" applicable in all armed conflicts).

3. Common Article 3(1), *supra* note 1, provides "persons taking no active part in the hostilities, including members of armed forces who have laid down their arms and those placed *hors de combat* by . . . detention."

4. Protocol Additional to the Geneva Conventions of 12 August 1949, and Relating to the Protection of Victims of Non-International Armed Conflicts, June 8, 1977, 1125 U.N.T.S. 609 [hereinafter Additional Protocol II].

5. *Id.*, art. 4 ("all persons who do not take a direct part or who have ceased to take part in hostilities"); art. 5 ("persons deprived of their liberty for reasons related to the armed conflict, whether they are interned or detained"); art. 6 ("this Article applies to the prosecution and punishment of criminal offences related to the armed conflict").

6. *See* CUSTOMARY LAW STUDY, *supra* note 2. *See also* Jean-Marie Henckaerts, *Study on Customary International Humanitarian Law: A Contribution to the Understanding and Respect for the Rule of Law in Armed Conflict*, 87 INTERNATIONAL REVIEW OF THE RED CROSS 175 (2005), *available at* http://www.icrc.org/eng/assets/files/other/irrc_857_henckaerts.pdf.

7. U.N. Human Rights Committee, Consideration of Reports Submitted by States Parties Under Article 40 of the Covenant: Comments by the Government of the United States of America on the Concluding Observations of the Human Rights Committee, Addendum, 2–7, U.N. Doc. CCPR/C/USA/CO/3/Rev.1/Add.1 (Feb. 12, 2008). *See also* Fourth Periodic Report of the United States of America to the United Nations Human Rights Committee Concerning the International Covenant on Civil and Political Rights ¶¶ 504–9 (Dec. 30, 2011).

8. Legality of the Threat or Use of Nuclear Weapons, Advisory Opinion, 1996 I.C.J. 226, ¶ 25 (July 8); Legal Consequences of the Construction of a Wall in the Occupied Palestinian Territory, Advisory Opinion, 2004 I.C.J. 136, ¶¶ 102–14 (July 9) [hereinafter Legal Consequences of the Construction of a Wall]; Armed Activities on the Territory of the Congo (Dem. Rep. Congo v. Uganda), 2005 I.C.J. 1, ¶ 216 (Dec. 19) [hereinafter Armed Activities on the Territory of the Congo]; U.N. Human Rights Committee, General Comment No. 31: Nature of the General Legal Obligation Imposed on States Parties to the Covenant ¶ 4, U.N. Doc. CCPR/C/21/Rev.1/Add.13 (May 26, 2004) [hereinafter General Comment 31].

9. GC III, *supra* note 1.

10. GC IV, *supra* note 1.

11. The International Court of Justice (ICJ) in the *Legal Consequences of the Construction of a Wall* judgment, *supra* note 8, in paragraph 106, stated:

> As regards the relationship between international humanitarian law and human rights law, there are thus three possible situations: some rights may be exclusively matters of international humanitarian law; others may be exclusively matters of human rights law; yet others may be matters of both these branches of international law. In order to answer the question put to it, the Court will have to take into consideration both these branches of international law, namely human rights law and, as *lex specialis*, international humanitarian law.

The Court, however, was not called upon to elaborate further in terms of detention.

In the *Armed Activities on the Territory of the Congo* decision, *supra* note 8, paragraph 216, the ICJ recalled its advisory opinion in *Wall*, stating,

> "[T]he protection offered by human rights conventions does not cease in case of armed conflict, save through the effect of provisions for derogation of the kind to be found in Article 4 of the International Covenant on Civil and Political Rights. As regards the relationship between international humanitarian law and human rights law, there are thus three possible situations: some rights may be exclusively matters of international humanitarian law; others may be exclusively matters of human rights law; yet others may be matters of both these branches of international law." It thus concluded that both branches of international law, namely international human rights law and international humanitarian law, would have to be taken into consideration. The Court further concluded that international human rights instruments are applicable "in respect of acts done by a State in the exercise of its jurisdiction outside its own territory," particularly in occupied territories (citations omitted).

12. For further details, see INTERNATIONAL COMMITTEE OF THE RED CROSS, INTERNATIONAL HUMANITARIAN LAW AND THE CHALLENGES OF CONTEMPORARY ARMED CONFLICTS 18–20 (2011), *available at* http://www.icrc.org/eng/assets/files/red-cross-crescent-movement/31st-international-conference/31-int-conference-ihl-challenges-report-11-5-1-2-en.pdf [hereinafter IHL AND THE CHALLENGES OF CONTEMPORARY ARMED CONFLICTS].

13. *See infra* pp. 353–58.

14. *See, e.g.*, U.N. Economic & Social Council, Commission on Human Rights, Sub-Commission on the Promotion and Protection of Human Rights, Final Report of the Special Rapporteur, *Specific Human Rights Issues: New Priorities, in Particular Terrorism and Counter-terrorism* ¶¶ 54–55, U.N. Doc. E/CN.4/Sub.2/2004/40 (June 25, 2004) (by Kalliopi K. Koufa); Laura M. Olson, *Practical Challenges of Implementing the Complementarity between International Humanitarian and Human Rights Law—Demonstrated by the Procedural Regulation of Internment in Non-International Armed Conflict*, 40 CASE WESTERN RESERVE JOURNAL OF INTERNATIONAL LAW 437, 450 (2009); LINDSAY MOIR, THE LAW OF INTERNAL ARMED CONFLICT 194 (2002).

15. For further details, see IHL AND THE CHALLENGES OF CONTEMPORARY ARMED CONFLICTS, *supra* note 12, at 14–15; Jelena Pejic, *Conflict Classification and the Law Applicable to Detention and the Use of Force*, *in* INTERNATIONAL LAW AND THE CLASSIFICATION OF CONFLICTS (Elizabeth Wilmshurst ed., forthcoming Aug. 2012).

16. *See, e.g.*, Common Article 3, *supra* note 1 ("Persons taking no active part in the hostilities, including . . . those placed hors de combat by . . . detention . . . shall in all circumstances be treated humanely."); IHL AND THE CHALLENGES OF CONTEMPORARY ARMED CONFLICTS, *supra* note 12, at 15.

17. IHL AND THE CHALLENGES OF CONTEMPORARY ARMED CONFLICTS, *supra* note 12, at 15–18.

18. *See, e.g*, Common Article 3, *supra* note 1; GC III, *supra* note 1, art. 13; GC IV, *supra* note 1, art. 27; Protocol Additional to the Geneva Conventions of 12 August 1949, and Relating to the Protection of Victims of International Armed Conflicts art. 75, June 8, 1977, 1125 U.N.T.S. 3 [hereinafter Additional Protocol I]; Additional Protocol II, *supra* note 4, art. 4(2); International Covenant on Civil and Political Rights arts. 6–7, G.A. Res. 2200A (XXI), U.N. Doc. A/6316 (Dec. 16, 1966), 999 U.N.T.S. 171; Convention against Torture and Other Cruel, Inhuman or Degrading Treatment or Punishment, Dec. 10, 1984, 1465 U.N.T.S. 85; American Convention on Human Rights arts. 4–5, Nov. 22, 1969, O.A.S.T.S. No. 36, 1144 U.N.T.S. 123; Convention for the Protection of Human Rights and Fundamental Freedoms arts. 2–3, Nov. 4, 1950, Europ. T.S. No. 5, 213 U.N.T.S. 222; CUSTOMARY LAW STUDY, *supra* note 2.

19. Cordula Droege, *Transfers of Detainees: Legal Framework, Non-refoulement and Contemporary Challenges*, 90 INTERNATIONAL REVIEW OF THE RED CROSS 669, 700 (2008), *available at* http://www.icrc.org/eng/assets/files/other/irrc-871-droege2.pdf.

20. *Id.* at 675.

21. GC III, *supra* note 1, art. 12(2) ("Prisoners of war may only be transferred by the Detaining Power to a Power which is a party to the Convention and after the Detaining Power has satisfied itself of the willingness and ability of such transferee Power to apply the Convention. When prisoners of war are transferred under such circumstances, responsibility for the application of the Convention rests on the Power accepting them while they are in its custody.").

22. GC IV, *supra* note 1, art. 45(3) ("Protected persons may be transferred by the Detaining Power only to a Power which is a party to the present Convention and after the Detaining Power has satisfied itself of the willingness and ability of such transferee Power to apply the present Convention. If protected persons are transferred under such circumstances, responsibility for the application of the present Convention rests on the Power accepting them, while they are in its custody. Nevertheless, if that Power fails to carry out the provisions of the present Convention in any important respect, the Power by which the protected persons were transferred shall, upon being so notified by the Protecting Power, take effective measures to correct the situation or shall request the return of the protected persons. Such request must be complied with.").

23. INTERNATIONAL COMMITTEE OF THE RED CROSS, STRENGTHENING LEGAL PROTECTION FOR VICTIMS OF ARMED CONFLICTS 11–12 (2011), *available at* http://www.rcrcconference.org/docs_upl/en/31IC_Strengthening_legal_protection.EN.pdf.

24. IHL AND THE CHALLENGES OF CONTEMPORARY ARMED CONFLICTS, *supra* note 12, at 16.

25. *See, e.g.*, GC III, *supra* note 1, arts. 21–38; GC IV, *supra* note 1, arts. 83–95; CUSTOMARY LAW STUDY, *supra* note 2, Rules 118–28.

26. *See* Additional Protocol II, *supra* note 4, art. 5; CUSTOMARY LAW STUDY, *supra* note 2, Rules 118–28.

27. *See* U.N. Economic & Social Council, Standard Minimum Rules for the Treatment of Prisoners, U.N. Doc. A/CONF/611 (Aug. 30, 1955) (adopted by the First United Nations Congress on the Prevention of Crime and the Treatment of Offenders), approved by U.N. Economic and Social Council, E.S.C. Res. 663 C (XXIV), U.N. Doc. E/RES/3048 (July 31, 1957), amended by E.S.C. 2076 (LXII), U.N. Doc. E/5988 (May 13, 1977); Principles for the Treatment of Prisoners, G.A. Res. 45/111, U.N. Doc. A/RES/45/111 (Dec. 14, 1990).

28. *See* Jelena Pejic, *The Protective Scope of Common Article 3: More Than Meets the Eye*, 93 INTERNATIONAL REVIEW OF THE RED CROSS 189, 216–19 (2011), *available at* http://www.icrc.org/eng/assets/files/review/2011/irrc-881-pejic.pdf.

29. STRENGTHENING LEGAL PROTECTION FOR VICTIMS OF ARMED CONFLICTS, *supra* note 23, at 10.

30. *Id.*

31. Additional Protocol I, *supra* note 18, art. 5(2)(a).

32. CUSTOMARY LAW STUDY, *supra* note 2, Rule 120.

33. Additional Protocol I, *supra* note 18.

34. *See, e.g.*, COMMENTARY ON THE ADDITIONAL PROTOCOLS OF 8 JUNE 1977 TO THE GENEVA CONVENTIONS OF 12 AUGUST 1949, ¶ 3092 (Yves Sandoz, Christophe Swinarski & Bruno Zimmermann eds., 1987) ("[m]ost of the guarantees listed in sub-paragraphs (a)–(j) [of Article 75(4)] are contained in the . . . Covenant on Human Rights"); MICHAEL BOTHE, KARL JOSEF PARTSCH & WALDEMAR A. SOLF, NEW RULES FOR VICTIMS OF ARMED CONFLICTS: COMMENTARY ON THE TWO 1977 PROTOCOLS ADDITIONAL TO THE GENEVA CONVENTIONS OF 1949, at 463 ¶ 2.17 (1982).

35. CUSTOMARY LAW STUDY, *supra* note 2, Rule 100.

36. IHL AND THE CHALLENGES OF CONTEMPORARY ARMED CONFLICTS, *supra* note 12, at 16.

37. *See infra* pp. 354–55.

38. *Id.*

39. International Commission of Jurists, The Berlin Declaration: Upholding Human Rights and the Rule of Law in Combating Terrorism, Principle 6 (Aug. 28, 2004), *available at* http://www.icj.org/dwn/database/BerlinDeclaration2004-ENG.pdf; U.N. Human Rights Committee, Consideration of Reports Submitted by States Parties Under Article 40 of the Covenant: Comments of the Human Rights Committee, ¶ 16, U.N. Doc. CCPR/C/79/Add.35 (Aug. 10, 1994); U.N. Human Rights Committee, Consideration of Reports Submitted by States Parties Under Article 40 of the Covenant: Comments of the Human Rights Committee, ¶ 21, U.N. Doc. CCPR/C/79/Add.44 (Nov. 23, 1994). In the European context, administrative detention is only possible if the State has derogated from Article 5 of the Convention for the Protection of Human Rights and Fundamental Freedoms, *supra* note 18, in accordance with Article 15. Lawless v. Ireland, 3 Eur. Ct. H.R. (ser. A) ¶¶ 13–20 (1961); Ireland v. United Kingdom, 2 Eur. Ct. H.R. (ser. A) ¶¶ 194–96, 214 (1978). Even in NIACs experts have adopted a view that internment is an exceptional measure. *See Expert Meeting on Procedural Safeguards for Security Detention in Non-International Armed Conflict*, 91 INTERNATIONAL REVIEW OF THE RED CROSS 859, 863–64 (2009), *available at* http://www.icrc.org/eng/assets/files/other/irrc-876-expert-meeting.pdf [hereinafter Expert Meeting on Procedural Safeguards]; Tyler Davidson & Kathleen Gibson, *Expert Meeting on Security Detention Report*, 40 CASE WESTERN RESERVE JOURNAL OF INTERNATIONAL LAW 315, 326–27 (2009).

40. IHL AND THE CHALLENGES OF CONTEMPORARY ARMED CONFLICTS, *supra* note 12, at 16.

41. *Id.* at 17.

42. *Id.*; Expert Meeting on Procedural Safeguards, *supra* note 39, at 866–68.

43. IHL AND THE CHALLENGES OF CONTEMPORARY ARMED CONFLICTS, *supra* note 12, at 17–18; Expert Meeting on Procedural Safeguards, *supra* note 39, at 880–81.

44. U.N. Human Rights Committee, General Comment No. 29, Statement of Emergency (Article 4), ¶ 16, CCPR/C/21/Rev.1/Add.11 (Aug. 31, 1994).

45. IHL AND THE CHALLENGES OF CONTEMPORARY ARMED CONFLICTS, *supra* note 12, at 18; Expert Meeting on Procedural Safeguards, *supra* note 39, at 881; Laura M. Olson & Marco Sassòli, *The Relationship between International Humanitarian and Human Rights Law Where It Matters: Admissible Killing and Internment of Fighters in Non-international Armed Conflicts*, 90 INTERNATIONAL REVIEW OF THE RED CROSS 599, 622 (2008), *available at* http://www.icrc.org/eng/assets/files/other/irrc-871-sassoli-olsen.pdf.

46. Pejic, *supra* note 15.

47. *See* General Comment 31, ¶ 10, *supra* note 8 ("States Parties are required by article 2, paragraph 1, to respect and to ensure the Covenant rights to all persons who may be within their territory and to all persons subject to their jurisdiction. This means that a State Party must respect and ensure the rights laid down in the Covenant to anyone within the power or effective control of that State Party, even if not situated within the territory of the State Party. . . . This principle also applies to those within the power or effective control of the forces of a State Party acting outside its territory, regardless of the circumstances in which such power or effective control was obtained, such as forces constituting a national contingent of a State Party assigned to an international peace-keeping or peace-enforcement operation."). *See also* Cordula Droege, *Elective Affinities? Human Rights and Humanitarian Law*, 90 INTERNATIONAL REVIEW OF THE RED CROSS 501, 510–13 (2008).

48. It should be noted, however, that the European Court of Human Rights has taken positions in the field of detention abroad, although it has been criticized for some of its findings.

49. U.N. Charter, ch. VII.

50. Expert Meeting on Procedural Safeguards, *supra* note 39, at 868–69. For practice on detention by multinational forces, see Ashley S. Deeks, *Security Detention: The International Legal Framework: Administrative Detention in Armed Conflict*, 40 CASE WESTERN RESERVE JOURNAL OF INTERNATIONAL LAW 403, 415–22 (2009), citing Press Release, Kosovo Force ['KFOR'], KFOR Detention Under UNSCR 1244, 04-28 (May 5, 2004), *available at* http://www.nato.int/kfor/docu/pr/2004/05/28.htm (stating KFOR derived the authority to detain individuals from UN Security Council Resolution 1244, which authorized KFOR to use all necessary means to maintain and secure a safe environment). The Danish Ministry of Foreign Affairs argued in a non-paper presented at the Copenhagen Conference on the handling of detainees in international military operations that although a legal basis for detention can be derived from a UN Security Council resolution giving a mandate to use all necessary means, it is preferable for the resolution to clearly establish such a legal basis in order to avoid different interpretations of the mandate. Ministry of Foreign Affairs Legal Service, *Non-Paper on Legal Framework and Aspects of Detention* 10 (Oct. 4, 2007), *available at* http://www.afghanistan.um.dk/NR/rdonlyres/F5364962-DC30-4333-9EFC-1B612B43DC28/0/NonpaperCopenhagenConference.pdf.

51. Droege, *supra* note 19, at 690–91.

52. The institutional guidelines were published as Annex 1 to an ICRC report, *International Humanitarian Law and the Challenges of Contemporary Armed Conflicts*, presented at the 30th International Conference of the Red Cross and Red Crescent, held in Geneva in 2007. The guidelines were also published in Jelena Pejic, *Procedural Principles and Safeguards for Internment/Administrative Detention in Armed Conflict and Other Situations of Violence*, 87 INTERNATIONAL REVIEW OF THE RED CROSS 375 (2005), *available at* http://www.icrc.org/eng/assets/files/other/irrc_858_pejic.pdf [hereinafter Procedural Principles and Safeguards for Internment/Administrative Detention).

53. *Id.* at 383.

54. Expert Meeting on Procedural Safeguards, *supra* note 39, at 864; Text of letters from the Prime Minister of the Interim Government of Iraq Dr. Ayad Allawi and United States Secretary of State Colin L. Powell to the President of the Council, annexed to S.C. Res. 1546, U.N. Doc. S/RES/1546 (June 8, 2004).

55. *See* IHL AND THE CHALLENGES OF CONTEMPORARY ARMED CONFLICTS, *supra* note 12, at 42–45. For a discussion of direct participation of hostilities, see NILS MELZER, INTERNATIONAL COMMITTEE OF THE RED CROSS, INTERPRETIVE GUIDANCE ON THE NOTION OF DIRECT PARTICIPATION IN HOSTILITIES UNDER INTERNATIONAL HUMANITARIAN LAW (2009), *available at* http://www.icrc.org/eng/assets/files/other/icrc-002-0990.pdf.

56. *See* IHL AND THE CHALLENGES OF CONTEMPORARY ARMED CONFLICTS, *supra* note 12, at 42–45.

57. *See supra* note 52.

58. Procedural Principles and Safeguards for Internment/Administrative Detention, *supra* note 52, at 380.

59. *Id.* at 382.

60. Pejic, *supra* note 15.

61. Procedural Principles and Safeguards for Internment/Administrative Detention, *supra* note 52, at 387.

62. *Id.* at 388.

63. For a discussion of the study process, see STRENGTHENING LEGAL PROTECTION FOR VICTIMS OF ARMED CONFLICTS, *supra* note 23, at 4–9. See *id.* at 4–5 and 8–24 for a discussion of the normative gaps.

64. *See id.* at 4, 24–29.

65. *Id.*

66. 31st International Conference of the Red Cross and Red Crescent, Resolution: Strengthening Legal Protection for Victims of Armed Conflicts, Res. 31IC/11/R1 (Nov. 28–Dec. 1, 2011), *available at* http://www.rcrcconference.org/docs_upl/en/R1_Strengthening_IHL_EN.pdf.

67. This paragraph indicated in general terms the possible ways of acting without expressing a preference with regard to the priority. The priority areas were identified later in the resolution.

PART VIII

ENFORCEMENT IN NON-INTERNATIONAL ARMED CONFLICTS

XVII

International Enforcement in Non-International Armed Conflict: Searching for Synergy among Legal Regimes in the Case of Libya

John Cerone*

In mid-February 2011, in the wake of popular uprisings in Tunisia and Egypt, members of the Libyan public began protesting against the decades-old regime of Libyan leader Muammar Gaddafi. The situation rapidly escalated as the government sought to forcibly suppress the demonstrations. By early March the situation had deteriorated into an armed conflict.

A number of international organizations responded to the crisis in Libya as it evolved. They utilized a variety of different tools, ranging from official statements and press communiqués to the adoption of sanctions and other legal measures. On March 19, 2011, a coalition of States initiated a bombing campaign in Libya. The United Nations Security Council authorized this enforcement action in response to reports of serious violations of international human rights law and the international law of armed conflict committed in Libya by persons acting on behalf of the Gaddafi regime.

* Professor of Law and Director, Center for International Law & Policy, New England Law | Boston.

This article provides an overview of applicable rules of international law through different phases of the situation in Libya and sketches out various modes of enforcement action employed by international organizations to respond to the crisis, analyzing several of the controversial legal issues that arise in that context. The article concludes with an analysis of the unresolved legal issues implicated by the evolving situation in Libya and by the international community's responses to it.

Applicable Law

Non-intervention

One of the foundational principles of the international legal order, and a corollary to the equally fundamental principle of the sovereign equality of States, the principle of non-intervention requires all States to refrain from interfering in the internal affairs of other States, or, in the words of the UN Charter, in "matters which are essentially within the domestic jurisdiction" of other States.[1] While the scope of this principle was traditionally understood to preclude international regulation of the way in which a State treated its own people, that understanding has evolved considerably since, at the latest, the advent of the UN Charter system.

In light of the human rights provisions of the UN Charter and the practice of Charter bodies, it is now generally accepted that serious human rights abuses, even if committed purely within a State (i.e., not involving aliens, foreign territory or any other material interests of other States), are no longer regarded as internal matters shielded by the principle of non-intervention. Most States are also parties to specific human rights treaties, further internationalizing the issue of how they treat their own people and correspondingly diminishing the scope of the principle of non-intervention. Nonetheless, mere political wrangling, even if it involves the failure to meet international expectations of good governance, remains a purely internal matter so long as it does not entail violations of international legal obligations.

The Use of Force/*Jus ad Bellum*

Another fundamental rule of international law is the prohibition on the use of force. Article 2(4) of the UN Charter provides that "[a]ll Members shall refrain in their international relations from the threat or use of force against the territorial integrity or political independence of any State, or in any other manner inconsistent with the Purposes of the United Nations." The two established exceptions to this prohibition are valid exercises of the right of self-defense and enforcement action taken in accordance with UN Security Council authorization.[2] These international rules on the use of force apply only between States. Thus, the prohibition on the use of force does not apply internally to a State.[3]

The Law of State Responsibility for Injury to Aliens

This body of international law regulates the way States treat foreigners. It provides for a baseline of humane treatment, essentially protecting foreigners against serious human rights abuses, denials of justice and other unjustified deprivations of liberty or property. Embedded in the traditional State-centric international legal system, the responsibility of the wrongdoing State, in general, may be invoked only by the State of nationality of the victim.[4]

The Law of Armed Conflict/*Jus in Bello*/International Humanitarian Law

The international law of armed conflict regulates the conduct of hostilities and provides legal protections for individuals not—or no longer—taking part in the hostilities. As such, the vast majority of its provisions apply only in times of armed conflict or occupation. Prior to World War II, the *jus in bello* generally applied to inter-State armed conflicts. Starting with the Geneva Conventions of 1949[5] it also began to regulate non-international armed conflicts, including purely internal armed conflicts. With the advent of international regulation of non-international armed conflict came the direct applicability of international humanitarian law to non-State, organized armed groups.[6] While international law still provides more extensive regulation of inter-State armed conflicts than of non-inter-State armed conflicts, the extent of difference has diminished.

International Criminal Law in the Strict Sense

International criminal law in the strict sense refers to those rules of international law the breach of which gives rise to individual criminal responsibility in international law.[7] These rules of international law directly bind individuals, as opposed to operating through the vehicle of domestic law (e.g., suppression treaties). The core crimes in international criminal law are war crimes, genocide, crimes against humanity and aggression. As Libya is not a party to the Statute of the International Criminal Court (ICC), Libyan nationals committing acts entirely within Libya are bound only by those international criminal prohibitions that have acquired the status of customary international law. Most, but not all, of the crimes prohibited by the ICC Statute were prohibited by customary international law during the relevant period.

International Human Rights Law

International human rights law, in general, regulates the way a State treats individuals under its control by requiring States to respect and ensure certain fundamental rights of the human person.[8] As noted above, the evolution of this relatively modern body of international law has greatly reduced the scope of the non-intervention principle in relation to a State's conduct toward its own people.

Unlike the areas of international law identified above, human rights law is principally treaty-based. Libya has been a party to several universal and regional human rights treaties since well before the 2011 unrest. Libya is a party to, *inter alia*, the International Covenant on Civil and Political Rights (ICCPR)[9] and its first Optional Protocol,[10] the International Covenant on Economic, Social and Cultural Rights,[11] the Convention on the Rights of the Child,[12] the Convention on the Elimination of All Forms of Racial Discrimination,[13] the Convention on the Elimination of All Forms of Discrimination Against Women[14] and the African Charter on Human and Peoples' Rights.[15]

The ICCPR is subject to derogation. Under Article 4 of the ICCPR, States parties may take measures derogating from certain obligations under the Covenant to the extent strictly necessary to respond to a "public emergency which threatens the life of the nation." Among the derogable rights are the rights to freedom of expression, to freedom of movement, to freedom from arbitrary detention and to a fair trial.[16] States parties must officially proclaim a state of emergency and must notify other States parties through the intermediary of the UN Secretary-General.[17] According to available UN records, at no time during the 2011 unrest did Libya lodge a notice of derogation with the Secretary-General.

Phases of the Conflict and Modes of International Enforcement

Prior to the February Unrest

Prior to the unrest, the applicable law included all of the above bodies of international law, except for the law of armed conflict, and those rules of international criminal law derived from the law of armed conflict since there was no armed conflict in existence. Libya was fully bound by its obligations under all of the human rights treaties to which it was a party and also by norms of customary human rights law.[18] Similarly, Libya was bound by the requirements of the law of State responsibility for injury to aliens in its relations with foreigners (particularly those within its territory). Libya and individuals within Libya were also under an obligation to refrain from committing the international crimes of genocide and crimes against humanity. Other States, in their relations with Libya, were bound by the prohibition on the use of force and the principle of non-intervention. States were obliged to refrain from interfering in the internal functioning of the Libyan political system, at least to the extent that its functioning did not contravene Libya's international obligations owed to those States.[19]

February Unrest

By mid-February a series of protests broke out across Libya. Once the unrest in Libya reached the point of a "public emergency which threaten[ed] the life of the nation," Libya could have claimed an authority to derogate from some of its obligations under the ICCPR to the extent "strictly required by the exigencies of the situation."[20] This would have permitted the Libyan government a freer hand in arrest and detention matters, as well as in restricting the freedom of expression, the freedom of movement and the freedom of association. As noted above, Libya did not provide notice of derogation to the treaty depositary. Nonetheless, there is some authority to suggest that the failure to notify does not of itself preclude the lawfulness of derogation.[21] While in principle most of the rights in the ICCPR are derogable, the burden would be on Libya to demonstrate the necessity for each restriction imposed.[22]

In any event, reports soon emerged of violations of non-derogable rights, such as the right to life and to freedom from torture. The gravity of the reported violations brought the matter beyond the internal sphere, and gave standing to other States and international organizations to invoke the international responsibility of Libya. Notwithstanding these violations, at this stage recognition of any entity other than the Gaddafi regime as the government of Libya would likely still have constituted a prohibited intervention in Libyan internal affairs. The use of force against Libya remained prohibited. Notwithstanding the emerging notion of the responsibility to protect, which may provide enhanced standing to take diplomatic measures or economic sanctions, the use of force remained precluded absent Security Council authorization.[23] The use of force could not be justified on the basis of collective self-defense since the protesters, as non-State actors, had no international legal right of self-defense under the *jus ad bellum*.

February 25: UN Human Rights Council Special Session

One of the first organizations to adopt operative measures was the UN Human Rights Council. On February 25, 2011, the Council convened a special session on the "situation of human rights in the Libyan Arab Jamahiriya." This was the fifteenth special session of the Council since its creation in 2006. One of the advances of the Council over its predecessor, the UN Commission on Human Rights, is the relative ease of convening special sessions. While the Commission required the support of a majority of members, the Council can convene a special session with the support of only one-third of its members.

Several others factors contributed to the convening of this special session. Libya was at the time a member of the Human Rights Council. In addition, as noted above, Libya is a party to a number of international human rights treaties. There was thus a clear legal basis for invoking Libya's international responsibility. Lastly, the Libyan ambassador to the Human Rights Council had by this time ceased to support the Gaddafi government and supported the convening of the special session.

In its Resolution S-15/1 of February 25, 2011, the Human Rights Council decided to establish an international commission of inquiry and to recommend that Libya be suspended from the Council.

After recalling official statements on the situation made by other UN bodies, the Arab League, the Organization of the Islamic Conference, the African Union and the European Union, the Human Rights Council strongly condemned the "gross and systematic" human rights violations being committed in Libya, and suggested that some of the abuses might rise to the level of crimes against humanity.[24] It also "strongly call[ed] upon" the government of Libya to fulfill its "responsibility to protect" its population; to comply with its human rights obligations, placing particular emphasis on the freedoms of expression, assembly and information;[25] and to "stop any attacks against civilians."[26]

The Human Rights Council urged the Libyan government to "respect the popular will, aspirations and demands of its people and to make [its] utmost efforts to prevent further deterioration of the crisis."[27] The Council also stressed the need to hold accountable "those responsible for attacks in [Libya], including by forces under Government control, on civilians."[28] In addition, it reminded Libya of its commitment, as a member of the Council, "to uphold the highest standards in the promotion and protection of human rights and to cooperate fully with the Council and its special procedures."[29]

The Council then decided to "urgently dispatch an independent, international commission of inquiry . . . to investigate all alleged violations of international human rights law in [Libya], to establish the facts and circumstances of such violations and of the crimes perpetrated and, where possible, to identify those responsible." Its express purpose was to ensure "that those individuals responsible are held accountable."[30]

Finally, the Council recommended to its parent body, the UN General Assembly, that Libya's "rights of membership" in the Council be suspended, "in view of the gross and systematic violations of human rights by the Libyan authorities."[31]

February 26: UN Security Council Emergency Meeting

On February 26, the day after the special session of the Human Rights Council, the UN Security Council convened an emergency meeting. The Security Council unanimously adopted Resolution 1970[32] under Chapter VII of the UN Charter and took binding measures under Article 41 of the Charter, including the imposition of an arms embargo, a travel ban and an asset freeze. It also referred the situation in Libya to the ICC.[33] As with the Libyan ambassador to the Human Rights Council, the ambassador of Libya to the United Nations had ceased to support the Gaddafi government and spoke in support of the Security Council resolution.

The preambular paragraphs of the Security Council resolution refer to the "gross and systematic violations of human rights" taking place,[34] as well as serious violations of "international humanitarian law."[35] The reference to "international humanitarian law" may indicate a perception that the situation in Libya had by this time evolved into an armed conflict.[36] Mirroring language employed by the Human Rights Council, the Security Council also recalled "the Libyan authorities' responsibility to protect its population,"[37] evoking the "responsibility to protect" concept and perhaps implying further consequences for continued failure to fulfill that responsibility.

The Security Council welcomed the work of the Human Rights Council and reiterated its call for accountability, emphasizing the responsibility of superiors.[38] It then recalled the Security Council's own power to defer ICC prosecutions, perhaps telegraphing an incentive to cooperate.[39] In this respect, Article 16 of the ICC Statute provides that the Security Council may defer an ICC prosecution for up to twelve months, with the possibility of renewal.

The resolution's operative language begins with the Council's demand for an immediate end to the violence and its call for steps to fulfill the "legitimate demands of the population."[40] It urges the Libyan authorities to comply with international human rights and humanitarian law,[41] to ensure the safety of foreign nationals, to ensure the safe passage of humanitarian supplies and workers, and to "[i]mmediately lift restrictions on all forms of media."[42]

The Security Council's referral of the situation to the ICC marks the first time that the referral power has been used with the unanimous support of Council members. The only other Security Council referral to date, that of the situation in Darfur, was not unanimously supported. Both China and the United States abstained in that vote. China had also been a holdout for the Libya resolution, but was ultimately persuaded to vote in favor of the resolution. The Chinese delegation indicated that it supported the resolution "taking into account the special circumstances in Libya."[43]

The ICC referral is followed by a jurisdictional exclusion similar to that included in the Darfur referral. It provides that

> nationals, current or former officials or personnel from a State outside the Libyan Arab Jamahiriya which is not a party to the Rome Statute of the International Criminal Court shall be subject to the exclusive jurisdiction of that State for all alleged acts or

> omissions arising out of or related to operations in the Libyan Arab Jamahiriya established or authorized by the Council, unless such exclusive jurisdiction has been expressly waived by the State.[44]

By its terms this provision would seem to exclude not only ICC jurisdiction, but any jurisdiction other than that of the non–State party. Some delegations have disagreed with this interpretation, opining instead that it only excludes ICC jurisdiction.

The resolution also provided that the ICC's expenses in this matter shall be borne by the ICC States parties and those States that wish to contribute voluntarily. The resolution created a new Sanctions Committee to, *inter alia*, monitor implementation of the sanctions, designate individuals subject to the measures, consider requests for exemptions and report back to the Council.

March 1: UN General Assembly Suspends Libya's Rights of Membership in the Human Rights Council

Acting on the recommendation of the Human Rights Council, the UN General Assembly on March 1, 2011, in Resolution 65/265, suspended Libya's "rights of membership" in the Human Rights Council.[45] This was the first time the General Assembly had used its authority to suspend a State.

March 3: ICC Prosecutor Opens Investigation

On March 3, 2011, the ICC Prosecutor announced his decision to open an investigation into alleged crimes against humanity committed in Libya since February 15.[46] In his statement, he also identified certain individuals with "formal or de facto authority, who commanded and had control over the forces that allegedly committed the crimes," and thus "put them on notice" that they could be held criminally responsible if forces under their command committed crimes. In particular, he singled out Muammar Gaddafi, the Minister of Foreign Affairs, the head of Regime Security and Military Intelligence, the head of Gaddafi's Personal Security and the head of the Libyan External Security Organization. He further indicated that members of opposition groups would also be subject to investigation if they committed crimes.

He concludes by stating, "It is important to avoid an armed conflict in Libya." One could read this statement to mean that the ICC Prosecutor's position at that time was that the situation in Libya had not yet reached the necessary levels of violence, organization and duration to constitute an armed conflict. There is no mention of war crimes in the March 3 statement.

Early March: Emergence of Armed Conflict

By early March, at the latest, at least some of the forces opposing the Gaddafi regime had constituted themselves as organized armed groups. In addition, the violence between the government and these groups became sufficiently protracted and intense to constitute armed conflict, leading to the application of the law of non-international armed conflict.[47] The application of the *jus in bello* also brings about the application of the relevant war crimes provisions of international criminal law.

March 12: Arab League Calls for the Use of Force

At its meeting in Cairo on March 12, 2011, the Council of the Arab League issued a statement on the implications of the events in Libya and the Arab position.[48] Most significantly, the Arab League called upon the UN Security Council to impose a no-fly zone and to create "safe areas." The members of the Security Council had already been discussing the possibility of the use of armed force. In this context, the political support of the Arab League was seen as a key factor.

In the preamble the League called for compliance with international law and an end to the fighting. It also called on the Libyan authorities to withdraw from the areas they "entered forcibly" and to ensure "the right of the Libyan people to fulfill their demands and build their own future and institutions in a democratic framework."[49]

The League Council then recalled its commitment "to reject all forms of foreign intervention in Libya," but emphasized "that the failure to take necessary actions to end this crisis will lead to foreign intervention in internal Libyan affairs."[50] It then decided to call upon the Security Council "to take the necessary measures to impose immediately a no-fly zone on Libyan military aviation, and to establish safe areas in places exposed to shelling as a precautionary measure that allows the protection of the Libyan people and foreign nationals residing in Libya . . . ."[51]

March 17: Security Council Authorizes the Use of Force

On March 17, 2011, the UN Security Council, again using its enforcement power under Chapter VII of the UN Charter, responded to the call by imposing a no-fly zone and authorizing the use of armed force to protect civilians and "civilian populated areas under threat of attack."[52] Resolution 1973 also expanded the existing sanctions and established a Panel of Experts to assist the Sanctions Committee.

The resolution was adopted with a vote of ten in favor and five abstentions. The abstentions came from the BRIC countries (Brazil, Russia, India and China) and Germany. The two permanent members that abstained—Russia and China—have traditionally espoused robust interpretations of the non-intervention principle.[53] The abstaining delegations cited a lack of information, the failure to exhaust diplomatic means, ambiguity as to how force would be used and by whom, and doubts as to whether the use of force would effectively achieve the Council's purposes.[54]

The operative text of the resolution begins with the Council's demand for the immediate establishment of a ceasefire and a "complete end to violence and all attacks against, and abuses of, civilians."[55] The Council also demanded that Libya comply with its obligations under international human rights law, humanitarian law and refugee law, and "take all measures to protect civilians and meet their basic needs," as well as to ensure the delivery of humanitarian aid.[56]

In operative paragraph 4, the Council authorized the use of armed force to protect civilians and civilian populated areas, while excluding military occupation. Specifically, it authorized

> Member States that have notified the Secretary-General, acting nationally or through regional organizations or arrangements, and acting in cooperation with the Secretary-General, to take all necessary measures . . . to protect civilians and civilian populated areas under threat of attack in the Libyan Arab Jamahiriya, including Benghazi, while excluding a foreign occupation force of any form on any part of Libyan territory.

This broad grant of authority was narrowed by the requirements of "acting in cooperation with the Secretary-General," the limitation to protection of "civilians"[57] and areas "under threat of attack,"[58] and the exclusion of occupation.[59]

The resolution also established a no-fly zone in Libyan airspace "in order to protect civilians," providing exemptions for humanitarian flights and authorizing member States to use armed force to enforce it.[60]

In addition to strengthening enforcement of the arms embargo, the resolution also expanded the asset freeze. Mindful that a new Libyan government would need these assets, the Council "[a]ffirm[ed] its determination to ensure that assets frozen . . . shall, at a later stage, as soon as possible be made available to and for the benefit of the people of the Libyan Arab Jamahiriya."[61]

Finally, the Security Council used its power to bind States to deprive the Libyan government, and those acting on its behalf, of legal remedies that might otherwise be available for breach of contract under domestic law. Operative paragraph 27 requires "all States"[62] to take "the necessary measures to ensure that no claim shall lie at the instance of the Libyan authorities . . . in connection with any contract or other transaction where its performance was affected by reason of the measures taken by the Security Council . . . ."

March 19: Coalition Airstrikes Begin

On March 19, armed forces of France, the United States, the United Kingdom and others initiated military strikes in Libya pursuant to Security Council Resolution 1973. The intervention of other States' armed forces brought into application the law of international armed conflict.[63]

On March 27, the North Atlantic Council decided that NATO would undertake enforcement action in Libya.[64] Control of the enforcement action in Libya was subsequently transferred to NATO under unified command.

March 25: African Court of Human and Peoples' Rights Orders Provisional Measures

On March 25, 2011, the African Court of Human and Peoples' Rights unanimously ordered provisional measures against Libya.[65] The proceedings were instituted by the African Commission on Human and Peoples' Rights, which lodged an application with the Court after receiving a number of complaints alleging violations of the African Charter on Human and Peoples' Rights by Libya, a State party.

The Commission did not request the Court to order provisional measures. Nonetheless, the Court recalled that it is "empowered to order provisional measures *proprio motu* 'in cases of extreme gravity and urgency and when necessary to avoid irreparable harm to persons' and 'which it deems necessary to adopt in the interest of the parties or of justice.'"[66]

After satisfying itself, *prima facie*, that it had jurisdiction, the Court reviewed statements and resolutions of relevant international organizations. In light of the condemnations of abuses contained therein, the Court concluded that "there is therefore a situation of extreme gravity and urgency, as well as a risk of irreparable harm to persons who are the subject of the application, in particular, in relation to the rights to life and to physical integrity of persons as guaranteed in the [African] Charter."[67]

The Court then found that the circumstances required it to order, "as a matter of great urgency and without any proceedings,"[68] the following provisional measures: (1) that Libya refrain from "any action that would result in loss of life or violation of physical integrity of persons, which could be a breach of the provisions of the Charter or of other international human rights instruments to which it is a party"; and (2) that Libya report to the Court within fifteen days on measures taken to implement the order.[69]

The first provisional measure ordered is somewhat unclear. Use of the term "could" introduces a degree of ambiguity. Further, it is unclear whether the dependent clause beginning with "which" describes or qualifies the preceding clause. It is likely that it qualifies the preceding clause, so that only those actions that constitute a breach (or "could" constitute a breach) of human rights law are encompassed by the order.

Mid-April: Concern about NATO Interpretation of Mandate

By mid-April, some States, including Security Council permanent members Russia and China, began to claim that the multinational force was exceeding the scope of its mandate.[70] In particular, they recalled that regime change was not authorized by Security Council Resolution 1973. According to some observers, NATO's airstrikes went beyond protection of civilians and potentially constituted a violation of the prohibition on the use of force.

May 4: ICC Prosecutor Presents Report to the Security Council

Pursuant to operative paragraph 7 of Security Council Resolution 1970, the ICC Prosecutor on May 4 reported to the Security Council on actions taken pursuant to the referral of the situation in Libya to the ICC.[71] In his report, the Prosecutor provided an overview of the preliminary examination of jurisdictional issues conducted by his office, the ongoing investigation and anticipated judicial activities.

The Prosecutor found that available information provided "reasonable grounds to believe that crimes against humanity have been committed and continue being committed in Libya,"[72] and he noted that there is also "relevant information concerning" war crimes "once the situation developed into an armed conflict."[73]

As to admissibility of the complaint, the Prosecutor indicated that his office had "not found any genuine national investigation or prosecution of the persons or conduct that would form the subject matter of the cases it will investigate."[74] He also found that the situation "clearly meets the threshold of gravity required by the ICC Statute, taking into account all relevant criteria."[75] He noted that there were no countervailing "reasons to believe that the investigation would not serve the interests of justice,"[76] and thus opened an investigation on March 3.

In describing the ongoing investigation, the Prosecutor stated that his office was pursuing those who bore the greatest responsibility. He also referred to cooperation activities and reported receiving "outstanding support from States Parties and non–States Parties alike."

After enumerating the type and quantity of evidence collected, he indicated that this evidence revealed two main types of "incidents": (1) "[s]ecurity forces allegedly attacking unarmed civilians constituting crimes against humanity," and (2) "[t]he existence of an armed conflict with alleged war crimes as well as other crimes against humanity that appear to have been committed by different Parties."[77] He then surveyed specific factual allegations supporting the existence of these types of crimes, including excessive use of force by security forces; "[s]ystematic arrests, torture, killings, deportations, enforced disappearances and destruction of mosques";[78] rape; and "unlawful arrest, mistreatment and killings of sub-Saharan Africans perceived to be mercenaries."[79]

As to the anticipated judicial proceedings, the Prosecutor indicated that his office would soon be submitting its first application for an arrest warrant. On May 16, the ICC Prosecutor requested a pretrial chamber to issue arrest warrants for three individuals, including Muammar Gaddafi.

June 1: Commission of Inquiry Issues Report

On June 1, 2011, the Commission of Inquiry, established pursuant to Human Rights Council Resolution S-15/1, issued its report.[80] The Commission opined that "a significant number of international human rights law violations have occurred, as well as war crimes and crimes against humanity." According to the Commission, the large majority of violations were committed by those acting on behalf of the Gaddafi regime "in the pursuit of a systematic and widespread policy of repression against opponents to his regime and his leadership." In addition, the report noted that "[t]here have also been violations by opponents to the regime."

As to methodology, the Commission "opted for a cautious approach in the present report by consistently referring to the information obtained as being distinguishable from evidence that could be used in criminal proceedings, whether national or international." Despite its findings of numerous violations of human rights, humanitarian and international criminal law, the "commission feels that, at this stage, it is not in a position to identify those responsible, as requested by the Human Rights Council in the resolution establishing its mandate."

June 27: ICC Pretrial Chamber Issues Arrest Warrants

On June 27, ICC Pre-Trial Chamber I issued arrest warrants for three senior Libyan officials, including Muammar Gaddafi. This was the second time that the ICC has issued an arrest warrant for a sitting head of State. The first was for Omar Al Bashir, the President of Sudan. As with the situation in Sudan, Libya is not a State party to the ICC Statute.

Unresolved Legal Issues

The international community employed a broad range of tools in responding to the situation in Libya: arms embargoes, economic sanctions, recognition/de-recognition, suspension of rights of membership, regional human rights mechanisms, a commission of inquiry, an ICC referral and, ultimately, the use of force. The unprecedented combination of these tools and the intersections of the various bodies of international law identified above have given rise to a number of unresolved legal issues.

Derogation under the ICCPR

The Human Rights Council and the Security Council both condemned Libya for violations of provisions of human rights law and humanitarian law. Among the rights invoked by both bodies were the rights to freedom of expression and freedom of assembly, both of which are subject to limitation and derogation.

As noted above, States parties to the ICCPR may take measures derogating from some of their obligations in the event of a "public emergency which threatens the life of the nation." While no clear threshold has been established for determining when this standard has been met, the jurisprudence of the Human Rights Council indicates that the possibility of derogation arises only in situations of the utmost gravity. In any event, this standard was clearly met by the time the situation in Libya erupted into armed conflict.

In this context, two derogation-related issues arise. The first is the significance of Libya's failure to notify the other States parties to the ICCPR via the UN Secretary-General of any derogation. The second is whether Libya's legal ability to derogate is impeded by the Libyan government's role in creating the emergency situation.

As noted above, the failure to notify the Secretary-General does not necessarily preclude the lawfulness of derogation.[81] The notification nonetheless serves important purposes. It is an important procedural safeguard in that it puts other States parties on notice of the derogation and presents them with an opportunity to assess the situation. More significantly, it also requires the State party derogating from its obligations to specify "the provisions from which it has derogated and . . . the reasons by which it was actuated."[82]

Apart from its failure to notify the Secretary-General, Libya also failed to provide any public statement concerning derogation. There was thus no indication that Libya intended to avail itself of the capacity to derogate. Nor was there any indication of what measures would be taken in derogation of its obligations, the degree of derogation or the extent to which such measures were necessary. More recent jurisprudence of the Human Rights Council supports the view that the complete failure to provide this information in any form may be fatal to the lawfulness of such measures.[83]

The second derogation-related issue is whether and to what extent a State's participation in creating a situation of public emergency might undercut its ability to derogate. There are at least two conceptual models for thinking about this issue.

The first is by analogy to the relationship between the *jus ad bellum* and the *jus in bello*.

It is a basic principle of the *jus in bello* that its application is independent of the *jus ad bellum*. The issue of which State violated the *jus ad bellum* in bringing about a situation of armed conflict is generally irrelevant to the application of the *jus in bello*. Once an international armed conflict has begun, the law of armed conflict applies equally to all parties, regulating the conduct of hostilities and providing protections for individuals not—or no longer—taking part in the hostilities. Nonetheless, a State that violates the *jus ad bellum* would still bear international responsibility for that violation, and would be obliged to make reparation for all of its harmful consequences.

Applying this model to the issue of derogation, one could argue that the cause of an emergency situation should not affect the ability to derogate once that situation has arisen. Thus, once the threshold of "public emergency which threatens the life of the nation" has been met and the State has announced measures derogating from its obligations in conformity with Article 4, the applicable legal framework has been altered. Under this approach, international law would not look "behind" the then-prevailing facts on the ground. The issue of who caused the state of emergency would be irrelevant to the issue of derogation. At the same time, the State party would still bear responsibility for any human rights violations, including those in violation of derogable obligations, committed in the lead-up to the emergency situation.

Another approach would be to proceed from the principle of "unclean hands." This equitable principle, whereby actors are precluded from benefiting from their own wrongdoing, is arguably a general principle of law within the meaning of Article 38 of the Statute of the International Court of Justice,[84] and variations of it are reflected in several fields of international law, including the law of State responsibility and the law of treaties. Under this approach, a State party should not be able to avail itself of the possibility of derogation if the government of that State party created the emergency situation by committing serious violations of human rights law (e.g., in the context of a brutal crackdown against protesters).

There are strong arguments in favor of both approaches. The advantage of employing the former approach is that it avoids having to determine who was at fault in bringing about the new state of affairs. The importance of this principle in the context of the *jus ad bellum/jus in bello* dichotomy is particularly clear. States generally claim that their uses of force are lawful, and there is no standing judicial body with jurisdiction to determine otherwise. One could argue that the wisdom of remaining agnostic as to which party wrongfully caused a conflict would apply *a fortiori* in an internal context.

Moreover, States have agreed that irrespective of who started the armed conflict, certain rules must be followed by all parties in order to mitigate some of its effects. This raises, however, an important distinction with respect to the issue of derogation. In international law, the principle of the independence of the *jus ad bellum* and *jus in bello* ensures that the restrictions of the *jus in bello* will apply to any armed conflict. Derogation is in a sense the inverse. The consequence of a valid derogation is the removal of restrictions that would otherwise apply to the conduct of the State party. Another basis of distinction may be found in the nature and function of international human rights law. This body of law principally regulates the way a State treats its own people, formerly regarded as a purely internal matter. International human rights treaties also establish compliance bodies to monitor implementation of the obligations under those treaties, including in times of public emergency.

Application of International Human Rights Law during Armed Conflict

The issue of whether and to what extent international human rights law applies in situations of international armed conflict and occupation remains controversial. While international judicial bodies have found that international human rights law continues to apply in times of armed conflict,[85] some States consistently reject this position and instead argue that international human rights law ceases to apply or is otherwise entirely abrogated by the application of the *lex specialis* of the *jus in bello*.[86]

Despite this continuing controversy over the application of human rights law to international armed conflict, there now appears to be consensus that human rights law *does apply* in *internal* armed conflicts. Even the United States, which has been vocal in its rejection of the application of human rights treaty law to international armed conflicts and to transnational, non-international armed conflicts, has never objected to the application of human rights law to internal armed conflicts.[87] Indeed, the United States consistently exerts pressure bilaterally on States dealing with situations of internal armed conflict to comply with their obligations under international human rights law.

Thus, to the extent the conflict in Libya remained internal, the application of international human rights law to it was uncontroversial. This does not mean, however, that there is not continuing controversy over the interoperability of particular rules of human rights law and humanitarian law in this context. There are still divergent views on this subject.

As noted above, once other States began to use armed force in Libya, the law of international armed conflict began to apply to the conflict between those States and Libya. The applicability of international human rights law to international armed conflicts remains unsettled, though a consensus appears to be emerging in favor of application at least where the relevant party to the conflict is exercising a degree of control over territory or individuals.[88] In any event, if the role of the intervening States is limited to aerial bombing campaigns (i.e., in the absence of any direct control of individuals or territory), then most questions arising under international human rights law, even if applicable, would likely be resolved by reference to the rules of the *jus in bello* as *lex specialis*.[89]

Use of Force Issues

A number of controversial legal issues are implicated by the Security Council's authorization to use force in this context.

Some have suggested that the Security Council's authorization to use force to protect civilians was a manifestation of the responsibility-to-protect doctrine. To the extent this assessment is accurate, it underscores the political nature of the doctrine. The use of force was authorized by a vote of the Security Council, a vote that was enabled through a careful alignment of political factors, including Gaddafi's lack of allies in the Arab world. There is little indication that the response by the international community gave legal content to the responsibility-to-protect concept, except perhaps as a conceptual umbrella for independently existing obligations under human rights and humanitarian law.[90]

More controversial has been the way in which force was used by the intervening States and regional organizations. In particular, the international community's support for the mandate began to erode in the wake of concerns that NATO was exceeding the authorization granted by the Security Council in Resolution 1973.

The Security Council's grant of authority to use force to "protect civilians and civilian populated areas" seemed to sweep more broadly than the more limited establishment of "safe areas" called for by the Arab League. Presumably, the United Kingdom, France and the United States preferred not to have to go back to the Security Council again if an initial grant of authority proved inadequate. Nonetheless, the Security Council imposed limits on the authorization to use force, clearly envisioning a protective use of force. Thus, despite the breadth of the mandate, it would not seem to encompass regime change.[91]

Key to assessing the scope of the mandate is the interpretation of the term "civilian." To interpret this term in light of existing rules of international law,[92] one would naturally turn to the law of armed conflict. As the mandate was formulated against the backdrop of the internal armed conflict in Libya, the relevant body of law would be the law of non-international armed conflict.

There are divergent opinions as to the meaning of the term "civilian" in non-international armed conflict. Some authorities take the position that as civilians are traditionally defined as those who are not combatants, and as there are, strictly speaking, no combatants in non-international armed conflict, then all individuals in a non-international armed conflict are civilians. This would arguably even include Gaddafi himself, as well as the members of his security forces. On this interpretation, only purely defensive uses of force would be permissible, as any offensive use of force would necessarily target those who are to be protected.

Others reject such a broad application of the term "civilian," contending that those who take part in the hostilities are effectively combatants, styling them as unlawful combatants or unprivileged belligerents. This would include Qaddafi's security forces, rebel soldiers and, depending upon the breadth of interpretation, any other individual taking part in the hostilities. On this interpretation, protection of these individuals would fall outside the mandate. Noteworthy in this context is that the United States government over the past decade has advanced a relatively narrow conception of civilian status, excluding those taking part in the hostilities or even providing material support to the belligerents. In the present context, such interpretations narrow its authority to use force.

A further wrinkle is introduced by use of the term "civilian populated areas under threat of attack." Use of this phrase could expand the mandate to include protection of all places where civilians reside. In particular, it could be read to include within the mandate the use of force to protect all parts of Libya. Of course, it would also then apply to towns where Gaddafi loyalists resided.

Once the tide turned against Gaddafi and the rebels began to launch offensives against loyalist strongholds, the legality of continued NATO bombing in support of the rebels became questionable. Particularly difficult to justify under the mandate would be the NATO attacks against retreating convoys. While some have reasoned that protection of civilians in Libya necessitated regime change, and that dislodging Gaddafi from power was a justified means of fulfilling the mandate, such reasoning renders the limitations expressly set forth in Resolution 1973 almost meaningless.

If NATO's use of force exceeded the scope of the 1973 authorization, would that then constitute the crime of aggression within the definition for that crime adopted at the 2010 Review Conference of the International Criminal Court? The aggression amendment adopted at the Review Conference defines aggression as

> the planning, preparation, initiation or execution, by a person in a position effectively to exercise control over or to direct the political or military action of a State, of an act of aggression which, by its character, gravity and scale, constitutes a manifest violation of the Charter of the United Nations.[93]

The phrase "act of aggression" is then defined by reference to General Assembly Resolution 3314.[94] That resolution does not expressly refer to uses of force in excess of Security Council authorization. Nonetheless, it does provide an analogous category of conduct. It includes as an act of aggression "[t]he use of armed forces of one State which are within the territory of another State with the agreement of the receiving State, in contravention of the conditions provided for in the agreement or any extension of their presence in such territory beyond the termination of the agreement."[95] Thus, to the extent the definition of aggression includes *ultra vires* uses of force, it could be argued that certain offensive aspects of the NATO bombing campaign qualify as acts of aggression.

The definition of the *crime* of aggression under the ICC Statute, however, is somewhat narrower. In particular, the act of aggression would have to "by its character, gravity and scale, constitute[] a manifest violation of the Charter of the United Nations." Given the divergent interpretations of the mandate, it would be difficult to conclude that any violation was "manifest," or objectively evident.[96]

In any event, NATO's broad interpretation of the mandate seems to have set back the responsibility-to-protect doctrine as a political matter. Russia and China, States that have traditionally advocated robust interpretations of the non-intervention principle but were persuaded to acquiesce in the 1973 mandate, have since voted against even the mildest measures in relation to the situation in Syria.[97]

ICC Referral Issues

The ICC referral also raises a number of significant legal issues, including the applicability of head of State immunity and the principle of non-retroactive application of criminal law (or *nullum crimen sine lege*).

The Security Council referral was a necessary precondition to the exercise of ICC jurisdiction in this case because Libya is not a party to the ICC Statute.[98] Libya's non-party status is also relevant to the issues of head of State immunity and the application of *nullum crimen sine lege*.

As noted above, an ICC pretrial chamber issued an arrest warrant for Gaddafi in June 2011. As an incumbent head of State, Gaddafi was entitled to absolute immunity from foreign legal process under customary international law. Although Gaddafi's death rendered the issue moot, the question remains whether the issuance of the arrest warrant was a violation of international law, and if so, which entity, if any, bore responsibility for the violation.

The ICC has established for itself the lawfulness of issuing arrest warrants for sitting heads of State by reference to its own Statute. The Statute provides that "[i]mmunities or special procedural rules which may attach to the official capacity of a person, whether under national or international law, shall not bar the Court from exercising its jurisdiction over such a person."[99] Thus, those States that are parties to the treaty have effectively waived immunity claims. This is not true for States that are not parties to the treaty.[100] Nonetheless, in its decision authorizing the issuance of an arrest warrant for Sudanese President Omar Al Bashir, an ICC pretrial chamber found that the abrogation of immunity provided in the ICC Statute applied equally vis-à-vis the territorial States of situations referred to the Court by the Security Council irrespective of whether or not that State is a party to the ICC Statute.[101] It remains unresolved whether this decision is consistent with customary international law.

It may be argued that Security Council Resolution 1970, in deciding that "the Libyan authorities shall cooperate fully" with the Court, effectively abrogated any immunities. However, it is also arguable that any derogation of existing customary international law would have to be expressly stipulated.

In any event, even if the issuance of the arrest warrant conflicted with international law, it is unclear who would bear responsibility for the violation. Is the International Criminal Court a legal person bound by customary international law? Even if it is a legal person, and even if it violated customary international law, it remains unclear what remedy would be available to injured States or individuals.

Another issue related to Libya's status as a non–State party to the Rome Statute revolves around the principle of *nullum crimen sine lege*. According to this principle, an individual may not be prosecuted for conduct that was not proscribed by applicable law at the time the conduct took place.[102] As Libya is not a party to the Rome Statute, the criminal prohibitions set forth therein did not form part of the law applicable to Libyan nationals acting on the territory of Libya. Nonetheless, at the time the Rome Statute was adopted, there was broad agreement that most of the crimes included in the Court's subject matter jurisdiction had already acquired the status of customary law. It was also understood, however, that there was an element of progressive development in the Statute, particularly in relation to the war crimes provisions applicable in situations of non-international armed conflict.

Hardly a decade earlier, it was far from clear whether even the most serious violations of the law of non-international armed conflict would give rise to the individual criminal responsibility of the perpetrator in international law. By the mid-1990s, the International Criminal Tribunal for the former Yugoslavia had determined that serious violations of Common Article 3 of the 1949 Geneva Conventions were war crimes giving rise to individual criminal responsibility.[103] The Tribunal's pronouncements were not met with any significant opposition from States. By the time of the Rome Statute's adoption in the summer of 1998, it was already well accepted among States that serious violations of Common Article 3 constituted war crimes. The Rome Statute, however, provides a much more extensive elaboration of war crimes in non-international armed conflict, going well beyond the provisions of Common Article 3. Thus, in considering war crimes charges against the suspects, the Court will have to carefully examine whether the crimes were well established in customary international law in early 2011.[104]

Conclusion

In responding to the situation in Libya, the international community employed virtually every tool at its disposal, creating an unprecedented combination of force, embargoes, sanctions, and other legal and political mechanisms. The Human Rights Council convened a special session, issued a condemnation, established a commission of inquiry and ultimately sought the suspension of Libya's membership, which was effected by the General Assembly in a seminal exercise of its authority to do so. The UN Security Council, acting under Chapter VII of the UN Charter, imposed an arms embargo, a travel ban and an asset freeze. It also referred the situation to the ICC, which issued an arrest warrant for Muammar Gaddafi and two others for alleged crimes against humanity. Following the emergence of armed conflict in Libya, the Security Council authorized the use of force, which was initially carried out by a coalition of States, then taken over by NATO.

The combination of these tools in the Libyan context reveals the extent to which a number of important legal issues of human rights law, *jus in bello*, *jus ad bellum* and international criminal law are unresolved. Specifically, the availability and applicability of derogation from ICCPR obligations, absent notification to the Secretary-General, and in the context of a State-generated emergency situation need to be addressed, as does the application of international human rights law during times of international armed conflict, particularly in the context of aerial bombing campaigns. Also unresolved is the extent to which, if at all, NATO exceeded the scope of the Security Council's authorization of the use of force, and if so, whether the crime of aggression is thereby implicated. Additionally, it is uncertain if the ICC violated customary international law by issuing an arrest warrant for the head of State of a non–State party to the Rome Statute, who would be accountable if so, and whether the application of certain war crimes charges in this context would transgress the principle of *nullum crimen sine lege*.

Despite the significance of these questions, the political, ad hoc nature of the international community's response to the situation in Libya portends that many of these issues will likely remain unresolved for the foreseeable future.

Notes

1. U.N. Charter art. 2, para. 7.

2. *Id.*, arts. 51, 42, respectively.

3. The way in which force is employed within a State is regulated by other rules of international law that have evolved in the post–World War II era, including international human rights law and the law of non-international armed conflict.

4. See the ILC Articles on Diplomatic Protection, G.A. Res. 62/67, Annex, U.N. Doc. A/RES/62/67 (Dec. 6, 2007), which were commended to the attention of governments by the UN General Assembly in Resolution 65/27. G.A. Res. 65/27, U.N. Doc. A/RES/65/27 (Dec. 6, 2010).

5. Convention for the Amelioration of the Condition of the Wounded and Sick in Armed Forces in the Field, Aug. 12, 1949, 6 U.S.T. 3114, 75 U.N.T.S. 31; Convention for the Amelioration of the Condition of Wounded, Sick and Shipwrecked Members of Armed Forces at Sea, Aug. 12, 1949, 6 U.S.T. 3217, 75 U.N.T.S. 85; Convention Relative to the Treatment of Prisoners of War, Aug. 12, 1949, 6 U.S.T. 3316, 75 U.N.T.S. 135; Convention Relative to the Protection of Civilian Persons in Time of War, Aug. 12, 1949, 6 U.S.T. 3516, 75 U.N.T.S. 287.

6. John Cerone, *Much Ado about Non-State Actors*, 10 SAN DIEGO INTERNATIONAL LAW JOURNAL 335 (2009).

7. The qualifier "in the strict sense" is used to distinguish this body of law from the rules of international law regulating inter-State cooperation in criminal justice matters generally, such as suppression conventions and extradition treaties. Certain prohibitions, e.g., the prohibition of genocide, bind both the individual and the State, and also give rise to suppression obligations.

8. The scope of application of human rights treaties varies.

9. Article 2 of the International Covenant on Civil and Political Rights requires each State party to "respect and to ensure to all individuals within its territory and subject to its jurisdiction the rights recognized in the present Covenant. . . ." International Covenant on Civil and Political Rights, Dec. 16, 1966, 999 U.N.T.S. 171, *reprinted in* 6 INTERNATIONAL LEGAL MATERIALS 368 (1967) [hereinafter ICCPR]. Libya did not enter any substantive reservations upon acceding to the ICCPR. It did, however, state that "[t]he acceptance and the accession to this Covenant by the Libyan Arab Republic shall in no way signify a recognition of Israel or be conducive to entry by the Libyan Arab Republic into such dealings with Israel as are regulated by the Covenant." International Covenant on Civil and Political Rights, United Nations Treaty Collection, http://treaties.un.org/pages/ViewDetails.aspx?src=TREATY&mtdsg_no=IV-4&chapter=4&lang=en (then follow Libya hyperlink) (last visited Jan. 31, 2012).

10. Optional Protocol to the International Covenant on Civil and Political Rights, Dec. 16, 1966, 999 U.N.T.S. 302.

11. International Covenant on Economic, Social and Cultural Rights, Jan. 3, 1976, 993 U.N.T.S. 3.

12. Convention on the Rights of the Child, Nov. 20, 1989, 1577 U.N.T.S. 3.

13. International Convention on the Elimination of All Forms of Racial Discrimination, Mar. 7, 1966, 660 U.N.T.S. 195.

14. Convention on the Elimination of All Forms of Discrimination Against Women, Dec. 18, 1979, 1249 U.N.T.S. 13.

15. African Charter on Human and Peoples' Rights, June 27, 1981, O.A.U. Doc. CAB/LEG/67/3 Rev.5, 1520 U.N.T.S. 217.

16. The Human Rights Committee has opined that certain of these rights may become non-derogable when linked to a non-derogable right, such as the right to life. *See* U.N. Human Rights

Committee, General Comment No. 29, States of Emergency (Article 4), U.N. Doc. CCPR/C/21/Rev.1/Add.11 (2001) [hereinafter General Comment No. 29].

17. ICCPR, *supra* note 9, art. 4(3).

18. Libya entered very few reservations when expressing consent to be bound by the human rights treaties to which it is a party.

19. In this context, it is important to recall the *erga omnes* nature of at least the most fundamental obligations under international human rights law. *See* Barcelona Traction, Light and Power Company, Limited (Belg. v. Spain), 1970 I.C.J. 3 (Feb. 5). *See also* Articles on the Responsibility of States for Internationally Wrongful Acts, G.A. Res. 56/83, art. 48, U.N. Doc. A/RES/56/83 (Jan. 28, 2002).

20. ICCPR, *supra* note 9, art. 4.

21. *See* Salgar de Montejo v. Colombia, Communication No. 64/79, ¶ 10.3, U.N. Doc. CCPR/C/15/D/64/1979 (1982).

22. General Comment No. 29, *supra* note 14.

23. In 2005 the UN General Assembly declared its readiness to take collective action when States fail in their responsibilities. *See* STEPHEN MCCAFFREY, DINAH SHELTON & JOHN CERONE, PUBLIC INTERNATIONAL LAW: CASES, PROBLEMS, AND TEXTS 1294 (2010).

24. Human Rights Council Res. S-15/1, ¶ 1, U.N. Doc. A/HRC/S-15-1 (Feb. 25, 2011) [hereinafter Resolution S-15/1]. Under the Rome Statute of the International Criminal Court, a crime against humanity is defined as one of a list of enumerated inhumane acts "committed as part of a widespread or systematic attack directed against any civilian population," where the attack is "pursuant to or in furtherance of a State or organizational policy to commit such attack." Rome Statute of the International Criminal Court art. 7, July 17, 1998, 2187 U.N.T.S. 90 [hereinafter ICC Statute].

25. Resolution S-15/1, *supra* note 24, ¶ 2. As noted above, under the ICCPR the obligation to respect these rights is derogable. However, the Council points out that abuses are being committed against "peaceful" demonstrators.

26. *Id.*

27. *Id.*, ¶ 6.

28. *Id.*, ¶ 7.

29. *Id.*, ¶ 9.

30. *Id.*, ¶ 11.

31. *Id.*, ¶ 14. The resolution references the General Assembly resolution that created the Human Rights Council. G.A. Res. 60/251, ¶ 8, U.N. Doc. A/RES/60/251 (Apr. 3, 2006). Paragraph 8 provides that "the General Assembly, by a two-thirds majority of the members present and voting, may suspend the rights of membership in the Council of a member of the Council that commits gross and systematic violations of human rights."

32. S.C. Res. 1970, U.N. Doc. S/RES/1970 (Feb. 26, 2011).

33. Because Libya is not a State party to the ICC Statute and has not otherwise consented to ICC jurisdiction, the Security Council referral was necessary to satisfy the legal preconditions to the exercise of the Court's jurisdiction over the situation in Libya.

34. S.C. Res. 1970, *supra* note 32, pmbl. para. 2.

35. *Id.*, pmbl. para. 3.

36. International humanitarian law is the international law of armed conflict. However, it is possible that "international humanitarian law" is being used in a broader sense. This phrase is sometimes used to include the prohibitions of genocide and crimes against humanity, both of which may be committed in peacetime.

37. S.C. Res. 1970, *supra* note 32, pmbl. para. 9.

38. *Id.*, pmbl. para. 11.

39. *Id.*, pmbl. para. 12. Security Council referral of an ICC prosecution could be stopped by the veto of any permanent member. A continuing deferral would require the continued support of all five permanent members.

40. *Id.*, ¶ 1.

41. *Id.*, ¶ 2(a). The reference to both international human rights law and international humanitarian law may indicate the Security Council's position that these two bodies of law apply simultaneously to situations of internal armed conflict. But see note 36 *supra*.

42. *Id.*, ¶ 2(d).

43. Press Release, U.N. Security Council, In Swift, Decisive Action, Security Council Imposes Tough Measures on Libyan Regime, Adopting Resolution 1970 in Wake of Crackdown on Protesters (Feb. 26, 2011), *available at* http://www.un.org/News/Press/docs/2011/sc10187.doc.htm.

44. S.C. Res. 1970, *supra* note 32, ¶ 6.

45. G.A. Res. 65/265, U.N. Doc. A/RES/65/265 (Mar. 1, 2011).

46. Statement, Prosecutor of the International Criminal Court, Opening of the Investigation into the Situation in Libya (Mar. 3, 2011), http://www.icc-cpi.int/NR/rdonlyres/035C3801-5C8D-4ABC-876B-C7D946B51F22/283045/StatementLibya_03032011.pdf.

47. The standard for determination that the violence had reached a level such that it could be labeled "armed conflict" was addressed in *Prosecutor v. Tadić*, Case No. IT-94-1, Appeals Chamber Decision on the Defence Motion for Interlocutory Appeal on Jurisdiction, ¶ 70 (Int'l Crim. Trib. for the Former Yugoslavia Oct. 2, 1995) [hereinafter *Tadić*] ("we find that an armed conflict exists whenever there is . . . protracted armed violence between governmental authorities and organized armed groups").

48. Arab League, Res. No. 7360, The Outcome of the Council of the League of Arab States Meeting at the Ministerial Level on the Implications of the Current Events in Libya and the Arab Position (Mar. 12, 2011), *available at* http://responsibilitytoprotect.org/Arab%20League%20Ministerial%20level%20statement%2012%20march%202011%20-%20english.pdf.

49. *Id.*, pmbl. para. 6.

50. *Id.*, pmbl. para. 7.

51. *Id.*, ¶ 1.

52. S.C. Res. 1973, ¶ 4, U.N. Doc. S/RES/1973 (Mar. 17, 2011).

53. This attitude is further reflected in the votes of China and Russia during the subsequent special session of the Human Rights Council (HRC) on Syria. Both of these HRC members voted against the resolution adopted at that special session. In October 2011, they vetoed a draft Security Council resolution that would have contemplated measures being taken against Syria if it continued its heavy-handed response to protest movements.

54. Press Release, U.N. Security Council, Security Council Approves "No-Fly Zone" over Libya, Authorizing "All Necessary Measures" to Protect Civilians, by Vote of 10 in Favour with 5 Abstentions (Mar. 17, 2011), *available at* http://www.un.org/News/Press/docs/2011/sc10200.doc.htm.

55. S.C. Res. 1973, *supra* note 52, ¶ 1.

56. *Id.*, ¶ 3.

57. *Id.*, ¶ 4. Again, there is some ambiguity in the use of the terms "civilian" and "civilian populated area." Would this, for example, include civilians who directly participate in the hostilities? To what extent would individuals cease to be "civilians" for this purpose if they had a continuous combat function?

58. *Id.*

59. *Id.* This exclusion of military occupation, however, would not preclude the use of ground troops. It would preclude their establishment of authority over territory.

60. *Id.*, ¶¶ 6–8.

61. *Id.*, ¶ 20. This issue had become acute as States had become divided over whether to recognize the rebel authorities as the legitimate government of Libya.

62. Note that this provision is not limited to UN member States.

63. While some have suggested that the *jus in bello* does not apply to UN-authorized uses of armed force, this would contravene the basic principle that application of the *jus in bello* is independent of the *jus ad bellum* and does not reflect the majority position.

64. Ian Traynor & Julian Borger, *Military Mission: Nato Agrees to Take Over Air Campaign against Gaddafi*, THE GUARDIAN (London), Mar. 28, 2011, at 5.

65. In the Matter of African Commission on Human and Peoples' Rights v. Great Socialist People's Libyan Arab Jamahiriya, App. No. 004/2011, Provisional Measures, Afr. Ct. Hum. & Peoples' Rts. (Mar. 25, 2011), *available at* http://www.unhcr.org/refworld/pdfid/4da59c082.pdf.

66. *Id.*, ¶ 10.

67. *Id.*, ¶ 22.

68. *Id.*, ¶ 23.

69. *Id.*, ¶ 25.

70. *See, e.g.*, Yevgeny Shestakov, *Play by the Rules, Says Lavrov*, DAILY TELEGRAPH (London), Apr. 19, 2011, at 1 ("Russia reiterated its stance that the western alliance's Libya campaign has overstepped its UN mandate through use of excessive force.").

71. Office of the Prosecutor, International Criminal Court, First Report of the Prosecutor of the International Criminal Court to the UN Security Council Pursuant to UNSCR 1970 (2011) (May 4, 2011), *available at* http://www.icc-cpi.int/NR/rdonlyres/A077E5F8-29B6-4A78-9EAB-A179A105738E/0/UNSCLibyaReportEng04052011.pdf.

72. *Id.*, ¶ 11.

73. *Id.*, ¶ 12.

74. *Id.*, ¶ 14.

75. *Id.*, ¶ 16.

76. *Id.*, ¶ 21.

77. *Id.*, ¶ 31.

78. *Id.*, ¶ 34.

79. *Id.*, ¶ 36. The report also refers to abuses committed against "prisoners of war." *Id.*, ¶¶ 36, 38. To the extent this refers to Libyan detainees, or nationals of States not parties to the armed conflict in Libya, in the hands of the then Libyan government or rebels, the term "prisoners of war" is presumably used in a non-technical sense (e.g., as a way to refer to detained individuals who had been engaged in the hostilities), as this status does not exist in non-international armed conflict.

80. Report of the International Commission of Inquiry to Investigate All Alleged Violations of International Human Rights Law in the Libyan Arab Jamahiriya, U.N. Doc. A/HRC/17/44 (June 1, 2011), *available at* http://www2.ohchr.org/english/bodies/hrcouncil/docs/17session/A.HRC.17.44_AUV.pdf.

81. *See supra* text accompanying note 21.

82. ICCPR, *supra* note 9, art. 4(3).

83. *See* Adrien Mundyo Buyso et al. v. Democratic Republic of the Congo, Communication No. 933/2000, ¶ 5.2, U.N. Doc. CCPR/C/78/D/933/2000 (2003).

84. Statute of the International Court of Justice, June 26, 1945, 59 Stat. 1055, 33 U.N.T.S. 993.

85. *See, e.g.*, Armed Activities on the Territory of the Congo (Dem. Rep. Congo v. Uganda), 2005 I.C.J. 116, ¶ 216 (Dec. 19); *see also* John Cerone, *Jurisdiction and Power: The Intersection of Human Rights Law & the Law of Non-international Armed Conflict in an Extraterritorial Context*, 40 ISRAEL LAW REVIEW 396 (2007).

86. Françoise J. Hampson, *Direct Participation in Hostilities and the Interoperability of the Law of Armed Conflict and Human Rights Law*, *in* INTERNATIONAL LAW AND THE CHANGING CHARACTER OF WAR 187, 188 (Raul A. "Pete" Pedrozo & Daria P. Wollschlaeger eds., 2011) (Vol. 87, U.S. Naval War College International Law Studies) (citing the United States and Israel); *see also* U.S. Department of State, Second and Third Periodic Report of the United States of America to the UN Committee on Human Rights Concerning the International Covenant on Civil and Political Rights ¶ 130 (Oct. 21, 2005), *available at* http://www.state.gov/j/drl/rls/55504.htm.

87. It may be that this position simply reduces to rejection of extraterritorial application of human rights treaties, though the United States maintains that that is a separate and independent ground for non-application of human rights treaties.

88. Cerone, *supra* note 85, at 446.

89. *Id.*

90. While Security Council Resolutions 1970 and 1973 both refer to the "responsibility to protect," this phrase is used to refer to Libya's responsibility to protect its own population. This obligation clearly exists under the very broad spectrum of obligations under human rights and humanitarian law applicable to Libya.

91. *See also* Authority to Use Military Force in Libya, 35 Opinions of the Office of Legal Counsel of the Department of Justice (Apr. 1, 2011), *available at* http://www.justice.gov/olc/2011/authority-military-use-in-libya.pdf. In a footnote, the opinion states, "Although President Obama has expressed opposition to Qadhafi's continued leadership of Libya, we understand that regime change is not an objective of the coalition's military operations." It then quotes Obama's March 28, 2011 public address: "Of course, there is no question that Libya—and the world—would be better off with Qaddafi out of power. I . . . will actively pursue [that goal] through non-military means. But broadening our military mission to include regime change would be a mistake." *Id.* at 10 n.3.

92. Vienna Convention on the Law of Treaties art. 31(3)(c), May 23, 1969, 1155 U.N.T.S. 331 [hereinafter Vienna Convention].

93. Review Conference of the Rome Statute, 13th plenary meeting, June 11, 2010, I.C.C. Doc. RC/Res.6, Annex I, art. 8bis(1). The Court's jurisdiction over the crime of aggression is not yet operative.

94. G.A. Res. 3314, U.N. Doc. A/RES/3314 (Dec. 14, 1974).

95. *Id.*, art. 3(e).

96. See Article 46(2) of the Vienna Convention, *supra* note 92, for an indication of the meaning of the term "manifest."

97. Russia and China voted against the resolutions at both of the Human Rights Council's special sessions on Syria. They also vetoed a draft Security Council resolution that merely suggested the possibility of future sanctions.

98. The Court may also exercise jurisdiction over a case if it has the consent of the State of nationality of the alleged perpetrator or of the territory in which the crime occurred, even if these States are not parties to the Rome Statute. *See* ICC Statute, *supra* note 24, art. 12(3). As the crimes concerned were allegedly perpetrated by Libyans on Libyan territory, and as the consent of the Libyan government was not forthcoming at the relevant time, Security Council referral was the only means by which the Court could exercise its jurisdiction.

99. *Id.*, art. 27.

100. Vienna Convention, *supra* note 92, art. 34.

101. Prosecutor v. Al Bashir, No. ICC-02/05-01/09-3, Decision on the Prosecutor's Application for a Warrant of Arrest Against Omar Hassan Ahmed Al Bashir (Mar. 4, 2009).

102. The ICC Statute, *supra* note 24, incorporates a variation of this principle in Article 22, which states, "A person shall not be criminally responsible under this Statute unless the conduct in question constitutes, at the time it takes place, a crime within the jurisdiction of the Court."

103. *Tadić*, *supra* note 47, ¶¶ 131–34.

104. Crimes against humanity charges are less controversial. Crimes against humanity have been established rules of customary international law at least since 1946, when the Nuremberg Principles were unanimously affirmed by the UN General Assembly. *See* G.A. Res. 95(I), U.N. Doc. A/RES/95(I) (Dec. 11, 1946). In addition, the ICC Statute sets a higher bar for crimes against humanity than customary international law, at least as formulated by the ad hoc tribunals for the former Yugoslavia and Rwanda. The ICC Statute requires as a contextual element for crimes against humanity that the attack be "pursuant to or in furtherance of a State or organizational policy to commit such attack." ICC Statute, *supra* note 24, art. 7(2)(a). The Appeals Chamber of the International Criminal Tribunals for the former Yugoslavia and Rwanda has held that there is no such policy requirement under customary law. As the Rome Statute definition sets a higher bar than customary law, thus capturing a narrower category of conduct, the *nullum crimen* principle is not offended, at least with respect to these contextual elements.

PART IX

CLOSING ADDRESS

XVIII

Concluding Remarks on Non-International Armed Conflicts

Yoram Dinstein*

This Newport conference has covered a large number of issues pertaining to non-international armed conflicts (NIACs), as compared to international armed conflicts (IACs). In these concluding remarks, I shall focus on six main themes: (i) the proper definition of a NIAC; (ii) the thresholds of armed conflicts; (iii) the application of the *jus in bello* in a NIAC; (iv) the various types of recognition relevant to a NIAC; (v) intervention by a foreign country in a NIAC; and (vi) the interaction between NIACs and IACs.

I. Definition

A useful definition of a NIAC in international law appears in Article 1(1) of Additional Protocol II (AP II) of 1977: a NIAC must "take place in the territory of a High Contracting Party between its armed forces and dissident armed forces or other organized armed groups."[1] (The text goes on to add features that do not configure in the nucleus of the general definition; these will be spelled out below.)[2]

There are two constitutive elements in this definition:

* Professor Emeritus, Tel Aviv University, Israel.

(a) A NIAC must take place within the borders of a high contracting party, that is to say, a single State; and

(b) A NIAC has to be waged between the armed forces of the State (loyal to the central government) on the one hand, and organized armed groups (including dissident armed forces) on the other.

A. NIAC as an Internal Armed Conflict

The first vital ingredient of NIAC relates to its internal nature, i.e., that it is waged within a State. This characteristic is repeated in other texts, as illustrated in Article 19(1) of the 1954 Hague Convention on Cultural Property, which speaks of "an armed conflict not of an international character, occurring within the territory of one of the High Contracting Parties."[3] Virtually all commonly used definitions of a NIAC are restrictive in that the armed conflict is circumscribed to a single State[4] (the common locution in the past was "civil war").

Admittedly, a majority of the Supreme Court of the United States, in the *Hamdan* case of 2006, seems to have arrived at the conclusion that the post-9/11 transnational "war on terrorism" should be deemed a NIAC.[5] However, the idea that a NIAC can be global in nature is oxymoronic: an armed conflict can be a NIAC and it can be global, but it cannot be both. Cross-border action against terrorists, like the SEAL Team Six raid that took out Osama bin Laden in Pakistan, may be carried out as an "extraterritorial law enforcement" operation.[6] Ordinary military operations in Afghanistan, directed at Al-Qaeda terrorists, blend into an IAC waged in that country—against the Taliban—that, in my opinion, is still ongoing.[7] Repeated references have been made in the course of the present conference to the American alignment in Afghanistan against "Al-Qaeda and its associates." To my mind, the armed conflict in Afghanistan should rather be seen as conducted against "the Taliban and their associates." And, since the central issue in the legal (and public) debate on the subject is that of detention of captured enemy personnel, I must add that I fail to grasp the rationale behind the decision to incarcerate detainees outside of Afghanistan. Why is Guantanamo Bay preferable to Bagram?

B. Organized Armed Groups

The second component of the definition of NIAC postulates the existence of a clash of arms between the armed forces of a State (loyal to the central government) and organized armed groups (including dissident armed forces) rebelling against the powers that be. Several comments are called for in this context.

The phrase "organized armed group" is of pivotal significance. The rudiments of organization are immanent in any insurgency amounting to a NIAC. Without organization, there is no NIAC (as distinct from mere internal disturbances.)[8] The organized armed group may fall into two types. It may consist of (i) dissident (*viz.*, mutinous) units of the State's armed forces; or it may be formed by (ii) improvised groups of civilians who have coalesced in rebelling against the central government. The degree of organization of insurgent groups does not have a fixed pattern. Dissident military forces will naturally possess built-in structure and hierarchy. Other—improvised—organized armed groups are likely to be more loosely knit together (at least at the onset of the insurgency). But the emphasis is on the existence of some minimal organization, so that disconnected acts of violence committed by individuals will be excluded from the definition.

The insistence on insurgent organized groups being "armed" is principally designed to distinguish them from political opposition factions that challenge the central government without resorting to force. For sure, being "armed" does not imply that the armament employed by the insurgents has to be sophisticated.

The central government of the State in which a NIAC is raging is liable to become paralyzed—even to disintegrate and disappear altogether—either as a direct result of the NIAC or for other reasons. In extreme cases, such a phenomenon produces what is commonly called a "failed State." However, the removal from the scene of the central government does not have to put an end to the NIAC. Frequently, an existing NIAC may continue—or a new NIAC may be triggered—between two or more organized armed groups vying with each other for ascendance. Strictly speaking, hostilities between sundry organized armed groups—subsequent to the breakdown of governmental control—can no longer be viewed as an insurgency: after all, who is rebelling against whom? But the definition of NIAC must embrace such a state of affairs.

The add-on potential of a clash between two or more organized armed groups coming within the scope of a NIAC has been acknowledged by the Appeals Chamber of the International Criminal Tribunal for the former Yugoslavia (ICTY) in the *Tadić* case in 1995, which talked about "protracted armed violence between governmental authorities and organized armed groups *or between such groups* within a State" (emphasis added).[9] Article 8(2)(f) of the 1998 Rome Statute of the International Criminal Court follows in the same vein: "armed conflicts that take place in the territory of a State when there is protracted armed conflict between governmental authorities and organized armed groups or between such groups."[10] No doubt, this comprehensive version is the correct definition of a NIAC today.

C. Motives and Modalities

The motives propelling an organized armed group to an insurgency against the central government (or to a violent confrontation with other organized armed groups) may differ. These motives may be political, social, economic, ideological, religious, ethnic, etc. Whatever the motive, it does not impact on the definition of NIAC.

The modalities of NIACs are multiple; some are national and some regional:

(a) An organized armed group may have countrywide goals, the ultimate being to overthrow the central government, with the insurgents taking into their hands the helm of State throughout the territorial domain (the best illustration being that of the Franco rebellion in the Spanish Civil War, 1936–39). Alternatively, an organized armed group may have more limited national aims, such as effecting radical constitutional innovations, ensuring greater participation of underrepresented groups in the political process, securing fundamental freedoms or gaining certain specific concessions from the central government.

(b) The insurgents' aims may be confined to a particular region or locality, e.g., demanding autonomy within a portion of the State. The insurgents may even push for outright secession of a part of the country, with a view to creating a new sovereign State (the best example being that of the Southern Confederacy in the American Civil War, 1861–65) or uniting—on irredentist grounds—with an existing foreign State. There may be a more complex impetus for the insurgents' drive to wrest control over a particular district from the central government. Even criminal incentives (as in the case of narco-traffickers) cannot be ruled out.[11]

The long and short of it is that—irrespective of concrete objectives—when an organized armed group is rebelling against the central government of a State, there is a NIAC in progress.

II. Thresholds

The overall spectrum of violence is wide—ranging from ordinary crime and internal disturbances to NIACs and IACs—and it is necessary to bear in mind that different tiers of violence are subject to discrete legal regimes.[12] It is therefore useful to refer to three thresholds of armed conflicts—two relating to NIACs and one to IACs—plus a level of violence that is below the first threshold.

A. Below-the-Threshold Situations

Below-the-threshold violence fits a domestic law enforcement paradigm. Article 1(2) of AP II provides that the Protocol will not apply to "situations of internal disturbances and tensions, such as riots, isolated and sporadic acts of violence and other acts of a similar nature, as not being armed conflicts."[13] The same formula is reiterated in Article 8(2)(f) of the 1998 Rome Statute of the International Criminal Court,[14] in Article 22(2) of the 1999 Second Protocol to the 1954 Hague Convention for the Protection of Cultural Property[15] and in a 2001 Amendment to Article 1 of the 1980 Convention on Conventional Weapons (CCW).[16] By now, this uniform treaty definition of below-the-threshold violence seems to be universally accepted. The two signal adjectives are "isolated and sporadic," and the emblematic noun is "riots."

Riots, as well as other "isolated and sporadic" disturbances, are ordinarily handled by law enforcement agencies—namely, police forces (regardless of their domestic designation)—rather than by military contingents. Still, the intensity of riot-like disturbances may be such that military units are summoned to lend indispensable assistance to the police in stamping out the violence. This by itself does not alter the operation of the law enforcement paradigm.[17]

Below-the-threshold violence does not call for the application of the *jus in bello* (the law of armed conflict). The conduct of all concerned in below-the-threshold confrontations is governed by the domestic constitutional and criminal legal system of the State afflicted with the violence, subject to the strictures of international human rights law.

As a rule, law enforcement agents enjoy less latitude when it comes to opening fire on rioters during "isolated and sporadic" disturbances compared to the degree of latitude conferred on the armed forces when engaged in an IAC or even in a NIAC. Nevertheless, exceptionally, law enforcement agents—in below-the-threshold scenarios—may have more latitude in the use of certain weapons, when quelling an ordinary disturbance, compared to their counterparts in an armed conflict (either an IAC or a NIAC). Preeminently, in Article I(5) of the 1993 Chemical Weapons Convention contracting parties undertake not to use "riot control agents" (or, in plain language, tear gas) as a method of warfare, whereas Article II(9)(d) explicitly allows the employment of non-lethal chemical agents for law enforcement purposes, including domestic riot control.[18] Moreover, the use of expanding soft-nosed bullets (interdicted in armed conflicts)[19] is common when special weapons and tactics teams engage in counterterrorism activities, particularly when faced with hostage takers or suicide bombers.

B. Over the First Threshold

The first threshold of NIACs is established in Common Article 3 to the four Geneva Conventions of 1949 for the protection of war victims, which refers *tout court* to "armed conflict not of an international character occurring in the territory of one of the High Contracting Parties."[20] Common Article 3 of the Geneva Conventions paved the way for Article 19(1) of the 1954 Hague Convention for the Protection of Cultural Property, which employs the same formula.[21]

Common Article 3 has acquired a special status, since—in the 1986 *Nicaragua* case—the majority of the International Court of Justice held that it expresses "minimum rules applicable to international and to non-international conflicts";[22] in other words, that it reflects customary international law (applicable both in IACs and in NIACs). Yet, unfortunately, Common Article 3 does not shed light on the point at which the first threshold is crossed. Article 19(1) of the Hague Convention does not do that either.

The most authoritative attempt to fill the vacuum was made by the Appeals Chamber of the ICTY, which held—in the 1995 *Tadić* case—that there must be "protracted armed violence."[23] The adjective "protracted" is repeated in Article 8(2)(f) of the Rome Statute of the International Criminal Court.[24]

"Protracted" is obviously the antonym of AP II's "isolated and sporadic," but is it enough that the internal violence is prolonged for it to qualify as a NIAC? The ICTY Trial Chamber, in its *Tadić* judgment of 1997, added—as an extrapolation of the notion of "protracted" hostilities—the element of the "intensity" of the armed conflict, thereby "distinguishing an armed conflict from banditry, unorganized and short-lived insurrections, or terrorist activities."[25] Subsequent judgments of the ICTY have come up with "[v]arious indicative factors" in trying to assess the intensity of an armed conflict.[26]

C. Over the Second Threshold

The second threshold is laid down in Article 1(1) of AP II, which, after stating that a NIAC must "take place in the territory of a High Contracting Party between its armed forces and dissident armed forces or other organized armed groups," goes on to refer to organized armed groups that "under responsible command, exercise such control over a part of its territory as to enable them to carry out sustained and concerted military operations and to implement this Protocol."[27]

The salient element here, in comparison to the first threshold, is the control exercised by the insurgent organized armed group (under responsible command) over a part of the territory. The size of the area under insurgent control is not defined, but it must be sufficient (i) to allow "sustained and concerted military operations" to be carried out; and (ii) to enable the implementation of the Protocol (for example, caring for the wounded and sick).[28] The degree of control exercised by the insurgents in the area in question need not exceed these two conditions. In particular, there is no requirement that "any actual administration in a governmental sense" will take place.[29]

As for the first condition, any (military or quasi-military) operations carried out by insurgents in a NIAC over the second threshold must be "sustained and concerted." "Sustained" means that the operations are kept up continuously; "concerted" signals that they are carried out according to some plan.[30]

With respect to the second condition, it must be kept in mind that in any armed conflict control over certain areas may pass from one side to the other (possibly more than once). In the ebb and flow of a NIAC, an insurgent organized armed group may lose control over an area earlier seized by it. That by itself is inconsequential. For the second condition to be met, what is indispensable is that the insurgent organized armed group retains control over some territory at any given time.

The great advantage of the territorial control prerequisite is that it provides an acid test facilitating the ability to tell apart a NIAC from intense violence below the threshold. Thus, when one juxtaposes the settings in Libya and Syria in June 2011, it is noteworthy that the rising in Syria is no less protracted or intense than that in Libya. If Libya is different from Syria (apart from the element of foreign intervention with the *fiat* of the Security Council),[31] it is in the fact that the Libyan insurgents have gained control of large tracts of land, whereas in Syria there has been no similar development. The trouble, of course, is that the insistence on insurgents' control over territory excludes some cases of protracted and intense violence—e.g., the struggles by and against the Irish Republican Army in Northern Ireland or the Basque separatists in Spain.[32]

Once the second threshold is crossed, the treaty law of AP II comes into play for contracting parties.[33] Several provisions of AP II can currently be viewed as declaratory of customary international law.[34] Regardless, it must be perceived that all NIACs above the second threshold remain subject also to the customary *jus in bello*, which is applicable whenever the first threshold is crossed.

D. Over the Third Threshold

Whereas the gap between the first and the second thresholds is quantitative (the second threshold providing weightier evidence that a NIAC is actually occurring), the leap over the third threshold is qualitative: it is a move from a NIAC to an IAC. Many people are under the impression that a NIAC is *ipso facto* less intensive than an IAC, although this idea is not empirically corroborated by the historical record. In any event, it does not matter whether the fighting in an IAC is more or less intense than in a NIAC. The sole question is whether the fighting is intra-State (a NIAC) or inter-State (an IAC). The third threshold is crossed automatically once two or more States are taking part in the armed conflict, fighting each other.

Crossing the third threshold means that the *jus in bello* in its plenitude will be applicable to the armed conflict. The *jus in bello* applicable in a NIAC is sketchier,[35] and the entire gamut of the *jus in bello* is in play only when an IAC is going on.

More significantly, perhaps, IACs are subject to a *jus ad bellum*: international law (as entrenched both in the United Nations Charter and in customary international law) forbids the use of force in international relations, with only two exceptions, *viz.*, (i) self-defense, and (ii) enforcement action either mandated or authorized by a binding decision of the Security Council.[36] No parallel *jus ad bellum* exists as regards NIACs. "There is no rule in international law against civil wars."[37] While the domestic law of every State forbids an insurgency against the established order, international law turns a blind eye to the issue. International law neither prohibits an uprising against the central government nor denies the right of the central government to put down the insurrection by force.

III. Jus in Bello

The *jus in bello* regulating IACs started to develop in the nineteenth century, and has now become strongly anchored in both custom and extensive treaty law. Conversely, the *jus in bello* applicable in NIACs did not begin to develop until the adoption of Common Article 3 of the Geneva Conventions. Indeed, it took several decades for the urge to further develop NIAC *jus in bello* to become firmly implanted in the international legal mind-set.

NIAC *jus in bello* governs armed conflicts above either the first or the second threshold. When it does, it is applicable throughout the territory of the State affected, as long as the NIAC is going on. In the words of the Appeals Chamber of the ICTY, in the 2002 case of *Kunarac*, a violation of the NIAC *jus in bello* may "occur at a time when and in a place where no fighting is actually taking place."[38]

A. The Trend of Convergence

Contemporary developments in treaty law display a palpable trend of growing convergence between the *jus in bello* governing IACs and in NIACs. This trend is manifested in the following treaties:

(a) Article 8(c)–(e) of the 1998 Rome Statute of the International Criminal Court, which elaborates a list of NIAC war crimes (admittedly not as long as the comparable list of IAC war crimes)[39]

(b) Article 1(3) of the 1996 Amended Protocol II to the CCW, which applies the instrument (dealing with mines and booby traps) to NIACs[40]

(c) Article 22(1) of the 1999 Second Protocol to the Hague Convention for the Protection of Cultural Property, which does the same[41]

(d) The 2001 amendment to Article 1 of the CCW, which applies to NIACs all the Protocols annexed to the Convention.[42]

No doubt, we are also witnessing the emergence of a new customary law in this regard: some of it is already fully formed,[43] and some is probably in the process of formation.

B. The Impossibility of a Full Merger

Notwithstanding the increasing resemblance between the norms of the *jus in bello* applicable in IACs and in NIACs, it is unlikely that there will ever be a total merger of the law in the two discrete categories of armed conflicts. There have been some academic calls for conflating the law regulating the two types of armed conflicts.[44] Yet, at least three insurmountable obstacles stand in the way of such an amalgamation being effected in the practice of States:

(a) What might be termed a congenital trait of NIACs is that captured insurgents cannot claim the privileges of prisoners of war (POWs).[45] The rationale is that domestic law always considers insurgents to be criminals, perhaps even traitors.[46] When detained by government forces, insurgents are subject to prosecution and punishment for their criminal conduct by the domestic courts (military or civilian). For that and other reasons, insurgents in NIACs cannot be regarded as "combatants" (in contradistinction to civilians).[47] Accordingly, the 2006 *San Remo Manual on Non-International Armed Conflict* uses the term "fighters" instead.[48] The intrinsic asymmetry between well-organized (trained, disciplined, uniformed, etc.) members of the armed forces loyal to the central government and loosely organized insurgents (especially when they do not belong to dissident forces) creates lots of practical problems in the application of the *jus in bello* in a NIAC.

(b) The law of neutrality does not apply to NIACs.[49] This is due to the fact that in a NIAC solely one single State is embroiled in the armed conflict.[50] The construct of a neutral as a "third State" does not make sense when the nature of the armed conflict precludes the possibility of a second State being engaged (subject to the extraordinary setting of "recognition of belligerency").[51]

(c) The whole body of law relating to belligerent occupation is out of tune with NIACs,[52] since neither areas seized by insurgents nor those retained or liberated by the central government can be regarded as occupied territories in the sense of the *jus in bello*.[53]

I shall not dwell upon additional—less compelling—problems relating to the legality of certain means and methods of warfare, which have been raised during this conference.

C. Exceptional Situations

There are two exceptional situations when the *jus in bello* will apply in NIACs as if they were IACs. One—under customary international law—is "recognition of belligerency."[54] The other is confined to treaty law. Pursuant to Article 1(4) of Additional Protocol I of 1977, which is devoted to IACs, armed conflicts in the exercise of the right of self-determination are subject to the application of the Protocol and the Geneva Conventions, although they do not involve two opposing States.[55] It must be noted, however, that this is an exceedingly controversial provision which does not bind non-contracting parties to the Protocol.

IV. Recognition

A. "Recognition of Belligerency"

Sometimes, the central government of a State ravaged by a NIAC is compelled by circumstances to face a dire reality. This happens primarily when, by dint of their military successes in the field, the insurgents manage to capture large numbers of soldiers serving in the armed forces loyal to the central government. If the central government desires to ensure that its captive soldiers will benefit from POW privileges, it has no viable option except to confer on the insurgents "recognition of belligerency," which means that—on condition of reciprocity—the whole *jus in bello* governing IACs will become applicable to the NIAC.[56]

It is interesting to note that, in a regular IAC, a belligerent party is not required to grant POW status to its own nationals: an enemy soldier (serving in the armed forces of State B) owing allegiance to the captor State (State A)—mostly as a result of the link of nationality—is not regarded by the *jus in bello* as a lawful combatant entitled to POW status.[57] In a NIAC, members of the organized armed group fighting against the central government of State A are ordinarily nationals of that State. Once the central government proclaims a "recognition of belligerency," however, it is bound to treat insurgent captives as POWs despite their local nationality. What ensues is that the protection afforded to such insurgents in a NIAC—by virtue of the *jus in bello*—is actually wider in scope than the parallel protection available in an IAC.[58]

When "recognition of belligerency" is granted by the central government of State A, it means that the IAC *jus in bello* is applied to the NIAC not only in the relations between that government and the insurgents but also vis-à-vis all other States. The upshot is that the laws of neutrality will be in effect as far as States B, C, etc., are concerned. These States will then not be allowed to forcibly intervene in the armed conflict: neither in support of the insurgents nor even in support of the central government, notwithstanding the general rule under customary international law that intervention to assist the central government is permitted.[59]

"Recognition of belligerency" may be proclaimed not only by the central government of State A but by State B. Such recognition cannot affect the conduct of hostilities between the central government of State A and the insurgents (these hostilities will continue to be governed by the NIAC *jus in bello*). Nor does "recognition of belligerency" by State B affect the position of States C, D, etc. But "recognition of belligerency" by State B will alter its standing with respect to the NIAC.

The legal effect of "recognition of belligerency" by State B does not denote that that State is thereby entitled to forcibly intervene in the conflict in favor of the insurgents. To the contrary, State B is bound by its "recognition of belligerency" to observe total neutrality in the NIAC. That is to say, following "recognition of belligerency," State B will have to display impartiality toward both the central government of State A and the insurgents. Whereas—prior to "recognition of belligerency"—State B was allowed to forcibly intervene in the NIAC in favor of the central government of State A[60] and disallowed to do that in aiding and abetting the insurgents,[61] as from the turning point of "recognition of belligerency" State B is forbidden to assist any of the opposing sides. State B thus loses its pre-existing right to militarily assist the central government of State A, without acquiring a new right to militarily support the insurgents.

As a matter of fact, explicit "recognition of belligerency" is largely in "disuse" today.[62] But the basic concept of "recognition of belligerency" is as relevant as ever. There is no need for an express proclamation of "recognition of belligerency," inasmuch as it may be distilled from the actual conduct or official pronouncements of State B. Thus, "recognition of belligerency" may be tacitly inferred from a promulgation of neutrality issued by State B[63] (so that instead of such neutrality flowing from "recognition of belligerency," it is the other way around).

"Recognition of belligerency" may also be implied from the conduct of the central government of State A—for example, if it confers on insurgent captives the status of POWs (a clear-cut indication that the IAC *jus in bello* applies). Additionally, if the central government of State A wishes to close a maritime port seized and controlled by the insurgents, the only effective way to do this may be to impose a blockade.[64] The upside, from the central government's viewpoint, is that it can then interfere with freedom of navigation of international shipping on the high seas. The downside is that the imposition of a blockade on a port controlled by the insurgents implies "recognition of belligerency," inasmuch as a blockade is a means of warfare vouchsafed by IAC *jus in bello*—subject to certain conditions (preeminently, that the blockade is effective and does not exist on paper only)[65]—but not by NIAC *jus in bello*. If the central government of State A does not wish to bestow upon the insurgents (by implication) "recognition of belligerency," it has no choice but to avoid a proclamation of blockade as against a port controlled by them.[66]

B. Other Types of Recognition

"Recognition of belligerency" must not be confused with three other types of recognition: (i) "recognition of insurgency," (ii) recognition of a new government and (iii) recognition of a new State.

"Recognition of insurgency" in State A is issued by State B and has consequences that are less far-reaching than those attendant on "recognition of belligerency." "Recognition of insurgency" will usually come about when an organized armed group fighting the central government of State A gains effective control of some territory. By granting (explicitly or implicitly) "recognition of insurgency," State B merely indicates that it will maintain some de facto relations with the insurgents, in order to safeguard its own interests (and those of its nationals) in the territory actually under the sway of the insurgents.[67] In other words, State B will outflank the central government and deal directly with the insurgents in matters pertaining to the area subject to their control.

Recognition of the insurgents as the new central government of State A may be granted by State B "prior to, in the absence of, concurrently with, or subsequent to recognition of belligerency" by the central government of State A (or by State C).[68] The outcome of a recognition of the insurgents by State B as the new central government of State A is a dramatic *volte-face* in the political constellation. It means that, following the recognition, State B may extend military assistance to the new government (by consent/request) against the forces still loyal to the ancien régime, now looked upon as the insurgents against the reconstructed central authorities. I shall have more to say on this eventuality in the context of intervention.[69] It must be noted, however, that premature recognition of the new government is a breach of international law.[70]

Another possibility is recognition—issued by State B—of the entity created by the insurgents as a new State, X. What such recognition denotes is that State B regards the armed conflict not as an intra-State NIAC (between the central government and organized armed groups) but as an inter-State IAC (between States A and X). This is an even more radical reshuffle of the political cards. Still, in practice, the result of recognition of State X is similar to "recognition of belligerency" in that State B must then maintain neutrality regarding both belligerent parties.

V. Intervention

A. Forcible Intervention against the Central Government

State B is liable to forcibly intervene in the affairs of State A by fomenting an insurgency against the central government of State A. If State B has effective control over the insurgents, they may be regarded as its de facto organs.[71] There is no need to go here into the controversial issue of the degree of control required in order for it to be effective for this purpose. Suffice it to say that, if State B's control over the insurgents is effective, the armed conflict is internationalized.[72] In other words, what appears on the face of it to be a NIAC in State A would actually cross the third threshold and qualify as an IAC between States A and B.

Generally speaking, the issue of forcible intervention by State B in State A relates to a less flagrant scenario. The presupposition is that a genuine NIAC is taking place in State A, but State B extends military assistance to the insurgents against the central government of State A. Such military assistance may cross the third threshold and bring about an IAC between State A and B (side by side with the NIAC). However, State B has some elbow room before its action is considered to be crossing the third threshold. Thus, the majority of the International Court of Justice—in the *Nicaragua* case of 1986—did "not believe" that mere "assistance to rebels in the form of the provision of weapons or logistical or other support" rates as an armed attack.[73] Still, the degree of logistical support that can lawfully be extended by State B to insurgents in State A is not free of doubt.[74] At any rate, it is indisputable that—at a certain point—a forcible intervention by State B on behalf of the insurgents against the central government of State A will produce an IAC.

B. Forcible Intervention in Support of the Central Government

Under customary international law, State B is allowed to forcibly intervene in a NIAC in State A, as long as this is done on behalf of the central government—at its request or, as a minimum, with its consent—and against the insurgents. It is true that, under Article 2 of a 1975 resolution of the Institut de Droit International, "The Principle of Non-Intervention in Civil Wars," it is forbidden to extend foreign assistance to any party in a "civil war."[75] But this prohibition is irreconcilable with traditional international law;[76] it runs counter to the statement of the

International Court of Justice in the *Nicaragua* case that intervention is "allowable at the request of the government of a State";[77] and it is equally inconsistent with the more modern practice of States.[78] Contemporary international practice is replete with instances of detachments of armed forces sent by one State to another, at the latter's request, in order to help in restoring law and order in the face of intractable domestic turmoil.[79]

If State B forcibly intervenes on behalf of the central government of State A against the insurgents, the armed conflict still qualifies as a NIAC—even when State B deploys in State A an expeditionary force engaged in intense hostilities against the insurgents—inasmuch as the troops of State B are not battling another State, but operating jointly with that other State (State A) to quell the insurgency. The legal position remains the same notwithstanding effective control by the insurgents of large areas and despite large-scale casualties that the hostilities entail.

Surely, State B cannot dispatch troops into State A—in order to fight the insurgents within the latter's territory—against the will of the host government. Any forcible intervention by State B in a NIAC going on within State A must take place with the full consent of the central government of State A.[80] Such consent may be in the form of either (i) an ad hoc request for (or acceptance of) help after the NIAC has started; or (ii) a previous treaty (usually a military alliance or a regional arrangement) in which contracting parties confer on each other the right of intervention in prospective NIACs. (For an example, see the 2002 Durban Protocol of the African Union.)[81]

When consent is granted by State A to entry into its territory of armed forces of State B, in order to carry out military operations against the insurgents, it must be appreciated that—in the language of the International Court of Justice, in its 2005 judgment in the *Armed Activities* (Congo v. Uganda) case—State B is restricted by "the parameters of that consent, in terms of geographic location and objectives."[82] Moreover, as stressed by the Court, State A's consent can always be revoked (no formalities being required for revocation, in the absence of a treaty).[83] This is a crucial point. By revoking its consent, State A pulls the rug from under the legality of the presence of the foreign troops and State B must extract them without undue delay.

Any extension of the presence of the armed forces of State B in the territory of State A, beyond the termination of State A's consent to their presence (plus a reasonable space of time enabling their orderly departure), amounts to aggression,[84] and converts the armed conflict from a NIAC into an IAC between States A and B.

Naturally, there is a problem if the central government of State A disappears (State A thus becoming a "failed State"). In such circumstances, no party to the NIAC can express its consent to foreign intervention in the NIAC, and no revocation of consent can be issued. This scenario might invite application of the Institut's 1975 resolution concerning non-intervention in "civil wars."[85] The reason is that, should States B and C both intervene militarily in a NIAC in the "failed State" (A)—in support of two opposing organized armed groups[86]—they are likely to clash with each other, with an IAC between States B and C as the outcome.

C. Recognition of the Insurgents as the New Government

Recognition by State B of the leadership of an insurgency as the new central government of State A transforms everything:[87] the newly recognized central government is the one empowered to seek forcible assistance from State B; it is also the one competent to revoke the request for help. Such recognition was extended to the Benghazi authorities by a number of European countries intervening in the Libyan NIAC against the Tripoli government run by Moammar Qaddafi.

Evidently, if State B recognizes the leadership of an organized armed group of insurgents as the new central government of State A, and State C continues to recognize the original central government or recognizes the leadership of another organized armed group as the successor of that government, and if both States B and C militarily intervene in the NIAC in State A, this is likely to develop into an IAC between States B and C.[88]

The Security Council can always adopt a binding decision (under Chapter VII of the United Nations Charter), which will mandate or authorize forcible intervention by other States in a NIAC in progress in State A.[89] Such intervention will certainly be lawful, but (if directed against the central government of State A) it will either turn the NIAC into an IAC or bring about a separate IAC.

VI. Interaction

A. Armed Conflict and Criminal Activities

The outbreak of an armed conflict (whether an IAC or a NIAC) does not entail the cessation of ordinary criminal activities (within the ordinary bounds of the law enforcement paradigm). Indeed, the outbreak of an armed conflict may mean that ordinary crime is on the rise: this is commonly due to (i) psychological reasons linked to times of great tension; (ii) the omnipresence of weapons during an armed conflict; and even (iii) the emergence of numerous new crimes (such as black marketeering or trading with the enemy). In any event, ordinary crimes—even when committed in the course of an armed conflict—are governed not by the *jus in bello* but by the domestic criminal law, subject to the precepts of international human rights.

As noted earlier, a NIAC may have criminal motivations.[90] In such cases, it is patently difficult to draw the line between military operations executed against the insurgents in a NIAC and those directed at ordinary criminals. Colombia is a prime example. We heard at this conference that the Colombian armed forces are provided with multicolored cards telling them whether their operations come within the rubric of a NIAC or the law enforcement paradigm (below the threshold).[91] The idea is attractive, but I doubt its efficacy. After all, the two categories of situations are governed by different legal systems, and the training of forces required is by no means the same. The flip of a card may not be sufficient for the government units to adapt themselves instantly to an entirely disparate legal regime.

B. Simultaneous NIACs

More than one NIAC may be going on in a single country at any given time. This transpires when the central government has to contend—usually in distinct parts of a large territory—with assorted organized armed groups having diverse, and perhaps even clashing, aims. (As we heard at this conference, the Philippines presents a vivid illustration.)[92]

A NIAC in one country (State A) may spill over its borders and generate another NIAC within a neighboring country (State B). The situation in the Great Lakes region in Africa (in different time frames) is the most graphic example. In this scenario, insurgents against the central government of State A find temporary shelter within State B and ignite another NIAC, this time against the central government of State B. As long as the two central governments of States A and B (acting separately or in collaboration with each other) wage hostilities only against the insurgents, the two simultaneous conflicts—despite their cross-border effects—remain NIACs. But if the two central governments become embroiled in combat against each other, the armed conflict crosses the third threshold and becomes an IAC.

There is actually a parallel state of affairs in IACs. Two or more IACs between diverse belligerent parties may be going on simultaneously (perhaps in different parts of the world). These separate IACs may spread and even roll into one. Thus, the USSR was part of the Grand Alliance against Nazi Germany from June 1941 on, but it joined the war against Japan only in August 1945.

C. Combinations of NIACs and IACs

There may be multiple combinations of NIACs and IACs, both vertically (along an axis of time) and horizontally (along an axis of space).

Horizontally, the territory of a single State may be ravaged by hostilities that can be categorized as both an IAC (between two or more States opposing one another) and a NIAC (between the central government and an organized armed group or even between two or more rival organized armed groups vying for power within the State). The dual armed conflicts, international and internal, may commence simultaneously or consecutively (the IAC may be preceded by the NIAC or vice versa). But the point is that—whether synchronized or unsynchronized—the hostilities have separate inter-State and intra-State strands.[93] That is what happened, for instance, in Afghanistan in October 2001: the Taliban regime, having fought a long-standing NIAC with the Northern Alliance, got itself embroiled in a parallel IAC with the United States and its allies as a result of providing shelter and support to the Al-Qaeda terrorists who had launched the notorious attack against the United States on 9/11.[94]

Vertically, armed conflicts may be mixed in two ways. First, an armed conflict may commence as a NIAC but later segue into—or bring about—an IAC. We have already seen how a forcible intervention by State B on the side of insurgents against the central government of State A will trigger an IAC.[95] It should be added that if the central government of State A disappears—and if the insurgents assume control over State A, forming a new central government therein—continuation of the hostilities by State B against the erstwhile insurgents would convert the armed conflict from a NIAC into an IAC, since the armed forces of State B will now be pitted against the new central government of State A.

An alternative vertical scenario arises when an IAC is the outcome of the implosion of a State torn apart by a NIAC and the continuation of the hostilities between the several new sovereign States into which it has fragmented. Such implosion and fragmentation occurred in Yugoslavia in the 1990s. In 1997, the Trial Chamber of the ICTY held in the *Tadić* case that, from the beginning of 1992 until May of the same year, an IAC existed in Bosnia between the forces of the Republic of Bosnia-Herzegovina on the one hand, and those of the Federal Republic of Yugoslavia (Serbia and Montenegro), on the other.[96] Yet, the majority of the Chamber (Judges Stephen and Vohrah) arrived at the conclusion that, as a result of the withdrawal of Yugoslav troops announced in May 1992, the conflict reverted to being a NIAC in nature.[97] The Presiding Judge (McDonald) dissented on the ground that the withdrawal was a fiction and that Yugoslavia remained in effective control of the Serb forces in Bosnia.[98] The majority opinion was reversed by the ICTY Appeals Chamber in 1999.[99] The original Trial Chamber's majority opinion had elicited much criticism from scholars;[100] and even before the delivery of the final judgment on appeal, another Trial Chamber of the ICTY took a divergent view in the *Delalić* case of 1998.[101] Still, the essence of the disagreement must be viewed as factual in nature. Legally speaking, the fundamental character of an armed conflict as an IAC or a NIAC can indeed metamorphose—more than once—from one stretch of time to another.

Obviously, as far as fighters in the field are concerned, it may not always be easy to detect at what exact time frame a NIAC has morphed into an IAC: if the ICTY judges—with the advantages of legal expertise and hindsight—could not readily agree on an analysis of the situation in Bosnia in 1992, one can only imagine how much more confusing the position looked from the battlefield perspective. It is therefore easier to wrestle with the situation when a clear-cut interval can be detected between the NIAC and the IAC. The template is Eritrea. This country declared its formal independence from Ethiopia—following a protracted NIAC and a referendum—in 1993. Then, after a period of several years, border disputes between Eritrea and Ethiopia triggered a full-scale IAC in 1998–2000 and reignited further hostilities in 2003. The dividing line here between the NIAC and the IAC (unlike in the former Yugoslav provinces) is easy to delineate.

Just as a NIAC may turn into an IAC, an IAC may turn into a NIAC. Iraq is a good illustration. After the fall of Baghdad in an IAC between the American-led coalition and the Baathist regime, a newly elected government was installed, at which point a NIAC evolved between it and the remnants of the Baathists. The NIAC in Iraq was waged concurrently with the coalition's IAC pursued against the same foe.[102] The IAC came to an end after fierce fighting upon the official termination of American combat operations in Iraq in 2010, but the NIAC does not appear to be over yet.

VII. Conclusions

There is no need to belabor the point that NIACs are taking place all over the world with startling frequency and with alarming intensity. NIACs are certainly more common today than IACs, and the trail of devastation that they leave behind is sometimes colossal. Winning domestic peace subsequent to a sanguinary NIAC may take decades.

These self-evident truths are not always registered in the official gazettes. The reason is that governments are often "in denial," doing their utmost to ratchet down the applicable threshold of violence. That is to say, when governments are engaged in an IAC, they tend to go one step below, claiming that the armed conflict is under the third threshold. When they are caught in a NIAC, they are reluctant to concede that they are facing an insurgency and are inclined to cling to the fiction that the violence (however protracted and intense) is sporadic and constitutes merely a disturbance below the first threshold.[103] Still, it is the duty of international lawyers to make the right call when IACs or NIACs are taking place, without making concessions to "political correctness" in the eyes of this or that government. We must constantly bear in mind that correct taxonomy lays the foundation for the application of the right legal regime.

Notes

1. Protocol Additional to the Geneva Conventions of 12 August 1949, and Relating to the Protection of Victims of Non-International Armed Conflicts, June 8, 1977, 1125 U.N.T.S. 609, *reprinted in* THE LAWS OF ARMED CONFLICTS: A COLLECTION OF CONVENTIONS, RESOLUTIONS AND OTHER DOCUMENTS 711 (Dietrich Schindler & Jiri Toman eds., 4th ed. 2004) [hereinafter Additional Protocol II].

2. *See infra* text accompanying note 27.

3. Convention for the Protection of Cultural Property in the Event of Armed Conflict art. 19, May 14, 1954, 249 U.N.T.S. 240, *reprinted in* THE LAWS OF ARMED CONFLICTS, *supra* note 1, at 999, 1007.

4. *See* Rogier Bartels, *Timelines, Borderlines and Conflicts: The Historical Evolution of the Legal Divide between International and Non-International Armed Conflicts*, 91 INTERNATIONAL REVIEW OF THE RED CROSS 35, 39 (2009).

5. Hamdan v. Rumsfeld, 548 U.S. 557, 724 (2006), *reprinted in* 45 INTERNATIONAL LEGAL MATERIALS 1130, 1195 (2006).

6. On extraterritorial law enforcement, see YORAM DINSTEIN, WAR, AGGRESSION AND SELF-DEFENCE 268–77 (5th ed. 2011).

7. *See* Yoram Dinstein, *Terrorism and Afghanistan*, *in* THE WAR IN AFGHANISTAN: A LEGAL ANALYSIS 43, 51–52 (Michael N. Schmitt ed., 2009) (Vol. 85, U.S. Naval War College International Law Studies).

8. *See infra* Part II.A.

9. Prosecutor v. Tadić, Case No. IT-94-1, Appeals Chamber Decision on the Defence Motion for Interlocutory Appeal on Jurisdiction, ¶ 70 (Int'l Crim. Trib. for the Former Yugoslavia Oct. 2, 1995), *reprinted in* 35 INTERNATIONAL LEGAL MATERIALS 35, 54 (1996) [hereinafter Tadić Appeals Chamber Decision].

10. Rome Statute of the International Criminal Court, July 17, 1998, 2187 U.N.T.S. 90, *reprinted in* THE LAWS OF ARMED CONFLICTS, *supra* note 1, at 1314, 1320 [hereinafter Rome Statute].

11. *See* Sylvain Vité, *Typology of Armed Conflicts in International Humanitarian Law: Legal Concepts and Actual Situations*, 91 INTERNATIONAL REVIEW OF THE RED CROSS 69, 78 (2009).

12. *See* UNITED KINGDOM MINISTRY OF DEFENCE, THE MANUAL OF THE LAW OF ARMED CONFLICT 17 (2004).

13. Additional Protocol II, *supra* note 1, at 777.

14. Rome Statute art. 8(2)(f), *supra* note 10, at 1320.

15. Second Protocol to the Hague Convention of 1954 for the Protection of Cultural Property in the Event of Armed Conflict, Mar. 26, 1999, 38 INTERNATIONAL LEGAL MATERIALS 769 (1999), *reprinted in* THE LAWS OF ARMED CONFLICTS, *supra* note 1, at 1037, 1045.

16. Amendment to the Convention on Prohibitions or Restrictions on the Use of Certain Conventional Weapons Which May Be Deemed to Be Excessively Injurious or to Have Indiscriminate Effects, Doc. No. CCW/CONF/II/2 (Dec. 21, 2001), *reprinted in* THE LAWS OF ARMED CONFLICTS, *supra* note 1, at 184, 185 n.4 [hereinafter 2001 Amendment].

17. The assumption is that the military units conduct themselves within the ambit of the law enforcement paradigm. If these military units use force in a manner inconsistent with that

paradigm, they bring about a crossing of the first threshold. *See* Arne W. Dahl & Magnus Sandbu, *The Threshold of Armed Conflict*, 45 MILITARY LAW AND LAW OF WAR REVIEW 369, 380 (2006).

18. Convention on the Prohibition of the Development, Production, Stockpiling and Use of Chemical Weapons and on Their Destruction, Jan. 13, 1993, 1974 U.N.T.S. 45, *reprinted in* THE LAWS OF ARMED CONFLICTS, *supra* note 1, at 239, 242, 244.

19. *See* YORAM DINSTEIN, THE CONDUCT OF HOSTILITIES UNDER THE LAW OF INTERNATIONAL ARMED CONFLICT 69–70 (2d ed. 2010).

20. Convention for the Amelioration of the Condition of the Wounded and Sick in Armed Forces in the Field, Aug. 12, 1949, 6 U.S.T. 3114, 75 U.N.T.S. 31, *reprinted in* THE LAWS OF ARMED CONFLICTS, *supra* note 1, at 459, 461–62; Convention for the Amelioration of the Condition of Wounded, Sick and Shipwrecked Members of Armed Forces at Sea, Aug. 12, 1949, 6 U.S.T. 3217, 75 U.N.T.S. 85, *reprinted in id.* at 485, 487–88; Convention Relative to the Treatment of Prisoners of War, Aug. 12, 1949, 6 U.S.T. 3316, 75 U.N.T.S. 135, *reprinted in id.* at 507, 512–13; Convention Relative to the Protection of Civilian Persons in Time of War, Aug. 12, 1949, 6 U.S.T. 3516, 75 U.N.T.S. 287, *reprinted in id.* at 575, 580–81.

21. *See supra* quotation in text accompanying note 3.

22. Military and Paramilitary Activities in and against Nicaragua (Nicar. v. U.S.), 1986 I.C.J. 14, ¶ 219 (June 27) [hereinafter *Nicaragua*].

23. *See supra* full quotation in text accompanying note 9.

24. Quoted *supra* in text accompanying note 10.

25. Prosecutor v. Tadić, Case No. IT-94-1-T, Judgment, ¶ 562 (Int'l Crim. Trib. for the Former Yugoslavia May 7, 1997), *reprinted in* 36 INTERNATIONAL LEGAL MATERIALS 908, 920 (1997) [hereinafter Tadić Judgment]. The words "banditry, unorganized and short-lived insurrections" are borrowed from COMMENTARY TO GENEVA CONVENTION I FOR THE AMELIORATION OF THE CONDITION OF THE WOUNDED AND SICK IN ARMED FORCES IN THE FIELD 50 (Jean S. Pictet ed., 1952).

26. *See especially* Prosecutor v. Boškoski & Tarčulovski, Case No. IT-04-82-T, Judgment, ¶ 177 (Int'l Crim. Trib. for the Former Yugoslavia July 10, 2008).

27. Additional Protocol II, *supra* note 1, at 777.

28. COMMENTARY ON THE ADDITIONAL PROTOCOLS OF 8 JUNE 1977 TO THE GENEVA CONVENTIONS OF 12 AUGUST 1949 ¶¶ 4464, 4466 (Yves Sandoz, Christophe Swinarski & Bruno Zimmermann eds., 1987) [hereinafter AP COMMENTARY].

29. LESLIE C. GREEN, THE CONTEMPORARY LAW OF ARMED CONFLICT (2d ed. 2000).

30. AP COMMENTARY, *supra* note 28, ¶ 4469.

31. *See infra* text accompanying note 89.

32. *See* GARY D. SOLIS, THE LAW OF ARMED CONFLICT: INTERNATIONAL HUMANITARIAN LAW IN WAR 131 (2010).

33. It has been argued that AP II does not apply in the "failed State" scenario where organized armed groups are fighting each other. *See* A.P.V. ROGERS, LAW ON THE BATTLEFIELD 221 (2d ed. 2004).

34. *See* Emily Crawford, *Blurring the Lines between International and Non-International Armed Conflicts—The Evolution of Customary International Law Applicable in Internal Armed Conflicts*, 15 AUSTRALIAN INTERNATIONAL LAW JOURNAL 29, 47–48 (2008).

35. *See infra* discussion Part III.

36. *See* DINSTEIN, *supra* note 6, at 87–91.

37. *See* PETER MALANCZUK, AKEHURST'S MODERN INTRODUCTION TO INTERNATIONAL LAW 318 (7th ed. 1997).

38. Prosecutor v. Kunarac et al., Case No. IT-96-23 & IT-96-23/1-A, Judgment, ¶ 57 (Int'l Crim. Trib. for the Former Yugoslavia June 12, 2002).

39. *See* Rome Statute, *supra* note 10, at 1319–20.

40. Amended Protocol on Prohibitions or Restrictions on the Use of Mines, Booby-Traps and Other Devices (Amended Protocol II), May 3, 1996, S. Treaty Doc. No. 105-1 (1997), *reprinted in* THE LAWS OF ARMED CONFLICTS, *supra* note 1, at 196.

41. Second Protocol to the Hague Convention, *supra* note 15, at 1045.

42. 2001 Amendment, *supra* note 16, at 185 n.4.

43. *See supra* text accompanying notes 22 & 34.

44. *See* Emily Crawford, *Unequal before the Law: The Case for the Elimination of the Distinction between International and Non-International Armed Conflicts*, 20 LEIDEN JOURNAL OF INTERNATIONAL LAW 441, 449–52 (2002).

45. *See* THE HANDBOOK OF INTERNATIONAL HUMANITARIAN LAW 627 (Dieter Fleck ed., 2d ed. 2008).

46. There is an interesting question relating to the treatment of captured personnel in a NIAC fought between organized armed groups in a "failed State." Since there is no central government left, and all the organized armed groups in the field are equally shorn of any authority to cloak themselves with the mantle of the State—all of them operating on the same unconstitutional footing vis-à-vis each other—the construct of treason cannot be factored into the equation. Hence, none of the groups can justifiably claim that its opponents are rebelling against the State's authority. That being the case, why should the diverse groups not apply to the captured personnel of their foes the rules pertaining to the status of prisoners of war?

47. *See* Jann K. Kleffner, *From "Belligerents" to "Fighters" and Civilians Directly Participating in Hostilities—On the Principle of Distinction in Non-International Armed Conflicts One Hundred Years after the Second Hague Peace Conference*, 54 NETHERLANDS INTERNATIONAL LAW REVIEW 315, 321 (2007).

48. MICHAEL N. SCHMITT, CHARLES H.B. GARRAWAY & YORAM DINSTEIN, THE MANUAL ON THE LAW OF NON-INTERNATIONAL ARMED CONFLICT WITH COMMENTARY ¶ 1.1.2 (2006).

49. HARVARD PROGRAM ON HUMANITARIAN POLICY AND CONFLICT RESEARCH, COMMENTARY ON THE HPCR MANUAL ON INTERNATIONAL LAW APPLICABLE TO AIR AND MISSILE WARFARE 305 (2010).

50. *See supra* Part I.A.

51. *See* discussion *infra* Part IV.A.

52. *See* ROGER O'KEEFE, THE PROTECTION OF CULTURAL PROPERTY IN ARMED CONFLICT 98 (2006).

53. *See* YORAM DINSTEIN, THE INTERNATIONAL LAW OF BELLIGERENT OCCUPATION 34 (2009).

54. To be examined *infra* Part IV.A.

55. Protocol Additional to the Geneva Conventions of 12 August 1949, and Relating to the Protection of Victims of International Armed Conflicts, June 8, 1977, 1125 U.N.T.S. 3, *reprinted in* THE LAWS OF ARMED CONFLICTS, *supra* note 1, at 715.

56. *See* STEPHEN C. NEFF, WAR AND THE LAW OF NATIONS: A GENERAL HISTORY 258–59 (2005).

57. See the decision of the Privy Council in *Public Prosecutor v. Koi*, [1968] A.C. 829, 856–58 (P.C. 1967).

58. *See* Richard R. Baxter, Ius in Bello Interno: *The Present and Future Law, in* LAW AND CIVIL WAR IN THE MODERN WORLD 518, 529 (John N. Moore ed., 1974).

59. *See infra* Part V.B.

60. *Id.*

61. *See infra* Part V.A.

62. *See* ANTHONY CULLEN, THE CONCEPT OF NON-INTERNATIONAL ARMED CONFLICT IN INTERNATIONAL HUMANITARIAN LAW 22–23 (2010).

63. *See* Vernon A. O'Rourke, *Recognition of Belligerency and the Spanish War*, 31 AMERICAN JOURNAL OF INTERNATIONAL LAW 398, 402 (1937).

64. See the Arbitral Award of 1903, between Britain and Venezuela, in the *Compagnie Générale des Asphaltes de France* case. Here the umpire, F. Plumely, stated the law as follows:

> To close ports which are in the hands of revolutionists by governmental decree or order is impossible under international law. It may in a proper way and under proper circumstances and conditions in time of peace declare what of its ports shall be open and what of them shall be closed. But when these ports or any of them are in the hands of foreign belligerents or of insurgents, it has no power to close or to open them, for the palpable reason that it is no longer in control of them. It has then the right of blockade alone, which can only be declared to the extent that it has the naval power to make it effective in fact.

Compagnie Générale des Asphaltes de France (Gr. Brit. v. Venez.), 9 REPORTS OF INTERNATIONAL ARBITRAL AWARDS 389, 394.

65. *See* INTERNATIONAL INSTITUTE OF HUMANITARIAN LAW, SAN REMO MANUAL ON INTERNATIONAL LAW APPLICABLE TO ARMED CONFLICTS AT SEA 176–78 (Louise Doswald-Beck ed., 1995).

66. *See* L.H. Woolsey, Editorial Comment, *Closure of Ports by the Chinese Nationalist Government*, 44 AMERICAN JOURNAL OF INTERNATIONAL LAW 350, 353–54 (1950).

67. 1 OPPENHEIM'S INTERNATIONAL LAW 166 (Sir Robert Jennings & Sir Arthur Watts eds., 9th ed. 1992).

68. *See* Norman J. Padelford, *International Law and the Spanish Civil War*, 31 AMERICAN JOURNAL OF INTERNATIONAL LAW 226, 228 (1937).

69. *See* discussion *infra* Part V.C.

70. *See* HERSCH LAUTERPACHT, RECOGNITION IN INTERNATIONAL LAW 95 (1947).

71. On this issue, and the controversy surrounding it, see DINSTEIN, *supra* note 6, at 221–24.

72. *See* Christine Byron, *Armed Conflicts: International or Non-International?*, 6 JOURNAL OF CONFLICT AND SECURITY LAW 63, 81 (2001).

73. *Nicaragua*, *supra* note 22, ¶ 195.

74. *See* dissenting opinions of Judges Schwebel and Jennings, *id.* at 349, 543.

75. Institut de Droit International, Resolution, *The Principle of Non-Intervention in Civil Wars*, 56 ANNUAIRE DE L'INSTITUT DE DROIT INTERNATIONAL 545, 547 (1975) [hereinafter Institut de Droit International Resolution].

76. *See* James W. Garner, *Questions of International Law in the Spanish Civil War*, 31 AMERICAN JOURNAL OF INTERNATIONAL LAW 66, 67–69 (1937).

77. *Nicaragua*, *supra* note 22, at 246.

78. *Cf.* Louise Doswald-Beck, *The Legal Validity of Military Intervention by Invitation of the Government*, 56 BRITISH YEAR BOOK OF INTERNATIONAL LAW 189–252 (1985).

79. *See* 1 OPPENHEIM'S INTERNATIONAL LAW, *supra* note 67, at 435–36.

80. *See* DINSTEIN, *supra* note 6, at 119.

81. Protocol Relating to the Establishment of the Peace and Security Council of the African Union (AUPSC), July 9, 2002, *reprinted in* AFRICA: SELECTED DOCUMENTS ON CONSTITUTIVE, CONFLICT AND SECURITY, HUMANITARIAN, AND JUDICIAL ISSUES 161, 163 (Jeremy I. Levitt ed., 2003).

82. Armed Activities on the Territory of the Congo (Dem. Rep. Congo v. Uganda), 2005 I.C.J. 168, ¶ 52 (Dec. 19).

83. *Id.*, ¶ 47.

84. *See* Article 3(e) of the 1974 General Assembly Definition of Aggression resolution. G.A. Res. 3314 (XXIX), U.N. GAOR, 29th Sess., Supp. No. 31, U.N. Doc. A/9890 (Dec. 14, 1974), *reprinted in* 29(1) RESOLUTIONS OF THE GENERAL ASSEMBLY 142, 144 (1974). Such conduct is now a crime. See Article 8 *bis* (2) of the Rome Statute of the International Criminal Court, as amended in Kampala in 2010. Res. RC/Res.6, Annex I ¶ 2, U.N. Doc. RC/Res.6 (June 11, 2010), *reprinted in* 49 INTERNATIONAL LEGAL MATERIALS 1334, 1335 (2010).

85. Institut de Droit International Resolution, *supra* note 75.

86. For an example, see CHRISTINE D. GRAY, INTERNATIONAL LAW AND THE USE OF FORCE 96 (3d ed. 2008).

87. *See supra* text accompanying notes 68 & 70.

88. *Cf.* with *supra* text accompanying note 86 of circumstances when two States militarily intervene in a NIAC in a "failed State."

89. For an illustration, see UN Security Council Resolution 1973 concerning the situation in Libya. S.C. Res. 1973, U.N. Doc. S/RES/1973 (Mar. 17, 2011).

90. *See supra* text accompanying note 11.

91. Juan Carlos Gomez, *Twenty-First-Century Challenges: The Use of Military Forces to Combat Criminal Threats*, which is Chapter XIII in this volume, at 279.

92. *See* Raymundo B. Ferrer & Randolph G. Cabangbang, *Non-International Armed Conflicts in the Philippines*, which is Chapter XII in this volume, at 263.

93. *See* Christopher Greenwood, *The Development of International Humanitarian Law by the International Tribunal for the Former Yugoslavia*, 2 MAX PLANCK YEARBOOK OF UNITED NATIONS LAW 97, 117 (1998).

94. *See* Christopher Greenwood, *International Law and the 'War against Terrorism,'* 78 INTERNATIONAL AFFAIRS 301, 309 (2002).

95. *See* Jelena Pejić, *Status of Armed Conflicts*, *in* PERSPECTIVES ON THE ICRC STUDY ON CUSTOMARY INTERNATIONAL HUMANITARIAN LAW 77, 92 (Elizabeth Wilmshurst & Susan Breau eds., 2007).

96. Tadić Judgment, *supra* note 25, ¶ 569.

97. *Id.*, ¶ 607.

98. *Id.*, ¶ 7 (McDonald, J. dissenting).

99. Tadić Appeals Chamber Decision, *supra* note 9, ¶ 157.

100. *See, e.g.*, Theodor Meron, *Classification of Armed Conflict in the Former Yugoslavia:* Nicaragua*'s Fallout*, 92 AMERICAN JOURNAL OF INTERNATIONAL LAW 236–42 (1998).

101. Prosecutor v. Delalić et al., IT-96-21-T, Judgment, ¶¶ 199–234 (Int'l Crim. Trib. for the Former Yugoslavia Nov. 16, 1998), *reprinted in* 38 INTERNATIONAL LEGAL MATERIALS 57, 58 (1999).

102. *See* Yoram Dinstein, *Concluding Observations: The Influence of the Conflict in Iraq on International Law*, *in* THE WAR IN IRAQ: A LEGAL ANALYSIS 479, 482 (Raul "Pete" Pedrozo ed., 2010) (Vol. 86, U.S. Naval War College International Law Studies).

103. For a list of cases in which governments refused to admit that internal violence had crossed the first threshold, see EVE LA HAYE, WAR CRIMES IN INTERNAL ARMED CONFLICTS 42 (2008).

APPENDIX

CONTRIBUTORS

Contributors

Editors' Note: In order to most accurately portray the events of the conference, the biographical data in this appendix reflect the positions in which the authors were serving at the time of the conference, as set forth in the conference brochures and materials.

Air Commodore Bill Boothby is the Deputy Director of Legal Services for the Royal Air Force. A legal officer since 1981, he has served in Germany, Hong Kong, Cyprus and Croatia, and at the Ministry of Defence in London. He received a PhD degree in international law at the Europa-Universität Viadrina in Frankfurt (Oder), Germany. A participant in the Program on Humanitarian Policy and Conflict Research at Harvard University, Air Commodore Boothby was a participant in the process that produced the *HPCR Manual on International Law Applicable to Air and Missile Warfare* and is participating in the NATO Cooperative Cyber Defence Centre of Excellence project to prepare a manual on the law of cyber warfare. He is the author of *Weapons and the Law of Armed Conflict* published in 2009 and is coauthoring with Professor Michael N. Schmitt *The Law of Targeting* (forthcoming).

Lieutenant Colonel Randolph G. Cabangbang (INF), Philippine Army, is the Chief, Unified Command Staff for Civil Military Affairs and Public Information Officer, Western Mindanao Command, both located in Zamboanga City. He graduated from the Philippine Military Academy in 1991 and has served assignments as a platoon leader, company commander, intelligence officer, civil-military affairs officer, operations officer and public affairs officer. His awards include bronze cross medals, the gold cross medal, the wounded personnel medal for wounds sustained in an encounter with New People's Army insurgents, military merit medals and military commendation medals. Lieutenant Colonel Cabangbang has also received the International Military Student Officer's Badge for training undertaken at the U.S. Army John F. Kennedy Special Warfare Center and School and the U.S. Army National Guard Commendation Medal for assistance provided to Joint Special Operations Task Force–Philippines.

Professor John Cerone is Professor of International Law and Director of the Center for International Law and Policy at New England Law | Boston. He has been a fellow at the Max Planck Institute for Comparative Public Law and International

Law and a visiting scholar at the International Criminal Court. He has also been a Fulbright scholar at both the Danish Institute for Human Rights and the Tokyo University of Foreign Studies. Before joining the New England faculty in 2004, Professor Cerone was executive director of the War Crimes Research Office at American University Washington College of Law, where he served as a legal adviser to various international criminal courts and tribunals. As a practicing international lawyer, Professor Cerone has worked for a number of different intergovernmental and nongovernmental organizations, including the United Nations, the Organization for Security and Cooperation in Europe, the International Secretariat of Amnesty International, and the International Crisis Group. He also has extensive field experience in conflict and post-conflict environments, such as Afghanistan, Kosovo, Sierra Leone and East Timor. He is accredited by the United Nations to represent the American Society of International Law before various UN bodies and is an elected member of the International Institute of Humanitarian Law. In 2009 he served as special adviser to the first U.S. delegation to the UN Human Rights Council. He is the author of several articles and book chapters on international law, as well as the casebook *Public International Law: Cases, Problems, and Texts* (with Dinah Shelton and Stephen McCaffrey).

Professor Geoffrey S. Corn is professor of law at South Texas College of Law. He spent twenty-one years on active duty in the Army, retiring in the rank of lieutenant colonel. In his last assignment, Professor Corn served as the Special Assistant for Law of War Matters to the U.S. Army Judge Advocate General, the Army's senior law of war adviser and representative to the Department of Defense Law of War Working Group. He is the author of more than thirty articles focused on the law of armed conflict, national security law criminal procedure and criminal ethics. He is the lead author of *The Laws of War and the War on Terror*, coauthor of *Principles of Counter-Terrorism* and lead author of the textbook *The Law of Armed Conflict: An Operational Perspective*. A graduate of Hartwick College, Professor Corn earned his JD degree from The George Washington University School of Law and his LLM degree from the U.S. Army Judge Advocate General's Legal Center and School. He is also a graduate of the Army Command and Staff College.

Professor Yoram Dinstein is Professor Emeritus of International Law at Tel Aviv University (Israel). He is a former President of the University, as well as former Rector and former Dean of the Faculty of Law. Professor Dinstein served two appointments as the Charles H. Stockton Professor of International Law at the Naval War College. He was also a Humboldt Fellow at the Max Planck Institute for Comparative Public Law and International Law at Heidelberg (Germany), a Meltzer

Visiting Professor of International Law at New York University and a Visiting Professor of Law at the University of Toronto. Professor Dinstein is a Member of the Institute of International Law and has written extensively on subjects relating to international law, human rights and the law of armed conflict. He is the founder and Editor of the *Israel Yearbook on Human Rights*. He is the author of *War, Aggression and Self-Defence*, now in its fourth edition (2005), and *The International Law of Belligerent Occupation* (2009). His latest book is *The Conduct of Hostilities under the Law of International Armed Conflict* (2nd edition, 2010). Professor Dinstein is frequently cited by the Supreme Court of Israel. He has also been cited by judges of the International Court of Justice, the International Criminal Tribunal for the former Yugoslavia, the House of Lords and the Supreme Court of Canada.

Doctor Knut Dörmann is the Head of the Legal Division of the International Committee of the Red Cross (ICRC) and has served in that position since December 2007. Prior to that, he was the Deputy Head of the Legal Division from 2004 to 2007 and a legal adviser in the Legal Division from 1998 to 2004. He was a member of the ICRC delegation to the Preparatory Commission of the International Criminal Court. He holds a Doctor of Laws degree from the University of Bochum in Germany (2001). He was Managing Editor of *Humanitäres Völkerrecht—Informationsschriften* from 1991 to 1997. Prior to joining the ICRC, he was a Research Assistant (1988–93) and a Research Associate (1993–97) at the Institute for International Law of Peace and Armed Conflict, University of Bochum. Doctor Dörmann is and has been a member of several groups of experts working on the current challenges of international humanitarian law. He has extensively spoken and published on the international law of peace, international humanitarian law and international criminal law. He received the 2005 Certificate of Merit of the American Society of International Law for his book *Elements of War Crimes under the Rome Statute of the International Criminal Court.*

Lieutenant General Raymundo B. Ferrer, Philippine Army, is the Commander of Western Mindanao Command in the southern Philippines. He has served continuously in various assignments in the southern Philippines from 2006 to the present. He began his military career when he joined the Philippine Military Academy as a cadet, graduating in 1977 with a BS degree. During his military service, Lieutenant General Ferrer has served as a platoon leader, company commander, battalion commander, brigade commander and division commander, and in staff positions at various military units in the Luzon, Visayas and Mindanao regions. He is the recipient of numerous military and civilian awards, which he earned for both peacetime and combat service. His military awards include distinguished service stars, bronze cross medals, military merit medals, military commendation medals and civic action medals, and Luzon, Visayas and Mindanao campaign medals. He received the Presidential Legion of Honor Award for the successful implementation of the state of emergency and martial law in Maguindanao Province in December 2009, and the Mindanao Peace Champion Award by the United Nations Action for Conflict Transformation for Peace Programme in December 2010 for his contributions to peace building in Mindanao.

Professor Charles Garraway CBE retired in 2003 after thirty years in the United Kingdom Army Legal Services, initially as a criminal prosecutor and then as an adviser on the law of armed conflict and operational law. In that capacity, he represented the Ministry of Defence at numerous international conferences and was part of UK delegations to the First Review Conference for the 1981 Conventional Weapons Convention, the negotiations on the establishment of an International Criminal Court and the Diplomatic Conference that led to the 1999 Second Protocol to the 1954 Hague Convention on Cultural Property. He was also the senior Army lawyer deployed to the Arabian Gulf during the 1990–91 Gulf conflict. Since retiring, Professor Garraway spent three months in Baghdad working for the Foreign Office on transitional justice issues and six months as a senior research fellow at the British Institute of International and Comparative Law. He was the 2004–5 Charles H. Stockton Professor of International Law at the Naval War College. He is currently a Visiting Fellow in the Department of Human Rights, University of Essex, and an Associate Fellow at the Royal Institute of International Affairs (Chatham House) in the International Security Programme. In 2006, he was elected as a member of the International Humanitarian Fact Finding Commission, established under Article 90 of Additional Protocol I to the Geneva Conventions of 1949. Professor Garraway is a member of the teaching faculty at the International Institute of International Law, San Remo, Italy, and has lectured extensively on the law of armed conflict and international criminal justice. He is a widely published author.

Colonel Juan Carlos Gomez, Colombian Air Force, is the Director of the Colombian Air Force Postgraduate School in Bogotá. He has served on active duty for twenty-six years. He has two thousand five hundred flight hours as a combat navigator in combat, intelligence and transport aircraft. He is also a lawyer who specializes in administrative law. He earned an MA degree in National Security and Civil Military Relations from the U.S. Naval Postgraduate School in 2001. During the last twelve years, Colonel Gomez has worked in the fields of human rights law and international humanitarian law, while also giving operational advice to Colombian military commanders in military operations. He was the coauthor of the

Colombian Ministry of Defense's *Human Rights and International Humanitarian Law Policy*, published in 2008, and the first *Manual of Operational Law for the Colombian Military*, published in 2009. He has authored multiple articles, as well as two chapters regarding the use of force and application of the law of war in responding to non-traditional threats. In 2009, Colonel Gomez concluded a five-year assignment as the Director of the Human Rights and International Humanitarian Law office in the Colombian Ministry of Defense. Until May 2011, he served as a visiting professor at the Center for Hemispheric Defense Studies at the U.S. National Defense University.

Colonel David E. Graham, U.S. Army (Ret.), is the Executive Director of the U.S. Army Judge Advocate General's Legal Center and School. He is a graduate of Texas A&M University (BA), The George Washington University (MA) and the University of Texas School of Law (JD). He is also a Distinguished Graduate of the National War College. Colonel Graham has over thirty years of experience as an Army judge advocate. He has an extensive background in both international and operational law, with a mix of assignments in the United States, Europe, Latin America and the Middle East. During his last eight years on active duty, he served as the Chief of International/Operational Law, Office of The Judge Advocate General, Department of the Army. Mr. Graham has a long-standing relationship with the Legal Center and School, where he served as a professor, a department head and Academic Director, as well as the Director of the Center for Law and Military Operations. Colonel Graham is a published author in multiple legal and professional journals, and has lectured extensively in both U.S. and international fora on international and operational law topics.

Professor Dr. Wolff Heintschel von Heinegg is Professor of Public Law, especially public international law, European law and foreign constitutional law, at the Europa-Universität Viadrina in Frankfurt (Oder), Germany. From October 2004 to October 2008 he was the dean of the law faculty of the Europa-Universität. Since then he has served as the university's Vice President. Prior to his association with the Europa-Universität, he served as Professor of Public International Law at the University of Augsburg. In academic year 2003–4 he was the Charles H. Stockton Professor of International Law at the U.S. Naval War College. He had been a visiting professor at the Universities of Kaliningrad (Russia), Almaty (Kazakhstan), Santiago de Cuba (Cuba) and Nice (France). He was the Rapporteur of the International Law Association Committee on Maritime Neutrality and was the Vice President of the German Society of Military Law and the Law of War. He is a member of the Council of the International Institute of Humanitarian Law in San

Remo, Italy. Professor Heintschel von Heinegg was among a group of international lawyers and naval experts who produced the *San Remo Manual on International Law Applicable to Armed Conflicts at Sea*, and in 2002 he published the German *Humanitarian Law in Armed Conflicts Manual.* Professor Heintschel von Heinegg is a member of several groups of experts working on the current state, and progressive development, of international humanitarian law. He is a widely published author of articles and books on public international law and German constitutional law.

Colonel Richard B. "Dick" Jackson, U.S. Army (Ret.), is the Special Assistant to the U.S. Army Judge Advocate General for Law of War Matters. He has served in that position since 2005, when he retired from the U.S. Army after over thirty years in uniform. Colonel Jackson has extensive experience in the law of war and international and operational law. He served in infantry, special forces, joint and coalition commands during his military career, spending most of the last ten years as the principal legal advisor at a U.S. Army division, Multinational Division North in Bosnia; U.S. Army Special Operations Command; U.S. Army Pacific; and Joint Forces Command–Naples, a NATO headquarters. He served in military operations in Panama, Haiti, Bosnia, Kosovo and Iraq. He was also the Chair of the International and Operational Law Department of the U.S. Army Judge Advocate General's Legal Center and School. He has written extensively in professional publications and lectured around the world on law of war matters. Colonel Jackson has represented the U.S. government at several international conferences and negotiations regarding arms control, the law of war and protection of cultural property.

Mr. William K. Lietzau is the Deputy Assistant Secretary of Defense for Detainee Policy in the U.S. Department of Defense. In this capacity, he is responsible for developing policy recommendations and coordinating global policy guidance relating to individuals captured or detained by the Department of Defense. Mr. Lietzau is a retired Marine Corps officer who served primarily as a judge advocate. His last assignment on active duty was at the White House as Deputy Legal Adviser to the National Security Council, where he addressed a variety of legal issues dealing with subjects such as international criminal law, counter-narcotics, interdictions, piracy, counterterrorism, weapons of mass destruction, non-proliferation, missile defense, foreign assistance and treaty implementation. Mr. Lietzau was initially trained as an infantry officer. As a judge advocate, he was stationed in Japan, Germany and numerous locations within the United States. As a legal adviser, he served as Staff Judge Advocate to U.S. European Command, Chief of the Law of War Branch for the Department of the Navy's International Law Division, Deputy Legal Adviser to the Chairman of the Joint Chiefs of Staff and Special Adviser to the

General Counsel in the Office of the Secretary of Defense. Mr. Lietzau served on several U.S. delegations in multilateral treaty negotiations, including those adopting the Terrorist Bombing Convention, the Ottawa Convention banning anti-personnel landmines, the Second Protocol to the Hague Cultural Property Convention and the Rome Statute for the International Criminal Court. Mr. Lietzau led the U.S. negotiating team responsible for defining war crimes for the International Criminal Court. He has also taught international law as an adjunct professor in Georgetown University Law Center's LLM program and published several articles on international, criminal and constitutional law subjects.

Captain Rob McLaughlin, Royal Australian Navy, is currently an associate professor of law at the Australian National University. Previously, he was Director of Operations and International Law in the Department of Defence Legal Division and Director, Naval Legal Service. His previous appointments include as counsel assisting the Chief of Defence Force Commission of Inquiry into the loss of *HMAS Sydney II*, and service as the Strategic Legal Adviser, the Fleet Legal Officer and Executive Officer of *HMAS Wollongong*. He joined the Australian Defence Force (Army Reserve) in 1986 as a rifleman, and was commissioned into the Navy in 1990 as a seaman officer, serving in patrol vessels, landing craft, frigates and destroyer escorts, before subspecializing in submarines. He served as Chief of Maritime Operations for the United Nations Transitional Administration in East Timor Peacekeeping Force in 2001–2, and as the Plans Officer and Legal Officer to the Naval Task Group Commander in Iraq in 2003. He is a graduate of the University of Queensland and holds an MA (history) degree from Brown University. Captain McLaughlin obtained his LLB degree at the University of Queensland, an LLM (international law) degree at the Australian National University and MPhil (international relations) and PhD degrees at Cambridge University.

Professor John F. Murphy is professor of law at Villanova University School of Law. In addition to teaching, Professor Murphy's career includes a year in India on a Ford Foundation Fellowship; private practice in New York City and Washington, D.C.; and service in the Office of the Assistant Legal Adviser for United Nations Affairs, U.S. Department of State. He was previously on the law faculty at the University of Kansas and has been a visiting professor at Cornell University and Georgetown University. During academic year 1980–81, Professor Murphy was the Charles H. Stockton Professor of International Law at the U.S. Naval War College. He is the author of numerous articles, comments and reviews on international law and relations, as well as the author or editor of various books or monographs. Most recently, he has authored *The Evolving Dimensions of International*

Law: Hard Choices for the World Community (2010). His casebook (with Alan C. Swan), *The Regulation of International Business and Economic Relations* (2nd edition, 1999), was awarded a certificate of merit by the American Society of International Law in 1992. Professor Murphy has served as a consultant to the U.S. Departments of State and Justice, the ABA Standing Committee on Law and National Security, and the United Nations Crime Bureau, and has testified before Congress on several occasions.

Mr. Stephen Pomper is Assistant Legal Adviser for Political Military Affairs in the Office of the Legal Adviser at the U.S. Department of State. Mr. Pomper's areas of expertise include the international law of armed conflict, use of force and U.S. national security law. He has served as the Assistant Legal Adviser for Afghanistan, Pakistan, and South and Central Asia, and as an attorney adviser with responsibility for counterterrorism issues in the Legal Adviser's Office of Law Enforcement and Intelligence. Prior to joining the Department of State in 2002, Mr. Pomper practiced law at Cleary, Gottlieb, Steen, and Hamilton. He is a graduate of Harvard College and Yale Law School.

Professor Michael N. Schmitt holds the Chair of Public International Law, Durham University in the United Kingdom. He was previously Dean of the George C. Marshall European Center for Security Studies in Garmisch-Partenkirchen, Germany, where he had served as Professor of International Law. During academic year 2007–8, he occupied the Charles H. Stockton Chair of International Law at the U.S. Naval War College. Before joining the Marshall Center faculty, Professor Schmitt served as a judge advocate in the U.S. Air Force for twenty years. During his military career, he specialized in operational and international law, and was senior legal adviser to multiple Air Force units, including units conducting combat operations over northern Iraq. He is the General Editor of the *Yearbook of International Humanitarian Law* and serves on the editorial boards of the *International Review of the Red Cross, Journal of International Peacekeeping*, the *Journal of Military Ethics, Connections, Journal of International Humanitarian Legal Studies* and the *International Humanitarian Law Series*. The author of many scholarly articles on law and military affairs and contributing editor for multiple volumes of the Naval War College's International Law Studies series, his works have been published in Belgium, Chile, Germany, Israel, Italy, Norway, Peru, Sweden and Switzerland. Professor Schmitt became the Chairman of the International Law Department, U.S. Naval War College, on October 1, 2011.

Professor Kenneth Watkin is the Charles H. Stockton Professor of International Law at the U S. Naval War College. He retired in April 2010 as the Judge Advocate General for the Canadian Forces after thirty-three years of military service, including twenty-eight years as a military legal officer. During his military service, in which he attained the rank of Brigadier-General, he served as the Deputy Judge Advocate General/Operations, Special Assistant to the Judge Advocate General and the Assistant Judge Advocate General/Atlantic Region. He was the director of offices dealing with human rights and information law, operational law, claims and civil litigation, and training. His operational law experience included service as a legal adviser to the Canadian Navy, adviser to Canadian commanders in Bosnia and as the Deputy Judge Advocate General/Operations at the time of the terrorist attacks on September 11, 2001, and during a significant portion of the subsequent deployments in connection with the "Campaign Against Terrorism." He was the legal adviser to a 1993 Canadian military/civilian board of inquiry that investigated the activities of the Canadian Airborne Regiment Battle Group in Somalia. From 1995 to 2005, he was counsel in various investigations and inquiries arising from the 1994 genocide in Rwanda. Professor Watkin is a widely published author on a variety of operational law topics, including the law of armed conflict, discipline and human rights.

Professor Sean Watts is an assistant professor of law at Creighton University Law School, where he teaches constitutional law, federal courts, federal habeas corpus, international criminal law and military law. Additional teaching experience includes service as a lecturer at the University of Virginia School of Law and at The Judge Advocate General's Legal Center and School of the U.S. Army. He has also provided law of war instruction at a wide range of domestic and international governmental agencies and educational institutions. His primary research interest is legal regulation of evolving forms of warfare. Prior to teaching, Watts served as an Army officer for fifteen years in legal and operational assignments, including chief of claims, trial defense counsel, chief of international and operational law, funded legal education program student, tank company executive officer, and tank platoon leader. Professor Watts was recently awarded Creighton Law School's Outstanding Faculty Member of the Year and received the 2010 American Society of International Law Francis Lieber Military Prize for his article "Combatant Status and Computer Network Attack."

Index

A

B

C

I

R

S

T

V

W

Y

PREVIOUS "BLUE BOOKS"*
International Law
Studies/Documents/Situations/Decisions/Topics/Discussions

VOL 87

INTERNATIONAL LAW AND THE CHANGING CHARACTER OF WAR (Raul A. "Pete" Pedrozo & Daria P. Wollschlaeger eds., 2011) (Vol. 87, U.S. Naval War College International Law Studies).

VOL 86

THE WAR IN IRAQ: A LEGAL ANALYSIS (Raul A. "Pete" Pedrozo ed., 2010) (Vol. 86, U.S. Naval War College International Law Studies).

VOL 85

THE WAR IN AFGHANISTAN: A LEGAL ANALYSIS (Michael N. Schmitt ed., 2009) (Vol. 85, U.S. Naval War College International Law Studies).

VOL 84

INTERNATIONAL LAW AND MILITARY OPERATIONS (Michael D. Carsten ed., 2008) (Vol. 84, U.S. Naval War College International Law Studies).

VOL 83

GLOBAL LEGAL CHALLENGES: COMMAND OF THE COMMONS, STRATEGIC COMMUNICATIONS AND NATURAL DISASTERS (Michael D. Carsten ed., 2007) (Vol. 83, U.S. Naval War College International Law Studies).

VOL 82

THE LAW OF WAR IN THE 21ST CENTURY: WEAPONRY AND THE USE OF FORCE (Anthony M. Helm ed., 2006) (Vol. 82, U.S. Naval War College International Law Studies).

VOL 81

INTERNATIONAL LAW CHALLENGES: HOMELAND SECURITY AND COMBATING TERRORISM (Thomas McK. Sparks & Glenn M. Sulmasy eds., 2006) (Vol. 81, U.S. Naval War College International Law Studies).

VOL 80

ISSUES IN INTERNATIONAL LAW AND MILITARY OPERATIONS (Richard B. Jaques ed., 2006) (Vol. 80, U.S. Naval War College International Law Studies).

VOL 79

INTERNATIONAL LAW AND THE WAR ON TERROR (Fred L. Borch & Paul S. Wilson eds., 2003) (Vol. 79, U.S. Naval War College International Law Studies).

VOL 78

LEGAL AND ETHICAL LESSONS OF NATO'S KOSOVO CAMPAIGN (Andru E. Wall ed., 2002) (Vol. 78, U.S. Naval War College International Law Studies).

VOL 77

LILLICH ON THE FORCIBLE PROTECTION OF NATIONALS ABROAD (Thomas C. Wingfield & James E. Meyen eds., 2002) (Vol. 77, U.S. Naval War College International Law Studies).

---

* Copies of selected editions of the "Blue Book" series may be obtained commercially from William S. Hein & Co., Inc. This does not constitute government endorsement of either William S. Hein & Co., Inc. as a commercial source and no official endorsement is intended or implied. Electronic copies of this volume and volumes 59–87 may be located at the following website: http://www.usnwc.edu/Publications/Studies-Series.aspx.

VOL 76

COMPUTER NETWORK ATTACK AND INTERNATIONAL LAW (Michael N. Schmitt & Brian T. O'Donnell eds., 2002) (Vol. 76, U.S. Naval War College International Law Studies).

VOL 75

INTERNATIONAL LAW ACROSS THE SPECTRUM OF CONFLICT: ESSAYS IN HONOUR OF PROFESSOR L.C. GREEN ON THE OCCASION OF HIS EIGHTIETH BIRTHDAY (Michael N. Schmitt ed., 2000) (Vol. 75, U.S. Naval War College International Law Studies).

VOL 74

GEORGE K. WALKER, THE TANKER WAR, 1980–88: LAW AND POLICY (2000) (Vol. 74, U.S. Naval War College International Law Studies).

VOL 73

ANNOTATED SUPPLEMENT TO THE COMMANDER'S HANDBOOK ON THE LAW OF NAVAL OPERATIONS (A.R. Thomas & James C. Duncan eds., 1999) (Vol. 73, U.S. Naval War College International Law Studies).

VOL 72

THE LAW OF MILITARY OPERATIONS: LIBER AMICORUM PROFESSOR JACK GRUNAWALT (Michael N. Schmitt ed., 1998) (Vol. 72, U.S. Naval War College International Law Studies).

VOL 71

THE LAW OF ARMED CONFLICT: INTO THE NEXT MILLENNIUM (Michael N. Schmitt & Leslie C. Green eds., 1998) (Vol. 71, U.S. Naval War College International Law Studies).

VOL 70

LEVIE ON THE LAW OF WAR (Michael N. Schmitt & Leslie C. Green eds., 1998) (Vol. 70, U.S. Naval War College International Law Studies).

VOL 69

PROTECTION OF THE ENVIRONMENT DURING ARMED CONFLICT (Richard J. Grunawalt, John E. King & Ronald S. McClain eds., 1996) (Vol. 69, U.S. Naval War College International Law Studies).

VOL 68

READINGS ON INTERNATIONAL LAW FROM THE NAVAL WAR COLLEGE REVIEW 1978–1994 (John Norton Moore & Robert F. Turner eds., 1995) (Vol. 68, U.S. Naval War College International Law Studies).

VOL 67

LEGAL AND MORAL CONSTRAINTS ON LOW-INTENSITY CONFLICT (Alberto R. Coll, James S. Ord & Stephen A. Rose eds., 1995) (Vol. 67, U.S. Naval War College International Law Studies).

VOL 66

J. ASHLEY ROACH & ROBERT W. SMITH, EXCESSIVE MARITIME CLAIMS (1994) (Vol. 66, U.S. Naval War College International Law Studies).

VOL 65

TARGETING ENEMY MERCHANT SHIPPING (Richard J. Grunawalt ed., 1993) (Vol. 65, U.S. Naval War College International Law Studies).

VOL 64

THE LAW OF NAVAL OPERATIONS (Horace B. Robertson ed., 1991) (Vol. 64, U.S. Naval War College International Law Studies).

VOL 63

ALFRED P. RUBIN, THE LAW OF PIRACY (1988) (Vol. 63, U.S. Naval War College International Law Studies).

VOL 62

READINGS IN INTERNATIONAL LAW FROM THE NAVAL WAR COLLEGE REVIEW 1947–1977, II *The Use of Force, Human Rights and General International Legal Issues* (Richard B. Lillich & John Norton Moore eds., 1980) (Vol. 62, U.S. Naval War College International Law Studies).

VOL 61

READINGS IN INTERNATIONAL LAW FROM THE NAVAL WAR COLLEGE REVIEW 1947–1977, I *Role of International Law and an Evolving Ocean Law* (Richard B. Lillich & John Norton Moore eds., 1980) (Vol. 61, U.S. Naval War College International Law Studies).

VOL 60

DOCUMENTS ON PRISONERS OF WAR (Howard S. Levie ed., 1979) (Vol. 60, U.S. Naval War College International Law Studies).

VOL 59

HOWARD S. LEVIE, PRISONERS OF WAR IN INTERNATIONAL ARMED CONFLICT (1977) (Vol. 59, U.S. Naval War College International Law Studies).

VOL 58

WILLIAM T. MALLISON JR., STUDIES IN THE LAW OF NAVAL WARFARE: SUBMARINES IN GENERAL AND LIMITED WARS (1966) (Vol. 58, U.S. Naval War College International Law Studies).

VOL 57

(Not Published)

VOL 56

NEILL H. ALFORD JR., MODERN ECONOMIC WARFARE: LAW AND THE NAVAL PARTICIPANT (1963) (Vol. 56, U.S. Naval War College International Law Studies).

VOL 55

CARL Q. CHRISTOL, THE INTERNATIONAL LAW OF OUTER SPACE (1962) (Vol. 55, U.S. Naval War College International Law Studies).

VOL 54

NATO AGREEMENTS ON STATUS: TRAVAUX PRÉPARATOIRES (Joseph M. Snee ed., 1961) (Vol. 54, U.S. Naval War College International Law Studies).

VOL 53

CARL M. FRANKLIN, THE LAW OF THE SEA: SOME RECENT DEVELOPMENTS (WITH PARTICULAR REFERENCE TO THE UNITED NATIONS CONFERENCE OF 1958) (1959–60) (Vol. 53, U.S. Naval War College International Law Studies).

VOL 52

ROLAND J. STANGER, CRIMINAL JURISDICTION OVER VISITING ARMED FORCES (1957–58) (Vol. 52, U.S. Naval War College International Law Studies).

VOL 51

BRUNSON MACCHESNEY, SITUATION, DOCUMENTS AND COMMENTARY ON RECENT DEVELOPMENTS IN THE INTERNATIONAL LAW OF THE SEA (1956) (Vol. 51, U.S. Naval War College International Law Situation and Documents).

VOL 50

ROBERT W. TUCKER, THE LAW OF WAR AND NEUTRALITY AT SEA (1955) (Vol. 50, U.S. Naval War College International Law Studies).

VOL 49

HANS KELSEN, COLLECTIVE SECURITY UNDER INTERNATIONAL LAW (1954) (Vol. 49, U.S. Naval War College International Law Studies).

VOL 48

INTERNATIONAL LAW DOCUMENTS 1952–53: *Peace Treaties; Defense Agreements; European Unions* (Manley O. Hudson ed., 1954) (Vol. 48, U.S. Naval War College International Law Documents).

VOL 47

INTERNATIONAL LAW DOCUMENTS 1950–51: *The Protection of Victims of War (Part I: Conventions before 1949; Part II: Geneva Conventions of 1949)* (Manley O. Hudson ed., 1952) (Vol. 47, U.S. Naval War College International Law Documents).

VOL 46

INTERNATIONAL LAW DOCUMENTS 1948–49: *International Organization; Trials of War Criminals; Rights Claimed by Littoral States in Adjacent Seas; et al.* (Manley O. Hudson ed., 1950) (Vol. 46, U.S. Naval War College International Law Documents).

VOL 45

INTERNATIONAL LAW DOCUMENTS 1946–47: *The Treaties of Peace of 1947; Instrument of Japanese Surrender; et al.* (Manley O. Hudson ed., 1948) (Vol. 45, U.S. Naval War College International Law Documents).

VOL 44

INTERNATIONAL LAW DOCUMENTS 1944–45: *Contraband of War; The Crimea Conference; Act of Chapultepec; et al.* (Payson S. Wild Jr. ed., 1946) (Vol. 44, U.S. Naval War College International Law Documents).

VOL 43

INTERNATIONAL LAW DOCUMENTS 1943: *Visit and Search; Destruction of Prizes; War Zones; Defense Zones; et al.* (Payson S. Wild Jr. ed., 1945) (Vol. 43, U.S. Naval War College International Law Documents).

VOL 42

INTERNATIONAL LAW DOCUMENTS 1942: *Orders to American Military Forces in India; Crimes against Civilian Populations in Occupied Countries; et al.* (Payson S. Wild Jr. ed., 1943) (Vol. 42, U.S. Naval War College International Law Documents).

VOL 41

INTERNATIONAL LAW DOCUMENTS 1941: *Freezing of Japanese and Chinese Assets in the United States; The Atlantic Charter; et al.* (Payson S. Wild Jr. ed., 1943) (Vol. 41, U.S. Naval War College International Law Documents).

VOL 40

INTERNATIONAL LAW DOCUMENTS 1940: *Proclamations and Regulations Concerning Neutrality of the United States in the War between Germany and Norway; et al.* (Payson S. Wild Jr. ed., 1942) (Vol. 40, U.S. Naval War College International Law Documents).

VOL 39

INTERNATIONAL LAW SITUATIONS 1939: *Neutral Duties and State Control of Enterprise; Neutrality Problems; Contiguous Zones; et al.* (Payson S. Wild Jr. ed., 1940) (Vol. 39, U.S. Naval War College International Law Situations).

VOL 38

INTERNATIONAL LAW SITUATIONS 1938: *Belligerent and Neutral Rights in Regard to Aircraft; Force Short of War; et al.* (Payson S. Wild Jr. ed., 1940) (Vol. 38, U.S. Naval War College International Law Situations).

VOL 37

INTERNATIONAL LAW SITUATIONS 1937: *Protection by Vessels of War; Naval Protection during Strained Relations; et al.* (George G. Wilson ed., 1939) (Vol. 37, U.S. Naval War College International Law Situations).

VOL 36

INTERNATIONAL LAW SITUATIONS 1936: *Insurrection, Belligerency, Statehood; Visit by and Internment of Aircraft; et al.* (George G. Wilson ed., 1937) (Vol. 36, U.S. Naval War College International Law Situations).

VOL 35

INTERNATIONAL LAW SITUATIONS 1935: *Vessels and Neutral Ports; Action during Civil Strife; et al.* (George G. Wilson ed., 1936) (Vol. 35, U.S. Naval War College International Law Situations).

VOL 34

INTERNATIONAL LAW SITUATIONS 1934: *Transfer and Capture; Interference with Ships; et al.* (George G. Wilson ed., 1936) (Vol. 34, U.S. Naval War College International Law Situations).

VOL 33

INTERNATIONAL LAW SITUATIONS 1933: *Contraband and Blockade; Independent Philippine Islands; et al.* (George G. Wilson ed., 1934) (Vol. 33, U.S. Naval War College International Law Situations).

VOL 32

INTERNATIONAL LAW SITUATIONS 1932: *Belligerents in Neutral Waters; Artificial Structures and Maritime Jurisdiction; et al.* (George G. Wilson ed., 1934) (Vol. 32, U.S. Naval War College International Law Situations).

VOL 31

INTERNATIONAL LAW SITUATIONS 1931: *Neutrality and Aircraft; Neutrality and Territorial Waters; Belligerency and Maritime Jurisdiction* (George G. Wilson ed., 1932) (Vol. 31, U.S. Naval War College International Law Situations).

VOL 30

INTERNATIONAL LAW SITUATIONS 1930: *London Naval Treaty; Absence of Local Authority; Belligerent Aircraft; et al.* (George G. Wilson ed., 1931) (Vol. 30, U.S. Naval War College International Law Situations).

VOL 29

INTERNATIONAL LAW SITUATIONS 1929: *Neutrality and Vessels; Status of Islands in Pacific Ocean; Neutral Obligations* (George G. Wilson ed., 1931) (Vol. 29, U.S. Naval War College International Law Situations).

VOL 28

INTERNATIONAL LAW SITUATIONS 1928: *Maritime Jurisdiction; Carriage of Mail in Time of War; Enemy Persons on Neutral Vessels* (George G. Wilson ed., 1929) (Vol. 28, U.S. Naval War College International Law Situations).

VOL 27

INTERNATIONAL LAW SITUATIONS 1927: *Goods on Neutral Merchant Vessels; Visit and Search; Armed Merchant Vessels* (George G. Wilson ed., 1929) (Vol. 27, U.S. Naval War College International Law Situations).

VOL 26

INTERNATIONAL LAW SITUATIONS 1926: *Continuous Voyage; Submarines; Angary; Aircraft in Neutral Ports* (George G. Wilson ed., 1928) (Vol. 26, U.S. Naval War College International Law Situations).

VOL 25

INTERNATIONAL LAW DOCUMENTS 1925: REGULATION OF MARITIME WARFARE (George G. Wilson ed., 1926) (Vol. 25, U.S. Naval War College International Law Documents).

VOL 24

INTERNATIONAL LAW DOCUMENTS 1924: INTERNATIONAL AGREEMENTS (*Five Power Limitation of Naval Armament; Nicaraguan Canal Route; Danish West Indies; et al.*) (George G. Wilson ed., 1926) (Vol. 24, U.S. Naval War College International Law Documents).

VOL 23

INTERNATIONAL LAW DECISIONS 1923: *Vessels (The Haelen, etc.); Armed Vessels (Submarine E14, etc.); Search in Port (The Bernisse, etc.); et al.* (George G. Wilson ed., 1925) (Vol. 23, U.S. Naval War College International Law Decisions).

VOL 22

INTERNATIONAL LAW DECISIONS 1922: *The Berlin; The Miramichi; The Maria; et al.* (George G. Wilson ed., 1924) (Vol. 22, U.S. Naval War College International Law Decisions).

VOL 21

INTERNATIONAL LAW DOCUMENTS 1921: CONFERENCE ON THE LIMITATION OF ARMAMENT (George G. Wilson ed., 1923) (Vol. 21, U.S. Naval War College International Law Documents).

VOL 20

INTERNATIONAL LAW DOCUMENTS 1920: THE TREATIES OF PEACE WITH AUSTRIA AND WITH HUNGARY AND PROTOCOLS AND DECLARATIONS ANNEXED THERETO (George G. Wilson ed., 1922) (Vol. 20, U.S. Naval War College International Law Documents).

VOL 19

INTERNATIONAL LAW DOCUMENTS 1919: THE TREATY OF PEACE WITH GERMANY (George G. Wilson ed., 1920) (Vol. 19, U.S. Naval War College International Law Documents).

VOL 18

INTERNATIONAL LAW DOCUMENTS 1918: NEUTRALITY, CONDUCT AND CONCLUSION OF HOSTILITIES (George G. Wilson ed., 1919) (Vol. 18, U.S. Naval War College International Law Documents).

VOL 17

INTERNATIONAL LAW DOCUMENTS 1917: NEUTRALITY; BREAKING OF DIPLOMATIC RELATIONS; WAR (George G. Wilson ed., 1918) (Vol. 17, U.S. Naval War College International Law Documents).

VOL 16

INTERNATIONAL LAW TOPICS 1916: NEUTRALITY PROCLAMATIONS AND REGULATIONS (George G. Wilson ed., 1917) (Vol. 16, U.S. Naval War College International Law Topics).

VOL 15

INTERNATIONAL LAW TOPICS 1915: DOCUMENTS ON NEUTRALITY AND WAR (George G. Wilson ed., 1916) (Vol. 15, U.S. Naval War College International Law Topics).

VOL 14

INTERNATIONAL LAW TOPICS AND DISCUSSIONS 1914: *Classification of Public Vessels; Regulations Relating to Foreign Ships of War in Waters under the Jurisdiction of the United States; et al.*

(George G. Wilson ed., 1915) (Vol. 14, U.S. Naval War College International Law Topics and Discussions).

VOL 13

INTERNATIONAL LAW TOPICS AND DISCUSSIONS 1913: *Marginal Sea and Other Waters; Commencement of Hostilities; Limitation of Armaments; et al.* (George G. Wilson ed., 1914) (Vol. 13, U.S. Naval War College International Law Topics and Discussions).

VOL 12

INTERNATIONAL LAW SITUATIONS 1912: *Merchant Vessels and Insurgents; Air Craft in War; Cuba Neutral; et al.* (George G. Wilson ed., 1912) (Vol. 12, U.S. Naval War College International Law Situations).

VOL 11

INTERNATIONAL LAW SITUATIONS 1911: *Asylum in Neutral Port; Protection to Neutral Vessels; Destruction of Neutral Vessels; et al.* (George G. Wilson ed., 1911) (Vol. 11, U.S. Naval War College International Law Situations).

VOL 10

INTERNATIONAL LAW SITUATIONS 1910: *Coaling within Neutral Jurisdiction; Declaration of War; Days of Grace; et al.* (George G. Wilson ed., 1911) (Vol. 10, U.S. Naval War College International Law Situations).

VOL 9

INTERNATIONAL LAW TOPICS 1909: THE DECLARATION OF LONDON OF FEBRUARY 26, 1909 (George G. Wilson ed., 1910) (Vol. 9, U.S. Naval War College International Law Topics).

VOL 8

INTERNATIONAL LAW SITUATIONS 1908: *Termination of Liability for Breach of Blockade; The Twenty-Four Hour Rule; Sequestration of Prize; et al.* (George G. Wilson ed., 1909) (Vol. 8, U.S. Naval War College International Law Situations).

VOL 7

INTERNATIONAL LAW SITUATIONS 1907: *Fugitive from Cuban Justice at Guantanamo; Status of United States Auxiliary Collier in Foreign Harbor; et al.* (George G. Wilson ed., 1908) (Vol. 7, U.S. Naval War College International Law Situations).

VOL 6

INTERNATIONAL LAW TOPICS AND DISCUSSIONS 1906: *Use of False Colors; Transfer of Flag of Merchant Vessels during or in Anticipation of War; et al.* (George G. Wilson ed., 1907) (Vol. 6, U.S. Naval War College International Law Topics and Discussions).

VOL 5

INTERNATIONAL LAW TOPICS AND DISCUSSIONS 1905: *Inviolability of Private Property at Sea; Contraband of War; Restriction of Visit and Search; et al.* (George G. Wilson ed., 1906) (Vol. 5, U.S. Naval War College International Law Topics and Discussions).

VOL 4

INTERNATIONAL LAW SITUATIONS 1904: *Merchant Vessels Adapted for Conversion into Auxiliary Cruisers; Rights of Foreigner under Martial Law; Asylum for Insurgent Troops on War Vessel; et al.* (George G. Wilson ed., 1905) (Vol. 4, U.S. Naval War College International Law Situations).

VOL 3

INTERNATIONAL LAW DISCUSSIONS 1903: THE UNITED STATES NAVAL WAR CODE OF 1900 (George G. Wilson ed., 1904) (Vol. 3, U.S. Naval War College International Law Discussions).

VOL 2

INTERNATIONAL LAW SITUATIONS 1902: *Submarine Telegraphic Cables in Time of War; Asylum on Ships of War; Waters of Leased Territory; et al.* (George G. Wilson ed., 1903) (Vol. 2, U.S. Naval War College International Law Situations).

VOL 1

INTERNATIONAL LAW SITUATIONS 1901: *Coast Warfare; Contraband; Transportation of Military Persons; et al.* (John B. Moore ed., 1901) (Vol. 1, U.S. Naval War College International Law Situations).